RARE MASTERPIECES
OF PHILOSOPHY AND SCIENCE
EDITED BY DR. W. STARK

★

ON THE SYLLOGISM
And Other Logical Writings

ON THE SYLLOGISM

and Other Logical Writings

by

AUGUSTUS DE MORGAN

Edited, with an Introduction
by

PETER HEATH

ROUTLEDGE & KEGAN PAUL
LONDON

First published in 1966
by Routledge & Kegan Paul Limited
Broadway House, 68–74 Carter Lane
London, E.C.4

Printed in Great Britain
by Butler & Tanner Limited
Frome and London

CONTENTS

INTRODUCTION[1]

The author of these papers was born in 1806, at Madura, India, where his forebears, of Huguenot origin, had for three generations been army officers in the service of the East India Company. The father, Colonel John De Morgan, married Elizabeth Dodson, daughter of a custom-house official and grand-daughter of James Dodson, a mathematician well-known in his day. Augustus, the fifth child, was born with a defective right eye, and thus had no prospect of following the family career. Brought to England in infancy, he lost his father at the age of ten, Colonel De Morgan dying at St. Helena on his way home from a further tour of duty out East. Thereafter the family lived at various places in the West of England, where the boy attended private schools of no note and acquired a solid classical education, though little was done to observe or cultivate his talent for mathematics. At fourteen, a friend found him trying to solve a Euclidean problem by drawing, and introduced him to the concept of proof. From this point on he made rapid progress, read his school algebra 'like a novel', and on entering Trinity College, Cambridge, at sixteen-and-a-half, soon abandoned classics for a course of mathematical and philosophical reading, varied by novel-reading and flute-playing, which, had it been less discursive, would doubtless have gained him a higher place than the Fourth Wranglership he obtained in 1827. The main effects of his stay in Cambridge were to imbue him with a lasting distrust of examinations, and to furnish him with friendships, some of which, like those with his teachers, Airy, Peacock and Whewell, were to last him for much of his life.

The elder De Morgans had both been stern evangelicals, and the narrowly religious atmosphere of his early upbringing produced in the son a predictable reaction. Despite his mother's anxieties, he became and remained what he called a 'Christian unattached', disclaiming any open profession of faith because, as he afterwards said in his will, 'in my time such confession has always been the way up in the world'. The immediate result was to prevent his subscription to the religious

[1] The chief sources for De Morgan's life are: the *Memoir*, by his wife (1882); obituary notices in the *Athenaeum* (25 March 1871) and *Monthly Notices* of the Royal Astronomical Society (February 1872); *William De Morgan and his Wife*, by A. M. W. Stirling (1922); and articles by Leslie Stephen and Stanley Jevons in the *Dictionary of National Biography* and *Encyclopaedia Britannica*, respectively. The account of him in *Ten British Mathematicians*, by A. Macfarlane (1916), also deserves mention.

tests then in force at Cambridge, and thus to exclude him from any chance of a fellowship, or even of the M.A. degree. He contemplated medicine, and then law; but in 1828 the founding of the new and non-denominational University of London (now University College) re-opened the possibility of an academic career. At the age of twenty-two, the youngest of thirty-two candidates, he was elected to the mathematical professorship, and remained in this post intermittently for the rest of his working life. De Morgan is possibly unique among professors in having twice resigned his chair, each time on a point of principle. In 1831 he headed a revolt among his colleagues against the high-handed treatment of the professoriate by the governing body, and retired for five years into the wilderness, until the accidental death of his successor led to his unanimous recall. In 1853 he nearly resigned again, when acceptance by the college of a legacy with religious conditions attached seemed to him to imperil the principle of non-discrimination on which it had been founded. Finally, in 1866, the refusal to appoint James Martineau to the chair of mental philosophy, on the ground that he was too prominent a Unitarian to be suited to the post, led De Morgan to protest once more against the betrayal of principle involved, and to quit with reluctance an institution he had served with great energy and distinction for more than thirty years. The distress of this affair affected his health, and may well have contributed to his comparatively early death.

De Morgan was unsurpassed as a teacher, and delighted many generations of students with lectures at once eloquent, lucid, humorous and profound. Of the many good mathematicians who sat under him, the best known are probably Sylvester, Todhunter and E. J. Routh; Lady Lovelace, the daughter of Lord Byron and authoress of a celebrated account of Babbage's analytical engine, was a private pupil; while others who later achieved fame included Sir George Jessel, Master of the Rolls, Stanley Jevons (who 'adored' him), R. H. Hutton and Walter Bagehot. De Morgan had strong views on the teaching of mathematics, insisted on a philosophical approach to the subject, and did all in his power to discourage cramming. He quarrelled occasionally with his students, generally over late arrival in class, but retained their affection; after his retirement, it was his old pupils who obtained, and with difficulty persuaded him to accept, a small government annuity.

In addition to his academic duties, De Morgan was often in demand as an actuarial consultant to various insurance companies, and thereby came to know his neighbour, William Frend, a fellow-mathematician and sometime tutor of Trinity, whose daughter, Sophia Elizabeth, he married in 1837. By her he had three sons and four daughters, of whom the eldest son, William, after limited success as a painter and ceramic artist, was later to become known as a novelist. Another son, George

Campbell, who died young, was a promising mathematician and co-founder of the London Mathematical Society, of which he induced his father to be first president. Though shrewd enough in practical matters, De Morgan—'the most ungregarious animal living', as he once described himself—was generally anything but an organization man. He refused to seek election to the Royal Society, as 'too much open to social influences', and took no part in the activities of the British Association. He 'got as far as' joining the decimal coinage agitation of the 1850s, and served on a committee for the establishment of a standard pitch; but the only bodies to engage his lasting allegiance were the Royal Astronomical Society, of which he was for many years secretary and vice-president, and Brougham's Society for the Diffusion of Useful Knowledge. For the latter he wrote a number of tracts and treatises, including his elaborate work on the *Differential and Integral Calculus* (1842), and contributed an enormous number of articles (about seven hundred) to the *Penny*, later the *English, Cyclopaedia*. De Morgan's mathematical and literary output was very extensive, probably the largest of any mathematician of his time. In addition to original works, such as the *Trigonometry and Double Algebra* (1849) and a considerable sheaf of papers in the scientific journals, a series of first-rate elementary text-books on arithmetic, algebra and the theory of probabilities, and a long line of articles, on the most diverse subjects, in the annual *Companion to the Almanac*, he was an indefatigable reviewer, preface-writer, obituarist, journalist and pamphleteer. Much of his work in this line lies buried in the columns of the *Athenaeum*, though a serial miscellany he contributed thereto in the 1860s was assembled posthumously by his wife into possibly the most entertaining of all his works, the famous *Budget of Paradoxes*.[1] De Morgan collected cranks as other men collect postage stamps, and his *catalogue raisonné* of their efforts to upset Newton, square the circle and so forth, still makes diverting reading. Characteristically, he included in it an ironical review of a book on spiritualism, written anonymously by his wife, with an equally anonymous preface by himself.[2] Of the latter it has been said that 'for ingenuity and sceptical suggestiveness, as well as wit, . . . there is nothing in the "Literature of Spiritualism" comparable to this brief essay'.[3] Mrs De Morgan, as the *Memoir* of her husband shows, was herself a lady of talent, and helped to bring him into contact with a variety of literary and scientific people, including many of the leading nonconformists of the day. Brougham, Whewell, Sir John Herschel, Sir Frederick Pollock and John Stuart Mill were regular or intermittent

[1] First published in 1872; 2nd edn (by D. E. Smith), 1915; reprinted, with a preface by E. Nagel, 1954.

[2] *From Matter to Spirit*, by C. D., with a Preface by A. B., 1863.

[3] David Masson: *Recent British Philosophy*, 3rd edn. (1877), p. 184.

correspondents; Henry Crabb Robinson (of whom he wrote an amusing memoir) was a valued friend; Sir William Hamilton (of whom more anon) an equally valued enemy. To confuse matters[1]—and though they met only once—he also had a life-long postal crony in Sir William Rowan Hamilton, one of the few mathematicians of the time whose interests lay close to his own.[2] Nor should it be forgotten that he was among the first to discern the genius of George Boole, then an unknown schoolmaster, and that he not only encouraged and obtained a hearing for his work, but was instrumental in securing for Boole his first and only academic post, as professor at Queen's College, Cork.

De Morgan's generosity and lack of self-interest, his high principles and honest indignation at all worldly shams and expediencies, were somewhat reminiscent of Mr Pickwick, whom he came to resemble in appearance, and whose creator he greatly admired. Such qualities, allied to a certain natural pugnacity, were apt to involve him in controversy, made him something of a foe to the Victorian 'Establishment', and led, indeed, to his refusal even of such conventional honours as would ordinarily have come his way. He declined Brougham's offer of an honorary doctorate from Edinburgh, saying that he 'did not feel like an LL.D.'. He refused, similarly, his old pupils' request to have his portrait painted for presentation to University College. Though pleased at Mill's election to Westminster, his general attitude to politics was one of total indifference: '. . . I never gave a vote in my life,' he told Hamilton;[3] '. . . I hate the system. Given two persons of whom I know nothing; required, which is the best qualified to manage matters of which I know next to nothing. The presumption is that 5000 incompetent persons, by a contest of opposite incompetencies, will produce a competent decision. This absurdity fills the House of Commons.' He had no greater respect for the Lords, and took little interest, indeed, in personages or places of any description: 'I never saw a king or a queen in my life, except Louis Philippe. . . . I never was in the House of Commons, or in the Tower, or in Westminster Abbey. I spent only 1¾ hours in the Great Exhibition. . . . I never got further north than Cambridge, and never while at Cambridge penetrated to the northern extremity of the town. . . .'[4] An inveterate Londoner, to whom country holidays with his family were a penance, and even Blackheath a scene of 'desolation', his scant resources and scantier leisure were spent in haunting the bookstalls, where extensive learning and a curious eye

[1] As it has; the two Hamiltons have long stood confounded in the *Britannica* (Art. De Morgan); and the mistake is repeated at least twice in the index.

[2] The correspondence between them forms the bulk of volume III of R. P. Graves' *Life of Sir William Rowan Hamilton* (1889).

[3] Graves, op. cit., pp. 377, 384–5.

[4] Ibid., p. 462

assisted him in building up an excellent small library, whose remains are now in the possession of London University.[1]

The erudition and good sense of De Morgan's writings would not have kept them alive without other qualities, of which the most obvious is their quaint and endearing wit. Witty in himself, he was also a great collector of other men's jests, anecdotes, puzzles and puns, which enliven even his most forbidding passages, and season what is in any case a notably vigorous and individual prose style. This humour, and fondness for the humorous, never left him, either in the heat of controversial battle, or even under the shadow of the personal misfortunes which darkened the final years of his life. His departure from University College was followed soon after by the death of his son George, and of a daughter; by the loss of nearly all his old friends; and by a stroke from which he never fully recovered. He declined slowly, and died of nervous prostration and kidney disease in March 1871.

De Morgan's mathematical achievement, though primarily that of a great teacher, is enough to give him a place in the history of the subject, the nature of which can only briefly be mentioned here. As an algebraist, he belongs to the school of Peacock, Gregory and other Cambridge 'reformers' of the early years of the century, whose object it was to formalize the subject, as a pure science of (uninterpreted) symbols and their laws of combination, and thereby to free it from its old dependence, as 'universal arithmetic', upon interpretation in terms of the real positive number system. De Morgan's contribution was to define the basic notions and to give a fairly complete tabulation of the laws of operation, though he could not eliminate all content from the sign of equality, and naturally had some trouble with the (non-commutative) index laws. His approach was largely accepted, however, by the British algebraists who succeeded him, and in this aspect foreshadows the procedure of later formalists. (It also influences his logic, as may be seen in his endeavours to formalize the copula as a general sign of transitive relation.) By extending this treatment to 'double algebra', he also did something to clarify the then controversial status of 'imaginary' and complex numbers; and though his attempts to develop a consistent 'triple algebra' were unsuccessful, the failure was itself of some importance in throwing light on the true interpretation of the quaternion calculus discovered by his friend Rowan Hamilton. Hamilton himself paid tribute to De Morgan's work in this field, as materially assisting his own.

De Morgan's first incursion into logic was a small and now rare

[1] His *Arithmetical Books* (1847) is a classic of mathematical bibliography, and (as any antiquarian bookseller's catalogue will testify) still in daily use.

pamphlet, *First Notions of Logic* (1839), whose primary object was to equip his own students with sound habits of mathematical reasoning. His second, *On the Structure of the Syllogism* (1847), was the first of five important papers contributed to the *Transactions* of the Cambridge Philosophical Society; and with it, he immediately fell foul of Sir William Hamilton of Edinburgh, and so became embroiled in a controversy that lasted for well-nigh a quarter of a century, with effects apparent in nearly all his later work. Sir William, at this time, was Professor of Logic and Metaphysics at Edinburgh, and 'the first logical name in Britain, it may be in the world'.[1] This reputation he owed to a masterful critical article, dating from 1833, in the *Edinburgh Review*;[2] apart from that he had published nothing in logic, save the prospectus of a never-to-be-completed work on a 'New Analytic of Logical Forms', appended to his edition of Reid (1846). But the fame of his teaching, and the infiltration of his pupils and followers into leading academic positions in Britain and America, had conferred on the Hamiltonian logic a prestige rivalled only by that of Mill, and reinforced by the appearance of his doctrines in such standard textbooks as Thomson's *Outline of the Necessary Laws of Thought* (1st edn, 1842).

From 1839 or thereabouts, Hamilton had been teaching from his chair the principle of a quantified predicate, yielding eight propositional forms instead of the traditional four, and enabling all such propositions to be treated as equations, or statements of identity. De Morgan, however, knew nothing of this when, in 1846, on completion of his paper, he applied to Hamilton for historical information, and thereby initiated a friendly, if guarded, correspondence about their respective innovations in the theory of the syllogism. At the end of the year, this led to Hamilton's sending (2 November) the *Requirements* for a prize essay set to his class the previous June, and (28 December) the *Prospectus* already alluded to. He also referred his correspondent to the class-notes of a common pupil, William Shaen, who provided them a few days later. De Morgan had made virtually nothing of the *Requirements*, but on receipt of the *Prospectus* he concluded, wrongly, from a veiled remark or two about quantity in the predicate, that Hamilton had anticipated his treatment of the 'numerically definite' syllogism, which involved assigning numerical values to the middle term. He at once returned the *Prospectus*, underlining those parts of it to which he 'felt able to subscribe' on his own terms, and followed it with letters showing himself to have the whole method already committed to paper, and acquainting Hamilton with much of its detail,

[1] Unpublished, and possibly unsent letter from De Morgan to Spalding, 26 June 1857.

[2] Reprinted in *Discussions on Philosophy, etc.*, 1852.

together with the gist of his still unpublished Cambridge paper. Shaen's notes, when they arrived, proved to be of no great relevance, based as they were on material dating from 1837, before the novelties in Hamilton's teaching had begun.

Still unaware of their exact nature, De Morgan's next step, at the end of February 1847, was to send in an *Addition* to his paper, setting out in full the material communicated to Hamilton, with due acknowledgement to the latter as having possibly forestalled him. Hamilton received an offprint of the whole, but not till 30 March. In the meantime, the underlinings of his prospectus, and so much as he could understand of the letters that went with it, had aroused in him the suspicion that De Morgan, having extracted from the *Requirements* the idea of quantifying the predicate, was now about to publish it as his own. On 13 March he accordingly addressed to his correspondent the 'acrimonious charge of plagiarism'[1] which precipitated the quarrel between them: '. . . it appears, that you claim for yourself the independent re-discovery of the fundamental doctrine of the syllogism, which I privately communicated to you. . . . This claim, though it be only to secondary originality, I am altogether unable to admit. To me it is manifest, that, for the principle of the doctrine, you are wholly indebted to my information; and I cannot but think, that if you (though recognizing always my priority), give forth that doctrine as a speculation of your own, you will be guilty—pardon the plain speaking—both of an injurious breach of confidence towards me, and of false dealing towards the public.'

De Morgan, 'the most upright of men, and almost morbidly scrupulous',[2] was justifiably incensed, and demanded an immediate and public withdrawal, or substantiation, of this 'odious charge': '. . . I beg to inform you that I shall wait till the 10th of next month for one of two things—your retractation—or the announcement of the specific time and manner in which you will publicly maintain the truth of the accusation which—excuse the expression—you have dared to bring against me. If I do not receive one of these two things by the date above specified, I shall then at once proceed to draw up a statement, of the publication of which, I need not say, you shall be duly apprised.'

Hamilton must have been taken aback by this, and by what he learnt thereafter of the defendant, for, after further correspondence, and on receipt of the Cambridge paper, he wrote a comparatively polite and conciliatory letter, acknowledging among other things that De Morgan had preceded him in the use of the 'ultra-total' quantification ('most'). This letter was transmitted, however, *via* an Edinburgh surgeon and professor of physiology, Dr Allen Thomson, whose one-time associate,

[1] W. S. Jevons, in *The Contemporary Review*, 1873.
[2] Ibid.

Dr Sharpey, was by this time De Morgan's fellow-professor in London. De Morgan declined to receive it, nor did he see a second letter, offering a retractation on terms. Sir William wrote directly, on 13 April, undertaking to withdraw his charge, and seeking only an explanation of the matter; but the irate De Morgan was by now determined on a public show-down. The two logicians 'agreed to have a battle', and the outcome was a pair of pamphlets, Sir William's *Letter to Augustus De Morgan, Esq.* (containing, *inter alia*, the whole previous correspondence), and De Morgan's *Statement in Answer to an Assertion made by Sir William Hamilton, Bart.* Owing to a strike among the Edinburgh printers, De Morgan got his blow in first. But the delay enabled Hamilton to add a 'Postscript' and 'Note' in answer to his adversary's defence.

In the main body of his *Letter*, Hamilton expressly withdrew the charge of wilful plagiarism, but maintained, what was little better, that De Morgan had published the substance of his (Hamilton's) quantification, under the mistaken and vainglorious impression that it was his own discovery. He argues at length, in a hectoring, forensic style, that the so-called 'second view' contained in De Morgan's *Addition* was derived from his own *Requirements*; that nothing had been said of any new view for three months after receipt of this latter document, which De Morgan had professed 'not to comprehend at all'; that the period alleged for its excogitation was improbably located in a single week in early October, after the completion of the Cambridge paper, and before the *Requirements* had been sent; and that it was in any case highly unlikely that the same important advance should have been made independently by two persons already known to, and in communication with, each other.

De Morgan's *Statement* shows that he had by this time realized, what Hamilton never fully grasped, that the pair of them were not on the same track at all. His case, briefly, is that his own new matter is all contained in the body of the Cambridge paper; that no intelligible communication was thereafter made to him; and that he had, in any event, acted with complete propriety in furnishing Hamilton, on receipt of the *Prospectus*, with a full account of what he claimed to have done. Though there was 'something racy', he allows, in Hamilton's proposal to compare notes before entering into public controversy, he remains firm in refusing to accept the withdrawal of the main charge in exchange for any admission of possible mistake. Reprinting extracts (first seven paragraphs of Section III, and the last but one of Section IV) from his original paper, from Hamilton's letter and *Requirements* of 2 November, and from the *Addition* (first five paragraphs), he shows that his own concern was, not with any general quantification of the predicate, but with the assignment of definite quantity to the middle term in syllogisms with two particular premisses, thereby permitting a valid conclusion, in spite of the appearance of an undistributed middle. In reasoning that if most men have coats, and most men waistcoats, some must have both, he claims to have produced a non-Aristotelian form of argument having nothing in common with Hamilton's procedure, which merely assigned the traditional quantities, universal or particular, to the predicate throughout.

The lengthy reply to this in Hamilton's *Postscript* does not, in fact, add anything to his case. Still preoccupied with the belief that *something* must have been stolen from him, he labours to prove: that the Cambridge paper proceeds only on the traditional scheme of quantification; that the *Addition* contains *his* scheme, together with that based on numerical definition of the middle term; and that De Morgan is guilty of a 'wretched confusion' between them. After insisting once more on his own priority, he repeats the attempt to convict De Morgan of error in dating his 'second view' before perusal of the *Requirements.* In the *Note* following, he claims, for his own part, to have already lighted earlier upon the 'ultra-total' quantification, but to have discarded it as a 'useless and cumbrous subtlety'; thereby resigning to De Morgan whatever credit might attach to the discovery.

De Morgan took note of Hamilton's pamphlet in a short but defiant letter in the *Athenaeum* (29 May), and received an equally belligerent answer to it the following week. Hostilities, for the moment, then ceased. The consensus of De Morgan's correspondents, and of fair-minded persons generally—so far as they professed to understand the issue—was that Sir William had had a good deal the worst of it, and that the whole affair was unseemly and should never have arisen. It had, however, one notable consequence, in the appearance (on the same day[1] as De Morgan's *Formal Logic*) of Boole's celebrated essay, *The Mathematical Analysis of Logic*—inspired, so the author averred, by this very same quarrel, which had induced him 'to resume the almost-forgotten thread of former inquiries', and which was thereby indirectly responsible for the birth of modern logic.

The publication of *Formal Logic*, in the autumn of 1847,[2] gave De Morgan a further opportunity of vindicating himself against Hamilton. The work itself is in large part a résumé of his logical achievement to date; the early *First Notions* reappears without much change as Chapter I, while Chapters IV, V, VIII and X represent an enlarged and amended version of the first Cambridge paper. Appendix I gives an 'Account of a Controversy . . .', relating the whole affair in some detail. In

[1] So De Morgan (2 December 1867), in communicating Boole's posthumous 'Of Propositions Numerically Definite' to the Cambridge *Transactions* (Vol. XI, 1868).

[2] 2nd edn (by A. E. Taylor), 1926. The impossibly garbled and inaccurate bibliographical note prefixed to the text is presumably by another hand.

reconstructing the Hamiltonian quantification, and the eight propositional forms resulting, De Morgan draws attention to a fatal flaw in the scheme: two of the forms, 'All *A* is all *B*' and 'Some *A* is not some *B*', are anomalous in having no contradictories. The first, he argues, is really a complex proposition, while the second says so little as to be, for all practical purposes, useless. The rest of the Appendix deals at length with the *Athenaeum* letters and reprints the extracts already referred to; but it is more 'for the record' than for the sake of adding anything new. Appendix II unearths some earlier quantifiers in Lambert, Thomson, Ploucquet, Drobitsch and Solly. The latter had actually given the eight Hamiltonian forms in 1839; but it is curious that neither party should seemingly have been aware that they had been stated even earlier, for English readers, by George Bentham, nephew to Jeremy, whose *Outlines of a System of Logic* was published in 1827. Bentham's claim was championed in the *Athenaeum* (December 1850) by a Mr Warlow from Haverfordwest; the subsequent discussion (in which Hamilton and others joined) brought out the even more curious fact that this had been one of the books under review in Sir William's celebrated article of 1833. De Morgan had more excuse, since it was only on thus hearing of it that he first examined the book.

In November 1847, De Morgan sent a copy of *Formal Logic* to Hamilton. It was returned within a week, almost uncut, the recipient finding it 'impossible to accept what . . . I must needs, if I ever notice it, characterize in painful terms'. The flyleaf carries the inscription: 'Sir William Hamilton, Bt., from the Author', followed by 'The Author, from Sir William Hamilton, Bt.'; 'simple conversion' was De Morgan's comment on the transaction. He interleaved the copy and used it, around 1850, in preparing a second edition, which was never published;[1] his notes for the work contain the following, which might well serve (and was perhaps so intended) as an epigraph for the whole encounter: 'Two French squadrons at B—— cannonaded each other—why? Because each took the other for *Russians*. "Then why did they fight?" said a little girl.'

The controversial passages in *Formal Logic* do more, however, than merely rebut the charge of plagiarism; they mark the beginning of a systematic polemic on De Morgan's part against certain technical deficiencies in the Hamiltonian logic, which he was among the first to notice and proclaim.[2] The next shots in this direction were fired in his second Cambridge memoir, *On the Symbols of Logic* . . . (January

[1] It is now in the University of London library.

[2] For a recent account of this new phase of the debate, cf. A. N. Prior: *Formal Logic* (2nd edn, pp. 148 ff.). The best of the earlier discussions is in J. Venn: *Symbolic Logic* (1881). W. Bednarowski has investigated the Hamiltonian quantification in *Arist. Soc. Proc.* 1955–6, but without specific reference to De Morgan.

1850, with an *Addition* in July). Apart from numerous minor criticisms, it is there proposed to remedy the defects already pointed out in Hamilton's forms by reading his quantifiers in an 'exemplar', or distributive, sense ('any one'), rather than in the usual 'cumular', or collective, sense ('all'). The reaction was immediate. 'Your papa', wrote Lady Hamilton on 7 August, 'is busy cutting up De Morgan'[1]—the first result of which was another letter in the *Athenaeum* (24 August),[2] irritably repudiating the cumular reading as either usual or used by him, and counter-criticizing his critic on the use of the word 'any'.

By this time, at least, the lineaments of the Hamiltonian system were beginning to emerge into public view. Thomson's *Outline* had reached a second edition, with a note by Hamilton, in 1849, and the year following the prize dissertation by his English pupil, T. S. Baynes, *An Essay on the New Analytic of Logical Forms*, appeared under Hamilton's *imprimatur*, and gave the system as explicit a form as it was ever destined to obtain. Other Hamiltonians also became active in its defence. In May 1851, the *North British Review* carried an article, *Recent Extensions of Formal Logic*, by Mansel of Oxford,[3] in which *Formal Logic* and the second Cambridge paper were subjected to lengthy and unappreciative criticism. Mansel disliked De Morgan's apparent reduction of logic to algebra, and inveighed, on Kantian grounds, against the intrusion of material elements into the science, in the shape of relational copulas, numerical syllogisms, and the like. He also came to the rescue of 'All *A* is all *B*', on lines later to be endorsed by Hamilton himself. The opening pages of De Morgan's third memoir are an answer to Mansel, though he is not mentioned directly. They clashed again later, but were amicable enough behind the scenes, and occasionally conspired in staging them.[4]

Hamilton himself had meanwhile been preparing his *Discussions*, a reprint of his *Edinburgh Review* articles,[5] which appeared in the spring of 1852. Appendix II(B) of this work is a long rampageous counterblast to the second paper on syllogism, in the author's highest style. Boole, for one, thought it went too far. 'I think you are unjustifiably severe', he wrote, 'upon my friend Mr De Morgan'; though, having made no study of the 'peculiarities' of the latter's system, he did not presume to 'pass any opinion upon the correctness or mutual consistency of his views'.[6] De Morgan, however, seems to have been delighted. 'For a cut-and-thrust, might-and-main, tooth-and-nail, hammer-and-tongs assault', he wrote afterwards, 'I can particularly recommend it.

[1] J. Veitch: *Memoir of Sir William Hamilton*, p. 327.
[2] Reprinted in *Discussions*, pp. 673–80 (references are to the 3rd edn).
[3] Reprinted in *Letters, Lectures and Reviews* (1873).
[4] Graves, op. cit., III, p. 562.
[5] 2nd edn, 1853; 3rd edn, 1866.
[6] Veitch, op. cit., p. 344.

I never knew, until I read it, how much I should enjoy a thundering onslaught on myself, done with racy insolence by a master hand. . . .'[1] The fact was, that all this hue-and-cry was doing much to bring his name and opinions into notice among logicians. Hamilton, from this point of view, was 'one of the best friends and allies I ever had',[2] and the permanence of the present attack was especially gratifying. 'Your namesake', he told Rowan Hamilton, 'has fired another shot at me—to my great joy—in a printed book which will last.'[3] So far from returning his presentation copy, he addressed to the donor a brief disquisition upon the etiquette of retaining it, enclosing two small works of his own by way of repayment for its non-controversial residue, which Hamilton had the grace to accept.[4]

The Appendix itself opens with a fiery commination of the enemy and all his works: '. . . there is not, in the whole compass of Mr De Morgan's "logical systems", a single logical novelty which is not a logical blunder. . . . If, as has been said, Mr De Morgan's Memoir may represent the Transactions, the Transactions the Society, and the Society the University of Cambridge, then either is the knowledge of Logic . . . in that seminary now absolutely null, or I am publicly found ignorant of the very alphabet of the science I profess. The alternative I am unable to disown; the decision I care not to avoid; and the discussion, I hope, may have its uses.'[5]

The Appendix proper begins by reprinting the *Athenaeum* letter, wherewith Hamilton signalizes anew his rejection of De Morgan's 'general and gigantic error' in misreading his forms of predication. These, he says, are not arbitrary, nor is his canon of inference insufficient. De Morgan's own rule, of erasing the middle term, is purloined from Ploucquet. The subsequent defence of his own disputed forms is more forcible than convincing, complicated as it was by the fact that certain Hamiltonians—notably Thomson—had already repudiated the notorious 'Some *A* is not some *B*'. In this connexion, Hamilton attributes to Aristotle the belief that 'some' may actually mean 'none', and himself argues that it fluctuates in meaning between 'some at most' and 'some at least', thereby excluding or including the case of 'all'. This was later to provide a further bone of contention. The next section finds him 'doing battle' at length for the doctrine of breadth and depth —his own names for extension and intension—which he endeavours to treat, in both cases, as quantities reciprocal to each other. In denying Leibniz to be Newton, we deny to the one *all* the attributes possessed by the other—but only to the extent that he actually possesses them. The claim (*Syllogism II*, p. 49 n.) that he had admitted his own scheme to be

[1] *Budget* (2nd edn), I, p. 339.
[2] Ibid., p. 335.
[3] Graves, op. cit., p. 627.
[4] *Budget*, I, p. 340 f.
[5] *Discussions*, pp. 672–3.

contained in the despised 'numerically definite' system of his rival, naturally meets with indignant dismissal; the latter, says Hamilton, is in any case taken from Lambert. As for the alleged identity of De Morgan's notation, 'horrent with mysterious spiculae' and his own, 'easy, simple, compendious, all-sufficient, consistent, manifest, precise, complete'—as he elsewhere describes it,[1] the very suggestion enrages him to the point of apoplexy. The piece ends with a comparison of the mathematician to an 'owl in daylight', and with a warning to his opponent that 'mathematics and dram-drinking tell, especially in the long run. For a season, I admit, Toby Philpot may be the Champion of England; and Warburton testifies,—"It is a thing notorious, that the *oldest mathematician* in England is the *worst reasoner* in it." So much for Mathematical Logic; so much for Cambridge Philosophy.'[2]

De Morgan had every reason for replying to this outburst, but he chivalrously did not do so. Hamilton was known to be in failing health —he had been partially paralysed since 1846—and the excitement of further controversy might well have been injurious to him. Open warfare was at an end, therefore, nor did De Morgan publish anything more on logic in Hamilton's lifetime, apart from the two small papers *On Indirect Demonstration* and *Some Suggestions in Logical Phraseology*,[3] neither of which has any connexion with the issues in question. Hamilton died in May 1856, and received a brief obituary notice from his old opponent in the *Athenaeum*.[4] De Morgan was not yet ready, however, to bury Hamilton the logician. The third memoir, *On the Syllogism* . . . ., completed in August 1857, with a Postscript dated in June of the following year, consists of two parts: the second is a summary account of the author's system, on the lines of the later *Syllabus*; but the first is largely polemic, directed, not at Mansel only, but also to some extent with him, against the weaknesses of Hamilton's extensional approach to logic, when applied to the problems of intension. In common with such followers as Baynes and Spalding,[5] Hamilton had denied, in effect, the traditional view, that the individual contains, embodies or

[1] 'The corresponding antithetic adjectives', says Venn, 'being freely expended in the description of the schemes of those who had gone before him.' Op. cit., p. 432.

[2] *Discussions*, pp. 705–6. This was an old hobby of Sir William's. He had long since annoyed all Cambridge by his strictures on mathematical education (op. cit., pp. 260–336).

[3] *Philosophical Magazine*, December 1852, and *Proceedings of the Philological Society*, February 1853. The first is addressed to mathematicians; the second outlines some distinctions later reproduced in *Syllogism III*.

[4] 10 May 1856. For Hamilton's life and character, see the *Memoir* by Veitch, already cited; for an interesting shorter account of him, cf. also T. S. Baynes in *Edinburgh Essays 1856*.

[5] Like Veitch, a predecessor of Baynes in the Logic chair at St. Andrews. His *Introduction to Logical Science* (from the *Encyclopaedia Britannica*, 8th edn) appeared in 1857.

exemplifies the whole of each of the various attributes predicated of him; maintaining, rather, that he is merely the sum of some part of each of them. De Morgan argues at length against the notion that concepts can be partitioned and aggregated in this way; his own account of the matter is more complicated than satisfactory, but there can be little doubt of its superiority to the interpretation in dispute. The postscript is concerned with rebuttal of the more personal accusations occurring in Hamilton's *Appendix*, of plagiarism, incompetence, misrepresentation and the like. It draws attention, among other things, to the mathematical absurdity of Hamilton's assertion that breadth and depth are identical quantities, which nonetheless vary in inverse proportion to each other. De Morgan was apt to harp on this mistake, in season, and sometimes out; as when a casual reference to it provoked inquiries, and eventually the need for a full explanation, to the baffled readers of *Notes and Queries* (11 September 1858).

1859 saw the completion of two important additions to De Morgan's logical output; the *Syllabus of a Proposed System of Logic*, and the fourth Cambridge memoir, *On the Syllogism, IV, and on the Logic of Relations*. The latter stands almost alone among his major writings in having (and making) no reference to the Hamiltonian quarrel. Though modestly described by its author as a 'crabbed conglomerate',[1] it is generally agreed to be his most original contribution to logic.[2] The young Charles Peirce (who received a complimentary copy) 'at once fell to upon it; and before many weeks had come to see in it, as De Morgan had already seen, a brilliant and astonishing illumination of every corner and every vista of logic'. 'No decent semblance of justice', he adds, 'has ever been done to De Morgan, owing to his not having brought anything to its final shape. . . . He stood indeed like Aladdin (or whoever it was) gazing upon the overwhelming riches of Ali Baba's cave, scarce capable of making a rough inventory of them.'[3] Peirce, in his 'logic of relatives', was himself the first to appreciate and exploit these riches. No writer, indeed, of the succeeding generation, had a clearer understanding of De Morgan's general merits, or—for that matter—a more informed disdain for the pretensions of Hamilton and his school.

The *Syllabus*, though it contains a few characteristic digs at Hamilton, is for the most part a valuable, if congested, survey of the author's later views, and more especially of the developments already outlined in *Syllogism III*. As such, it forms one of the best points of entry to the

[1] *Budget*, I, p. 334.

[2] For summaries of its content, cf. C. I. Lewis: *A Survey of Symbolic Logic*, p. 45 f.; J. Jørgensen: *Treatise of Formal Logic*, I, p. 96; and A. N. Prior, op. cit., p. 152 f.

[3] C. S. Peirce: *Collected Papers*, 1. 562.

study of his work.[1] The same may be said of the *English Cyclopaedia* article on Logic, published in July of the same year (1860); though here too, the temptation to 'fire some more shot'[2] at his old antagonist, and at Mansel, was not to be (or at least was not) resisted. The polemical character of this article is doubtless to be accounted for by De Morgan's awareness that Hamilton's posthumous *Lectures*, on metaphysics and on logic, were on the verge of publication at the hands of Mansel and Veitch. He reviewed both sets of volumes in the *Athenaeum* (10 and 24 November 1860), dwelling, as his wont was, on Hamilton's failings as a mathematician. Mansel rose promptly to the defence, and, after a brief exchange, retired worsted. De Morgan himself made no doubt, however, as he told Rowan Hamilton, that the *Lectures* were 'very well worth reading'.[3] On a later occasion, to the same correspondent, he speaks of Hamilton as 'a most interesting writer—even in logic, when quantity is not in question. On this point his head is a curious one. But as to other things the freshness of his mind, loaded as it was with learning, is unique'.[4]

These expressions of regard are worth noting, if only because later writers (including Peirce) have too often been led, by their justified assessment of Hamilton's long-term unimportance as a logician, to underrate the contemporary reverence accorded to his opinions, and the consequent difficulty of overthrowing them. De Morgan could have no illusions on that score, and no scruples, therefore, in continuing to vex his ghost. In the latter half of 1861, four letters from him on *Hamiltonian Logic* appeared in the *Athenaeum*.[5] Their purpose was to redirect attention to Hamilton's peculiar use, in the *Discussions* article and the *Lectures*, of the word 'some', and to provoke his supporters into defending, or at least clarifying, his assertions on the matter. Hamilton, says De Morgan, imputed to Aristotle the view that 'some' may include 'all', or even 'none', and himself held that it may mean 'some, but not the rest'. On the latter interpretation, many of his syllogisms become invalid; in particular, the 'Gorgon syllogism' appears to imply that all men other than lawyers are men of stone. Though willing to attribute these mistakes to hurry and ill-health, De Morgan still wanted to know what Hamilton had actually taught; but for the moment he had run out of assailants, and could get no public answer. In the autumn of 1861, he even applied to Boole:[6] '. . . Being always grubbing at logic in some shape or other, I have been at Sir W. H.—my best friend,

[1] Cf. Lewis, op. cit., p. 38.
[2] Letter to Boole, 13 July 1860.
[3] Graves, op. cit., p. 561.
[4] Ibid., p. 616 (5 July 1864).
[5] 13 July, 17 August, 2 November and 28 December 1861.
[6] Letter to Boole, 16 November 1861.

whom I treat with prepense ingratitude—and you may see by the *Athenaeum* that I convict him of actually forging invalid syllogisms. His friends are quite silent. Can you do anything for him? I mean in the way of suggesting a possible meaning for his quantifications which will make his syllogisms valid. Dr Mansel, who rushed in so boldly to the defence of his mathematical blunders, and left me the field at last, was wise enough, when I wrote my *first* letter in the *Athenaeum* to write me a private note, saying that he had intended to write to the *Athenaeum*—but thought it was really so simple a thing to answer that he must have mistaken my meaning. *He* thought that it was, etc. I gave him a *spicilegium* of what I should think—and he abandoned his intention. That I should be allowed to advance without contradiction, that the great reformer—who blew his own trumpet so very loud—has committed actual paralogisms, is so strange, that I really want an opponent for the sake of the case and the subject. . . . Besides, I am personally in want of a row: as the Irishman said, I am dry-moulded for want of a bating. . . .'

Boole, with a rare flicker of humour, replied from Cork:[1] '. . . I very much fear that though I am in the land in which a disposition to fight is supposed most to bloom, I shall not be able to find you an antagonist. You could not contrive to bring in the Pope or Garibaldi or the Queen's Colleges—and without something of the kind I fear I can do nothing for you here. If I entered the lists myself it would be on your side, and that would only make your case worse. Shade of Duns Scotus, arise!'

This conjuration proving ineffective, De Morgan was left to conduct unaided his final *Auseinandersetzung* with the Hamiltonian school. The opening pages of *Syllogism V*, sent in to the Cambridge society in May of 1862 (though not read until a year later), contain a thorough investigation of all the main points in dispute. It is shown in detail how, on the 'doubly partitive' interpretation ('some but not the rest'), valid syllogisms can be constructed which are debarred by Hamilton's canon of inference, while, of those which *are* allowed, no fewer than 15 out of 36 are either false or incomplete. After indicating the sources of the error, De Morgan proceeds to restate the system properly, pointing out that, so understood, the eight Hamiltonian forms of predication reduce to five exhaustive possibilities of relationship between two classes (the so-called Euler or Gergonne relations), plus three indeterminate cases, which cannot, without further information, be assigned to any particular one of them. Thus Hamilton's forms, in spite of their apparent verbal symmetry, correspond to no genuine scheme of relation among classes; or rather, they merely exhibit, inadequately, a part of a larger system, including negative terms and based on an exemplar reading of the quantifiers, which is thereupon outlined in detail.

[1] 21 November 1861.

'Final and unanswerable' as Peirce declared this paper to be,[1] it was not quite the end of the affair. While it was still in the press, a further letter from De Morgan in the *Athenaeum* was at last successful in goading Baynes, 'the pupil, the prizeman, the substitute, and the accredited expounder',[2] into breaking a lance on his old master's behalf. Though tolerably effective in extricating him from the charge of having misconstrued Aristotle, and in exonerating him from having actually taught the impugned system of syllogism from his chair, Baynes inevitably found himself in difficulty when he argued that Hamilton's restricted use of 'some' had never been intended for employment within the syllogism. The exchanges again became personal; and De Morgan again had the last word in the *Addition* appended to his paper at the end of 1862.

This was, for all practical purposes, the last to be heard of the matter. De Morgan returned to it briefly, in a letter to *Notes and Queries* (6 August 1864), on Hamilton's qualities as a bibliographer, and duly found a niche for him in the *Budget of Paradoxes*. Neither piece is of much importance, though the latter is an amusing, and sufficiently magnanimous, popular account of the whole tangled business. With it, De Morgan's interest in logic is generally assumed to have ended; but there are good reasons for thinking that this was not the case. The University of London library contains, in manuscript, a *sixth* memoir on the syllogism, dated 27 August 1868, and what appear to be two earlier drafts of the same, conflated under the title *On some Logical Difficulties of Language*. Unpublished, and perhaps unpublishable, these lengthy and discursive papers seem to have escaped the notice of bibliographers. The material in them represents a technical development of themes occurring in *Syllogism V*, interspersed with historical notes on such matters as the origin of the mnemonic verses, at that time generally, though as De Morgan suspected, wrongly, attributed to Peter of Spain. Hamilton's name appears with fair regularity throughout, confirming that, to the very last, De Morgan's thinking on logic still owed much of its impetus to his collisions with the 'Edinburgh Aristotle', and to the struggle for supremacy between them that had started twenty-one years before.

A final echo of the encounter was heard only after De Morgan's death, when, in 1873, *The Contemporary Review* published an article by Herbert Spencer, in which he alluded to Bentham, rather than Hamilton, as having been the first to quantify the predicate. Hamilton's claim was immediately championed by Baynes, but the only effect of this was to bring in Jevons, who re-established the titular priority of Bentham,

[1] *Collected Papers*, 2. 533; a view from which few subsequent writers have ventured to differ.

[2] Letter to Boole, 20 September 1862.

and again put on record De Morgan's part in the affair. There seems little doubt, by now, that the true position on this not very important question of fact was simply this, that whatever may have been done by European logicians, Bentham was the first writer in English to quantify the predicate, Hamilton the first to make any extensive use of it, and De Morgan the first to grasp what it was all about. Since the result of his investigation was to expose the hollowness of the claims that had been made for it, the dispute over priority has ceased, in any case, to be a matter of serious concern.

De Morgan's own logic, as presented in these papers, is by no means a finished edifice; though its main outlines appear quite early, his ingenuity was constantly at work in correcting, improving and expanding the structure—and occasionally spent itself in unprofitable enterprises, or in complication for its own sake. His devotion to the traditional lore of the subject, and his admirable insight into its workings, were liable, unfortunately, to restrict his outlook, and to prevent him from attaining to any radically novel point of view. Unlike Boole, he remains therefore—with Hamilton—in most things a reformer of the old logic, rather than the creator of a new one.

For all that, he shares with both the writers just mentioned a conception of logic that clearly points forward rather than back. Like them, he sees it as a formal science, having nothing to do, directly, with questions of empirical psychology or abstract metaphysics. Its forms are forms of possible thinking, rather than of actual thought. Within these terms of reference, he also recognizes a contrast between what he calls the objective and the subjective sides of logic—a contrast associated with the mediaeval distinction between terms of first and second intention. In the former and more elementary capacity, its concern is with particular objects (including objects of thought), and with the individual qualities, or *qualia*, they possess; in the latter, with classes of such objects, and with the attributes, or universals, they have in common. On both views, the elements consist of terms, copulative relations, propositions and syllogisms. Objectively considered, the term is a mere name or mark attached to an object; the proposition, a mere pair of names connected by a copula; while the function of the latter —in what he calls the 'arithmetical view' of the subject—is merely to formulate the result of an enumeration of similar instances. Sometimes, as in the 'numerically definite' proposition, the precise number of such instances is stated, and various non-traditional forms of valid inference are possible as a result;[1] more generally, in the common logic, it matters only that the quantity should be definitely given, as 'all' or 'none', or vaguely so, as 'some', meaning 'not none; at least one,

[1] pp. 17-19.

and possibly all'. In this respect, logical notions are more formal, because less specific, than those of mathematics.

De Morgan's first real departure from orthodoxy occurs with his introduction of negative (or 'contrary') terms, symbolized by lowercase letters instead of capitals. To limit the scope of these, he also proposes the useful convention of a 'universe of discourse'.[1] '*X*' and '*x*' between them exhaust this universe, whatever it may be, and it is assumed that there always *are* objects, be it only objects of thought, in either category. One consequence of this thoroughgoing 'qualification of the subject' is that problems about nonentities, empty classes and the 'existential import' of universal propositions are firmly evicted at the outset. A second is, that the *ex facie* distinction between affirmative and negative propositions disappears, and a special rule becomes necessary for identifying them.[2]

The admission of negative terms immediately engenders eight basic forms of proposition, in place of the traditional four:

A.	(1) All *X*s are *Y*s	(5) Some *X*s are *Y*s
	(2) All *x*s are *y*s	(6) Some *x*s are *y*s
	(3) All *X*s are *y*s	(7) Some *X*s are *y*s
	(4) All *x*s are *Y*s	(8) Some *x*s are *Y*s

By applying familiar rules for double negation and distribution, these can be rewritten, without negatives, as follows:

B.	(1) All *X*s are *Y*s	(5) Some *X*s are *Y*s
	(2) All *Y*s are *X*s (Some *X*s are all *Y*s)	(6) Some things are neither *X*s nor *Y*s
	(3) No *X*s are *Y*s	(7) Some *X*s are not *Y*s
	(4) Everything is either *X* or *Y*	(8) Some *Y*s are not *X*s (All *X*s are not some *Y*s).

Some care must be taken over propositions (4) and (6) in the second list. Their curious verbal forms disguise, what is apparent in the earlier table, that the first is a universal negative proposition, and the second a particular affirmative. One has to resist the temptation, whereby Hamilton fell—and which De Morgan's symbolism does nothing to discourage—to read them respectively as 'Some *X*s are not some *Y*s' and 'All *X*s are all *Y*s'. At the price of this awkwardness, De Morgan is able, however, as Hamilton was not, to provide contradictories for all his propositions, the pairing of (2) and (8), along with the two just mentioned, being all that is needed to supplement the *A–O* and *E–I* oppositions of the traditional scheme.

A word should be said of De Morgan's symbolism, at which he tinkered a good deal without ever quite achieving finality. Having tried

[1] p. 2. [2] pp. 156-7.

and abandoned the systems of diacritical marks employed in *Syllogism I* and *Formal Logic*, he confined himself, after his second paper, to variations on the 'spicular' notation, which had there excited Hamilton's derision.[1] Though versatile enough in its way, and superior to Hamilton's in compactness and ease of printing, it harbours ambiguities in practice, and perhaps blinded its author to weaknesses in his notion of distribution which he might otherwise have been acute enough to detect. The spicula (or bracket) is turned inwards to indicate that the term it accompanies is distributed, and outwards to show that it is not. A dot between the brackets marks a negative proposition (though *not* the denial of the corresponding form without dots). Two dots cancel one another. Table *B* above may thus be written:

C.	(1) *X*))*Y*	(5) *X*()*Y*
	(2) *X*((*Y*	(6) *X*)(*Y*
	(3) *X*).(*Y*	(7) *X*(.(*Y*
	(4) *X*(.)*Y*	(8) *X*).)*Y*

Subject, again, to the rules of distribution, these forms can be converted by merely reading them backwards. 'Contraversion' (or obversion) proceeds by replacing a term by its contrary, while changing both its distribution and the quality of the proposition, i.e., reversing the bracket and adding or subtracting a dot. 'All *X*s are *Y*s' [*X*))*Y*] becomes, in turn, 'No *X*s are *y*s' [*X*).(*y*], 'Some *x*s are all *y*s' [*x*((*y*], and 'Everything is either *x* or *Y*' [*x*(.)*Y*]. Each of the eight propositions can thus be written in four different ways, making 32 forms in all.

Armed with this apparatus, De Morgan is able to give a clear and symmetrical account of syllogistic reasoning involving either singular propositions (unit-syllogisms), or collections of these ('cumular' forms). Four basic patterns of syllogism emerge, namely:

(1)))))))	(3) ((() ()
(2) ())) ()	(4) (( )) ().

Since the three terms, *X*, *Y* and *Z*, and their negative counterparts, can be taken in threes, one from each pair, in eight different combinations, their application to each pattern yields 32 valid syllogisms, half of which have two universal premisses, and eight a universal conclusion.[2] There are similarly 32 invalid forms, also generated from four archetypes, which violate the rule that either both premisses should be universal, or, if only one is, that the middle term should be distributed once. Subject to these conditions, and arranging the premisses (as can always be done) with minor term first and major term last, inference is obtained by simply erasing the middle term and its attendant spiculae: *X*((*Y* and *Y*()*Z* yield *X*()*Z*.

[1] The two notations are compared on pp. 35, 158.

[2] pp. 160–1.

In comparison with the traditional system, De Morgan's can be seen to have several advantages. The distribution of each term being shown throughout, conversion *per accidens* becomes unnecessary; distinctions of figure serve no purpose; and redundant forms, such as 'No *Y*s are *X*s' and 'Some *Y*s are *X*s', can be readily eliminated. A complication arises, however, in that, owing to the indefinite meaning of 'some', universal propositions leave the distribution of one term undecided. 'All *X*s are *Y*s' is consistent equally with some or all of the *Y*s being *X*s. To eliminate this 'terminal ambiguity', De Morgan conjoins his elementary forms into 'complex propositions', in which the various possibilities are distinctly set forth.[1] There are six of these, and their contradictories are disjunctions of the contradictories of their constituents—a principle also employed in his treatment of complex terms, and which has since been generally, if not quite justly, commemorated as 'De Morgan's rule'.[2]

Reference has already been made to Hamilton's system, with its eight fully quantified forms, and to De Morgan's efforts to mend it by substituting the 'exemplar' readings, 'any one' and 'some one', for the 'cumular' quantifiers, 'all' and 'some'. This also generates eight forms, which differ chiefly in that Hamilton's objectionable interpretations of *X*)(*Y* and *X*(.)*Y* are now rendered 'Any one *X* is any one *Y*' and 'Some one *X* is not some one *Y*', which do form a contradictory pair. 36 syllogisms result, the same number as in Hamilton's scheme, but unblemished by the errors he fell into, through neglect of the ambiguities of 'all', 'any', 'every' and 'some'. The exemplar system is asserted to be an extension of the type of reasoning employed by Euclid, and, if the truth were known, by Aristotle himself.[3]

De Morgan was a friend to other forms of reasoning giving inference of the syllogistic type, but despised or ignored by orthodox logicians, due to want of conformity with their one standard model. His development of the numerically definite syllogism is one example, and others may be found in his discussion of syllogisms of undecided assertion,[4] and of transposed quantity.[5] In the one, a premiss expressing indecision about something transfers the doubt to the conclusion; in the other, the quantity in one premiss is transposed into the other, as in: 'Some *X*s are not *Y*s; for every *X* there is a *Y* which is *Z*'; from which it follows, though not by an Aristotelian route, that 'Some *Z*s are not *X*s'.

More important than these is his recognition that the 'is' of identity in the traditional syllogism performs its function only in virtue of possessing the more general properties of being transitive and convertible (or symmetrical), and hence that any other relation similarly endowed would serve equally well. Inconvertible copulae require the introduction

[1] pp. 124, 165. [2] pp. 119, 182. [3] pp. 289 ff. [4] pp. 302–3.
[5] pp. 242–6.

of converse relations, but once this is allowed for, many other kinds of argument, hitherto stigmatized as 'material', can be brought under logical control. It is no great step from this to a formalization of the ordinary copula, as but a special case of the judgment that 'there is the probability α that X is in the relation L to Y'. A pair of such propositions, with a middle term in common, yield a joint probability that X and Z stand in the composite relation L of M, formed by uniting the two.[1]

Consideration of such complexes already belongs to the 'subjective' logic of second intentions, in which terms stand for classes or attributes, both of which may be formed from others of their kind by taking the logical sums or products, as the case may be (aggregation and composition). Aggregation of attributes, or, more generally, classes, increases the extension; composition of classes, or, more generally, attributes, the intension (comprehension) of the resultant complex term.[2]

De Morgan's analyses of complex terms and their contraries lead him to some interestingly archaic versions of theorems familiar, in another guise, to students of elementary propositional logic; for example, that the contradictory of 'X and Y or x and y' is 'x and Y or X and y'; that if anything that is X or Y is Z, then anything that is X is, but not anything that is W or X or Y—and so on.[3] His treatment of the matter is somewhat perplexed, however, by his attempt to run extension and intension, of both classes and attributes, in double harness throughout, as the 'mathematical and metaphysical sides of logic'. The distinction between the two—between class logic and attribute logic—itself turns on the interpretation given to a more ultimate system, that of 'onymatic' relationship among terms considered purely as terms. At this level (which is that of the older logic), the only question that arises is whether a pair of terms (XY, Xy, xY or xy) have, or have not, joint application to some objects or other. When they do, a particular proposition results; when not, a universal; and, as usual, there are eight possibilities in this regard. Into such a system, quantity does not enter, and inference is dependent solely on the fact that concomitancy of application is a transitive affair.[4] Once it is assumed that the terms apply to individual objects, the objective, or 'arithmetical' interpretation follows; when classes are the subject-matter, it is the 'mathematical' version of the subjective view that results; and when attributes are in question, it is the equally subjective 'metaphysical' view. In the one case, the relations are those of class-inclusion and exclusion; in the other, of the composition or decomposition of attributes. Two mixed readings,[5] the 'physical', in which an attribute is predicated of the whole of a class, and the 'contraphysical', in which the class is alleged to

[1] pp. 80, 218. [2] pp. 104 f., 182. [3] pp. 182, 202, 268. [4] pp. 188, 304 f. [5] pp. 96 ff.

harbour an attribute, do not get much further notice; and even of the main classification it may be felt that it does not succeed too well. At all events, it has not gained acceptance, any more than has the elaborate system of nomenclature[1] devised to express the various possible relationships between classes, or attributes, on which the syllogisms, in either *genre*, depend. The fact is, that the logic of intension, whether applied to individuals, classes or attributes, turns out to be too amorphous to yield very much to any purely mechanical line of attack. In particular, the subdivision of an attribute into its components does not terminate in individuals, as it does with classes, so that the attempt to make the 'metaphysical' reading of terms into a sort of mirror-image, parallel in all respects with the 'mathematical' reading, inevitably comes to grief. De Morgan, to his credit, recognized the difficulty, though he underrated its importance.[2] The later development of logic has steered clear of it, by concentrating almost entirely on the extensional viewpoint, and so has had comparatively little to learn from him here.

Altogether more successful is his treatment of relations. In this area, he was the first to penetrate where many others have followed, and, as he predicted, their labours have done much to improve understanding of the logical foundations of mathematics. De Morgan's own motive for enquiry lay in the desire to obtain a more abstract view of syllogistic reasoning, and to provide a general rubric from which the Aristotelian forms, and many others, could be derived. These aims are now outmoded; but the theorems he established *en route* are still of fundamental importance, though no longer expressed in his again rather makeshift symbolism.

In that symbolism, X and Y stand for singular terms, and L, M, N for relations. $X..LY$ signifies the assertion that X is an L of Y (e.g., a lover of Y, though the relation may, of course, be a transitive one); $X.LY$ denies this; $X..lY$ asserts the contrary relation; while $Y..L^{-1}X$ gives the converse, which may be the same, in which case the relation is convertible. $X..LMY$ informs us that X is an L of an M of Y—the notion of a combined relation (or relative product); L alone stands (with systematic ambiguity) for that which has the relation, as well as the relation itself; and LY, similarly, for any X having that relation to Y. For syllogistic purposes, quantification of the relation is also needed, and LM' stands accordingly for an L of every M, L, M for an L of only (or none but) Ms, L, M' for an L of every M and none but Ms, and so on.

Given these conventions, De Morgan proceeds to state a number of equivalences, as, for example, that the contrary of the converse is the converse of the contrary—not (L^{-1}) is l^{-1}—and that a quantified compound relation, LM' or L,M, is identical with that formed from the

[1] pp. 107 f., 123 f. [2] pp. 97, 104 f., 200.

contraries of its components by altering and shifting the sign of quantity (*l,m* or *lm'*). He gives rules for finding the contraries and converses of compound relations, tabulating the results,[1] and discusses the situation where one relation is 'contained in', or implies, another (symbolized by *L*))*M*). In this connexion he proves what he calls 'theorem *K*',[2] viz. that if *LM*))*N*, then $L^{-1}n$))*m* and nM^{-1}))*l*: if every master of a parent is a superior, then every servant of an inferior is a non-parent, and every inferior of a child a non-master. He goes on to notice that a relation may be symmetrical without necessarily being exclusively reflexive, and that a transitive relation has a transitive converse, but not necessarily a transitive contrary. A further table summarizes the relations of implication between transitive relations, and prepares the way for a treatment of the relational syllogism, in which figure regains its importance, though not in the old way.[3] From this, in turn, the quantified propositions and syllogisms of the common system are derived, and De Morgan's claim to have set them on a more general foundation is seen to be justified. He might, indeed, have claimed more, since his principles could equally have been extended to inferences involving doubly or multiply quantified propositions, of the type later studied by Peirce, Mitchell and Johnson. But this was beyond him. His preoccupation with syllogism did not delude him as to its importance in everyday reasoning; but it did set limits to his own perception of what his logic could do.

De Morgan is not the easiest of writers to summarize, and so slight a sketch as the foregoing can give little idea of the powers that led Jevons to describe his Cambridge memoirs as 'a great treatise on logic', and Peirce, in a moment of enthusiasm, to call him 'the greatest formal logician that ever lived'. That verdict—so far as it rests upon evidence—must be justified from the text. The assembly of his treatise, a hundred years late, can hardly be expected to do so much for what was always a minority view. But it can at least hope to ensure henceforward that he is no longer treated merely as the author of a theorem he did not invent, and that—to borrow from Peirce again—some 'decent semblance of justice' will at last be done to his name.

EDITORIAL NOTE

De Morgan was in the habit of annotating his writings after publication, and sometimes used more than one offprint to do so. Amended versions of almost all the papers in this volume are to be found in the University

[1] p. 224. [2] pp. 186 f., 224. [3] pp. 231 ff.

of London library, and a few others at University College. Most of this extra matter has been incorporated in the text, its occurrence being marked by bold square brackets. The printed amendments added to some of the papers have also been silently inserted in their appropriate place.

I am indebted to the Librarians of both the above-mentioned institutions for access to these documents, and other unpublished material. I am also under obligations to Dr P. S. Ardal, Dr G. E. Davie and Mr R. H. Stoothoff, all of Edinburgh University, who have given me the benefit of their advice.

SELECT BIBLIOGRAPHY

Mrs De Morgan's *Memoir* of her husband contains an extensive, though not complete, list of his writings. Secondary sources worth mention include the following:

BAIN, A. *Logic: Part I, Deduction* (1870).
BAYNES, T. S. *Essay on the New Analytic of Logical Forms* (1850).
BEDNAROWSKI, W. 'Hamilton's Quantification of the Predicate'. *Arist. Soc. Proc.*, 1955–6.
COUTURAT, L. *La logique de Leibniz* (1901).
DE MORGAN, S. E. *Memoir of Augustus De Morgan* (1882).
GARDNER, M. *Logic Machines and Diagrams* (1958).
GEACH, P. T. *Reference and Generality* (1962).
GRAVES, H. P. *Life of Sir William Rowan Hamilton*, vol. III (1889).
HALSTED, G. B. 'De Morgan as Logician'. *J. of Specul. Phil.*, 1884.
JØRGENSEN, J. *Treatise of Formal Logic*, vol. I (1931).
KEYNES, J. N. *Formal Logic*, 4th edn (1906).
KNEALE, W. & M. *Development of Logic* (1962).
LADD-FRANKLIN, C. 'Some Proposed Reforms in Common Logic'. *Mind*, 1890.
LEWIS, C. I. *Survey of Symbolic Logic* (1918).
LIARD, L. *Les logiciens anglais contemporains* (1907).
MACFARLANE, A. *Ten British Mathematicians* (1916).
MANSEL, H. L. *Letters, Lectures and Reviews* (1873).
PASSMORE, J. *100 Years of Philosophy* (1957).
PEIRCE, C. S. *Collected Papers* (1931–5).
PRIOR, A. N. *Formal Logic*, 2nd edn (1962).
SHEARMAN, A. T. *Development of Symbolic Logic* (1906).
SPALDING, W. *Introduction to Logical Science* (1857).
THOMSON, W. *Outline of the Necessary Laws of Thought*, 2nd edn (1849).
VENN, J. *Symbolic Logic* (1881).

ON THE SYLLOGISM: I

On the Structure of the Syllogism, [and on the Application of the Theory of Probabilities to Questions of Argument and Authority][1]

[Read 9 November 1846]

Since the time when the Aristotelian syllogism ceased to be regarded as an all-sufficient instrument of inquiry, it has remained precisely in the state in which those who are called the *schoolmen* left it. I have never heard[2] of any attempt to ascertain whether the forms which his followers derived from the writings of the great master were the perfection of system and simplicity which they were supposed to be. The uninquiring adherence of all writers on logic to the model of the middle ages, proves one of two things: either that the model is human perfection, or that the authority of the ancients has been followed as of course in the forms of logic long after it has been abandoned in every other part. With such an alternative, it is not presumption to venture upon the examination: and this is the more apparent when we consider that the general impression among writers seems to be that there cannot exist *any* other theory of the syllogism except that derived from Aristotle. If another can be produced, which is but self-consistent, true, and comprehensive, the tacit assertion of all writers is overthrown, whether that system be or be not judged superior to the one handed down.

I here venture to propose a derivation and classification of the forms of the syllogism, differing very widely from that in use.

I. On the meaning of the simple term

A term, or name, is merely the word which it is lawful to apply to any one of a collection of objects of thought: and, in the language of Aristotle, that name may be *predicated* of each of those objects. He uses this word predicate only as 'that which *can* be said of.' When in later times the negative proposition 'X is not Y' was said to have Y for its *predicate*, the word ought to have been *non-predicate*, or some

[1] [An additional paper, independent of the first, and here omitted.—Ed.]

[2] See the Addition to this paper [p. 17].

equivalent. The proper predicate is not-*Y*, which I shall call the *contrary* of *Y*.

When we use a term, such as 'man,' we predicate, in Aristotle's sense of the word, of every individual *which the notion can suggest*, of John, Thomas, William, &c. If we extend the word, and allow *Y* to be called the predicate of '*X* is *not* *Y*,' we must then affirm that the word 'man' predicates of *every* object of thought, either affirmatively or negatively: affirmatively of John or Thomas, negatively of a certain tree, or quadruped, or book. Every name then, in this sense, predicates of every thing: '*X* is either *Y* or not-*Y*' is a proposition of universal identity.

The express introduction and consideration of contraries ought, I think, to have followed the extension of the word predicate. Aristotle rejects and then admits: not-man, he says, is not a name; and then he calls it an *aorist* name, which can be predicated both of existent and non-existent things. I deny the justice of this distinction, for two reasons.

Names in logic are used subjectively; they are the representations of the notion in the mind. Now *man* and *not-man* are equally the names of things which, objectively speaking, are non-existent. *Not-man*, Aristotle would say, is a name which can be predicated of the speaking bird and the singing tree in the eastern fable: but surely, with as much justice, *man* may be predicated of the Shakespeare who wrote Paradise Lost, or the Caesar who conquered Darius.

In the next place, it is not true that the aorist or indefinite character of the mere contrary actually exists in the use which we make of language. Writers on logic, it is true, do not find elbow-room enough in anything less than the whole universe of possible conceptions: but the universe of a particular assertion or argument may be limited in any matter expressed or understood. And this without limitation or alteration of any one rule of logic. Let every one of the possible points of space have one or more of the names *X*, *Y*, &c.: then if we can say, 'No *X* is *Y*,' of course we can say 'No *Y* is *X*.' But this is equally true if, by an understanding to that effect, the universe of our proposition be one square described in a certain plane. Divide the points of this square into *X*s and not-*X*s, and the not-*X* is no more an aorist term than the *X*.

By not dwelling upon this power of making what we may properly (inventing a new technical name) call the *universe* of a proposition, or of a name, matter of express definition, all rules remaining the same, writers on logic deprive themselves of much useful illustration. And, more than this, they give an indefinite negative character to the *contrary*, as Aristotle did when he said that not-man was not the name of anything. Let the universe in question be 'man:' then *Briton* and *alien* are simple contraries; alien has no meaning of definition except not-Briton. But we cannot say that either term is positive or negative, except correlatively. As to a claim of right to be considered a prisoner of war, for instance, alien is the positive term, and Briton the negative one. We separate formal logic from language, if we refuse to admit this. In many cases, the language has the term which signifies the contrary, and wants the direct term: as in the word *parallels*, for example. To this day the word *intersectors* has not found its way into the idiom of geometry. In one case we give a name to the thing of course, and define the exception by means of a contrary: in another we find it more convenient to reverse the process. I hold that the system of formal logic is not well fitted to our mode of using language, until the rules of direct and contrary terms are associated: the words direct and contrary being merely correlative. Those who teach Algebra know how difficult it is to make the student fully aware that a may be the negative quantity, and $-a$ the positive one. There is a want of the similar perception in regard to direct and contrary terms.

Throughout this paper, I shall use the small letters x, y, z, &c. for names contrary to those represented by the capitals X, Y, Z, &c. Thus 'every thing *in the universe* is either X or x,' 'No X is x,' &c. are identical propositions.

II. On the simple proposition

There is no need to dwell on the usual matters given as to the distinction of universal and particular, or of positive and negative. But, I think it cannot be denied, that the distinctions may, for logical purposes, be considered as accidents of language. Any proposition which is either of the four in one language, may be either of the others in another. Our language has, say the names X and Y, and suppose that 'Every X is Y' is true. Another language translates X by X', but has no term for Y, but only y' for its contrary; the proposition is then 'No X' is y'.' In a third language Xs have no specific name; they appear but as individuals of the name X'': the proposition is then 'Some X''s are Y''s.' But if the last language had only possessed the name y'', it would have been 'Some X''s are not y''s.'

Very often, having established such a proposition as 'Some Xs are Ys,' we, for that reason, distinguish *those* Xs by a separate name, Z: and then we have '*Every* Z is Y.' If language were copious enough, particular propositions would seldom occur: and the idioms of every tongue are probably influenced by its power of supplying universal terms, or of converting particulars into the form of universals.

I shall use, as is usual, the letters A and E to signify positive and negative universals: and I and O for the corresponding particulars: but with a modification presently noticed. I shall also use the following notation, without which I should hardly have had patience for the many hundreds of cases which this paper has required.

$P)Q$	signifies	Every P is Q.
$P.Q$	......	No P is Q.
PQ	......	Some Ps are Qs.
$P{:}Q$	......	Some Ps are not Qs.

I have taken for the convertible propositions, the symbols $P.Q$ and PQ, which the algebraist is accustomed to consider as identical with $Q.P$ and QP: the same thing is true under these meanings. But $P)Q$ and $P{:}Q$, which are also used in arithmetic and algebra, convey no idea of convertibility.

All expressions that have any meaning can of course be reduced to one of these forms. Aristotle denies this, and divides all expression into significative and enunciative, meaning by the latter that in which there is truth or falsehood. Thus prayer, he says, is speech, but neither true nor false. This is surely not correct:—*Deliver us from evil* may be either 'To be delivered from evil is our prayer,' or 'We are of those who pray to be delivered from evil,' or 'Evil is a thing we pray to be delivered from.' Or, as the text, it would be 'Deliver us from evil, is the passage on which I mean to comment:' and the sermon would probably give all the enunciations above. In a request, command, inquiry, or announcement, the tone[1] of voice predicates.

In classifying all possible predications by means of two names Y and X, their contraries must be included. We must therefore consider all the relations that may exist between Y and X, X and y, y and x, x and Y. Between each of these there are six modes of enunciation: thus between P and Q we have

$$\underset{1}{P)Q},\quad \underset{2}{Q)P},\quad \underset{3}{P.Q = Q.P},\quad \underset{4}{PQ = QP},\quad \underset{5}{P{:}Q}\quad \underset{6}{Q{:}P}$$

But it will be best to arrange these by contradictories, or propositions one of which must be true and the other false: as $P)Q$ and $P{:}Q$, $Q)P$ and $Q{:}P$, $P.Q$ and PQ. These six modes applied to each of the four variations of subjects, give twenty-four varieties, which are reducible to eight, being identical three and three, as follows:

$$\begin{array}{lcl} X)Y = X.y = y)x & \qquad & X.Y = X)y = Y)x \\ X{:}Y = Xy = y{:}x & & XY = X{:}y = Y{:}x \\ Y)X = Y.x = x)y & & x.y = x)Y = y)X \\ Y{:}X = Yx = x{:}y & & xy = x{:}Y = y{:}X \end{array}$$

Though the use of the great and small letters may suit the eye, these

[1] To call a person by his name is a proposition, perhaps more. There is certainly the full meaning of a syllogism in it. When a person calls—John! no one can say that any part of the following is not implied: 'John is the person I want to speak to; you are John; therefore, you are the person I want to speak to.' The least that can be said is, that he states the premises, and leaves John to draw the conclusion.

lines should be read thus: 'Every *X* is *Y*' is identical with 'no *X* is not-*Y*,' and 'every not-*Y* is not-*X*,' and so on. These eight modes may all be derived from the four Aristotelian modes by changing both terms into contraries; which suggests the following notation:

$$
\begin{array}{llll}
(A) & X)Y & x)y = Y)X & (a) \\
(O) & X{:}Y & x{:}y = Y{:}X & (o) \\
(E) & X.Y & x.y & (e) \\
(I) & XY & xy & (i)
\end{array}
$$

This notation is established with reference to the order *XY*: the inversion of the order interchanges small and large letters.

The propositions (*A*) and (*O*) are the assertion and denial of complete inclusion of the first name in the second. And (*a*) and (*o*), the assertion and denial of complete inclusion of contrary in contrary, are, as appears, equivalent to the assertion and denial of complete inclusion of the second in the first. Again, (*E*) and (*I*) are the assertion and denial of complete non-interference, or that each name is wholly contained in the contrary of the other. But (*e*) and (*i*), the propositions which I propose to add to those commonly received, may be explained as follows:

The proposition (*i*) or *xy*, affirming that there are individuals in the universe of the proposition which are neither *Xs* or *Ys*, merely affirms that *X* and *Y* are *not* contraries, and do not between them contain the universe. The contradiction of this, (*e*), or *x.y*, affirming that it is false that there are any individuals which are neither *X* or *Y*, might seem at first sight to declare that *X* and *Y* *are* contraries. But it is not so, since the preceding is perfectly consistent with there being individuals which are both *Xs* and *Ys*. In fact, to express that *X* and *Y* are contraries we must have both *x.y* and *X.Y*.

The following tables show the relations of these propositions.

	Denies	Contains or is contained in	Can exist with or without		Denies	Contains or is contained in	Can exist with or without
A	*OEe*	*Ii*	*ao*	*E*	*IAa*	*Oo*	*ei*
O	*A*	*Ee*	*Iaio*	*I*	*E*	*Aa*	*Oeio*
a	*oeE*	*Ii*	*AO*	*e*	*iaA*	*Oo*	*EI*
o	*a*	*Ee*	*iAIO*	*i*	*e*	*Aa*	*oEIO*

Or each universal proposition denies, besides its own contradictory, the two universals of a different name; contains both particulars of the same name; and is independent of the other universal of the same name and its contradictory. Each particular proposition denies only its own contradictory; is contained in both the universals of the same name; and is independent of either of the other three particulars, as well as of the other universal (not its own contradictory) of a contrary name.

It is usual in modern works to say that a term which is universally spoken of is *distributed.* But in truth every proposition distributes, wholly or partially, among the individuals of the predicate, or of its contrary. It will be sufficient to call a term universal or particular, according to the manner in which it is spoken of. It will then be found that every proposition speaks in different ways of each term and its contrary; making one particular or universal, according as the other is universal or particular. The manner in which the subject is spoken of is expressed; as to the predicate, it is universal in negatives but particular in affirmatives. And of the two terms and their contraries, each proposition speaks universally of two, and particularly of two.

Let *S* signify that the subject is changed into its contrary, *P*, the same of the predicate. Let *C* signify that the copula is changed, from positive to negative, or *vice versa.* Let *T* denote transformation or interchange of subject and predicate: to avoid confusion, either this must be done last, or the original subject and predicate are to retain those names after the transformation. Then we have the following tables, *L* standing for letting the proposition remain unaltered:

L	*T*	*SP*	*SPT*	*L*
PC	*SCT*	*SC*	*PCT*	*PC*

P	*PT*	*S*	*ST*	*P*
C	*SPCT*	*SPC*	*CT*	*C*

Changes and combinations of changes that are written under one another, are *in all cases* of the same effect: thus by writing *PT* and *SPCT* under one another, I mean that change of subject, predicate, copula, and order, are always of the same effect as change of predicate and order only. Thus the operation *SPTC* performed upon *X*)*Y* gives *y.x*. But *PT* only gives *y*)*X* and *y.x* = *y*)*X*, as appears above. Further, when a *single* line separates two vertical pairs, the two pairs are identical when performed upon *inconvertible* propositions: when a *double* line, the same with respect to *convertible* propositions. Thus, as to convertible propositions, *L*, *PC*, *T*, *SCT* are all of the same effect: as to inconvertible propositions, *T*, *SCT*, *SP* and *SC*.

There is a point which develops itself very strongly when we come to consider the transformations upon instances; namely, the distinction between the assertion of a proposition subjectively and objectively. The former mode is that which is always presumed: but in actual use of logic the distinction must be drawn.

When we say, Every *X* is *Y*, as a proposition with meaning, and with or without truth as the case may be, we treat neither *X* nor *Y* as having any other existence except that which our minds give them: but we imply that if *X* have any such other existence, so has *Y*. But the syllogism '*X*)*Y* and *Y*)*Z* therefore *X*)*Z*' is not valid merely by understanding *X* and *Z* to be taken in the conclusion as in the premises. The middle term *must exist*: not necessarily objectively, but it must have a positive existence. It is no syllogism to say that *X* is *Y*, if there be such a thing, and *Y* (if &c.) is *Z*; therefore *X* is *Z*. And yet there is no offence against any of the ordinary rules of logic: the middle term is strictly *middle*; it is '*Y*, on the condition that *Y* exists' in both. Thus 'Homer was a perfect poet (if ever there were one); a perfect poet (if &c.) is faultless in morals; therefore Homer was &c.' The premises will sometimes be admitted; but they do not prove the conclusion: the proper conclusion is a dilemma, 'Either Homer was faultless in morals, or there never was a perfect poet.' The existence here spoken of is objective: but the same thing applies to purely subjective cases. The terms of the conclusion may be conditional: but inference requires that the middle term should be unconditional. Every *X* (if ever *X* existed) is *Y*; every *Y* is *Z* (if ever *Z* existed): therefore every *X* (if ever *X* existed) is *Z* (if ever *Z* existed). This is a good syllogism: but *Y* is here absolute.

When the syllogism can be converted into another, having for its middle term the contrary of the first middle term, the same absolute existence must be claimed for the contrary. And here again I remind the reader that the absolute existence spoken of is existence within the *universe* of the propositions. Thus $X)Y$ and $Y)Z$ give $X)Z$, or $y)x$ and $z)y$ give $z)x$. A positive existence is then required both for *Y* and *y*. There is an extreme case; *y* may not exist, that is, *Y* may contain the universe; but then *Y* and *Z* are identical, and the conclusion $X)Z$ is identical with $X)Y$ and $z)x$ contains nothing.

Whatever sort of existence is spoken of is tacitly claimed for the terms of a proposition by the proposition itself: the refusal of this claim, or the denial by assertion of non-existence, being a distinct thing from denial by contradiction. A certain meadow (the universe of the proposition) is flooded during the hay-harvest: the proposition 'No part of the crop that was not flooded was not saved' (of the form $x.y$) means logically that all which was not flooded || was saved, that all which was not saved || was flooded, and that part may have been both flooded and saved. Some reflexion (for want of habit of dealing with triple negatives makes the proposition rather complicated) will shew that a person who is apt to think objectively of propositions, as all do who are not trained in logical considerations, is much more likely to require the insertion of the words (*if any*) in two places (||) than he would be if the proposition were presented in the more simple form, 'All the dry crop was saved.' Probably such a person would not require the conditional words here, merely because he would take it that the proposition asserts that some *was* dry: reserving the right to deny by non-existence if there were none.

I suppose it is hardly necessary to remark that, in propositions, asserted as true, the same sort of existence is claimed for both terms: for instance, that there is no objective first term with a subjective second one. In such a proposition as 'he is good' we may certainly say that 'good' by itself is a purely subjective notion; a state of the mind in regard to an external object. But good is not the term of the proposition; it is 'he (an external object) is one of these external objects to which the mind attaches the idea of good'. I can conceive opposition to this: what I say is that the opposition is not to me, but to the universal maxims of technical logic. For all writers admit that *YX* necessarily follows from *XY*: which cannot be if *Y* be a name of the state of the mind and *X* of an external object. Most of the Romans were brave; therefore some brave [men] were Romans. No hint is ever given by writers on logic of the necessity, previously to conversion, of attaching the subjective notion to an object.

III. On the quantity of propositions

The logical use of the word *some*, as merely 'more than none,' needs no further explanation. Exact knowledge of the extent of a proposition would consist in knowing, for instance in 'some *X*s are not *Y*s', both what proportion of the *X*s are spoken of, and what proportion exists between the whole number of *X*s and of *Y*s. The want of this information compels us to divide the exponents of our proportions into 0, more than 0 not necessarily 1, and 1. An algebraist learns to consider the distinction between 0 and quantity as identical, for many purposes, with that between one quantity and another: the logician must (all writers imply) keep the distinction between 0 and a, however small a may be, as sacred as that between 0 and $1 - a$: there being but the same form for the two cases. We shall now see that this matter has not been fully examined.

Inference must arise from bringing each two things which are to be compared into comparison with a third. Many comparisons may be made at once, but there must be this process in every one. When the comparison is that of identity, of *is* or *is not*, it can only be, in its ultimate or individual case, one of the two following;—'This *X* is a *Y*, this *Z* is the very same *Y*, therefore this *X* is this *Z*;' or else 'This *X* is a *Y*, this *Z* is not the very same *Y*, therefore this *X* is not this *Z*.' And collectively, it must be either 'Each of these *X*s is a *Y*; each of these *Y*s is a *Z*; therefore each of these *X*s is a *Z*;' or else 'Each of these *X*s is a *Y*, no one of these *Y*s is a *Z*, therefore no one of these *X*s is a *Z*.'

All that is essential then to a syllogism is that its premises shall mention a number of *Y*s, of each of which they shall affirm either that it is both *X* and *Z*, or that it is one and is not the other. The premises may mention more: but it is enough that this much can be picked out; and it is in this last process that inference consists.

Aristotle noticed but one way of being sure that the same *Y*s are spoken of in both premises: namely, by speaking of all of them in one at least. But this is only a case of the rule: for all that is necessary is *that more Ys in number than there exist separate Ys shall be spoken of in both premises together*. Having to make $m + n$ greater than unity, when neither m nor n is so, he admitted only that case in which one of the two m or n, *is* unity and the other is anything except 0. Here then are two syllogisms which ought to have appeared, but do not: and there are others;—

Most of the *Y*s are *X*s	Most of the *Y*s are *X*s
Most of the *Y*s are *Z*s	Most of the *Y*s are not *Z*s
∴ Some *X*s are *Z*s	∴ Some of the *X*s are not *Z*s.

And instead of most, or $\frac{1}{2} + a$, of the *Y*s, may be substituted any two fractions which have a sum greater than unity. If these fractions be m and n, then the *real* middle term is *at least* the fraction $m + n - 1$ of the *Y*s. It is not really even necessary that each *Y* should enter in one premise or the other: for more than the fraction $m + n - 1$ of the whole may be found in each.

And in truth it is this mode of syllogizing that we are frequently obliged to have recourse to; perhaps more often than not in our universal syllogisms. '*All* men are capable of some instruction; all who are capable of any instruction can learn to distinguish their right and left hands by name; therefore all men can learn to do so.' Let the word *all* in these two cases mean only *all but one*, and the books on logic tell us with one voice that the syllogism has particular premises, and *no conclusion can be drawn*. But in fact, idiots are capable of no instruction, many are deaf and dumb, some are without hands: and yet *a* conclusion is admissible. Here m and n are each very near to unity, and $m + n - 1$ is therefore near to unity. Some will say that this is a probable conclusion: that in the case of any one person it means there is the chance m that he can receive instruction, and n that one so gifted can be made to name his right and left hand: therefore $m \times n$ (very near unity) is the chance that this man can learn so much.

But I cannot see how in this instance the probability is anything but another sort of inference from the demonstrable conclusion of the syllogism, which must exist, under the premises given. Besides which, even if we admit the syllogism as only probable with regard to any one man, it is absolute and demonstrative in regard to the whole number of men with which it concludes.

This is not the only case in which the middle term need not enter universally: this however is matter for the next Section: see also the Addition [p. 17].[1]

[1] [Some paragraphs, on probability theory, are here omitted.—Ed.]

On the Syllogism: I

IV. On the syllogism

There is much that is elegant and instructive about the theory of the four figures of the syllogism, three of which belong to Aristotle. And the magic words *Barbara*, *Camestres*, etc. are models of notation, almost every letter of the moods in the three latter figures being a rule of direction. The following old epitaph on a schoolman selects, I think, one of the best parts of the system for ridicule:

Hic jacet magister noster
Qui disputavit bis aut ter
In *Barbara* et *Celarent*
Ita ut omnes admirarent
In *Fapesmo* et *Frisesomorum*
Orate pro animis eorum![1]

In proposing another system of classification, in connexion with the use of contraries, I remark, first, that the ordinary method has two points of redundancy. The distinct use of the two forms of a convertible proposition, *X.Y* and *Y.X*, *XY* and *YX*, is made for the system of figures, rather than the figures for it. It is desirable I think to confound them as much as possible; so that each may never fail to suggest the other. In the next place, if the use of contraries be introduced, every one of the twenty-four modes of predicating would claim admission into a system of figures, and their number would be increased to thirty-two.

Again, the first followers of Aristotle, in adopting the rule that no syllogism should be admitted in which the conclusion was not the strongest the premises would allow—in rejecting for instance '*X*)*Y* and *Y*)*Z* therefore *XZ*,' because *X*)*Z* also follows—did not adopt the equally obvious rule of admitting no syllogism in which a weaker premise would lead to as strong a conclusion. They retained, for instance, '*Y*)*X* and *Y*)*Z* therefore *XZ*', though *Y*)*X* and *YZ* would produce the same conclusion. Now I think it desirable to adopt the rule of producing the strongest conclusion with the weakest premises, not only because it will turn out that by so doing the number of forms is diminished, even when contraries are considered, but also because a better and clearer distinction is drawn between the necessary and the contingent.

I also drop the distinction of *minor* and *major* terms and premises. Aristotle meant them to apply only to affirmative propositions, in which the predicate includes the subject. But the use of them was extended, to the utter destruction of the meaning in negative propositions, or worse, to the danger of carrying a false meaning to the last

[1] [Quoted by Gabriel Naudé: *Sur les frères de la Rose-Croix*, Paris, 1623. Magister noster = D.D. Bis aut ter = (in American vernacular) 'he disputed a few'.—From *Syllogism VI.*]

named. The consequence of the distinction is that these four syllogisms,

	$X)Y$	$Z.Y$	$Y.Z$	$X)Y$
	$Z.Y$	$X)Y$	$X)Y$	$Y.Z$
	$Z.X$	$X.Z$	$X.Z$	$Z.X$
Figure	2	2	1	4
Name	*Camestres*	*Cesare*	*Celarent*	*Camenes*

which are identical in sense and effect, are made separate objects of study. In fact, as is known, all the figures are in the first, the fourth being occasionally brought into it by a reduction which deserves the name of *Barbara* in every case, and which the simplest use of contraries avoids.

For syllogisms I shall adopt such notation as

$$X)Y + Y)Z = X)Z.$$

Or if a weaker conclusion be taken,

$$X)Y + Y)Z > XZ.$$

As there are eight modes of predicating between X and Y, and between Y and Z, it follows that there are sixty-four combinations which may give conclusions. Of these, all but eight are distributable two and two into counterparts, in which X and Z are interchanged, everything else remaining the same; giving eight single, and twenty-eight pairs of counterparts. Of these, exactly half, (four single, and fourteen pairs) are wholly inconclusive. Of the conclusive cases, two single ones and two pairs are rejected, because as strong a conclusion can be obtained from a weaker premise. There remain two single ones and twelve pairs, to which a systematic classification is to be given. Instead of enumerating, I shall state a mode of deriving all the cases from a common principle.

Since every proposition is, but for accidents of language, a universal affirmative, as before noticed, it will follow that there are really no forms of syllogism except those in which the premises and conclusion are universal affirmatives, or can be made so by use of contraries and invention of subgeneric terms. Now the only universal affirmative syllogism is

$$X)Y + Y)Z = X)Z$$

considering the counterpart $Z)Y + Y)X = Z)X$ as identical in form. If we take universal affirmative premises only, we have one which will have a particular conclusion, with respect to the names X and Z,

$$Y)X + Y)Z = XZ,$$

which must be used in discovery of forms, (and will in fact give the two single syllogisms of this system) though it will only ultimately enter as

$Y)X + YZ = XZ$. Now if we change one or more of the terms X, Y, Z into their contraries, we have eight modes of transformation, according as we use

$$XZY, \quad XZy, \quad xzy, \quad xzY, \quad XzY, \quad Xzy, \quad xZY, \quad xZy.$$

First take the syllogisms

$$X)Y + Y)Z = X)Z \text{ and } XY + Y)Z = XZ;$$

the latter of which is only the first, with the premise $X)Y$ weakened, and would be reduced to the first form by inventing a subgeneric name for the Xs there spoken of. Apply each of these to the eight varieties just named, transforming premises and conclusion, when necessary, to one of the eight standard forms of predication:

$$X)Z \quad X{:}Z \quad Z)X \quad Z{:}X \quad X.Z \quad XZ \quad x.y \quad xz.$$

To each result I attach a letter of notation, derived from the nature of the conclusion, with letters subscript indicative of the premises. Thus A_{Aa} signifies a syllogism with a conclusion A derived from premises of the forms A and a. The order of reference is XY, ZY, XZ, the middle term being the predicate of both premises *in the references*.

Universal Syllogisms

First Form	*Transformation*	*Description*
$X)Y + Y)Z = X)Z$	$X)Y + Y)Z = X)Z$	A_{Aa}
$X)y + y)Z = X)Z$	$X.Y + z.y = X)Z$	A_{Ee}
$x)y + y)z = x)z$	$Y)X + Z)Y = Z)X$	a_{aA}
$x)Y + Y)z = x)z$	$x.y + Z.Y = Z)X$	a_{eE}
$X)Y + Y)z = X)z$	$X)Y + Z.Y = X.Z$	E_{AE}
$X)y + y)z = X)z$	$X.Y + Z)Y = X.Z$	E_{EA}
$x)Y + Y)Z = x)Z$	$x.y + Y)Z = x.z$	e_{ea}
$x)y + y)Z = x)Z$	$Y)X + z.y = x.z$	e_{ae}

Of these forms four are distinct and the others are their counterparts. Writing each with its counterpart, we have

$$A_{Aa} \text{ and } a_{aA}, \quad A_{Ee} \text{ and } a_{eE}, \quad E_{AE} \text{ and } E_{EA}, \quad e_{ea} \text{ and } e_{ae}.$$

Particular Syllogisms

First Form	*Transformation*	*Description*
$XY + Y)Z = XZ$	$XY + Y)Z = XZ$	I_{Ia}
$Xy + y)Z = XZ$	$X{:}Y + z.y = XZ$	I_{Oe}
$xy + y)z = xz$	$xy + Z)Y = xz$	i_{iA}
$xY + Y)z = xz$	$Y.X + Z.Y = xz$	i_{oE}
$XY + Y)z = Xz$	$XY + Z.Y = X{:}Z$	O_{IE}
$Xy + y)z = Xz$	$X{:}Y + Z)Y = X{:}Z$	O_{OA}
$xY + Y)Z = xZ$	$Y{:}X + Y)Z = Z{:}X$	o_{oa}
$xy + y)Z = xZ$	$xy + z.y = Z{:}X$	o_{ie}

But though the eight universal syllogisms are counterparts, two and two, they admit of another division into pairs, in each of which the terms are the *contraries* of those of the other. Thus A_{Aa} is connected with a_{aA} in this manner, and A_{Ee} with a_{eE}: and these are counterparts. And E_{AE} and e_{ae} and E_{EA} and e_{ea}, which are not counterparts, have the same connexion. The eight particular syllogisms, which contain no counterparts, are divisible into four pairs with the same connexion. Thus I_{Ia} is changed into i_{iA}, I_{Oe} into i_{oE}, O_{IE} into o_{ie}, and O_{OA} into o_{oa}. It is also worth notice that when the conclusion is negative, the premises are always of contradictory forms, and when positive, of consistent ones: and that the substitution of the contradictory *forms* in the premises is equivalent to that of contrary *terms* in the conclusion. Thus from $XY + Y)Z = XZ$; if we substitute contradictories in the premises, we have $X.Y + Y{:}Z$, the conclusion of which is xz.

Before proceeding further it may be worth while to endeavour to impress the notation upon the reader. The letters, *A, E, I, O*, have the well-known meanings, thus restricted, that they belong to a particular order of the terms, or a particular choice of subject and predicate. Thus, *X* and *Y* being the terms, in the order *XY*, or *X* being the subject and *Y* the predicate, the four capitals stand for $X)Y$, $X.Y$ ($=Y.X$), XY ($= YX$) and $X{:}Y$. And *a, e, i, o* stand for the same propositions when both subject and predicate are changed into contraries: that is, they stand for $x)y$, $x.y$ ($= y.x$), xy ($= yx$), $x{:}y$. In these last, system is sacrificed to simplicity in using $Y)X$ and $Y{:}X$ for $x)y$ and $x{:}y$. The following table shows what transformation takes place when the terms and orders are successively *XY, Xy, xy, xY, YX, yX, yx, Yx*.

XY	*Xy*	*xy*	*xY*	*YX*	*yX*	*yx*	*Yx*
A	*E*	*a*	*e*	*a*	*E*	*A*	*e*
O	*I*	*o*	*i*	*o*	*I*	*O*	*i*
a	*e*	*A*	*E*	*A*	*e*	*a*	*E*
o	*i*	*O*	*I*	*O*	*i*	*o*	*I*
E	*A*	*e*	*a*	*E*	*a*	*e*	*A*
I	*O*	*i*	*o*	*I*	*o*	*i*	*O*
e	*a*	*E*	*A*	*e*	*A*	*E*	*a*
i	*o*	*I*	*O*	*i*	*O*	*I*	*o*

Here we mean, for instance, that *E* of the order (*X, Y*) is the same thing as the *A* of (*X, y*) or the *e* of (*x, y*) &c.; or that $X.Y$, $X)y$ are the same. As to the *e* of (*x, y*) it is identically $X.Y$. The eight operations by which the transformations of headings are made are those which I have denoted by *L, P, SP, S, T, PT, SPT,* and *ST*, of which the simplest readings are

For inconvertibles	*L*	*P*	*T*	*S*	*T*	*S*	*L*	*P*,
For convertibles	*L*	*P*	*SP*	*S*	*L*	*P*	*SP*	*P*.

Taking the terms *XY, YZ, ZX*, for the premises and conclusion, and the order of reference *XY, ZY, XZ*, the notation given defines the syllogism.

Thus, valid or not, the syllogism O_{eA} can be nothing but $x.y + Z)Y = X{:}Z$. In turning the fundamental syllogism into the form $X)Y + Y)Z = X)Z$, I have altered Aristotle's order of the premises, which would give $Y)Z + X)Y = X)Z$. Reasoning direct from his *dictum de omni et nullo*, namely, that what is true or false of all is true or false of every some, it would seem natural first to ascertain the fact relating to the whole, and then to introduce the part which is to be considered. But in another point of view it may be more natural to reverse this order. If there be three boxes *P*, *Q*, and *R*, of which I want to ascertain by means of *Q* whether *P* will go into *R*, it seems to me more natural to try first whether *P* will go into *Q*, and then whether *Q* will go into *R*. But if the question be whether *R* will hold *P*, then perhaps it may be more natural to try first whether *R* will hold *Q*, and then whether *Q* will hold *P*. It must be mere matter of opinion which should be taken; and the idioms of the language which people speak produce the associations on which they will decide.

The syllogisms which we have got as yet, four universal and eight particular, contain all those of Aristotle. Six of them indeed are enough for this purpose: that is to say, every syllogism of Aristotle is either one of these six, or one of them with a premise converted or strengthened, or both. The six really distinct syllogisms of the old system, with the order *XZ* established in the conclusion, are as follows, with the scholastic names of the forms which they have or can be made to have:

A_{Aa}	$X)Y + Y)Z = X)Z$	*Barbara.*
I_{Ia}	$XY + Y)Z = XZ$	*Darii, Darapti, Disamis, Datisi, Bramantip, Dimaris.*
E_{AE}	$X)Y + Z.Y = X.Z$	*Celarent, Cesare, Camestres, Camenes.*
O_{IE}	$XY + Z.Y = X{:}Z$	*Ferio, Festino, Felapton, Feriso, Fesapo, Fresison.*
O_{OA}	$X{:}Y + Z)Y = X{:}Z$	*Baroko.*
O_{ao}	$Y)X + Y{:}Z = X{:}Z$	*Bokardo.*

If we wish to have a notation which neglects the premises, we may call these A, I, E, O_1, O_2, O_3, which may be separated into two connected sets, thus. The contradiction of a conclusion coupled with either premise must give the contradiction of the other premise. It will be found that if we call A, O_2, and O_3 *opponents*, and also E, I, and O_1, each syllogism can be produced from either of its two opponents, by coupling the denial of their conclusions with the affirmations of their premises.

The six new syllogisms, reduced to the same order, will be

$$\begin{array}{ll} A_{Ee} & X.Y + z.y = X)Z \\ i_{iA} & xy + Z)Y = xz \\ I_{Oe} & X{:}Y + z.y = XZ \\ i_{oE} & Y{:}X + Z.Y = xz \\ e_{ea} & x.y + Y)Z = x.z \\ O_{ei} & x.y + zy = X{:}Z. \end{array}$$

The correlation of these two sets is by no means simple. Before examining it, observe that an interchange of X and Z, though it alters A into a and O into o, does not alter E and I, nor e and i. The counterpart of a syllogism, made by this interchange, is represented by simply inverting the letters of the premises, and interchanging A and a, O and o, in the letters of the conclusion. Thus the counterpart of i_{oE} is i_{Eo}: that of A_{Ee} is a_{eE}. Now if we take the six Aristotelian syllogisms, and make all the changes, and tabulate the results, we shall have as follows:

XYZ	xYZ	xyZ	xyz	xYz	XYz	Xyz	XyZ
A_{Aa}	$\boldsymbol{e_{ae}}$	$\boldsymbol{e_{ae}}$	a_{aA}	$\boldsymbol{a_{eE}}$	E_{AE}	E_{EA}	$\boldsymbol{A_{Ee}}$
I_{Ia}	o_{oa}	$\boldsymbol{o_{ie}}$	$\boldsymbol{i_{iA}}$	$\boldsymbol{i_{oE}}$	O_{IE}	O_{OA}	$\boldsymbol{I_{Oe}}$
E_{AE}	$\boldsymbol{a_{eE}}$	a_{aA}	$\boldsymbol{e_{ae}}$	$\boldsymbol{e_{ea}}$	A_{Aa}	$\boldsymbol{A_{Ee}}$	E_{EA}
O_{IE}	$\boldsymbol{i_{oE}}$	$\boldsymbol{i_{iA}}$	$\boldsymbol{o_{ie}}$	o_{oa}	I_{Ia}	$\boldsymbol{I_{Oe}}$	O_{OA}
O_{OA}	$\boldsymbol{i_{iA}}$	$\boldsymbol{i_{oE}}$	o_{oa}	$\boldsymbol{o_{ie}}$	$\boldsymbol{I_{Oe}}$	I_{Ia}	O_{IE}
O_{ao}	$\boldsymbol{i_{Eo}}$	$\boldsymbol{i}_{Ai}$	o_{AO}	o_{EI}	I_{aI}	$\boldsymbol{I_{eO}}$	$\boldsymbol{O_{ei}}$

The syllogisms written under each heading[1] are those which that written under the first becomes, when the variation shown in the heading is made. Thus if X and Z be changed into x and z, O_{IE} becomes o_{oa}, or

$$XY + Z.Y = X{:}Z \text{ becomes } xY + z.Y = x{:}z, \text{ or } Y{:}X + Y)Z = Z{:}X.$$

The new syllogisms have their letters in Bold Italics. Each form, old or new, or its counterpart, occurs four times: but though the first column contains old syllogisms only, there is no column which contains none but new ones. So that it cannot be said that the new syllogisms are, on any one hypothesis, views of the old ones: though, in the column xyZ, five of them are so.

The following are the sets of opponents in the old and new system.

Old system	A_{Aa}	O_{OA}	O_{ao}	E_{AE}	O_{IE}	I_{Ia}
New system	A_{Ee}	I_{Oe}	i_{oE}	e_{ea}	O_{ei}	i_{iA}

But we have not yet closed our investigation; for we have to examine the remaining syllogism of universal premises, or $Y)X + Y)Z = XZ$. If we go through the cases, in the last order of headings, we shall find as follows.

[1] The order of the headings follows a recurring law, the next step of which would give XYZ again. If there be any *odd* number, n, of assertions, any one or more of which may be changed into its contrary, giving 2^n varieties, all the varieties may be gained as follows: write them in order, change the first, in that the second, in that the third, and so on to the end. Then go backwards with the same process, and then forwards and so on until 2^n have been made. Thus, if there were five, the changes would be made thus, 0 indicating no change, 0, 1, 2, 3, 4, 5, 4, 3, 2, 1, 2, 3, 4, 5, 4, 3, 2, 1, 2, &c. In the case of three, it is

0	1	2	3	2	1	2	3	2
XYZ	xYZ	xyZ	xyz	xYz	XYz	Xyz	XyZ	XYZ

First Form	Transformation	Description	Remarks
$Y)X + Y)Z = XZ$	$Y)X + Y)Z = XZ$	I_{aa}	Derived from I_{Ia}
$Y)x + Y)Z = xZ$	$Y.X + Y)Z = Z{:}X$	o_{Ea}	,, ,, o_{oa}
$y)x + y)Z = xZ$	$X)Y + y.z = Z{:}X$	o_{Ae}	,, ,, o_{ie}
$y)x + y)z = xz$	$X)Y + Z)Y = xz$	i_{AA}	Not yet obtained
$Y)x + Y)z = xz$	$Y.X + Y.Z = xz$	i_{EE}	Derived from i_{oE}
$Y)X + Y)z = Xz$	$Y)X + Y.Z = X{:}Z$	O_{aE}	,, ,, O_{IE}
$y)X + y)z = Xz$	$y.x + Z)Y = X{:}Z$	O_{eA}	,, ,, O_{ei}
$y)X + y)Z = XZ$	$y.x + y.z = XZ$	I_{ee}	Not yet obtained.

The derivation here mentioned is merely strengthening a premise. We thus obtain the only two remaining forms

$$i_{AA} \quad X)Y + Z)Y = xz \quad | \quad I_{ee} \quad y.x + y.z = XZ.$$

These cannot be derived from the twelve previously established by strengthening a premise, though their equivalents (the other six) can. These two last syllogisms differ from all the rest in having no counterparts, and may therefore be called *single* syllogisms.

The old rules are of course true as to the old syllogisms: but most of them are inapplicable to the new ones. Particular premises, indeed, never gave a conclusion, as yet: but premises both negative may, and in the case of i_{AA}, the middle term is universal in neither premise. Again, both premises may be negative, and may give a positive form of conclusion. The following rules, however, will be found to hold good.

From premises both particular, nothing follows. The middle term cannot be particular in both, except in i_{AA}: nor can its contrary be universal in both, except in I_{ee}. One negative premise always yields a negative conclusion, and two negative premises an affirmative. When one premise is particular, the conclusion is particular. When *e* is in the premises the conclusion is never in *i*.

I now take the two cases in which particular premises may give a conclusion: namely

$$I_{II} \quad XY + ZY = XZ \qquad XY + Y{:}Z = X{:}Z \quad O_{Io}$$

on the suppositions that the *Y*s mentioned in both premises are in number more than all the *Y*s. If Y_1 and Y_2 stand for the fractions of the whole number of *Y*s mentioned or implied in the two premises, and y_1 and y_2 for the fractions of the *y*s implied or mentioned, we shall by a repetition of the process on $YX + YZ = XZ$ (the other being obtained

Designation	Syllogism	Condition of its validity
I_{II}	$YX + YZ = XZ$	$Y_1 + Y_2$ greater than 1
O_{Io}	$YX + Y{:}Z = X{:}Z$	,, ,, ,,
i_{oo}	$Y{:}X + Y{:}Z = xz$	,, ,, ,,
O_{oi}	$X{:}Y + yz = X{:}Z$	$y_1 + y_2$ greater than 1
i_{ii}	$yx + yz = xz$	,, ,, ,,
O_{oi}	$X{:}Y + yz = X{:}Z$	,, ,, ,,
I_{oo}	$X{:}Y + Z{:}Y = XZ$	,, ,, ,,

in the course of the process) arrive at the following results or their counterparts: remembering that $Y_1 + Y_2$ is greater or less than 1, according as $y_1 + y_2$ is less or greater. (See the Addition [below].)

There are many remarks to be made on the demonstrative connexion of the parts of this system with one another, and on the explanations in general language of the new varieties of syllogism. The length of this paper, however, is a sufficient reason for stopping here.[1]

Addition [*Dated* 27 *February* 1847]

Since this paper was written, I found that the whole theory of the syllogism might be deduced from the consideration of propositions in a form in which *definite quantity* of assertion is given both to the subject and the predicate of a proposition. I had committed this view to paper, when I learned from Sir William Hamilton of Edinburgh, that he had for some time past publicly taught a theory of the syllogism differing in detail and extent from that of Aristotle. From the prospectus of an intended work on logic, which Sir William Hamilton has recently issued, at the end of his edition of Reid, as well as from information conveyed to me by himself in general terms, I should suppose it will be found that I have been more or less anticipated in the view just alluded to. To what extent this has been the case, I cannot now ascertain: but the book of which the prospectus just named is an announcement, will settle that question. From the extraordinary extent of its author's learning in the history of philosophy, and the acuteness of his written articles on the subject, all who are interested in logic will look for its appearance with more than common interest.

The footing upon which we should be glad to put propositions, if our knowledge were minute enough, is the following. We should state how many individuals there are under the names which are the subject, and predicate, and of how many of each we mean to speak. Thus, instead of 'Some *X*s are *Y*s,' it would be, 'Every one of *a* specified *X*s is one or other of *b* specified *Y*s.' And the negative form would be as in 'No one of

[1] [In the memoir in the Cambridge Transactions, I gave the first account of what has since grown into Chapters IV, V, VIII, and X, of [*Formal Logic*]. With reference to the subject of chapter V, I may note the following defects of that memoir: 1. That only one arrangement of *X* and *Z* as premises being taken, only half the system is given, and many correlative arrangements are not obtained (see *F.L.*, p. 140). 2. That owing to my not seeing distinctly that each universal proposition has *two* weakened forms, the syllogisms *A,A'I'* and *E'E'I,* are considered as a class apart. 3. That much of the power of forming easy rules is not gained, by the order of reference being made *XY, ZY, XZ*, instead of *XY, YZ, XZ*. The former appears at first the more natural order, and is certainly more easily described; namely, to refer each of the concluding terms to the middle term, with which both are compared; but the other is by an immense deal more convenient in its results, as I think I have shown.
—from *Formal Logic*, pp. 324–5.]

a specified *X*s is any one of *b* specified *Y*s.' If propositions be stated in this way, the conditions of inference are as follows. Let the *effective number* of a proposition be the number of mentioned cases of the *subject*, if it be an affirmative proposition, or of the *middle term*, if it be a negative proposition. Thus, 'Each one of 50 *X*s is one or other of 70 *Y*s,' is a proposition, the effective number of which is always 50. But 'No one of 50 *X*s is any one of 70 *Y*s' is a proposition, the effective number of which is 50 or 70, according as *X* or *Y* is the middle term of the syllogism in which it is to be used. Then two propositions, each of two terms, and having one term in common, admit an inference when (1) They are not both negative. (2) The sum of the effective numbers of the two premises is greater than the whole number of existing cases of the middle term. And the excess of that sum above the number of cases of the middle term is the number of the cases in the affirmative premise which are the subjects of inference. Thus, if there be 100 *Y*s, and we can say that each of 50 *X*s is one or other of 80 *Y*s, and that no one of 20 *Z*s is any one of 60 *Y*s;—the effective numbers are 50 and 60. And 50 + 60 exceeding 100 by 10, there are 10 *X*s of which we may affirm that no one of them is any one of the 20 *Z*s mentioned.

The following brief summary will enable the reader to observe the complete deduction of all the Aristotelian forms, and the various modes of inference from *specific particulars*, of which a short account has already been given.

Let a be the whole number of *X*s; and t the number specified in the premise. Let c be the whole number of *Z*s; and w the number specified in the premise. Let b be the whole number of *Y*s; and u and v the numbers specified in the premises of X and Z. Let X_tY_u denote that each of t *X*s is affirmed to be one out of u *Y*s: and $X_t{:}Y_u$ that each of t *X*s is denied to be any one out of u *Y*s. Let $X_{m,\,n}$ signify m *X*s taken out of a larger specified number n: and so on. Then the five possible syllogisms, on the condition that no contraries are to enter either premises or conclusion, are as follows:—

1. $X_tY_u + Z_wY_v = X_{t+w-b,\,t}Z_w = Z_{t+w-b,\,w}X_t.$
2. $X_tY_u + Y_vZ_w = X_{t+v-b,\,t}Z_w = Z_{t+v-b,\,w}X_t.$
3. $Y_uX_t + Y_vZ_w = X_{u+v-b,\,t}Z_w = Z_{u+v-b,\,w}X_t.$
4. $X_tY_u + Z_w{:}Y_v = X_{t+v-b,\,t}{:}Z_w.$
5. $Y_uX_t + Z_w{:}Y_v = X_{u+v-b,\,t}{:}Z_w.$

The condition of inference expresses itself; in the $X_{m,\,t}$ of the conclusion, m must neither be 0 nor negative. The first case gives no Aristotelian syllogism; the middle term never entering universally (of necessity) into any of its forms, under any degree of specification which the usual modes of speaking allow. The other cases divide the old syllogisms among themselves in the following manner: they are written so as to show that there is sometimes a little difference of amount of specification between the results of different figures, which amount may change in the reduction from one figure to another. The Roman numerals mark the figures.

2.	$t = a,\ v = b$	$Y)Z_w + X)Y_u = X)Z_{u,\,w}$	*Barbara* I.
	$t = a,\ v = b$	$X)Y_u + Y)Z_w = Z_{u,\,w}X$	*Bramantip* IV.
	$t < a,\ v = b$	$Y)Z_w + X_tY_u = X_tZ_{u,\,w}$	*Darii* I.
	$t < a,\ v = b$	$X_tY_u + Y)Z_w = Z_{t,\,w}X_t$	*Dimaris* IV.
3.	$u = b,\ v = b$	$Y)X_t + Y)Z_w = Z_{b,\,w}X_{b,\,t}$	*Darapti* III.
	$u < b,\ v = b$	$Y_uX_t + Y)Z_w = Z_{u,\,w}X_{u,\,t}$	*Disamis* III.
	$u = b,\ v < b$	$Y)X_t + Y_vZ_w = Z_{v,\,w}X_{v,\,t}$	*Datisi* III.
4.	$t = a, v = b, w = c$	$Y.Z + X)Y_u = X.Z$	*Celarent* I.
	$t = a, v = b, w = c$	$Z.Y + X)Y_u = X.Z$	*Cesare* II.
	$t = a, v = b, w = c$	$X)Y_u + Z.Y = Z.X$	*Camestres* II.
	$t = a, v = b, w = c$	$X)Y_u + Y.Z = Z.X$	*Camenes* IV.
	$v = b, w = c$	$Y.Z + X_tY_u = X_t{:}Z$	*Ferio* I.
	$v = b, w = c$	$Z.Y + X_tY_u = X_t{:}Z$	*Festino* II.
	$t = a, v = b,$	$X)Y_u + Z_w{:}Y = Z_w{:}X$	*Baroko* II.
5.	$u = b, v = b, w = c$	$Y.Z + Y)X_t = X_{b,\,t}{:}Z$	*Felapton* III.
	$u = b, v = b, w = c$	$Z.Y + Y)X_t = X_{b,\,t}{:}Z$	*Fesapo* IV.
	$v = b, w = c$	$Y.Z + Y_uX_t = X_{u,\,t}{:}Z$	*Feriso* III.
	$v = b, w = c$	$Z.Y + Y_uX_t = X_{u,\,t}{:}Z$	*Fresison* IV.
	$u = b,\quad w = c$	$Y_v{:}Z + Y)X_t = X_{v,\,t}{:}Z$	*Bokardo* III.

This system is complete in itself, if contraries be excluded. That in the body of this paper is also complete, if all specification be excluded, except which is contained in the usual words *some* and *all*. An attempt to combine the two systems would be useless, because its forms of expression would not be those of common language. For instance, the following must be one form of an affirmative proposition in the combined system 'Of t Xs and t' xs every one is one or other of u Ys and u' ys.' It would be useless to investigate the conditions of inference as to forms which are not those of speech in any language.

But at the same time there is a certain approach to the preceding forms, if we take in not merely the logical force of our common propositions, but also what is usually implied. He who says, 'Some Xs are Ys,' is generally held to mean that the other Xs are not Ys. The complex syllogisms, in which the alternatives left by the common forms are supposed to be definitely settled, are worthy of attention: and their theory is as follows.

With respect to the name Y, the name X may be of seven different kinds, distinguishable without numerical specification. These are as follows: neither term containing the whole universe.

(I.) The two terms may be *identical*, or $Y)X$ and $X)Y$. Let this be denoted by D. Taking the order XY, we have, to constitute D, the proposition A, a. And denoting coexistence by $+$, as before, we may write $D = A + a$.

(II.) X may be entirely contained in, but not repletive of, Y, or we may have $X)Y$ and $Y{:}X$. Let X be now called a *subidentical* of Y, and let $D_,$ denote this form. We have then $D_, = A + o$.

(III.) X may entirely contain Y, and more; or $Y)X$ and $X{:}Y$. Let X be now called a *superidentical* of Y, and let D' denote this form. We have then $D' = a + O$.

(IV.) X may be the *contrary* of Y, both together filling up the universe of the proposition without anything in common; or $X.Y$ and $x.y$. Let this form be called C: we have then $C = E + e$.

(V.) X and Y may have nothing in common, but may not together fill up the universe of the proposition; or $X.Y$ and xy. Let them be called *subcontraries*, and let $C_,$ denote this form. We have then $C_, = E + i$.

(VI.) X and Y may have something in common, and may together fill up the universe; or XY and $x.y$. Let these be called *supercontraries*, and let C' denote the form. We have then $C' = e + I$.

(VII.) Each of the two may have something in common with the other and something not in common, both together not filling up the universe; or XY, xy, $X{:}Y$, $Y{:}X$. I cannot propose any name for this case with which I am in any degree satisfied: but as all the particular forms are here concerned, I will for the present call X and Y in this case *complete particulars* each of the other. Let P represent this form; we have then $P = I + O + i + o$.

In arranging for a syllogism, let the order be XY, ZY, XZ, the conclusion being described by what X is as related to Z, X coming from the first premise; and both terms of the conclusion being described with respect to the middle term, Y. On examining the cases in which complete premises give a complete conclusion, I find as follows.

1. If one of the concluding terms be a complete particular of the middle term, there is no complete conclusion except when the other concluding term is either identical with or contrary to the middle term. And then each concluding term is a complete particular of the other.

2. The following table shows the result of all the other cases.

		Z					
		D,	*D*	*D'*	*C,*	*C*	*C'*
X	*D,*	(*CC'*)	*D,*	*D,*	*C,*	*C,*	(*DD'*)
	D	*D'*	*D*	*D,*	*C,*	*C*	*C'*
	D'	*D'*	*D'*	(*C,C*)	(*D,D*)	*C'*	*C'*
	C,	*C,*	*C,*	(*DD'*)	(*CC'*)	*D,*	*D,*
	C	*C,*	*C*	*C'*	*D'*	*D*	*D,*
	C'	(*D,D*)	*C'*	*C'*	*D'*	*D'*	(*C,C*)

This is a table of double entry, in which from the description of *X* and *Z* with respect to *Y*, we see set down that of *X* with respect to *Z*, when one can be affirmed: and, when nothing can be affirmed, all that can be denied, in parentheses. Thus, if *X* be a supercontrary of *Y*, and *Z* a subcontrary, *X* must be a superidentical of *Z*. But if *X* and *Z* be both subidenticals of *Y*, it may be denied that *X* is either the contrary or a supercontrary of *Z*.

I will not lengthen this addition by putting down in words all the rules which are expressed in the preceding table.

ON THE SYLLOGISM: II

On the Symbols of Logic, the Theory of the Syllogism, and in particular of the Copula, [and the application of the Theory of Probabilities to some questions of evidence.][1]

[Read 25 February 1850]

Three years ago I communicated to the Society some developments of the theory of the Syllogism, which I have since embodied, with additions, in a work[2] on *Formal Logic.* I now proceed to consider the subject still further, with particular reference to the application of symbols, and the tendency which such application has to develop what I must call the *algebra* of the laws of thought.

It will be necessary for me to refer, in various ways, to the literary topics of a controversy in which the paper above-mentioned involved me: and this I can do without dwelling on the part of it which is personal to myself or to my opponent. That controversy turned upon the connexion between two systems of syllogism. The first, Sir William Hamilton's alteration of the Aristotelian system by the *invention* of forms of predication, so as to assign either of the two modes of quantity, universal or particular, to either of the terms of a proposition, subject or predicate, in either of the different species of propositions, affirmative or negative. The second, my own *numerically definite* system, in which the number of objects of thought that are spoken of, whether under subject or predicate, and also all that exist, are numerically signified, either by the specific or general symbols of arithmetic. But in the present paper I have nothing to do with the numerically definite system, except as it may be alluded to in illustration of the others. Still, I shall have to compare two systems. The first, that of Sir William Hamilton above alluded to. The second, the other and prior of my own two systems, in which the extension of the Aristotelian system is made by the application of *contrary terms* to all the usual forms of predication, without any *direct* invention of modes of applying quantity.

And I may further state, that the methods of this paper have nothing in common with that of Professor Boole, whose mode of treating the forms of logic is most worthy the attention of all who can study that

[1] [An independent paper, here omitted—Ed.]
[2] Referred to, throughout this paper, by the initials *F. L.*

science mathematically, and is sure to occupy a prominent place in its ultimate system.

I. On the approximation of logical and algebraical modes of thought

Throughout this paper I use the word logic in the purely technical sense. The progress of algebra as distinguished from arithmetic, is marked by the gradual approach to the following theorem, that *every pair of opposite relations is undistinguishable from every other pair, in the instruments of operation which are required.* So early did this principle gain some practical acceptance, that no attempt was ever persisted in (even if made, which is more than I know) to signify different oppositions by different pairs of symbols: + and − were found instrumentally adequate to all the wants of the mechanism of the science. I do not say that this was a benefit: I only state it as a fact. An algebraist, who may be required, should the proper problem occur, to interpret $-(-(+(-a)))$ as the *removal* from an expression of all traces of a *loss* incurred in an *ascent* made at a time *prior* to a certain epoch—may have gained the power of making such interpretation very slowly, in consequence of never having sufficiently distinguished differences, as a preliminary to, or a concurrent with, abstraction by observation of resemblances. There may be many for whom it would have been better that the above symbol had been −(*(†(‡*a*))), or the like, until identity of rules had suggested identity of symbols: and I am sure that I was of the number.

The forms of thought which have not immediate relation to magnitude have been otherwise treated: consideration of differences has predominated, that of resemblances has been almost ignored. In the single case in which algebra was forestalled, the old maxim that *two negatives make an affirmative*, so loose was the treatment that the penalty of algebra was incurred. The two negatives, which are only instrumentally the equivalent of an affirmative, are two signs as different in origin and character as the two negative signs in $-(-a)$. In 'man is not (not-animal),' the first negative disconnects, the second describes the predicate disconnected.

In many cases, the difference of symbols, so much wanted by the beginner in algebra, far from encouraging abstraction of resemblances, stimulated differences of interpretation, as in 'not unwilling,' which means less than willing: the double negative has, in common language, deteriorated into an affirmative of a lower degree.

The suggestions of symbolic notation have led me to more recognition than is usually made of harmonies which exist among various pairs of opponent notions common in logical thought. I select the following; —affirmative and negative—universal and particular—the subjective distinction of possible and impossible—the objective distinction of existent and non-existent—necessary and not necessary—sufficient and insufficient—conjunctive and disjunctive—convertible and inconvertible —conclusive and inconclusive—singular and plural—definite and indefinite: omitting *true and false*, the most general of all, as most obviously capable of forming one element of the distinctive definition of any pair. I believe that any of these oppositions might be interchanged and used for each other: but not always without what would be called *forcing*. This, however, is not a conclusive objection: a forced analogy may only deserve that name because we have not been accustomed to the comparisons which it suggests, or to the language, or to the order of ideas, &c. The following phrase of Sir William Hamilton's system, 'All *A* is not some *B*,' is very forced, both in order and phraseology; one who sees it for the first time finds it hard to make either English or sense of it. The meaning is, 'Each *A* is not any one among certain of the *B*s:' and in its place in the system alluded to, the uncouth expression helps to produce system, and the perception of uniform law of inference.

I now take an instance from the preceding list, in which it will appear that an obscurity of expression, if not absolute error, which has often occurred, would have been avoided if the mind had been *forced* to an analogy or an analogy had been *forced* until the mind readily saw it. I say that the distinction of *universal* and *particular* may be replaced by that of *conclusive* and *inconclusive*. In comparing 'every *X* is *Y*' and 'some *X*s are *Y*s,' the first is conclusive with respect to every case which can be brought to the proposition for settlement by it. Certain *X*s, determinable or indeterminable, are proposed; are they *Y*s, or not? The universal is conclusive on this point, the particular inconclusive. Had this comparison been always made, we should not have had so many[1] writers who have expressed themselves as if the 'some' of a particular proposition excluded every other some.

I will now go through all the cases I have named, making *universal and particular* the standard case which is to be compared with all the rest.

1. The distinction of universal and particular may be replaced by that of affirmative and negative. The universal *affirms* the right to

[1] No small number of the elementary writers do this. But that their leaders had no such error in their heads, is clear enough. Ludovicus Vives, speaking of the maxim that *Differentia et proprium non accipiunt magis et minus*, remarks that to be fit for a physician or a sailor are *propria* of man, and yet one man may have *more fitness* for either than another. But this is wrong, and the error consists in introducing into the *proprium* that which is not part of it, as *proprium*: for one beast is *more fit* for a sailor than another; and the *proprium* of man is to have as much as is wanted. The same maxim, *non accipit magis et minus*, was practically and consistently applied to particular quantity, though not stated of it, that I am aware of: but the writers I speak of use language which, but for their subsequent proceedings, would lead any one to suppose that they accepted *magis et minus* as indefinitely applicable to particulars, and definitely to the relation of universal and particular.

assign one or other or both of two names to every object of thought in the universe of the proposition: the particular *denies* it. Thus, x being the contrary name of X, the proposition 'Every X is Y' affirms that Y and x fill the universe; and 'some Xs are not Ys' denies it.

2. The distinction of universal and particular is that of possible and impossible, or of existent or non-existent, according as the proposition speaks subjectively or objectively. Let PQ signify the name compounded of P and Q, and belonging to every object which has a right to both names. Then 'every X is Y' sets down Xy as impossible or non-existent, and 'some Xs are not Ys' sets down Xy as possible or existent.

3. On the connexion of universal and particular with necessary and not-necessary (contingent) see the doctrine of modals, *passim*: on the correlative connexion with sufficient and not-sufficient, see *F. L.* p. 73.

4. The distinction of universal and particular is that of conjunctive and disjunctive; the universal speaks conjunctively, the particular disjunctively, of the same set. The Xs being distinguished as X_1 X_2 X_3 &c., the universal 'Every X is Y' affirms that X_1 is Y, *and* that X_2 is Y, *and* that X_3 is Y, *et caetera.* But the particular 'some Xs are not Ys' only declares that *either* X_1 is not Y, *or* that X_2 is not Y, *or* that X_3 is not Y, *aut caetera.* Nor do I here narrow the meaning of the particular: as used in logic, this species of proposition does not necessarily affirm nor deny of more than one.

5. The distinction of universal and particular may be made that of convertible and inconvertible. This is the only case in which I have had to search for a meaning to make the system good: in all the other cases, perception of the instance preceded that of the general analogy; I believe my work on logic will shew this of nearly all. Now convertibility and inconvertibility are only expressions of identity and non-identity: and it may be easily shewn that the universal is the identity of (followed by the right to convert) two names; and the particular the non-identity. Let U be the name of everything in the universe of the proposition: and let X,Y be a name which includes everything that is either X, or Y, or both. Then the universal 'Every X is Y' affirms the convertibility of x,Y and U; while 'some Xs are not Ys' denies it.

6. On the connexion of universal and particular with conclusive and inconclusive, I have already spoken.

7. The distinction of universal and particular is that of singular and plural. All books of logic affirm that the singular proposition is universal. But the manner in which logicians have treated the *universal* proposition as *singular*, in effect, if not in name, will be the material of a curious chapter in the history of logic, when written. Some of them have seen their own tendency, and have made 'Man is animal' to be a proposition of a distinct species from '*Every* man is *an* animal.' The

universal proposition treats the subject collectively, and makes one singular notion of the whole: the particular makes, or may make, two groups, of indefinite proportions to the whole, and affirms or denies of one, neither affirming nor denying of the other.

8. Sir William Hamilton has very effectively forced the attention of logicians to the manner in which their universal and particular are *definite* and *indefinite*. I shall presently insist on this same distinction as that of *indefinite* and *definite*, and that with particular relation to Sir William Hamilton's system.

If, instead of taking universal and particular as the standard relation, I had chosen affirmative and negative, the principle for which I contend would have appeared more clearly, perhaps: but at the same time it would have appeared to state nothing but what everybody knows. Surely, one would remark, all oppositions stand to one another in an affirmatory and negatory relation, so that affirmation and negation are the root of them all, and as things which are connected with the same are connected with one another, it follows that all opposite relations are connected with one another. This is perfectly true, and fully admitted: nevertheless, true and easy as it is, writers on logic are not yet masters of it, nor were writers on algebra till recently. In this last science, all oppositions are instrumentally reducible to addition and subtraction: let gain, ascent, prior time, . . . give or require addition, then loss, descent, posterior time, . . . give or require subtraction. This easy key to the generalization of the meanings of + and −, is modern as to clear perception and full acceptance: D'Alembert denied its universality.

I think it reasonably probable that the advance of symbolic logic will lead to a calculus of opposite relations, for mere inference, as general as that of + and − in algebra. On the advantages or disadvantages of its introduction it would be vain to speculate beforehand. I now proceed to another point of the approximation of logic and algebra.

When the dry and lifeless instrumental forms of syllogism are placed before a student who has already familiarized himself with their use without thinking about them, it may easily happen that they are received with disgust, and it often *has* happened. That the noble act of the mind called by us *inference*, should be defined as consisting in mere transformation and substitution, appears[1] ridiculous. And the definition is truly so, unless it be confined to the *instrumental* part of inference, the part of the process which might be done by a machine. Algebra might be just as unworthily treated, by confining it to those few general rules in which its operative part really consists, and elevating this part to the dignity of a whole. At the highest, we can but compare the forms of

[1] The two propositions *Omnis dives est sapiens* and *Solus sapiens est dives* are *logical equivalents*!

logic in reasoning with the laws of linear perspective in painting: and the presence of these forms with the incidental lines which perspective requires, and which are rubbed out, not merely before the design is finished, but before the higher art of the process begins. And the parallel holds still further. Many great painters have disfigured their work by too much neglect of the instrumental laws of perspective; many have wilfully and skilfully violated them to produce the effect they wanted;—and so has it been with reasoners.

Speaking instrumentally, what is called *elimination* in algebra is what is called *inference* in logic. If there be four $\left\{\begin{matrix}\text{equations}\\ \text{assertions}\end{matrix}\right.$ in $\left\{\begin{matrix}\text{algebra}\\ \text{logic}\end{matrix}\right.$ involving any number of objects of $\left\{\begin{matrix}\text{equation}\\ \text{assertion}\end{matrix}\right.$, it is possible from the four to produce one $\left\{\begin{matrix}\text{equation}\\ \text{assertion}\end{matrix}\right.$, excluding three objects of $\left\{\begin{matrix}\text{equation}\\ \text{assertion}\end{matrix}\right.$ from among those in the originals. The $\left\{\begin{matrix}\text{resulting equation}\\ \text{inference}\end{matrix}\right.$ is free from the three $\left\{\begin{matrix}\text{eliminated quantities}\\ \text{middle terms}\end{matrix}\right.$.

The logicians confine themselves in the first instance to the simple syllogism, which is the elimination of one middle term between two assertions. In like manner the algebraist asserts that all elimination may be reduced to successions of eliminations of one quantity between two equations. And just as all direct power of elimination, exclusive of what are called *artifices*, depends upon our being able to find one quantity in terms of others with which it is involved in an equation—so all our power of expressing inference depends upon our being able to describe one object of thought in terms of others, by means of an assertion in which they are all involved. When I say ' "John met Thomas in the street"—"John shook hands with Thomas"—that is, "John shook hands with what John met in the street" '—there is an elimination of 'Thomas' perfectly answering in process to '$a + x = b$, $y = c + x$, therefore $y = c + b - a$'.

Several remarkable matters connected with inference may be made to arise out of this view, of which some will be noticed. But I now proceed to observe that this perfect sameness of logical and algebraical process does not continue. Whenever close resemblances exist which are rarely or never noted, we may be pretty sure that the attention has been diverted by differences as remarkable or more so. In algebra, in which the result is quantity, equations are perfect identities. If x be 10, every x that can be produced under precisely the same circumstances, is entitled to the copular sign ($=$) in connexion with any abstract 10 that we can imagine. The consequence is, that a complete conversion of all the processes of elimination can always be made. If $y = \phi x$, $z = \psi x$ give

$z = \chi y$, then $z = \psi x$ and $z = \chi y$ always give $y = \phi x$ as one at least of certain alternatives. From $y = c + x$, $y = c + b - a$, we can recover $a + x = b$, with which we began; but from 'John shook hands with Thomas' and 'John shook hands with what he met in the street', we cannot of right recover 'John met Thomas in the street' [because $x > y$, &c. does not give conversions].

When an assertion becomes complicated, we may be, as in algebra, in the position of finding the reduction impossible: or else we may make the beginner's mistake of disentangling the subject (solving the equation) by the process of *ignotum per ignotum*. For instance 'John met Thomas near his own house:' if we describe John as '*a man* who met Thomas near *his own* house,' we may not have a solution, for the *pronoun* is logically the *noun*. But we have one if we refer '*his own*' to '*a man*.'

The following is an imitation of an elimination of two quantities between three equations:

John met Thomas; John and Thomas live in the same street;

John is richer than Thomas. The elimination gives either of three forms, of which this is one; the algebraic process is here fully imitated.

'A person who met one not so rich as him whom he met' and 'that same person not so rich as him whom he met' live in the same street.

These assimilations may appear ludicrous, but it will be presently seen that the ideas which they suggest may help to free logic from being to the higher processes of thought what algebra would have been to its present state if it had discussed no forms more complicated than $x = y$, $y = z$, &c. The world at large is more advanced in constructive process than the books on logic; in which arbitrary separations are declared by old authority to contain all the forms of thought.

There are many processes of inference which are not syllogisms nor reducible to them, and they all belong to a form of elimination which is not precisely that of *common* algebra. In this last science we use identities because we can command identities. We have not much occasion to employ $x > y$ or $x < y$, because, from our experience of identities, we find it more convenient to suppose $x = y - b$, or $x = y + b$; making the indeterminate character of b supply the want of precision which appears in $x > y$, as compared with $x = y$. Nevertheless, elimination between *inequalities* is sometimes required: and then we know that in $x > y$ our right of substitution is, that we may for x write an equal or a greater, for y an equal or a less. In $x > y$, y is used after the manner of a universal term in logic, x after the manner of a particular. We must know the whole of y; but we may be enabled to make the assertion by knowing a part of x. A little consideration suggests as a necessary rule of inference, the right to substitute a larger term used particularly for a smaller one, however used, and a smaller, used in either way, for a larger used universally. What we may affirm or deny of *some* or *all* men, we may affirm or deny of some *animals*: what we may affirm or deny of *all* animals, we may affirm or deny of *all* or *some* men. The second part of the rule is the *dictum de omni et nullo*; the first part has not, within my reading, been added to it: both might well be incorporated in one under the name of the *dictum*[1] *de majore et minore*. Observing that every inference was frequently declared to be reducible to syllogism, with no exception unless in the case of mere transformation, as in the deduction of 'No *X* is *Y*' from 'No *Y* is *X*,' I gave a challenge in my work on formal logic to deduce syllogistically from 'Every man is an animal' that 'every head of a man is the head of an animal.' From the total absence of attempt to answer this challenge, I conclude[2] that no one has succeeded in whose way it has fallen.

I shall presently have occasion to pursue this subject a little further: I now proceed to a new section.

II. On the formation of symbolic notation for propositions and syllogisms

The commonly received method of denoting the affirmative and negative universals by *A*, *E*, and the particulars by *I*, *O*, is rather mnemonical than instrumental: it suggests to nothing but the memory. Of all the systematic deductions of the valid forms of syllogism, not one came into general use: inductive selection and exclusion were employed, when anything more than a mere declaration of results was given. The figure being given, the above symbols are sufficient: thus *AEI* in the first figure can be nothing but the invalid mode 'Every *Y* is *Z*, no *X* is *Y*, therefore some *X*s are *Z*s.'

In my former paper, and in my work since published, I borrowed from the above notation the use and meaning of *A*, *E*, *I*, *O*, and added symbolic distinctions. So far I have nothing to change: any system must use some mode of expressing its relation to the language of so many centuries. *I also adopted a more detailed mode of expressing propositions:* and here it would have been better if the *detail*[3] had been greater at first, that it might have been ultimately made still less.

A *fundamental* symbol should not be of compound meaning: that is, should not expressly signify more than one thing. Composite expres-

[1] Every syllogism in the Aristotelian system is a direct use of this dictum.

[2] This would be a very unsafe conclusion from the absence of printed answer. But any one who writes on a controverted subject gains a number of private correspondents, with and without names. When I advanced, in my discussion with Sir William Hamilton, that a person kept close to Aristotle's forms could not prove that some must have both coats *and* waistcoats, if a majority have coats, and a majority waistcoats, I had various ingenious attempts to disprove my assertion.

[3] [Italics added in MS.]

sions should be reserved for symbols which are avowedly in abbreviation of combinations of fundamental symbols. Again, the complex symbol should not be prior in invention to the simple ones; nor should it be invented until the simple ones have had their chance of good suggestion.

For instance, in the old notation, the letters *A*, &c. are of compound meaning; *A* is universal and affirmative. If *A* and *E* had stood simply for affirmative and negative, and two consonants, as *B* and *N*, for universal and particular, the distinction of figure might have been symbolized. *Barbara* does not suggest the first figure, nor *Camestres* the second, except by memory. But if the premise-consonants had been made to imitate the middle term in location, the figure would have been seen in the word which would have resulted, whether unmeaning letters had been added for euphony or not. Thus *AE* occurring as premises in the second figure, in which the middle term is predicate of both premises, would have given *ABEBE*; and so on. If some choice of liquids had been allowed for designation of particulars, and of other consonants for designation of universals, euphonic words might have been invented, which would have been, by this time, as venerable as *Bokardo* or *Felapton*. Nor would it have been difficult to have fitted on letters symbolic of the method of reduction into the first figure.

This suggestion, however, comes a few centuries too late: the following one is more to our purpose.

Symbols in which *relative position* is the whole or part of the symbol, whatever their advantages may be in other respects, lie under one great disadvantage: abstraction is not suggested, and can only be done awkwardly. The exponential symbol in algebra has this defect: we cannot describe it independently of others, except by $()^{()}$, or some such contrivance. In the more detailed notation of my former paper this fault was committed: thus *XY*, by mere position of the letters, was made to indicate 'Some *X*s are *Y*s.'

The distinctive characters of the proposition are made to be, usually, the terms, the copula (affirmative or negative), and the quantity of the subject. But if the quantity of the *predicate* be also symbolized, notice of the terms is not *distinctively* necessary: for every proposition used has neither more nor less than two terms, and a term need not enter except to have its quantity noted. The symbols of the terms, in fact, are only pegs on which to hang distinctions: so that it is desirable that they should not be essential, though capable of introduction.

The quantities of the terms give name to the proposition: which is usually called universal or particular after its subject. This is arbitrary; and it is open to us, by the same license, to make the proposition take the name of its predicate. The enlargement of the proposition, whether Sir William Hamilton's or my own, will probably require a new word to express the distinction of propositions: for both have their double universals, and their double particulars, which are not in the Aristotelian set. At present, however, I am not prepared to suggest a term which would apply to both systems.

Let the subject and predicate, when specified, be written before and after the symbols of quantity. Let the inclosing parenthesis, as in *X*) or (*X*, denote that the name-symbol *X*, which would be inclosed if the oval were completed, enters universally. Let an excluding parenthesis, as in)*X* or *X*(, signify that the name-symbol enters particularly. Let an even number of dots, or none at all, inserted between the parentheses, denote affirmation or agreement; let an odd number, usually one, denote negation or non-agreement. Thus *X*)) *Y* means that all *X*s are *Y*s; *X*(.(*Y* means that some *X*s are not *Y*s; but)) and (.(specify the characters of the propositions; as do also ((and).). We must conceive ourselves at liberty to read either way: thus *X*)) *Y* and *Y*((*X* both denote that every *X* is *Y*.

A syllogism may be denoted by juxtaposition of the symbols of the premises, taking the order *XY*, *YZ*, *XZ*. Thus 'Every *X* is *Y*, some *Z*s are not *Y*s, therefore some *Z*s are not *X*s' may be stated thus,

X)) *Y*).)*Z* gives *X*).)*Z* or))).) gives).).

In the Aristotelian system, and in my extension, the canon of formation of the inference, when there is one, is;—*Erase the symbols of the middle term, the remaining symbols shew the inference*. Thus, if there be a valid inference from).((.) it is)..) or)). Thus also *X*() *Y*))*Z* expresses the premises 'Some *X*s are *Y*s, and every *Y* is *Z*:' erase *Y* and its accompaniments, and we have *X*()*Z* for the conclusion, or 'Some *X*s are *Z*s.' In Sir William Hamilton's system, this law is not quite universal in the symbolic deduction of the inference; but a certain variation, which I shall presently suggest, will make it so.

If we wish to read by *distinction* of figure, that is, by Aristotelian figure, we may contrive it thus. Let the subject of each proposition have its quantity denoted by a thicker or larger parenthesis. Then the first figure, in which we read *through* the concluding terms, would present the appearance |||; remembering that when the distinction of major and minor term of conclusion is preserved, we read the second premise first. Thus

X)) *Y*))*Z* = *X*))*Z*, which is now symbolized in the first figure,
is *Y*))*Z* + *X*)) *Y* = *X*))*Z*.

The second figure, in which we read *to* the middle term, is as seen in |||; the third, in which we read *from* the middle term, is as seen in |||; and the fourth, in which we read *through* the middle term, is as seen in |||.

All notation, no doubt, is both pictorial and arbitrary: nevertheless there are cases in which one or the other character decidedly predominates. The arbitrary character decidedly predominates in the preceding notation: but the syllogism admits of a graphical representation which is as suggestive as a diagram of geometry. This was partially adopted by Lambert and Euler (*F. L.* p. 323), and may be more completely shewn, and without new types or woodcuts, in the following way.

Let all the instances in the *universe* of the syllogism be represented by the points of a definite straight line: but to avoid confusion, let this straight line be repeated as often as it is necessary to introduce a name. Let the division of this straight line into a continuous and a dotted portion signify the distribution of the universe into a name and its contrary. When a proposition is asserted, let a second line run over so much of the extent of each name as is declared by the proposition to be in agreement or disagreement with the whole or part of the other: extents which fall *under* one another being taken as in agreement. Thus in the following diagrams we see the propositions 'Every *X* is *Y*,' and 'Some things are neither *X*s nor *Y*s,'

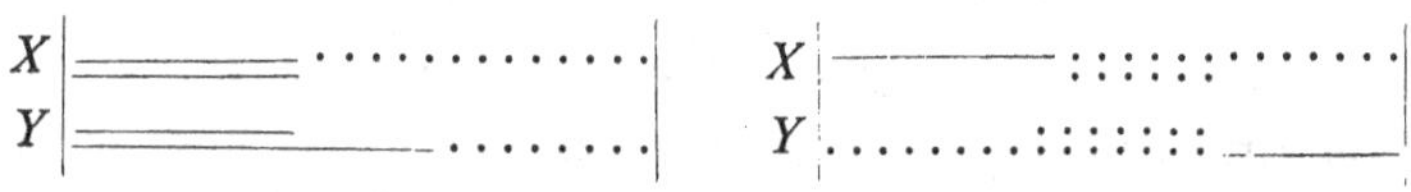

Let the middle name of a syllogism be placed in the middle, and when the two premises are formed, let the extents which enter into the conclusion be signified by thicker lines, or thicker dots. Thus it will appear what the conclusion is, and also whether the quantities in the conclusion be those which entered into the premises, or whether, by the character of the inference, either be curtailed. Thus in the diagram before us

(·))·) = ()

we see the pictorial and arbitrary notation for the following syllogism:—Everything is either *X* or *Y*; some *Z*s are not *Y*s; therefore some *Z*s (as many as entered the premise) are *X*s (not necessarily as many as in the premise). We also see that the real middle term of agreement is a portion (or what may be only a portion) of the extent of *y*: and that the affirmative form of the syllogism is *X*((*y*()*Z* = *X*()*Z*. References to figure might easily be added.

I should here close this section, if it had not been that Sir William Hamilton's scheme of notation has been published by an acute writer, with such commendations,[1] that I must not appear to shun the comparison. This system is certainly so simple, that a person who knows the premises *and inference* well, would write down any case of it immediately. I exhibit one case of it in the three figures: premising that Sir William Hamilton rejects the distinction of major and minor, and draws two conclusions in the second figure and in the third: but does not permit the fourth figure to append itself to the first, nor to appear in any way.

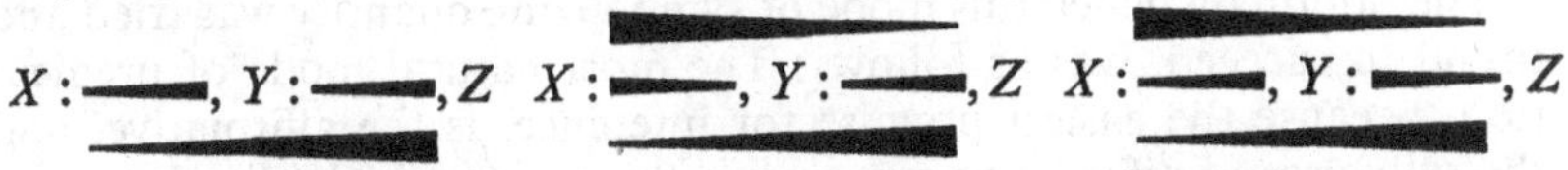

First Figure		*Second Figure*		*Third Figure*
Some *Y* is all *X*.		All *X* is some *Y*.		Some *Y* is all *X*.
Some *Z* is all *Y*.		Some *Z* is all *Y*.		All *Y* is some *Z*.
∴		Some *Z* is all *X*.		Some *Z* is all *X*.
Some *Z* is all *X*,	or	All *X* is some *Z*,	or	All *X* is some *Z*.

Negation is expressed by drawing a vertical line through the sign of predication. When the thin end of this sign is made the subject, the syllogism is read by *intension*.

It would appear at first that this notation is almost identical with what I have proposed above, as to principle. Leave out the lines of predication, and the above syllogism would be $X{:},\ Y{:},\ Z = X{:},\ Z$, instead of $X))\,Y))Z = X))Z$. And I am bound to attribute[2] to Sir William Hamilton the expression of the two distinct quantities, universal and particular, as two distinct matters of phraseology and thence of notation, *when the quantities are not numerically conceived and expressed.* (*F. L.* p. 301.)

If then the preceding notations were as much alike as they appear to be, I should call mine (which was first used in trying Sir W. Hamilton's system, *F. L.* p. 302), so far as affirmative syllogisms are concerned, Sir William Hamilton's with what I judge to be a more convenient mode of expression. But there is, in fact (independently of the omission of

[1] 'A mode of notation proposed by Sir William Hamilton, is, beyond doubt, one of the most important contributions to pure Logic which has ever been made since the science was put forth; and I am fortunate in being permitted to annex it. Its excellences are—that it is very simple, that it shews the equivalent syllogisms in the different figures at a glance, that it shews as readily the convertible syllogisms in the same figure, that it enables us to read each syllogism with equal facility according to extension and intension, . . .' *Outline of the Necessary Laws of Thought.* By William Thomson, M.A. (2nd Edition, 1849, p. 265.) A work to be strongly recommended.

[2] And I may also note an inaccuracy of expression used by Mr. Thomson (pp. 265, 266): 'Many of the different elements of the notation are not new, but the novelty lies in the completeness and simplicity of the whole scheme.' Not so; for though the notation had failed entirely both in completeness and simplicity, there would have remained the most remarkable novelty which there now is, namely, notation of quantity in both subject and predicate.

term-symbols), a very material difference, and one which makes the notation I have given more suggestive,[1] and its symbolic rules more easy to some extent in my own system, to a greater in Sir William Hamilton's. In his mode of notation, the symbols of universal and particular are absolute (: and ,): in mine, the *universality of the subject* has the same symbol as the *particularity of the predicate*, and *vice versâ*: thus in *X*)) *Y*, the same symbol [ )] is applied to the universal subject, and the particular predicate.[2]

The notion on which this mode of symbolizing quantity was tried and found to succeed, was as follows: The most natural mode of predication, because the easiest premise for inference, is the affirmative, and the syllogism of affirmative premises is the one to which all other cases are naturally reduced. And here the predicates are always particular, while the subjects are either universal, or, which is the same reality in inference, take the whole extent named in the premise into the conclusion. Whenever this is the case, the invention of a name will shew that the inference is of the same kind as one in which the term of the premise and of the conclusion are both universal. In representing 'All *X* is in *Y*, all *Y* is in *Z*, therefore all *X* is in *Z*' by *X*)) *Y*))*Z* there is something pictorial, and the particular character of the predicate has its symbol of particularity invented out of the relation to the subject from which we deduce that character.

III. On the symbolic forms of the extension of the Aristotelian system in which contraries are admitted.

This system is, *by consequence, not by assumption*, one in which any term, be it subject or predicate, may have either kind of quantity, universal or particular, in any proposition, affirmative or negative. Sir William Hamilton's system has the same peculiarity, as the *basis of invention for the forms of predication*: that is, the accidental form of my system is the substantial form of his, so far as these terms are applicable.

I did not make this point of agreement between the two systems prominent in my work on formal logic, for the following reasons. In the memoir printed by this Society, in which all my interest in *novelty* of quantification was directed to the algebraical form of numerically

[1] It would seem that the forms given by Sir William Hamilton have not suggested any rules. 'In the negative modes the distribution of terms will remain exactly the same as it was in the affirmatives from whence they were respectively formed, with some few exceptions in which the conclusion has a term distributed which was not when it was affirmative.' Thomson, op. cit. p. 267. Under a suggestive notation, the rule which regulates the exceptions will be visible; and it will be seen that these so called exceptions are in the rule, and that cases of the *affirmative* syllogism are the exceptions.

[2] [But I had not seen H's when this was made: in fact H's had not been printed. (21 March 1860).]

definite propositions, this complete distribution of all the quantifications, existing in the system of contraries, was overlooked. So much so, that no one could conclude from my words[1] more than that, with *eight* forms of predication, and knowledge of the doctrine of combinations, I must have seen the necessity of this alternative—either two forms of predication with the same terms and the same quantities, or a distribution of all possible pairs of quantifications. But I have no remembrance of even this alternative suggesting itself.

When the discussion with Sir William Hamilton turned all my attention to the question whether he had or had not the numerical system, and, subsequently, to the comparison of his system (*F. L.* pp. 300–2) with the numerical one, it became evident of course, that the complete distribution of quantifications is incidental to the system of contraries. But I did not mention this explicitly in my work (pp. 63, 293): because, as the controversy was then unfinished, I neither wished to dwell upon an irrelevant quantification (that which is assumed and constructed, not that which can be derived, being the subject-matter of the dispute), such as might mislead the reader of the controversy, nor to appear as insinuating that I had published to the Society, before I had had any correspondence with my opponent, a system containing by derivation the whole extent of quantification, the invention of which was in the subject-matter of the discussion. Such insinuation would have been untrue: for though the system I now write upon *does* contain that extent of quantification, and though it *was* published (to the Society) before I had any knowledge even of the fact of Sir William Hamilton having a system of his own, yet I can most distinctly affirm that all my perception of complete quantification of both terms was derived from the algebraical form of numerical quantification.

The universal and particular affirmative may be made the bases of all the modes of predication: the others arising out of the various substitutions of contraries in them. The following are then the eight forms, with reference to the order *XY*.

Universals

Notation of my			*Notation now proposed*	*Proposition expressed in common language*
Former Memoir	*Work on Logic*	*Both*		
A	*A,*	*X*)*Y*	*X*))*Y*	Every *X* is *Y*
a	*A′*	*x*)*y* or *Y*)*X*	*x*))*y* or *X*((*Y*	Every *Y* is *X*
E	*E,*	*X*)*y* or *X*.*Y*	*X*))*y* or *X*).(*Y*	No *X* is *Y*
e	*E′*	*x*)*Y* or *x*.*y*	*x*))*Y* or *X*(.)*Y*	Everything is *X* or *Y* or both.

[1] As follows, in the fourth page of my paper '. . . every proposition speaks in different ways of each term and its contrary; making one particular or universal, according as the other is universal or particular. . . . And of the two terms and their contraries, each proposition speaks universally of two, and particularly of two.'

Particulars

I	*I*,	*XY*	*X*()*Y*	Some *X*'s are *Y*s
i	*I'*	*xy*	*x*()*y* or *X*)(*Y*	Some things are neither *X*s nor *Y*s
O	*O*,	*Xy* or *X*:*Y*	*X*()*y* or *X*(.(*Y*	Some *X*s are not *Y*s
o	*O'*	*xY* or *Y*:*X*	*x*()*Y* or *X*).)*Y*	Some *Y*s are not *X*s.

I think that the words universal and particular can be better described for this system than in the usual way, both as to terms and propositions. A *term* enters *universally*, when, in order to verify the proposition by induction, every instance of the name *must* be examined: *particularly*, when the verification *may* be attained without it. A *proposition* is *universal*, when every instance in the *universe* must be examined before it can be inductively verified: *particular*, when the verification *may* be attained without. So that the phrases 'universal proposition,' and 'particular proposition,' refer to all things in the universe of the proposition; while 'universal term' and 'particular term' refer to all things contained in a term, or portion of that universe. The introduction of contraries does, in fact, introduce a third term into the proposition; the *universe*, or *summum genus*, be it the whole universe of thought, or a conceivably separable portion of it. And it is to be particularly remembered, that every term is supposed to be *part* only of the universe: that is, to have an existing contrary in that universe.

In the inductive examination above alluded to, we suppose that we do not know beforehand which instances of the universe are *X*s and which are *Y*s; nor, in selecting[1] an instance from the universe, can we say that that instance is not an *X*, till we have examined it with all the *X*s. In verifying *X*))*Y*, we have then to examine every instance of the universe to see whether it be *X*, but only when it is *X* need we examine further to see whether it be *Y*: *Y*s may never be ascertained to be such, since, by reason of their not being *X*s, the examination may never take in those *Y*s. Hence *X*))*Y* is a universal proposition in which *X* is universal and *Y* particular. Again, in *X*)(*Y* or 'some things are neither *X*s nor *Y*s,' the *first* instance of the universe which is carried through all the *X*s and all the *Y*s, and found to agree with no one instance of either, verifies all that the proposition asserts: hence the proposition is particular, and its terms both universal.

I can now correct a symbolic want of my former writings, though the

[1] That is, we do not suppose, as it were, that every instance is ticketed in its place in the universe as *X* or *x*, *Y* or *y*, but that each instance taken from the universe has its own universe-mark, and that we must then, in order to find if that instance be an *X*, examine a separate index of *X*s, to see if that mark occur. The ticketing of the instances, first mentioned, is the representative of the supposition on which some have discovered that the syllogism concludes in what was already known before the premises could be asserted.

thing to be signified was often matter of explanation. Expression for the *contrary* of a *contrary* was wanting in the *subject* of the proposition: whence it arose that only three equivalents appeared in the *detailed symbols*, though four existed in thought and in the more compressed symbols. Thus I had $A_{\prime}$ of XY, $E_{\prime}$ of Xy, A' of xy, E' of xY, as equivalents: while only $X)Y = X.y = y)x$ appeared in the detailed symbols. I now have

$$X))Y = X).(y = x((y = x(.)Y$$
$$X(.(Y = X()y = x).)y = x)(Y.$$

The rule of transformation is:—To use the contrary of a term, without altering the import of the proposition, alter the curvature of its parenthesis, and annex or withdraw a negative point.

We may now say that the *quantitative contrary* of 'every X' is 'some xs,' and of 'some Xs,' 'every x.' Thus, when I say, 'some Xs are Ys' I deny something of every x: namely, that any one of them is one of those Ys. Again, 'Every X is Y' denies of some xs that they are Ys: for Ys must not fill the universe. And so on.

The distinction of affirmative and negative, in the usual sense, is abandoned: for any affirmative proposition, as $X()Y$, is also negative, as seen in its equivalent $X(.(y$. My two new forms of predication were properly called, (.) negative, and)(affirmative, and were derived in the forms $x).(y$ and $x()y$ as 'no not-X is not-Y' and 'some not-Xs are not-Ys.' Nevertheless, stated in reference to X and Y, the first appears affirmative, 'Everything is either X or Y', and the second negative, 'Some things are neither Xs nor Ys.' But the first obeys the rules for the indisputable negatives, and the second those for the affirmatives. There enters an extension of an old maxim;—it is that *three negatives make a negative.* There are three positive ideas, X, Y, affirmation; opposed to the three correlative negatives, x, y, negation. Negative propositions present an *odd* number of the negatives; positive ones an even number (or none). Thus in all the equivalent forms of $X(.)Y$, nothing but an odd number of the negatives will occur; as seen in

$$X(.)Y = x))Y = X((y = x).(y.$$

There is yet one more opposition; the quantitative parentheses may turn the same or different ways: which are to be considered as positive and negative cases. By this, and the opposition of affirmation or negation, the extent of the proposition is determined. When these oppositions are none or two, the proposition is universal: when one, particular. Thus $X))Y$ having none, and $X(.)Y$ having two, are universals: but $X()Y$ having one, is particular.

In a universal proposition, any *one* quantity may be altered, either from universal to particular, or from particular to universal; and the result is always a true deduction, though not an equivalent. Thus *X*)) *Y* gives both *X*() *Y* and *X*)(*Y*.

Contrary propositions (usually called *contradictory*), of which one must be true and one false, differ both in quantities and copula. Thus *X*)) *Y* and *X*(.(*Y* are contraries. The *concomitants* of a universal, to which it is perfectly indifferent, differ from it in quantities, or in copula, not in both. Thus *X*)) *Y* coexists either with *X*((*Y* or *X*).) *Y*. The superior universals of a particular, or the inferior particulars of a universal, are made by altering one quantity only: thus *X*)(*Y* has *X*((*Y* and *X*)) *Y* for its superior universals; and *X*(.) *Y* has *X*).) *Y* and *X*(.(*Y* for its inferior particulars. The alteration of one quantity, and the copula, turns a universal into another and inconsistent universal, and a particular into another and a consistent particular: as *X*)) *Y* into *X*(.) *Y*, or *X*(.) *Y* into *X*).) *Y*. An alteration of either of the terms into its contrary, must count as alteration of the quantity of that term, and the copula.

To carry this a little further, observe that though all the particulars consist with one another, or may exist together, yet they take distinctions, when looked at as to probability, which have some resemblance to those existing among the universals either as probabilities or as certainties. Take the universal *X*)) *Y*, and change both quantities: it becomes *X*((*Y*. If the latter be true, it is in favour of *X*)) *Y* rather than otherwise. Do the same with *X*() *Y*, it becomes *X*)(*Y*: if the second be true, it is also rather a presumption for *X*() *Y* than otherwise. The more things there are which are neither *X* nor *Y*, the smaller the number of instances of the universe within which all the *X*s and all the *Y*s are contained; and the greater the probability of *X*() *Y*. Now take the universal *X*)) *Y* and alter one quantity and the copula: we have *X*(.) *Y* and *X*).(*Y*, both absolutely inconsistent with *X*)) *Y*. Do the same with *X*() *Y*: we have *X*).) *Y* and *X*(.(*Y*, neither inconsistent with *X*() *Y*, but both diminishing its probability. This observation is of some worth in classification: it may justify us in extending the general name of concomitants to particulars in which both quantities differ, and opponents to those in which one quantity and the copula differ; and will help us to system.

Now let a proposition be considered as having two sides, on each of which a change of quantity counts as *one*, and a change of copula as *one* for each side. Changes of quantity then may be represented by 1|0 and 0|1, change of copula is 1|1, and changes of term are 2|1 and 1|2. The utmost amount of change is 4|4, which restores the original: thus *x*(..(*y* is *X*)) *Y* affected by 4|4, and it is *X*)) *Y* itself. And it will be found that 1|0 and 0|1 always produce a superior universal or an inferior particular, that 1|1 produces a concomitant, 2|1 or 1|2 an opponent, 2|2 a contrary; and so on.

When contraries are allowed, all inference may be made to consist in declaration of agreement. The disagreement of two things, because one agrees and the other disagrees with a third, may be made to fall under the other and more simple case; not indeed, as the easiest rule of thought, but as the best basis of a classification. This *X* agrees with this *Y*; this *Z* does not agree with this *Y*; therefore this *X* does not agree with this *Z*—may be stated as, This *X* agrees with this *Y*, something not this *Z* agrees with this *Y*, therefore this *X* agrees with something not this *Z*. And the universe, explicitly divided into this *Z* and other things, is a provision for the definite understanding of the manner in which the second proposition is transformed.

Accordingly, agreement between *X*s and *Y*s, *Y*s and *Z*s leads to agreement between *X*s and *Z*s, if the number of agreements be altogether more than there are *Y*s. Restricted as we are now to the case of the universal and the indefinite particular, one of the propositions must mention all the *Y*s. So that the fundamental syllogisms, from which all the rest are derived by every introduction of contraries, seem to be

A,A,A, X))*Y*))*Z* = *X*))*Z* or)))) =))	*X*()*Y*))*Z* = *X*()*Z* or ()))= () *I,A,I,*
A′A′A′ X((*Y*((*Z* = *X*((*Z* or ((((= ((	*X*((*Y*()*Z* = *X*()*Z* or ((() = () *A′I,I,*

A′A,I, X((*Y*))*Z* = *X*()*Z* or (()) = ().

But in truth this basis is excessive, in three distinct ways.

1. ((((and)))) really belong to one of the sets which is to be formed; and the proceeds of the two will be identical. One only of them should be taken.

2. The sets from ())) and ((() only differ in respect to the species of figure[1] which I employ. I keep to *XY*, *YZ*, *XZ*; and one of these sets is the other referred to *ZY*, *YX*, *ZX*: the refusal of all distinction of figure obliges me to retain both sets.

3. In (()) = () we see only a *strengthened* syllogism: that is, stronger in the premises than is required to produce the conclusion. It is either ())) or ((() with the particular middle term universalized.

The number of variations produced by combining *X* or *x*, *Y* or *y*, *Z* or *z*, is eight, taking one out of each pair. And as these variations do not affect the character of the proposition, we must have as follows. *Eight universal* syllogisms, with two universal premises and a universal

[1] I thought I had sufficiently expressed this in my work by stating that I abandoned the *distinction* of figure. But I suppose it was hardly clear: for a learned reviewer observes, 'That is not new—but is Sir William Hamilton's avowed rule.' This is not correct: Sir William Hamilton's method is equally indifferent to all figures [but recognizes the distinction, were it only in saying that figure is an 'unessential variation']; mine holds by one, and recognizes no other, in its classifications. I have one establishment, and tolerate no distinction of sect. Sir William Hamilton has none, but tolerates three sects: Aristotle had three state-churches, Galen (they say) founded a sect of dissenters, which, after some centuries of toleration, was made a fourth establishment.

conclusion, derived from)))) =)). *Sixteen particular* syllogisms, each with a particular conclusion, derived from one universal and one particular premise; *eight* commencing with a particular, from ()))=(); *eight* commencing with a universal, from ((( ). *Eight strengthened* syllogisms, in which two universals conclude with a particular, derived from (()) =().

The canon of *validity* is as follows. The change of *Y* into *y* will alter the middle parentheses by changing them both, and therefore will not affect their relative character. Consequently, if the middle parentheses turn the same way, ((or)), any two propositions which give this arrangement allow of an inference, if one at least be universal; that is, if the number of oppositions in the parentheses, and the number of negative dots, put together, be an odd number in all, or an even number (0 included) in each proposition. But when the middle parentheses turn contrary ways, there need but be two universals, or an even number (0 included) on each side.

The canon of *inference* is merely this;—Strike out the middle parentheses, and *two* negative dots, if there be two; the remaining symbol shews the inference.

In the following table, the syllogisms are arranged in the manner described in the headings.

The universal and strengthened syllogisms appear twice, once from each set of particular syllogisms. The *contranominals*, or those in which all the terms used are contraries, are written together: they are formed from each other by alteration of all the parentheses.

Altering one quantity in a particular proposition, even though a universal term be changed into a particular one, *strengthens* the proposition, or converts it into a universal. In fact, in this system strength and weakness are terms which, like affirmation and negation, have nothing but opposition of character left: the less the strength of a proposition with respect to a term, the greater with respect to its contrary: so that what I have called strengthening a proposition, is only altering the distribution of strength.

The *opponents* of a syllogism, meaning those in which one premise and the contrary of the conclusion produce the contrary of the other premise, are thus formed. Substitute the contrary of the conclusion for one premise and change the order of reading in the other, or let the symbol of the other revolve about an axis. Thus the two opponents of).)).(are (.((.) and (.)).(; and those of ())) are ()).(and).(((.

The opponents of the strengthened syllogisms are universals weakened in their conclusions.

The change of the figure from *XY YZ XZ* to *ZY YX ZX* is merely the writing of the symbol from the other end; it turns)))) into ((((and ())).(into).((). Those syllogisms which agree in their parentheses and differ only in their affirmations and negations are the *concomitants* of my

Terms employed	*Particular syllogism* with first *premise particular*	*Universal syllogism strengthened by the* first *quantity of the particular*	*Particular syllogism strengthened by the second quantity of the particular*
X Y Z	*I,A,I,* ())) = ()	*A,A,A,*)))) =))	*A'A,I,* (()) = ()
x y z	*I'A'I'*)(((=)(	*A'A'A'* ((((= ((	*A,A'I'*))((=)(
x Y Z	*O'A,O'*).))) =).)	*E'A,E'* (.))) = (.)	*E,A,O'*).()) =).)
X y z	*O,A'O,* (.(((= (.(	*E,A'E,*).(((=).(	*E'A'O,* (.)((= (.(
X y Z	*O,E'I,* (.((.) = ()	*E,E'A,*).((.) =))	*E'E'I,* (.)(.) = ()
x Y z	*O'E,I'*).)).(=)(	*E'E,A'* (.)).(= ((	*E,E,I'*).().(=)(
X Y z	*I,E,O,* ()).(= (.(	*A,E,E,*))).(=).(	*A'E,O,* (().(= (.(
x y Z	*I'E'O'*)((.) =).)	*A'E'E'* (((.) = (.)	*A,E'O'*))(.) =).)

Terms employed	*Particular syllogism with* second *premise particular*	*Universal syllogism strengthened by the* second *quantity* of *the particular*	*Particular syllogism strengthened by the first quantity of the particular*
X Y Z	*A'I,I,* ((() = ()	*A'A'A'* ((((= ((	*A'A,I,* (()) = ()
x y z	*A,I'I'*)))(=)(	*A,A,A,*)))) =))	*A,A'I'*))((=)(
x Y Z	*E,I,O'*).(() =).)	*E,A'E,*).(((=).(	*E,A,O'*).()) =).)
X y z	*E'I'O,* (.))(= (.(	*E'A,E'* (.))) = (.)	*E'A'O,* (.)((= (.(
X y Z	*E'O'I,* (.)).) = ()	*E'E,A'* (.)).(= ((	*E'E'I,* (.)(.) = ()
x Y z	*E,O,I'*)(.(.(=)(	*E,E'A,*).((.) =))	*E,E,I'*).().(=)(
X Y z	*A'O,O,* (((.(= (.(	*A'E'E'* (((.) = (.)	*A'E,O,* (().(= (.(
x y Z	*A,O'O'*))).) =).)	*A,E,E,*))).(=).(	*A,E'O'*))(.) =).)

work (pp. 88, 89, 94), or the *coexistents* in a complex syllogism. Thus *A,A,A,, O'A,O'* and *A,O'O'* are))))).))) and))).). These syllogisms coexist in my complex syllogism *D,D,D,*; and *perhaps*, then, the best notation for this last might be derived from).)).), indicative of the only one of the four combinations which is *not* valid as a simple syllogism.

I need not enter further into this subject, as what is here given on notation may be easily applied throughout my work.

IV. On the symbolic forms of the system in which all the combinations of quantity are introduced by arbitrary invention of forms of predication

This system, which belongs to Sir William Hamilton, has not yet been published in detail by its learned author, except in lectures; in which, I believe, it was first published in 1840 or 1841. There is some account of its forms, communicated by him, and printed with his sanction, in Mr Thomson's *Outlines*, already cited. See also *F. L.* pp. 300–2.

The modes of predication in this system, are, by hypothesis, as follows, at least when the language of *extent*, preferred by Sir William Hamilton, is changed into that of numeration of instances. The symbols attached are dictated by the quantities of the terms, with reference to the order *XY*.

All *X*s are all *Y*s	)(	$A_, + A'$.	No *X*s are *Y*s	).(	$E_,$.
Some *X*s are some *Y*s	()	$I_,$.	Some *X*s are not some *Y*s	(.)	—.
All *X*s are some *Y*s	))	$A_,$.	No *X*s are some *Y*s	).)	O'.
Some *X*s are all *Y*s	((	A'.	Some *X*s are no *Y*s	(.(	$O_,$.

Some authors had gone so far (*F. L.* Appendix II.) as to adapt expressed quantity to the predicate, for the purpose of procuring convertible forms: and Mr Thomas Solly (*Syllabus of Logic*, 1839, p. 47) gave the above eight forms, with his reasons for reducing them to four. But Sir William Hamilton is the first who published the idea of taking all phases of usual quantification, and making them the basis of a system of syllogism.

It will be observed that I have not called this system an *extension* of that of Aristotle. That it is more extensive, in one sense, I admit; namely, in so far as it includes all which Aristotle included, and more. But a mathematician cannot therefore call it an extension, accustomed as he is to a very precise use of that term. With him enlargement is not extension, unless the wider extent be governed by the laws of the narrower one. The name *multiplication*, conceived by aid of integer numbers, is properly allowed to be *extended* to fractional ones, because, among other reasons, in every problem in which integers demand integer multiplication, fractional data demand what is *thence* called fractional multiplication. Botany was once agriculture, but in its present state it cannot properly be called an extension of agriculture: the union of England and Scotland was not an *extension* of England. This refusal to use the word extension, in the present case, is not the assertion of any defect in the system, but rather the contrary: it is quite open to inquiry whether the best form of syllogism be what I call an extension of Aristotle, or contain the incorporation of new fundamental principles.

Perhaps some may ask why I have called my own system an *extension* of Aristotle. I answer that no new laws are propounded, though the application of the old ones to an enlarged subject-matter of predication introduces some new forms of expression, and some striking points of view from which to look at the old ones. Every one of my syllogisms can be reduced to an Aristotelian form, without any addition except that of contraries to the matters of predication. For example, one of my new syllogisms,))((=)(, or 'All *X*s and all *Z*s are *Y*s, therefore some things (namely, all that are not *Y*s) are neither *X*s nor *Z*s—is reducible to ordinary form. With *X Y Z* it is new: but with *X y z* it is *Fesapo*, being

$$X).(y))z = X).)z.$$

The syllogism))((=)(can thus be made Aristotelian: but in my system, a plain man who sees clearly that some things are proved to be neither men nor mice, were it only because they do not eat cheese, may rest content that his knowledge, even in the form of the light of nature, can be made science, without the necessity of having recourse to the following very venerable, but very unsatisfactory, form:

No man is a non-eater of cheese
All non-eaters of cheese are other things than mice
Therefore some other things than mice are also not men.

Now take one of Sir William Hamilton's peculiar syllogisms:—

Some men are soldiers, Some animals are not men,
Therefore some soldiers are not some animals.

This syllogism cannot in any way be made Aristotelian, either with the terms as they stand, or with any others derived from them by a method independent of the syllogism itself; for instance, the derivation of the contrary from the direct term. Sir William Hamilton's system is therefore an independent addition to that of Aristotle; and the addition must be discussed on its own merits.

The forms)) (( ).) (.(()).(exist in the old system, in that of contraries, and in that of invention of predicates. The peculiar propositions of the second and third may therefore be compared as follows, and under the same[1] symbols:

Introduction of Contraries	*Invention of predicates*
(.) Universal negative, with particular terms, and affirmative form in common language. *All things are either Xs or Ys.*	(.) Particular negative with particular terms, not used in common language. *Some Xs are not some Ys.*
) (Particular affirmative, with universal terms, and negative form in common language. *Some things are neither Xs nor Ys.*	) (Universal affirmative with universal terms, being declaration of identity in common language. *All Xs are all Ys.*

[1] Looking at the fact that the system of contraries admits premises both negative, and that of invention of predicates admits premises both particular, with other analogies which I do not describe here,—I strongly suspect that the two systems have some correlative formation in which the distinction of affirmative and negative appears in the first with the same laws of form under which that of universal and particular appears in the second; and *vice versa*. If this be the case, then (·) though it have a particular form in common language, will be a universal, and)(a particular. This is a hint for the consideration of the reader: I have not been able to make anything out of it, as yet.

My objections to this system as promulgated by Sir William Hamilton (*F. L.* p. 302) may be developed as follows:

First, the fundamental propositions of a logical system should be independent of each other, so that no one of them should be a compound of two others. Now *X*)(*Y*, or '*X* and *Y* are identical names,' is really compounded of *X*)) *Y* and *X*((*Y*. If we once grant a *complex* proposition, why this one only, when there are others, out of which, as I have shewn, a separate system of complex syllogism may be constructed?

To say that the mode of inventing propositions yields no other, is not an answer: for it is the mode itself which is attacked in its results. Every syllogism in which)(occurs, is either a strengthened form, or the resultant of *two* other syllogisms.

Secondly, one object of *formal* logic being to provide form of enunciation for all truth, and form of denial for all falsehood, it is clear that every falsehood which can be enunciated as a truth should be deniable within the forms of the science. Now the simple denial of)(is the disjunctive assertion ').) or (.('. Though it happen that I can prove one of these to be true, without knowing which, yet the power of denying in an elementary form the elementary proposition)(is refused me. A philologist asserts the Greek words *A* and *B* to be identical in meaning: he says 'All *A* is all *B*.' One passage of Homer, and one of Hesiod, both contain the doubtful word *C*, having two possible explanations, the first of which makes Homer assert that some *A*s are not *B*s, while the second makes Hesiod assert that some *B*s are not *A*s. The premises being admitted, the resulting denial of the *simple proposition* of Sir William Hamilton's system is only obtainable by a *dilemma*, or, as it were, *metasyllogism*.

Thirdly, the proposition (.), or 'Some *X*s are not some *Y*s,' has no fundamental proposition which denies it, and not even a compound of other propositions. It is then open to the above objection: and to others peculiar to itself. It is what I have called (*F. L.* p. 153) a *spurious* proposition, as long as *either* of its names applies to more than one instance. And the denial is as follows: 'There is but one *X*, and but one *Y*, and *X* is *Y*.' Unless we know beforehand that there is but one soldier, and one animal, and that soldier the animal, we cannot deny that 'some soldiers are not some animals.' Whenever we know enough of *X* and *Y* to bring forward 'Some *X*s are not some *Y*s' as what *could be conceived* to have been false, we know *more*, namely, 'No *X* is *Y*,' which, when *X* and *Y* are singular, is true or false with 'Some *X*s are not some *Y*s.'

These difficulties[1] lie on the surface; and the first objector is sure to

[1] Sir William Hamilton is, I have no doubt, the first *advocate* of the form (·): but it, and the peculiar syllogism derived from it (with two particular premises) have been seen and *rejected*, by myself at least, probably by others. I mention the following as a curious coincidence. Sir William Hamilton states that he had in his own mind

seize them. I expect a powerful consideration of them in Sir William Hamilton's forthcoming work, from the known learning and acuteness of the author, with some weight given to his assertion that his system has been 'adequately tested and matured.' And I should not be surprised at a *successful* explanation: for, though I cannot give one myself, as long as the system stands on its inventor's ground, yet I can prevent the appearance of the objections by shifting that ground.

The occurrence of eight forms, corresponding in their modes of quantification with those which I had obtained, and by coincidence which did not arise from any sameness in the path of investigation, struck me as exceedingly remarkable. I could not entirely declare against the possibility of sufficient reason for a system which, independently of the habitual acquaintance of its promulgator with the logician's mode of thinking in every age, had, as we shall see, strong symbolic claims to being *something*. Symbolic language gives the expression of the laws of thought in their purest forms: and it has never deceived those who were willing to be its servants before they claimed to be its masters. In the present case, there seemed something resembling a system of algebra with a singular form in it. Formal Logic must teach how to enunciate all definitely conceivable truth and falsehood, just as symbolic algebra must teach how to enunciate all definitely expressible quantity: and 'some *X*s are not some *Y*s' appeared to partake very much of the indeterminateness of $\frac{0}{0}$. An algebraist has not profited by the history of his science, if he dogmatically reject what appears incapable of interpretation in connexion with the rest of its system. Thinking on this, I tried whether there might not be some view of predication which would make Sir William Hamilton's eight forms self-consistent: that is, make them contradict each other four and four. The thing required is that)), ((,).), (.(,).(, and () should remain related to each other as at present: and that)(and (.) should be a double universal and a double particular, destructive each of the other.

We might put this question to any person, When you say 'every man is an animal,' do you speak of *all* men, or of *one* man, of as many animals as there are men, or of *one* animal? Is your proposition

arrived at the form, 'most *Y*s are *Z*s, most *Y*s are *X*s, therefore some *X*s are *Z*s' before me, and thrown it away, unpromulgated, as a cumbrous and useless subtlety. He had thus made the approach of a single instance towards the numerically definite syllogism. Now I, on my part, had made and published, as a true inference, but not within the forms of predication, one syllogism in the new part of Sir William Hamilton's system; in the following words: 'The weakest syllogism from which such an inference [particular negative] can be drawn would then seem to be as follows. Some *X*s are *Y*s, some *Z*s are not *Y*s, therefore some *Z*s are not *X*s. . . . But here it will appear on a little consideration, that the conclusion is only thus far true, that those *X*s which are *Y*s cannot be *those* *Z*s which are not *Y*s. . . .' (*First Notions of Logic*, 1839, reprinted (with slight alteration) as the introductory chapter of *F. L.*)

cumular, or what I will call *exemplar*? I apprehend the general first answer would be in favour of the cumular view, but not the universal one. Some would say, I speak of *one* man, being *any one I can select*, and of one animal, but not *any one I please*, for upon *what man* I select, depends *what animal* I select. Some would say that the article *an*, which denotes one animal, confines the subject to one man: how else can every man be *an* animal? And in truth they are etymologically right, for *every* is *each*, not *all*, in meaning. Some would be inclined to say they were sometimes cumular, and sometimes exemplar: and a great many would hesitate to affirm perfect identity of mode of thought as existing between 'Every man is an animal' and '*all* men are *animals*;' and would admit, when it was put to them, that there is more or less of this difference—the former *tells off*, the latter *sums up*: the former is a completed *induction*, the latter a transformation preparatory to *deduction*.

The next question would be, Are the general propositions of any science, *as actually proved*, cumular or exemplar: and here the answer must be, that what is proved is the exemplar proposition. Euclid, meaning to prove that *all* isosceles triangles have equal angles at the bases, fulfils his meaning by proving that *any one* isosceles triangle is so, and the perception of the goodness of his proof is entirely dependent on the perception of the force of the word *any* before *one*. A student who looks at the definition of proportion sees nothing but a hopeless heap of conditions between him and the knowledge of any possible proportion, until he sees a case established in which *any one* multiple of the first is shewn to lie among the multiples of the second as *that same* multiple of the third lies among those of the fourth.

If the cumular proposition can, generally speaking, only be proved by the help of the exemplar, it follows that the exemplar proposition must precede in order of thought: and it is justifiable to propose it as the basis of a logical system. The distinction of the two modes exists in every language in which I can form the sentence: if there be one in which both forms do not exist, the study of the minds of those who speak that language would be curious.[1]

Of our language and many, I suppose most, others, it must be obvious that the exemplar and cumular forms of expression are much more apt to be confounded as to subject than as to predicate, as to affirmation than as to negation. The logician, who must have *forms*, has to make a choice; and he has invented cumular expressions which do not suit the genius of common thought or common language. 'All man is not fish' is the form in which a logician denies that any man is a fish: Sir William Hamilton says, 'All man is not all fish.' Common language would deny the first by saying, 'No, nor any part of him.' Even 'All men are not fishes' only means, in common language, 'some men are not fishes,'

[1] [*Omnis*—each or every; *Omnes*—all.—MS note.]

with emphasis upon the great number that are implied to be so; and would therefore be held false. The predicate of a negative must be exemplar: it is, 'Every man is not any one fish.' The examination of the following table will shew that there is much less forcing of common expression in a list of nothing but exemplars, than in a list of nothing but cumulars.

Quantity now becomes *mode of selection of the example*: *universal* is replaced by *wholly indefinite*, particular by *not wholly indefinite*, having some, no matter how much nor how little, limitation on the right of selection, under conditions known or unknown. The oppositions of logic must always be mere contradictions, of which one must exist (*F. L.* p. 59). Accordingly, *definite* is to mean *not wholly indefinite*. The terms of selection may be *any one* and *some one*.

Now apply the two selective forms in every way, and the following exemplar forms of predication will occur, arranged in contrary pairs and presenting a system of predication free from the objections which I have urged against the cumular forms, so far as contradiction is concerned.

$A'_{,}$	)(	Any one X is any one Y	*giving*	There is but one X and one Y, and X is Y.
$O'_{,}$	(.)	Some one X is not some one Y	*giving*	There can be found some one X and some one Y which are not the same.
$A_{,}$	))	Any one X is some one Y	*giving*	All Xs are Ys.
$O_{,}$	(.(	Some one X is not any one Y	*giving*	Some Xs are not Ys.
A'	((	Some one X is any one Y	*giving*	Every Y is X.
O'	).)	Any one X is not some one Y	*giving*	Some Ys are not Xs.
$E'_{,}$	).(	Any one X is not any one Y	*giving*	No X is Y.
$I'_{,}$	()	Some one X is some one Y	*giving*	Some Xs are Ys.

The detailed notation needs no explanation. The form given to the old notation may be explained thus. In the system of contraries, the accents refer to the relation of standard terms and contraries. Thus $O_{,}$ being X(.(Y, O' is y).)x or Y(.(X. In the exemplar system, the accent refers to the example, *sub*accent to *sub*ject, superaccent[1] to predicate. Every accent which occurs shews that its term is named after the proposition. Thus in $I'_{,}$ both subject and predicate are, like the proposition, particular or not wholly indefinite: but in $A_{,}$ only the subject is, like the proposition, universal or wholly indefinite. The E' and I' of the system of contraries cannot exist here, but $E'_{,}$ and $I'_{,}$ have double accents, and we have the new propositions $A'_{,}$ and $O'_{,}$, which have similar selective forms in both terms.

The non-entrance of contraries keeps the following rules of syllogism

[1] Subject, as used in reference to a proposition, is liable to some objections. He would be a bold man who would dare to substitute *subdict* and *superdict* for subject and predicate: or, retaining *subject*, to call the predicate the *superject*: but a word on the rashness of this imaginary individual may help the reader in remembering the use of the accents.

intact. The middle term must be indefinite in one of the premises—negative premises give no conclusion. But on the other hand, the system of contraries acknowledges the rule that particular premises give no conclusion—which is not a rule of the exemplar system—and does not acknowledge the two first named.

Taking the 64 cases of combination of premises, in any one figure, we must then reject 16 cases of negative premises, and 12 others in which, the premises not being both negative, both the middle terms are not indefinite. There remain 36 cases for examination, *and all admit of inference*: so that the canon of validity is;—one affirmative premise and one indefinite middle term. This is also the case when exemplar forms are abandoned in favour of cumular ones: but the conclusions in the second (or Sir William Hamilton's) form are not always the same as those in the first.

The validity of every case in which there is one indefinite middle and one premise is affirmative, immediately appears: the *any one* Y of one premise may be taken to be the *some one* Y of the other: and the same is then compared with two others, both giving agreement, or one agreement and one disagreement. Further it will appear that in every case, the selective forms of the terms of the conclusion are the same as they had in the premises. Thus 'any one X is some one Y, any one Y is some one Z' gives 'any one X is some one Z,' for whatever some one Y the first premise can allow, the second premise makes it some one Z: and similarly of others. Hence the symbolic canon of inference is the same as in the system of contraries, namely, the erasure of the middle parentheses gives the symbolic form of the conclusion.

But in the cumular system, this canon of inference is modified. In the exemplar system, the proposition $X)(Y$ or 'Any one X is any one Y,' though it appear to be of the widest character, is restricted by its *double* indefiniteness: doubly indefinite produces doubly singular. This will explain the mode in which conclusions are admissible in the exemplar form which are not admissible in the cumular. For example, in the former,)))(gives)(or 'Any one X is some one Y, and any one Y is any one Z,' gives 'Any one X is any one Z.' Here, if all we knew were that Y and Z are identical, all we could infer would be, 'Any one X is *some* one Z;' but because we know from $Y)(Z$ that there is but one Z, we may say that any one X is *any* one Z. In the cumular system, then,)))(gives)): and the modification of the canon of inference which the cumular system requires is;—Erase the middle parentheses, but when they both *turn one way*, any parenthesis of indefiniteness which turns the *other* way must itself be turned, unless it be *protected* by a negative point. Thus ())(gives (), but))).(gives).(.

To collect the syllogisms, we may observe that there are two doubly indefinite forms $A'_,$ and $E'_,$, each of which has three less indefinite varieties; the first $A_,$, A', and $I'_,$; the second, $O_,$, O' and $O'_,$. A syllogism then in which both premises are double, admits, in original and weakened forms, of 16 varieties; and there are three such double syllogisms which are valid. Classifying the syllogisms by the degrees of relaxation in their forms, we have the following list:

A',A',A',)()(=)(	***A,A',A',***)))(=)(	***I',A',A'*** ())(= ((	*I',A,I',* ())) = ()
	A'A',A' (()(= ((	*A,A,A,*)))) =))	*A'I',I',* ((() = ()
	A',A,A,)()) =))	*A'A,I',* (()) = ()	
	A',A'A',)(((=)(	*A'A'A'* ((((= ((	
		A',I',A,)(() =))	
A',E',E',)().(=).(	***A,E',E',***))).(=).(	***I',E',O,*** ()).(= (.(	***I',O'O',*** ()).) = (.)
	A'E',O, (().(= (.(	*A,O'O'*))).) =).)	*A'O',O',* (((.) = (.)
	A',O'O')().) =).)	*A'O'O',* (().) = (.)	
	A',O,E',)((.(=).(	*A'O,O,* (((.(= (.(	
		A',O',O')((.) =).)	
E',A',E',).()(=).(	***O'A',E',***).))(=).(	***O',A,O,*** (.))(= (.(	*O',A,O',* (.))) = (.)
	O,A',O, (.()(= (.(	*O A,O'*).))) =).)	*O,I',O',* (.(() = (.)
	E',A,O').()) =).)	*O,A,O',* (.()) = (.)	
	E',A'E',).(((=).(	*O,A'O,* (.(((= (.(	
		E',I',O').(() =).)	

The cases in which the cumular system requires the above-mentioned modification of the law of inference have their capital letters in bold italics. The three fundamental syllogisms give, each of them, four cases with one relaxation, five with two, and two with three. Many different rules of formation might be produced, and many analogies, but it is not necessary for my present purpose to examine them.

One however may be mentioned, as giving the mode of arrangement preferred by Sir William Hamilton. The preceding is a table of double entry, and the passage from compartment to compartment in the same column shews that all the negative syllogisms are formed from the affirmative ones by simple insertion of the negative distinction into one or the other premise and the conclusion. Thus, in the second column, at the head of the three compartments, stand)))(=)(and))).(=).(and).))(=).(. In the cumular system, the modified modes of inference occur with certain *affirmative* propositions, which are therefore exceptional.

Looking at the preceding as one way of meeting the formal difficulties of Sir William Hamilton's system, it will easily be conceived possible that there may[1] be others, for one or more of which we are to look to its

[1] Of course I might instance my own numerically definite system, which, as Sir William Hamilton acknowledges, contains his system, and which is not open to any charge of inconsistency. The acknowledgment was made in the assertion that my numerical system, so far as it gives expressed quantity of all kinds to the predicate, was *derived from information furnished by him.* I am still waiting for two *citations*: one from Sir William Hamilton's communication, containing information; one from my own subsequent writings, containing use made of it. I want, in fact, an exemplar proposition of the form)(: having hitherto obtained nothing but)), or (): I have had enough of single indefiniteness, and want an instance of the *double* character which gives singularity to the things to be compared.

inventor, and one more of which I shall presently give myself. But, in the manner in which it has been given out, up to the present time, the defects which I have pointed out exist unanswered.

The exemplar system and that of contraries have 21 syllogisms in common. Of the remaining 15 of the first, 7 correspond to 7 of the syllogisms with both premises negative in the second. The remaining 8 of the first belong, a pair to each of the four syllogisms of the second which have both middle terms particular, one of them being the remaining syllogism with premises both negative. When a symbol taken from the exemplar system is invalid if read in the other, first try it by annexing the negative sign to each premise which is affirmative: if this do not make it valid, alter the curvature of both the middle parentheses, and then either the addition or removal of a negative symbol will make it valid.

V. On the theory of the copula and its connexion with the doctrine of figure

The analysis of the so called *simple* proposition, or judgment, shews that it is, in every one of its particulars, of a complex character. This is readily admitted in regard to the terms, and to the quantity in its connexion with them. But the copula has always been considered as the extreme both of simplicity and generality; and any attempt at the resolution of the copular relation into its elements, is likely to be misunderstood.

In algebra, as it now stands, the *forms* born and educated in arithmetic have left their parent and set up for themselves. Any meanings which obey certain specified laws may be adopted as the means of giving expression to the forms: and the results must be accepted as true in every instance in which the combinations used are consistent and intelligible under the meanings given. Thus we may have, and have, a calculus in which the symbols are in frequent cases not magnitudes at all, but directions how to operate: and though this calculus, when pushed beyond a certain point, has, for the present, its unintelligible symbols, which play the part of the impossible quantities of the older algebra, we have good reason to think that some day the victory over these will be cited as encouragement under the difficulties of a yet more advanced stage of progress.

In my work on *Formal Logic* (pp. 46–54) I followed the hint given by algebra, and separated the essential from the accidental characteristics of the copula, thereby shewing the conditions of invention for a copula different from the ordinary one, or for a copula which, being substituted for the ordinary one, shall leave all the forms and conditions of inference unaltered. On this a learned critic remarks that I claim the abstract copula as an improvement: adding, that some of my modes of making the copula are less abstract, none more so, than *is* and *is not*. As this remark either embodies or suggests the whole, or nearly the whole, of what would be said by a logician, technically so called, it will be worth while to dwell upon it.

By an 'abstract copula' of course is meant a formal mode of joining two terms which carries no meaning, and obeys no law except such as is barely necessary to make the forms of inference follow. Any concrete or actual copula, fulfilling other conditions, is, to the extent of those conditions, less abstract. The best proof of the perception of an abstraction, is the invention of an abstract designation, which must be a technical symbol, if convenience be to dictate. The mode of denoting terms by *letters* fully shews us that the abstract *term* is arrived at: but as there is no symbol for the copula except the verb *is*, we are left to ascertain from the use of that word how the matter stands with respect to the copula.

If an abstract copular symbol had been used, the copular conditions would have been expressly laid down. They are two in number; together sufficient for all forms of inference, but not both necessary in all. The first is what I shall call *transitiveness*, symbolized in

$$X\text{——}Y\text{——}Z = X\text{—}Z;$$

meaning that if X stand in the relation denoted by — to Y, and Y to Z, X therefore stands in that relation to Z. Very many copulae exist in which this transitive relation is seen; as—is,—rules,—lifts,—draws,—leads to,—is superior to,—is ancestor of,—is brother of,—joins,—depends upon,—is greater than,—is equal to,—is less than,—agrees with (in a given particular), &c.

The second condition is *convertibility*, symbolized in

$$X\text{——}Y = Y\text{——}X,$$

in which the relation is its own correlation. Of those mentioned above, convertible relation is seen in—is,—is brother of,—joins (if a middle verb),—is equal to,—agrees with. As instances of the convertible without the transitive character we may take—converses with,—is in the habit of meeting,—is cousin of,—is in controversy with, &c. &c.

The connexion between the affirmative and negative copula is merely that of contrariety: in $X\text{—}Y$ and $X\text{- -}Y$ it is supposed that one or the other must be. It is not necessary that one should be the denial of the other, as I may say, over the whole universe of thought: it is enough if within the universe of the syllogism, either $X\text{—}Y$ or $X\text{- -}Y$ must be true. Thus 'agrees in colour,' 'agrees in size,' may be alternative copulae in a universe the alternative of which is that any X is either of the colour or of the size of some Y.

When contraries are introduced, the copular condition further required is that either X—Y or X—y should hold for any X.

The least abstract of all copulae is the *is* and *is not* of the logicians, when employed, whether subjectively or objectively, in the sense of identity. But logicians rarely confine it to that sense. It takes many meanings in their modes[1] of speaking and in their examples: and perhaps may be stated as generally signifying agreement in some understood and, *pro vice*, unvarying particular. I have never seen it carried further, formally at least: and I feel safe in affirming that *is*,—used as merely satisfying the transitive and convertible conditions, with a consequent right, for example, to treat it as standing for 'is brother to,'—is a more abstract copula than the *is* of the logicians.

I should almost presume this from the silence of the writers who distinguish between reading the *extension* and reading the *intension* of a proposition, as to any other change of the copula being possible. 'Every man is an animal' is read either in extension, 'All man is animal,' or in intension, as by saying that the notion of animal forms part of the notion of man; every attribute of an animal is an attribute of man. Without at all denying the existence of the distinction, or its *metaphysical* value, I feel convinced that it is not another reading of the proposition, but another proposition, derived *inferentially*, though not *syllogistically*, by aid of the *dictum de majore et minore*. For a term used universally we may substitute a lesser term; and the attribute of *all* animals is the attribute of all *men*. The proposition only says that man is the lesser term; and intensive reading is thus derived from the *dictum*. Invent a substantive, *A*, such that *ex vi termini*, the '*A* of an animal,' is one in which the word *animal* must be construed universally; and then we may affirm that '*A* of an animal' is '*A* of a man.' And though, undoubtedly, the word *attribute*, used metaphysically, will be the one most often employed in place of *A*, yet the formal process of reading by intension will be only a case of that principle on which we say that 'Englishman who does not use tobacco' is included in 'European who does not take snuff,' obtained by enlargement of the particular and diminution of the universal.

Formally speaking, the change from extension to intension is as

[1] But not in their formal definitions and enunciations. The *substantive verb* is the most common definition. The Port Royal Logic, which I choose from those lying before me, as a work which dares to differ, or to revive, at pleasure, makes its definition very distinct. 'Non sufficit hos duos termines percepisse; sed debent mente vel conjungi vel separari. Et haec mentis Operatio in Propositione notatur verbo, *Est*. . . .' To take two extremes of the part of time in which scholastic logic and printing flourished together, we have *Paulus Venetus* (1474), 'Copula semper est verbum substantivum scilicet sum, es, est,'—and *Crackanthorp* (4th ed., 1677), 'Et haec [*sc*. copula] est in omni Propositione Verbum hoc Substantivum, *Sum, es, fui*, aut aliqua persona illius.'

follows; and it will be seen that a new distinction is introduced, and further, that the two modes of reading are not convertible; the extensive mode gives the intensive, but not *vice versa* in all cases.

Extension given	*Intension deduced*
Every *X* is *Y*.	Every *existing* part of *all Y*s is an *existing* part of *all X*s.
No *X* is *Y*.	No *sufficient*[1] part of any *Y* is an *existing* part of any *X*.
Some *X*s are *Y*s.	Every *existing* part of all *Y*s is an *existing* part of some *X*s.
Some *X*s are not *Y*s.	No *sufficient* part of any *Y* is an *existing* part of some *X*s.

Intension given	*Extension deduced*
A *sufficient* part of some one *Y* is an existing part of every *X*.	Every *X* is *Y*.
An existing part of any *Y* is not an existing part of any *X*.	No *X* is *Y*.
A sufficient part of some *Y*s is an existing part of some *X*s.	Some *X*s are *Y*s.
An existing part of any *Y* is not an existing part of some *X*s.	Some *X*s are not *Y*s.

By treating the predicate itself as one attributive notion, the modes of reading both kinds of propositions intensively may be assimilated: but not without losing sight of an important distinction. In the affirmative, any portion of the intension of the predicate may be affirmed of the subject; in the negative, it is not true that *any* portion of the intension of the predicate may be denied of the subject. Thus 'no planet moves in a circle' gives us a right to deny any *constitutive* attribute of circular motion to that of a planet, but not *any* attribute; not, for instance, the progression through every longitude.

Leaving the distinction of extensive and intensive reading entirely out of view, as not connected with the theory of the copula, I proceed to inquire into the connexion of the doctrine of figure with that of the copula; a connexion which I take to be the most important part of the former doctrine. And first, I take the system from which contraries are excluded. Looking at the two copular conditions, the transitive and the convertible, I ask what inferences hold good when *only* the transitive condition holds: for this one must hold, as long as there is but one species of copula; we shall presently see that it is the *condition of permanence* of the copula. As a representative of a transitive but inconvertible copula, let us take the verb *give*, assuming that he gives who gives that which gives. Then '*X* gives *Y*, *Y* gives *Z*, therefore *X* gives *Z*' is legitimate, being the mere expression of the transitive hypothesis. And

[1] Meaning part sufficient to determine it to be *Y*. I do not say *attribute*, because the inference does not depend upon the metaphysical meaning of that word.

the opponent forms of this must be legitimate. Thus '*X* gives *Y*, *X* does not give *Z*' leads to '*Y* does not give *Z*': for if *Y* gave *Z*, *X* giving *Y*, *X* would give *Z*: this is in the third figure. Again, '*X* does not give *Z*, *Y* gives *Z*' leads to '*X* does not give *Y*:' for if *X* gave *Y*, *Y* giving *Z*, *X* would give *Z*: this is in the second figure. When these propositions are made cumulative, with quantities proper for inference, the usual inferences are obtained. Accordingly, + meaning affirmative, and − negative, all + + syllogisms in the first figure, + − syllogisms in the second figure, and − + syllogisms in the third figure (reading premises in the Aristotelian order) do not need a convertible copula. They are

I.		II.		III.	
Barbara	))))	*Camestres*	).(((	*Felapton*	(().(
Darii	())))	*Baroko*	(.(((	*Ferison*	()).(
				Bokardo	(.(((

Turning to Sir William Hamilton's system, I find that his peculiar syllogisms will not follow this rule: but in the *exemplar* system it is preserved throughout. The fourth figure is incapable of inference, as long as one *inconvertible* copula, and that only, is used.

The copula being inconvertible, we may complete the modes of inference by allowing the correlative copula; as '*X* gives *Y*' '*Y* is given by *X*'. That is, whenever conversion is necessary to turn the syllogism into + + of the first figure, + − of the second, or − + of the third, the correlative copula must somewhere be introduced.

The following addition to the poetry of logic may be euphonized by any one to his own taste: the letter *g*, following a vowel, denotes that the premise (or conclusion) denoted by that vowel takes the correlative copula.

Barbara, Celagrent, Darii, Ferigoque prioris
Cesareg, Camestres, Festinog, Baroko secundae
Tertia Darapgi, Disagmis, Datigsi, Felapton
Bokardo Ferison habet. Quarta insuper addit
Bramantigp, Camegnes, Dimarigs, Fegsapo, Fregsison.

This means, for example, that *Fesapo* may be read in the *fourth* figure under the additional condition seen in *Fegsapo*, namely, that the copula of the first premise is to be correlative of that used in the second premise and conclusion: and Darapgi in the third, if the second copula used be correlative of the other two. Thus 'all the piles supported arches; all the piles were supported on gravel, therefore gravel did then support arches' is a good syllogism, and not capable of reduction to an Aristotelian syllogism. The proposition 'support of support is support' is necessary to the inference, which inference can only be obtained from a sorites, and not then except by help of the *dictum* already quoted. It may be said that this is *more* than an Aristotelian syllogism; I maintain it to be *less, if either*. The outstanding copular relation (always implied) of an Aristotelian syllogism is '*is that which is*, gives *is*:' of the preceding case, 'support of support is support.' The former demands transitive and convertible meaning for *is*, or that *is* shall be its own correlative: the latter demands transitive meaning for *support*, and the allowance of its correlative.

The following table shews the way in which any combination of premises is to be read in any figure, it being presumed, as in Sir William Hamilton's system, that every syllogism may be read in any figure.

$$\begin{array}{llll} \text{I.} & + \; + \; + & (+) - \; - & - \; (+) \; - \\ \text{II.} & (+) \; + \; + & + \; - \; - & - \; + \; (-) \\ \text{III.} & + \; (+) \; + & + \; - \; (-) & - \; + \; - \\ \text{IV.} & + \; + \; (+) & + \; (-) \; - & (-) \; + \; - \end{array}$$

These cases may be remembered as follows. Let $+ +$, $+ -$, $- +$, and $- -$, be called the *primitive forms* of the four figures: the fourth figure taking its root in an inconclusive form. In every primitive form the correlative copula need not appear. When *one* premise of a primitive form is altered, the necessity of a correlative copula is thrown upon *the other*: when *both*, upon the *conclusion*.

The principles laid down in Section I. enable us to make a still further enlargement. The logician, followed by the algebraist, has restricted himself to one copula: the former uses *is*, the latter $=$; and both are used in some variety of sense. The algebraist, indeed, sometimes goes a little further, and introduces the correlatives $>$ and $<$, which might be generalized for the purposes of logic into symbols of correlative copulae in general. In every kind of logic, formal and applied, the transitive copula is insisted on. This however is not necessary: inference may be seen without it. The perception of relations by means of relations does not require us to use only one relation. If I can see that

Every X has a relation to some Y
and Every Y has a relation to some Z,

it follows that every X has a compound relation to some Z. Be the premised relations what they may, there is a concluding relation, which may or may not be expressible by one word. Thus if John can persuade Thomas, and Thomas can command William, we cannot infer that John can either persuade or command William: but if we express by one word the process of gaining an end by persuading one who can command—say we choose to use the word *control*[1] for this purpose—then John can

[1] This is not an improper word; for the compound relation, as well as the original ones, enters in a particular, not a universal, manner. It is enough that persuading

control William. We have then a bicopular syllogism, in which the intransitiveness of the individual copulae is supplied by the invention of a compound copula for the conclusion. This is the step by which we ascend to the general theory of the copula: but those who proceed from a general copula to a particular one, will merely see how to read the general conditions in the particular case.

Can a bicopular syllogism be reduced to a compound process of unicopular syllogism? In the case before us the conditions are:

Postulate. Control includes the influence exerted over the governed by one who can persuade the governor.

Premises. John can persuade Thomas.
Thomas can command William.

Conclusion. John can control William.

The only way in which this can be reduced to unicopular syllogism is by the following sorites.

Given premise. John is {one who can persuade Thomas}.

Postulate. {One who can persuade Thomas} is {one who can control all whom Thomas commands.}

Second given premise, and dict. de maj. et min. {One who can control all whom Thomas commands.} is {One who can control William}.

Conclusion. John is {one who can control William}.

The algebraical equation $y = \phi x$ has the copula $=$, relatively to y and ϕx: but relatively to y and x the copula is $= \phi$. This is precisely the distinction of 'John can persuade Thomas' and 'John is {one who can persuade Thomas.}' The deduction of $y = \phi\psi z$ from $y = \phi x$, $x = \psi z$ is the formation of the composite copula $= \phi\psi$. And thus may be seen the analogy by which the instrumental part of inference may be described as *the elimination of a term by composition*[1] *of relations.* For though in ordinary inference the concluding copula is usually identical with those premised, yet it is no less true that the composition must have taken place: X is Y, Y is Z, therefore X is that which is ($=$ is) Z.

[1] Or *composition and resolution*, but these two words never finally mean more than one. Composition of an opponent is resolution. Whether the words shall both occur or not depends upon whether we begin on a narrow or a wide basis. Arithmeticians begin with *multiplication* and *division*, and end by declaring them identical. The old geometers began with *composition* of ratios, and never arrived at *resolution*, for they had all resolutions in their compositions.

---

one who can command is *one* of the ways of controlling. And let there be any number of forms of persuasion, and of command, it is enough that one of the forms of persuasion procuring one of the forms of command, should be one form of control. And thus it may happen that, legitimately, the copular word of the conclusion may be that of the premise in a different sense; a very common thing in the logic of common life. But in the negative copula, the copular word must be universal.

Upon two given relations, there is but one species of affirmative syllogism, and two species of opposing negative syllogisms; that is, if the alternative relation be merely negative, and no correlative be permitted. If —— and ...... be the copular symbols, and $\overline{\ldots\ldots}$ that of the compound relation; and if — — and ... ... and $\overline{\ldots}\ \overline{\ldots}$ represent the negatives of the first relations, the three syllogisms are

First figure	*Second figure*	*Third figure*
$\left\{\begin{array}{l} Y\text{——}Z \\ X\ldots\ldots Y \end{array}\right.$	$\left\{\begin{array}{l} Z\text{——}Y \\ X\overline{\ldots}\ \overline{\ldots}Y \end{array}\right.$	$\left\{\begin{array}{l} Y\overline{\ldots}\ \overline{\ldots}Z \\ Y\ldots\ldots X \end{array}\right.$
$X\overline{\ldots\ldots}Z$	$X\ldots\ \ldots Z$	$X\text{— —}Z$

The terms are here singular: if we make them cumulative, we introduce the usual laws of quantity. And the three figures shew their primitive forms $++$, $+-$, $-+$. If the correlative copulae be introduced, the preceding theory of figure may be extended to the bicopular syllogism. And we now see as follows:—

First, the fourth figure is dependent for its existence upon the entrance of the *copular correlative*. I have always looked with surprise upon the arguments for and against the fourth figure. If the inferences therein made be good inferences—if the man who can establish the premises, *does* establish the conclusion, of *Dimaris* or *Camenes*, how can it be said that the fourth figure is not to be used? *there it is*, and it cannot be reasoned out of existence. But in the above system, the fourth figure yields no *true inference* until the copular correlative is allowed: this may be excluded from *data* by hypothesis, but on what principle of reason can true consequences of data be excluded by hypothesis, and what is the correct English of the word hypothesis, in such case? There ought to be no bounds to any science, except such as are determined by its data.

Secondly, it appears that the affirmative syllogism gains its conclusion by composition, the negative by resolution: *the negative premise has a compound copular relation, which is to be resolved.* We see this plainly when *different* relations are compounded: just as a beginner in algebra sees properties of $a \times b$ which would be much clouded by taking his initial examples from $a \times a$. Indeed, the forms of logic, stinted down to the Aristotelian syllogism, much resemble those of an algebra in which all the letters are equal, and all equal to unity. For example, taking our previous instance of composition, from '*Z* can command *Y*, *X* cannot control *Y*' we deduce *X* cannot persuade *Z*. And we must deduce it by resolving control into persuasion to command; and saying '*X* cannot persuade any one who can command *Y*' or *X* cannot persuade *Z*.

But, it may be said, this cannot be shewn on the ordinary syllogism '*Z* is *Y*, *X* is not *Y* therefore *X* is not *Z*;' nor on any syllogism in which the negative premise is not expressly composite. This objection I proceed to examine.

When the copula *is* means pure identity, as in 'that horse *is* that horse' (in which case I shall write it in capitals) I own that the resolution is so purely formal, and the reality represented under the compound form so elusive of our attempts to mean something more than was meant by the simple form, that I should compare the resolution to that of 1 into 1×1 in arithmetic. And though this arithmetical resolution be often useful, and even requisite, as a preliminary to clear notion of some higher development of thought, yet the logical type of it might well wait until the time comes when the same may be said of *it*.[1] 'That horse "IS that which IS" that horse' may therefore be abandoned to the objector. But when, as more frequently happens, the copula *is* only denotes some agreement, or something[2] transitive and convertible which is not pure identity, I maintain the actual resolution to be part of the process of inference. Let us take a material instance, which may represent anything objective, as will be admitted: and I think that the process may find its analogue in purely subjective matters. Let *is* represent agreement in *colour*. Then it will be instantly admitted that '*Z* is *Y*' and '*Z* is that which is *Y*' are two different propositions. The question is, how do we infer from '*Z* is *Y*, *X* is not *Y*.' Our second premise is *X* has not 'the colour which *Y* has:' and for the last words we substitute, as an *identity*, 'the colour which *Z* has,' the identity being purely subjective. Here the resolution was made: our second premise became '*X* is not that which *Y* is'.

Logical writers do not collect their copulae: and their processes seem reducible to common form in no way but this. They postulate that the copulae they use (which they take good care shall be transitive and convertible) have the inferential force of the identity IS: they examine and dwell upon syllogisms of identity, thereby giving the opponents of logic some reason for their scoffs at the syllogism, and return with their results to other copulae, by aid of the postulate. To this there can be no objection as to the truth of its results, but much in every other way. This subject however is too wide a one; and requires the preliminary consideration of the manner in which the *term* has been used, and a disentanglement of the confusion of ideas under which logicians speak, in one sense, of man as a part[3] of the notion animal, and in another of

[1] [Bentley: *Phalaris* preface, citing Plato's *Phaedrus*: *τοῦτον δὲ τὸν Θεύθ πρῶτον ἀριθμόν τε καὶ λογισμὸν εὑρεῖν* (2 August 1860).]

[2] In the *IS* of identity, the transitive and convertible relations are a kind of zero forms. There is not much transition in travelling from York to York and from thence to York: nor much to see, in spite of the Italics, in the proposition that from York to *York* is the same distance as from *York* to York.

[3] In all that relates to quantity, there is no occasion for the mathematical logician to pay the least deference to the Christian followers of Aristotle; the master himself

animal as part of the notion man. The 'integrate or mathematical whole' which, according to Sir William Hamilton, 'the philosophers contemned,' and which is seen in 'All men are animals', must take its proper place: and 'philosophy', which 'tends always to the universal and the necessary' must be taught that the *universal* belongs to the mathematical whole, as surely as the *necessary* to the metaphysical whole.

The admission of relation in general, and of the composition of relation, tends to throw light upon the difference between the invented syllogism of the logicians and the natural syllogism of the external world. The logician, tied to a verb of identity, from which if he wander it is never quite out of sight, is bound to subject and predicate of the same class; objective both, or subjective both. He cannot say the rose *is* red, for his *is* would require the inference that some red is the rose. He has nothing but a method of reducing his predicate to an object: the rose is a red thing; some red thing is a rose. The common man uses a copula which ties the object up in relation to a more subjective predicate; not reading inversely by intension, not dwelling on redness as an attribute of the rose, but directly by extension, thinking of the family *rose* as his external object, and the sensation red as one condition under which it appears to his senses. Again, an ordinary person says that the rose is red,

---

was a mathematician, as were some of his Greek successors. Those who could contentedly put *number* and *speech* together, as discrete *quantity*, in opposition to *length*, as continuous, do not deserve to be listened to, as quantitarians. But this it will be said is in the writings of the master. It is so; but the question is, whether it be not an obvious interpolation. The case stands thus: In the sixth chapter of the Categories, quantity is made discrete or continuous; the discrete is ἀριθμὸς καὶ λόγος, the continuous is length, surface, &c. Farther on, λόγος is changed into φωνή—λέγω δὲ αὐτὸν τὸν μετὰ φωνῆς λόγον γινόμενον—and the reason given is that it is *measured* by long and short syllables. On this I say first, that Aristotle would probably have seen what his determined disciple Crackanthorp afterwards saw, that the *time of speaking* is not *speech*; secondly, that it is incredible that he should have used a wrong word and have afterwards corrected himself by a synonyme instead of an erasure; thirdly, that ἀριθμὸς καὶ λόγος, in the language of the time, are integer number, and fractional ratio or ratio of commensurables. An editor who was not a mathematician, seeing λόγος, which to him was only communication in its most general sense, may have excogitated the absurdity above alluded to, by help of φωνή. Proclus has been used in a similar way. Barocius makes him inform us that the predecessors of Euclid had written on inexplicables (*quae non explicari possunt*): Proclus says ἄλογα, and means incommensurables.

But how can λόγος be called discrete? Before Euclid it must have been so. Euclid's definition, which brings incommensurables under the same law with commensurables, gives the term ratio a title to continuity, which it had not before: just as in modern times, the interminable decimal, when admitted as a distinct conception of arithmetic, gives continuity to *number*.

[Smiglecius (*Disp.* 9, *quaest.* 6) notes that Aristotle does not count speech as quantity in the 5th book of the *Metaphysics*. He argues against, and says that Aristotle has made it a quantity here '*vulgarem ea de re opinionem secutus*' (30 July 1860).]

and red is pretty, so that the rose is pretty. The logician's pupil, when not far advanced, will interpret him as saying that 'The rose is a red thing; a red thing is a pretty thing, &c.' thus committing him to an opinion upon red cabbage which perhaps was not within his meaning. The logician himself will substitute another process: 'The colour of the rose is red colour; red colour is pretty colour; therefore the colour of the rose is pretty colour:' he thus reduces it to the equation of two terms by comparison with a third; when most probably the real form of thought (and logic professes to be the study of existing forms) is nothing but the composition of relations. The rose *is* (in its relation to one sense) red; red *is* (in the relation of the perceptions to the judgment) pretty; therefore the rose is (to one sense that which is to the judgment) pretty. This distinction of copulae is more nearly present to the mind than any one of the transformations by which the technical form is arrived at: it is visible, more or less distinctly, that the first premise is matter of *fact*, the second matter of *taste*; here is a recognition of difference between *is* of the first premise and *is* of the second; which leads, with proportionate strength, to the recognition of the composite character of *is* in the conclusion. Nor does the logician's form avoid it, except by a pure assumption that the copulae are the same; an assumption not true in fact. Nor can an answer be given by saying that logic takes no cognizance of the matter, but only of the form; for it is bound, by the laws of form, not to represent differences by agreements, except when it is formally shown that the differences cannot affect the object to be gained.

In one very material consideration, the logicians have evidenced the manner in which their copula '*is*' partakes of the verb of identity on which, as above remarked, they test all their inferences. When the copula of identity is employed, it is of necessity that one subject example can only agree with one predicate example: any one man IS, merely because he IS *one* man, only *one* animal. Extend the copula to a meaning short of perfect identity, and the copular relation may belong, in an affirmative, to more than one example of the predicate. For instance, when the copula is agreement in colour, 'Every X is Y' may mean that each X is of the colour of one or more of the Ys. The particular character of the predicate, that is, the description of its extent as being 'one or more, possibly all' may belong to it, independently of the number of instances of the subject, in right of, and by derivation from, *one* instance of the subject. And the proposition 'one X——Every Y' may be true without our being obliged to say that there is therefore only one Y in existence, by reason of the relation indicated by —— existing between that one X and every Y in existence.

Hence follows an extended mode of interpreting Sir William Hamilton's system into consistency. Let the quantity of the predicate be determined by the least number of instances of the predicate which are declared to stand in the copular relation to each instance of the subject: it being understood that the declaration of the copular relation existing between a certain *X* and a certain *Y* does not deny that the relation may exist between that *X* and other *Y*s, or between other *X*s and that *Y*. Thus, 'All *X*s——all *Y*s,' or *X*)(*Y*, now means that every *X* stands in the copular relation to each and every *Y*. If there were ten *X*s and ten *Y*s, Sir William Hamilton's proposition would assert ten agreements: the form here proposed declares a hundred. And it is now contradicted by *X*(.)*Y* or 'some *X*s - - some *Y*s:' for either each *X* and each *Y* agree, or some *X*s do not agree with some of the *Y*s.

This view of the subject meets another objection of mine to the system as proposed. It can no longer be asserted that *X*)(*Y* is a proposition compounded of two others of the system, *X*))*Y* and *Y*))*X*: for each *X* may agree with some of the *Y*s, and each *Y* with some of the *X*s, without every *X* agreeing with every *Y*.

There is however a distinction to be drawn. When the quantity of the affirmative predicate is determined solely by the number of instances which *each* instance of the subject is related to, let us say that the predicate has *exemplar quantity*. But in the common system, in which the quantity of the predicate is cumulated from all the instances of the subject, let us say that it has *cumular quantity*: this second system permitting, like the first, each instance of the subject to be related to more than one instance of the predicate. Thus, quantity being exemplar, we must say of 'Every man IS an animal' that the predicate is singular: quantity being cumular, that the predicate is arithmetically coextensive with the subject. But when it is 'Every man—agrees with in being carnivorous—a brute,' the predicate is not singular, even when its quantity is exemplar.

[An extension of the numerically definite system here arises, which I shall not stop to investigate the consequences of. If ξ be the whole number of *X*s in the universe, η the number of *Y*s, and n the number of *Y*s (at least) to which each of m*X*s is related; then mn is the least number of relations asserted. If mn be greater than $(\xi - 1)\eta$, then $mn - (\xi - 1)\eta$ at least of the η *Y*s must be related to ξ *X*s, that is, to all the *X*s. Now as n cannot exceed η, m must be ξ: and a necessarily convertible proposition may then exist, if n exceed $\eta - \eta \div \xi$.]

By merely allowing a complete exemplar form of quantification we procure the extension of Sir W. Hamilton's system which I have described in the last section: we now annex to this admission, a predicate quantity of more than one example.

And the forms with their meanings are as follows, each universal with its particular contradiction.

⎧ *X*)(*Y*	Each *X* is related to all the *Y*s.
⎩ *X*(.)*Y*	Some *X*s are not related to some of the *Y*s.

⎧ $X))Y$	Each X is related to one or more Ys.
⎩ $X(.(Y$	Some Xs are not related to any Ys.
⎧ $X((Y$	Some Xs are (among them) related to all the Ys.
⎩ $X).)Y$	No X is related to some one or more Ys.
⎧ $X).(Y$	No X is related to any one Y.
⎩ $X()Y$	Some Xs are related to some one or more Ys.

This system as it stands, is free from all objections which I can raise. Every proposition has its contradictory, the form (.) is not generally spurious, no numerical dictum is established[1] by the mere assertion of a proposition. The symbolic law of inference does not present any modified cases; and, transitive copular relation existing, though inconvertibly, the use of the correlative relation, in the places previously marked out, will allow of inference. The manner in which the introduction of more general copular relation allows of more general inference, and the alterations in the import of the forms)(and (.), with the value of those alterations in the expression of the forms of thought, would admit of considerable discussion, if the length to which this paper has attained did not forbid.

Taking the predicate as both exemplar and cumulative in quantity, the copular relation as both transitive and convertible, we see a system which differs from that of Sir William Hamilton only in the admission of a wider alternative of copular agreement: instead of 'one Y or no Y at all' it is 'one or more Ys or no Y at all.' Circumstances require me, I think, to point out my reasons for concluding that this extension of alternatives has *not* been made by Sir William Hamilton. They are first, his description of his own use of quantity, made in terms[2] so technical, that it is impossible to suppose he varies from the ancient *modes* of quantity, in extending the *application* of them: secondly, that the author of the 'Outlines,' an accredited expounder of the details of this system, not only does not give the smallest hint to the contrary, but adopts the conclusions[3] suggested by the old modes, as 'of course.'

[1] If indeed we were to declare that the number of correlated instances should never exceed 10, then)(would imply that there are not more than 10 Xs nor more than 10 Ys. It is the refusal to admit of more than one instance of each in relation which reduces)(to double singularity in the exemplar form first discussed.

[2] 'The *first* scheme is that which logically—confines all expressed quantity to the *Subject*, presuming the *Predicate* to be taken—in *negative* propositions, always determinately in its *greatest* and *least* extension (universally and singularly), in *affirmative* propositions, always indeterminately in *some part* of its extension (particularly). The *second* scheme is that which logically—extends the expression of quantity to *both* the propositional terms, and allows the *Predicate* to be of *any quantity*, in propositions of *either quality*. . . . The first doctrine is the common or Aristotelic; the second is mine; . . .' 'Letter, &c.' subsequent to my 'Statement,' pp. 31, 32.

[3] Mr Thomson agrees with me as to the *spuriousness* of 'Some Xs are not some Ys' in Sir Wm Hamilton's system, except 'of course' as a denial of singularity and identity: 'Except of course they represent individuals.' 'Outlines, &c.' pp. 188, 189.

I shall now proceed to the application of correlative copulae to the system of predication by contraries. I insert a slight and preliminary notice of this extension more as an example of the study of extension than because of its representation of any very common modes of thought. At the same time it should be remembered that we cannot appeal to existing modes, and to their agreement with the Aristotelian forms, as conclusive evidence of the natural character of those forms, or of any restriction which results from their use. For many centuries, and in particular during those centuries which saw the relations of the modern and ancient languages finally settled, every man who learnt to read was alphabetically drilled in the Aristotelian syllogism. If technical forms could produce such an effect as either to supplant more natural ones, or to prevent the natural growth of the most natural ones, the Aristotelian forms have had every advantage given them, and may have done it. Consequently, no modes of thinking which are not easily reconcilable with the Aristotelian forms ought to be suppressed because they do not seem to have any usage in their favour.

The copula to be extended is the word *is*, in its widest sense: the extended copula may be said to be *has relation to*, the relation being expressed or understood, but distinctly conceived as *transitive*. The correlative copula may be expressed by *has correlation to*: and it is demonstrable, or is rather seen to accompany than to follow, that all transitive relations have transitive correlatives. As a short mode of speaking, we may say that our relations are *gives to* and *receives from*. The terms *active* and *passive* might be generalized into words of description for the correlatives; and *middle* into a word of description for relations which are their own correlatives.

In the common system, if a certain *X* be a certain *Y*, that *Y* is that same *X*: but the correlative (then called converted) relation need not be much dwelt upon. Of the two '*X* is *Y*' and '*Y* is *X*,' either may be called direct, and the other inverted. In the extension, each instance may stand both in direct and inverted relation to something: so that every *X* gives something, every *Y* gives something; every *X* receives from something, every *Y* receives from something. And it must be that no *X* gives to nor receives from, any contrary, *x*, either directly or by transition. If, for instance, a certain *X* give to one or more *Y*s, no one of those *Y*s can give to any *x*: but as each of those *Y*s must *give*, and either to *X*s or *x*s, it must be that they give to *X*s, but not necessarily to those from which they received. Nor must the same *X* give to both *Y* and *y*, &c.

We have then for any one *X* either X,Y' and Y,X' or X,y' and y,X': meaning that either an *X* selected gives to *Y*s, and each of those *Y*s to *X*s; or to *y*s, and each of those *y*s to *X*s. And the subscript and superscript accents may be applied to the parentheses: thus $X,))'Y$ may stand for 'every *X* gives to one or more *Y*s.'

[Accordingly[1], if we adopt this hypothesis, namely, that a direct and inverted relation always exists, it follows that all syllogisms are valid, put what marks of relation we may. For $X,))'Y$ never exists without $X')),Y$: and the same of all the other forms. And $X,))'Y$ has $X,).('y$ and $y,))'x$ and $x,(.)'Y$ among its equivalents. From this most complete of all possible assignments of relation, we may descend by two steps.

First, we may dismiss the condition that every existing relation has its correlative: and then we may ask under what relations each syllogism is valid, there being one existing between each of the pairs XY, YZ, and one (inferred) between XZ. Here each relation is supposed to extend over the terms and their contraries: thus from $X,))'Y$ we are to infer $X,).('y$, and may use it. Secondly, we may dismiss the condition that the relation extends over the contrary, and then we arrive at the modification of the common or Aristotelian syllogism, already discussed: in this case, the inference can be obtained without any use of the contrary, or extension of the relation.

I now give the heads of the results which arise from the hypothesis that one of the correlations is assigned or inferred, and the other not admitted. The equivalent propositions are those of the ordinary system, with the relations unaltered: thus

$$X,))'Y = X,).('y = x,(('y = x,(.)'Y$$
$$X,()'Y = X,(.('y = x,)('y = x,).)'Y$$

Here $x,(.)'Y$ must be read as follows; in every instance, either x gives, or Y receives, or both: and $x,).)'Y$ means that there are some instances in which neither x gives, nor Y receives.

These equivalences may be easily proved by those who remember the meaning of the relative symbol. The assertion $X,))'Y$ is that of a relation in which every X and every x is a giver, and every Y and every y is a receiver; but so that no Y nor y can receive both from a X and from a x, no X nor x can give both to a Y and to a y. Accordingly, $x,(('y$ immediately follows: for every y receives either from a x or from a X, but not from the latter, because then a Y and a y would both receive from that X.

The law of entrance of the relations is as follows. When the syllogism is read in an Aristotelian figure (the first or the third) which begins with the middle term, all that is requisite is that the major and concluding relation should be the same: when in a figure (the second or the fourth) which does not begin with the middle term, all that is requisite is that the major and concluding relation should be correlatives. Each syllogism therefore can be read in two ways, according as the major and minor relations are the same or correlative.

[1] The paragraphs between [] are substituted for those originally given: their date is 1 July 1850.

For example, the syllogism

$$A,A'I', \quad \text{or} \quad))((=)($$

read in the first figure, is

$$Y((Z + X))Y = X)(Z,$$

which may be either

$$Y,(('Z + X,))'Y = X,)('Z, \quad \text{or} \quad Y,(('Z + X')),Y = X,)('Z.$$

To prove the first, remark that since *every X* supplies a Y, there are but the xs to supply the remaining Ys and all the ys. But since the Zs are all supplied by Ys, all the ys supply zs, being themselves supplied by xs. Hence, by the transitive character of the relation, we have $x,()'z$, or $X,)('Z$. To prove the second, observe that every y supplies a x, and if any such x supply a Z, the y which supplies that x also supplies that Z; but every Z is supplied by a Y. Consequently $x,()'z$, or $X,)('Z$, as before.

In each syllogism, one or other of its two cases must involve the direct entrance of contraries: so that the Aristotelian form never allows two cases. For instance,

$$Y,))'Z + X,))'Y = X,))'Z$$

is obviously true without consideration of contraries; every X supplies a Y, and every Y a Z. But $Y,))'Z + X')),Y = X,))'Z$ must be proved thus. If any X supplied a z (here the contrary enters), a Y would supply that z, and would therefore supply both a Z and a z.

The remarkably simple modification which occurs in the Aristotelian forms depends upon those forms being confined to particular predicates in affirmatives, and universal ones in negatives. When all relations have their correlatives, the *reading by figure is a matter of indifference*[1]; when the two correlatives are not allowed *in the same proposition*, the figures are grouped in pairs, the first and third, the second and fourth; when no term is allowed its alternative, or contrary, the four figures become distinct in their properties.

The primitive forms of the four figures being $+\,+$, $+\,-$, $-\,+$, $-\,-$, the mode of reading by thickened parentheses may be connected with them as follows:

	+ − + −		+ − + −		+ − + −		+ − + −
I.	**❙** | **❙** |	II.	**❙** | | **❙**	III.	| **❙** **❙** |	IV.	| **❙** | **❙**

in which, over the thick lines in I, occur $+\,+$; in II, $+\,-$; in III, $-\,+$; in IV, $-\,-$.

All these relations may, no doubt, be connected; but a general demonstration of the law of relations, when two correlatives are not admitted in one proposition, would be requisite: this demonstration is very easy.

[1] [Yes, for figure of position. (Italics added in MS.)]

In my written communication to the Society, having seen that the + +, + –, and – + syllogisms of the first three figures required no correlative, I concluded that, on investigation, the – – syllogisms of the fourth figure would require none. And as this turned out to be true, I looked no further at the time. But I afterwards found that, though this be all correct, the entrance of the contraries under which alone a – – syllogism gains existence, gives rise to the validity of *every* syllogism without any correlative.]

When an intermediate relation exists, which is equally related to both the correlatives, as in the case of *greater*, *equal*, and *less*, that intermediate relation may be employed for either. The effect, if any, upon the conclusion, is easily connected with the law by which the strengthening or weakening one of the premises produces its effect on the conclusion. But the length of this paper compels me to omit the detail of this and other points. The combination of the system of invention of predicates with that of contraries remains for consideration.

Addition

[Dated 3 July 1850]

It may be useful to advert to the manner in which logicians, who all contend more or less explicitly for the sufficiency of ordinary syllogism, meet the cases in which premises give inference which cannot be reduced to one ordinary syllogism *with those premises*. I pass over the following, as extra-logical. First, giving the inference a bad name, as calling it a subtlety, or the like; logic is the science of the *necessary* laws of thought, subtle and not subtle. Secondly, affirming that the inference is very easy: which is just as much the case with the favoured modes of syllogism. I proceed to one which is both logical and sufficient, but which again applies just as much to the ordinary syllogism as to the cases which will not fall under it.

In every inference, there is an act of the mind, which we may perform with or without consciousness of reference to the general, self-evident, and indemonstrable postulate under which the validity of that act might be maintained. Useful as reference to the postulate may be, it is not, or need not be, formally necessary, since the act of the mind by which we refer the instance of inference to the postulate is, logically considered, of the same kind as that by which we draw the inference at once from the premises. Nevertheless, the formal syllogism, in the first case, is never anything but that easiest of all cases, the syllogism of *principle and example*, (*F. L.* p. 257). And thus we have for the ordinary syllogism, two forms of argument: the common one, and the reference to the postulate. Now this postulate always has had, [certainly] always must have, a *composition of relations*, such as I have generalized in Section V.

Consequently, I assert that the logicians have, when compelled to declare the ordinary syllogism incapable, had recourse to instances of the composition of relations out of which I have constructed the bicopular syllogism; though in truth they have not seen the extension of the theory, merely because their reference of the example to the principle may be made under the form *Barbara*.

First, I take a common syllogism, say *X*)) *Y*).(*Z* = *X*).(*Z*. Using the terms of my work (*F. L.* ch. xiv., in which every syllogism is thus reduced, though composition of relations is not, as it ought to have been, the leading idea,) we see that *X* is a species of *Y* which is an external of *Z*, so that *X* is a species of an external of *Z*. Now if we merely compound the relations, we see that species of external is external; whence *X* is an external of *Z*. If we choose to make our last step in the greatest form, we have

Every species of an external (of any notion) is an external (of that notion),
X is a species of an external of *Z*;
Therefore *X* is an external of *Z*.

If I were to attack the syllogistic theory in a manner analogous to that in which logicians have, in certain isolated cases, supplied its deficiencies, the attack would involve the assertion that the preceding transformation is the legitimate form.

I now give instances of the supplementary use of this method. Reid justly remarks that '*A is equal to B, and B to C*, therefore *A is equal to C*, cannot be brought into any syllogism in figure and mode.' On which Sir W. Hamilton's note (p. 702) is as follows;—'Not as it stands; for, as expressed, this reasoning is elliptical. Explicitly stated, it is as follows:—

What are equal to the same, are equal to each other;
A and C are equal to the same (B);
Therefore, A and C are equal to each other.'

I am quite at a loss to see how the second is an *expanded* form of the first. But I see distinctly the composition of relation, 'equal of equal is equal,' expressing the transitiveness of the copula *equals*, which, with its convertibility, renders it of equal validity with *is* as the copula to be employed in a syllogism.

Again, a recent and learned editor of Aldrich, the Rev. H. L. Mansel, observes of the preceding, that 'the reasoning is elliptical, and therefore, *as it stands*, material; though owing to the suppressed premise being self-evident, its deficiency is apt to be overlooked.' This suppressed premise is the major given above. But does it not then follow that the ordinary syllogism is elliptical? Is there not always the suppressed premise (as I feel bound, on these authorities, to call it), 'What *are* the same *are* each other?'

There is some want of distinctness in the use of the word *material*, as distinguished from *formal*. When the last named writer makes it 'material and therefore extra-logical' that Alexander was the son of Philip because Philip was his father, he uses the word historically. The formal connexion of relation and correlation exists, though Aristotle did not recognize it as copular except when the relation is its own correlation, and then only in a limited case. Certainly the matter, in the case of *father* and *son*, supplies the knowledge of the correlative relation existing, but not the mode of using it in inference, when known to exist. In this and a great many other instances, matter is opposed by writers, not to form, but to what is recognized as form in the school of Aristotle: the assumption of course being that that school exhausts the forms of thought. Historically speaking, the copula has been material to this day: this I must continue to believe until it be pointed out where the formal conditions have been separated from the matter, and made the instruments of inference, independently of the separated matter.

A certain indifference to close description of the copular relation is manifest in many logical works, accompanied by negligence in its application; and this may produce strange consequences in literal translations. The proposition '*X* is *Y*,' may bear expression in French as '*X* doit être *Y*,' and in Latin as '*X* debet esse *Y*,' though both are rather negligent forms for a strict work: but the English '*X* ought to be *Y*' is of a different signification. Both[1] the English translations of the *Port Royal Logic* give a paralogism for the instance cited in illustration of the definition of the word *reasoning*: 'having judged that true virtue ought to be referred to God, and that the virtue of the heathens was not referred to him, we thence conclude that the virtue of the heathens was not true virtue.' Had the copula been as fully treated of as the terms, such inaccuracies could hardly have occurred.

[1] A new one has recently been published by T. S. Baynes, Edinburgh, 1850.

SOME SUGGESTIONS IN LOGICAL PHRASEOLOGY

From the 'Proceedings of the Philological Society', 11 February 1853

Among the most unfortunate ambiguities of language only, unaccompanied by any confusion of thought, are those expressions which we so frequently qualify by the words *exclusive* and *inclusive*. Whether the termini or extreme cases are to be both taken in, both left out, or one taken in and one left out, is a matter which often requires an additional sentence. In mathematics, no ambiguity is more common than a statement about *greater* or *less*, which leaves it uncertain whether the extreme case, namely *equality*, is or is not included. In logic, the same thing occurs in the propositional forms. 'Every *X* is *Y*' would be commonly understood as meaning that *X* is not coextensive with *Y*, though the extreme case, that in which there are no more *Y*s than *X*s, would not be held formally excluded. The distinction of these two cases led Aristotle to what have since been called the *predicables*. Returning to the master himself, and not attending to his followers, we find the distinction of *genus*, of *definition* or *property* (words the distinction of which is extra-logical), and of *accident*. When all the *X*s are some (only) of the *Y*s, *Y* is the genus of *X*; when all the *X*s, and no other things, are *Y*s, *Y* is the definition or property of *X* (Thomson: *Outlines of the Laws of Thought*, p. 146).

Similar ambiguities exist as to negative propositions; but Aristotle does not take notice of them, as he would have done, if he had admitted contrary or privative terms. The *universe* of the proposition being either the whole universe of thought, or a given portion of it, all that is not *X* may be called the *contrary* of *X*. If *Y* be a name entirely external to *X*, so that no *X* is *Y*, then *Y* may either apply to the whole contrary of *X*, or only to a part of it. We owe to this omission of Aristotle the want of clear phraseology by which to express relations of disagreement, in terms as familiar to us as genus, species, and property. I dissent from the general opinion that Aristotle confined himself to the common modes of thought, and maintain that it was the common mode of thought which confined itself to Aristotle. We owe the capability of our modern languages, as vehicles of abstract science of all kinds, to the scholastic followers of the Greek philosopher; and I, for one, am persuaded that the difficulty of certain existing and therefore possible forms of thought is due solely to neglect of cultivation; and that this neglect has been most injurious to the progress of mental power.

My present object is to invite criticism and suggestion with respect to an attempt to construct language expressive of extension, and of distinction: of extension to privative or contrary notions, and of distinction between what, relatively to each other, we may call unambiguous and ambiguous predication.

In my work on Logic I designated terms which are coextensive as *identical*, and the contained and containing terms as *subidentical* and *superidentical*: while terms which are contained in and contain the *contrary* were called *subcontrary* and *supercontrary*. With these terms, as expressing the relations of *extent*, I am well satisfied. Any one who will learn to recall their meaning will very easily make axioms of those compositions of relations on the perception of which the complex syllogism depends. For instance, in the assertion 'A sub-contrary (or contrary) of a supercontrary of *Z* is a subidentical of *Z*', will be seen the mode of inference contained in the following:—'If no *X* be *Y* (whether there be other things or not which are not *Y*s), and if *Y* contain all that is not *Z* (and also some things that are *Z*s), then *X* (and other things besides) must always be *Z*'. Reserving this language for comparison of *extents*, I now propose the following extended table of predicables, to express every way in which we can predicate or deny one notion of another, in which *some* is *not all.*

Let that which can be said of all be an *attribute*; of some and some *only*, an *accident*; of none, an *excludent*. Observe that the *accident* is also, by definition, *non-accident*: the former in relation to the part of which it can be said; the latter in relation to the part of which it cannot. Let each of these be divided into *universal*, *generic*, and *specific*. Let any predicable be *universal* when it applies in the same manner both to the subject of predication and to its contrary. Let it be *generic* when, not being universal, by enlarging the subject of predication from a species into some higher genus, the additional extent contains matter to which the predicable is applicable, or which contributes towards the name. Let it be *specific* when no such thing can happen in any genus into which the subject of predication can be enlarged. The application of the three adjectives to each of the three substantives will give nine predicables, which are all that can be, so long as we do no more than annex the privative notion to the form of thought on which Aristotle distinguished genus, property, and accident.

I take a descriptive example of each, the universe in question being *animal*, that is, all the names of which we predicate being species of animals, and each species having all other animals in its contrary.

1. *Universal attribute.*—The term *organized*, as applied to *man*, in the

universe *animal*, is a universal attribute, because, besides applying to all men, it applies to all the contrary, or to all other animals.

2. *Generic attribute* (superidentical).—The term *warm-blooded*, as applied to all men, is a generic attribute, because, without being an attribute of all the contrary, it is of some, so that a larger genus, containing man, can be formed, of which the term in question shall still be an attribute.

3. *Specific attribute* (identical).—The term *rational* is a specific attribute of man, because, applying to all men, it applies to nothing else, so that no additional extent contained in any genus of which man is a species, has anything to which it is applicable.

4. *Specific accident* and *generic non-accident* (subidentical).—The term *lawyer* is a specific accident of man, inasmuch as no genus of man contains it except as man contains it. The species is called an accident of the genus even by Aristotle.

5. *Universal accident* and *universal non-accident*.—The term *dark-coloured*, an accident of man, is a universal accident, because it is an accident of the class not-man. The word *universal*, it must be remembered, is used strictly according to definition. The *universe*, animal, is divided, as a subject of predication, into man and not-man, and the predicable which applies *in the same manner* to both man and not-man, is *therefore* called universal. But the phrase 'universal accident,' sounds like 'total part', or 'permanent casualty'. One of the questions to which I wish to draw attention is the following:—When a word applies in a natural and vernacular sense to all subdivisions except one, which should be preferred—the extension of the word to that one exceptional subdivision, which we are obliged to do in mathematics, or the introduction of another and, for the present time, more natural, expression?

6. *Generic accident* and *specific non-accident* (supercontrary).—The term *unclothed* (by art) is a generic accident of man, because, being an attribute of some races, and not being universal (for it is not an accident, but an attribute, of the contrary), a genus containing man can be formed, of which genus the term is still an accident, the term applying also to the part of the genus which is not man.

7. *Specific excludent* (contrary).—The term *dumb* (in the sense of not capable of speaking and understanding language) is, as predicated with respect to man in the universe animal, a specific excludent; because, not applying to man at all, but to all other animals, it cannot be predicated excludently of any genus of which man is a species.

8. *Generic excludent* (subcontrary).—The term *quadruped* is a generic excludent of man, because it is also an excludent of genera in which man is contained.

9. *Universal excludent*.—The term *mineral* is a universal excludent of man, because it excludes also every animal which is not man.

The preceding cases include all the forms in which one term can be predicated of another without terminal ambiguity in the meaning of the word *some*. Here, some means *not none* and *not all*. In the sense in which it is used in the common proposition, it only means *not none*.

And in passing to this common proposition, we see that the mode of predication affirms, not one of the preceding, but one of two. There are eight modes of connexion, for which eight distinct terms are absolutely requisite: these must be of that degree of clearness which will make axioms of the compositions of relations which take place in inference. In applying the terms *genus* and *species* here, instead of in the former enumeration, I consider them as having become vernacular, and as having taken a purely relative sense. When Aristotle mentions the genus, it is not so much with relation to species, as in connexion with *property* and *accident*. I could not, in the preceding list, have used the word *genus* instead of *attribute*, merely because the word *genus*, in common language, is no more than a correlative of *species*, and is not usually thought of in opposition to accident or excludent.

I signify the four universals as follows:—

Every *X* is *Y*. . . . . *X* is a *species* of *Y*.
Every *Y* is *X*. . . . . *X* is a *genus* of *Y*.
No *X* is *Y*. . . . . *X* is an *external* of *Y* (and *Y* of *X*).
Everything is either
  X or *Y* or both. . . . . *X* is a *complement* of *Y* (and *Y* of *X*).

The species, then, is either the specific accident or the specific attribute. The genus is either the specific or generic attribute. The complement is either the specific excludent or the generic accident. The external is either the specific or generic excludent. The name of the particular proposition which denies one of the preceding universals, can in no case be a familiar term, so far as I can find. Not a species, is partly (at least) external, and may be called *exient*. Not a genus, that is, not entirely filling up, may be called *subtotal*. Not external, and therefore partly, at least, internal, may be called *partient*. Not a complement, and therefore not filling up the whole contrary, may be called a *subremainder*, or *subremnant* (the word *subcontrary* being already appropriated). Thus we have

Some *X*s are not *Y*s. . . . . *X* is an *exient* of *Y*.
Some *Y*s are not *X*s. . . . . *X* is a *subtotal* of *Y*.
Some *X*s are *Y*s . . . . *X* is a *partient* of *Y* (and *Y* of *X*).
Some things are
  neither *X*s nor *Y*s. . . . . *X* is a *subremainder* of *Y* (and *Y* of *X*).

With little practice, any one will be enabled to reduce a compound relation to a simple one, when it can be done. That a species of a species is a species is self-evident at once, from our familiarity with this one word. That the complement of a subtotal is partient will perhaps give a few seconds' thought, at first. It is the axiom on which the inference of the following syllogism depends:—Everything is either *X* or *Y*, some *Z*s are not *Y*s; therefore some *Z*s are *X*s,—in which *X* is the complement of *Y*, the subtotal of *Z*.

All that precedes has been admitted into logic, so far as it can be done without direct admission of the contrary, or privative term. The cases I have brought forward are exhaustive of all the modes of predication which can be applied to one term by means of another, when the logical quantities employed are either none, some (not all), and all, or none, some (it may be all), and all. The question I raise is one of language entirely; can we propose any words instead of those I have given, which combine with sufficient system such an amount of ordinary meaning as will enable those who use them to do it with facility in a short time?

ON THE SYLLOGISM: III

and on Logic in general

[Read 8 February 1858]

I put this paper under the title here given, for the sake of continuity of reference: in scope, however, it is more extensive than those which precede. It will best be disposed under two heads. I shall first put together remarks on the object of logic; on its present state; on the opinion of the world with respect to it; on the views which I take of it, in opposition to the world at large as to its advantages, and to the writers upon it as to its details. I shall incidentally answer some objections to my former paper; objections, not objectors: and I would gladly do something, be it ever so little, to hasten the time when logic shall again be a part of education in the University of Cambridge. I am satisfied that there is no study, however useful, no exercise of the intellect, however essential, but has its own short-comings which can only be made good by the study of mind as mind, psychology; and induces its own bad habits which can only be eradicated by the study and practice of thought as thought, logic. But psychology and logic, in their turn, require other studies even more than other studies require them.

In the second part, I shall present the elementary points of the system which I advocate. Which of the two parts should be taken first is a question which each reader must decide for himself.

I. General considerations

1. Eleven years ago, when I began to put together details on which I had been thinking during several previous years, I had not the encouragement which would have arisen from a knowledge of what was then going on in the logical world. In my own mind I was facing Kant's[1] assertion that logic neither has improved since the time of Aristotle, nor of its own nature can improve, except[2] in perspicuity, accuracy of expression, and the like. I did not know that very high authority was then teaching its *alumni* to assert that logic had always been one sided, deprived of

[1] There is an intelligible translation of Kant's logic, and, as I judge by comparison with Tissot, a good one, by John Richardson. London, 1819, 8vo.

[2] Of Lambert's additions Kant says that like all legitimate subtilties, they *sharpen the intellect*, but are of no material use. Logic thinks about thought: what for? that we may think the better, that we may sharpen the intellect. Consequently, every part of logic which makes us think more acutely conduces to the very use of logic

much scientific truth, encumbered with much scientific falsehood, perverted and erroneous in form, and given, in some of its doctrines, to impeach the truth of the laws of thought on which it is founded. In one extreme of opinion, logic, language, and common sense are never at variance: in another, Aristotle exhibits the truth partially, not always correctly, in complexity, and even in confusion. Between these opinions I am not obliged to choose. I am satisfied, with the satisfaction of one long used to the distinction between demonstrated and probable conclusion, that the old logic is, so far as it goes, accurate in method and true in result; that is, as to the *quod semper, quod ubique, quod ab omnibus*: but without affirming that all that is called necessary is necessary, or that all that is called natural is natural. I feel equally sure that it is only a beginning; that it contains but a small part of the whole which it arrogates to itself in its old aspirations and its modern definition; and that the low estimation in which a large part of the educated world now holds it is to be traced to consequences of this incompleteness.

2. Logic inquires into the form of thought, as separable from and independent of the matter thought on. To every proposal for a new introduction there is but one answer;—You outstep the bounds of logic, you introduce material considerations. On this point the first question is, What is the distinction of form and matter?—the second, Who are best able to judge of it?

The *form* or *law* of thought—asserted differences between these words being of no importance here—is detected when we watch the machine in operation without attending to the matter operated on. The form may again be separable into form of form and matter of form: and even the matter into form of matter and matter of matter; and so on. The *modus operandi* first detected may be one case of a limited or unlimited number, from all of which can be extracted one common and higher principle, by separation from details which are still differences of form.

Take a nut-cracker, two levers on a common hinge. Put a bit of wood between the levers to represent filbert, walnut, beechnut, almond, or any other kind of nut. We have here what a logician would call the *form of nut-cracking*: and, imitating his practice of insisting that he has obtained pure form so soon as he has effected one separation, we may say that we have got the *pure form* of nut-cracking. But when we come to consider the screw, the hammer, the teeth, &c. we begin to apprehend that the pure form of nut-cracking is strong pressure applied to opposite sides of the nut, no matter how; and this even though we may detect in all the instruments the *principle*, as we call it, of the hinged levers.

itself. No part of logic is of any *material* use, in Kant's sense of the word. The scaffolding by which the house was built is of no use to the inhabitants, except indeed when repairs or additions are wanted. But the main question of the utility of logic refers to education, during which the scaffolding is up.

The logician is not much accustomed to the working presence of his own great distinction: the mathematician deals with it unceasingly, though with little apprehension of its existence, in most cases. Though logic has been in waking life for at least fifteen hundred years, its real definition has not been in recognized existence during the fifteenth part of that time: this definition has indeed been obeyed in many points, it has been caught for a minute and let go again, it has been seen through a glass darkly,—at any time from Aristotle inclusive: it is only in very modern days that it has been seized, stript of its coverings, and firmly fixed in its place. And the first imperfect introduction, and the perfect recognition, have been the work of mathematicians.

Of the two philosophers who might have made the distinction of form and matter exercise a strong influence over their systems, Aristotle did it, and Plato did not. Plato's writings do not convince any mathematician that their author was strongly addicted to geometry; they shew at most that he may have been well versed in it: I have no objection to say that geometry helped him in his colouring. We know that he encouraged mathematics, that his followers form a school, and that the reputation of the school has given the character of a geometer to the founder. But if—which nobody believes—the *μηδεὶς ἀγεωμέτρητος εἰσίτω* of Tzetzes had been written over his gate, it would no more have indicated the geometry within than a warning not to forget to bring a packet of sandwiches would now give promise of a good dinner. But Aristotle was a mathematician, versed in that science and addicted to it: geometry aided him in the tracing of his outline. This appears throughout his writings, even after rejection of those which are doubtful, some of which, supposing him to be only a putative father, show that a very positive mathematical character was assigned to him by his successors. To him we owe such perpetual indication of the distinction of form and matter that many, including some who should have known better, have assigned the *form of thought* to him as his definition of *logic*, giving him the word into the bargain. But the definition was never distinctly conceived in that character until the last century, when it was propounded by a philosopher whose earliest studies had been in mathematics, which he had taught in conjunction with logic for fifteen years before he gave himself up to the study of the pure reason. If, between Kant[1] and Aristotle, there were one leader of philosophical opinion who more

[1] It is only of late years that, in this country at least, Kant's definition has been clearly apprehended, and its truth sincerely felt. If the inquirer will look out for English works preceding 1848, or thereabouts, which state Kant's definition as an existing thing, not to speak of adopting it, he will have some difficulty in finding one. In some old notes of my own, made after comparison of Aristotle, some of the mediaevals, and Kant, I find the following sentence: 'I should say [of formal and material] that the great leader *saw* the distinction, that the schoolmen *made* the distinction, and that Kant *built upon* the distinction.'

nearly than another caught the conception, it was the mathematician Leibnitz. And the history of man in species analogizes with what we have seen of man in individuals: we trace our mathematics to the Greeks and the Hindoos, the two independent cultivators of systems of logic in which form is investigated for its own sake, though the separation is indistinctly conceived by both. Of the Romans, we only know that they originated nothing, either in mathematics or in logic: and it is just worth notice here that Boethius, the only Roman who gave us [so much as] a summary of Aristotle, was the only Roman who gave us a summary of Euclid.[1]

The separation of mathematics and logic which has gradually arrived in modern times has been accompanied, as separations between near relations generally are, with a good deal of adverse feeling. Great names in each have written[2] and spoken contemptuously of the other; while those who have attended to both are aware that they have a joint as well as a separate value. This alienation of the two sciences has furnished two magazines to those who would put down all education except that which immediately conduces to production of wealth: in fact, if what either party has advanced against the other be true, the common opponent has a good case against both, provided only mathematics enough for a higher kind of land-surveyor be exempted from the common doom, and made a part of professional education.

There never was in history the time at which mathematics, in any branch, wanted a palpable separation of form and matter: and mathematicians have always seen the separation, though they have not always rightly apprehended the relation of the components. They have spoken much of *abstraction*, a word truly applied to their function: but they have not duly distinguished between abstraction of colleague qualities from each other, and abstraction of the instrument from the material. They have also dwelt much on *generalization*, a word so truly descriptive of what is always taking place within the precinct, that they have oftentimes made it give name to the fence.

The first element of mathematical process is the separation of space from matter filling it, and [of abstract *quantum*] from the material *quantum*: whence spring geometry and arithmetic, the studies of the laws of space and number. Distinctions which are of form in arithmetic

[1] I ought not to have used words implying that Boethius gave Aristotle *only* in summary, as he did Euclid [25 June 1858].

[2] There is no occasion to refer to any of the ordinary exhibitions, whether dissertations in favour of ignorance, or orations in contempt of knowledge. But there is one which deserves preservation for its humour, and which may be lost with an ephemeral pamphlet, if not elsewhere recorded. An Oxford M.A. writing on education, about ten years ago, advocated some pursuit of mathematics: for, said he, man is an arithmetical, geometrical, and mechanical animal, as well as a rational soul.

become material in algebra. The lower forms of algebra become material in the algebra of the functional symbol. The functional form becomes material in the differential calculus, most visibly when this last is merged in the calculus of operations. But, though the distinction of form and matter be very certainly present to those who can see it, it is equally certain that many followers of the mathematics have their ideas of the distinction as dark as those of any of the old logicians. The difference is that the mathematician cannot help dealing with the thing in question, though under a name of too little intension: he cannot but be sensible of *abstraction*; but he may be unused to remember that he abstracts *form* from *matter*. The logician on the other hand may, as often was the case, have his system cast in so material a mould, that he is hardly sensible even of abstraction: and when the fault is not palpably committed in the treatise, the individual reader may, of his own inaptitude to abstract except under symbolic compulsion, convert formal logic into material. Accordingly, the separation of form is often learned language to the logical student, with a bad dictionary to read it by: to the mathematician it is as often M. Jourdain's prose, and nothing more. To the logician it is a collect for certain holidays; it is the paternoster of the mathematician, who may run it over without thinking of the meaning, if he ever knew it. And these tendencies, large in amount in the learner, have their sway even in the books he learns from, and in the discussions of the highly informed: the great distinction of form and matter is more in the theory[1] of the logician than in his practice, more in the practice of the mathematician than in his theory.

3. Logic bears on its modern banner, The form of thought, the whole form, and nothing but the form. It has been excellently well said that whatever is operative in thought must be taken into account, and consequently be overtly expressible, in logic: for logic must be, as to be it professes, an unexclusive reflex of thought, and not merely an arbitrary

[1] I am fully aware of the boldness of my comparison of the logician and mathematician, and of the audacious appearance which it is likely to present to a class of inquirers who have hitherto been allowed to distribute functions to the branches of human knowledge pretty nearly in their own way. My averments are of that kind which nothing but success will justify: and about which controversy is useless. It is not competent to those who are only logicians, and to those who are only mathematicians, to settle a question in which the alleged unfitness of either to decide is a part of the matter to be decided: still less is it competent to the few who unite both characters to demand of the others that they shall see this. Time must settle it; and I believe this will be the way. As joint attention to logic and mathematics increases, a logic will grow up among the mathematicians, distinguished from the logic of the logicians by having the mathematical element properly subordinated to the rest. This *mathematical* logic—so called *quasi lucus a non nimis lucendo*—will commend itself to the educated world by showing an actual representation of their form of thought—a representation the truth of which they recognize—instead of a mutilated and onesided fragment, founded upon canons of which they neither feel the force nor see the utility.

selection,—a series of elegant extracts,—out of the forms of thinking.[1] Whether the form that it exhibits be stronger or weaker, be more or less frequently applied, that, as a material and contingent consideration, is beyond its purview. Nevertheless, so soon as a form of thought is exhibited which does not come within the arbitrary selection, the series of elegant extracts, it is forthwith pronounced material:—

St Aristotle! what wild notions!
Serve a *ne exeat regno* on him!

The proper reply to every accusation of introducing the material where all should be formal, is as follows. You say this thought or process is material: now every material thinking has its form: therefore this thought has its form. Logic is to consider the whole form of thought: *your* logic either contains the form of this thought, or it does not. If it contains[2] the form of this thought, shew it: if not, introduce it. I shall now state three instances of the objection.

In my last paper, as in my work on *Formal Logic*, I separated form from matter in the copula of the common syllogism. The copula performs certain functions; it is competent to those functions; it is competent because it has certain properties, which are sufficient to validate its use, and, all cases considered, not more than sufficient. The word '*is*,' which identifies, does not do its work because it identifies, except[3] in so

[1] [Sir W. H., *Lectures*, ii, 293, 294, 263!]

[2] When I see a chapter in a book of logic headed *On material and formal consequence*, distinguishing '$A = B$, $B = C$, therefore $A = C$' as *material* from 'A is B, B is C, therefore A is C' as *formal*, I am at first inclined to think that the distinction of formal and material is that of contained and not contained—in Aristotle. But when the title-page shews me an author whose mind is as free from the sway of that distinction as my own, I am compelled to have recourse to the difference between the ideas of form belonging to the mathematician and to the logician. Is there any *consequence* without *form*? Is not *consequence* an action of the machinery? Is not logic the science of the action of this machinery? Consequence is always an *act* of the mind: on every consequence logic ought to ask, What kind of act? what is the *act*, as distinguished from the *acted on*, and from any inessential concomitants of the action? For these are of the form, as distinguished from the matter. What is the difference of the two syllogisms above? In the first case the mind acts through its sense of the transitiveness of '*equals*:' in the second, through its sense of the transitiveness of '*is*.' Transitiveness is the common form: the difference between *equality* and *identity* is the difference of matter. But the logician who hugs identity for its transitiveness, cannot hug transitiveness: let him learn abstraction.

[3] I again call the reader's attention to the pure form of nut-cracking, with which I began. The syllogism is the nut to be cracked. I believe I have got to the pure form, which equally applies to two levers, a screw forced into a receptacle, Nasmyth's steam-hammer, the collision of a couple of planets, as the case may be: the common form of all being pressure enough applied to opposite sides of the nut. The logician insists upon it that the pure form is a couple of metallic levers, with friction-studs, if that be the proper name, to prevent the nut from slipping aside, and such a hinge that, according to the way we turn it, the levers give convenient entrance to a common

far as identification is a *transitive* and *convertible* notion: 'A is *that which is* B' means 'A is B'; and 'A is B' means 'B is A'. Hence every transitive and convertible relation is as fit to validate the syllogism as the copula '*is*,' and by the same proof in each case. Some forms are valid when the relation is only transitive and not convertible; as in '*give*.' Thus if X—Y represent X and Y connected by a transitive copula, *Camestres* in the second figure is valid, as in

Every Z—Y, No X—Y, therefore No X—Z.

For if any one X—Z, this with Z—Y, gives X—Y, which is excluded by the second premise.

To this the objection is that the process is material, for that it is of the matter of the proposition whether *give* will or will not do: that *touch*, for instance, will not do. Does not this,—from a living writer who in combination of logical learning and logical acumen is second to none—corroborate my assertion that the logician has the distinction of form and matter more in his theory than in his practice? I might as well say that 'Every X is Y' is a material proposition: it is of the matter of X and Y whether it be true or no. In the following chain of propositions, there is exclusion of matter, form being preserved, at every step:—

		Hypothesis
(Positively true)	Every man is animal	
————————	Every man is Y	Y has existence
————————	Every X is Y	X has existence
————————	Every X—Y	—— is a *transitive* relation
————————	α of X—Y	α a fraction $<$ or $= 1$
(Probability β)	α of X—Y	β a fraction $<$ or $= 1$

The last is *nearly* the purely formal judgment, with not a single material point about it, except the transitiveness of the copula. But '*is*' is more intense than the symbol —, which means only transitive copula: for '*is*' has transitiveness, and more. Strike out the word *transitive*, and the last line shews the pure form of the judgment.

The same objection has been raised to the law of inference when the middle term is definitely quantified. If the fractions α and β of the Ys be severally As and Bs, and if $\alpha + \beta$ be greater than unity, it follows that some As are Bs. To this it is objected that whether $\alpha + \beta$ be or be not greater than unity, is material. No doubt it is; and so is the case of the logician's canon of syllogism, that the middle term must be universal in one or both premises. The logician demands $\alpha = 1$, or $\beta = 1$, or

nut or a walnut. All his additions to the pure form I admit to be usual and convenient: but I affirm and maintain that whatever can crack a nut, and does crack a nut, is a nut-cracker; and being a nut-cracker, must be considered as a nut-cracker, and included among nut-crackers, in every treatise on the whole form of nut-cracking.

both: he can then infer; but only because he knows that when more in number have been named than there are separate things to name, some must have been named twice. But he does not know this better of $1 + \beta$ than of $\frac{2}{7}$ + (more than $\frac{5}{7}$): or if he did, the difference of form and matter is not merely difference of arithmetical facility. The writer against whom I am contending declares that, as a logician, he cannot know that 2 and 2 make 4. I do not ask him for so much: I do not ask him to know that there *are* cases in which $\alpha + \beta > 1$. What I say is this, that in every case in which it shall happen (if ever it do happen, which is by hypothesis more than we know) that $\alpha + \beta > 1$, in each of these cases he is bound, as a logician, to infer that some *A*s are *B*s. And this instance is another corroboration of my assertion that the distinction of form and matter is more in the theory of the logician than in his practice.

As a third instance, I note that the limited universe, and its division into two contraries, are pronounced material, because it *is not by logic* we learn that when *property* is the universe, *real* and *personal* are contraries. Neither by logic do we learn that every man is animal; but by logic we analyse our use of this proposition in conversion, in inference &c. Similarly, by logic we learn how we use contraries in inference &c. But what things *are* contraries, logic no more needs to inquire than law needed to inquire who wore the crown before she settled whether writs should run in the name of the King *de facto* or of the Pretender.

A little consideration will shew us that every inference which is anything more than pure symbolic representation of inference is due to the presence of something material: even a derived or compound symbol, *representing* inference, shews the presence of something material. Here are two purely formal propositions, in which *P, Q, R, S*, represent individual objects of thought, and *–A–* indicates a relation *A*:—

P –A– Q   *R –B– S*

P stands in *A*-relation to *Q* and *R* in *B*-relation to *S*. What are we to infer? Now rub out *R*, and for it write *Q*. This is *material*: it is now seen to be of the matter of our system that the second subject is the first predicate. And now we have *P –A– Q*, and *Q –B– S*. Can we infer anything? With the form of combination of relations in our thoughts, we may symbolize it, and say *P –AB– S*. Now make the relations material: let *–A–* and *–B–* each be '*is*:' then we have a material inference; *P* is *Q*, *Q* is *S*, therefore *P* is *S*. In common logic, the objects of inference, being terms expressed in general symbols, are void of matter; the relations between them, and the modes of inference, are material: I speak of logic as it is. Many relations have a common form: the logician cannot yet see that when many cases, no matter what, proceed upon a common principle, his concern is with that principle. It is his business to apprehend the principle and to shew, as to the *modus operandi* of the mind, how containing cases severally contain it, and apply it, [in the same manner in all].

I am charged with maintaining that thought is a branch of algebra, instead of algebra a branch of thought. The answer is easy enough. Logic considers, not *thought*, but the *form* of thought, the law of action of its machinery. Psychology herself does not know what thought *is*: and the odds are that if she did she would not feel bound to tell logic. Thought, the genus, has parts of its machinery, usually under cover, which work by daylight in algebra, the species, to every one who has meditated on the principles of algebra. He who makes me confound all other thought with algebra, because I call attention to what is more visible in algebra than in other thought, though it exists in all thought, must make his own logic responsible for the inference, not mine. He may hire a soldier to cook his victuals, because both soldier and cook cut flesh with steel: but neither Mr Boole, the greater culprit, nor I, the lesser[1] one, have done anything to deserve an invitation to the feast.

I might with much more justice charge the logician with affirming all thought a branch of geometry, instead of geometry a branch of thought. By processes nearly resembling those which led Descartes to affirm that space is *all* the essence of matter, he reduces all thought of comparison to the assertion or denial of containing and contained. These are originally terms of space-relation: and his only syllogism, his universal includent of all argument, can be fully symbolized by areas: a practice which many logicians dislike, and with reason, for it tells tales. I have pointed out, in my second paper, the syllogism in which the copulae may be any relations whatever. The copula of cause and effect, of motive and action, of all in which *post hoc* is of the form and *propter hoc* (perhaps) of the matter, will one day be carefully considered in a more complete system of logic. The cases in which *A*, simultaneous with *B*, is either cause or effect according to the attribute considered, will be duly symbolized. For instance, it is disputed whether men dive for pearls because pearls fetch a high price, or whether pearls fetch a high price because men dive for them: it is one or the other, according to the attribute of the actions held in view. Considered as *volitions*, the diver is *willing* to dive because the lady is *willing* to pay dear for her necklace. As *necessities*, the lady *must* pay dear because the diver *must* dive. The word *because* is the heading of a chapter in the *form* of thought, of which many a complexity is yet unanalysed, simply because it is possible to reduce relation to class, by throwing '*X* has *A*-relation to *Y*' into the form '*X is* in the class of objects having *A*-relation to *Y*.' Hence, to the world at large, logic is neither the form of their thought, nor the matter, nor the junction of both. The *judgment* of the logician is only *one* of the judgments of mankind.

[1] Not meant for extenuation: I wish I were the greater one.

When a common person says 'Achilles killed Hector,' his objects of thought are the two heroes: his mode of thinking them is in the relation of slayer and slain in time past. The logician demands that he shall think himself to be identifying by the verb '*is*'—either Achilles with the former slayer of Hector, or Hector with the former slain of Achilles, or slaughter with the former action of Achilles on Hector, or time past with the date of that action. All these forms are unquestionably co-existent and coextensive with the relation affirmed: out of any one all the others may be evolved; they are different dichotomies and reintegrations of a coexistence of four things. But neither reintegration represents the manner in which the relation is held in thought. Each dichotomy makes it possible that a contradiction may step in, which the reintegration denies: one of them shews a front to the assertion that *Patroclus* killed Hector, another to the assertion that Achilles was Hector's *defender*, &c. And so it always happens: a person who wants to signify that 'Achilles was the person who killed Hector' will take care, on the principle of not saying one thing when another is meant, to avoid the phrase 'Achilles killed Hector,' or else to supply 'was the person who' by emphasis on *Achilles*: unless it be a person who has been long in the hands of Giant Maul.[1] In all propositions, existence is predicated of the terms in the fact of predication. When I say *X* is *Y*, I do not mean 'if *X* exist and *Y* exist, then *X* is *Y*:' I mean that *X* and *Y* do exist, and that they are the same. Accordingly, when I am told that 'Achilles *is* the former slayer of Hector,' it is as if it could not be disputed that Hector *was* slain, so that the only question remaining is, Who killed him? For the books of logic give no way of denying '*X* is *Y*' except '*X* is not *Y*.' But should I be told 'Achilles killed Hector' I should not receive it in this way, nor should I believe it was so intended. I should receive it as an equally balanced combination of elements, in which the dichotomy is left to myself, to be made according to my own mode of assent or denial, including a right given to me to preserve the existing balance. I see great difference in the *propositum* between 'This house was built by Jack' and 'This is the [or even *a*] house that Jack built.' Granting it true that either of the logician's forms will give as much inference as the simple relation, it does not follow that the logician's form *is* the form of thought we actually employ in inference. It is one thing to say, I can shew you by such and such reductions how to demonstrate the only inference these premises will give; and quite another thing to add, Therefore this is the way you infer.

[1] According to incomparable John Bunyan, this worthy lived at the end of a dark valley and 'did use to spoil young pilgrims with sophistry.' What was hinted at appears in this, that Mr Greatheart and the giant settle the *quaestio* before they begin to fight, and the opponent objects to the respondent, 'These be but generals, man, come to particulars.' Maul was the most difficult giant to kill of Bunyan's whole troop.

4. Logic is both science and art: and the art, the *logica utens*, ought to be a preparation for sure and rapid material application. The proposition of the world at large is highly complex: it is loaded with what I shall call *charges*. It has complex terms, conjunctive and disjunctive; it introduces allusions, for reinforcement, for explanation, for justification of its appearance, for colouring and effect. It gives reasons, takes syllogisms into the description of terms, and implies assertions in giving reasons, leaving the assertions to be supplied from their reasons. It is a tapestry, of which the logical form is only the original web. It undergoes conversions in which idiom demands synonymes: but the *logica docens* keeps clear of the whole theory of complex terms by throwing the proposition into disjunctive or dilemmatic forms which the actual form of thought does not recognize. Is the student of logic, generally speaking, prepared *rapidly* to analyse the two following propositions, and to say whether or no they must be identical, if the identity of synonymes be granted?

The suspicion of a nation is easily excited, as well against its more civilized as against its more warlike neighbours; and such suspicion is with difficulty removed.

When we see a nation either backward to suspect its neighbour, or apt to be satisfied by explanations, we may rely upon it that the neighbour is neither the more civilized nor the more warlike of the two.

This, under the symbols I have used and shall use, is the conversion of the form *A, B))CD* into *c, d))ab*. The world would have treated logic with more respect, if it had led up to such conversions as the above. But it lands us and leaves us, as to conversion, in 'Some tyrant is cruel' turned into 'Some cruel is tyrant,' or the like: a needful commencement, but a lame and impotent conclusion.

I will now take a syllogism, *one syllogism*, well charged[1] certainly, but

[1] Of all the writers on logic whom I have examined, John Milton is the one who delights in extracting the syllogism from its loading: his instances are almost entirely from the Latin poets, which he probably needed no sight to recall. Milton's logic was published two years before his death. 'Joannis Miltoni, Angli, Artis Logicae plenior institutio, ad Petri Rami methodum concinnata' (London, Impensis Spencer Hickman, Societatis Regalis Typographi, 1672, 12mo, portrait). The logic of Ramus was adopted by the University of Cambridge, probably in the sixteenth century. George Downame, or Downam, who died Bishop of Derry in 1634, was praelector of logic at Cambridge in 1590. His 'Commentarii in P. Rami . . . Dialecticam. . . .' (Frankfort, 1616, 8vo,) is an excellent work. The Cambridge book then most in use was the *Dialectica* of John Seton, first published (Ames) in 1563, and repeated down to 1611 at least: it is noticed by Dr Peacock as the book to some editions of which (from 1570 onwards, if not before, I find) Buckley's arithmetical verses are appended. It is not a Ramist book: the presumption is that Downam was the Cambridge apostle of his doctrine. Ramism fixed a mark upon Cambridge which it has never lost to this

only with charges which are incessantly used. I insert it for the consideration of those who, for want of advice to the contrary, imagine that the logical gymnastic can afford no higher exercise than the perception of 'No cruel is kind, some cruel is tyrant, therefore some tyrant is not kind', duly chronicled as *Ferison*[1] of the third figure, cousin by the conversion side to *Ferio* of the first. The following *single*, though not *simple*, syllogism is an extract from a letter to a person who had supposed, from some circumstances of character and fact, that a common friend of his own and of the writer must have been the person who had figured in the narrative of a very silly proceeding:—

'We both see clearly enough that he [the hero of the narrative] must

[1] I think as I always did of the admirable ingenuity of these words, for their purpose: they are the most *meaning* words ever made.

day; that is, if the acts in divinity, &c. be still kept in the old form. The distribution of the syllogism into three conditionals, 'Si *A* sit *B*, cadit quaestio; sed *A* est *B*, ergo cadit quaestio, &c.' is pure Ramism, both as to form and phrase. Never having paid any attention to Ramist logic, I never could understand this form. No one could inform me: even a question sent to the *Notes and Queries* produced no reply except an ingenious conjecture that the *casus quaestionis* explains Shakspeare's meaning of the obscure words 'loss of question' in *Measure for Measure*, act ii. scene 4: a phrase on which commentators were so far to seek that Johnson proposed 'toss of question.' And so it stood until I happened to propose the difficulty to Prof. Spalding of St Andrews, who replied that an explanation might be presumed if we knew, or could assume, that this form was introduced by *Ramists*. Though cognizant of Cambridge Ramism, I had never had the sense to put the two things together.

I greatly regret the abolition of the *act* for the B.A. degree. It was the most useful of the exercises, and the most *trying*.

[25 June 1858] I may add that it must not be inferred that the Ramist logic long prevailed at Cambridge to the exclusion of all other. It is likely that its complete predominance did not long outlive the personal career of Downam in the University. Of his work I cannot even trace a Cambridge edition. Of all the books used by Newton when very young, no one, as it happens, is recorded [Conduitt] except Sanderson's *Logic*: which he read so attentively (Brewster, I. 21), that, when it was lectured on in College, he was found to know it better than his tutor. Such are the scraps from which, for lack of historians, we collect what we can about the old studies of the University: though a contemporary comedy will give us more than a dozen subsequent biographies. Thomas Randolph, Ben Jonson's son in the Muses, and Fellow of Trinity College, who died in 1634, not aged thirty, must have written his *Aristippus*, the scene of which is laid in Cambridge, about or before 1630. The writers on logic then current in the University are told off as follows:—

> Hang Brerewood and Carter in Crackenthorp's garter,
> Let Keckerman too bemoan us:
> Ile be no more beaten for greasie Jack Seaton,
> Or conning of Sandersonus.

The last verse may mean that Sanderson was then *forbidden*, and *sub poena*. In 1680 was published at Cambridge a neat edition (8vo) of the Logic of Burgersdicius, with Heereboord's Synopsis.

It would be very desirable that such scraps should be noted by those who casually pick them up. I will undertake to arrange any that may be sent to me, and to deposit them in *Notes and Queries*.

have been rich, and if not absolutely mad, was weakness itself subjected either to bad advice, or to most unfavourable circumstances. How then can you persist in identifying him with the friend of whom we are now speaking; who was indeed very rich, and easily swayed, and so far, we will say, not distinguishable from our hero; but who was conspicuous for clearness of head and sobriety of fancy; who never sought serious counsel except from his father's old friends, and you know what men they were; and who passed his youth in severe study varied only by useful exertion, and his manhood in domestic life and country occupations.'

Says the man of the world to the logician, I am very clear that two men who are proved to be different cannot be the same: but all I learnt at college about identity and difference, and excluded middle into the bargain, has done nothing towards putting me into a condition *rapidly* to assert or deny that the advocate has put the principle of difference between the rich fool and his rich friend. Here are two complex descriptions one of which contradicts the other. The description of the rich fool excludes him from either of three classes: the description of the rich friend places him in one of those classes: the two cannot then be the same. In the symbols I use—and symbols will one day be the scaffolding of logical education, though useless then, as now, to all who have not mastered them—the argument is expressed as follows. *H* is the rich fool; *h* any other person; *H'* the rich friend; *R* rich, *r* not rich; [*M* mad, *m* not mad;] *W* weak, *w* not weak; *A* badly advised, *a* not so; *C* unfavourably circumstanced, *c* not so.

H)) *R*[*M*, *W*(*A*, *C*]; contrapositively, *r*, *m* (*w*, *ac*))) *h*;
or *r*, *mw*, *mac*)) *h*; but *H'*)) *mac*; whence *H'*)) *h*; or *H'*)·(*H*.

The syllogism itself is the web of an argument, on which the tapestry of thought is woven; the *primed* canvas on which the picture is painted. The logician presents it to the world as the tapestry or the picture: he does this in effect by the position he makes it occupy; for he sends the primed canvas to the exhibition. And the world does not see that, though the syllogism be a mere canvas, it stands to the thinker in a very different position from that in which the canvas stands to the painter. Call the historian or the moralist a practised artist at a thousand a year, and I am well content that his structure of the canvas shall be valued at ten shillings a week: it would not hurt my argument if it were valued at a halfpenny. For the painter can and does delegate the preparation of the canvas; the historian cannot *put out* his logic. He must do it himself as he goes on; and he must do it well, or his whole work is spoiled.

I will take an example from one of the unusual forms of syllogism. Say 'The time is past in which the transmission of news can be measured by the speed of animals or even of steam; for the telegraph is not approached by either.' Is this a syllogism? Many would say it is not; but wrongly. Throw out the *charges*, the modal reference to past falsehood and present truth, the advantage of the telegraph, its *superior* speed, the reference to progress conveyed in *even*—and we rub off the whole design of the picture. But the ground which carried the design is a syllogism. In old form it is *Darapti*, awkwardly.

All telegraph speed is (not steam speed)
All telegraph speed is (not animal speed)
Therefore Some (not animal speed) is (not steam speed).

In the system which admits contraries it is a syllogism with two negative premises, and a form of conclusion unknown to Aristotle: it is, in the symbols I use, the deduction of)(from)·()·(

No animal speed is telegraph speed
No steam speed is telegraph speed
Therefore Some speed is neither animal nor steam speed.

When this is presented, a person would naturally ask, What then? The answer to this question is seen when the charges are restored, and the sentence takes its proper place in the whole argument.

5. A great objection has been raised to the employment of mathematical symbols: and it seems to be taken for granted that any symbols used by me must be mathematical. The truth is that I have not made much use of symbols actually employed in algebra; and the use which I have made is in one instance seriously objectionable, and must be discontinued. But it has been left to me to discover this mistake, into which I was led, as I shall shew, by the ordinary school of logicians. If A and B be the premises of a syllogism, and C the conclusion, the representation $A + B = C$ is faulty in two points. The premises are compounded, not aggregated; and AB should have been written: the relation of joint premises to conclusion is that (speaking in extension) of contained and containing, and $AB < C$ should have been the symbol. Nevertheless, $A + B = C$, with all its imperfections, made a suggestion of remarkable character to an inventive friend of mine: while $AB < C$ was both a *suggestio veri* and a *suppressio falsi* to myself. For these things see the second part of this paper.

As to symbols in general, it is not necessary to argue in their favour: mine or better ones will make their way, under all the usual difficulties of new language. There was a time when logic had more peculiar symbols than algebra. Every system of signs, before it has become familiar, as we all remember when we look back to *ABC*, is repulsive, difficult, unmeaning, full of signs of difference which are practical synonymes[1] by combination of want of comprehension with ignorance of the want. But it is too certain to need argument that the separation of form and matter requires as many symbols as there are separations.

In the opinion of Hegel, we are told, Ploucquet's logical *calculus* was the bitterest libel ever vented against the science. So far as this refers to one particular calculus I need say nothing: but, looking on the opinion as one having a general direction against symbols, it ought to be noticed that every exact science is only so far exact as it knows how to express one thing by one sign. Every science that has *thriven* has thriven upon its own symbols: logic, the only science which is admitted to have made no improvements in century after century, is the only one which has *grown no symbols*. To be presented with new marks by which to learn new combinations is to be libelled, because there is a charge of imperfection, tending to destroy credit. But both truth and utility may be pleaded to the indictment. Every little boy has this libel vented against him, when he is first presented with his *ABC*: he does not feel it, because he is not come to his dignity. If logic, in her maturity, must be vexed with a horn-book, the fault does not rest with those who offer it now, but with those who did not teach her the alphabet when she was young. And I cannot help suspecting that the stern and decided opposition which the follower of the ancients makes to the first introduction of symbols is the feeling of the urchin whose chief objection to saying *A* was that he knew if he said it he should be made to say *B*, as no doubt he would.

6. I shall now proceed to fundamental points, and to some criticism of the common doctrines. Should I appear too free[2] in my remarks, I

[1] A Cambridge tutor of high reputation was once trying to familiarize a beginner with the difference between na and a^n. After repeated illustration, he asked the pupil whether he saw the point. 'Thank you very much, Mr [Peacock]', was the answer; 'I now see perfectly what you mean: but, Mr [Peacock], between ourselves, now, and speaking candidly, *don't* you think it's a *needless refinement*.'

[2] In this country, the study of logic has been, for a long time past, and almost up to the present time, either the traditional practice of an old university, or the taste of an isolated individual. A great amount of reaction in its favour, all things considered, has taken place in the last twelve years, as evidenced by the publications on the subject. The consequence is, even at Oxford, a commencement of considerable diversity of opinion, and of plan of teaching: but, in the bulk of the writings, we see the old system, variously patched, except where a wider meaning is given to the word *logic* than it usually bears, and it is taken for a science in which all human knowledge is surveyed in its mode of acquisition. In such a state of things, nothing is more desirable than the most decided and uncompromising attack from without, conducted on the principle that a useful logic may exist, and directed to the details of the common system, not to the question of its general character. The dispute which has lasted so long has assumed that if there be anything worth having, the common books have it all; a basis on which both sides have agreed that this or nothing is their alternative. A change of question is gradually, but far too gradually, taking place: any assault which tends to expedite the fulness of this change must be a benefit to the science.

desire it may be remembered that my former self is one of the parties assailed. In developing the opinion that all the writers on logic have kept themselves too exclusively within what I now call the *logico-mathematical* field, I do not claim to be an exception, save in a sentence here and there which may contain a germ of my present views. I am especially to deal with the great distinction which is gradually forcing its way into its proper place, usually called the distinction of *extension* and *comprehension*. I do not adopt these terms. First, because, like *denotation* and *connotation*, they are kindred words which might change places with the least possible violence. Secondly, because the distinction of *extension* and *intension* occurs both in what is called extension, and in what is called comprehension. Nor can *objective* and *subjective* be made the basis of the distinction, for both are again in both, though the subjective rather predominates[1] in one and the objective in the other. I distinguish the two sides of logic as the *logico-mathematical* and the *logico-metaphysical*, frequently dropping the prefix *logico*.

I symbolize *extension* and *intension* as follows. Let A, B, C, be names, no matter how conceived; let X be a name containing *all* that is signified by A, by B, and by C; let Y be a name of *no more than* is contained under the three, A and B and C. That is, let $X = A, B, C$; let $Y = A\text{-}B\text{-}C$, in which the hyphens are frequently dropped. Then I say that X has more *extension* than A, unless by casualty B and C be both contained in A: also that Y has more *intension* than A, is more descriptive, more discriminative, more *intense*; unless, by casualty, B and C should only be components of A. I call (A, B, C) an *aggregate*, and A one of its *aggregants*; $A\text{-}B\text{-}C$ a *compound*, and A one of its *components*. And (A, B) is not $A + B$, but $A + B - AB$; as pointed out by Mr Boole. The distinction may also be made as follows:—If A and B be aggregants of X, it means that X contains both: if components, that X is contained in both.

A name may belong to an individual object of thought, objectively considered, or to the class in which that object is placed by possession of a *quality*, objectively considered as inhering in it. The name may also belong to the quality itself, and also to the *class-mark*, or *attribute*, the subjective quality, the possession of the mind, by which it can think of the class subjectively. These distinctions are fundamental parts of thought. Thus one name has no fewer than four separate uses: and the battle of the four senses is a large part of the history of logic. There are two reductions of plurality to unity, that of objects to class, that of qualities to attribute. Both are often denied; some maintain that we cannot think of class without the individual object, nor of attribute without an object to qualify by it. But perhaps it is more common in the

[1] I speak here only of the *subjective* distinction of subject and object. With the true *objective*, Logic has nothing to do.

general world implicitly to deny the subjective unity of class, and the objective plurality of quality. However others may be constituted, I find myself conscious of full and clear possession of both class and attribute, as *second intentions*. Illustration will be useful, and none is better than the oldest. We are in a warehouse full of packages of all kinds: each package has one or more seal-impressions on it, its *qualities*, by which alone we see the existence of the packages. These packages represent, some the material, some the mental substrata about the existence of which so much discussion has arisen: they are perfectly dark, and the seal-impressions shine by a light of their own. We can put together all which have one seal-impression, and so form a class, the members of which might be scattered among other classes, if we sorted by other seal-impressions. Perhaps all the impressions of one design come from one original seal, *universale ante rem*: but this is the question of [scholastic] realism, and is purely metaphysical: our affair is with the sorting &c. of the packages. Certain it is that for our own use we take off on what we call *memory* a seal from each class of impressions, an inverse process, that we may have the means of testing new impressions when we come to them, and that we may always recall the design when we want it. Thus we make the quality, *universale in re*, give us an attribute, *universale post rem* [image and concept (3 January, 1864)].

The denial of unity in plurality is made by saying that *man*, for instance, thought of as a class, means only the conception of an *individuum vagum* from among the class individuals, who must be tall or short, fair or dark, &c.: also that *attribute* is only *quality* thought of as appertaining to this individual. All but this, they say, is only grasping a name: the conception of a class is only the imagination (calling up an *image*) of an individual. I do not know how it is with others, except from their own report, which I cannot question. But it is not so with me. Procrustes has hitherto been, in most cases, one of the names of a psychologist; a speculator who stretches or shortens the rest of his species to his own pattern, having previously stretched or shortened himself to the pattern of Aristotle, Plato, Kant, or another.

I believe men in general to be true realists, *post rem* at least. They speak attributively: they allow the *same* feeling to different persons, the *same* quality to different things. This many affirm to be an incorrect mode of speaking: they aver that two persons cannot have the same feeling in the sense in which they can sit at the same table. This assumes that a table is more than a *collection of feelings*. For myself, if I may not say that two persons who die of a stroke of the sun, or two strokes of the sun, are killed by the *same disorder*, neither will I be inveigled by the *usual hypothesis* of matter into saying that they were killed by the *same sun*. It would be easy to frame hypotheses which no one can, of knowledge, deny, under which attributes in the brain should be as real as the sun in the heavens or the rocks on the earth: and this without denying either the existence of matter, or the separate existence of mind; and so that the question whether *A* gives the *same* attribute, roundness, to both sun and moon, should be the very same question as whether *A* and *B* both see the *same* sun.

7. A man may be allowed to ignore, as a logician, what he admits as a metaphysician: but he must not *deny* it. Some logicians have controverted the plurality in unity, in order to base logic wholly on what I shall presently describe as the *mathematical* notion. One chief object of this paper is to reinforce the assertion that the mathematical branch of logic, the part which has a mathematical principle, has been allowed to overgrow the metaphysical part, and deprive it of light and air. This begins to be admitted, though not in my words: but those who make the admission seem to be trying to grow another branch of the mathematical: which is most conspicuous in the attempt to introduce, by postulation of its universal existence in thought, a complete quantification of the predicate, as a part of the notion of enunciation. It is said that all that enters into the predicate notion is denied of the subject when the predicate is denied, and that in this matter there is no difference between the constitutive and the attributive. This is a hard saying, so long as that which enters a notion enters in the way of the world at large. *Man* is denied of *Bucephalus*, and *animal* enters the notion of *man*; is *animal* denied of *Bucephalus*? No, answers the pluralist, only that part of the notion which belongs to man. The truth is that, to make the whole fit on the mathematical abacus, the unity of attribution is denied, and there is left but a class of qualities, distributed, one a piece, among the individual class objects. Alexander of Macedon, Newton, and Leibnitz, have three human natures. Leibnitz is not Newton: therefore every attribute *comprehended* in our thought of Newton is virtually denied of Leibnitz, be it his humanity, be it the *wearing of his wig awry*.[1] Now all this is in the form of thought, because it can be thought: it is therefore a part of logic. The qualities of Newton are not the qualities of Leibnitz, because Newton is not Leibnitz. It is however a part of the mathematical side. The class may be divided into individuals, the attribute, or class-mark, may be made to give thought of a class of individual qualities, as much separated as the individuals of the class of objects in which they inhere. Nay, even the perception of the desirableness of putting on the right class-mark may be made to generate a class, a class of *desirablenesses*: one perception of the propriety of placing Newton in the class man; another for Leibnitz; and so on. But the very logician who thus lays down all thought on a meagre abacus will—at least I see from his writings that he always *does*—return to

[1] [Cf. Hamilton's *Discussions*, p. 693.—Ed.]

unity the moment he drops the counters with which he was acting his *professional* part. The distinction which he played at abrogating, the distinction between the genus in species of metaphysical composition, and the species in genus of mathematical aggregation, will recur to his nature before the pitch-fork is well out of his hand. The attribute of humanity will then be in his mind common to Newton and Leibnitz, and so will that of *phenacostrepticism,* if he must needs suppose that the wigs which covered those vast masses of thought were given to unseemly rotation about their polar axes.

8. I now come to the strongest of the differences between my own views and those which have been recently propounded. A clear detail of the point is due to the eminence of those from whom I differ: and all the remainder of this paper will contain very frequent illustrations of a distinction which I am confident has been wholly misconceived.

Aristotle saw that though the genus contains more than the species, more extent, more *things*, yet the species also contains more than the genus, each *thing* takes more *description*, more fulness of quality. Our own language will make the distinction expressively:—animal is more than man; *and* there is more in a man than in an animal: animal is horse, dog,[1] &c. as well as man, but a man has reason, which an animal other than man has not. All the attributes make up the *οὐσία*, and accordingly (*Categories*, cap. 5) the species has more *substance* than the genus; *τὸ εἶδος τοῦ γένους μᾶλλον οὐσία.* Again, (*Metaphysics*, lib. iv. or v. cap. 25) the genus is called part of the species, but otherwise the species is part of the genus; *διὸ τὸ γένος τοῦ εἴδους καὶ μέρος λέγεται· ἄλλως δὲ τὸ εἶδος τοῦ γένους μέρος.* In the *Physics* (lib. v. cap. 5) various illustrations are given. The sense of this is very clear; as follows:

Species in genus. All man is in animal: whole class *man* part of class *animal.*

Genus in species. All animal is in man: whole *attribute* animal component of attribute *man.*

The whole of man is in animal, European, Asiatic, &c. The whole of animal is in man, body, organization, sentience, want of food, power to get it, instinct of reproduction, &c. But *man* is not all *animal,* witness horse, dog, &c.: nor is *animal* all *man,* witness all the attributes which make up the distinction of *reason.* Hence we may say, in one reading, that man is universal, animal particular: in the other, that animal is universal and man particular. And this is the great distinction, to the

[1] Since putting down these instances, I happened to see in the recent English translation of Aristotle's metaphysics (l. iv. c. 26) that man, horse, *god,* are *animals.* I took it for granted that a transposition of letters had taken place in the last word; but on looking at Aristotle, I found *θεός*. The confusion arises from the practice of translating *ζῷον* by *animal*: it should be *living being*; the English word *animal* agrees with the middle Latin word in meaning *corpus animatum.*

[Patricius charges Aristotle with maintaining that God is an animal—(1863).]

sides of which it was always intended to give the words *extension* and *comprehension*.

This distinction was very little attended to. It always had its scholastic name: the species as part of the genus was a part of the *logical* whole; the genus as part of the species was a part of the *metaphysical* whole. The schoolmen were no mean proficients in the art of saying what they meant: and they meant to keep 'species in genus' within logic, and to drive 'genus in species' into metaphysics.

The *Port Royal Logic* is said to be the first modern work in which the distinction is insisted on; the use made of it is not very extensive. But it is correctly conceived. It is said, for example, that the attribute (predicate) of an affirmative proposition is affirmed according to its *whole* comprehension: and also that the negative proposition does not separate from the subject *all* the parts contained in the comprehension of the attribute: meaning, for instance, that to say *Bucephalus* is not *man* does not separate *animal* from *Bucephalus*. I do not think that many works carry on this distinction: for, had there been many, I suppose my own research, limited as it is, would have detected more than one. But I have only[1] found it in the *Institutiones Philosophicae* of J. Bouvier of Mans (third edition, Mans, 1830, 12mo).

The logicians who have recently contended for the revival, or rather the full introduction, of the distinction of extension and comprehension, have completely passed over the *change of the quantity*, and, so far as I see, make it only the distinction of number of objects in a class, and number of *marks of class*, or concrete qualities, one to each. So that, with them, quantity of comprehension is the same thing as quantity of

[1] Since this was written I find—or rather *refind*, for I must have seen it—that a learned reviewer of myself and others [Mansel] has hinted an objection to the growing theory of his day, in a manner which implies that he inclines to the old view. I find also that he admits it *is* the old view. But his objection is hesitatingly given, and with an avowed expectation of refutation; though this I suspect to be rather deference than doubt.

[It is hardly right to say that the distinction of extension and comprehension was wholly lost, till revived by the Port-Royal authors. It always existed as a metaphysical distinction, and, though not fundamentally laid down in logic, made no infrequent appearance. I think Occam, but I cannot now refer to his work, expressly applies the *whole* predicate to the whole subject; and whoever does so must think of the comprehension of the predicate. In speaking of the works which 'carry on' the Port Royal distinction, I mean only to include those in which the *change of the quantity*, so well laid down by Arnauld, is distinctly stated, in some of its cases at least. Thus though William Duncan of Aberdeen speaks of extension and comprehension, I cannot find that he lays down anything on quantity. But Isaac Watts, in his excellent and much underrated work, which I call the English Port-Royal Logic, both lays down the distinction, and the universal comprehension of the predicate of an affirmative: this I have found only recently. But Watts says nothing about the predicate of a negative, as to comprehension. Nor have I anywhere found it laid down that in *all* terms of *all* propositions, the quantities in extension and in comprehension are of different names.—(25 June 1858).]

extension: six of one, half-a-dozen of the other. For example, when one of them reads in extension 'all metals are some shining things' he converts it into a proposition of comprehension as follows—'The notion of *some shining things* attaches to the notion of *all metals.*' It ought to be said that the *whole* notion of *shining*, with *all* its components, badness of radiation, hurtfulness to the eye if too long continued, fitness for mirrors, difficulty of good imitation in painting, &c. &c. all form a part, and, as it happens (but this is not necessarily contained in the proposition), a part *only*, of the notion *metal*: which contains besides, hardness, conduction of electricity, &c. &c.

Another powerful writer sets out a table of descent from the *summum genus A*, which contains species *E*, which contains *I*, which contains *O*, which contains *U*, which contains *Y*, which contains the individuals z, z', z'', &c. As in animal, mammal, man, European, Greek, Athenian (*i.e.* Socrates, Plato, &c. &c.). Beginning with *z*, we are told this subject is (contains *in* it the inherent attribute) *some Y*. Here Plato contains in himself as an attribute, *some* Athenian. Now he is contained in the class as *some* (one) Athenian: but he contains in himself *all* attributes essential to an Athenian. As an individual, he helps to make up Athenian (class of men): but *all* that goes to the composition of an Athenian man is in him, the *whole* of every attribute must be awarded to him as a quality. If an Athenian must talk Attic Greek, so must Plato; if an Athenian must look down on a Spartan as a fellow not fit to talk to nor to dine with, so must Plato. The next step is 'All *Y* is some *U*,' or 'All Athenian is some Greek.' But it should be:—All the attribute Greek is part of what we think of under the attribute Athenian. Any one would suppose my quotations were meant for class readings; but it is not so: the readings in extension are given as 'Some *Y* is *z*' and 'Some *U* is all *Y*,' &c.

It seems that by a strong bias in favour of the mathematical side of logic, the decomposition of the attribute has been discarded in favour of the disaggregation of a class of qualities. But whether this be done avowedly, in opposition to the ancient distinction of logical and metaphysical whole, or whether those who do it imagine themselves in accordance with the old writers, is a point which I have not seen settled, nor even alluded to, by those to whom alone belongs the power of deciding it. Except so far as this. The preceding table of descent, from the *summum genus* to the individuals, was partly written in answer to passages of my second paper in which the view of the *Port Royal* logic was taken; that is, the affirmative proposition was made intensively universal in the predicate, the negative proposition intensively particular. I and some others were declared to be wrong: but whether the *Port Royal* authors were among those others was not stated, though I suspect that my reviewer mentioned in the previous note is included.

Of course no one can object to the truth of the proposition that some individual instances of the quality animal are distributed, one a piece, among all men. This proposition can be thought, and is thought: and it is not quite the same thought as 'All men are so many animals.' But this very subordinate distinction is not the one which Aristotle laid down, and which he obtained from the necessities of human thought. He meant that animal contains man, for animal is aggregate of man and brute: but (ἄλλως) man contains animal, for man is compound of animal and reason.

9. The quantification of the predicate has been the guide under which the school against which I contend has been led to take a reduplication of the mathematical side of logic for an introduction of the metaphysical side. This quantification they justify by the postulate that logic ought to be allowed to find language for all that *is* contained in thought. Whether usual thought does quantify the predicate may be doubted: but this does not matter: for the postulate should have had *can be* instead of *is*. It is the business of logic, as a mental[1] gymnastic, to put into activity all the powers, if any, which ordinary life allows to lie dormant. Of every mode of thinking, as of every mode of using the muscles, it is certain that it was meant for a purpose, and for a purpose which cannot be so well accomplished without it. Accordingly, the syllogism of the predicate quantified by postulation has its proper place: I believe that place to be, as I shall point out, in company with the common form of syllogism, and the numerically definite syllogism, in the *arithmetical whole*, or whole of *first intention.*

But there is one mode of thought, very often expressed in common life, and almost always implied, which logic has wilfully neglected, to the serious curtailment of her field of operation. Her pictures are not bounded by a frame, with landscape and sky definitely painted up to the sides of the rectangle; but have only a foreground with an indefinite back shading, equally signifying, under the type of an exclusion, the distant hill and the intermediate river. The *contrary* of the name or term, the not-*X* of the *X*, is made only aorist, indefinite, standing for more or less, no matter which, of the whole universe of thought. But not only is common thought conducted in a limited universe, but this so

[1] A learned writer [Mansel] denies it this character, in its primary purpose. He says that logic is no more designed primarily to give men facility in the practice of reasoning than a treatise on optics is intended to improve their sight. The parallel is imperfect. Suppose that optics neither had, nor could have, other subject-matter than spectacles; that men did nothing in their waking moments without making spectacles; that religion and morals, life and manners, food and clothing, &c. &c. all depended in the highest degree upon every man, or most men, making those spectacles well which they must all make well or ill. In such a case 'Optics, or the art of improving defective vision' would be no very absurd title: nor, as man *is* constituted, is there any great objection to 'Logic, or the art of reasoning.' It would be better to say 'Optics, or the form of spectacle-making, with a view to the improvement of vision' and 'Logic, or the form of thought, with a view to the improvement of reason.'

palpably that express mention is seldom needed. A person strikes into a conversation to deny the first he has heard of it, and is instantly put down by, We were talking of ——. A proposition, false in the whole universe of thought, is true in the universe of the speaker's argument. The first sentence in Euclid is a marked instance: a point is that which has no part. My firm conviction that Euclid was a man and not a myth *has no part*: I cannot dichotomize it; is it then a point? Any one can answer that Euclid was talking of space, not of historical beliefs and convictions: space and its laws are the universe of his book. The definite universe, the duality of every classification, exclusion as definite as inclusion, should be of the *logica docens* because it is possible, and of the *logica utens* because it is actual: and fundamental in both.

10. We think by class, or by attribute, under relations. The relation which must take precedence of all others, *because it must be present in the mere idea of nomenclature*, is that of whole and part, of containing and contained. This relation, and its concomitants, I call *onymatic* relations: and it appears to me that, onymatic being absent, *formal*[1] has supplied its place. There is a fourfold mode of thought, which logicians confound into one by a fourfold use of the word '*is*'. I denote and symbolize the four modes as follows, proceeding only by an instance, and leaving the full description of the relations for the summary in the second part.

(*a*) *Logico-mathematical*; class aggregant of class. The class *man* included in the class *animal.* Always intended where symbols are both common parentheses, as)) () &c.

(*b*) *Logico-physical*; attribute predicated of class. Animal a quality of every man, an attribute of the class. Symbols)] (] &c.

(*c*) *Logico-metaphysical*; attribute component of attribute. The notion animal a component part of the notion human. Symbols]] [] &c.

(*d*) *Logico-contraphysical*, attribute[2] subjected to class. Human, an attribute to be looked for within the class animal. Symbols]) [) &c.

a. *Mathematical.* The logicians excluded—or rather tried to exclude —all predication except reference of class to class: accordingly, genus as an aggregate of species they called the *logical* whole. The name is good so long as the exclusion lasts, and no longer. Aggregation of individuals into species, they called the *mathematical* whole: I call it the

[1] The more I read of the common statements about form and matter, with the word *onymatic* in my mind, the more does the conviction grow upon me that logicians have taken the distinction between forms which are and which are not onymatic to be the distinction between formal and material.

[2] *Nec quarta loqui persona laboret.* It seems to be a rule that every quaternion of logic shall contain one member who is to be considered a disgrace to the family, if not entirely disowned. Of the four universal propositions, one, marked by me (·), is unknown to the logicians; the same of one particular,)(. We all know what a bad character the fourth figure has had, ever since it got a footing as a poor relation.

arithmetical. And aggregation of species into genus I call the *mathematical* whole: mathematical, because summation of parts is a mathematical process; but not necessarily *arithmetical,* or proceeding by enumeration of *similars.* The difference between species and individual is, in some points, extralogical. The logician, as such, never knows whether he has or has not specified down to an individual, or even down to nonexistence, at each or any step of the process. His stoppage at an *infima species,* composed of many individuals, was his own fiction. Begin from animal, and compound successively the *differentiae,* human, Roman, ancient, general, conqueror of Gauls, writer of his own campaigns. No one knows whether we have or have not specified down to Julius Caesar. Add *surviving author,* and we are safe enough: add *composer for the pianoforte,* and we are morally certain we have an empty box. But logic takes no account of the actual effect of differences upon the numerical strength of the species.

Extension and intension both exist, but extension predominates. We often think of class as aggregate of classes, seldom as compound or common part of classes. We hardly reconcile ourselves to the idea of the common part of two classes as a *compound*: by habit we slip into the notion of the attribute of the common part as compounded of the attributes of the two. Thus *marine* is a joint class, both *soldier* and *sailor*: but we rather say the marine, the individual, unites both *characters.*

b. Physical. This is the most common mode of thought in man's *nature,* as well as in *physics*: and my use of the word is not far from that made in the old *totum physicum.* I mean that this reading is the most common use of the word *is*: especially in controversy, which is most often about the attributes of things and actions. Man is born and educated a mathematician as to the subject of his propositions, a metaphysician[1] as to the predicate: he thinks attributively of class in every wrong way and some right ones. His universals are necessities,

[1] Contending as much as any one for the distinction between logic and metaphysics, I must yet remind my reader that logic is concerned with the *whole form of thought.* The *necessary* form of thought for all practical teaching, is any form which all men *actually have,* whether we can imagine them to be without it, or not. If every man, saint, savage, or sage, have a certain form of thought, it is the business of logic to teach him to use that form correctly. Now it is a fact that, in their daily thoughts and judgments, all men are metaphysicians, and always have been: and the uneducated more than the educated, and children more than grown people. We have all our ideas, which we are constantly applying, about natural and unnatural, necessary and not necessary, essential and not essential, repugnant and not repugnant, cause and effect, dependence and independence, possibility and impossibility, &c. &c. &c. These are our strong points. We set out in all our inquiries with clear ideas of the naturally possible and impossible: we sometimes feel our ignorance as to what *is* and *is not,* but never as to what *can be* and *cannot be.* Now whether our metaphysics be true or false, it is the business of logic to take care that it be logical. Even if it be the truth that no notions have either essential connexion, or necessary repugnance, it is a law of our minds to *envisage* them as having both, and it is a law of our

whether of inclusion or exclusion, not enumerated individual facts. One great use of logic is to teach him the mathematical mode: that is, to make it more of a habit: one great use of natural history in liberal education is to bring down the metaphysical habit, and raise up the mathematical one, until they are more nearly equipollent. The natural *historian* predicates of class in class, arranges facts by facts: he savours of the *physiologist* so soon as his predicate becomes attributive. The logician attempts to point out the human fault and mend it in much the same way as a social reformer would attempt to improve a rude and dirty peasantry, if he should begin by the assurance that they had always lived, and were living, in neat glazed cottages, into which no pig had ever presumed to thrust his snout; and that all they had to do was to become aware of the fact. He assures the beginner that when he said snow is white, he had not in thought a necessary attribute, for he never had any attribute at all: he meant that snows are *some* white objects, with a distinct reference of possibility to others unnamed. Logic would have been of greater use if it had been distinctly announced that one of its great aims is the abatement of *natural philosophy*, the increase of the power of referring thing to thing, and of inferring from classes, the majesty of ignorance having been accustomed only, or chiefly, to the assignment of attributes. Common thought deals mostly in double universals: the metaphysical whole applied to the mathematical whole. And so the old logicians often phrased it: they said that in a universal affirmative the whole predicate is applied to the whole subject. Some logicians deny the existence of this form, in logic at least. Declaring that the word '*is*' shall be, ought to be, the only copula, in its meaning of *identification*, they declare that attribute can only be predicated of attribute, or class of class. With this I have nothing to do, except to appeal to the world at large whether by '*is*' they do not intend to convey predication of attribution and subjection of class, at least as often as any other sense. To me the 'elegant extracts' of the logicians are no answer: I deny their right to exclude any form under which men *do think*; and I contend for the *whole form* of thought.

c. Metaphysical. This is an old and well-known use of the word, appropriate both to its etymology and to its derived meaning. If chemistry had been known as it is now, that which was called the metaphysical whole would have been called the *chemical* whole. The manner in which the concept man is composed in our thoughts of animal and

---

language to talk of them as having both. But many a man who is metaphysician enough to know that reason is essential to man, is not logician enough to avoid the inference that it is *therefore* repugnant to the nature of brute. A man may, in his closet, be both an idealist in philosophy and a mathematician in logic: but the moment his foot is on the pavement and his eye on the world, realism and metaphysics resume their sway.

reason is a very different thing from that in which animal is made up of man and brute. The logicians say that a concept is the *sum*[1] of the attributes which it comprehends: the mathematician easily corrects them. *Animal* is the *sum* of *man* and *brute*: withdraw *brute*, and the notion *animal* is not destroyed; *man* remains, and some *animal* is left. In fact, *animal* is made up of human-*animal* and brute-*animal*. But in *comprehension*, to use his own term, being the view of which the logician was speaking, man is a *compound*, not a *sum*, of *animal* and *reason*: withdraw *reason*, and the notion *man* ceases to exist. *Man* is not added up of *animal-in-man* and *reason-in-man*. Again, in aggregating animal, we may conceive all man to be in Europe, and all brute in Asia: but in compounding man we cannot conceive all the animal to be in Europe, and all the rational in Asia. Put an impossible species into the genus, and the rest are not affected: put an impossible component into the notion, and it ceases to be a notion. A black-white horse is a subjective nonentity: nevertheless, if we divide horses into black, white, and black-white, the genus is still usable; it is only a three-stall stable with one stall locked up and the key lost, or never made.

Extension and intension both exist in the metaphysical, but intension predominates. The attribute human may be extensively subdivided into attributes, and also into individual qualities. The misconception of the logicians which I have discussed at length consists in seizing the extension of an attribute, and missing the intension.

When the old logicians puzzled themselves with what they called the *indefinite* proposition, Man is animal, and tried to make out whether it should be universal or particular, they were dealing with the metaphysical form of speech, attribute predicated to be component of attribute. Nor is this the only instance in which the metaphysical intruded itself within the mathematical boundary. To me the old books read like a running fight between the two modes of conception: not a pitched battle between regimented ranks under the banners of *quid* and of *quale*; but a mob-scuffle in which there is neither front nor rear. It has been said that logic ought to be the uncovered skeleton: this was said of the mathematical view. The old logicians clothed the bones with a little

[1] The illustrations which follow are familiar to the mathematician in the distinctive properties of $a + b$ and ab. Such a mistake as that made by the logicians would be, in mathematics, equivalent to substitution of logarithms in place of their primitives. This mistake was made by the old geometers, when they styled *composition* of ratios *addition* of ratios: it appears in Euclid's *duplicate* and *triplicate* ratio. But here it was not all mistake. The logarithmic idea was present in an undefined and uncomprehended form: and, when the time arrived, the *measure of the ratio* was easily accepted as the definition of the *logarithm*. Those who have affirmed that Archimedes invented logarithms, were right so far as this, that Archimedes or a predecessor invented the *integer* part of the notion, if indeed it be not more correct to say that the integer part of the notion invented itself. Napier invented the fractional part of the notion, and applied all.

metaphysical muscle: so that, instead of presenting the examination of a skeleton in one compartment of a museum, and of muscular fibre in another, logic looked like an inquest on a starved pauper in the workhouse.

d. Contra-physical. This form is rarely in use. In human thought, the more frequently one of two inverse forms occurs, the more rare is the other. But it is only in a result to be expressed that this reading is a rarity. When the old metaphysician was hunting the species in a genus by a *differentia* which was *of the essence*, he was engaged in a contra-physical process.

All these words express distinctions which are purely formal. The *logico-metaphysical* is only the form, law, mode of entrance, of the *metaphysical* notion, so long as humanity and phenacostrepticism are equally admissible as attributes of Newton and Leibnitz. I shall make no other answer to the charge of *materialism*, except this, and a reference to what I have already said. If all that precedes contain any matter, find the form of it, and either point it out as existing, or introduce it. If the phrases savour too much of the material, either sublimate them into formalism by mental chemistry, or find better phrases.

Even the words *necessary* and *contingent* must be allowed a formal sense, which has an eye to the mode of action common to two kinds of matter. Real necessity only exists in the laws of thought, applied to matter of which we form judgments *à priori*: popular necessity exists where contingence has never shown two different kinds of result. Instead therefore of widening the bounds of logic to introduce the consideration of true metaphysical necessity, it is to be part of logic that the necessity which can be seen *à priori* or from *à priori, the three angles of a triangle make two right angles*, is not of the same material as the necessity inferred from uncontradicted contingency, *man is biped*, but that the two have a common form in thought, or set the machinery in action in the same way. The same may be said of other notions of pure meta-physics: the subjective and the objective are of one form of process in logic.

11. The only copula which logicians provide, for all the modes of reading, is the substantive verb '*is*.' Nor is another wanted, so long as one relation only is used: but more must now be found. To express in language all that is contained in thought, is to divide in language all that is divided in thought. We must have definite *words of relation, anaphorical* or *schetical* terms: and these I shall presently propose. But an ambiguity, to which I now proceed, nipped the use of schetical words in the bud.

Dichotomy, in mathematics, has an extreme case which is always included. If $c = a + b$, the terminal instance $c = a + 0$ is admitted and accounted for, or else excluded under the showing of the particular problem. Logical dichotomy, class into two classes, has the well-known quantitative division of *all* into two *somes*. The word *some*, in mathematical meaning, ranges from *none* to *all*, both ends included. But in logic, the exclusion of the terminus *none* is an absolute necessity: its inclusion would bring under one word existence and non-existence, would make falsehood the extreme case of truth. But it is otherwise at the second terminus. Ambiguity here exists in thought and in usage. Accordingly, logic has always recognized [the consequences of *Buffon*] two kinds of *some*; that of *terminal ambiguity*, some-it-may-be-all; and that of *terminal precision*, some-not-all, the *some* of common life.

Some-not-all, separated by specific difference, and *all*, are in the relation of species and genus; a relation which is lost when *some* becomes *all*, in the old sense of the words species and genus. But in 'All *X* is *Y*' the force of *Y* is 'some or all *Y*, as it may happen.' It is 'All *X* is some-it-may-be-all *Y*.' The logicians frequently define some as not-all in the outset, and then proceed to use it with an ambiguous terminus, by expressly laying down that 'Some *X* is *Y*' does not allow inference of 'some *X* is not *Y*.' This confusion still continues. We have been assured that 'All *X* is some *Y*' is contradicted by 'All *Y* is some *X*,' a proposition which cannot be made good except by *some* being declared *not all*.

This distinction totally prevented the expression of any syllogism as a combination of relations. No one could say that the process in *Barbara* is expressed by 'Species of species is species.' This last expresses the act of mind in one of what I have called complex syllogisms, each containing three simple syllogisms. The process in *Barbara* is as follows:—That which is either species or coextensive of that which is either species or coextensive of *Z* is itself either species or coextensive of *Z*. Add to this that while the propositional forms were more of the mathematical character, the predicables were more of the metaphysical.

12. I now come to the proposition, its form, quality, and quantity. For the distinction which I draw between the technical sense of *affirmation* and *negation*, and the general words *assertion* and *denial*, I refer to the second part of this paper.

A beginner in logic, on hearing the propositions 'Omnis homo est animal,' 'Aliquis homo est doctus,' not only as first examples of predication, but as the ultimate instruments of syllogism, might be expected to say—I was told that logic was chiefly, if not wholly, conversant with *second intentions*; Pray what has become of them? The fact is that philosophy, in spite of her proud tendency towards the universal and the necessary, and her contempt for what I call the arithmetical whole, as vague, partial, and contingent, actually proceeded in this arithmetical whole, not merely in the convenient expression, but in the scientific structure, of her propositions. Her forms were *all* and *some*, as fundamental discriminators of propositional enunciations. Her good intentions as to second intentions—in adopting which she took a course worthy of herself—were rendered of no effect, partly by the habit of the arithmetical whole, partly by the want of the definite universe, partly by a preference for the affirmative over the negative; the first of a tendency towards the contingent, the second and third of a tendency towards the necessary and universal. She saw, I suspect, that omniscience need never use form of denial, because it is in possession of the counter-affirmation. All denial is ignorance: no one need rest in 'No *A* is *B*' if his knowledge will allow him to say 'Every *A* is *C*' where *C* and *B* are of essentially and visibly repugnant attributes. Or, to descend to common life, no one replies by a simple negative to 'Does he live at No. 42?' if he knows that No. 43 is the true number. Vieta, an accomplished pupil of the schools, caught the dislike to negation, and did his best to avoid subtraction: he used artifices *contra vitium negationis*; but algebra beat him.

Philosophy, again, which scorned the idea of the *εἶδος εἰδικώτατον* descending to the individual, as savouring of the arithmetical whole, had to work in this whole through all the syllogism, partly because she insisted on raising the *γένος γενικώτατον* up to the whole universe of thought. When *all* and *some* were selected as the exponents of quantity, no reason was ever given for the exclusion of *most* and *fewest*, or of any of the signs of definite ratio of part to whole called fractions. A reason could have been given, and I shall come to it; but philosophy never gave it, within my[1] reading: the light of second intention shone but dimly into the arithmetical whole. The considerations which I shall proceed to offer are destructive of the right of the numerical syllogism to a place in the logic of the two opposed wholes: but they equally destroy the right of the common form of syllogism, under both quantifications, natural and postulated. All go together to the arithmetical whole, in which all are formed, whether the *some* be more or fewer, vague or definite, all, some perhaps all, some not all, most, nearly all, two-sevenths exactly, two-sevenths or more, two-sevenths or thereabouts. I cannot see how it is possible, under any effective understanding of the difference between first and second intentions, to deny that the common proposition *speaks* by first intention; though of course those who use it may *think* of class or attribute. The arithmetical whole is subordinated, though with

[1] There is hardly an imaginable speculation on thought which is not to be found in the vast number of large volumes by powerful authors which have descended to us. It is not an uncommon mode of replying to a claim for the introduction of this or that into logic, that some Optimus Albinus or Pessimus Niger—as the case may be—mentioned the matter at some date preceding 1600. With this I have nothing to do. That an opinion has been held before now, and has not gained room in the *quod semper*, &c. is no argument at all: and if it were, it would come with no effect from those who are now pressing the point that the whole of one side of logic, though known to and hinted at by both the illustrious writers above mentioned, has never been put in its proper place.

[There *was* an Albinus—(1863).]

different degrees of affinity, both to the mathematical and to the metaphysical wholes: but the habit is to refer it to the former, and for a reason we shall see.

13. Taking the mathematical form first, and dichotomizing the universe in two ways, by classes *X* and not-*X* (*x*), and *Y* and *y*, the onymatic relations of class to class can be predicated without any explicit dichotomy of class, whether vague or definite. The *relations* are *inclusion* and *exclusion* (inclusion in *contrary*); the judgments, *assertion* and *denial.*

	Mathematical Form	*Arithmetical Form*
A	I assert the inclusion of *X* in *Y*	Every *X* is *Y*
O	I deny the inclusion of *X* in *Y*	Some *X*s are not *Y*s
E	I assert the exclusion of *X* from *Y*	No *X* is *Y*
I	I deny the exclusion of *X* from *Y*	Some *X*s are *Y*s

Here the classes *X* and *Y* are treated in their philosophical unity: the common reading represents objective verification. What is your right to deny the exclusion of *X* from *Y*? Answer, this *X* is a *Y*, and this, and this, &c.

Quantity is here of no fundamental account: but if not a root, it must be a branch. The objective verifications tell us in the common way the story of universal and particular terms. But the objective and enumerative character has led to much extra-logical discussion on the syllogism. The common form seems to make the whole prove no more than must have been proved in establishing the part. It is only an appearance: but there is substantial neglect in omitting to notice that the syllogism, as logical, has nothing to do with the sort of vindication under which its premises are advanced. If there be a logical necessity that every *Y* is *Z*, then *X* being *Y*, *X* is *Z*. Let the necessity be from *à priori* deduction, let it be the imperfect necessity of induction of the past made deduction of the future, or let it be the *à posteriori* necessity of a complete induction, the syllogism is one and the same act of mind in all cases. The full mathematical form includes all these cases, and shews their inclusion.

The above forms leave only a contingent place for the additional propositions which enter when the predicate is quantified by postulation of every distribution of *all* and *some*. It *may* come out that *X* and *Y* are identical in extent: this is one case of *A*. It *must* come out that some *X* is not some *Y*, unless *X* and *Y* be singular and identical. The first is to be referred to the forms of terminal precision, the second to a notiòn antecedent to propositional enunciation, and connected with the purposes and distinctions of nomenclature.

14. The idea of enumeration of individuals does not afford the most satisfactory basis for a doctrine of logical quantity which shall put the counter wholes, mathematical and metaphysical, into complete correlation.

In the mathematical whole, the logicians often conceal enumeration by speaking of *extent* instead of *number*: not 'every man is one of the animals,' but 'All man is part of animal.' Very strange is it to a beginner to hear of the *extent* of the term man, and of parts of that extent, as if the notion were capable of continuous accretion, and each new birth put a little bit more man into the extent. To me, when I first heard this language, it seemed as if the notion *man* had been treated after the manner of a dish of potatoes *de-individualized* by being skinned and then mashed together. There is perhaps in the geometrical idea some help towards the expression of class as a unit, because number is connected with the notion of partition in a closer way than area. Still, the attribute compounded of attributes does not seem at once, and without effort, to correlate with the class aggregated of classes.

If we subdivide a class into four others, there is an amount of information in the four, as four, which we are not conscious of when we see four attributes in an individual object. If the worthy Jesuit Gaspar Schott had announced that the number of beatified existences on whose aid man could rely was the 256th power of 2, there would have been an intelligible basis of comparison with other things: how many to each man, what reduction by probable increase of population in a given time, &c. would be matters of approximation for an actuary. But when Schott announced 2^{256} as the number of graces and glories of the Virgin, no comparison could well exist within the limits of attractive speculation. For aught we can say, there may be 2^{256} distinct powers in human reason, developed or undeveloped.

In classification, we know that we arrive at a true *infima species*, the individual: for from the individual we start, and therefore to the individual we can regress. But in an attribute we begin with the compound; and our knowledge of simple substances is not yet attained, far less our atomic theory. In the case of a simple perception, as *white*, we may just distinguish brightness and tint, but we can go no further: the prism which decomposes the cause does not decompose the effect, does not give separate perceptions of which we were perceptively conscious in the compound. Again, in disaggregating[1] a class, we have a distinct

[1] At first sight we might imagine that one of the fundamental distinctions between class and attribute is this, that a composition of classes introduces no new individuals, and puts no individual into any class in which it was not before: but a composition of attributes may introduce a new attribute, not belonging to either alone. Thus to the attribute *metallic brilliancy* belongs the attribute *destructible by oxidation*, which neither belongs to *metallic* alone, nor to *brilliancy* alone: to *mortal reason* belongs the attribute of capability to believe in a *future state*, in the common sense of the words; which capability belongs neither to mortality without reason, nor to reason without mortality. But this, as happens in so many other cases, is of the usual tendency of thought, and not of necessity. Speaking in extension, we have but been saying that the class *AB* may be wholly contained in classes which wholly contain neither *A* nor *B*.

idea of *incopartient aggregants*: but in decomposing attribution, we are seldom sure of *incommunicant components. Human* is compounded of rational and animal: here we are sensible of a true dichotomy; according to our notions of these terms, the animal demands no essential component of the rational, nor the rational of the animal. But into what two certainly incommunicant attributes shall we divide *rational*? *Capable of abstraction* is one attribute; but what is the other? Psychology cannot answer. When the controversy about decomposition of reason begins, thick darkness rises about the wrath of the combatants, and veils the unutterable fight, as in the case of Yamen and Kehama[1]: with this difference, however, that the mist does not clear off at the end, and shew us which has won the drink of immortality. Again, in phrenology, I hold it established that parts of the brain are separate machineries having their modes of connexion with different feelings or modes of mental existence. But who can name these parts? Grant that three of them are known to exist in *veneration, combativeness*, and *tune*, what are the components of human power which belong to all the three states, or to any two? A certain style of music conduces to the action of veneration, another style to that of combativeness: what component unit-faculty in the organ of music conspires with a correspondent unit in the organ of veneration by which the *organ*—now meaning what the old Presbyterians, of whose organs of veneration it drew out the wrong stop, called the 'kist fu' o' whistles'—acts upon both? All these are questions which can only be asked in illustration of the difference between composition of attribution and aggregation of extent. We go as far as we can, and we try to see what we can: to ask a question is a step in knowledge, and even if there be no answer it is a preparation for an answer. In the present case we realize the false analogy of the assertion that a concept is the sum of its attributes; and, perceiving how truly metaphysical is the process of decomposition of attribute, we raise a contrast which throws light on the exclusively mathematical character of the disaggregation of genus into species.

We want different words to signify quantity of extension and quantity of intension: the difference is that of *quantitas* and *copia*. The world is in possession of the word *force*: it speaks of a term used in its complete force. In fact, as I found out after I had completely organized the second part of this paper, the world has got beyond the logician's abacus in this point, as in others. Corresponding to quantity particular and universal, I shall, in metaphysical enunciation, use the terms complete and incomplete force.

Before illustrating this matter, I must observe that there are two forms of quantity: the extensive, used in common logic, the intensive, not used. Either quantity is universal when its element, be it aggregant or

[1] [Southey: *The Curse of Kehama*, XXIV, 4.—Ed.]

component, may be thrown away at pleasure: particular, when it may not. Thus, the class man is contained in the class animal: man is extensively universal, because we speak of its aggregants separately; each aggregant is animal. Throw out any class of man, and the proposition is only crippled, not falsified. But animal is particular, extensively: we cannot throw out any arbitrary formation of class we please, savage animal for instance, because men may be among them, and it need not be true that All man is (in what is left of) animal. Now pass to intensive quantity (which we shall call force when we speak of attributes) mathematically considered. The quantities change names; and this always happens: the extensive universal is always the intensive particular, &c. *Man* is intensively particular, and *animal* is intensively universal, in the proposition above. We may reject any component of *animal*: man is in the class indicated by the remaining compound. But we may not at pleasure reject any component of *man*: for in so doing we may reject a restricting class which takes the common part of the remaining compounded classes out of *animal* in some part of its extension. Speaking metaphysically, *animal* is a component of *man*: *animal* enters in its complete force, but not man: all the attributes of *animal* compound into a component of *man*.

As another instance, suppose 'I deny the co-exclusion of *X* and *Y*.' When a relation is convertible, it is convenient that the word should denote it: so, instead of saying that *X* is an external of *Y*, I say that *X* and *Y* are co-externals. Here *X* and *Y* are both extensively particular: we cannot make the denial of any aggregant of either, necessarily. For this reason they are both intensively universal: I deny that any component of *X* is excluded from any component of *Y*. In the metaphysical reading, it will be 'I deny the repugnance of the notions *X* and *Y*'; and both have complete force. Speak thus of metallic and fluid, to both of which belongs mercury: in thus speaking, I deny that brilliancy is repugnant to equality of pressure; I deny that high specific gravity is repugnant to mobility: either of these repugnances would create repugnance between *metallic* and *fluid*.

15. The following symbols will be used:—

Mathematical Reading		*Metaphysical Reading*	
X) or (*X*	*X* Extensively universal or intensively particular	]*X* or *X*[	*X* of complete force
X(or)*X*	*X* Extensively particular or intensively universal	[*X* or *X*]	*X* of incomplete force

I call this notation *spicular*, a name first given in derision, but not the worse for that: it is better than *parenthetic*, which has a derived meaning.

16. In the old use of the word intension, it referred to intensity of degree, a kind of extension, since there was more or less of the same;

but continuous, not increasing by individuals. We may distinguish, when needful, between intensity of degree and intensity of composition: the two kinds are of the same logical power. We may dissect class until we come down to the individual, either by successive intensifications of composition, or of degree: some do one thing, some the other, and dispute arises on the result. Thus one man arrives at his highest member of any class, poet, artist, general, &c. by the greatest intension of degree of the attribute on which he most admires the merit of the class; another by greatest intension of composition of constitutive attributes; a third balances the two.

17. I have stated that I consider the ordinary form of the syllogism as belonging to the arithmetical whole, as dealing with first intentions and objective verifications. The syllogism of each of the opposed, or rather confronted, wholes of mathematical and metaphysical thought, is of second intention, and deals with the notions so called. It is, in fact, *combination of relations*: the act of mind by which we see that the *A* of (the *B* of Z), or the (*A* of *B*) of Z, is thinkable under one relation. Here the compound relation, or combined relation, may be represented by *AB*, but by no one except a mathematician who is used to the *functional* symbol, and to the idea of $\phi\psi(xy)$ in its distinction between the mode of composition of x, y, and that of ϕ, ψ. I use the word *combination* instead of *composition*, to avoid raising this question, and the more readily because, until we treat of sorites, *combination* is of *two*. We have seen, in the appendix to my second paper, how the logician, when he has a copula which does not give *his* syllogism, though it be transitive and convertible, has no resource except the combination of relation, thrown into a syllogism of *principium* and *exemplum*. Every thing depends upon our having words descriptive of second intentions, or *schetical* words, which shall, so far as may be, have the force we want in common usage. Four sets are wanted, for terminal precision and terminal ambiguity, both in the mathematical and metaphysical views. Tables of the terms which I adopt for the present, and on which I invite suggestion, are given in the second part. I shall now proceed to some description and remark.

(*a*) *Terminal ambiguity, mathematical view.* Naming the universal first, and its contrary particular second, I say that *X* is either *species* or *exient* of *Y*; either *genus* or *deficient*; either *coexternal* or *copartient*; either *complement* or *coinadequate*. When class is treated as a philosophical unit, we have seen that the distinction of the universal and particular proposition is an emergence from that of assertion or denial of inclusion, or of exclusion. But it consists better with the actual form of thought, as trained by existing logic, not to fashion the terms upon the more philosophical basis. To make them stand on the idea of universal and particular I found impracticable: I have therefore taken them upon no basis at all except the aptness of the several words themselves.

Genus and species. I use these words under terminal ambiguity: thus the species may be the whole genus. They have acquired much of this force in common language, by the *subsidence of knowledge.* In old time it was necessary that *man* should not be a species of *rational animal,* but the whole genus: the earth was the only abiding place of animals. But since it has come into thought that animals may possibly reside in stars and planets, it is in thought that man may be no more than a species of the genus. Other planets may contain organized, sentient, &c. bodies which have a thinking faculty and which name, abstract, &c. but in which the whole combination is so different from our own, that we should not call the compound a man. A snake's body, for instance, with a man's mind. The subsidence, or possible subsidence, of genus into species, and the erection of species into genus, by alteration of knowledge or opinion, leave the terms very nearly indeed, if not quite, in possession of terminal ambiguity.

Exient and *deficient.* I have been obliged to coin the first word, of which the only fault is that it is an *active* participle. *Emergent* is wanted to describe the character of results; *extravagant* and *transcendent* have their derived meanings. *Deficient* usually applies to that which is all used, but all is not enough: there is no word which signifies a deficiency arising, it may be, from a sufficiency being bestowed elsewhere. In the language I use, *X* is a deficient of *Y*, if there be any part of *Y* which *X* is not.

On *coexternal* and *copartient,* I need say nothing. The word *complement* means either *contrary*, or *supercontrary* (containing all the *contrary* and also *copartient*).

As to *coinadequate,* I may observe that if the earlier logicians had studied the relations of exclusion with any amount of sustained attention, we should have been provided with names to express many relations which are perhaps not so much, certainly not so clearly, in thought as they ought to be, chiefly for want of names. The notion of combination is confined to what is positive: things may conspire to produce, cause, be sufficient, &c., but they do not, in usual idiom, conspire to be insufficient. When it is denied that the contraries of *X* and *Y* are coexclusive of each other, so that some things are neither *X*s nor *Y*s, that is, *X* and *Y* do not together fill the universe, we see that they are not together adequate, conspire to be inadequate, are *coinadequate.* This may introduce the word, but it was not of my making, nor formed by such a deduction. I asked a friend [Dr Sharpey] who was likely to give an answer, What, supposing *A* and *B* to be areas not together large enough to make *C*, he would say *A* and *B* were to one another in reference to this joint insufficiency: his almost immediate answer was, *Coinadequate.*

(*b*) *Terminal ambiguity, metaphysical view.* Not being here restricted by usage but, on the contrary, supported by common idiom, I make the distinction of universal and particular to be merely that of assertion and denial of completeness. Accordingly, *X* is either an *essential* or an *inessential* of *Y*; either a *dependent* or an *independent*; either a *repugnant* or an *irrepugnant*; either an *alternative* or an *inalternative*. The four last words may have the sign of convertible relation, *Co-*, prefixed when wanted.

Essential and Dependent. Compare these words with *genus and species*, and the habits of thought of the world at large are well illustrated. The common substantive is of the mathematical type; the common adjective of the metaphysical. The common proposition being physical, the world has a good hold on the substantive *species* and the adjective *essential* [coessentials $X \parallel Y$ etc.]: but it knows much less of the substantive *genus*, or of the adjective *dependent*, as here used. Nevertheless, the word *dependent* is common enough: as in, Cleanliness is essential to comfort; comfort depends upon cleanliness. The logician has only the abacus, 'All comfortable is clean.' On the remaining words there is no especial remark to make, except the one which this very dismissal suggests: namely, that it is easy to pick out of common usage a moderately good set of logico-metaphysical words of relation, while as good a set of logico-mathematical words does not exist in the common dictionary. I believe that this phenomenon does not give much countenance to common logic as an exponent of actual thought, though it bears testimony to the science as, in one particular, an improver of it.

(*c*) *Terminal precision, mathematical view.* The phrases used are those which are found in my *Formal Logic*: and need no especial remark here. The only addition is the distinction of extension and intension: thus the subidentical in extension is the superidentical in intension, &c. This distinction is so easily made that I have not thought it worth while to tabulate it.

(*d*) *Terminal precision, metaphysical view.* All the schetical words yet used might be called *predicables*: but it will be historically more convenient to confine that name to the set now before us. I gave them in the *Philological Transactions*, Vol. vi. No. 129 (1853).[1] The predicables of Aristotle savour strongly of the metaphysical view. I here use the adjectives *generic* and *specific*, which, being adjectives, have retained a metaphysical use, and that even with reinforcement. In treating exclusion as well as inclusion, in a definite universe, and with terminal precision, we require three substantive ideas, all attributive, or denoting *attributes*, though that word is technically applied only to one. There is the *attribute*, said of all [*inherent postea*]; the *accident*, of some and some only (which is therefore *non-accident* as to what it cannot be said of, the

[1] [Cf. p. 70 f.—Ed.]

term being equally positive and negative); and the *excludent*, or *excluse*, said of none. Each of these exists in a three-fold distinction; *universal, generic, and specific*.

Looking at the notion predicated of, say X, in extension, a *universal* predicable is one which applies in the same manner both to X and to x, attribute of both, accident (= non-accident) of both, excludent of both. These are of no value in syllogism. The universal attribute and universal excludent are helps to definition, positive or negative, of the universe: the universal accident, which is independent, inessential, irrepugnant, and inalternative, to both X and x, is what we should suppose of an attribute taken at hazard, with reference to a notion taken at hazard. A predicable is *generic*, when it applies to wider genera of the subject notion, in all the additional extent of those genera: it is *specific*, when it does not apply to any wider genera, nor gain any new extent of application from the additional extent of the wider genus. Here the subject notion has been treated as a class, or the proposition has been made logico-physical: it will be nearly as easy to treat the subject as an attribute, as well as the predicate.

18. On the various names which one relation receives, the following remarks may be made. Since every reading in one view has its reading in the other, the mathematical names will so often and so easily pass into the metaphysical, and *vice versa*, that it is almost as if we gave all the schetical words of either reading to both. To put different, but concomitant, notions under *one name* is clearness, or at least facility, at the beginning of a subject: but the more progress the more confusion, unless it be prevented by checking development. To put them under *different names* is confusion, or at least difficulty, at the commencement: but the more progress, the more clearness, and development without confusion. The question which it concerns me to answer, as to the number of names, goodness apart, is but this:—Have I made any divisions in language which are not divisions in thought? If the answer be in the negative, there is an end of all objection. If logic must take account of n real dichotomies, there may be 2^n desirable distinctions to draw: in fact, 1, 2, 4, 8, &c. is the logician's progression, rather than 1, 2, 3, 4, &c.

The want of a distinct name for a distinct notion may affect the mode of thought, must affect the mode of expression, of educated men. Shortly after I had first distinguished by name the *supercontrary* from the *contrary*, I happened to look at several pieces of controversial theology, written by Oxonians versed in the common logic and distinguished by the name of *Tractarians*. Their *universe* was the Anglo-Irish Christian world, consisting of *churchmen* and *heretics*, variously named. I was amused by the frequent protection from difficulty which I received from my own nomenclature: for the distinction of contrary and supercontrary was either indistinctly conceived by the writers, or, which is more likely, their habits of phraseology had been fashioned in youth upon a logical discipline which did not bring out the distinction in its living force, so that their words were not separatively adequate to their thoughts. Accordingly, though *churchman* and *heretic*, or the synonymes, were clearly meant for supercontrary terms, that is, every man in their universe was one or the other, and *some* (I think it was *many*) were *both*, yet sometimes the words had the contrary, and sometimes the supercontrary, sense, in a manner which would have perplexed a person incognizant of the source of confusion. The comparison of one couple of pages seemed to give the right to infer 'Some churchmen are dissenters:' while another couple seemed to allow us to conclude that *orthodox* and *heretic* are not repugnant attributes.

In connexion with the supercontrary relation, I have the following words:—*Mathematical*, Extensively supercontrary, intensively subcontrary, copartient complement; *Metaphysical*, Intensively subcontrary, generic accident, specific non-accident, irrepugnant alternative. Now I observe that when a compound name exists, the blame of its existence, if any, must be thrown upon the components. If the relations of terminal ambiguity may have names, I cannot choose but call the supercontrary a *copartient complement*, because it *is*[1] *so*. This disposes of the apparent superfluity of names. And we thus draw attention to some much-wanted distinctions. The common word alternative frequently means 'one or the other or both' and more frequently 'one or the other but not both.' There is no word in common use to mark the distinction; nor have educated logicians yet introduced the distinction of repugnant alternative and irrepugnant alternative.

19. By accustoming the mind to the combination of relations, under the clearness of well-understood language, we dispense with the logician's abacus, even in the most complicated cases. For example, take the following syllogism: 'We must not say that either bodily strength or meanness is a necessary alternative, for courage and meanness are incompatible, while courage does not depend on bodily strength.' Compare it with the following: 'Health is essential to comfort and comfort to full use of the faculties, whence health is essential to full use of the faculties.' The second is a very obvious consequence, while the first, as given, is either a very dark one, or a *non sequitur* of mine, as a trap. Will the reader say which, honestly, without going to

[1] The honest sailor's mistake is no mistake at all about composition of names to which meaning has been previously attached. He scorned the French for calling a cabbage a shoe (*chou*): why, said he, can't they call it a cabbage, when they must know it *is* one? A word with a meaning to it is a thing, or has the privileges of a thing; one of which is a right to combine whenever combination can be. Hence when the names *A* and *B* have been attached to meanings, the only question about the introduction of *AB* is, does the compound exist or not?

the abacus? A full and clear notion, such as practice only gives, of the meanings of alternance, repugnance, and dependence, would answer the question of itself.

The educated world, though not so far advanced in combination of relation as it would be under instruction in the logic of second intentions, has made far too much progress to need the abacus as a means of power, in usual cases; accordingly, it laughs at the abacus and those who use it. It does not value the instrument as an analyser, because it derives no power from the analysis, as commonly made. In like manner, one who could perform division in his head, when the divisor does not exceed 10, would look down on a *calculator*, a user of pebbles on all occasions, in spite of the manner in which the pebbles would assist fundamental explanations. This is no proof of wisdom: but we may as well wait to teach a boy his letters until he can read his way to school by the corners of the streets as expect to teach the world on a basis which requires it to have philosophical acuteness before it can make up its mind to want the teaching. The mathematics made their modern way, not as the philosophy of space, time, and number, but as the instrument of surveying, navigation, commerce, &c.: and in this day, more than ever, they have a crowd[1] of followers who have no idea of any other use. Let logic be taught so as to sharpen the intellect as well as to analyse its processes, and logic will thrive as much as mathematics: while the abacus will become, as it ought to be, the starting-point of little boys and girls, instead of being at the top of a column of psychology.

20. In the metaphysical words of relation we have seen that *necessity* is of the purely logical form, as explained. But all reference to causation must be absolutely thrown away from each relation. This is not merely a logical demand: even the *material* meaning of the words ought to be independent of causation. Thus, health and intemperance are repugnant. We do not mean that intemperance is *the* cause of ill-health, or even *one* cause: we may know this, but the proposition in hand does not state it; and in fact, ill-health frequently leads to intemperance, not the converse. Another form is, temperance is an essential of health: not

[1] There is a strong impression in the world of physical inquiry that a mathematician is almost bound, whatever his pursuit may be, to make his science the means of investigating or registering some facts connected with the material world. A *teacher* of mathematics for example, whose business it is to study the mind and its discipline, that he may make his teaching permanently useful to those who will not, in nineteen cases out of twenty, ever have any need to apply it professionally, would be thought quite in the right way if he should take to investigating the force of steam, or the strength of beams, or the orbits of binary stars: they would call him a *practical man*. I should give him quite another name if he took up steam or star for anything beyond relaxation, supposing his taste to turn that way. The disposition to hold material application to be *always* practical is one of the consequences of the want of psychological thought, and will vanish before sound logical training, with other myopisms.

a cause, there may be temperance without health; ill-health often leads to temperance. Another equivalent is, health is dependent on temperance; but not on temperance alone. Lastly, ill-health and temperance are alternatives, but not *repugnant* alternatives. This branch of logic would help to drive out the idea of causation which lurks in that of connexion. In the logical form, necessary and sufficient cause is dependent (in the form of thought) upon its effect, as well as effect upon cause: effect is essential to cause, as well as cause to effect. If the attributes gravity and weight be never separate either from the other, they are *logico*-metaphysically identical, and each is an *essential dependent* of the other. When our reputed *cause and effect* are not precedent and consequent, but strictly simultaneous, a question arises whether these words be rightly applied. Their real sense may be of a much more subjective character than physical philosophers take them in. Force and change of momentum are always simultaneous: our predetermination to employ force is only in consciousness: we say that change of momentum will follow; but the two things go together, and in fact we change one momentum in producing what we call the force which changes another momentum. Would higher knowledge teach us to say that change of momentum evolves force, not *vice versa*? This is one of those questions which it is very important to ask because they cannot be answered. We ought however to think it *possible* that we have made a converse to the Irishman's blunder,

> For though one went *before* and the other *behind*, Sir,
> They set off *cheek by jowl* at the very same time, Sir.

21. I have had much occasion to point out that the logician is, by his own choice, no more[1] than a mathematician: not too mathematical, in fact not mathematician enough, if he will be nothing more. One error forces a metaphysical notion within the mathematical boundary, as a concept the *sum* of all its attributes. One is the presentation of a mere transformation—'Some animal is all man' from 'All man is some animal'—as transition from the mathematical to the metaphysical. One grand error[2] yet remains, though not, I judge, so widely received. Before

[1] From the thesis that the mathematics contain a sufficient study of logic, and the answers which have been made to it, I equally dissent. But the discussion would require a volume. Every branch of learning certainly grows a crop of logical habits, that is, of habits of the form of thought: a majority good, a minority bad. Nothing but the study of logic as a science, simultaneously with other studies, will prevent tares from growing up with the wheat.

[2] I might dwell on some strange uses of mathematical language: but there is only one which really makes a difficulty; it is the use of the word *numerical*. Many writers on logic call the distinction between one thing and another—their not being the same thing—a *numerical* distinction. Thus they say that a perception is numerically

proceeding to it I remark that the logician, in thus making mathematics a present of his science, does it under protest that the mathematician is not to plant it, and make it grow: above all, that he is not to use any symbol-manure. Those who make a concept the *sum* of its attributes are indignant at the appearance of $A + B$: though, had they had a mathematician's power over the distinction of $A + B$ and AB, they would never have fallen into the mistake.

The attachment to mathematical quantity has become so strong that this Aaron's rod has swallowed up all the others. We are told that predication is nothing *more or less* than the expression of the *relation of quantity* in which notions stand to one another; that we think *only* under determinate quantity; that *all* thought is comparison of *less and more* (*Achilles killed Hector*, for example); that an affirmative proposition is *merely* an *equation of the quantities* of its subject and predicate, and the *consequent* declaration of the coalescence of terms in a single notion; that a negative proposition is a *non-equation*—whatever that may mean—of quantities, and an announcement of non-identity of terms. The word *equation* is often followed by *identification*, in a manner which would lead us to suppose that the two words are taken as convertible.

Quantity, to confront the old logicians with the new ones, was left undefined by Aristotle for several reasons: the first, that it is a *summum genus*, and therefore cannot be defined; we may excuse them all the rest. The followers gave various definitions, one of which would palliate the preceding use of the word equation: it is *res per se divisibilis in partes*, which confounds quantity with its subject of inhesion.[1] Others, passing to another extreme, made *quantitas* the abstract notion on which we say of anything that it is or has *quantum*: and thus they announced a maxim which bewilders those who have not the key; *Quantitas non suscipit magis et minus*.[2]

They meant that a thing which has one amount of *quantum* is not a thing of which we have more perception of its having *quantitas* than another thing of another amount of *quantum*. Nevertheless, even in the hands of the old logicians, quantity came to have the meaning which we

[1] [Smiglecius: *Disp.* IX, *qu.* 5: De essentia quantitatis est habere *partes intra partes*].

[2] [True in intension, not in extension. *Suarez.*—MS. note].

different from the thing perceived; and that the hunger of to-day is numerically different from the hunger of yesterday. Now though it may be true that first, second, third, &c. are called by grammarians ordinal *numbers*, it is equally true that the phrase will not stand the smallest reflexion. The seventh, the twentieth, are not numbers: the distinctions are ordinal, because they are arranged in order; but they are not numerical distinctions; they do not allow predication of more and less. The ordinal numbers, so called, are of a pronominal character: this, that, the other, supply the place of the first three.

now[1] give it, that which exists where it is possible to conceive of answer to the question How much? or How many?—measured solely by the *quantum* of the answer. Accordingly, to *equate* two quantities, is to assert them to be the same quantities: a furlong of the wall of China is the same quantity of length as 220 yards of the pier at Brighton. The *res divisibilis* is a frequent use of the word in common life. Thus a person may buy a *quantity* of timber, and may sell that *quantity* again, meaning the very same planks, not as many cubic feet out of what he had before. To *equate* quantities, even if the word be thus restricted, can only mean to *identify* them in a very loose and inaccurate acceptation. If a person should be tried for stealing the timber just spoken of, his counsel could not properly ask the prosecutor, even when speaking concretely of quantity, 'Now, Sir, on your oath, can you equate the quantity found on the prisoner's premises to the quantity you bought at the yard?'[2]

The singular theory of predication above described seems to depend, not merely on the adoption of the *res divisibilis* by persons unpractised in mathematical thought, though this must have had some share; but also on a tendency, fostered by an invented quantification, to confusion between two attributes of the relation of *whole and part*; one, the notion of *containing and contained*, the other, the notion of *more and less*. *Containing and contained* is convertible with *whole and part*, if

[1] The mathematician becomes so accustomed to the abstract *quantitas* that he often forgets—and some have even denied—the quantitative science of the *res divisibilis* itself. This science, to which the curious in words may refuse the name of arithmetic in its *addition* or *subtraction*, until *concrete number* is expressly introduced, becomes arithmetic in its *multiplication* and even takes from abstract arithmetic: for the multiplier must be an abstract number. In its *division*, either magnitude divided by magnitude gives an abstract quotient, or magnitude divided by abstract number gives a magnitude as quotient. So that, granting application of magnitude to magnitude, addition and subtraction may be treated independently of any notion of number, and number itself may be *learnt* in the quotient of division, made antecedent to multiplication. When we come to fractions in abstract arithmetic, which we cannot do without making an abstract *res divisibilis* of the unit, we see a cognate distinction. Addition, subtraction, and division with integer quotient can be fully conceived and reduced to rule so soon as the common denominator is obtained, or the modes of dividing the unit all reduced to one: multiplication remains inconceivable until the idea of *part of a time* is introduced.

Euclid's system of proportion is a specimen of the arithmetic of the *res divisibilis*. When it is abandoned, and what is called an *arithmetical* definition is introduced, elementary writers generally leap the difficulty of expressing magnitudes numerically, and start from the expressed magnitudes, taken merely as numbers. But the way of bridging this chasm involves some matters which are of great importance. The connexion of number and magnitude should not be left to mother wit.

[2] [Smiglecius: Loc. cit.: Qui negunt numerum esse unum per se, negunt consequenter esse veram speciem quantitatis: Primo: Quia species quantitatis est quantitas: numerus autem, cum sit multitudo quantitatum, non est quantitas sed quantitates, et sicut cumulus lapidum non est species substantiae, cum non sit substantia sed multitudo substantiarum, ita et numerus quantorum (2 August 1860).]

terminal ambiguity be conceded to both, or denied to both: but *more and less*, though contained in either on the same terms, is not convertible with either. The mathematicians, to whom *more and less* frequently constitutes the whole matter of thought for which they introduce the relation of whole and part, do very often use the name of the whole relation for the name of the component which they are considering: thus a problem may occur in which a bottle of sherry in London in 1857 may be (quantitatively only) part of a cask of claret at Bordeaux in 1800. The mathematicians thus speak of the compound where they mean only the component: the logicians whom I am now describing insist that the compound shall mean no more than the component.

There is no use[1] in the arithmetically definite syllogism: to this there is almost unanimous agreement. But the study of it would have prevented such mistakes as that on which I am now writing. For it is an exercise in the study of the relations of quantity as part, *and part only*, of the study of the coalescence and non-coalescence of notions. It shows that quantification of the predicate is a superfluity, an excrescence which disappears in the elaboration of rules of inference: and that the only entrance of comparison of quantity into negatives is through the limitation of the universe by which those negatives are but other affirmatives.

I now proceed to the second part of this paper, the first elements of the system on which the preceding remarks are made. Some part of the groundwork of its higher developments is contained in my second paper.

II. First elements of a system of logic

22. A *name* is a sign by which we distinguish one object, process, or product of thought from another.

A name has four applications: two *objective*, signs of what the mind can (be it right or wrong in so doing) conceive to exist though thought were annihilated; two *subjective*, signs of what the mind cannot but conceive to be annihilated with thought. (§ 6.)

The objective applications are:—first, to individual *objects* external to the mind; secondly, to individual notions attaching to or connected with objects, called *qualities*, which are said *and thought* to inhere in

[1] It is, I find, at the utmost, worth doing once or more as a school-exercise. This is exactly the view I take, and have always taken, of all that I now call the *arithmetical* whole of logic, including the common form of syllogism. Nineteen years ago I wrote my *First Notions of Logic*, intended, as the preface states, ultimately to become an appendix to my *Arithmetic*. I had not then any glimpse, so far as my memory serves, of the numerical syllogism: and I doubt if I could have given any very distinct account of my reason for appending the common syllogism to a book of numbers. But it may be that my now confirmed notion of the usual form of syllogism being arithmetical was germinating.

the objects. The object itself is but a compound of qualities. The *quality* is, in logic, any appurtenance whatever: thus to be called Caesar is a quality.

The subjective applications are:—to designate *class*, collection of objects having similar qualities, or put into one notion by some similar *class-mark*; and a class may consist of one individual only, if only one have the mark; secondly, to designate *attribute*, the class-name of *quality*, the notion of quality in the mind.

Class and *attribute* are two modes of thinking many in the manner of one; two reductions of plurality to unity. The class *man* is one notion in the mind, the receptacle of many individuals: the attribute *human* is also one in thought, being the notion derived from similar qualities possessed by many individuals. *Class* is a noun of multitude, but not a multitude of nouns, nor even one noun selected from a multitude.

Quality, as a class name, may be distributed over any number of individuals. But it has a division peculiar to itself. As merely an appurtenant notion, it may be the compound of several notions. And similarly, attribute may be the compound of several attributes.

In grammar, class is often a substantive capable of designating the individual also, and used in both ways, as man, the man Plato. Quality is often an adjective, as *human*; attribute is often an abstract substantive, as *humanity*, which cannot designate an individual. Language would be more perfect if these distinctions were made by inflexion in all cases: logic would do well to think of introducing such[1] words as *X*-ic and *X*-ity.

The class is an aggregate of individuals; the individual is a compound of qualities; the attribute is a compound of attributes.

Objective names, representing objects and qualities, were once called names of *first intention* or *first notions*, as being used according to the mind's first *bent* towards names. Subjective names, representing classes and attributes, were names of *second intention*, or *second notions*. Thus, 'every crow is black' considered merely as a collation of cases, is of first intention: but 'the class crow has the attribute black' is of second intention. Nevertheless, the first sentence, spoken or written, may be thought under the second form. (§ 12.)

Logic is the science and art, the theory and practice, of the form of thought, the law of its action, the working of its machinery; independently of the matter thought on. It considers different kinds of matter only when, if ever, and so far as, they necessitate different forms of thought. It must deal with names, and therefore should deal with all

[1] The boldest symbolic word ever made was proposed—I think in print, but I cannot find the reference and I am not sure—by one of the young analysts (I speak of 1813, or thereabouts) who first cultivated the continental analysis in England. It was such as 'iso-x-ical,' to signify that in which x has always one value. Thus every circle which has its centre at the origin is iso-$(x^2 + y^2)$-ical. When the crude form is not too complicated, the word might be useful.

the forms of thought demanded in the four uses of names. It has no right to reject any use of a name: for every such use appertains to a form of thought. (§§ 2, 3.)

Logic considers both first and second intentions, because both are forms of thought; but the first chiefly as leading to the second: and in both it considers *quae non debentur rebus secundum se, sed secundum esse quod habent in anima*. That is, logic belongs to psychology, not to metaphysics.

It is not to be assumed that the practice of the logic of first intentions is the common property of mankind, and that second intentions form a science to which the student is to be led. The actual form of thought is an unanalysed mixture of first and second intention, with the latter in decided predominance.

A name may be formed from other names as follows. First, by *extension*, symbolized in $X = (A, B, C)$ where the *aggregate* X includes as much as can be spoken of under each and all of the *aggregants* A, B, C. Secondly, by *intension*, symbolized in $X = A\text{-}B\text{-}C$, or ABC, where the *compound* X includes *no more than* can be spoken of under *all* the *component* names A, B, C. Thirdly, by combinations of the two.

Increase of extension is generally diminution of intension, never increase: and diminution of extension is generally increase of intension, never diminution. And *vice versa*.

The disjunctive particle, *or*, expresses aggregation: 'either A or B' means 'in the class (A, B).'

Class is most connected with extension, and attribute with intension. Extended attribute is merely class of qualities, and there is some effective use in the distinction between class and its subdivisions on the one hand, and the whole class-mark and its subdivision into qualities on the other hand. These two forms of thought, though closely related, must not be confounded with the relations arising out of comparison of extension and intension. (§ 8.)

Aggregation of the impossible does not destroy the notion; composition of the impossible does. (§ 10.)

The universe is the whole sphere of thought within which the matter in hand is contained: usually not the whole possible universe of thought, but a limited portion of it. In the last syllogism of § 4, the universe is *speed of transmission of news*. The universe being U, the class X introduces with itself the class not-X (or x). Let X and x be called *contraries* or *contradictories* (I make no distinction between these words). It is understood that every class is only *part* of the universe. The symbol (X, x) is equivalent to U: in extension, it contains everything; in intension, it belongs to everything. Thus A, if in the universe, is in (X, x); and A is $A\text{-}(X, x)$, aggregate of $A\text{-}X$ and $A\text{-}x$. The universe is the maximum of extension, and the minimum of intension. (§ 9.)

The contrary of an aggregate is the compound of the contraries of the aggregants: the contrary of a compound is the aggregate of the contraries of the components. Thus (*A*, *B*) and *AB* have *ab* and (*a*, *b*) for contraries.

23. When two objects, qualities, classes, or attributes, viewed together by the mind, are seen under some connexion, that connexion is called a *relation*. To make very perfect parallelism, we should say that *relation* may be either of the four: that a boat towed by a ship, for instance, has the tow-rope for an *object* of relation. But relation, for all useful logical purposes, is a word of second intention, used only of class and attribute.

A *proposition* is the presentation of two names under a relation. A *judgment* is the sentence of the mind upon a proposition, true, false, more or less probable. The distinction of judgments, other than the simple *true* or *false*, is referred to the theory of probabilities, as a matter of practical convenience. The absolute exclusion of this distinction from logic is an error: the difference between certainty and uncertainty is of the form of thought; the amount of uncertainty is of the matter of this form. Full belief is a logical whole, which is divided into parts in the theory of probabilities: and the division of a logical whole into parts is of logic, whether it be convenient or not to treat it in the same book which treats the syllogism.

The distinction of *subject* and *predicate* is the distinction between the *notion in relation* and the *notion to which it is in relation.*

Every relation has its counter-relation, or *converse* relation: thus if *X* be in the relation *A* to *Y*, *Y* is therefore in some relation *B* to *X*: and *A* and *B* are converse relations, and the propositions are converse propositions. Every proposition has its converse, of meaning identical with itself.

When a relation is its own converse, the *proposition* is said to be *convertible*: meaning that the converse exhibits no change of relation. It is the *terms* (subject and predicate) which are convertible, strictly speaking.

When *X* has a relation (*A*) to that which has a relation (*B*) to *Y*, *X* has to *Y* a *combined* relation: the *combinants* are *A* and *B*. Relations have both extension and intension. Thus, to take one of those *relations* which have appropriated the word in common life, the relation of *first-cousin* is the *aggregate* of son of uncle, daughter of uncle, son of aunt, daughter of aunt. The relation of the minister to the crown is the *compound* of *subordinate* and *adviser.*

24. Certain relations take precedence of all others, because they are presented by the notion of naming, and spring out of its purpose, if indeed they do not themselves constitute the purpose. They may be called *onomatic* or *onymatic* (*nominative* and *nominal* being engaged).

The excessive importance of these relations has enabled them to drive all others out of common logic, on the pretext of every other relation being expressible in terms of these: as must be the case, since these relations exist wherever names exist which apply to the same object.

The onymatic relations, to which in *this* paper I confine myself, are those of *whole and part* in the two aspects of *containing and contained* and *compounded and component*; and also the relations which the notion of contraries, and the notion of true and false, introduce in connexion with them.

Subordinate to, and necessarily compounded in, the notion of whole and part, is that of *more and less*, in the matter of which are the incidents of *quantity*. But *more and less* is only a component of *whole and part*, in the form of thought: and except as such component, is of no logical import. Thus *infusorium* is no doubt a larger class than *man*, and no doubt for reasons: but if we knew the extent of superiority, and the reasons, neither would be of any logical effect, for our present purpose; because the more and less is not that of containing and contained, and the relation is not onymatic.

The distinction of *aggregation* and *composition* is the most important distinction in the subdivisions of logic. Our knowledge does not suffice to define it by full description: we can only illustrate it. To the mathematician we may say that it has the distinctive character of $a + b$ and ab: to the chemist,[1] of mechanical mixture and chemical combination: to the lawyer it appears in the distinction between 'And be it further enacted' and 'provided always.'

25. The notion of whole and part presents itself in three different ways, giving rise to three *logical wholes*.

Arithmetical whole. The class as an aggregate of individuals; the attribute as an aggregate of qualities of individuals. This whole is objective, of first intention, enumerative of individuals in process, collative of individuals in result. It *numbers*, whether the numerical result be definite or vague; and always either answers the question *How many?* or permits that question as a pertinent supplement. As in, 200 men were on board the packet, Every man is animal, Some men are learned, Some men are not some men, &c. Inductive verification is conducted in this whole, which is subordinated to both the other wholes, but in different ways. It is the essential character of this whole that it aggregates *similar things*, things only distinguishable as this, that, and the other, of the same name applied in first intention to all separately. And so it can only be a whole of aggregation. Composition of similars is unmeaning: a human human human being[2] is only a human being; we cannot subdivide a class by its own name.

[1] The chemist will some day be aware of the great mistake he has made in using the sign + to denote *chemical combination*.

[2] This is Mr Boole's equation $x^3 = x$.

The two other wholes are of second intention, subjective in character, enumerative only, and collative only, upon the ideas of class and attribute considered as philosophical units. They number, then, but the numerical total is of no interest, or only of infrequent and accidental interest, in the form of thought: just as in common life, the junction in thought of a general, a battle, a site, a result, and a despatch, offers no interest in its *quinary* character. The *mathematical* whole, or whole of *class*, thinks, most frequently, of class aggregated of classes; less frequently, rarely in comparison, of class compounded of classes. The *metaphysical* whole, or whole of *attribute*, thinks, almost always, of attribute compounded of attributes: sometimes, but very rarely, of attribute aggregated of attributes. Extension, then, predominates in the mathematical whole; intension in the metaphysical.[1]

[1] [25 June 1858] The doctrine of *modals* may, I think, be regarded as virtually incorporated into any system which acknowledges the distinction of the mathematical and metaphysical sides of logic. I never had the curiosity to examine the old modal proposition closely until long after the present paper was written: I now add a brief account of the difficulty of this subject, and of one reason of it.

There are *three* ways in which one extent may be related to another, definite expression of ratio being forbidden: they are, complete inclusion, partial inclusion with partial exclusion, and complete exclusion. This trichotomy would have ruled the forms of logic, if human knowledge had been more definite; if, for instance, whenever complete inclusion is deniable, it had been known which form of denial is the true one, denial by affirmation of partial inclusion with partial exclusion, or denial by affirmation of total exclusion. As it is, we know well the grounds on which predication is not a trichotomy, but two separate dichotomies. Nevertheless, when we come to speak metaphysically, when our propositions are made to convey our impressions as to the nature of things, the trichotomy demands establishment. How indeed could beings who know *why* and *how* so soon as they know *what* imagine themselves incapable of choosing between two forms of denial? Accordingly, must be, may or may not be, cannot be, are the great distinctions of ontology: necessity, contingency, impossibility. This was clearly seen by the logicians. But it was not so clearly seen that this mode of predication tallies, not with the four ordinary forms *A*, *E*, *I*, *O*, but with the three forms *A*, (*OI*), *E*. As in the following:—Every *X* is *Y*, which is the consequence of necessity; Some *X*s are *Y*s and some are not, which is the consequence of contingency; and No *X* is *Y*, which is the consequence of impossibility.

Accordingly, an attempt was made to pack up the trichotomy with the dichotomies. It ought to have been done in the following way, in which the proper modal description follows the form of predication; it being assumed that the categorical form which exists has its reason in the nature of things.

A. Every *X* is *Y*. Necessity.

O. Some *X*s are not *Y*s. Non-necessity, i.e. either contingency or impossibility.

E. No *X* is *Y*. Impossibility.

I. Some *X*s are *Y*s. Non-impossibility, or possibility, i.e. either contingency or necessity.

(*O-I*). *Both* Some *X*s are *Y*s and some not. Contingency.

(*A*, *E*). *Either* Every *X* is *Y* or No *X* is *Y*. Non-contingency, i.e. either necessity or impossibility.

Instead of this, however, *possibility* was pressed into the list to make a fourth,

Every proposition, at least of the onymatic character, may be thought in either whole: and practical logic slips out of one into the other, as

---

but without any need; for the *contingens* was divided into the *contingens esse*, and the *contingens non esse*, and applied to the forms *I* and *O*; while the *possibile* was similarly applied, under the distinction of *possibile esse* and *possibile non esse*. But some separated the *possibile* and the *contingens*, applying the *possibile* to the form *I*, and the *contingens* to the form *O*. With them, *contingens* was equivalent to *possibile non esse*, and *possibile* to *contingens non esse*.

It must not be supposed that any of the objections I have hinted at were unseen or unnoticed. What, indeed, did the schoolmen not discuss? Two contiguous paragraphs of the minute Cologne commentary on Aristotle collected from Thomas Aquinas, Gilbert Porretanus, and others, address themselves to the questions why Aristotle did not introduce a single *mode* contradictory of *necessary*, as he had done in the case of *possibile* and *impossibile*; and why, since *possibility* and *contingency* are convertible, they are to be looked upon as distinct modes. The answers are too deep for me at present: but I have in so many instances found meaning in the schoolmen where I thought there was none, and sense where I thought there was nonsense, that I will not answer for the results of further consideration. Nevertheless, I cannot but hold the choice and distribution of the modal forms to have been a real lapse, as well in Aristotle as in his followers: and it seems that the later philosophers of the middle ages had come to something like the same conclusion. Those who would see the modal system in its full perfection of confusion, should, if they will trust Crackanthorpe, consult the Jesuit Peter Fonseca, *qui totis quinque prolixis capitibus de Modalibus agens, implicat se misere hisce spinis, nec tamen rem ipsam ullo modo explicat, sed velut alter Sisyphus, versat saxum sudans nitendo, neque proficit hilum: et propemodum facit ut lector intelligendo nihil quidquam intelligat.*

The application of the ideas of *necessary* and *impossible* to universals, and of contingent to particulars, was a mistake. It made a *truly* metaphysical conclusion the consequence of a mathematical form. *Omnis homo est animal*, taken to be a necessity because no exception was ever noticed, might have been a contingency: that is to say, it might have been, for aught the logicians knew, not merely *possible* for the Creator to have placed on earth—in a literal sense—rational and accountable vegetables, which they admitted, but even possible within the limits of the actual plan. And this mistake led to paralogisms. Thus, it was affirmed that a syllogism with a modal major might give a modal conclusion, though the minor was not modally given, but categorically. Thus from—It is necessary an animal should feel; every man is animal; they inferred it to be necessary a man should feel. Here one particular modality of the minor is tacitly assumed from its form: or else *conclusio sequitur partem deteriorem* was strangely forgotten. In what I have called the metaphysical form of the proposition, the question of necessity or contingency is left open. As the intention of thought in the premises, so also in the conclusion: necessary or contingent as the case may be. And any form may be thought as necessary, or as contingent: thus the *irrepugnance* of two notions may be either, as well as their *repugnance*.

I was not at all aware, when I forwarded to the Society on one day two papers so different in their subjects as the present one and that on the beats of imperfect consonances, that both had some relation to the antagonism of the numbers 3 and 2. The inequality of 2^{19} and 3^{12} is the source of a great part of the difficulties of temperament: and it may be that the ill success of the attempt to assimilate a ternary and binary mode of subdivision was a large part of the reason why a fair and consistent juxtaposition of the mathematical and metaphysical forms of predication did not become a recognized part of logic.

facility will require. All consequences which spring out of onymatic relations may be obtained in any whole. To insist that all thought *is* in one whole, is a mistake: that it *ought* to be, an absurdity.

Each onymatic proposition has two terms, and each term may be thought in either of the two ways. This gives four *readings*:—

		Subject	*Predicate*	*Notation*
Logico-	Mathematical	Class	Class	))
	Physical	Class	Attribute	)]
	Metaphysical	Attribute	Attribute	]]
	Contraphysical	Attribute	Class	])

On these see § 10. I shall here specially consider the first and third, from which all that is peculiar to the second and fourth easily follows.

In the relation of containing and contained, there may be *terminal precision*, or *terminal ambiguity*. If, when *X* is contained in *Y*, we mean that *X* is part only, leaving another part, there is terminal precision; but if we mean that possibly *X* may be as large as *Y*, there is terminal ambiguity. The distinction is that of part-not-whole, and part-or-whole. (§ 11.)

The first table following contains the various relations which may exist between the *classes X* and *Y*, as to inclusion or exclusion, under terminal ambiguity, with the readings in the arithmetical whole, and the notation of my last paper, presently noticed further. This is all condensed in the heading: and the other tables are as described.

26. *Logico-mathematical reading. Terminal ambiguity* (§§ 13, 17)

Proposition of assertion or denial	*X subjected to Y as*	*Y predicated of X as*	*Reading in arithmetical whole*	*Notation*
Assertion of *X* contained in *Y*	Species	Genus	Every *X* is *Y*	*X*))*Y*
Denial of *X* contained in *Y*	Exient	Deficient	Some *X*s are not *Y*s	*X*(·(*Y*
Assertion of *X* excluded from *Y*	Coexternal	Coexternal	No *X* is *Y*	*X*)·(*Y*
Denial of *X* excluded from *Y*	Copartient	Copartient	Some *X*s are *Y*s	*X*()*Y*
Assertion of *x* contained in *Y*	Complement	Complement	Everything is either *X* or *Y*	*X*(·)*Y*
Denial of *x* contained in *Y*	Coinadequate	Coinadequate	Some things are neither *X*s nor *Y*s	*X*)(*Y*
Assertion of *x* excluded from *Y*	Genus	Species	Some *X*s are every *Y*	*X*((*Y*
Denial of *x* excluded from *Y*	Deficient	Exient	No *X*s are some *Y*s	*X*)·)*Y*

27. *Logico-mathematical reading. Terminal Precision*, § 11

Proposition of Assertion	*X subjected to Y as*	*Y predicated of X as*	*Compounded of*	*Notation*
X and more contained in *Y*	Subidentical *Deficient Species*	Superidentical *Exient Genus*	$X))Y$, $X)\cdot)Y$	$X)\circ)Y$
X contained in and containing *Y*	Identical *Species Genus*	Identical *Genus Species*	$X))Y$, $X((Y$	$X\Vert Y$
X containing *Y* and more	Superidentical *Exient Genus*	Subidentical *Deficient Species*	$X((Y$, $X(\cdot(Y$	$X(\circ(Y$
X and more contained in *y*	Subcontrary *Coinadequate External*	Subcontrary *Coinadequate External*	$X)\cdot(Y$, $X)(Y$	$X)\circ(Y$
X contained in and containing *y*	Contrary *External Complement*	Contrary *External Complement*	$X)\cdot(Y$, $X(\cdot)Y$	$X\vert\cdot\vert Y$
X containing *y* and more	Supercontrary *Copartient Complement*	Supercontrary *Copartient Complement*	$X(\cdot)Y$, $X()Y$	$X(\circ)Y$

Here $X)\circ)Y$ is a compound of $X))Y$ and $X)\cdot)Y$, coexisting. We deny it by denying either $X))Y$ or $X)\cdot)Y$, or by asserting *either* $X(\cdot(Y$ *or* $X((Y$. Let this aggregate be represented by $X(,(Y$. Then $X)\circ)Y$ is denied by $X(,(Y$, $X(\circ(Y$ by $X),)Y$, $X)\circ(Y$ by $Y(,)Y$, $X(\circ)Y$ by $X),(Y$. And identity, $X\Vert Y$, is denied by either $X(\cdot(Y$ or $X)\cdot)Y$; and contrariety, $X\vert\cdot\vert Y$, by either $X()Y$ or $X)(Y$. When we read in mathematical intension, the prepositions *sub* and *super* change places.

The words subidentical &c. may also be introduced, in metaphysical sense, referring to intension, from the second table, with inversion of

28. *Logico-metaphysical reading. Terminal ambiguity*, § 17(*b*)

Proposition of Assertion or Denial	*Y predicated of X as*	*X subjected to Y as*	*Reading in arithmetical whole (by intension only)*	*Notation*
Assertion of *Y* a component of *X*	Essential	Dependent	*Y* always in *X*	$X]]Y$
Denial of *Y* a component of *X*	Inessential	Independent	*Y* sometimes not in *X*	$X[\cdot[Y$
Assertion of *Y* incompatible with *X*	Repugnant	Repugnant	*Y* never in *X*	$X]\cdot[Y$
Denial of *Y* incompatible with *X*	Irrepugnant	Irrepugnant	*Y* sometimes in *X*	$X[]Y$
Assertion of *Y* a component of *x*	Alternative	Alternative	In everything either *X* or *Y*	$X[\cdot]Y$
Denial of *Y* a component of *x*	Inalternative	Inalternative	In some things neither *X* nor *Y*	$X][Y$
Assertion of *Y* incompatible with *x*	Dependent	Essential	In *Y* always *X*	$X[[Y$
Denial of *Y* incompatible with *x*	Independent	Inessential	In *Y* sometimes not *X*	$X]\cdot]Y$

29. *Logico-metaphysical reading. Terminal precision*, § 17(*d*)

Proposition of Assertion	*Y predicated of X as*	*X subjected to Y as*	*Notation*
Y an attribute of the universe	Universal Attribute	—	—
	Essential Alternative	*Dependent Alternative*	
Y and others components of *X*	Generic Attribute	{Specific Accident {Generic Non-accident	$X]\circ]Y$
	Independent Essential	*Inessential Dependent*	
Y component and compound of *X*	Specific Attribute	Specific Attribute	$X\|\|Y$
	Dependent Essential	*Dependent Essential*	
Y compound of *X* and others	{Specific Accident {Generic Non-accident	Generic Attribute	$X[\circ[Y$
	Inessential Dependent	*Independent Essential*	
Y neither component nor compound of either *X* or *x*	Universal Accident and Non-accident *Inessential, Irrepugnant, Inalternative, Independent*	Universal Accident and Non-accident *Inessential, Irrepugnant, Inalternative, Independent*	—
Y and others components of *x*	{Generic Accident {Specific Non-accident	{Generic Accident {Specific Non-accident	$X[\circ]Y$
	Irrepugnant Alternative	*Irrepugnant Alternative*	
Y component and compound of *x*	Specific Excludent	Specific Excludent	$X\|\cdot\|Y$
	Repugnant Alternative	*Repugnant Alternative*	
Y compound of *x* and others	Generic Excludent	Generic Excludent	$X]\circ[Y$
	Inalternative Repugnant	*Inalternative Repugnant*	
Y an excludent of the universe	Universal Excludent	—	—

prepositions. Thus $X]\circ]Y$ means that *X* is a superidentical of *Y*, and *Y* a subidentical of *X*.

30. I shall now proceed to some remarks and developments:—

Arithmetical whole. In the third table, in this reading, *X* and *Y* are treated as qualities; and '*Y* is always in *X*' means that the quality *Y* is always recognized as a component of the quality *X*. Thus in the more objective side of this whole we read 'Every (object) man is (object) animal:' in the more subjective side we read 'Some (instance of quality) animal is in every (instance of quality) human.' This constitutes the whole of what many writers in this country now accept as the distinction between extension and comprehension: but, as to the distinction which I have called that of extension and *intension*, this distinction is only that of *object* and *quality*, both in extension. See § 8.

Those who supply complete terms of quantification make a mixture of what I called in my second paper *exemplar* and *cumular* reading; as in '*All X* is some *Y*' and 'No *X* is *any Y*.' When it is postulated that propositions shall be formed by every possible distribution of the terms of quantity, *all* and *some*, the two propositions 'All *X* is all *Y*' and 'Some *X* is not some *Y*' arise. The first is $X\|Y$ of the second table; the other has no place in the propositions of second intention. I hold by the opinion that the true[1] way of reading this system into consistency is the *exemplar* method, as explained in my last paper. I insist on it that a set of logical forms in which some propositions enter without possibility of contradiction *within the forms* is wholly inadmissible. For right and wrong, true and false, are the ultimate ends of applied logic; and a system which does not point out the false belonging to every true case, and the true case belonging to every false one, may defend itself, if it like, by saying that the difference between truth and falsehood is *material*: but one would almost suppose it held that difference to be *immaterial*.

31. *Relation of the two precisions*. The precise proposition is a compound of two ambiguous ones: the ambiguous proposition is an aggregate of two precise ones. The subidentical is both species and deficient; the species is either subidentical or identical. Either may be made a simple act of the form of thought: but, with reference[2] to the other, either is complex.

[1] There is another, to which I was led by a passage in a review of my last paper. It was advanced that the contradiction of 'All *X* is all *Y*' is 'All *X* is not all *Y*': which, if the second form be properly understood, is correct. Why then was this not introduced among the forms? Perhaps because there would then have been *two* negatives with both terms universal: one 'All *X* is not all *Y*'; the other 'Any *X* is not any *Y*'. And having thus introduced 'all' into the negatives, the following, 'Some *X* is not all *Y*', must have been examined. This should contradict 'Some *X* is all *Y*' or 'All *Y* is *X*'. So that 'Some *X* is not all *Y*' should have 'Some *Y* is not any *X*' for its equivalent. This is correct. And the principle of demanding contradiction introduces 'Any *X* is any *Y*' as the contradiction of 'Some *X* is not some *Y*': and *any*, thus introduced among the affirmatives, must be carried through. Let this be done, and there are three quantifiers; *all* (unbroken collection), *any*, and *some*. The chain of propositions and their contradictories does exist: and it is as follows. The bracketed propositions are equivalents:

Affirmative Proposition	*Contradicting Negative*
Any *X* is any *Y* }	{ Some *X* is not some *Y*
Any *X* is all *Y* }	{ Any *X* is not all *Y*
All *X* is any *Y* }	{ All *X* is not any *Y*
Any *X* is some *Y* }	{ Some *X* is not any *Y*
All *X* is some *Y* }	{ All *X* is not some *Y*
Some *X* is any *Y* }	{ Any *X* is not some *Y*
Some *X* is all *Y* }	{ Some *X* is not all *Y*
All *X* is all *Y*	All *X* is not all *Y*
Some *X* is some *Y*	Any *X* is not any *Y*.

This is the complete system of quantification by postulation, when it is open to entrance of cumular terms and bound to exhibition of contradictories. In affirmatives, *all* is *any* when it occurs only once; and *any* is *all*. When *any* occurs twice, either or both give *all*: for '*all* is *all*' follows from '*any* is *any*,' though not the converse. In contradiction, the occurrence of *all* has the effect of an individual term: when either *P* or *Q* is individual, '*P* is *Q*' and '*P* is not *Q*' are contradictions. When *all* is absent, *any* is changed into *some*, and some into *any*.

[2] This duality will surprise the logician, but not the geometer. A point determined by planes is a complex notion, the common intersection, or sole point determined,

Any digested system of propositional forms which gives a mixture of precise and ambiguous forms offends against all sound classification. Even if habit of thought should use such a system, this only proves that thought should be instructed to use the whole of both systems, instead of throwing away some of each, and joining the rest into a hybrid.

32. *Extreme cases.* The table of terminal precision joins two ordinary propositions together, in every useful case. What do the other cases mean? First, *X*)) *Y* and *X*)·(*Y* express the utmost contradiction possible. But it is to this effect: *X* does not exist in the universe. For *X*)) *Y* is a reading of *X*)·(*y*, which with *X*)·(*Y*, excludes *X* altogether. This answers to the way in which a mathematician examines a symbolic impossibility, and finds out the species of impossibility which it belongs to. Again, *X*)) *Y* and *X*(·) *Y*, incompatible when *X* is part of the universe, become compatible when *X* and *Y* are coextensive with the universe. Again, (),)(, (·(,)·), may all coexist. Any other junctions give only parts of the propositions we already have. The three junctions noted answer to the *universal* predicables in the fourth table, which are introduced to give completeness of language: the correspondents of the second table are hardly worth setting down. For the explanation of the terms of the fourth table see § 17(*d*).

33. *Affirmative and negative propositions.* With me these are technical terms, not wholly corresponding to *assertion* and *denial.* A proposition is affirmative which is always true of identicals and false of contraries: a proposition is negative which is always false of identicals and true of contraries. Thus)), ((, (),)(, are affirmatives;)·), (·(,)·(, (·), are negatives: the inserted dot indicates a negative; if an express symbol be required for an affirmative, it may be two dots, or)) may be)··). We see that *X*(·) *Y* is negative, though in common[1] language, it is an

[1] The disjunctive form in which the proposition (·) is most clearly enunciated, that is, 'Everything is either *X* or *Y*,' instead of 'No not-*X* is not-*Y*'—has been made the occasion of an assertion that I, in ignorance, introduce disjunctive syllogisms among categorical ones. This I do, beyond doubt: for, in adopting categorical syllogisms, I cannot avoid adopting disjunctive ones. Contraries once allowed, every categorical syllogism is also disjunctive. Thus the old instance, 'Every man is animal; *Sortes* (so Socrates was at last written) is man; therefore Sortes is animal,' can be identified with the following: 'Everything is either animal, or not-man; Sortes is not not-man; therefore Sortes is animal.'

by three planes. But so is a plane determined by points: three points determine one plane. The cultivators of geometry know this law of *duality*, with its marvellous consequences: the logician has yet to study it as a law of thought. But there are false dualities, as well as true ones. A circle which rolls upon another may be looked at as in simple motion: and will be so looked at by many, especially by those accustomed to the turning of trochoidal lines. But geometry knows that the rolling circle has a twofold rotation. The difficulty which so many have found in the moon's rotation depends upon this conversion of duality into unity, which compels them to consider unity as duality. We cannot allow water to be a simple substance, without declaring oxygen a compound.

assertion, 'Every thing is either *X* or *Y*.' But it has the *properties* of the other negatives.

34. Previously to entering upon the subject of *quantity* the following considerations are conveniently inserted here.

Proof of a proposition is the acquisition of necessary assent: and it must consist in ascertaining, first, that the names are rightly applied, secondly, that the relation between them is truly stated.

Inductive proof, or *induction*, or proof *à posteriori*, is the aggregation of separate verifications, whether upon individual qualities or objects, or species or component attributes, in number enough to make assent to the proposition an unavoidable necessity of thought.

Deductive proof, or *deduction*, or proof *à priori*, is the *composition* of separate previous propositions, from which the same unavoidable necessity follows.

The name depends upon the *immediate* character. Thus a deductive proof may have its components, or some of them, furnished by separate inductions, or may be a compound of inductions; and an inductive proof may be an aggregate of deductions. For instance, as often occurs in mathematics, an inductive proof may have every aggregant a compound of deduction from all those which precede.

Probable or *physical* induction is where the number of cases verified is so large, without any failure, that the mind feels the sort of necessity called *moral certainty* that no failure ever can occur within any limited experience. Where or why this proof is wanted, we are not to inquire: it is enough that this kind of proof is one of the forms of thought. All these cases come under the word *proof* in logic, because, under all these cases, the mind works with and from the proposition in one and the same way: be it with more of certainty, or less; with one ground of certainty, or another.

When a proposition proves of *all*, let it be called *necessary*. Logical necessity does not distinguish the preceding cases from one another. When a proposition proves of some only, not all, or not known to be all, it is *contingent*.

Inference differs from *proof* in having reference only to the perception of the purely logical part, the validity of the mode of junction of the propositions, or of the combination into one of the relations they propound.

35. In verification of names, we must imagine what I may call *registers*. One register answers, in every case, the question whether this or that object, species, attribute, is within the universe. This register is used in ordinary logic: existence is supposed to be ascertained before use of a name; and *all existence* is the universe of the propositions. I substitute existence in a given sphere of thought. Another register points out, for each name, the cases in which that name applies, and in which its contrary.

A proposition is *universal*, when inductive verification requires the examination of every part of extension of the universe (the maximum of extension and minimum of intension) or of every augmentation of intension which takes place within it: otherwise, the proposition is *particular*. A proposition is universal both extensively and intensively, or both ways particular. The universals are)), ((,)·(, (·); the particulars are (),)(,)·), (·(.

Keeping within the universe, by hypothesis, we cannot go beyond a certain extension, or below a certain intension: we never decompose the intension of the whole universe, or treat its intension as a compound; we never add to the whole universe, or make its extension an aggregant. Hence it is that extensively and intensively universal propositions are the same. But *terms* are examined, not from a maximum downwards in one case, and a minimum upwards in the other, but from a maximum downwards in both cases; and the effect of this difference is so marked that it might perhaps be desirable the words universal and particular should not be applied to both propositions and terms.[1]

A term is *universal*, extensively or intensively, when the verification by induction requires examination of the whole extension, or of the whole intension, of the term: otherwise it is *particular*. Thus in the particular proposition '*X* and *Y* are coinadequate' both terms are extensively universal: for though a part of the universe may furnish verification, that part must be ascertained to be out of the whole extent, both of *X* and *Y*. But both terms are intensively particular: for if any component classes of *X* and *Y* be together inadequate, so must be any compounds of those classes: consequently, a pair of components may settle the matter. Speaking metaphysically, the proposition is '*X* and *Y* are inalternative:' if any one component attribute of *X*, and one of *Y*, be not necessary alternatives, neither are *X* and *Y*.

The extensively universal is always intensively particular; and the extensively particular is always intensively universal; and their converses. Both descriptions exist in both readings. I shall use the phrases *quantity universal and particular* for mathematical reading, and *force complete and incomplete* for the metaphysical reading: both having their *extensive and intensive*. But, though all this distinction be in thought and nature, it is not all in habit or *second nature*. The extensive is almost exclusively limited to the mathematical; the intensive to the metaphysical: so that universal and particular quantity of extension, complete and incomplete force of intension, will be the great working distinctions.

In the notation for mathematical reading *X*) and (*X* denote *X* taken *universally in extension* and particularly in intension: and *X*(and)*X* denote *X* taken *particularly in extension* and universally in intension.

[1] [Propositions: Universal and particular. Terms: Total and partial in extension; complete and incomplete in intension.—15 May 1859.]

In metaphysical reading $X]$ and $[X$ denote complete force in extension, and *incomplete force in intension*: $X[$ and $]X$ denote *complete force*. Our usual habit, then, will be to consider $X)$, $(X$, $X[$, $]X$, as universals; $X($, $)X$, $X]$, $[X$, as particulars.

A proposition is determined so soon as its quantities and quality (affirmative or negative) are determined: this is inductively derived from the lists. Hence the proposition is completely symbolized by terms, quantities, and quality. To say 'I speak in extension, affirmatively, universally of X, particularly of Y' must be to say 'X is a species of Y,' and is denoted by $X))Y$, or $X)\cdot\cdot)Y$.

When a term is changed into its contrary, the spicula must be changed, and the mark of quality. Thus $X))Y$ is $X)\cdot(y$, and $x(\cdot)Y$ and $x((y$. A term and its contrary[1] have always opposite quantities, and opposite forces.

A term used particularly may be replaced by a stronger of its own *tension* (extension or intension): a term used universally may be replaced by a weaker of its own tension. Deductive truth remains, though not equivalence. We have here the whole principle of common, or onymatic, syllogism.

We may state it thus, and more widely.

In *universal terms* of either tension, elements of that tension are *dismissible* and *inadmissible*. Thus $A, B))CD$ gives $A))C$: but $A))C$ does not give $A, B))C$.

In *particular terms* of either tension, elements of that tension are *indismissible* and *admissible*. Thus $A))B$ gives $AC))B$: but $A))B, C$ does not give $A))B$.

In universal *propositions*, *indismissibles* are *transposible*, directly in negatives, by contraposition in affirmatives. But dismissibles are intransposible. Thus in $AB))Y$, A is indismissible, but transposible by contraposition; $AB))Y = B))Y, a$. But in $AB)\cdot(Y$, the indismissible A is directly transposible; $AB(\cdot(Y = A)\cdot(BY$.

In particular *propositions*, *dismissibles* are *transposible*, directly in affirmatives, by contraposition in negatives. But indismissibles are intransposible. Thus in $A, B()Y$, where A is indismissible, it is intransposible: but in $AB()Y$, the dismissible A is directly transposible; $AB()Y = A()BY$. And in $AB(\cdot(Y$, we have $B(\cdot(Y, a$.

[1] When a universal is converted into a particular merely by inserting or withdrawing a symbol of negation, the particular so obtained, joined to the universal, limits the extent of the universal, as in the following cases:

$))$, a species;	$)\cdot)$, but not the largest possible.
$)\cdot($, an external;	$)($, ...
$(($, a genus;	$(\cdot($, but not the smallest possible.
$(\cdot)$, a complement;	$()$, ...

The distinction thus drawn between $))$ and $)\cdot($, on the one hand, and $(($ and $(\cdot)$, on the other, might be worded in many ways.

The root of these distinctions may be clearly seen in the distinction of propositions as either affirming or denying coexistence. But I defer the consideration[1] of this point to a subsequent paper.

36. The *syllogism* is inference of the relation which exists between two terms, as a necessary consequence of their relations to the same third, or *middle*, term. When the relations are *onymatic*, so may be called the syllogism.

The perception of the validity of a syllogism is the perception of the combination of two relations into one. This is frequently the case even in the common mode of stating a syllogism, in which *premises* (the two expressions of simple relation) and *conclusion* (the expression of the compound relation) are stated in the arithmetical whole. If the common form be not compelled to accept the name of a syllogism of *first intention*, it is because the act of mind in forming the conclusion may be based on notions of second intention.

Some pairs of relations combine into one relation. Thus a species of a species is a species: but a species of a copartient may be any one of the eight relations.

The *major term* of a syllogism is that term of the conclusion to which the other is related, or the predicate: the subject of the conclusion is the minor term. The *major* term is the one to which the *action* of the syllogism points: in this way. We see that $X))Y$ and $Y)\cdot(Z$ give $X)\cdot(Z$, which may be expressed thus:—the species of an external of Z is an external of Z: here Z is the major term. But in reading backwards, as 'The external of a genus of X is an external of X,' we see that X is the major term.

The natural character of the *first figure* will now be seen, as the most simple expression of the combination of relations: but it is somewhat obscured by the usual order of writing the premises. The fourth figure is less natural, because it converts the expected relation. The second

[1] I hope at some future time to treat of a pure form of opposition which runs through all contraries. In my last paper I gave some account of the way in which various words may be made to replace each other, at least so far as this, that either may be described in terms of any one of the others. An eminent critic [Hamilton] thereupon says that I 'formally identify' these terms. If this mean that I say, *in form*, that they *are* identical, he is not correct: but if it mean that I contend for a *common form* running through all logical oppositions, he is correct so far as this, that I ventured to predict the future establishment of such a form. My critic adds that my system is a *witches' cauldron*: I accept the phrase. Algebra *is* a witches' cauldron. It has two handles, + and −. By these we lift on the fire, at once, the distinctions of addition and subtraction, multiplication and division, up and down, north and south, east and west, loss and gain, before and after, gravity and levity, attraction and repulsion, &c. &c. &c. They all boil together, and the results are magical. The spell was impaired by the long time which certain roots (of negative quantities) took to boil; but they are now quite done. The logical cauldron, of which I have some further knowledge, I hope to set boiling at some future time.

and third figures are less natural, because they do not present the relations to be combined, but one of them and the converse of the other.

Every syllogism may be read, with reference to one set of terms, in sixteen ways. For any term may be changed into its contrary, and the proper change of relation made: this gives eight ways of reading; and inversion of order gives eight more. But when we drop the terms, and consider merely combination of relation, the sixteen are only two repetitions of the same eight, when both premises are universal.

Two universal premises always give a conclusion, universal when the middle term is of different quantities in the two premises, particular, when of the same. A universal premise coupled with a particular always gives a conclusion when the middle term is of different quantities in the two; and not otherwise. But universal premises with a particular conclusion would allow as strong a conclusion if either premise be properly weakened into a particular: hence I called such a syllogism *strengthened*. A syllogism with a premise stronger than needful for the conclusion, or with a conclusion weaker than needful from the premises, is a logical argument, but one which should not be allowed to stand in the same class with the *fundamental*[1] syllogism which has all that can be got from premises which are no stronger than is necessary. How completely the entrance of such syllogisms has defaced the Aristotelian system, will easily appear: it has been well said that Aristotle commenced his synthesis before he had completed his analysis; a thing which is almost always done by the first organizer of any science or branch of science.

If the relations *A* and *B* combine into *C*, it is clear that *A* without *C* following means that there is not *B*; and that *B* without *C* following means that there is not *A*. This important principle, known only to the old logicians, in their practice, as a mode of reducing two obstinate malcontents into the first figure, might have led to such a classification[2] of syllogism as the following.

Throw out all needlessly strengthened or weakened forms, and there remain four syllogisms in each of the first three figures. These divide into four cycles of three each, one out of each figure: and in each cycle

[1] Had this distinction been made from the beginning, it would have been seen that it is as necessary to a fundamental syllogism that the middle term should enter once particularly, as that it should enter once universally. And it would have been seen that if there be any rule at all on the subject, it must be this one. For every syllogism may have the middle term changed into its contrary: it cannot be the rule, then, that the middle term should enter universally twice; for then there would be a class of syllogisms in which it enters particularly twice; and *vice versâ*. Consequently the rule must be, if a rule there be, that the middle term has one universal and one particular entry.

[2] This was communicated to me by my friend Sir William Rowan Hamilton (14 Febuary 1856), as a consequence of my mode of expressing the connexion of premises and conclusion.

each syllogism is what I have called an *opponent* of each of the others; that is, has the form in which one premise admitted, and the conclusion denied, denies the other premise. As follows:

		Figures	
	I	II	III
Cycles	1 Barbara.	Baroko.	Bokardo.
	2 Celarent.	Festino.	Disamis.
	3 Darii.	Camestres.	Ferison.
	4 Ferio.	Cesare.	Datisi.
Figure IV.	Camenes.	Dimaris.	Fresison.

The fourth figure, always marked by the rest with some symptom of dislike, is here absolutely excluded. It has three syllogisms which form a cycle by themselves.

37. I shall not repeat the details of my former paper on the relations of the syllogistic forms. It will however be worth while to state the following arrangement of the forms, which is, I think, the best I have given.

	VVP	*PVP* *VPP*	*VVV*	*VPP* *PVP*	*VVP*	
FFF	(())	.())) :((()	.)))): :((((.	)))(:)(((.	))((	*FFF*
NNF	(.)(.)	.(.((.) :(.)).)	.).((.): :(.)).(.	).((.(:).)).(.	).().(	*NNF*
FNN	(().(	.()).(:(((.(	.))).(: :(((.)	))).):)((.).	))(.)	*FNN*
NFN	(.)((	.(.(((:(.))(	.).(((: :(.))).	).(():).))).	).())	*NFN*
	VVP	*PVP* *VPP*	*VVV*	*VPP* *PVP*	*VVP*	

F, affirmative; *N*, negative; *V*, universal; *P*, particular. The compartment *NFN* contains all the syllogisms in which the first (minor) premise negative and the second premise affirmative give a negative conclusion. The columns (*PVP*), (*VPP*) contain all in which the one premise is particular and the other universal. The middle column contains all the universal syllogisms. It is flanked by four compartments of six each: and each one compartment contains all the syllogisms of one particular conclusion. Thus all in the upper left flank give the conclusion (). The canon[1] of validity is as follows:—Every pair of universals

[1] There are various ways in which the symbols may be put together so as to give all the syllogistic forms by consecutive pairs. Thus the following set

)))))·((·)

taken cyclically, that is, the first and last being considered as neighbours, give all the eight universal syllogisms in consecutive pairs, if we read both backwards and

gives a conclusion: and every universal and particular in which the middle terms are of different quantities. The canon of inference is:—Erase the symbols of the middle term, and what is left shews the conclusion. Thus ())·(gives (·(, by which I signify that the *copartient of an external* is *exient*: or reading metaphysically, []]·[gives [·[, the *irrepugnant of a repugnant* is *independent*. Supplying the terms, we have *X*()*Y*)·(*Z* gives *X*(·(*Z*; or, on the *abacus*, 'Some *X*s are *Y*s, no *Y* is *Z*; therefore some *X*s are not *Z*s.'

38. Thirty-two combinations give valid syllogisms; and as many are invalid. Sixteen of these invalid combinations, of which eight repeated twice, in conjunction with eight of the valid forms, thirty-two in all, have a meaning of their own, as follows. The form of our syllogism is, *A*, *B*, *C* being relations:—

Every *A* of *B* is a *C*.

Now there are[1] also thirty-two truths of this form, derivable as follows:—

Every *A* is a *C* of every (converse of *B*).

Thus every complement of every *species* is a complement: therefore every complement is a complement of every *genus*. Again, every genus of every *partient* is a partient: therefore every genus is a partient of every *partient*. The symbolic rule is as follows:—Choose any one of the thirty-two combinations in which the middle spiculae are of *different*

[1] If $\phi\psi x < \chi x$ for all values of x, which is the proper analogy for the composition of relations in the syllogism, then $\phi x < \chi\psi^{-1}x$, but we must not say $\psi x < \phi^{-1}\chi x$.

Let $P + Q = R$ express that P and Q, coexisting, give R: let $-P$ represent the contrary of P (or contradictory); let 0 be the symbol of impossibility of coexistence. If then P, Q, R be three propositions which cannot coexist, so that $P + Q + R = 0$, we have three modes of inference $P + Q = -R$, $Q + R = -P$, $R + P = -Q$. Now *Barbara* may be expressed thus

	X))*Y* + *Y*))*Z* + *X*(·(*Z* = 0	
whence	*X*))*Y* + *Y*))*Z* = *X*))*Z*	*Barbara* I.
	Y))*Z* + *X*(·(*Z* = *X*(·(*Y*	*Baroko* II.
	X))*Y* + *X*(·(*Z* = *Y*(·(*Z*	*Bokardo* III.

This process is carried through all the syllogisms of the first figure.

---

forwards. And under the same rule, eight particular syllogisms are seen in each of the two following cycles:

)))·))·(()
)·))))((·)

The following conceit gives a kind of *zodiac of syllogism*. Put round a circle the twelve symbols here consecutively written, distinguishing the universals by the thicker parentheses;

)))·))·) **))**)( )·) **)·(** ())(**(·)**)·) ()

Any two consecutive universals give a universal syllogism: any universal with a *contiguous* particular gives a particular syllogism. And these whether we read forwards or backwards. [Cf. p. 163.]

quantities. Reject a universal followed by a particular. In any other case, strike out the middle spiculae, and if the result be a universal, either let it stand, or change the second spicula: but if the result be a particular, there is no choice but to change the second spicula.

Thus (·) () is inoperative: there is no relation *A* of which we can say —Every *A* is a complement of every partient. Now take () (·) which, the middle spiculae being erased, gives (·), a universal; changing the second spicula, (·(

Every complement is a partient of every complement
Every exient is a partient of every complement.

The first is only a strengthened form of the second. Syllogisms being combinations, these relations may be called *decombinations.* From the strengthened syllogisms proceed the strengthened decombinations: from the syllogisms in which universals give universals the decombinations in which a universal gives two universals. The sixteen remaining cases arise from the particular syllogisms. The sixteen pairs, such as (·) () &c., and the eight)·))·) &c. which are not decombinations, are no doubt of some logical import which I do not now see. These decombinations are the contrapositives of the combinations. Thus 'Every external of any genus is an external' gives every non-external (partient) is a non-external (partient) of any genus, or () gives () ((, as from the rule.

39. The full stops and colons in the table denote that one of the syllogisms between which they stand is formed from the other (proceeding from the middle column) by altering the first or second premise. Thus (·))·) is formed from (·))·(by weakening the universal)·(into)·). But (·)(·) is formed from (·))·) by strengthening the second premise)·) into (·). Accordingly, the eight strengthened syllogisms are those which are under *VVP.*

I shall write down and illustrate one syllogism in the three readings: namely)·((·(which gives)(.

Arithmetical	*Mathematical*	*Metaphysical*
X).(*Y* No *X* is *Y*.	*X* co-external of *Y*.	*X* repugnant of *Y*.
Y(.(*Z* Some *Y*s are not *Z*s.	*Y* exient of *Z*.	*Y* independent of *Z*.
X)(*Z* Somethings neither *X*s nor *Z*s, i.e. as many at least as there are *Y*s which are not *Z*s.	*X* external of exient of *Z*, or coinadequate of *Z*, by all the extent at least by which *Y* is exient of *Z*.	*X* repugnant of independent of *Z*, or inalternative of *Z*, by at least all the force of *Z* which is not in *Y*.

Take the instance of metaphysical reading previously given, 'Courage (moral) and meanness are inconsistent ideas, and courage is not dependent on personal strength, so that strength and meanness are not necessary alternatives.' Courage does not depend on strength: a man wanting strength may therefore have courage, which puts meanness out of the question, so that a man may have neither strength nor meanness, or we must not say he must have one or the other or both. It is said that the force of this proposition is all the force of the word *strength* which is not in *courage*. Courage not depending on strength; the latter has attributes which are not in the notion of courage: say health. Ill-health is a field of intensive force for the verification of the proposition: the want of strength may arise from ill-health, which is consistent with courage, &c.

It is impossible that the logician can fully represent this case of common thought in his syllogism:—'All courageous is not mean, some courageous is not strong; therefore some not strong is not mean.'

40. When quantity or force is particular or incomplete in a term of the conclusion, that quantity or force is derived as follows:—

(*a*) *VVV*. If there be only one particular term in the conclusion, that term takes the whole quantity or force of the other term: but if there be two particular terms, one has the quantity or force of the middle term, the other of its contrary.

(*b*) *VVP*. The particular term, or both if there be two, takes quantity or force from the whole middle term, if the middle term be universal in both premises; and from the whole contrary of the middle term, if the middle term be particular in both premises.

(*c*) *PVP* and *VPP*. The particular term or terms in the conclusion take quantity or force from the particular term in the premise.

For example, let $X))Y))Z$ give $X))Z$ in the form $x(\cdot)Z$, with both terms particular. Everything is either x or Z. What extent of x are we sure of? an extent equal to that of y. And of Z, to fill up the universe, there remains the whole extent of Y.

Again, to apply symbols to a material example.

health]] temperance]] sobriety gives health].[excess in liquor.

The conclusion has both terms intensively particular. The forces of the repugnant terms health and [habit of] intoxication, are merely those of temperance and intemperance: health is a more intensive term than temperance, but we have not, in the argument, to do with any essential of health except temperance; or with any essential of intoxication except intemperance. Or, as people will sometimes say, 'to shew that health and intoxication are repugnant, it is enough to say that temperance is not intemperance.' This seems to many to be only a metaphorical heightening of contrast by substitution of explicit force of verbal *contrariety* for things which are *as repugnant as* contraries. But it is not so: it means that the intensive forces of a conclusion are in thought, and ought to have been in logic. The world sees—without knowing precisely what it sees—that the abacus process—'All healthy is temperate; all temperate is sober; therefore all healthy is sober: but no sober is drunken; therefore no healthy is drunken'—does not express its form of thought, though it be *Barbara* and *Celarent* in one.

41. The first figure is the most commodious: the fourth is nothing but the first with its conclusion read backwards; both these have been completely canonized. The symbolic rules for the second and third figures are very easily deduced: but I shall not swell this paper with them. If we consider premises only, there are but three figures. Each conclusion reads in two orders, which is no variation in two of the figures, and makes all the distinction between the first and the fourth. Now if we remember that premises are imposed upon us, but order of conclusion is our own choice, we see that the fourth figure is our own doing.

When both premises are mathematical, or both metaphysical, figure is a truly unessential variation, if the mind be equally accustomed to all modes of perceiving validity. All the duties which have been appropriated to the several figures seem to me to be fictions, so long as there is but one kind of reading. When the two propositions are of different readings, there is then a difference in the form of thought in different figures. The cases in which this occurs must be those in which the middle term is of the same reading in both, a mode of thought which must come first or last.

In the physical and contraphysical forms, it is not necessary to invent more schetical words: any term may be carried to another by its own reading. Thus we may call class a *species* of attribute and attribute an *essential* of class, in physical reading: and attribute a dependent of class, or class a genus of attribute, in contraphysical reading. We might even, on occasion, join the words of the two readings, in an order reverse of what we come from and what we are going to. Thus class may be a *dependent species* of attribute, and attribute a *genus essential* of class, in physical reading: while attribute may be a *class dependent* of class, and class an *essential genus* of attribute, in contraphysical reading. But no advice can be given on this point: such a familiarity with all the schetical words as we have with *species,* will dictate the form of mixed reading.

When both premises are physical, the first figure does not exist. In the second figure we compare classes by reference to a common attribute: in the third figure we compare attributes by reference to their relation with a common class. In the Aristotelian system, that is, confining ourselves to propositions in which we do not expressly deal with the whole universe, the second figure has no affirmative conclusion: that is, partience or inclusion cannot be inferred of two classes by reference to one attribute. And the third figure has no universal conclusion; that is, essentiality or repugnance of two attributes cannot be inferred by their relations to one class. This is more than technical knowledge; or would be, if duly expanded.

When the premises are of different kinds, with middle terms of the same reading, we have as follows, if we exclude the contraphysical form. The first figure yields only physical conclusion, from premises mathematical and physical, or physical and metaphysical. The second figure yields only physical conclusion, from premises physical and mathematical. The third figure yields only physical conclusion, from premises mathematical and physical.

The fourth figure, when both the premises are not of the same reading, and the middle term of the same reading in both, cannot exist without a contraphysical proposition, either in one premise or in the conclusion.

Postscript

Throughout this paper I have abstained from all mention of the name of any opponent of my views. This omission would have been an unpardonable affectation if there had not been a good reason for it: consequently it would appear in that light but for a good explanation. Had I taken the usual course, the name of a personal opponent and accuser would have struck the eye so often, that I should have been liable to serious misconstruction: not indeed from those who should carefully read my paper, but from the much larger number who would look over its pages on the way to other matter. Had I given one name its due frequency of mention, I should have been supposed by the turner of the pages to be continuing that kind of controversy which death should always interrupt: had I made an exception of that[1] name only, I should have appeared to the *reader* as ignoring, from personal motives, a memory which cannot be ignored in a branch of psychology from any worthy motives whatsoever.

I need hardly say that I allude to the late WILLIAM HAMILTON—a name which I hold entitled to the honour of losing its conventional accompaniments. And first, I take this opportunity of acknowledging the essential benefit which he conferred on my speculations. A mathematician might have written long enough upon logic before he would have attracted the attention of the readers of Aristotle. John Bernoulli and James Bernoulli (as I discovered by accident five years ago) both wrote on the subject, and so did Lambert: and all three on the proposition. But I doubt if Hamilton himself—the most omnivorous of readers—ever knew of the Bernoullis as writers on logic: and it is clear that he had no particular knowledge of Lambert before 1850 or

[1] This must be my apology to Mr Baynes, Mr Mansel, Mr Mill, Mr Spalding, Dr Thomson, and perhaps others, for my omission of direct allusion to them in my production of and remarks on their opinions.

thereabouts. Accordingly, my views might easily have remained the sole possession of the few mathematicians who study thought as thought. But when the most eminent teacher of logic of the century not only put himself in opposition to me at the outset, but affirmed his conviction that important parts of my views were derived from his own private communication to me, he gave me such an introduction[1] to his fellow-students as I should not have had the wit to contrive for myself, though the ordering of events had been unreservedly placed in my own hands. And what is the consequence? The writer of a manual omits to mention my name or to allude to my views—only, as afterwards stated, to avoid controversial description—and he is put upon the dilemma of culpable suppression or almost incredible ignorance in the very first journal which notices his book. And for this I have entirely to thank my opponent, who was well entitled to say of me,

> Iste tulit pretium *jam nunc* certaminis hujus,
> Quo cum victus erit, mecum certasse feretur.

It is due to the Society as well as to myself that some notice should be taken of the *Discussions on Philosophy* (first edition, from page 621* following 620 to page 652* preceding 621, second edition, pp. 676–707). There I find accusations of (unconscious) plagiarism, ignorance of elementary logic, and misrepresentation, coupled with reflections on the Society, extended even to the University, for the admission of such matter into their *Transactions*. I can afford to supply the word *unconscious*. First, because the charge is not made in terms which necessarily impute knowledge, while the retraction of a previous accusation, so far as wilful taking was concerned, leaves me at liberty to think that the second accusation was of the minor offence. Secondly, because I never knew of any journal, nor of more than one individual, who held that I had, even unconsciously, derived anything from the communications made to me, which have now been ten years before the world. I shall, in the briefest manner, take all necessary notice of the three things mentioned.

Unconscious plagiarism. Lambert unquestionably gave the definite quantification of the middle term. I never saw his *New Organon* till long after my first paper was published. When I saw it, I did not look at the part[2] which treats of this quantification: of which I first knew the

[1] To the discussion which followed it is due that Mr Boole turned his thoughts again to his old notes, and put his system into a form for publication. I need hardly say that this system is the true exhibition of the onymatic form of thought in the language of algebra.

[2] It is in the part of the book which treats of *probabilities*, in a different volume from the syllogism; and I dare say some will have found it difficult to believe that I, of all persons, should neglect that part of the *Neues Organon*. But I had both a subjective and an objective reason for abstaining. My acquaintance with German is

existence from Mr Baynes's *New Analytic* (1850, July). Ploucquet gave, according to my critic, the following rule: *Deleatur in premissis medius: id quod restat indicat conclusionem* (pp. 630*, 685); but in what work is not stated, nor whether Ploucquet used *symbols*. My rule is:—Erase the symbols of the middle term; the remaining symbols shew the inference. It is assumed that I derived this rule from Ploucquet. I answer that, in the second appendix to my *Formal Logic* (p. 323) I gave what then[1] was 'all I know of any attempt to deal with the forms of inference otherwise than in the Aristotelian method.' I had one borrowed work of Ploucquet in my hands for a few weeks; the only one of that writer I ever saw: I gave all I got from it. If the *methodus calculandi* described by me in page

[1] I add, so far as notes or recollections serve, what I have arrived at since. First, it is stated by Hamilton that Frommichen gave the numerical quantification of the middle term: but whether from Lambert, or independently, is not stated. Secondly, George Bentham, in his *Outlines of a new system of Logic*, (1827) made a universal quantification: but it is clear that he misunderstood some of its forms. A discussion arising out of this work, between Mr Warlow of Haverfordwest, the promoter, Hamilton, Dr Thomson, Mr Baynes, and others, took place in the *Athenaeum* Journal (December 1850—March 1851, Nos. 1208–1218). Thirdly, Mr Solly did the same, as noted in my last paper. Fourthly, Christopher Sturm, in his *Universalia Euclidea* . . . printed by Adrian Vlacq (Hague, 1661, 8vo. small) gave 12 forms of syllogism in which, the premises being Aristotelian, the contrary of one of the terms in the premises is allowed to be the *subject* of the conclusion. Thus from *A*)·(*B* and *B*)·(*C* he deduces *c*(·(*A*.

[25 June 1858—On this proposal of Sturm's Leibnitz, who describes it, remarks that the difference between a positive and privative term, or, what I call a term and its contrary, is of the matter of the term and not of the form of the proposition. Had he said that the distinction is of the *form* of the term, as distinguished from the form of the *proposition*, he would have been right: but there would have been no objection to take. Both Leibnitz and my critics should have objected to contrapositive conversion as material. But here, as in other cases, it is only the new introduction which is material: the established usage is formal. And this illustrates what I remarked in my second paper, namely, that the opposition really made is not of form to matter, but of what has been usually recognized as formal to that which has not.

It may be that the earliest attempt to augment the Aristotelian moods was that of *John* Hospinian (the Genevan divine was *Rodolph*) mentioned by Leibnitz as having appeared in a work published at Basle, 1560, 8vo. By pressing into the service

---

just enough to spell out mathematics, in which a person used to the subject reads in almost any European language. Again, the copy I used was borrowed, and was bound with marbled edges by an owner who had never used it. Many must know that when the older German paper is marbled, the leaves stick together at the edges in such manner that not the smallest crevice can be found for the end of a paper knife: and liberties which may be taken with an oyster must not be taken with a borrowed book; which put very serious difficulties in the way, and prevented even a cursory glance at all parts which I did not open. When I borrowed the book for the second time, after seeing Mr Baynes's work, I found that all the part on probabilities had never been opened. Had I opened this portion the first time, I could have learnt nothing more than the Society had published by reading more than a year before, and by printing six months before: but it would have been my duty to have stated what I had found.

333 be what[1] was meant, it will be seen to have not even a remote resemblance to my method: if not, I never saw what was meant. My *quantum*—very far from *sufficit*—of research in logical bibliography does not, at this moment, bear the most remote comparison to what some of my writings prove as to mathematical bibliography: and in 1849 it was much less than now.

Ignorance of elementary logic. To the general charge my writings must reply. But there are especial instances, which are quoted or referred to in three of the critic's writings. I have never been able to find the source of more than one of these instances. In giving an account of it, I cannot but express my conviction that the author of the imputation had lost

[1] My opponent had not my work before him, by his own act. He returned me the copy which I sent to him, in displeasure at my comments on his own accusation and its consequences; apparently denying, or at least not apprehending, that the copies of controversial works which pass between antagonist writers are no more *favours* than the gloves which used to pass between combatants of another kind. From this circumstance, and from internal evidence, I conclude that when he (pp. 649*, 704) pronounced me acquainted with the *logical writings* of both Ploucquet and Lambert, he spoke from vague recollection of my appendices, which were returned cut open.

---

indefinite and singular terms, and by admitting syllogisms of weakened conclusion (as *Cesaro* in the second figure) Hospinian obtains 512 possible moods, of which all but 36 are rejected as either useless or invalid. Some one, I know not who, or how, obtained 9210 moods. This I learn from an old disputation, *de Arte Syllogistica*, held at Leipsic in 1675, in which the young respondent, Christian Ihlius, after alluding to the 512 and the 9210, proceeds thus:—*Verum hi ipsi peccant tum in Deum tum in proximum: in Deum, dum dona concessa tam male impendunt; in proximum, dum ingenia discentium magis onerant quam juvant.*

Leibnitz himself worked out the 512 moods so soon as he saw Hospinian's title-page, and has given his account of them in the dissertation I have been citing. It is *de Arte Combinatoria*, first published at Leipsic in 1666, when Leibnitz was twenty years old. He approves of Hospinian's syllogisms of weakened conclusion, but attacks his treatment of the singular proposition as particular: *Titio omnes vestes quas habeo do lego, quis dubitet etsi unicam habeam ei deberi?* Wallis had maintained the same in a disputation at Emmanuel College in 1631, being then not sixteen years old. Leibnitz's dissertation *de Arte Combinatoria* must have been written as a university thesis, whether so read or not.]

I have already mentioned the Bernoullis. Their logical papers are heads of theses, in which both, but especially James Bernoulli, import the algebraical mode of thought into logic. They both take the distinction of extension and comprehension from the Port-Royal Logic, of which both were readers. James Bernoulli compares the common attribute of two notions to the common measure of two numbers, thus confirming my assertion that a mathematician would, of course, compound attributes, and not aggregate them. (Joh. B. *Works* i. 79; James B. *Works* i. 177, 213, 228.)

Lastly, while writing this note, accident led me to a paper by Louis Richer, in the volume for 1760–1761 of the Turin Memoirs (the one which contains Lagrange's celebrated paper on sound). This paper contains, among others, the very symbols I have used to distinguish propositions: but the object is to symbolize the notions of metaphysics. Thus (·) is necessity, (·) when positive, (·) when negative; and (··) is contingency.

some of his habit of deliberate reading, and that the misinterpretation of my meaning, and the indisposition to refer back, are to be attributed to ill-health.

The assertion is that I had confounded the *middle term* of a syllogism with its *conclusion*. The ground of this assertion is the following sentence in my *Statement in Answer* &c.: the word *former* referring to my first paper on syllogism:—'In the former I have expressed the quantity of my conclusion, there called *the* middle term, being as much as is really *middle*, by $m + n - 1$ . . .' My critic made what I call a wrong[1]

[1] [25 June 1858—I should have left the cause of this *wrong hyphenism* to the conjecture of my reader if I had not, while this paper was in proof, noticed the juxtaposition and opposition of the two passages given below. I have long been satisfied that I knew why a metaphysician who, right or wrong, was seldom weak, proclaimed the quantitative sciences of space and time to be mental nuisances; but, except for the passages now given, I could not have pointed to the explanation without much collation and laboured inference. I hope the reader will verify for himself, first, the following quotations, next, my assertion that the context would not reconcile them in the slightest degree. In both editions of the *Discussions*, within eight lines of each other, and as parts of the same train of thought, occur the following sentences (1st. ed. p. 644*; 2nd. ed. p. 699). The 'table' and the 'diagram' are one.

'This being understood, the Table at once exhibits the *real* identity and *rational* differences of Breadth and Depth, which, though denominated *quantities*, are, in reality, one and the same quantity, viewed in counter relations and from opposite ends. Nothing is the one which is not, *pro tanto*, the other.'

'The two quantities are thus, as the diagram represents, precisely the inverse of each other. The greater the Breadth, the less the Depth; the greater the Depth, the less the Breadth; and each, within itself, affording the correlative differences of whole and part, each, therefore, in opposite respects, *contains* and *is contained*.'

Of two quantities, then, which are 'one and the same quantity,' the less the one, the greater the other! ['My grief is great because it is so small—Then t'would be greater were it none at all'—MS. note.] The writer of these passages never failed to convey anything he really had to convey, by want of power over language: when the Bank ran short, he knew the way to the Mint. But he was here suffering under an insufficiency of notion. He wanted to grasp the idea that of his two quantities one *determines* the other. The conception of functional relation was struggling in a mind which could not furnish it with a *locus standi* for want of an adequate conception of quantity. A little further on he proceeds thus:—'Though different in the order of thought (*ratione*), the two quantities are identical in the nature of things (*re*). Each supposes the other; and Breadth is not more to be distinguished from Depth, than the relations of the sides, from the relations of the angles, of a triangle.' Had 'identical' here had its meaning, it would have been absurd to say that Breadth and Depth are 'not more' distinct than the relations of the sides and the relations of the angles of a triangle: it ought to have been 'not so much by a great deal.' But, as it is, and choice of word apart, my eminent critic is right: Breadth and Depth have relations each to the other. The word 'identical,' as used by him, symbolizes his aspiration after the notion of mutual dependence, which mathematicians call functional relation. He has pushed to an extreme a liberty with the word *identical* which is not uncommon among logicians. They start from '*X is X*' as the expression of *identity*; and their extensions of the verb involve extensions of the substantive. But they do not handle simultaneous extensions of cognate words with as much facility as the mathematicians, to whom the process is of constant occurrence, sometimes forced upon

hyphenism: he read it 'quantity of my conclusion-there-called-*the*-middle-term' instead of 'quantity-of-my-conclusion, there called the middle term.' If two leaves had been turned back, so that the extracts from 'the former' should have met the eye, there would have been seen—'If these fractions be m and n, then the middle term is *at least* the fraction $m + n - 1$ of the *Y*s.' The meaning is clear. If the fraction m of the *Y*s be *X*s, and the fraction n of the *Y*s be *Z*s, then the extent 'the fraction $m + n - 1$ of the *Y*s' is really in both terms, and is 'as much as is really *middle*.' I defend the grammar of my phrase, though not its sufficient completeness: but it is well enough for an allusion to matter of four pages back. In 'the *A* of my *B*, there called *C*,' *C* refers to *A*, unless context make it very apparent that the writer is not correct. If I had wanted to refer *C* to *B*, I should have said, 'the *A* of my *B*, which *B* is there called *C*.'

[25 June 1858—In my second paper I took some part of that distinction between extension and intension which I have developed in the present paper. On this point my eminent opponent (*Discussions*, 1st ed. p. 643*, 2nd ed. p. 698), speaking of his own maxim that 'the predicate of the predicate is, with the predicate, affirmed or denied of the subject,' proceeds thus: 'In fact, if this principle be not universally right, if Mr De Morgan be not altogether wrong, my extension of the doctrine of Breadth and Depth, in correlation, from notions to *propositions and syllogisms*, has been only an egregious blunder.' I do not rejoin that of this I put myself upon the country, for two reasons. First, because the last phrase is not one in which I should like to join issue with such an opponent, alive or dead. Secondly, because there lurks in the sentence I have quoted a *fallacia plurium descriptionum*, which prevents it from conveying no more than the point at issue. Sir W. Hamilton's principle

---

them by the progress of their science, sometimes excogitated, *pro re nata*, to forward that progress.

Quantity, in the mind of my critic, was the *res divisibilis* (§ 21); and not correctly conceived even in this sense. We may now see how it comes to be affirmed, in the dissertation I have quoted, that *equation of quantities* is convertible with *coalescence of notions*, and *equation* with *identification*: that a competent notation must 'sublimate into one' identical quantities: that though a proposition be 'merely' equation of quantities,—two Breadths, or two Depths,—it may, at will, be considered in neither quantity. No one of these assertions wants truth, provided that clear meaning be given by reduction of 'quantity' within its true limits, and restoration of 'coalescence' to its proper place. Other writings of the same author contain phrases illustrative of the theory on which I account for those already produced. Such as that moods are *numerically equal* in all figures; meaning that all figures have the same numbers of moods: such again as the phrase *amplification of number*; meaning the addition of other number to it: such again as *addition* to the *number* of things described as *increase* in the *things* themselves. And lastly, *quantity* of the conclusion not merely confounded with the conclusion itself, but the confusion attributed to a mathematician. (Cf. also *Notes and Queries*, 2nd Series, VI, p. 209—Ed.)]

is universally right, in its own meaning and in its proper place; but it is not contradictory of any thing brought forward by me; so that it does not make me altogether wrong. No one can dispute the principle when it is affirmed of qualities, distributed and separately residing in their subjects of inhesion. The difference between me and my opponent begins when he affirms or implies that his principle is, appertains to, or is in any way connected with, or even opposed to, the form of thought on which, from Aristotle downwards, has been based the distinction between extension and comprehension, denotation and connotation, logical whole and metaphysical whole, or whatever it may be called. This true and ever-abiding distinction is affirmed by Sir W. Hamilton, and denied by me, to be identical with that drawn by himself between *Breadth* and *Depth*. And this is the point on which issue is joined.]

Misrepresentation. In my second paper, speaking of complete quantification, I presumed that, as had been done by various writers who quantify the predicate, the words *some* and *all* would be made the words of quantity: so that, when quantity is expressly given, 'No *X* is *Y*' would become 'All *X* is not all *Y*,' and the like. Not that I complained of this awkward language: on the contrary, though I called it forced in order and phraseology, hard to make either English or sense of, I said that in its place in the system alluded to, the uncouth expression helps to produce system, and the perception of uniform law of inference. So I thought, and so I think still. The entrance of the exemplar *any* into the negatives, while *all* is used in the affirmatives, appears to me a symbolic blemish, though no doubt it is a grammatical propriety.

But as the system really does not proceed as I said it did, there is misrepresentation. My affair with it now is to shew that I had presumptive grounds for making the statement in my second paper. They were as follows:

In the prospectus of a work on logic, not yet[1] published, which prospectus appeared in 1846, my critic describes universal quantity as an *extensive maximum undivided*, and *universal* quantity is called *definite*. Now the maximum of extension, undivided, and definite, is *all*; the word *any* both indicates division, and is indefinite. No hint is given that in negatives the universal is represented by a maximum of extension divided by a word of indefinitely selective import.

In my work on logic (p. 302), forming the system from conjecture, I attributed the phrases afterwards repudiated by my critic; and this part

[1] It is to appear under the editorship of the Rev. H. L. Mansel, but I am afraid the state in which the papers were left will cause some delay. I understand that all which relates to *quantity* is left in a scattered state. The technical phrases of logic had been worn and torn until they were almost unintelligible. Hamilton's remarkable power over language gave some new life to almost every subject he touched: and logic will, I believe, not be found among the exceptions.

of my work I knew to have been seen by himself. Opportunity of correction subsequently offered itself in the statement of the system furnished to Dr Thomson, for the second edition of his *Laws of Thought* (1849). But no such correction was made; the explicit propositional forms were not given; and the only hint on the subject which this work contains is the hint in the notation, more fully spoken of immediately, in reference to another work.

In July 1850, just after the last revise of my second paper had been sent to Cambridge, but in time to have recalled it, I received Mr Baynes's *New Analytic*. I looked at all parts of this, at once, with a view to correction. I found no propositional forms, but only such an account of the syllogistic notation as would allow no other phraseology except what I had used. We are told, in more places than one (pp. 76, 151, 155) the last in a note by Hamilton himself, that the colon (:) denotes *all*, and no other rendering is given. Thus 'there is denoted by the sign [:] *all*' and 'the colon (:) to denote "all" (definite quantity)' and 'the colon denotes universal *quantity* "all."' In the notation, *A*:——:*B* is intended to be read 'All *A* is all *B*,' and *A*:+—:*B*, the symbol +— denoting negation, cannot, *according to directions*, be read in any other way than 'all *A* is not all *B*.' Most of the instances in the body of the work are material, and common words and elisions are employed. I did afterwards find a negative form (I believe such a thing occurs only once) thus—'No *C* is any *B*:' but even had I noticed this in the first examination, I could not have accepted, as a formal component of that system which rests entirely on explicit announcement of every quantity, a form in which the semi-copular, semi-quantitative word 'no' is used.

Lastly, in proof that I might have avoided the misrepresentation, my critic referred me to certain mnemonic verses which he had published in 1847, of which the first stanza is

> *A* it affirms of this, these, all,
> Whilst *E* denies of *any*:
> *I* it affirms, whilst *O* denies,
> Of some (or few or many).

But it is clear that, all other things put together with this, I could only look upon *any* as preferred for the convenience of rhyming; to say nothing of the word *any* referring only to the subject [and of the verses referring only to the old system].

Thus I have, I think, established a reasonable right, then existing, to assume the 'extensive maximum undivided' as intended to be expressed by the word *all*, wherever and however it occurred.

I trust I have now done with the personal part of this controversy. Enough remains of scientific assault, as amply shewn in the preceding pages. But this concerns the living: and enough remain, again, to defend what is capable of defence, and to surrender what must be surrendered. For all else, I select two names from the rolls of fame in which my late opponent is now inscribed, and I join to Morhof's description of Julius Scaliger—*Totus nervosus est et rerum plenus, vehemens ipsi ingenium, audax, acre, judicium penetrans, nonnunquam etiam cavillatorium, ut solent viri etiam summi aliqua in re labi*—the question asked by Erasmus concerning Laurentius Valla—*Adeo nihil ignoscendum putamus ei qui tot modis profuit?*

SYLLABUS OF A PROPOSED SYSTEM OF LOGIC [1860]

Διπλοῦν ὁρῶσιν οἱ μαθόντες γράμματα

Ὁ γραμμάτων ἄπειρος οὐ βλέπει βλεπων

PREFACE

The matters collected in this Syllabus will be found in those of my writings[1] of which the titles follow:—I. *On the Structure of the Syllogism.* . . . II. *Formal Logic, or the Calculus of Inference, necessary and probable* (London, Taylor and Walton, 1847, 8vo). III. *On the Symbols of Logic, the Theory of the Syllogism, and in particular of the Copula*, . . . IV. *On the Syllogism*, No. iii, *and on Logic in general.* Of these works the formulae and notation of the first are entirely superseded; the notation only of the second (the *Formal Logic*) may be advantageously replaced (see § 24) by that of the third and fourth and of the present tract. There is very little in the first three writings on which my opinion has varied; but of all three it is to be said that they are entirely based on what I now call the *arithmetical* view of the proposition and syllogism (§ 8, 173, 174), extending this term not merely to the *numerically definite* syllogism, but to the ordinary form, to my own extension of it, and to Sir W. Hamilton's departure from it.

The relations of my work on *Formal Logic* to the present syllabus are as follows. Chapter I, *First Notions*, may afford previous knowledge to the student who has hitherto paid no attention to the subject. Chapter III, On the *abstract form of the Proposition*, may be consulted at § 93 of this syllabus. Chapters IV, *On Propositions* and V and VI, *On the Syllogism*, are rendered more easy by the notation of this syllabus, and are

[1] The writings which oppose any of my views at length are the following, so far as my memory serves. I. *A letter to* Augustus De Morgan, Esq. . . . *from* Sir William Hamilton, Bart. London and Edinburgh, 1847. II. *Review of my Formal Logic*, signed *J*[oseph] *S*[ortain], *in the* Biblical Review, 1848. III. *Review of my Formal Logic* (since acknowledged by Mr Mansel, the author of the *Prolegomena Logica*) *in the* North British Review *for May* 1851, No. 29. IV. *Discussions on Philosophy* by Sir W. Hamilton [pp. 621*–652* (1st edn.); 676–707 (2nd edn.)].

partially superseded. Chapter XIV, *On the verbal Description of the Syllogism*, is entirely superseded. All the rest of the work may be read as the titles of the chapters suggest.

A syllabus deals neither in development nor in diversified example: and does not make the space occupied by any detail a measure of its importance as a part of the whole. I have omitted many subjects which are to be found in all the books, or dwelt lightly upon them: partly because more detail is contained in my *Formal Logic*, partly because any one who masters this tract will be able to judge for himself what I should have written on the omitted subjects. I have also endeavoured to remember that as a work of this kind proceeds, less detail of explanation is necessary.

I should suppose that a student of ordinary logic would find no great difficulty in understanding my meaning: and that those who are accustomed to symbolic expression, mathematical or not, would, even though unused to logical study, find no more difficulty than an ordinary student finds in Aldrich's *Compendium*. Either of these classes, I should think, would not fail to come to the point of understanding at which a reflecting mind can allow itself to meditate acceptance or rejection without latent fear of over-confidence. Whether a beginner who is conversant neither with ordinary logic nor with symbolic language will comprehend me is another question: and one on which those who try will divide into more than two classes. Such a reader, making concrete examples for himself as he goes on, and never leaving any article until he has done this, will either get through the whole tract, or will stop at the precise point at which he ought to stop, upon the principle of the next paragraph.

Every spoon has some mouths that it can feed; and some that it cannot. Every writer has some readers who are made for him, and he for them; and some between whom and himself there is a great gulph. I might prove this, in my own case, by a chain of discordant testimonies running through thirty years, if I had leisure and liking to hunt up extracts from reviews. I will content myself with a couple which are at hand: observing that I have no acquaintance with the authors. In 1830, I published my treatise on *Arithmetic*, and the following sentences speedily appeared in reviews of it:—

This book appears to us to mystify a very simple science.	It is as clear as Cobbett in his lucid intervals.

In 1847, I published my *Formal Logic*, and two opponents of my views wrote as follows:

Mr De Morgan is certainly not a lucid writer.[1]

This is an undeniably long extract, and yet we would, did our limits allow, continue it . . . . We beg the reader's notice to the exquisite precision of its language; to the definiteness of every line in the picture; for though it is a description of a profound mental process, still it is a luminous picture, the light of which does not interfuse its lineaments . . . . We are at very solemn issue with Mr De Morgan upon this argument . . .[2]

These antagonisms remind us of the stork and the fox, and of the failure of their attempts to entertain each other at dinner. When an author's dish and a reader's beak do not match, they must either divide the blame, or agree to throw it [entire] on that exquisite piece of atheism, *the nature of things*.

The points on which I differ from writers on logic are so many and so fundamental, that I am among them as Hobbes among the geometers, and, *mutato nomine*, may say with him of Malmesbury:—*In magno quidem periculo versari video existimationem meam, qui a* logicis *fere omnibus dissentio. Eorum enim qui de iisdem rebus mecum aliquid ediderunt, aut solus insanio ego aut solus non insanio; tertium enim non est, nisi (quod dicet forte aliquis) insaniamus omnes.*

Hobbes was in the wrong: the question of parallel or contrast must be left to time. But though some writers on logic explicitly renounce me and all my works, yet one point of those same works is adopted here and one there; so that in time it may possibly be said that

Mahometans eat up the hog.

All these differences are not about the truth or falsehood of my neologisms, but about the legitimacy of their adoption into *logic*, the study of the *laws of thought*. And I cannot imitate Hobbes so far as to write *contra fastum logicorum*, seeing that, *oblitis obliviscendis*, I have personally nothing but courtesy to acknowledge from all the writers of known name who have done me the honour of alluding to my speculations. In return, I endeavour to tilt at their shields and not at their faces. Should I make any one feel that I have missed my attempt, I will pray the introduction into these lists of the old practice of the playground. When I was a boy, any offence against the rules of the game was held to be nullified if the offender, before notice taken, could cry

[1] [*Douglas Jerrold's Weekly Newspaper*, 1 April 1848.]
[2] [Joseph Sortain, *Biblical Review*, 1848.]

Slips!—as I now do over all, to meet contingencies. As to the *matter* of our differences, I neither give nor take quarter: it is

'I will lay on for Tusculum,
Do thou lay on for Rome!'

as will sufficiently appear in my notes.

Now to another topic. I produce a fragment of a well-known conversation: those who choose may fill up the chasms.

'. . . I therefore dressed up three paradoxes with some ingenuity . . . . The whole learned world, I made no doubt, would rise to oppose my systems: but then I was prepared to oppose the whole learned world. Like the porcupine, I sat self-collected, with a quill pointed against every opposer. Well said, my boy, cried I, ... you published your paradoxes; well, and what did the learned world say to your paradoxes? Sir, replied my son, the learned world said nothing to my paradoxes; nothing at all, sir. Every man of them was employed in praising his friends and himself, or condemning his enemies; and unfortunately, as I had neither, I suffered the cruellest mortification, neglect.' [1]

A friend of the author just quoted remarked that a shuttlecock cannot be kept up unless it be struck from both ends. I was spared all the mortification of neglect by the eminence of the player who took up the other battledore. Of this celebrated opponent I can truly say that, so far as I myself was concerned, I never looked with anything but satisfaction upon certain points of procedure to which I shall only make distant allusion. For I saw from the beginning that he was playing my game, and raising the wind which was to blow about the seeds of my plant. The mathematicians who have written on logic in the last two centuries have been wholly unknown to even the far-searching inquirers of the Aristotelian world: to the late Sir William Hamilton of Edinburgh I owe it that I can present this tract to the moderately well informed elementary student of logic, as containing matters of which he is likely enough to have heard something, and may possibly be curious to hear more.

In controversy—and controversy was to him an element of life and a spring of action—Sir William Hamilton was too much the fencer of the moment, too much the firer of to-morrow's article: his impulses sometimes leap him over the barrier which divides philosophy from philosophism. Root the proofs of this out of his pages, and we have before us a man both learned and ingenious, profound and acute, weighty and flexible, displaying a most instructive machinery of thought as well when judged right as when judged wrong, save only when cause of regret arises that Oxford did not demand of his youth two books of Euclid and

[1] [Goldsmith: *Vicar of Wakefield*, Ch. XX.—Ed.]

simple equations. In describing a character some points of which are at tug of war—especially when liking for quotation was one of them—Greek may meet Greek. He showed more fondness than was politic in one so plainly destined to survive the grave for a too literal version of the motto.

> *Οὗτος κράτιστός ἐστ' ἀνὴρ ὦ Γοργία*
> *"οστις ἀδικεῖθαι πλεῖστ' ἐπίσταται βροτῶν.*

But on the other hand, though too much inclined to rule the house, he was *οἰκοδεσπότης ὅστις ἐκβάλλει ἐκ τοῦ θησαυροῦ αὐτοῦ καινὰ καὶ παλαιά*. And this as to words as well as things. Magnificent command of language, old terms rare enough to be new, and new terms good enough to be old, mask defects and heighten merits. In his writings against me, it delighted him to enliven the statements of the accuser by portraits of the mind of his opponent: colouring his notion of the mathematician from the darkness of his want of notion of the mathematics, his great and admitted defect as a psychologist. I dealt with the statements in my last Cambridge paper: I now oppose my sketch of him to his sketch of me, without the least misgiving as to which of the two will be pronounced the best likeness.

12 November 1859.

CONTENTS

*** The references are to the sections.

1. Logic[1] analyses the *forms*, or *laws of action*, of thought.

2. Logic is *formal*, not *material*: it considers the law of action, apart from the matter acted on. It is not *psychological*, not *metaphysical*: it considers neither the mind in itself, nor the nature of things in itself; but the mind in relation to things, and things in relation to the mind. Nevertheless, it is so far *psychological* as it is concerned with the results of the constitution of the mind: and so far *metaphysical* as it is concerned with the right use of notions about the nature and dependence of things which, be they true or be they false, as representations of real existence, enter into the common modes of thinking of all men.[2]

3. The study of elementary logic includes the especial consideration of—

1. The *term* or *name*, the written or spoken sign of an object of thought, or of a mode of thinking.

[1] Logic has a tendency to correct, first, inaccuracy of thought, secondly, inaccuracy of expression. Many persons who think logically express themselves illogically, and in so doing produce the same effect upon their hearers or readers as if they had thought wrongly. This applies especially to teachers, many of whom, accurate enough in their own thoughts, nourish sophism in their pupils by illogical expression.

It is very commonly said that studies which exercise the thinking faculty, and especially mathematics, are means of cultivating logic, and may stand in place of systematic study of that science. This is true so far, that every discipline *strengthens* the logical power: that is to say, strengthens most of what it finds, be the same good or bad. It is further true that every discipline corrects *some* bad habits: but it is equally true that every discipline tends to confirm *some* bad habits. Accordingly, though every exercise of mind does much more good than harm, yet no person can be sure of avoiding the harm and retaining only the good, except by that careful examination of his own mental habits which most often takes place in a proper study of logic, and is seldom made without it. This being done, and the house being built, the scaffolding may be thrown away if the builder please: though in most cases it will be advisable to keep it at hand, for use when inspection or repairs are needed. Some persons make the argument about the utility of logic turn on the question whether disputation is or is not best conducted [in technically formed syllogisms]: on which I hold—waiving the utter irrelevancy of the question—that those who cannot so argue need to learn, while those who can have no need to practise. It is just the same with spelling.

As to the difficult word *form*, and the variations of it, I refer to Dr. Thomson's *Outlines of the Necessary Laws of Thought*, § 11–15. By a form of thought I mean a necessary law of action, considered independently of any particular matter of thought to which it is applied.

[2] [Hamilton: *Lectures*, i, 43. 'In this respect (certainty) Logic and Mathematics stand alone among the sciences, and their peculiar certainty flows from the same source.'

Discussions (pp. 622,* 673). 'Reason and experience concur in showing that Mathematics and Logic, like Love and Majesty,

Haud bene conveniunt . . .'

Logic has always been *learning*; mathematics, *science*.—August 1860.]

2. The *copula* or *relation*, the connexion under which terms are thought of together.
3. The *proposition*, terms in relation with one another; and the *judgment*, the decision of the mind upon a proposition: usually joined in one, under one or other of the names.
4. The *syllogism*, deduction of relation by combination of other relations.

4. The thing which is not of the mind, and can be imagined to exist without the mind, is the *object*: the mind itself is called the *subject* of that object. Thus even a relation between two minds may be an *object* to a third mind. Logic considers only the connexion of the subjective and objective: it treats of things *non secundum se, sed secundum esse quod habent in anima*.

5. The consideration of names, *as names*, may be made to furnish the key to the mechanical, or instrumental, treatment of the ordinary proposition and the ordinary syllogism.

6. For this purpose a name is a mere mark, attached to an object: a letter painted on a post would do as well for explanation as the name of a notion or concept in the mind attached in thought to an external object. In this part of the subject, the assertion 'Every man is an animal' is treated as if it were merely 'Every object which has the name m-a-n has also the name a-n-i-m-a-l.' It answers[1] to 'Every post on which *X* is painted has also *Y* painted on it.'

7. The *proposition*, in this view, is no more than the connexion of name with name, as marks of the same object: the *judgment* is no more than assertion or denial of that connexion. The word *is* asserts the connexion: the words *is not* deny it.

8. This kind of proposition belongs to the *arithmetical* view of logic: there is in it result of enumeration of similar instances: as in 'Every *X* is *Y*', '50 *X*s are not *Y*s', i.e. there are 50 (or more) instances in which the name *X* occurs unassociated with the name *Y*.

9. The first-mentioned name is called the *subject*: the second the *predicate*.

10. The logical *quantity* (i.e. number of instances) is either *definite*, or *more or less vague*.[2]

11. *Definite* quantity is either *absolutely* or *relatively* definite: absolutely, as in '50 *X*s (and no more) are *Y*s'; relatively, as in '2-sevenths

[1] Remember that in producing a name, the *existence* of things to which it applies is *predicated*, i.e. asserted: and (§ 16) existence in the universe of the propositions. There is no *conditional* proposition intended, as Every *X* is *Y* (if *Y* exist). Every proposition is a conceivable or imaginable truth, when its terms are conceivable or imaginable, except only when it announces a contradiction, as 'Some men are not men,' or when it is its own subject-matter and denies itself, as 'What I now say is false,' a proposition which is false if it be true, and true if it be false.

[2] [*Perfect* vagueness makes every proposition true.]

(and no more) of all the *X*s are *Y*s', and in 'All the *X*s are *Y*s', and in "None of the *X*s are *Y*s', which last is both absolutely and relatively definite.

12. Quantity may be definite at one end, and vague at the other: as in '50 (or more) *X*s are *Y*s'; 'at least 2-sevenths of all the *X*s are *Y*s'; 'most of the *X*s (i.e. more than half) are *Y*s', which, however, is *limited* at one end, not *definite*.[1]

13. The only perfect definite quantities in ordinary use are *all* and *none*. The materials for other absolute or relative numerical definiteness are but seldom found in human knowledge. The words *all* and *none* are signs of *total* quantity, and make propositions *universal*, as 'All *X*s are *Y*s', 'No *X*s are *Y*s'.

14. The *contrary* (usually called *contradictory*) propositions of the last are 'Some *X*s are not *Y*s', and 'Some *X*s are *Y*s'. Here 'some' is a quantity entirely vague in one direction: it is *not-none*; one[2] at least; or more; all,[3] it may be. *Some*, in common life, often means both *not-none*

[1] [Quantity, as quantity, does not particularize individuals. *One* is neither this one, nor that one. Hamilton called the quantification *one half*, *semi*-definite—definite as to how much, indefinite as to which much. 'Never believe more than half of what you hear.—Yes, but *which* half?' Semi-definite maxim.—MS. note.]

[2] Remember that *some* does not guarantee more than *one*. There is much distinction between *none* (no one) as the logical contrary of *some* (one or more), and *nothing* as the limit of *some quantity*. In passing from the proposition 'no man can live without air' to 'there is one man at least who can live without air' we make a transition which alters the notions or concepts attached to man: the word man no longer represents entirely the same idea. But in passing from an indenture of apprenticeship with *no premium at all* to one with a premium of *one farthing*, we make no change of notion. An Act was once passed exempting such indentures from duty when the premium was under five pounds sterling: the Court of King's Bench held that the exemption did not apply when there was *no premium at all*, because 'no premium at all' is not 'a premium under five pounds.' That is, the judges gave to *nothing*, as the terminus of continuous quantity, the force of *none*, as the logical contrary of *some*; and violated to the utmost the principle of the Act, which was intended as a relief to those who could only pay small premiums, and *à fortiori*, or rather *à fortissimo*, to those who could pay none at all. Lawyers ought to be much of logicians, and something of mathematicians.

[3] *Some* may be *all*. In common language this is or is not the case according to the speaker's state of knowledge. But in logic there are no implications which depend upon the matter. When a logician says that 'Every *X* is *Y*' he means that 'All the *X*s are some *Y*s' and that 'some *Y*s are all the *X*s'. Whether he have or have not exhausted all the *Y*s he does not here profess to state, even if he know. Again, when he says 'Some *X*s are *Y*s' he does not mean to imply 'Some *X*s are not *Y*s': that is, his *some* may be *all*, for anything he asserts to the contrary. But when *two* propositions, each of which contains the vague *some*, are conjoined, the mere meaning may render the conjunction an absurdity unless *some* take the force of *all*. Just as in algebra an equation having two unknown quantities has the values of those quantities vague; but when two such equations are conjoined, those values become definite: so in logic, in which the same thing occurs. Thus the two propositions 'All *X*s are some *Y*s', and 'All *Y*s are some *X*s', when true together, force the inference that *some* must in both cases be *all*. Forget that *some* is that which *may be* all, and these two

and *not-all*; in logic, only *not-none*. *Some* is the mark of *partial* quantity; and the propositions which commence with it are *particular*. The *contrary* (usually *contradictory*) forces of the pairs are seen in 'Either all *X*s are *Y*s, or some *X*s are not *Y*s; not both'; and in 'Either no *X*s are *Y*s, or some *X*s are *Y*s; not both.'

15. In 'All *X*s are *Y*s', *Y* is partially spoken of; there may or may not be more *Y*s besides: the same of 'Some *X*s are *Y*s'. In 'No *X*s are *Y*s', and in 'Some *X*s are not *Y*s', *Y* is totally spoken of; each *X* spoken of is not any one of all the *Y*s.

16. By the *universe* (of a proposition) is meant the collection of all objects which are contemplated as objects about which assertion or denial may take place. *Let every name which belongs to the whole universe be excluded as needless:* this must be particularly remembered. Let every object which has not the name *X* (*of which there are always some*) be conceived as therefore marked with the name *x*, meaning not-*X*, and called the *contrary* of *X*. Thus every thing is either *X* or *x*; nothing is both: 'All *X*s are *Y*s' means 'No *X*s are *y*s': 'No *X*s are *Y*s' means 'All *X*s are *y*s': 'Some *X*s are not *Y*s' means 'Some *X*s are *y*s': 'Some *X*s are *Y*s' means 'Some *X*s are not *y*s'.

17. The following enlarged definitions include the definitions above given, and apply to all the uses of terms and relations in this work. Let a TERM be *total* or *partial* according as every existing instance must or need not be examined to verify the proposition. Thus in 'Everything is either *X* or *Y*', *X* and *Y* are both partial: an object being examined and found to be *X*, the proposition is made good so far as that object is concerned; that object may also be *Y*, but if so, it need not be ascertained: consequently, *Y* is partially spoken of; and the same may be said of *X*. But in 'Some things are neither *X*s nor *Y*s', *X* and *Y* are both total: we can only verify it by an object which is not any one of the *X*s and not any one of the *Y*s.

18. Let a PROPOSITION be *universal* or *particular*, according as the whole universe of objects must or need not be examined to verify it. Thus 'Everything is neither *X* or *Y*' is plainly universal: but 'Some things are neither *X*s nor *Y*s' is particular: the first object examined may settle the truth of the proposition.

19. Let a PROPOSITION be *affirmative* which is true of *X* and *X*, false

propositions appear to contradict one another: very distinguished logicians have asserted that they do so. Sir W. Hamilton (*Discussions*, 2nd edition, p. 688) calls them *incompossible* propositions, meaning propositions which cannot be true together. The word is an excellent one, and much wanted: but not here. These two propositions are not *incompossible*, unless *some* take into its meaning *not-all* as well as *not-none*: and *some* is never allowed by logicians to mean *not-all*. It is needless to argue things so plain: it would have been needless to state them twice, except for the eminence of the writers who deny them upon occasion.

of *X* and not-*X* or *x*; *negative*, which is true of *X* and *x*, false of *X* and *X*. Thus 'Every *X* is *Y*' is affirmative: 'Every *X* is *X*' is true; 'Every *X* is *x*' false. But 'Some things are neither *X*s nor *Y*s' is also *affirmative*, though in the form[1] of a *denial*: 'Some things are neither *X*s nor *X*s' is *true*, though superfluous in expression; 'Some things are neither *X*s nor *x*s' is false. Again, 'Everything is either *X* or *Y*' is *negative*, though in the form of an *assertion*: 'Everything is either *X* or *X*' is false; 'Everything is either *X* or *x*' is true.

20. Affirmative and negative propositions are said to be of different *quality*.[2]

21. Let *X*, totally spoken of, be *X*) or (*X*: let *X*, partially spoken of, be)*X* or *X*(. Let a negative proposition be denoted by one dot; an affirmative proposition by two dots or none, at pleasure. I follow Sir William Hamilton in calling this notation *spicular* (see § 216, note). So far as yet appears, we have propositions with the following symbols,—

Contraries	*A*	Universal Affirmative	*X*))*Y*	All *X*s are some *Y*s.
	O	Particular Negative	*X*(·(*Y*	Some *X*s are not (all) *Y*s.
Contraries	*E*	Universal Negative	*X*)·(*Y*	All *X*s are not (all) *Y*s.
	I	Particular Affirmative	*X*()*Y*	Some *X*s are some *Y*s.

22. These forms have been denoted by the letters *A*, *O*, *E*, *I*, for many centuries; *A* and *I* from the vowels in ***affirmo***; *E* and *O* from the vowels in ***nego***. The word (all), in parentheses, is not grammatical: the word *any* should be substituted for *all*. The reason why, for the present, I do not use '*any*' will appear in the sequel.

23. Take the four pairs, *X*, *Y*; *X*, *y*; *x*, *Y*; *x*, *y*; and apply the four forms above to all four. Sixteen results appear; of which eight are but a repetition of the other eight. Of the eight[3] which are distinct, we have four written above: the remaining four appear among the following,—

From)) we have *X*))*Y*, *X*))*y*, *x*))*Y*, and *x*))*y*. Of these *X*))*y* is

[1] When contrary terms are introduced, it is impossible to define the opposition of quality by assertion or denial: for every assertion is a denial, and every denial is an assertion. The denial 'No *X* is *Y*' is the assertion 'All *X*s are *y*s.' The necessary distinction between *affirmative* and *negative* is therefore drawn as in the text: these technical terms are retained, though perhaps they are hardly the right ones for *me* to use.

[2] [What is quality except as above? The ordinary method makes a selection of propositions, among which distinction of quality is but that of affirmative and negative.—MS. note.]

[3] Any one who wishes to test himself and his friends upon the question whether analysis of the forms of enunciation would be useful or not, may try himself and them on the following question:—Is either of the following propositions true, and if either, which? 1. All Englishmen who do not take snuff are to be found among Europeans who do not use tobacco. 2. All Englishmen who do not use tobacco are to be found among Europeans who do not take snuff. Required immediate answer and demonstration.

obviously $X)\cdot(Y$. And $x))Y$ is $x)\cdot(y$, a new form: no not-X is not-Y; nothing is both not-X and not-Y; everything is either X or Y [or both]. This being a universal proposition with both terms partial, and also a negative proposition, let it be marked $X(\cdot)Y$. Again, $x))y$ is $x)\cdot(Y$, or $Y)\cdot(x$, or no Y is not-X, or every Y is X, or some Xs are all Ys, or $X((Y$.

From () we have $X()Y$, $X()y$, $x()Y$, $x()y$. Here $X()y$ is $X(\cdot(Y$; and $x()Y$ is $Y()x$, some Ys are not Xs, or all Xs are not some Ys, or $X)\cdot)Y$. And $x()y$ is a new form, Some not-Xs are not-Ys; some things are neither Xs nor Ys. This is a particular proposition, affirmative, with X and Y both total: let it be marked $X)(Y$.

24. The eight distinct[1] forms in which X and Y appear are as follows; the ungrammatical introduction (all) being made as [in § 21, and the quantity of a term being always expressed],—

	Universal propositions		*Contrary particular propositions*
$X))Y$	All Xs are some Ys	$X(.(Y$	Some Xs are not (all) Ys
$X)\cdot(Y$	All Xs are not (all) Ys	$X()Y$	Some Xs are some Ys
$X(\cdot)Y$	[All things are] either some Xs or some Ys (or both)	$X)(Y$	Some things are not either (all) Xs nor (all) Ys
$X((Y$	Some Xs are all Ys	$X)\cdot)Y$	All Xs are not some Ys

For symmetry, $X)\cdot(Y$ might be read '[All things are] either not (all) Xs, or not (all) Ys'; and $X()Y$ as 'Some things are both some Xs and some Ys'. This will be better seen when we come to § 206. At present, however, I preserve the ordinary reading.

25. The thirty-two forms which arise from application of contraries are as now written, all the eight cases above being used: the four in each line are of identical meaning.

[1] The following is the comparison of the notation in my *Formal Logic* with that used in my second and third papers in the *Cambridge Transactions*, and in this syllabus [see also § 57].

For $X))Y$, $X)Y$ and A,	For $X()Y$, XY and I,
For $X((Y$, $X(Y$ and A'	For $X)(Y$, xy and I'
For $X)\cdot(Y$, $X.Y$ and E,	For $X(\cdot(Y$, $X{:}Y$ *and* O,
For $X(\cdot)Y$, $x.y$ and E'	For $X)\cdot)Y$, $Y{:}X$ and O'
For $X)\circ)Y$, D, and $A, + O'$	For $X)\circ(Y$, C, and $E, + I'$
For $X\Vert Y$, D and $A, + A'$	For $X\vert\cdot\vert Y$, C and $E, + E'$
For $X(\circ(Y$, D' and $A' + O$,	For $X(\circ)Y$, C' and $E' + I$,

These comparative notations being fixed in the mind, any part of my *Formal Logic* may be read in illustration of the present work. And the *detailed character* (§ 64, note) of the latest notation is, if I may judge, so much of a facilitation, that any reader of the *Formal Logic* will find it easier to translate the notation as he goes on than to confine himself entirely to the notation of that work: and this especially as to the tests of validity and the assignment of the symbol of inference.

Universals				*Particulars*			
X))Y,	X)·(y,	x(·)Y,	x((y,	X(·(Y,	X()y,	x)(Y,	x)·)y
X)·(Y,	X))y,	x((Y,	x(·)y,	X()Y,	X(·(y,	x)·)Y,	x)(y
X(·)Y,	X((y,	x))Y,	x)·(y,	X)(Y,	X)·)y,	x(·(Y,	x()y
X((Y,	X(·)y,	x)·(Y,	x))y,	X)·)Y,	X)(y,	x()Y,	x(·(y

26. The rule of *contraversion*—changing a name into its contrary without altering the import of the proposition—is, Change also the *quantity* of the term, and the *quality* of the proposition. Thus *X))Y* is *X)·(y* and *x(·)Y*. When both names are contraverted, change both quantities, and preserve the quality: thus *X(·)Y* is *x)·(y*.[1]

27. The rule of *conversion*[2]—making the names change places, without altering the import of the proposition—is, Write or read the proposition backwards. Thus *X))Y* is *Y((X*; or *X))Y* may be read backwards, Some *Y*s are all *X*s. That is, make both the terms and their quantities change places.

28. Each universal is inconsistent with the universals of different qualities, and indifferent to the universal of different quantities. Thus *X))Y* is inconsistent with *X)·(Y* and *X(·)Y*, and neither affirms nor denies *X((Y*. Each universal affirms the particulars of the same quality, contradicts the particular of different quantities, and is indifferent to the particular of the same quantities. Thus *X))Y* affirms *X()Y* and *X)(Y*, contradicts *X(·(Y*, and neither affirms nor denies *X)·)Y*.

	Affirms		*Contradicts*	*Is inconsistent with*		*Neither affirms nor denies*	
))	()	)(	(·(	)·(	(·)	((	)·)
)·(	)·)	(·(	()	))	((	(·)	)(
(·)	(·(	)·)	)(	((	))	)·(	()
((	)(	()	)·)	(·)	)·(	))	(·(
	Is affirmed by		*Contradicts*	*Is neither affirmed nor denied by*			
(·(	)·(	(·)	))	((	)·)	()	)(
()	((	))	)·(	(·)	)(	(·(	)·)
)(	))	((	(·)	)·(	()	)·)	(·(
)·)	(·)	)·(	((	))	(·(	)(	()

29. Contrary names, in identical propositions, always appear with different quantities. We cannot speak of *some X*s without speaking about *all x*s; nor of *all X*s without speaking about *some x*s.

[1] [Double contraversion is called *contraposition.*]

[2] Writers on logic have nearly always meant by *conversion* merely the change of place in the terms, without change of place in the quantities. Accordingly, when the quantities are different, (common) logical conversion is illegitimate. Thus *X))Y* and *Y))X* are not the same: but *X()Y* and *Y()X* are the same. There is this difficulty in the way of using the word *conversion* in the sense proposed in the text: namely, that common logic has rooted it in common language that 'Every *X* is *Y*' is the converse (true or false as the case may be) of 'Every *Y* is *X*.' Leaving the common idioms for the student to do as he likes with, I shall, if I have occasion to speak of a proposition in which *terms* only are converted, and not *quantities*, call it a *term-converse*.

30. A particular proposition is *strengthened* into a universal which affirms it (and more, may be) by altering *one* of the quantities: thus)·) is affirmed in (·) and in)·(. Remember § 16.

31. In a universal proposition, if *one* term be partial, it has the amount, not the character, of the quantity of the other: if *both*, the quantities of the two terms together make up the whole universe, with the part common to both, if any, repeated twice.

32. In a particular proposition, the quantity of a partial term is vague, but remains the same through all forms. And when both terms are total, the partial quantity still remains expressed: as in *X*)(*Y*, or *Some things* are neither *X*s nor *Y*s; which some things are as many as the *x*s or *y*s in the equivalents *x*()*y*, *X*)·)*y*, and *x*(·(*Y*.

33. If a proposition containing *X* and *Y* be joined with a proposition containing *Y* and *Z*, a third proposition containing *X* and *Z* may necessarily follow. In this case the two first propositions (*premises*) and the proposition which follows from them (*conclusion*) form a *syllogism*.

34. If an *X* be a *Y*, if that same *Y* be a *Z*, then the *X* is the *Z*. This is the *unit-syllogism* from collections of which all the syllogisms of this mode of treating propositions must be formed. At first sight it seems as if there were another: if an *X* be a *Y*, if that same *Y* be not any *Z*, then the *X* is not any *Z*. But this comes under the first, as follows: the *X* is a *Y*, that *Y* is a *z*, therefore the *X* is a *z*, that is, is not any *Z*. The introduction of contraries brings all denials under assertions.

35. Two premises have a valid conclusion when, and only when, they necessarily contain unit-syllogisms; and the conclusion has one *item* of quantity for every unit-syllogism so necessarily contained.

36. And all syllogisms may be derived from the following combinations:—

)))) or *X*)) *Y Y*))*Z*, or All *X*s are *Y*s and all *Y*s are *Z*s. The conclusion is *X*))*Z*, All *X*s are *Z*s: there is the unit-syllogism, This *X* is a *Y*, that same *Y* is a *Z*, repeated as often as there are *X*s in existence in the universe. Or, *X*)) *Y*))*Z* gives *X*))*Z*, or)))) gives)).

())) or *X*() *Y Y*))*Z*, or Some *X*s are *Y*s, all *Y*s are *Z*s. The conclusion is *X*()*Z*, Some *X*s are *Z*s: there is the unit-syllogism so often as there are *X*s in the first premise. Or, *X*() *Y*))*Z* gives *X*()*Z*, or ())) gives ().[1]

((() or *X*((*Y Y*()*Z*, or Some *X*s are all *Y*s, some *Y*s are *Z*s. The conclusion is *X*()*Z*, Some *X*s are *Z*s: this case is, as to form, nothing but the last form inverted. Or, *X*((*Y*()*Z* gives *X*()*Z* or ((() gives ().

(( )) or *X*((*Y Y*))*Z* or Some *X*s are all *Y*s, All *Y*s are *Z*s. The conclusion is *X*()*Z*, Some *X*s are *Z*s, as many as there are *Y*s in the universe. Or, *X*((*Y*))*Z* gives *X*()*Z*, or (( )) gives (). But this case gives no stronger conclusion than ())) or than (((), though it has *both* premises universal.

[1] [So far as contained in contained—contained. Either contained of contained is contained, or—containing some—partient of each other.—MS. note.]

These are all the ways in which affirmative premises produce a conclusion in a manner which has no need to take cognizance of the existence of contrary terms. And since all negations are contained among affirmations about contraries, we may expect that application of these cases to all combinations of direct and contrary will produce all possible valid syllogisms.

37. Apply the form)))) to the eight varieties *XYZ*, *xYZ*, *xyZ*, *xyz*, *xYz*, *XYz*, *Xyz*, *XyZ*, and contravert *x*, *y*, *z*, whenever they appear. Thus)))) applied to *x y Z* is *x*))*y*))*Z*, or *X*((*Y* combined with *Y*(·)*Z* or *X*((*Y*(·)*Z* or (((·). The conclusion is *x*))*Z* or *X*(·)*Z*. That is, *X*((*Y*(·)*Z* gives *X*(·)*Z*; or, if some *X*s be all [make up all the] *Y*s, and everything be either *Y* or *Z*, then everything is either *X* or *Z*. This process applied to the eight varieties gives the following eight forms of *universal* syllogism, that is, *universal premises with universal conclusion.*

))))   (·)))   (((·)   (((((·))·(   )))·(   )·(((   )·((·)

Here are all the ways in which two *universals* give *different* quantities to the middle term.

38. Apply ( ))) to the eight varieties and we have eight *minor-particular* syllogisms, *particular conclusion with the* minor (or first) *premise particular.*

( )))   )·)))   )((·)   )(((   )·))·(( ))·((·((((·((·)

Here are all the ways in which a particular followed by a universal give *different* quantities to the middle term.

39. Apply ((( ), and we have eight *major-particular* syllogisms, *particular conclusion with the* major (or second) *premise particular.*

((( )   )·(( )   )))·)   )))(   )·((·((((·((·))((·))·)

Here are all the ways in which a universal followed by a particular gives *different* quantities to the middle term.

40. Apply (( )) and we have eight *strengthened particular* syllogisms, *universal premises with particular conclusion.*

(( ))   )·( ))   )) (·)   )) ((   )·( )·((( )·((·) (((·) (·)

Here are all the ways in which two universals give *the same* quantity to the middle term.

41. There are 64 possible combinations, of which the 32 enumerated give inference. The remaining 32 may be found by applying the eight varieties to ( ) ((,)) ( ), ( ))(and ( ) ( ): and in no case does any inference follow. Thus *X*( ) *Y* and *Y*((*Z* are consistent with any of the eight relations between *X* and *Z*, which should be ascertained by trial.

42. The test of validity and the rule of inference are as follows,—

There is inference 1. When both the premises are universal; 2. When, one premise only being particular, the middle term has different quantities in the two premises.

The conclusion is found by erasing the middle term and its quantities. Thus)·((·) gives)··) or)) (§ 21). That is 'No *X* is *Y*, and Everything is either *Y* or *Z*' gives 'Every *X* is *Z*'.

43. Premises of *like* quality give an *affirmative* conclusion: of *different* quality, a *negative*. A universal conclusion can only follow from universals with the middle term differently quantified in the two. From two particular premises nothing can follow.

44. A particular premise having the *concluding* term strengthened, the conclusion is also strengthened, and the syllogism is converted into a universal: having the *middle* term strengthened, the conclusion is not strengthened, and the syllogism is converted into a strengthened particular syllogism. Thus if ())), with conclusion (), have the premise () strengthened into)), the syllogism becomes)))) and yields)). But if () be strengthened into ((, the syllogism becomes (( )) and yields only (), as before.

45. A universal conclusion affirms two particulars: if either of these be substituted in the conclusion of the universal syllogism, the syllogism may be called a universal of weakened conclusion or a *weakened universal*. Thus *X*)) *Y*))*Z*, made to yield only *X*()*Z* or *X*)(*Z*, instead of *X*))*Z*, is a universal of weakened conclusion. No further notice need be taken of this case [except as in § 49].

46. Of the 24 syllogisms of particular conclusion, the conclusions are equally divided among (),)(,)·), and (·(. The following table is one of many modes of arrangement of the whole.

Premises	*Strengthened Particular*	*Minor/Major Particular*	*Universal*	*Major/Minor Particular*	*Strengthened Particular*
Affirmative	(( ))	())) ((()	)))) ((((	)))( )(((	)) ((
Negative	(·) (·)	(·((·) (·))·)	)·((·) (·))·(	)·((·( )·))·(	)·( )·(
Affirmative Minor	(( )·(	())·((((·(	)))·((((·)	)))·))((·)	)) (·)
Affirmative Major	(·) ((	(·((((·))(	)·((((·)))	)·(())·)))	)·( ))

The middle column contains the universals: and each universal stands horizontally between the two particulars into which it may be weakened, by weakening one of the concluding terms. And each strengthened particular stands vertically between the two particulars from which it may be formed by altering the quantity of the middle term in the particular premise only.

47. If two propositions give a third, say *A* and *B* give *C*; then, *a*, *b*, *c*, meaning the contrary propositions of *A*, *B*, *C*, it follows that *A*, *B*, *c*, cannot all be true together. Hence if *A*, *c*, be true, *B* must be false, or *b* true: that is, if *A*, *B*, give *C*, then *A*, *c*, give *b*. Or, either premise joined with the contrary of the conclusion, gives the contrary of the other premise. And thus each form of syllogism has two *opponent forms*. But the order of terms will not be correct, unless the premise which is retained be converted. If the order of the terms in the syllogism be *XY YZ XZ*, we shall have in one opponent *XY XZ YZ*, which in our mode of arrangement must be *YX XZ YZ*, the retained premise changing the order of its terms.

Thus the opponent forms of)·))), which gives)·), are as follows. First, (·(, retained premise converted; ((, contrary of conclusion; (·(, contrary of other premise; giving (·(((and conclusion (·(. Secondly, ((, contrary of conclusion; ((, retained premise converted; ((, contrary of other premise; giving ((((and conclusion ((.

48. The universal and particular syllogisms can be grouped by threes, each one of any three having the other two for its opponents. And these groups can be collected in the following *zodiac*, as it may be called.

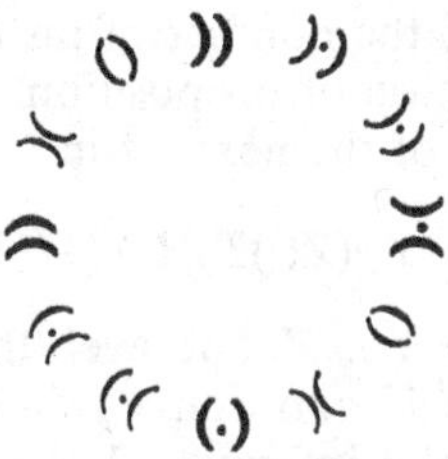

The universal propositions at the cardinal points are so placed that any two contiguous give a universal syllogism, whether read forwards or backwards, as)·(((,)))·(. Join each of these universals with its contiguous external particular, so as to read in a contrary direction to that in which the two universals were read, and a triad is formed each member of which has the other two members for its opponent forms. As in

)·((( )·() ())); or as in (·))))((((·))(.

49. The strengthened particulars have weakened universals (§ 45) for their opponent forms. Thus (( )) with the conclusion () has)))·(with the conclusion (·(and)·(((with the conclusion)·), for its opponents. And ((((with the conclusion () has)))·(with the conclusion).) and)·( ))) with the conclusion)·) for its opponents.

50. The partial terms of the conclusion take quantity in the following manner,—

In universal syllogisms. If one term of the conclusion be partial, its quantity is that of the other term: if both, one has at least the quantity of the whole middle term, and the other of the whole contrary of the middle term.

51. *In fundamental particular syllogisms.* The partial term or terms of the conclusion take quantity from the particular premise.

52. *In strengthened particular syllogisms.* The partial term or terms take quantity from the whole middle term or its whole contrary, according to which is universal in both of the premises.

53. These rules run through every form of the conclusion in which there is a particular term. Thus X)) Y))Z gives

1. X))Z in which Z has the quantity of X
2. x((z in which x has the quantity of z
3. x(·)Z, xs as many as ys, and Zs as many as Ys

Again, X(·) Y)(Z gives X(·(Z, X()z, and x)·)z, in which the quantities of X(and of)z are the number of instances in the 'some things' of Y)(Z.

Thirdly, X)·(Y)·(Z gives X)(Z, x(·(Z, x()z, and X)·)z, in which the quantities of x(and)z are the number of instances in Y.

54. A *sorites* is a collection of propositions in which the major term of each is the minor term of the next, as in

X)) Y)·(Z(·)T)) U)·(V((W

or All Xs are Ys, and No Y is Z, and everything is either Z or T, and every T is U, and No U is V, and Some Vs are all Ws.

55. A sorites gives a valid inference, 1. *Universal,* when all the premises are universal, and each intermediate term enters once totally and once partially; 2. *Particular,* when *one* (and one only) of the two conditions just named is broken *once*, whether by contiguous universals having an intermediate of one quantity in both, or by occurrence of *one* particular without breach of the rule of quantity.

56. The inference is obtained by erasing all the intermediate terms and their quantities, and allowing an even number of dots to indicate affirmation, and an odd number of dots to indicate negation.

Thus X)) Y)·(Z()T)·(U(·)V)) W gives X)·) W
X(·) Y((Z((T(·)U)·(V((W gives X(·(W
X((Y(·)Z)·(T(·)U)·(V gives X((V

57. We have seen that each universal may coexist with either the universal of altered quantities or with its contrary: which is a species of

terminal ambiguity. Thus X))Y may have either X((Y or X)·)Y true at the same time. All these coexistences may be arranged and symbolized as follows; giving propositions which, with reference to the ambiguity aforesaid, have *terminal precision*.

1.	X)∘)Y or both X))Y and X)·)Y	All Xs and some things besides are Ys
2.	X‖Y or both X))Y and X((Y	All Xs are Ys, and all Ys are Xs
3.	X(∘(Y or both X((Y and X(·(Y	Among Xs are all the Ys and some things besides
4.	X)∘(Y or both X)·(Y and X)(Y	Nothing *both* X and Y and some things *neither*
5.	X|·|Y or both X)·(Y and X()Y	Nothing both X and Y and every thing one or the other
6.	X(∘)Y or both X(·)Y and X()Y	Every thing either X or Y and some things both.

58. If any two be joined, each of which is 1, 3, 4, or 6, with the middle term of different quantities, these premises yield a conclusion of the same kind, obtained by erasing the symbols of the middle term and one of the symbols {°}. Thus X)∘(Y(∘)Z gives X)∘)Z: or if nothing be both X and Y and some things neither, and if every thing be either Y or Z and some things both, it follows that all Xs and *two lots* of other things are Zs.

59. In any one of these syllogisms, it follows that ‖ may be written for)∘) or (∘(in one place, or |·| for either)∘(or (∘) in one place, without any alteration of the conclusion, except reducing the *two lots* to one. But if this be done in both places, the conclusion is reduced to ‖ or |·|, and *both lots* disappear. Let the reader examine for himself the cases in which one of the premises is cut down to a simple universal.

60. The rules of contraversion remain unaltered: thus X(∘)Y)∘(Z is the same as X(∘(*y*(∘(Z &c.

61. The following exercises will exemplify what precedes. Letters written under one another are names of the same object. Here is a universe of 12 instances of which 3 are Xs and the remainder Ps; 5 are Ys and the remainder Qs; 7 are Zs and the remainder Rs.

X	X	X	P	P	P	P	P	P	P	P	P
Y	Y	Y	Y	Y	Q	Q	Q	Q	Q	Q	Q
Z	Z	Z	Z	Z	Z	Z	R	R	R	R	R

We can thus verify the eight complex syllogisms

X)∘)Y)∘)Z	P(∘)Y)∘)Z	P(∘(Q(∘)Z	P(∘(Q(∘(R
P(∘)Y)∘(R	X)∘)Y)∘(R	X)∘(Q(∘(R	X)∘(Q(∘)Z

In every case it will be seen that the two lots in the middle form the quantity of the particular proposition of the conclusion.[1]

62. The contraries of the complex propositions are as follows:

<table>
<tr><td></td><td></td><td>*Contraries*</td><td></td></tr>
<tr><td>*X*)∘)*Y*</td><td>Both *X*))*Y* and *X*)·)*Y*</td><td>*X*(·(*Y* or *X*((*Y* or both</td><td>*X*(,(*Y*</td></tr>
<tr><td>*X*||*Y*</td><td>—— *X*))*Y* — *X*((*Y*</td><td>*X*(·(*Y* - *X*)·)*Y* ——</td><td>*X*¦·¦*Y*</td></tr>
<tr><td>*X*(∘(*Y*</td><td>—— *X*((*Y* — *X*(·(*Y*</td><td>*X*)·)*Y* - *X*))*Y* ——</td><td>*X*),)*Y*</td></tr>
<tr><td>*X*)∘(*Y*</td><td>—— *X*)·(*Y* — *X*)(*Y*</td><td>*X*()*Y* - *X*(·)*Y* ——</td><td>*X*(,)*Y*</td></tr>
<tr><td>*X*|·|*Y*</td><td>—— *X*)·(*Y* — *X*(·)*Y*</td><td>*X*()*Y* - *X*)(*Y* ——</td><td>*X*¦¦*Y*</td></tr>
<tr><td>*X*(∘)*Y*</td><td>—— *X*(·)*Y* — *X*()*Y*</td><td>*X*)(*Y* - *X*)·(*Y* ——</td><td>*X*),(*Y*</td></tr>
</table>

63. The propositions hitherto enunciated are *cumular*: each one is a *collection* of individual propositions, or of propositions about individuals; *X*))*Y* is '*All X*s are some *Y*s'. This proposition is an aggregate of *singular* propositions [—the first *X* is a *Y*; the second *X* is a *Y*; etc.].

64. There is a choice between this *cumular* mode of [expression][2] and one which may[3] be called *exemplar*; in which each proposition is the

[1] [Let |∘| denote the combination of)(() (·( )·)
Just as || denotes ,, ,, ,,)) ((())(
And as |·| ,, ,, ,, ,, (·))·((·( )·).

Here |∘| means the utmost coexistence of the eight, which does not include either of the others; for (((·(())(includes (°(, etc.

We may make |∘| a *premise*, but it never appears in *conclusion*. Thus

)∘) |∘| gives)·))(, but not necessarily (·(().

In fact)∘) |∘| gives no more than)) |∘|; and this no more than))/)·))(, the combination of)))·) and)))(.—MS note, 27 February 1861.]

[2] [*Cumular* is meant to imply *distribution*. Only the *expression* is *cumular*.]

[3] The late Sir William Hamilton entertained the idea of completing the system of enunciation by making the words *all* (or when grammatically necessary, *any*) and *some* do every kind of duty. He thus put forward, as *the* system, the following collection:—

Affirmative		*Negative*	
1. All *X* is all *Y*	——	5. Any *X* is not any *Y*	*X*)·(*Y*
2. All *X* is some *Y*	*X*))*Y*	6. Any *X* is not some *Y*	*X*)·)*Y*
3. Some *X* is all *Y*	*X*((*Y*	7. Some *X* is not any *Y*	*X*(·(*Y*
4. Some *X* is some *Y*	*X*()*Y*	8. Some *X* is not some *Y*	——

Of the two propositions which are not in the common system (1 and 8) the first (§ 14, note) is *X*||*Y*, compounded of *X*))*Y* and *X*((*Y*: it is contradicted by *X*(·(*Y* and *X*)·)*Y*, either or both. The second (8) is true in all cases in which either *X* or *Y* has two or more instances in existence: its contrary is '*X* and *Y* are singular and identical; there is but one *X*, there is but one *Y*, and *X* is *Y*'. A system of propositions which mixes the simple and the complex, which compounds two of its own set to make a third in one case and one only, § 57, and which offers an assertion and denial which cannot be contradicted *in the system*, seems to me to carry its own condemnation written on its own forehead. From this system I was led to the exemplar system in the text. For Sir W. Hamilton's defence of his own views, and objections to mine, see his *Discussions on Philosophy*, &c. Appendix B. In making this reference, however, it is due to myself to warn the reader who has not access to the paper criticized

premise of a *unit-syllogism*: as 'this *X* is one *Y*', 'this *X* is not any *Y*'. The distinction is seen in '*All* men are animals' and '*Every* man is *an* animal', propositions of the same import, of which the first sums up, the second tells off instance by instance. In the second, *every* is synonymous with *each* and with *any*.

65. *Quantity* is now replaced by *mode of selection*. There is *unlimited selection*, expressed by the word *any one*: *vaguely limited* selection, expressed by *some one*. When we say *some one* we mean that we do not know it may be *any one*.

66. Let *X*) and (*X* now mean *any one X*: let)*X* and *X*(mean *some one X*.

67. The propositions are as follows: the first of each pair being a universal, the second its contrary particular.[1]

[1] [

Extension

In reading *X*)·(*Y*, there is no necessity to appeal directly to the idea of the universe; and the reading is most easily practicable without it.

No individual of *X* is an individual of *Y*.
There is no part of *extension* common to *X* and *Y*.

We can make a class of any individuals we please. We can imagine a quality by which to describe the class. Any individuals, however capriciously joined, are *logically* a class, let them be ontologically an unassimilating medley.

Intension

In reading *X*(·)*Y*, the usage of thought puts difficulty in the way of doing without the idea of appeal to the notion of the universe. Whereon we say:

No quality of *X* is a quality of *Y*.
There is no part of *intension* common to *X* and *Y*; we have not usage enough.

We do not see a correlative of the extensive reading 'Everything is either *X* or *Y*'. We must learn to imagine and dwell on the intensive right which corresponds to the extensive right. If any individuals may be constituted a class, then any individuals may be the exclusive possessors of a quality.

When we examine an instance, we begin to see that the exclusion of universal quality, made as explicitly as the exclusion of universal class, allows the intensive

that Sir W. Hamilton did not read with sufficient attention, partly no doubt from ill health. The consequence is that I must not be held answerable for all that is represented by him as coming from me. For example, speaking of my Table of exemplar propositions, he says 'And mark in what terms it [the table of exemplars] is ushered in:—as "*a system*. . . ." Nay, so lucid does it seem to its inventor, that, after the notation is detailed, we are told that it "*needs no explanation*".' The paragraph here criticized had *two* notations, one of which I called the *detailed* notation, because there is more *detail* in it than in the other: the other is the *old* notation, augmented. The first had been sufficiently explained in what preceded; the second was, as to the augmentations, new to the reader. Accordingly, the table being finished, I proceeded thus 'The detailed notation needs no explanation. The form given to the old notation may be explained thus . . .' Sir W. Hamilton represented me as saying that after the notation [all the notation, I suppose] is detailed, it [table or notation, I know not which] needs no explanation. I select this small point as one that can be briefly dealt with: there are many more, which I shall probably never notice, unless it be one at a time as occasion of illustration arises. A very decisive case is exposed in the postscript of my third paper in the *Cambridge Transactions* [p. 142 f.].

Exemplar form	*[Corresponding] Cumular form*
$X)(Y$ Any one X is any one Y	X and Y singular and identical
$X(\cdot)Y$ Some one X is not some one Y	Either X not singular, or Y not singular; or if both singular, not identical
$X))Y$ Any one X is some one Y	All Xs are some Ys
$X(\cdot(Y$ Some one X is not any one Y	Some Xs are not (all) Ys
$X((Y$ Some one X is any one Y	Some Xs are all Ys
$X)\cdot)Y$ Any one X is not some one Y	All Xs are not some Ys
$X)\cdot(Y$ Any one X is not any one Y	All Xs are not (all) Ys
$X()Y$ Some one X is some one Y	Some Xs are some Ys.

Six of the forms of this exemplar system are identical with six of the forms of the cumular system. And these six forms are the forms of the old logic, if we take care always to read $X((Y$ and $X)\cdot)Y$ backwards, and to count $X)\cdot(Y$ and $X()Y$ as each a pair of propositions, by distinguishing the reading forwards from the reading backwards.

68. The two new forms of the exemplar system (the first and second above) come under the same symbols as the two new forms of the cumular system, $(\cdot)$ and $)($: but the meanings are widely different. Both systems contain every possible combination of quantities, [the one of quantities, the other of selections] as well in universal as in particular propositions.

69. If the above propositions be applied to contraries, we have a more extensive system of propositions. I shall not enter on this enlargement, because the peculiar proposition of this system, $X)(Y$, is of infrequent[1] use in thought as connected with the consideration of X and Y in opposition to their contraries.

[1] All necessary laws of thought are part of the subject of logic: but a small syllabus cannot contain everything. The rejection *from logic*, and the rejection from a *book of logic*, are two very different things. It has not been uncommon to repudiate rare and unusual forms from the science itself, by calling them subtleties, or the like. This (§ 73) is not reasonable: but as to the contents of a work, especially of a syllabus, the time must come at which any one who asks for more must be answered by

Cum tibi sufficiant cyathi, cur dolia quaeris?

reading above to enter with as much clearness as our exclusion of the universal quality, and assumed power of giving *common quality* to any selection of individuals. In the universe property, for instance, 'no quality of real property is any quality of personal property'! What! not transmissibility by will? No—for this is a quality of property *qua* property, a universal quality: and is excluded in thought.

Again, $X)(Y$, Some things want either some qualities of X, or some qualities of Y; is, Some qualities of X are some qualities of Y. Here, X and Y being coinadequate, we can make classes containing both, and not universal: and these classes give common qualities.—7 February 1861.]

70. To make a syllogism of valid inference, it is enough that there be at least one unlimited selection of the middle term, and at least one affirmative proposition. And the inference is obtained by dropping all the symbols of the middle term. Thus *X*((*Y*(·)*Z* shows premises which give the conclusion *X*(·)*Z*: or 'Some one *X* is any one *Y* and Some one *Y* is not some one *Z*' giving 'Some one *X* is not some one *Z*'.

71. There are 36 valid[1] forms of syllogism, as follows, reading each symbol both backwards and forwards, but not counting it twice when it reads backwards and forwards the same, as in)( )(, (( )).

Fifteen in which)(is joined with itself or another,—

)( )(   )( ))   )(((   )( )·(   )( )·)   )((·(   )(()   )((·)

Fifteen in which the syllogism is but an exemplar reading of a cumular syllogism,—

))))   ()))   (( ))   )))·((( )·(())·(   )))·)   )·)))

Six which give the conclusion (·),—

(((·)   (( )·)   ())·)

72. The exemplar proposition is not unknown. It is of very frequent use in complete demonstration. When Euclid proves that Every triangle has angles together equal to two right angles, he selects, or allows his reader to select, a triangle, and shows that *any triangle* has angles equal to two right angles: and the force of demonstration is for those who can

[1] If Sir William Hamilton's system be taken, there are also 36 valid forms of syllogism, the same as in the text: but the law of inference is slightly modified, as follows. When both* the middle spiculae turn one way, as in)) and ((, then any spicula of universal quantity which turns the other way must itself be turned, unless it be protected by a negative point. Thus)((), which in the exemplar system gives)), in the cumular system gives ().

Exemplar system	*Cumular system*
Any one *X* is any one *Y*	All *X*s are all *Y*s.
Some one *Y* is some one *Z*	Some *Y*s are some *Z*s.
Therefore Any one *X* is some one *Z*	Therefore *Some X*s are some *Z*s.

This distinction will afford useful study. The minor premise of the exemplar instance implies that there is but one *X* and one *Y*.

* [This criterion is too complex: it is absurd that I should never have seen it before: if Hamilton had understood me, he must have pointed it out. How can)) be accompanied by (unprotected by a negative symbol, except by entrance of)(? Accordingly, the exceptional case is thus included:—let the main rule never be interpreted to the prejudice of *X*)(*Y* being a mere substitution of *X* in place of *Y*.—MS. note, 1860.]

As another example:—I have, § 16, required that no term shall be introduced which fills the whole universe. In common logic, with an unlimited universe, there is really no name as extensive as the universe except *object of thought*. But it is otherwise in the limited universes which I suppose. A short and easy chapter on names as extensive as the universe might be needed in a full work on logic, but not in a syllabus.

see that the selection[1] is not limited by anything in the reasoning. The exemplar form of enunciation, then, is of at least as frequent use in purely deductive reasoning as any other; and is therefore fitly introduced even into a short syllabus. In any case it is a subject of logical consideration, as [expressing] an actual form of thought.

73. The following passage, written by Sir William Hamilton himself, should be quoted in every logical treatise: for it ought to be said, and cannot be said better. 'Whatever is operative in thought, must be taken into account, and consequently be overtly expressible in logic; for logic must be, as to be it professes, an unexclusive reflex of thought, and not merely an arbitrary selection—a series of elegant extracts—out of the forms of thinking. Whether the form that it exhibits as legitimate be stronger or weaker, be more or less frequently applied;—that, as a material and contingent consideration, is beyond its purview.'

74. The heads[2] of the numerically definite proposition and syllogism are as follows;—

Let u be the whole number of individuals in the universe. Let x, y, z, be the numbers of *X*s, *Y*s, and *Z*s. Then $u - x$, $u - y$, $u - z$ are the numbers of *x*s, *y*s, and *z*s.

75. Let mXY mean that m or more *X*s are *Y*s. Then mXy means that m or more *X*s are *y*s, or not *Y*s. And mYX and myX have the same meanings as mXY and mXy.

76. Let a proposition be called *spurious* when it must of necessity be true, by the constitution of the universe. Thus, in a universe of 100 instances, of which 70 are *X*s and 50 are *Y*s, the proposition 20 XY is spurious: for at least 20 *X*s must be *Y*s, and 20 XY cannot be denied, and need not be affirmed as that which might be denied.

77. Let every negative quantity be interpreted as 0: thus (6–10) XY means that *none or more* *X*s are *Y*s, a spurious proposition.

78. The quantification of the predicate is useless. To say that m*X*s are to be found among n*Y*s, is no more than is said in mXY. To say that m*X*s are not any one to be found among any lot of n*Y*s is a spurious proposition, unless $m + n$ be greater than both x and y, in which case

[1] The limitation of the selection by some detail of process is one of the errors against which the geometer has especially to guard. I remember an asserted trisection of the angle which I examined again and again and again, without being able to detect a single offence against Euclid's conditions. At last, in the details of a very complex construction, I found two requirements which were only [compossible (§ 14n.)] on the supposition of a certain triangle having its vertex upon the base. Now it happened that one of the angles at the base of this triangle was the very angle to be trisected: so that the author had indeed trisected *an* angle, but not *any* angle; he had most satisfactorily, and by no help but Euclid's geometry, divided the angle 0 into three equal parts, 0, 0, 0. A modification of his process would have been equally successful with 180°, which Euclid himself had trisected.

[2] On this subject I have given only heads of result, the demonstrations of which will be found in my *Formal Logic*.

it is merely equivalent to both of the following, $(\boldsymbol{m} + \boldsymbol{n} - \boldsymbol{y})\ Xy$, and $(\boldsymbol{m} + \boldsymbol{n} - \boldsymbol{x})\ Yx$, which are equivalent to each other.[1]

79. In $\boldsymbol{m}XY$, the spurious part, if any, is $(\boldsymbol{x} + \boldsymbol{y} - \boldsymbol{u})\ XY$; the part which is not spurious is $(\boldsymbol{m} + \boldsymbol{u} - \boldsymbol{x} - \boldsymbol{y})\ XY$. For each instance in the last there must be an x which is y. The following pairs of propositions are identical.

$$\boldsymbol{m}XY \text{ and } (\boldsymbol{m} + \boldsymbol{u} - \boldsymbol{x} - \boldsymbol{y})\ xy$$
$$\boldsymbol{m}Xy \text{ and } (\boldsymbol{m} + \boldsymbol{y} - \boldsymbol{x})\ xY$$
$$\boldsymbol{m}xY \text{ and } (\boldsymbol{m} + \boldsymbol{x} - \boldsymbol{y})\ Xy$$
$$\boldsymbol{m}xy \text{ and } (\boldsymbol{m} + \boldsymbol{x} + \boldsymbol{y} - \boldsymbol{u})\ XY\text{[2]}$$

80.

Identical propositions		*Their contraries*	
$\boldsymbol{m}XY$	$(\boldsymbol{m} + \boldsymbol{u} - \boldsymbol{x} - \boldsymbol{y})\ xy$	$(\boldsymbol{x} + 1 - \boldsymbol{m})\ Xy$	$(\boldsymbol{y} + 1 - \boldsymbol{m})\ xY$
$\boldsymbol{m}Xy$	$(\boldsymbol{m} + \boldsymbol{y} - \boldsymbol{x})\ xY$	$(\boldsymbol{x} + 1 - \boldsymbol{m})\ XY$	$(\boldsymbol{u} + 1 - \boldsymbol{y} - \boldsymbol{m})\ xy$
$\boldsymbol{m}xY$	$(\boldsymbol{m} + \boldsymbol{x} - \boldsymbol{y})\ Xy$	$(\boldsymbol{u} + 1 - \boldsymbol{x} - \boldsymbol{m})\ xy$	$(\boldsymbol{y} + 1 - \boldsymbol{m})\ XY$
$\boldsymbol{m}xy$	$(\boldsymbol{m} + \boldsymbol{x} + \boldsymbol{y} - \boldsymbol{u})\ XY$	$(\boldsymbol{u} + 1 - \boldsymbol{x} - \boldsymbol{m})\ xY$	$(\boldsymbol{u} + 1 - \boldsymbol{y} - \boldsymbol{m})\ Xy$

81. From $\boldsymbol{m}XY$ and $\boldsymbol{n}YZ$ we infer $(\boldsymbol{m} + \boldsymbol{n} - \boldsymbol{y})\ XZ$, or its equivalent $(\boldsymbol{m} + \boldsymbol{n} + \boldsymbol{u} - \boldsymbol{x} - \boldsymbol{y} - \boldsymbol{z})\ xz$. The four following forms include all the cases of syllogism: the first two columns show the premises, the second two the identical conclusions,—

$\boldsymbol{m}XY$	$\boldsymbol{n}YZ$	$(\boldsymbol{m} + \boldsymbol{n} - \boldsymbol{y})\ XZ$	$(\boldsymbol{m} + \boldsymbol{n} + \boldsymbol{u} - \boldsymbol{x} - \boldsymbol{y} - \boldsymbol{z})\ xz$
$\boldsymbol{m}Xy$	$\boldsymbol{n}YZ$	$(\boldsymbol{m} + \boldsymbol{n} - \boldsymbol{x})\ xZ$	$(\boldsymbol{m} + \boldsymbol{n} - \boldsymbol{z})\ Xz$
$\boldsymbol{m}XY$	$\boldsymbol{n}yZ$	$(\boldsymbol{m} + \boldsymbol{n} - \boldsymbol{z})\ Xz$	$(\boldsymbol{m} + \boldsymbol{n} - \boldsymbol{x})\ xZ$
$\boldsymbol{m}Xy$	$\boldsymbol{n}yZ$	$(\boldsymbol{m} + \boldsymbol{n} + \boldsymbol{y} - \boldsymbol{x} - \boldsymbol{z})\ xz$	$(\boldsymbol{m} + \boldsymbol{n} + \boldsymbol{y} - \boldsymbol{u})\ XZ$

82. When either of the concluding terms is changed into its contrary, the corresponding changes are made in the forms of inference. Thus to find the inference from $\boldsymbol{m}xy$ and $\boldsymbol{n}yz$, we must, in the fourth form, write x for X, z for Z, X for x, Z for z, $\boldsymbol{u} - \boldsymbol{x}$ for $\boldsymbol{x}$, and $\boldsymbol{u} - \boldsymbol{z}$ for $\boldsymbol{z}$.

83. A spurious premise gives a spurious conclusion: and premises neither of which is spurious may give a spurious conclusion. A proposition is only spurious as it is *known* to be spurious: hence when $\boldsymbol{u}, \boldsymbol{x}, \boldsymbol{y}, \boldsymbol{z}$ are not known, there are no spurious propositions.

84. Every proposition has two forms, one of names contrary to the other, both spurious, or neither. Whenever *X*()*Y* is true in a manner which, by the constitution of the universe, might have been false, then *x*()*y*, or *X*)(*Y* is also true in the same manner. The ordinary syllogism would have two such *contranominal* forms of one conclusion, and, properly speaking, *has* two such forms. When the conclusion is universal, we *know* it has them: for *X*))*Z* is *x*((*z*, *X*)·(*Z* is *x*(·)*z*, &c. These

[1] [Demonstration as in *Syllogism IV*, Appendix [p. 243).]

[2] [Universal Form of Transformation:

$$\boldsymbol{m}AB = \left\{\begin{matrix} \boldsymbol{m} + \text{contrary of } \textit{either} \\ - \text{ number of } \textit{the other} \end{matrix}\right\} ab$$

—MS. note.]

we may see to be the contranominal conclusions of the numerical syllogism. For $X))Y$ is $\mathbf{x}XY$, and $Y))Z$ is $\mathbf{y}YZ$, whence $(\mathbf{x}+\mathbf{y}-\mathbf{y})\ XZ$ and $(\mathbf{x}+\mathbf{y}-\mathbf{y}+\mathbf{u}-\mathbf{x}-\mathbf{z})xz$, or $\mathbf{x}XZ$, which is $X))Z$, and $(\mathbf{u}-\mathbf{z})\ xz$, which is $x((z$. Again, let $X()Y$ be $\mathbf{m}XY$, then, $Y))Z$ being $\mathbf{y}YZ$, we have $(\mathbf{m}+\mathbf{y}-\mathbf{y})XZ$, or $\mathbf{m}XZ$, and $(\mathbf{m}+\mathbf{u}-\mathbf{x}-\mathbf{z})\ xz$, its equivalent. If $\mathbf{x}$, $\mathbf{z}$, $\mathbf{u}$, be known, then if $\mathbf{m}XZ$ be any thing except what must be, we have $\mathbf{m}+\mathbf{u}>\mathbf{x}+\mathbf{z}$, and $(\mathbf{m}+\mathbf{u}-\mathbf{x}-\mathbf{z})\ xz$ is $x()z$ or $X)(Z$. As it is, $\mathbf{x}$, $\mathbf{y}$, $\mathbf{u}$, being unknown, we have $\mathbf{m}XZ$ certainly true, be it spurious or not, and we can say nothing of $(\mathbf{m}+\mathbf{u}-\mathbf{x}-\mathbf{z})\ xz$.

85. Syllogisms with numerically definite quantity rarely occur, if ever, in common thought. But syllogisms of *transposed* quantity occur, in which the number of instances of one term is the *whole* possible number of instances of another term. For example;—'For every Z there is an *X* which is *Y*; some Zs are not *Y*s'. Here we have $\mathbf{z}XY$ and $\mathbf{n}yZ$; whence $(\mathbf{z}+\mathbf{n}-\mathbf{z})\ Xz$ and $(\mathbf{z}+\mathbf{n}-\mathbf{x})\ xZ$. The first is $\mathbf{n}Xz$, a case of $X(\cdot(Z$; some *X*s are not Zs. Thus, 'For every man in the house there is a person who is aged; some of the men are not aged': it follows, and easily, that some persons in the house are not men; but not by any *common* form of syllogism.

86. Of terms in common use the only one which can give the syllogisms of this [part of the subject] is 'most'. As in

Most *Y*s are *X*s; most *Y*s are Zs; therefore some *X*s are Zs.

Most *Y*s are *X*s; most *Y*s are not Zs; therefore some *X*s are not Zs.

Most *Y*s are not *X*s; most *Y*s are not Zs; therefore some things are neither *X*s nor Zs.

87. Each one of our syllogisms may be stated in eight different ways, each premise and the conclusion admitting two different orders. Thus $X))Y$, $Y))Z$, giving $X))Z$ may be stated as $Y((X$, $Y))Z$, giving $Z((X$, or as $X))Y$, $Y))Z$, giving $Z((X$, &c. All the orders are as follows—

I	II	III	IV
XY YZ XZ	*XY ZY XZ*	*YX YZ XZ*	*YX ZY XZ*
YX ZY ZX	*XY ZY ZX*	*YX YZ ZX*	*XY YZ ZX*

88. Whenever there is a first and a second, let them be called *minor* and *major*. Write the premises so that the *minor* premise shall contain the *minor* term of the conclusion (though it has long been most common to write the major premise first), and we have

I	II	III	IV
XY YZ XZ	*XY ZY XZ*	*YX YZ XZ*	*YX ZY XZ*

These orders are called the four *figures*. Thus $X))Y$ $Y))Z$ giving $X))Z$ is stated in the first figure; $X))Y$ $Z((Y$ giving $X))Z$ is stated in the second figure: $Y((X$ $Y))Z$ giving $X))Z$ is stated in the third figure; $Y((X$ $Z((Y$ giving $X))Z$ is stated in the fourth figure.

89. The first figure may be called the figure of *direct transition*: the fourth, which is nothing but the first with a *converted conclusion*, the figure of *inverted transition*; the second, the figure of *reference to* (the middle term); the third, the figure of *reference from* (the middle term).

90. The first figure is the one which has been used in our symbols; and it is the most convenient. The distinction of figure is wholly useless in this tract, so far as we have yet gone: it becomes necessary when we take a wider view of the copula.

91. A *convertible* copula is one in which the copular relation exists between two names *both ways*: thus 'is fastened to,' 'is joined by a road with,' 'is equal to,' 'is in habit of conversation with,' &c. are *convertible* copulae. If '*X* is equal to *Y*' then '*Y* is equal to *X*' &c.

92. A *transitive*[1] copula is one in which the copular relation joins *X* with *Z* whenever it joins *X* with *Y* and *Y* with *Z*. Thus 'is fastened to' is usually understood as a transitive copula: '*X* is fastened to *Y*' and '*Y* is fastened to *Z*' give '*X* is fastened to *Z*'.

93. The junction of names by appurtenance to one object, the copula hitherto used, is both convertible and transitive: and from these qualities, *and from these alone*, it derives the whole of its functional power in syllogism. Any copula which is both transitive and convertible will give precisely the syllogisms[2] of our system, and no others: provided always that if contrary names be introduced, no instance of a name can, either directly or by transition, be joined by the copula with any instance of the contrary name. For example, let the copula be some transitive and convertible mode of joining or fastening together, whether of objects in

[1] All the copulae used in this syllabus are *transitive*. The intransitive copula cannot be treated without more extensive consideration of the combination of relations than I have now opportunity to give: a second part of this syllabus, or an augmented edition, may contain something on this subject. [Cf. *Syllogism II*, for the simple decomposition.]

[2] The logicians are aware that many cases exist in which inference about two terms by comparison with a third is not reducible to *their* syllogism. As '*A* equals *B*; *B* equals *C*; therefore *A* equals *C*.' This is not an instance of common syllogism: the premises are '*A is* an equal of *B*; *B is* an equal of *C*.' So far as common syllogism is concerned, that 'an equal of *B*' is as good for the argument as '*B*' is a *material* accident of the meaning of 'equal.' The logicians accordingly, to reduce this to a common syllogism, state the effect of composition of relation in a major premise, and declare that the case before them is an example of that composition in a minor premise. As in, *A* is *an equal of an equal* (of *C*): Every *equal of an equal* is an *equal*; therefore *A* is an *equal* of *C*. [$Y = (\phi X)$, $Y(= \phi X)$.] This I treat as a mere evasion. Among various sufficient answers this one is enough: *men do not think as above*. When $A = B$, $B = C$, is made to give $A = C$, the word *equals* is a *copula* in thought, and not a *notion attached to a predicate*. There are processes which are not those of common syllogism in the logician's major premise above: but waiving this, logic is an analysis of the form of thought, possible and actual, and the logician has no right to declare that other than the actual is actual [or that if the actual do not please his system, he may replace it by a possible].

space or notions in the mind, &c.: so that no *X* is ever joined with any *x*, &c. The following are two instances of syllogism.

X)) *Y*)·(*Z*. Every *X* is joined to a *Y*; no *Y* is joined to a *Z*; therefore no *X* is joined to a *Z*. For if any *X* were joined to a *Z*, that *Z* would be joined to an *X*, and that *X* to a *Y*, whence that *Z* would be joined to a *Y*, which no *Z* is.

X(·) *Y*)(*Z*. Everything is joined either to an *X* or to a *Y*; Some things are joined neither to *Y*s nor to *Z*s; therefore Some *X*s are not joined to *Z*s. For if every *X* were joined to a *Z*, then every thing being (by the first premise) joined either to an *X* or to a *Y*, is joined either to a *Z* or to a *Y*, which contradicts the second premise.

94. The convertibility of the copula renders the inference altogether independent of figure.

95. Let the copula be *inconvertible*, as in '*X* precedes *Y*' from which we cannot say that '*Y* precedes *X*'. We must now introduce the *converse relation* '*Y* follows *X*', and the conversion of a proposition requires the introduction of the *converse* copula.

96. This extension, *when contraries are also introduced*, is almost unknown in the common run of thought: but it may serve for exercise, and also to give an idea of one of those innumerable systems of relation with which thought unassisted by systematic[1] analysis would probably never become familiar.

97. Let any two names be connected by transitive converse relations,

[1] The uneducated acquire easy and accurate use of the very simplest cases of transformation of propositions and of syllogism. The educated, by a higher kind of practice, arrive at equally easy and accurate use of some more complicated cases: but not of all those which are treated in ordinary logic. Euclid may have been ignorant of the identity of 'Every *X* is *Y*' and 'Every not-*Y* is not-*X*,' for any thing that appears in his writings: he makes the one follow from the other by new proof each time. The followers of Aristotle worked Aristotle's syllogism into the habits of the educated world, giving, not indeed anything that demonstrably *could not* have been acquired without system, but much that very probably *would not*. The modern logician appeals to the existing state of thought in proof of the completeness of the ordinary system: he cannot see anything in an extension except what he calls a *subtlety*. In the same manner a country whose school of arithmetical teachers had never got beyond counting with pebbles would be able to bring powerful arguments against pen, ink, and paper, the Arabic numerals, and the decimal system. They would point to society at large getting on well enough with pebbles, and able to do all their work with such means: for it is an ascertained fact that all which is done by those to whom pebbles are the highest resource, is done either with pebbles or something inferior. I have long been of opinion that the reason why common logic is lightly thought of by the mass of the educated world is that the educated world has, in a rough way, arrived at some use of those higher developments of thought which that same common logic has never taken into its compass. Kant said that the study of a legitimate subtlety (necessary but infrequent law of thought) sharpens the intellect, but is of no practical use. Sharpen the intellect with it until it is familiar, and it will then become of practical use. A law of thought, a necessary part of the machinery of our minds, of *no practical use*! Whose fault is that?

for an example say *gives to* and *receives from* (understanding that when *X* gives to *Y* and *Y* gives to *Z*, *X* gives to *Z*) in the following way,—

> [No *X* gives to any *X*, either directly or transitively, &c.]
> No *X* gives to another *X*, either directly or transitively, &c.
> Every *X* either gives to a *Y* or receives from a *y*, but not both.
> Every *x* either gives to a *Y* or receives from a *y*, but not both.
> Every *X* which gives to a *Y*, receives from *no other Y*, &c.

The same of all combinations of names, as *Y* with *X* and *x*, &c.

98. The following are the propositions used, with their symbols; and in a corresponding way for any other copula which may be used,—

X)′)Y	Every *X* gives to a *Y*	X))′Y	Every *X* receives from a *Y*
X(′·(Y	Some *X*s give to no *Y*s	X(·(′Y	Some *X*s receive from no *Y*s
X)′·(Y	No *X* gives to a *Y*	X)·(′Y	No *X* receives from a *Y*
X(′)Y	Some *X*s give to *Y*s	X()′Y	Some *X*s receive from *Y*s
X(′·)Y	In every relation, something either gives to an *X* or receives from a *Y* (or both)	X(·)′Y	In every relation, something either receives from an *X* or gives to a *Y* (or both)
X)′(Y	In some relations, nothing gives to any *X* nor receives from any *Y*	X)(′Y	In some relations, nothing receives from any *X* nor gives to any *Y*
X(′(Y	Some *X*s give to all the *Y*s	X((′Y	Some *X*s receive from all *Y*s
X)′·)Y	All *X*s do not give to some *X*s	X)·)′Y	All *X*s do not receive from some *Y*s

99. Propositions are changed into others identical with them by this addition to the rule in § 26:—When one term is contraverted, the relation is also converted: when both, the relation remains. In the following lists the four in each line are identical,—

X)′)Y	X)·(′y	x(·)′Y	x(′(y	X(′·(Y	X()′y	x)(′Y	x)′·)y
X)′·(Y	X))′y	x((′Y	x(′·)y	X(′)Y	X(·(′y	x)·)′Y	x)′(y
X(′·)Y	X((′y	x))′Y	x)′·(y	X)′(Y	X)·)′y	x(·(′Y	x(′)y
X(′(Y	X(·)′y	x)·(′Y	x)′)y	X)′·)Y	X)(′y	x()′Y	x(′·(y

The relations may be converted throughout.

100. To prove an instance, how do we know that X)′)Y is identical with x(·)′Y? If every *X* give to a *Y*, the remaining *Y*s, if any, do not give to any *X*s, by the assigned conditions of meaning: consequently those remaining *Y*s receive from *x*s. As to *y*s, none of them can give to *X*s, for then they would give to *Y*s: therefore all receive from *x*s. Conversely, if x(·)′Y, no *X* can receive from *y*, for then neither could that *y* receive from *x*, nor could that *X* give to *Y*: so that there would be a relation in which neither does any thing give to *Y*, nor receive from *x*. Consequently, every *X* gives to *Y*.[1]

[1] [Or thus:—If there be any thing which neither receives from an *X*, nor gives to a *Y*, that thing both gives to an *X*, receives from a *Y*, and is the medium through which *Y* gives to *X*, and thence to *Y*, which is against the conditions.—MS. note.]

101. Let the *phases* of a figure depend on the quality of the premises in the following manner: + meaning *affirmative*, and – *negative*, remember the phases in the following order,—

$$++ \quad -+ \quad +- \quad --$$

102. For the four figures, let these four phases be the *first* or *primary* phases: thus + – is the primary phase of the third figure. To put the other phases in order, read backwards from the primary phases, and then forwards.

	1	2	3	4
Figure I.	+ +	– +	+ –	– –
—— II.	– +	+ +	+ –	– –
—— III.	+ –	– +	+ +	– –
—— IV.	– –	+ –	– +	+ +

Thus + – is the third phase of the second figure.

103. In the primary phases, the direct copula may be used throughout. When *one* premise departs from the primary phase in quality, the converse copula must be used in *the other*; when *both*, in the *conclusion*. This addition is all that is required in the treatment of the syllogism of inconvertible copula.

104. Thus,[1] the premises being $X)\cdot(Y\ Z))\,Y$, we have the primary phase of the second figure, whence $X)\cdot(Z$ with the direct copula. That is, if no X give to a Y, and every Z give to a Y, no X gives to a Z. For if any X gave to a Z, that Z giving to a Y, that X would give to a Y, which no X does. Now contravert the middle term, and we have $X))y$ $Z)\cdot(y$, the phase of the second figure in which both premises differ from the primary phase. Hence Every X gives y, No Z gives y, yields no X *is given by* Z. For if any X were given by Z, a y would be given by that Z, which is given by no Z. But 'no X *gives* Z' will not do.

105. The common system of syllogism, which being nearly complete in the writings of Aristotle may be called Aristotelian, is as much as may be collected out of the preceding system by the following modifications,—

1. The exclusion of all idea of a limited universe, of contrary names, and of the propositions (·) and)(. 2. The exclusion of all right to convert

[1] The reader may exercise himself in the formation of more examples. The use of such a development as the one before him is this. Every study of a generalization or extension gives additional power over the particular form by which the generalization is suggested. Nobody who has ever returned to quadratic equations after the study of equations of all degrees, or who has done the like, will deny my assertion that *οὐ βλέπει βλέπων* may be predicated of any one who studies a branch or a case, without afterwards making it part of a larger whole. Accordingly, it is always worth while to generalize, were it only to give power over the *particular*. This principle, of daily familiarity to the mathematician, is almost unknown to the logician.

a proposition, except when its two terms have like quantities, as in)·(and (). Thus *X*)) *Y* must not be read as 'Some *Y*s are all *X*s'. But *X*)) *Y* may undergo what is called the conversion *per accidens*: that is, *X*)) *Y* affirming *X*() *Y*, which is *Y*() *X*, *X*)) *Y* may be made to give *Y*() *X*. 3. The exclusion of every copula except the transitive and convertible copula. 4. The addition of the consideration of the identical pairs *X*)·(*Y* and *Y*)·(*X*, *X*() *Y* and *Y*() *X*, as perfectly distinct propositions. 5. The introduction of the distinction of figure. 6. The writing of the major and minor propositions first and second, instead of second and first: thus *X*)) *Y*))*Z* is written '*Y*))*Z*, *X*)) *Y*, whence *X*))*Z*'.

106. There are four forms of proposition: ***A***, or *X*)) *Y* or *Y*)) *X*, not identical; ***E***, or *X*)·(*Y* or *Y*)·(*X*, identical; ***I***, or *X*() *Y* or *Y*() *X*, identical; ***O***, or *X*(·(*Y* or *Y*(·(*X*, not identical.

107. There are four fundamental syllogisms in the first figure, each of which has an opponent in the second, and an opponent in the third. There are three fundamental syllogisms in the fourth figure, each of which has the other two for opponents. Altogether, fifteen *fundamental* syllogisms. There are three strengthened particular syllogisms, two in the third figure, and one in the fourth: and one weakened universal, in the fourth figure. In all, nineteen forms.

108. Every syllogism has a *word* attached to it, the vowels of which are those of its premises and conclusion. In the first figure the consonants are all unmeaning; in the other figures some of the consonants give direction as to the manner of converting into the first figure. Thus *K* denotes that the syllogism cannot be directly converted into the first figure, though its *opponent* in the first figure may be used to force its conclusion. *S* means that the premise whose vowel precedes is to be simply converted. *P*, which occurs in all the strengthened particulars and the weakened universal, means that the conversion *per accidens* is to be employed on the preceding member. *M* means that the premises must be transposed in order. Each syllogism converts into that syllogism of the first figure which has the same initial letter. *G* is an addition of my own, presently described; it must be left out when the old system is to be just represented. *R*, *N*, *T*, have no signification. The following are the names put together in memorial[1] verse.

[1] The best attainable exposition of logic in the older form, with modern criticism, is Mr Mansel's edition of Aldrich's compendium. Should a reader of this work desire more copious specimens of old discussion, he may perhaps succeed in obtaining Crackanthorpe's *Logicae Libri quinque* (4to, 1622 and 1677). Sanderson's Logic is highly scholastic in character. For a compendium of mediaeval logic, ethics, physics, and metaphysics, I have never found anything combining brevity and completeness at all to compare with the *Precepta Doctrinae Logicae*, *Ethicae*, &c. of John Stierius, of which seven or eight editions were published in the seventeenth century (from 1630 to 1689, or thereabouts) and several of them in London. There is a large system of the older logic in the *Institutiones Logicae* of Burgersdicius, and a great quantity

109. Barbara, Celagrent, Darii, Ferigoque prioris:
Cesareg, Camestres, Festinog, Baroko secundae:
Tertia Daraptgi, Disagmis, Datigsi, Felapton,
Bokardo, Ferison habet. Quarta insuper addit
Bramantigp, Camegnes, Dimarigs, Fegsapo, Fregsison.

110. I leave the verification of what has been said as an exercise. As an example of reduction into the first figure take the syllogism *Camestres* from the second figure.

	II. *Camestres*		reduced into	I. *Celarent.*	
A	Every Z is Y		(m)	No Y is X	*E*
E	No X is Y	(s)		Every Z is Y	*A*
E	No X is Z	(s)		No Z is X	*E*

111. The letter G indicates (§ 103) the member in which, when a transitive but not simply convertible copula is used, the copula is to be the converse of the copula employed in the other members. Thus Celagrent shows that the minor premise must have the converse copula. Suppose, for example, that the copulae are *gives to* (transitively understood) and *receives from*. Then 'No Y gives to an X; every Z receives from a Y' yield 'No Z gives to an X'. For if any X received from a Z, which (second premise) receives from a Y, that X would receive from a Y, which contradicts the first premise.

112. In the preceding articles I have considered hardly anything but mere assertion or denial of *concomitance*, of any sort or kind whatsoever. I now proceed to more specially subjective views of logic.

113. A *term* or *name* may be in one word or in many. It describes, pictures, represents, but does not assert nor deny. Its object must exist, whether in thought only, or in external nature as well: and everything which does not contradict the laws of thought may be the object of a term. But sometimes the thinker's universe will be the whole universe of thought; sometimes only the objective universe of external reality; sometimes only a part of one or the other.

114. Terms are used in four different senses. Two *objective*, directed towards the *external* object, or to use old phrases, of *first intention*, or representing *first notions*. Two *subjective*, directed towards the *internal* mind, of *second intention*, or representing *second notions*.

115. In objective use the name represents, 1. The *individual object*,

of the metaphysical discussion connected with the old logic in Brerewood *de Predicabilibus et Predicamentis*. As all these books were printed in England, there is more chance of getting them than the foreign logical works, which are very scarce in this country. For more than usual information on parts of the history of logical *quantity*, a subject now exciting much attention, see Mr Baynes's *New Analytic*, in which will be found much valuable history so completely forgotten that it is as new as if he had invented it himself.

unconnected with, and unaggregated with, any other object of the same name; 2. The *individual quality*, forming part of, and residing in, the individual object, [but thought of apart]. One name may, at different times, represent both: thus *animal*, the name of an object, is the name of a quality of *man*. In fact, quality is but object considered as *component* of another object. The quality *white*, a component of the notion of an ivory ball, is itself an object of thought.

116. The objective[1] uses of names have been considered as the bases of propositions and syllogisms, in the preceding part of this tract.

117. In subjective use the name represents, 1. A *class*, a collection of individual objects, named after a quality which is in thought as being in each one: 2. An *attribute*, the notion of quality as it exists in the mind to be given to a class. Attribute is to individual quality what class is to individual object. Between the notion of a class, and the notion of an object, though the name be the same in both cases, there is this distinction. The class-name belongs to a number of objects: the object belongs to a number of class-names; for it may be named after any one of its qualities. We have classes aggregated *of many objects*: and objects compounded *of many classes*. But in this second case the object is said to have many *qualities*. The class is a whole of one kind: the object is a whole of another kind. This distinction emerges the moment a name begins to be a *universal*, that is, belonging to more than one object.

118. *Class* and *attribute* are units of thought: a noun of multitude is not a multitude of nouns. When we are fortunate enough to get four distinct names, we readily apprehend all these distinctions. This happens in the case of our own species: the objects *men*, all having the quality *human*, give to the thought the class *mankind*, distinguished from other classes by the attribute *humanity*. Should any reader object to my account of the four uses of a name, he can, without rejection of anything else in what follows, substitute his own account of the four words *man*, *human*, *mankind*, *humanity*.

119. With grounds of classification, and reasons for nomenclature, logic has nothing to do. Any number of individuals, whether yet unclassed, or included in one class, or partly in one class and partly in

[1] The ordinary syllogism of the logicians, literally taken as laid down by them, is objective, of first intention, arithmetical. I call it the *logician's abacus*. When the educated man rejects its use, and laughs at the idea of introducing such *learned logic* into his daily life, I hold his refusal to be in most cases right, and his reason to be entirely wrong. He has, and his peers always have had, some command of the *subjective* syllogism, the combination of relations to which I shall come. He has no more occasion—in most cases—to have recourse to the logical abacus for his reasoning, than to the chequer-board, or arithmetical abacus, for adding up his bills. I hold the combination of relations to be the actual organ of reasoning of the world at large, and, as such, worthy of having its analysis made a part of advanced education; the logician's abacus being a fit and desirable occupation for childhood.

another, may be constituted a new class, in right of any quality seen in all, by which an attribute is affixed to the class in the mind.

120. The term *X*, or *Y*, or *Z* may and does denote, at one time or another, the individual, the quality, the class, or the attribute. Any one who finds the distinction useful might think of the individual *X*, the quality *X*-ic, the class *X*-kind, and the attribute *X*-ity.

121. Identical terms are those which apply to precisely the same objects of thought, neither representing more than the other: so that identical terms are different names of the same class. Thus, for this earth, *man* and *rational animal* are identical terms. The symbol $X||Y$ will be used (§ 57) to represent that *X* and *Y* are identical. When of two identical terms one, the known, is used to explain the other, the unknown, the first is called the *definition* of the second.

122. The whole extent of matter of thought under consideration I call the *universe*. In common logic, hitherto, the universe has always been the whole universe of possible thought.

123. Every term which is used (§ 16) divides the *universe* into two classes; one within the term, the other without. These I call *contraries*: and I denote the contrary class of *X*, the class not-*X*, by *x*. When the universe is unlimited contrary names are of little effective use; not-man, a class containing every thing except man, whether seen or thought, is almost useless. It is otherwise in a limited universe, in which contraries, by separate definiteness of meaning, cease to be mere negations each of the other, and even [become separately[1]] positive names. Thus, the universe being property under English law, *real* and *personal* are contrary classes. Logic has nothing to do with the difficulties of allotment which take place near the boundary: with the decision upon those personals, for example, which, as the lawyer says, *savour of the realty*. The lawyer must determine the classification, and logic [studies the analysis and synthesis of] the laws of thought which then apply. If the lawyer choose to make an intermediate class, between real and personal, then real and personal are no longer logical contraries.

That *X* and *Y* are contrary classes is denoted (§ 57) by $X|\cdot|Y$.

124. Terms may be formed[2] from other terms,—

i. By *aggregation*, when the complex term stands for everything to

[1] The most amusing instance which ever came within my own knowledge is as follows. A friend of mine, in the days of the Irish Church Bill, used to discuss politics with his butcher: one day he alluded to the possible fate of the Establishment. 'Do you mean do away with the church?' asked the butcher. 'Yes,' said my friend, 'that is what they say'. 'Why, sir, how can that be?' was the answer; 'don't you see, sir, that if they destroy the church, we shall all have to be *dissenters*!'

[2] The reader must carefully remember that we are now engaged (§ 4) especially upon the *esse quod habent in anima*: and, if not accustomed to middle Latin, he must remember also that *esse* is made a substantive, *mode of being*. *Animal* cannot be divided into *man* and *brute* except *in a mind*. Logical composition must be distinguished from physical or metaphysical. Light [we suppose] always consisted of the

which *any one or more* of the simple terms applies. Thus *animal* is the *aggregate* of (the *aggregants*) *man* and *brute*.

ii. By *composition*, when the complex term stands but for everything to which *all* the simple terms apply. Thus *man* is *compounded* of (the *components*) *animal* and *rational*.

iii. By mixture of these two methods of formation.

125. The aggregate of *X*, *Y*, *Z* will be represented by (*X*, *Y*, *Z*): the term compounded of *X*, *Y*, *Z* will be represented by (*X*-*Y*-*Z*) or (*XYZ*).

126. The aggregate name belongs to each of the aggregants: but the compound name does not belong to each of the components, necessarily.

127. An aggregate is not impossible if either of its aggregants be impossible, or if two of them be contradictory: but a compound is impossible in either of these cases.

128. In these and all other formulae, care must be taken to remember that *the logical phrase implies nothing*: the phrases of ordinary conversation frequently *imply*, in addition to what they *express*. Thus 'some living men breathe' and 'every man is either animal or mineral' are colloquially false by what they imply, but logically true because the logical use implies nothing.

129. A class may be compounded of classes, as well as aggregated: thus the class *marine* is compounded of the classes *soldier* and *sailor*. An attribute may be aggregated of attributes, as well as compounded: thus Adam Smith's attribute *productive* is aggregated of land-tilling, manufacturing, &c. But composition of classes and aggregation of attributes are infrequent. Any name may be thought of either as a class, or an attribute (or *character*, as it is often called): and it is usual and convenient to think of class when aggregation is in question, and of attribute when composition is in question. So we rather say the *marine* unites the *characters* of the *soldier* and the *sailor*: the *productive* classes (as Adam Smith said) consist of farmers, manufacturers, &c. But all this for convenience, not of necessity: and the power of unlearning usual habits must be acquired. All modes of thought should be considered: the usual, because they are usual; the unusual, that they may become usual.

130. The words of aggregation are *either*, *or* [*or* both]: of composition, *both*, *and*. Thus (*X*, *Y*) is either *X* or *Y* (or both); (*XY*) is both *X* and *Y*.

131. The more classes aggregated, so long as each class has something

prismatic components; but, before Newton, it was not a logical quality of light that it is to be conceived as decomposible. Accordingly, a compound of qualities, though it may constitute a full distinctive *definition* of an object of thought, can never be accepted as a full *description*: there may be many more. The logician therefore must, in thinking of a compound, imitate the genial Dean Aldrich, the author of the *Compendium* of Logic to which so many have been indebted, in the structure of his fifth reason for drinking.

not contained in any of the others, the greater the *extension*[1] of the aggregate term. The more attributes compounded, so long as each attribute has some component not contained in the others, the greater the *intension*. *Animal* has more extension than *man*: *man* has more intension than *animal*.

132. The name of greatest extension, and of least intension, of which we speak, is the universe.

133. The contrary of an aggregate is the compound of the contraries of the aggregants: either one of the two X, Y, or both not-X and not-Y; either (X, Y) or (xy). The contrary of a compound is the aggregate of the contraries of the components; either both X and Y, or one of the two, not-X and not-Y; either (XY), or (x, y).

134. The following are exercises on complex terms,—

'Both or neither' and 'one or the other, not both', are contraries. That is (XY, xy) and (Xy, Yx) are contraries. Now the contrary of the first is (x, y)-(X, Y), which is (xX, xY, yX, yY), which is (xY, yX) since xX, yY, are impossible.

$X\|\|(A, B)\,C$	gives $x\|\|(ab, c)$	$X\|\|A, B\,(C, D)$	gives $x\|\|a\,(b, cd)$
$X\|\|(A, B)\,(C,D)$	— $x\|\|(ab, cd)$	$X\|\|(A, BC)\,(D, EF)$	— $x\|\|(ab, c), (de, f)$
$X\|\|AB, C$	— $x\|\|(a, b)\,c$	$X\|\|(A, B, aC)$	— $x\|\|abc$

Deduce these, and explain the last.

135. A term given in extension, as (A, B, C), has its contrary given in intension, (abc); and *vice versa*. Aggregates or components of either only enable us to deduce components or aggregates of the other.

136. A *proposition* is the presentation, for assertion or denial, of two names connected by a relation: as 'X in the relation L to Y.' A *judgment* is the sentence of the mind upon a proposition: certainly true, more or less probable, certainly false. Propositions without accompanying judgment hardly occur: so that *proposition* comes to mean, by abbreviation, *proposition accompanied by judgment*.

[1] The logicians have always spoken of 'all men' as constituting the 'extent' of the term *man*: thus the whole extent of *man* is part of the extent of *animal*. They have chosen that their more and less should be referred to by phrases derived rather from the notion of area than from that of number. Hence arise certain forms of speech which, when quantity is applied to the predicate, are not idiomatic; as 'All man is some animal'.

There are savage tribes which have not sufficient idea of number even for their own purposes: among them, when a dozen or more of men are to be indicated, an *area* sufficient to contain them is marked out on the ground. The speculative philosophers of the middle ages were in something like the same position: though the mercantile world was well accustomed to large numbers, the philosophical world, excepting only *some* of the mathematicians, was very awkward at high numeration. The works on theoretical arithmetic show this well. I have been straining my eye over the twelve books of the *Arithmetica Speculativa* of Gaspar Lax of Arragon (Paris, folio, 1515) to detect, if I could, a number higher than a hundred; and I have found only one, *the date* [which was more the printer's affair than the author's].

137. The distinction between certainty and probability is usually treated apart from logic, as a branch of mathematics. A few of the leading results, relative to authority and argument, will be afterwards given.

138. The purely formal proposition with judgment, wholly void of matter, is seen in 'There is the probability α that *X* is in the relation *L* to *Y*'. From the purely formal proposition no inference can follow. In all elementary logic, the terms are formal, the relation[1] material, and the judgment absolute assertion or denial (or, as a mathematician would say, the probabilities considered are only 1 and 0).

139. *Contrary* propositions are a pair of which one must be true and one false: as 'he did', 'he did not'; or as 'Every *X* is *Y*', 'Some *X*s are not *Y*s'. Contraries contradict[2] one another; but so do other propositions. Thus 'All men are strong' and 'all men are weak' contradict one another to the utmost: the second says there is not a particle of truth in the first. But the *contrary* merely says there is more or less falsehood: to 'all men are strong' the contrary is 'There are [man or] men who are not strong'.

140. Every proposition has its *contrary*: there is no assertion but has its denial: no denial but has its assertion. Every logical scheme of propositions must contain a denial for every assertion, and an assertion for every denial.

141. *Inference* is the production of one proposition as the necessary consequence of one or more other propositions. Inference from one proposition may be either an *equivalent* or *identical* proposition, or an *inclusion*. If from a first proposition we can infer a second, and if from the second proposition we can also infer the first, the two propositions are *logical equivalents* [as the words are understood]. Thus '*X* is the parent of *Y*' and '*Y* is the child of *X*' are logical equivalents: And also 'Every *X* is *Y*' and 'Every not-*Y* is not-*X*'. But from 'Every *X* is *Y*' we can infer 'Some *X*s are *Y*s', without being able to infer the first from the second: the second is only included in the first.

142. When inference is made from more than one proposition, the result is called a *conclusion*, and its antecedents *premises*.

[1] The logician calls 'Every man is animal' a material instance of the formal proposition 'Every *X* is *Y*'. He will admit no relation to be *formal* except what can be expressed by the word *is*: he declares all other relations *material*. Thus he will not consider '*X* equals *Y*' under any form except '*X is* an equal of *Y*'. He has a right to confine himself to any part he pleases: but he has no right, except the right of fallacy, to call that part the whole.

[2] In the usual nomenclature of logicians, what I call the contrary is called *the* contradictory, as if it were the only one. In common language, when two persons disagree, we say they are on *contrary* sides of the question: in the usual technical language of logic, this would mean that if one should say all men are strong the other says no man is strong. But in common language, the one who *maintains the contrary* is he who advocates *anything* which the other is opposed to.

143. Inference has nothing to do with the truth or falsehood of the antecedents, but only with the necessity of the consequence. When the inference from the antecedents is preceded by showing of their *truth*, the whole is called *proof* or *demonstration*.

144. *Deduction*, or *à priori* proof, is when the *compound* of the premises gives the conclusion. One false premise, and deduction wholly fails.

145. *Induction*, or *à posteriori* proof, is when the *aggregate* of the premises gives the conclusion. One false premise, and the induction partially fails.

146. *Absolute* or *mathematical* proof is when the conclusion is so established that any contradiction would be a contradiction of a *necessity*[1] of thought. [*Direct* and *indirect* proof.]

[1] Logic considers the *laws of action* of thought: mathematics applies these *laws* of thought to necessary *matter* of thought. That two straight lines cannot inclose a space is a necessary way of thinking, a proposition to which we must assent: but it is not a law of action of thought. That if two straight lines cannot inclose a space, it follows that two lines which do inclose a space are not both straight, is an example of a rule by which thought in action must be guided.

Mathematics are concerned with *necessary matter of thought*. Let the mind conceive every thing annihilated which it can conceive annihilated, and there will remain an infinite universe of space lasting through an eternity of duration: and space and time are the fundamental ideas of mathematics. Of course then the logicians, the students of the necessary *action* of thought, are in close intellectual amity with the mathematicians, the students of the necessary *matter* of thought. It may be so: but if so, they dissemble their love by kicking each other down stairs. In very great part, the followers of either study despise the other. The logicians are wise above mathematics; the mathematicians are wise above logic: of course with casual exceptions. Each party denies to the other the power of being useful in education: at least each party affirms its own study to be a sufficient substitute for the other. Posterity will look on these purblind conclusions with the smile of the educated landholder of our day, when he reads Squire Western's fears lest the sinking fund should be sent to Hanover to corrupt the English nation. A generation will arise in which the leaders of education will know the value of logic, the value of mathematics, the value of logic in mathematics, and the value of mathematics in logic. For the mind, as for the body, *Βίον πορίζου πάντοθεν πλὴν ἐκ κακῶν*.

This antipathy of necessary law and necessary matter is modern. Very many of the most illustrious names in the history of logic are the names of known mathematicians, especially those of the founders of systems, and the communicators from one language or nation to another. As Aristotle, Plato, Averroes (by report), Boethius, Albertus Magnus (by report), Ramus, Melancthon, Hobbes, Descartes, Leibnitz, Wolff, Kant, &c. Locke was a competent mathematician: Bacon was deficient, for the consequences of which see a review of the recent edition of his work in the *Athenaeum* for 11 and 18 September 1858. The two races which have founded the mathematics, those of the Sanscrit and Greek languages, have been the two which have independently formed systems of logic.

England is the country in which the antipathy has developed itself in greatest force. Modern Oxford declared against mathematics almost to this day, and even now affords but little encouragement: modern Cambridge to this day declares against logic. These learned institutions are no fools, whence it may be surmised that possibly they would be wiser if they were brayed in a mortar; certainly, if both were placed in the same mortar, and pounded together.

147. *Moral* proof is when the conclusion is so established that any contradiction would be of that high degree of improbability which we never look to see upset in ordinary life. Among the most remarkable of moral proofs is that common case of induction in which the aggregants are innumerable, and the conclusion being proved as to very many, without a single failure, the mind feels confident that all the unexamined aggregants are as true as those which have been examined. This is *probable induction*: often confounded with *logical induction*.

148. A proof may be mixed: it may be *deduction* of which some components are *inductively* proved: it may be *induction*, of which some aggregants are *deductively* proved.

149. Failure of proof is not proof of the contrary.

150. If any number of premises give a conclusion, denial of the conclusion is denial of one or more of the premises. If all but one of the premises be affirmed and the conclusion denied, that one premise must be denied. These two processes, conclusion from premises, and denial of one premise by denying the conclusion and affirming all the other premises, may be called *opponents* [contrapositives, really].

151. *Repugnant alternatives* are propositions of which one must be true, and one only. If there be two sets of repugnant alternatives, of the same number of propositions in each, and if each of the first set give its own one of the second set for its necessary consequence, then each of the second set also gives its own one of the first set as a necessary consequence. Thus if *A*, *B*, *C*, be repugnant alternatives, and also *P*, *Q*, *R*, and if *P* be the necessary consequence of *A*, *Q* of *B*, *R* of *C*, then *A* is the necessary consequence of *P*, *B* of *Q*, *C* of *R*. If *P* be true, neither *B* nor *C* can be true; for then *Q* or *R* would be true, which cannot be with *P*. But one of the three *A*, *B*, *C*, must be true: therefore *A* is true. And similarly for the other cases.

152. A relation is a mode of thinking two objects of thought together: a connexion or want of connexion. Denial of relation is another relation: and the two are contraries. The universe may have only a selection from all possible relations. [All names are in relation.]

153. The name in relation is the *subject*: the name to which it is in relation is the *predicate*. Thus in 'mind acting upon matter' *mind* is the *subject*, *matter* the *predicate*, *acting upon* is the *relation*. When the relation is convertible, subject and predicate are distinguished only by order of writing, as in § 9.

154. All *judgments* (asserted or denied relations) may be reduced to assertion or denial of concomitance by coupling the predicate and the relation into one notion. As in 'mind *is* a thing acting on matter' or 'mind *is not* a thing acting on matter'. In all works of logic, the consideration of relation in general is evaded by this transformation, and the development of the science is thereby altogether prevented.

155. If X be in some relation to Y, Y is therefore in some other relation to X. Each of these relations is the *converse* of the other. Converse relations are of identical effect, and neither exists without the other. In conversion the subject and predicate are transposed and usually change order of mention: as in 'X is master of Y; Y is servant of X'.

156. When a relation is its own converse, it is said to be *simply* convertible. As in 'X has nothing in common with Y' and 'Y has nothing in common with X'; or as in 'X is equal to Y' and 'Y is equal to X'.

157. When the subject of one relation is made the predicate of another, the first predicate may be made the predicate of a *combined* relation: as in the master[1] of (the-nephew-of-Y), that is, the-master-of-the-nephew of Y.

158. A combined relation may have a separate name, or it may not. Thus *brother of parent* has its own name, *uncle*: but *friend of parent* has no name which describes nothing else.

159. A combined relation may be of limited meaning, or it may not. Thus 'non-ancestor of a descendant of Z' has a limitation of meaning with reference to Z; he is certainly non-ancestor of Z. But 'ancestor of a descendant of Z' has no such limitation: any person may be the ancestor of a descendant of any other.

160. When a relation combined with itself reproduces itself, let it be called *transitive*: as *superior*; *superior of superior* is *superior*, the same sort of superiority being meant throughout. A transitive relation has a transitive converse: thus *inferior of inferior* is *inferior*.

161. Relations are conceivable both in extension and in intension (§ 131), both as aggregates and as compounds. Thus 'child of the same parents with' is aggregate of 'brother, sister, self': the relation of whole to part has among its components 'greater' and 'of same substance with'.

162. If two relations combine[2] into what is contained in a third relation, then the *converse* of either of the two combined with the *contrary* of the third, in the same order, is contained in the *contrary* of the other of the two. Thus the following three assertions are *identically the same*, superior and inferior being taken as contraries, that is, absolute equality not existing. Let the combination be 'master of parent' and the third relation 'superior'.

[1] The most familiar relations are those which exist between one human being and another; of which the *relations* of consanguinity and affinity have almost usurped the name *relation* to themselves. But hardly a sentence can be written without expression or implication of other relations.

[2] This theorem ought to be called theorem K, being in fact the theorem on which depends the process (§ 108) indicated by the letter K in the old memorial verses.

Every master of a parent is a superior
Every servant of an inferior is a non-parent
Every inferior of a child is a non-master.

From either of these the other two follow. This may be generally proved: at present it will be sufficient to deduce one of the assertions before us from another. Assume the second; from it follows that every parent is not any servant of an inferior, and therefore, if servant at all, only servant of superior, whence master of parent must be superior.

163. The relation in which an object of thought stands *to itself*, is called *identity*; to every thing else, *difference*. Every thing is itself: nothing is anything but itself: and any two things being thought of, they are either the same or different, and can be nothing except one or the other. These principles enter into the distinction between truth and falsehood: but cannot distinguish one truth from another. They are antecedent[1] to all nomenclature, and to all decomposition.

164. Identity is agreement in every thing and difference in nothing. Complex objects of thought usually agree in some things and differ in others. They get the same names in right of those points in which they agree, and different names in right of those points in which they differ. And thus, all resemblances or agreements giving an agreement of names, and all differences giving a difference of names, all the forms of inference [resulting from this head of relation] are capable of being evolved out of those forms in which nothing but concomitance or non-concomitance of names is considered (§ 5 to § 73).

[1] Many acute writers affirm that syllogism can be evolved from, and solely depends upon, three principles: *Identity*, *A* is *A*; 2. *Difference*, *A* is not not-*A*; thirdly, *excluded middle*, Every thing either *A* or not-*A*. Now syllogism certainly demands the perception of *convertibility*, '*A* is *B* gives *B* is *A*', and of *transitiveness*, '*A* is *B* and *B* is *C* gives *A* is *C*'. Are the *two* principles deducible from the *three*? If so, either by syllogism or without. If by syllogism, then syllogism, *before* establishment upon the three principles, is made to establish itself, which of course is not valid. Consequently, we must take the writers of whom I speak to hold that convertibility and transitiveness follow from the principles of identity, difference, and excluded middle, without *petitio principii*. When any one of them attempts to show *how*, I shall be able to judge of the process: as it is, I find that others do not go beyond the simple assertion, and that I myself can detect the *petitio principii* in every one of my own attempts. Until better taught, I must believe that the *two* principles of [convertibility] and transitiveness are not capable of reduction to consequences of the *three*, and must be assumed on the authority of consciousness.

Should I be wrong here: should any logician succeed, without assuming syllogism, in deducing the syllogism of the *identifying* copula 'is' from what may be called the three principles of *identification*, I shall then admit a completely established specific difference between the ordinary syllogism and others in which the copula, though convertible and transitive, is not the substantive verb. I should expect, in such an event, to deduce the transitiveness and convertibility of 'equals' from '*A* equals *A*', '*A* does not equal not-*A*' and 'every thing either equals *A* or not-*A*', where *A* is magnitude only [of some one given kind].

165. Relations which have immediate reference to, or are directly evolved from, the application of names and the mode of thinking about names in connexion with objects named, or with other names, may be called *onymatic*[1] *relations.*

166. The only relation in which a *name*, as a name, can stand to an *object*, is that of *applicable* or *inapplicable*.

167. Names may have many grammatical and etymological relations to one another, but the only relations which are of any logical import are the relations in which they stand to one another arising out of the relations in which they stand to objects. Accordingly we consider two names as having objects to which both apply, or as both applying to nothing whatsoever.

168. When *X*, *Y*, *Z*, are individual names, and we say '*X* is *Y*, *Y* is *Z*, therefore *X* is *Z*', we can but mean that in speaking of *X* and *Y* we are speaking of one object of thought, and the same of *Y* and *Z*, so that in speaking of *X* and *Z* we are speaking of one object. The law of thought which acts in this inference is the *transitiveness* (§ 160) *of the notion of concomitancy:* if *X* go with *Y*, and *Y* go with *Z*, then *X* goes with *Z*.

169. When names denote *classes*, the primary relation between them is that of containing and contained, in the sense of aggregate and aggregant (§ 124): other relations spring out of this, as will be seen. This relation is *mathematical* in its character: a class is made up of classes, just as an area is made up of areas. It is physically possible to connect the two aggregations: we can imagine all *men* on one area, and all *brutes* on another: the aggregate of the areas contains the class *animal*, the aggregate of *man* and *brute*.

170. When names denote *attributes*, the primary relation is that of containing and contained, in the sense of compound[2] and component

[1] The logician has hitherto denied entrance to every relation which is not onymatic; declaring all others to be *material*, not *formal*. When the distinction of matter and form is so clearly defined that it can be seen why and how no connexions are of the form of thought except those which I have called onymatic, it will be time enough to attempt a defence of the introduction of other relations. In the meantime, looking at all that is commonly said upon the distinction of form and matter, I am strongly inclined to suspect that there is nothing but a mere confusion of terms; that is, that when the logician speaks of the distinction of form and matter, he *means* the distinction of onymatic and non-onymatic. Dr Thomson, in his *Outlines, &c.* (§ 15, note), observes that the philosophic value of the terms matter and form is greatly reduced by the confusion which seems invariably to follow their extensive use. The truth is that the mathematician, as yet, is the only consistent handler of the distinction, about which nevertheless he thinks very little. The distinction of form and matter is more in the theory of the logician than in his practice: more in the practice of the mathematician than in his theory.

[2] It is not uncommon among logical writers to declare that an attribute is the sum of the attributes which it comprehends; that, for example, *man*, completely described

(§ 124). This relation is *metaphysical* in its character: the mode of junction of components is not mathematical, but is a subject for metaphysical discussion, though how that discussion may terminate is of no importance for logical purposes. The manner in which the sources of the notion *rational* are combined with those of the notion *animal* in the object which is called *man* has nothing to do with the laws of thought under which the compound and the components are and must be treated.

171. When the class X is *contained* in the class Y, as an aggregant, the attribute Y is *contained in* the attribute X, as a component. Thus the class man is contained in the class animal: the attribute animal is contained in the attribute man. These two apparent contradictions are both true in their different senses: say he is man, you say he is in animal; say he is man, you say animal is in him. Class *man* is in class *animal*, as aggregant in aggregate; attribute *animal* is in attribute *man*, as component in compound.

172. In all things which do not depend on ourselves, we learn to think of that which *always* happens as *necessarily* happening, of that which *always* accompanies as being *essential*,[1] part of the *essence*, part

1 Upon this word may be said, once for all, what is to be said concerning the use of metaphysical terms in logic. We have nothing to do with the way in which the mind comes *to* them; our affair is with the way in which the mind works *from* them. Thus it is absolutely essential to the fitness of three straight lines to be the sides of a triangle that any two should be together greater than the third; contradiction is inconceivable. It is naturally essential to an apple to be round; contradiction is unknown in nature. It is commercially and conveniently essential to a tea-pot to have a handle; any contradiction would be unsaleable and unusable. In all these cases, and whatever may be the force of the word *essential*, the mode of inference is the same: for the logical consequences of Y being an essential of X are but those of Y being always found whenever X is found. Why then do we not confine ourselves to this last notion, leaving the character of the conjunction, be it a necessity of thought, a result of uncontradicted observation, or a conventional arrangement, &c. entirely out of view? Simply because, by so doing, we fail to make logic an analysis of the way in which men *actually do think*. If men *will* be metaphysicians—and metaphysicians they will be—it must be advisable to treat the metaphysical views of the most common relations, the onymatic, in a system of logic. The metaphysical notion

---

by the notions *animal* and *rational* conjoined, is the *sum* of those notions. This is quite a mistake: let any one try to sum up *animal* and *rational* into *man*, in the obvious sense and manner in which he sums up *man* and *brute* into *animal*. The distinction of aggregation and composition, very little noticed by logicians, if at all, runs through all cases of thought. In mathematics, it is seen in the distinction of addition and multiplication; in chemistry, in the distinction of mechanical mixture and chemical combination; in an act of parliament, in the distinction between 'And be it further enacted' and 'Provided always'; and so on.

Hartley has more nearly than any other writer produced the notion of composition as distinguished from aggregation. His compound idea has a force and meaning of its own, which prevents our seeing the components in it, just as, to use his own illustration, the smell of the compound medicine overpowers the smells of the ingredients. But even Hartley represents the compound of A and B by $A + B$.

of the *being*. This *metaphysical* notion is always in thought, in one form or other, whenever undeviating concomitance of one notion with another is established or supposed.

173. Out of these onymatic relations arise five different modes of enunciating the same proposition. One of these, the *arithmetical*, already treated, merely states, or sums up, an enumeration of concomitances, or non-concomitances: as in 'Every man is an animal'; or as in 'No man is a vegetable'.

174. The four subjective modes of speaking which the notions of relation develop, are,—

i. *Mathematical*. Here both subject and predicate are notions of class: the *class* man contained in the *class* animal.

ii. *Physical*. The subject a *class*, the predicate an *attribute*. As in 'man is mortal': the class *man* has the attribute *subject to death*. [Most common in life.]

iii. *Metaphysical*. Both subject and predicate are notions of *attributes*. As in 'humanity is fallible': *fallibility* a component of the notion *humanity*.

iv. *Contraphysical*. The subject an attribute, the predicate a class. As[1] in 'All mortality in the class man', or 'none but men are mortal': that is, we must attribute mortality only in the class man; or, all of which mortality is the attribute is in the class man.

175. All these modes of reading are concomitant: each one of the five gives all the rest. If all the men in the *universe*[2] be so many animals, then the class man is in the class animal, and has the attribute animal

[1] I take a falsehood for once, to remind the reader that with truth or falsehood of matter we have nothing to do.

[2] According to the universe understood, so is the mode of taking the meaning of the onymatic terms. For example, if the universe be the universe of *objective reality*, then, all existing men being ascertained to be animals, it is of the nature of man, as actually created, to be animal: the attributes of animal are naturally essential to man. If the universe be the universe of all possible thought, then, if all men conceivable be animals, if, for whatever reason, it be impossible to think of man without thinking of animal, then the attribute animal is an essential of the attribute humanity. And now arises a question of words, with which logic has nothing to do. Those creatures of thought which occur in the fables, dogs and oxen, &c. which are rational as well as animal, are they *men*? Certainly not, according to the notion which the word represents. Consequently, the phrase *rational animal* is a larger term than man, when all the possibilities of thought are in question. But this is not a question of logic. The logician, as such, does not know what man is, nor what animal is: but he knows how to combine 'every man is animal' with other propositions, so soon as he knows that he is permitted to use that proposition.

is a natural growth of thought, and children and uneducated persons are more strongly addicted to it than educated adults.

[Essential refers to the universe. Universe of possible thought: ontological essence; universe of nature: natural essence; universe of commercial attributes, &c. &c.—MS. note.]

as one of its class marks; also, the attribute animal is an essential of the attribute humanity, and the attribute humanity is to be sought only in the class animal.

176. We have now to render the proposition and the syllogism into the four readings, mathematical, metaphysical, or mixed, inventing appropriate terms for all the relations which occur. It will be sufficient, however, to treat the first and third system, the wholly mathematical, and the wholly metaphysical.

177. When Every *X* is *Y*, *X*))*Y* or *Y*((*X*, let the class *X* be called a *species* of the class *Y*, and *Y* a *genus*[1] of *X*. In the contrary case, when some *X*s are not *Y*s, *X*(·(*Y* or *Y*)·)*X*, let *X* be an *exient of Y*, and *Y* a *deficient* of *X*.

178. When No *X* is *Y*, *X*)·(*Y* or *Y*)·(*X*, let each class be called an *external* of the other, or let the two be called *coexternals*. In the contrary case, when some *X*s are *Y*s, *X*()*Y* or *Y*()*X*, let each be called a *partient* of the other, or let the two be called *copartients*.

179. When every thing is either *X* or *Y*, *X*(·)*Y* or *Y*(·)*X*, let each class be called a *complement* of the other. In the contrary case, when some things are neither *X*s nor *Y*s, *X*)(*Y* or *Y*)(*X*, let each class be called[2] a *co-inadequate* of the other.

180. The spicular symbols may be made to stand for the relations themselves. Thus)) means *species* or *genus*, according as it is read forwards or backwards; ((, genus or species: and so on.[3]

181. *Genus* and *species* are *converse* relations; as also *exient* and *deficient:* of *external*, *partient*, *complement*, *coinadequate*, each is its own converse. *Genus* and *deficient* are contrary relations; as are *species* and *exient*, *external* and *partient*, *complement* and *coinadequate*.

182. *Genus* is both *partient* and *coinadequate*; as also is *species*. *External* is both *exient* and *deficient*, and so is *complement*.

[1] In the common use of these words, the *species* is a part only of the *genus*. As here used the species may be the whole genus. This is, to my mind, the greatest liberty I have taken with the ordinary terms of logic. [In the *Edinburgh Review*, 1860, Buffon is cited as saying a variety is *both species and genus*—a strong way of saying that it is too distinct from others to be made the other species of a genus with any.—MS. note.]

[2] Punsters are respectfully informed that the reading *coin-adequate*, and all jokes legitimately deducible therefrom, are already appropriated, and the right of translation reserved.

[3] [

Contradictory	*Partient*	*Plenary*
)·(by diminution	← () →	by augmentation ((
(·) by augmentation	)(	by diminution))
)) by diminution	(·(	by augmentation (·)
((by augmentation	)·)	by diminution)·(
	))	by augmentation ((
	)·(	by augmentation (·)

—MS. note.]

183. These are exercises in the meanings of the terms, and should be thought of until their truth is familiar; as also the following,—

The *genus* has the utmost *partience*, and may have the utmost *coinadequacy*. The *species* has the utmost *coinadequacy*, and may have the utmost *partience*. The *external* has the utmost *deficiency*, and may have the utmost *exience*. The *complement* has the utmost *exience*, and may have the utmost *deficiency*.[1]

184. These relations have *terminal ambiguity*, founded on the notion of *contained* having two cases, filling the whole, or filling only a part. Thus

> *Genus* is either *species* or *exient*
> *Species* is either *genus* or *deficient*
> *External* is either *complement* or *coinadequate*
> *Complement* is either *external* or *partient*.[2]

185. Read the identities in § 25 into this language, as in, Species is external of contrary, Contrary of species is complement, Contraries of species and genus are genus and species, &c.

186. The following are the combinations[3] of mathematical relation which take place in syllogisms.[4] Each triad in the first list contains a universal and two particular syllogisms, the three being opponents (§ 47), connected also by the theorem in § 162. The second list (§ 187) contains the strengthened syllogisms.

)))) Species of species is species [of genus]
(((·(Genus of *exient* is exient [of *deficient*]
(·(((Exient of genus is exient [of species]

((((Genus of genus is genus [of species]
)))·) Species of *deficient* is deficient [of *exient*]
)·))) Deficient of species is deficient [of genus]

[1] [The genus has no deficiency, and may have no exience;
The species has no exience, and may have no deficiency;
The external has no partience, and may have no coinadequacy;
The complement has no coinadequacy, and may have no partience.—MS. note.]

[2] [·((utmost () certainly: utmost)(possibly
·)) utmost)(certainly: utmost () possibly
·)·(utmost)·) certainly: utmost (·(possibly
·(·) utmost (·(certainly: utmost)·) possibly.—MS. note.]

[3] Note that when, and only when, one of the combining words is either *genus* or *species*, the other two words are the same; and this throughout [these] fundamental or unstrengthened syllogisms. What law of thought does this represent? And except when one of these words so occurs, the three words of relation are all different. [Accordingly, the three words are different when the two premises are both of the lower or weaker kind: that is, both negative, or a negative and a particular.—MS. note.]

[4] [Cf. table of syllogistic forms, p. 162.]

)·((·) External of [one] complement is species [of the other]
)·((·(External of *exient* is coinadequate [of *deficient*]
(·((·) Exient of [one] complement is partient [of the other]

(·))·(Complement of [one] external is genus [of the other]
(·))·) Complement of *deficient* is partient [of exient]
)·))·(Deficient of [one] external is coinadequate [of the other]

)))·(Species of [one] external is external [of the other]
((() Genus of [one] partient is partient [of the other]
())·(Partient of [one] external is exient [of the other]

(((·) Genus of [one] complement is complement [of the other]
)))(Species of [one] coinadequate is coinadequate [of the other]
)((·) Coinadequate of [one] complement is deficient [of the other]

)·(((External of genus is external [of species]
)·(() External of [one] partient is deficient [of the other]
())) Partient of species is partient [of genus]

(·))) Complement of species is complement [of genus]
(·))(Complement of [one] coinadequate is exient [of the other]
)(((Coinadequate of genus is coinadequate [of species].

187.

(( )) Genus of species is partient [of genus]
)) ((Species of genus is coinadequate [of species]
(·) (·) Complement of [one] complement is partient [of the other]
)·( )·(External of [one] external is coinadequate [of the other]
(( )·(Genus of [one] external is exient [of the other]
)) (·) Species of [one] complement is deficient [of the other]
(·) ((Complement of genus is exient [of species]
)·( )) External of species is deficient [of genus].

188. When we give what may be called, comparatively, *terminal precision*, as in § 57, we may use the following nomenclature,—

)∘) A deficient species may be called a subidentical
|| A species and genus is an identical
(∘(An exient genus may be called a superidentical

)∘(A coinadequate external may be called a subcontrary
|·| An external complement is a contrary
(∘) A partient complement may be called a supercontrary.

189. The complex syllogisms (§ 61) may be read as follows,—

)°))°) A subidentical of a subidentical is a subidentical
(°((°(A superidentical of a superidentical is a superidentical
)°((°) A subcontrary of a supercontrary is a subidentical
(°))°(A supercontrary of a subcontrary is a superidentical
)°))°(A subidentical of a subcontrary is a subcontrary
(°((°) A superidentical of a supercontrary is a supercontrary
)°((°(A subcontrary of a superidentical is a subcontrary
(°))°) A supercontrary of a subidentical is a supercontrary.

The following modes of connecting the symbols, as applied to the same two terms, may be useful,—

)°))), Species;)·), but not the greatest possible.
(°(((, Genus; (·(, but not the least possible.
)°( )·(, External;)(, but not the greatest possible.
(°) (·), Complement; (), but not the least possible.

190. I now proceed to the metaphysical relations[1] between *attribute* and *attribute*.

191. When *X*)) *Y* let the attribute *Y* be called an *essential* of the attribute *X*, and *X* a *dependent* of *Y*. In the contrary case, *X*(·(*Y*, let *Y* be called an *inessential* of *X*, and *X* an *independent* of *Y*. Remember that *dependent on* does not mean *dependent wholly on*, or *dependent only on*.

[1] The terms of metaphysical relation are picked up without difficulty in our common language: but those of mathematical relation had in several instances to be forged. This means that the world at large has more of the metaphysical than of the mathematical notion in its usual form of thought. But though the *unconnected* words *essential*, *dependent*, *repugnant*, *alternative*, are constantly on the tongues of educated people, the combinations of these relations are not made with any security, and when thought of at all, enter under a cloud of words: while the analysis by which precision of speech and habit of security might be gained is treated with contempt, as being *logic*. A whole drawing-room of educated men may be without a single person who can expose the falsehood of the assertion that the essential of an incompatible must be incompatible; a proposition which I have heard maintained, though not in those words, by persons of more than respectable acquirements; sometimes by actual error, sometimes by confusion between the essential of an incompatible, and that to which an incompatible is essential. But even of the persons who are not thus taken in, very few indeed, when told that the answer to 'the essential of an incompatible is incompatible' is 'not so much; *only* independent', will not be puzzled by the juxtaposition of incompatibility and independence as viewed in a relation of degree. In making these remarks, it will be remembered that I am not speaking of any words of my own, nor of any meanings of my own. The words are common, and I take them in their common meanings; but it is not generally seen that these common words, used in their common senses, are sufficient, in conjunction with their contraries, to express all the relations which occur in a completely quantified system of onymatic enunciation.

192. When $X)\cdot(Y$, let each attribute be called a *repugnant* of the other. When $X()Y$, let each be an *irrepugnant* of the other.

193. When $X(\cdot)Y$ let each attribute be called an *alternative* of the other. When $X)(Y$ let each be called an *inalternative* of the other.

194. When difference of symbols is desired, the square bracket may be used instead of the parenthesis: thus]] may denote *dependent* when read forwards, and *essential* when read backwards, &c.

195. *Essential* and *dependent* are converse relations; as are also *inessential* and *independent*. Of *repugnant*, *irrepugnant*, *alternative*, *inalternative*, each is its own converse. Essential and inessential are contrary relations; as are dependent and independent, repugnant and irrepugnant, alternative and inalternative. Compare § 181.

196. The *essential* is both *irrepugnant* and *inalternative*: as also is the *dependent*. The *repugnant* is both *independent* and *inessential*: as also is the *alternative*. Compare § 182.

197. The essential has the utmost irrepugnance, and may have the utmost inalternativeness. The dependent has the utmost inalternativeness, and may have the utmost irrepugnance. The repugnant has the utmost inessentiality, and may have the utmost independence. The alternative has the utmost independence, and may have the utmost inessentiality. Compare § 183.[1]

198. These relations also have terminal ambiguity (Compare § 184).

Essential is either dependent or independent
Dependent is either essential or inessential
Repugnant is either alternative or inalternative
Alternative is either repugnant or irrepugnant

199. Read the identities in § 25 into this language, as in Dependent is repugnant of contrary, contrary of dependent is alternative, contraries of dependent and essential are essential and dependent, &c.

200. The following are the combinations[2] in syllogism, arranged as in § 186.

)))) Dependent of dependent is dependent [of essential]
(((·(Essential of independent is independent [of inessential]
(·(((Independent of essential is independent [of dependent]

((((Essential of essential is essential [of dependent]
)))·) Dependent of inessential is inessential [of independent]
)·))) Inessential of dependent is inessential [of essential]

[1] [And half of note thereto, in phraseological identity. The essential has no inessentiality (of course!) and may have no independence, may be dependent (!), &c, &c.—(27 January 1861).]

[2] Note that when, and only when, one of the combining words is either *essential* or *dependent*, the other two words are the same; and this throughout the fundamental or unstrengthened syllogisms. What law of thought does this represent? And except when one of these words so occurs, the three words of relation are all different.

)·((·) Repugnant of [one] alternative is dependent [of the other]
)·((·(Repugnant of independent is inalternative [of inessential]
(·((·) Independent of [one] alternative is irrepugnant [of the other]

(·))·(Alternative of [one] repugnant is essential [of the other]
(·))·) Alternative of inessential is irrepugnant [of independent]
)·))·(Inessential of [one] repugnant is inalternative [of the other]

)))·(Dependent of [one] repugnant is repugnant of the [other]
((() Essential of [one] irrepugnant is irrepugnant [of the other]
())·(Irrepugnant of [one] repugnant is independent [of the other]

(((·) Essential of [one] alternative is alternative [of the other]
)))(Dependent of [one] inalternative is inalternative [of the other]
)((·) Inalternative of [one] alternative is inessential [of the other]
)·(((Repugnant of essential is repugnant [of dependent]
)·(() Repugnant of [one] irrepugnant is inessential [of the other]
())) Irrepugnant of dependent is irrepugnant [of essential]

(·))) Alternative of dependent is alternative [of essential]
(·))(Alternative of [one] inalternative is independent [of the other]
)(((Inalternative of essential is inalternative [of dependent].

201.

(( )) Essential of dependent is irrepugnant [of essential]
)) ((Dependent of essential is inalternative [of dependent]
(·) (·) Alternative of [one] alternative is irrepugnant [of the other]
)·( )·(Repugnant of [one] repugnant is inalternative [of the other]
(( )·(Essential of [one] repugnant is independent [of the other]
)) (·) Dependent of [one] alternative is inessential [of the other]
(·) ((Alternative of essential is independent [of dependent]
)·( )) Repugnant of dependent is inessential [of essential].

202. I now proceed to form metaphysical[1] terms expressing relations of terminal precision (compare § 188). Let an *inherent* be an attribute

[1] This new formation cannot be overlooked, since it is the extension of the Aristotelian system of *predicables*, *genus* and *species* (used in the old sense) and *accident*, to the system in which contrary terms are permitted. Otherwise, the relations of terminal ambiguity, compounded, might serve the purpose.

asserted; let an *excludent* be an attribute denied; let an *accident*, which is also *non-accident*, be an attribute affirmed of part and denied of the rest. Thus of man, *life* is an inherent, *vegetation* an excludent, *wisdom* an accident and a non-accident.

203. Each of these relations may be either *generic* or *specific*. Either is *generic* when it applies in as large or a larger degree to a larger genus: *specific*, when it does not so apply to any larger genus. This being premised, the following relations will be found correctly stated,—

)∘)	Inessential dependent	is	*Specific accident* / *Generic non-accident*
‖	Dependent essential	is	*Specific inherent*
(∘(	Independent essential	is	*Generic inherent*
)∘(	Inalternative repugnant	is	*Generic excludent*
|·|	Repugnant alternative	is	*Specific excludent*
(∘)	Irrepugnant alternative	is	*Generic accident* / *Specific non-accident*.[1]

[1] [

))))	Dependent of species is dependent of genus	1
(((·(	Essential of exient is independent of deficient	2
(·(((	Independent of genus is independent of species	1
((((	Essential of genus is essential of species	3
)))·)	Dependent of deficient is inessential of exient	2
)·)))	Inessential of species is inessential of genus	3
)·((·)	Repugnant of one complement is dependent of the other	4
)·((·(	Repugnant of exient is inalternative of deficient	5
(·((·)	Independent of one complement is irrepugnant of the other	4
(·))·(	Alternative of one external is essential of the other	6
(·))·)	Alternative of deficient is irrepugnant of exient	5
)·))·(	Inessential of one external is inalternative of the other	6
)))·(	Dependent of one external is repugnant of the other	7
((()	Essential of one irrepugnant is irrepugnant of the other	8
())·(	Irrepugnant of one external is independent of the other	7
)·(((	Repugnant of genus is repugnant of species	9
)·(()	Repugnant of one irrepugnant is inessential of the other	8
()))	Irrepugnant of dependent is irrepugnant of essential	9
(((·)	Essential of one complement is alternative of the other	10
)))(	Dependent of one coinadequate is inalternative of the other	11
)((·)	Inalternative of one complement is inessential of the other	10
(·)))	Alternative of species is alternative of genus	12
(·))(	Alternative of one coinadequate is independent of the other	11
)(((	Inalternative of genus is inalternative of species	12

204. The following are examples of each of these terms, the universe being *terrestrial animal,—*

Specific accident; generic non-accident. Lawyer is in this relation to man: *accident* and *non-accident*, because an attribute of some men, and not of others; *specific* accident, because not found in the additional extent of any genus larger than man; *generic* non-accident, for the same reason.

Specific inherent. Rational is in this relation to man: *inherent*, because an attribute of all; *specific*, because no attribute of the additional extent in a larger genus.

Generic inherent. Biped is in this relation to man; *inherent*, because an attribute of all; *generic*, because an attribute of the additional extent of a larger genus.

Generic excludent. Oviparous is in this relation to *man*; *excludent*, because an attribute to be denied of man; *generic*, because to be also denied of the additional extent of some larger genera.

Specific excludent. Dumb (wanting articulate language with meaning) is in this relation to man; *excludent*, because to be denied of man; *specific*, because not to be denied of the additional extent of any larger genus.

Generic accident; specific non-accident. Naked (not artificially clothed) is in this relation to man; *accident* and *non-accident*, because some are and some are not; *generic* accident, because an accident of the additional extent of larger genera; *specific* non-accident, because not non-accident of any such additional extent.

205. When either of the relations belongs equally to a term and its contrary, it may be called *universal.* Thus an attribute of both term and contrary is a *universal inherent*; an accident and non-accident of both term and contrary is a *universal accident and non-accident*; an excludent of both term and contrary is a *universal excludent.* But the first and third of these terms are chiefly of use in defining the universe: the second is that relation which we suppose until some contradiction is affirmed.

206. With the arithmetical reading in *extension* may be joined that in *intension*, § 115, 131. In extension, the unit of enumeration is one of the objects all of which aggregate into the class: in intension, the unit of

---

(( )) Essential of species is irrepugnant of genus
)) ((Essential of genus is inalternative of species
(·) (·) Alternative of one complement is irrepugnant of the other
)·( )·(Repugnant of one external is inalternative of the other
(( )·(Essential of one repugnant is independent of the other
)) (·) Dependent of one complement is inessential of the other
(·) ((Alternative of genus is independent of species
)·( )) Repugnant of species is inessential of genus.

—12 November 1860.]

enumeration is one of the qualities all of which compose the object.[1] The following is the system of arithmetical reading in intension: naturally connected (§ 129) with the metaphysical mode of viewing objects of thought. The inversion of the quantities, presently further described, will be easily seen; namely, that)*X* and *X*(now indicate that *X* is taken completely, in all its qualities; while *X*) and (*X* indicate that *X* is taken incompletely, in some (some or all, not known which) of its qualities. The term *any* (§ 22) is here introduced when grammatically desirable.[2]

Symbol	*Metaphysical reading*	*Arithmetical reading in intension*
X)) *Y*	*X* dependent of *Y*	All qualities of *Y* are some qualities of *X*[3]
X(·(*Y*	*X* independent of *Y*	Some qualities of *Y* not any qualities of *X*[4]
X)·(*Y*	*X* repugnant of *Y*	All things want either some qualities of *X*, or some qualities of *Y*
X() *Y*	*X* irrepugnant of *Y*	Some things want neither any quality of *X*, nor any quality of *Y*
X(·) *Y*	*X* alternative of *Y*	All things have either all the qualities of *X* or all the qualities of *Y*
X)(*Y*	*X* inalternative of *Y*	Some things want either some of the qualities of *X*, or some of the qualities of *Y*
X((*Y*	*X* essential of *Y*	Some qualities of *Y* are all the qualities of *X*
X)·) *Y*	*X* inessential of *Y*	Any qualities of *Y* are not some qualities of *X*.

207. I now proceed to further consideration of the subject of quantity. No new results can appear, but it will be necessary both to adapt the old results to the more subjective view of logical process, and also to consider the distinctions of quantity from new points of view.

208. The distinction of the two *tensions*, *extension* and *intension* (§ 131), or, for brevity, *extent* and *intent*, may for clearness (§ 129) be applied only to classes and attributes. The extent of a class embraces all the classes of which it is aggregated: the intent of an attribute embraces all the attributes of which it is compounded.

[1] [It should have been more distinctly expressed that the individual object is as completely expressed by the composition of *all* the qualities, as the class by the aggregation of all the individuals.—MS. note.]

[2] [Cf. note to § 67 above.]

[3] [Every class containing *Y* contains *X*
Every class-mark of *Y* is a class-mark of *X*.—MS. note.]

[4] [We understand here that class may be qualified down to an individual.—MS. note.]

209. A class may be subdivided down to the distinct and non-interfering individual objects of thought of which it is composed: and here subdivision must stop. But it is not for human reason to say what are the simple attributes into which an attribute may be decomposed: the decomposition of the notion *rational*, for example, into distinct and non-interfering component notions, is the subject of an old controversy which will perhaps never be settled. But this difficulty is of no logical importance.

210. The relation of quantity as exhibited in the arithmetical view of the proposition (§ 13, 14), giving the distinction of *universal* and *particular* quantity, as it is commonly expressed, or of *total* and *partial* quantity, as I have expressed it, may be in this part of the subject most conveniently attached to other names. Let the terms *full extent*[1] and *vague extent* be used to replace *total extension* and *partial extension*: and let *full intent* and *vague intent* replace *total intension* and *partial intension*.

211. Additional extent can only be gained by a new aggregant containing extent which is not in the collective extent of the others: additional intent only by a new component which is not in the joint intent of the others. Thus the extent of the class *animal* is not augmented by the aggregation of the class *having volition*, if the universe be the *visible earth*. Again, the intent[2] of the notion *plane triangle* is not augmented

[1] These terms are convenient from their brevity: *full extent* is shorter than *universal extension*. But they are still more useful as avoiding the ambiguity of the words *some*, *particular*, *partial*, which, as we have seen (§ 14, note [2]), misleads even the highest writers. The logical opposition of quantity is not *quantity universal* and *quantity not universal*, but *quantity asserted to be universal* and *quantity not asserted to be universal* [Sir W. Hamilton's 'definite']. Two words cannot be found which express the opposition of undertaking to assert and not undertaking to assert universality. We may therefore be content with *full* and *vague*, which, if they do not *express opposition*, at least do not, like *universal* and *particular*, express the *wrong* opposition.

[2] There is a remarkable difference between extent and intent, which, though logically nothing at all, is psychologically very striking. Say we discover extent hitherto unknown, without the necessity of reducing intent to include it within a class thought of. Columbus did this when he first was able to add the class *American* to the classes then known under *man*. [Augmentation means *non*-diminution.] Here is nothing beyond what was possible in previous thought, which could people the seas to any extent. But when we add intent without diminishing extent, which knowledge is doing every day, we cannot conceive beforehand what kind of additions we shall make. A beginner in geometry gradually adds to the [composition] of *triangle*, which at first is only rectilinear three-sided figure, the components—can be circumscribed by a circle—has bisectors of sides meeting in a point—has sum of angles equal to two right angles—and other properties, by the score. The distinction is that class aggregation joins *similars*—but that composition of attributes joins things perfectly distinct, of which no one can predicate anything merely by what he knows of another thing. When the old logicians threw the notion of intent out of logic into metaphysics, they were guided by the material differences *of* qualities, and did not apprehend their similarity of properties *as* qualities.

by the junction of the notion *capable of inscription in a circle*. The distinction between these real and apparent augmentations is of the matter, not of the form: and is of no logical import except this, that when we say that a new aggregant increases extent, and a new component increases intent, we must be prepared, with the mathematicians, to reckon 0 among the cases of quantity.

212. The distinction of extent and intent has found its way into common language, in the words *scope*[1] and *force*, which I shall sometimes use. Thus in 'every man is animal' the term *man* is used in all its scope, but not in all its force; a person incognizant of some of the components of the notion *man*, that is, of the whole *force* of the term, might have the means of knowing this proposition. But *animal* is used in all its force, and not in all its scope. This answers to saying that in 'Every *X* is *Y*', the term *X* is of full extent and vague intent; the term *Y* is of full intent and vague extent.

213. The quantity considered in the arithmetical view of logic (§ 5–111) was entirely quantity of extent. I now proceed to the comparison of extent and intent.

214. In every use of a term, one of the tensions[2] is full, and the other vague: the full extent and the full intent cannot be used at one and the same time; and the same of the vague extent and the vague intent. Thus *X*) and (*X* must stand for *X* used in full extent and vague intent: and)*X* and *X*(for vague extent and full intent.

[1] The logicians, until our own day, have considered the *extent* of a term as the only object of logic, under the name of the *logical whole*: the *intent* was called by them the *metaphysical whole*, and was excluded from logic. In our own time the English logical writers, and Sir William Hamilton among the foremost, have contended for the introduction of the distinction into logic, under the names of *extension* and *comprehension*: Hamilton uses *breadth* and *depth*. Now I say that in the perception of the distinction between scope and force, as well as in other things, the world, which always runs after quack preparations, has ventured for itself out of the logical pharmacopoeia. This certainly in a rude and imperfect way: and without apprehension of any *theorems*. I have not found, though I have looked for it, any such amount of recognition that the greater the scope the less the force as I could present without suspicion of the *aut inveniam aut faciam* bias. But I think it likely enough that some of my readers may casually pick up passages which show a *feeling* of this theorem.

[2] The logicians who have *recently* introduced the distinction of extension and comprehension, have altogether missed this opposition of the quantities, and have imagined that the quantities remain the same. Thus, according to Sir W. Hamilton 'All *X* is some *Y*' is a proposition of comprehension, but 'Some *Y* is all *X*' is a proposition of extension. In this the logicians have abandoned both Aristotle and the laws of thought from which he drew the few clear words of his dictum: 'the genus is said to be part of the species; but in another point of view (ἄλλως) the species is part of the genus'. *All animal* is in *man*, notion in notion: *all man* is in *animal*, class in class. In the first, all the notion *animal* part of the notion *man*: in the second, all the class *man* part of the class *animal*. Here is the opposition of the quantities.

The proof of this proposition is as follows. When a term is full in extent, we can abandon or dismiss any aggregant of that extent we please: the proposition, though reduced or crippled by the dismissal, is true of what is left: but we may not annex an aggregant at pleasure. When a term is vague in extent, we cannot dismiss any aggregant whatever: for we know not by what aggregant the proposition is made true: but we may annex any aggregant at pleasure: for we do not thereby throw out what makes the proposition true, even if we annex no additional truth; and we do not, when speaking vaguely, affirm or deny of any one selected aggregant. And as the extent must be full or vague, and we must be either competent or incompetent to dismiss an aggregant taken at pleasure, and must be either competent or incompetent to annex one, the converses follow (§ 151), namely, that when we are competent to dismiss, the extent is full, and when we are incompetent the extent is vague: and also that when we are competent to annex, the extent is vague, and when not, the extent is full. Precisely the same proposition may be established upon the intent of a term, and its components.[1]

Now let a term be of *full* extent. In diminishing the extent, which we may do, we can so do it as to augment the intent: and if we be competent to augment the intent, that intent must be *vague*, as just proved. Similarly, if a term be of *vague* extent, we are competent to annex an aggregant, that is, to diminish the intent; whence the intent must be *full*. And the same may be proved in like manner when either kind of intent is first supposed instead of extent; though by use of § 151 this case may be seen to be contained in that already treated. And the learner may gather the whole from instances. Thus $A,B))PQ$ gives $A))PQ$, and $A))P$; but not $A, B, C))PQ$, nor $A, B))PQR$. But $PQ))A, B$ does not give $P))A, B$, nor $PQ))A$, though it does give $PQR))A, B$ and $PQ))A, B, C$; and so on. And further, from § 133, this proposition can be made good of all universals when it is known of one: and the same of all particulars.

215. It appears then that the *elements* of a tension (aggregants of an

[1] [If $P = A(B + C + D)$, A is a factor of P, P is a *factum* of A.
If X be a factum of Y, every factum of X is a factum of Y.
$X = PY.\ MX = MPY.$
Every factor of Y is a factor of X.
The first answers to 'Every aggregant of X is an aggregant of Y'. For X is made up of XA, XB, XC . . .
Imagine $ABCD$ . . . non-communicant classes which make up the universe

$$A + B + C + D + \ldots = 1$$
$$AX + BX + CX + DX + \ldots = X$$

Factum = aggregant:
Factor = component.

—17 February 1861.]

extent, components of an intent) may be *dismissed* from the term used *fully*, but cannot be introduced; may be *introduced* into a term used *vaguely*, but cannot be dismissed. The dismissible is inadmissible: the indismissible is admissible.

216. Elements of either tension may, under the limitations of a rule to be shown, be transposed from one term of a proposition to the other, either directly, or by contraversion, *without either loss or gain of import to the proposition.* Thus $AB)\cdot(Y$ is the same proposition as $A)\cdot(BY$, and $X))A, B$ is the same as $Xa))B$. The demonstration of this may best be seen by observing that every universal is a declaration of *incompossibility*,[1] and every particular a corresponding declaration of *compossibility.* Thus $X)\cdot(Y$ is an assertion that X and Y, as names of one object, are incompossible; and $X()Y$ that they are compossible. Again, $X))Y$ declares X and y to be incompossible; and so on.

Now it will be seen that $AB)\cdot(Y$ is merely a statement that the three names A, B, Y, are incompossible; and so is $A)\cdot(BY$. Hence $AB)\cdot(Y$ and $A)\cdot(BY$ are identical. Similarly $AB()Y$ and $A()BY$ are identical, both declaring the compossibility of A, B, Y: or thus, if two propositions be identical, their contraries must be identical. Hence we learn that in $Y))a, b$ we have $YB))a$ &c. Carrying this through all transformations,[2] we arrive at the following rules:—

i. In universal propositions, vague elements (the elements of terms of either vague tension) are transposible; directly in negatives, by contraversion in affirmatives. But full elements are intransposible.[3]

ii. In particular propositions, full elements (the elements of terms of either full tension) are transposible; directly in affirmatives, by contraversion in negatives. But vague elements are intransposible.[4]

[1] These good words are Sir William Hamilton's (see § 14, note[2]), to whom, in matters of language, I am under what he would have called obligations general and obligations special. His occasional writing of the adjective after the substantive is a useful revival of an old practice, tending much to clearness. As to my obligations special, he, finding the word *parenthesis* not enough to erect his reader's hair, described my notation as 'horrent with mysterious spiculae'. This was the very word I wanted, § 21: for *parenthesis* has come to mean, not the punctuating sign, but the matter which it includes: and *parenthetic* notation would have been ambiguous.

[2] [$AB))Y = A))Yb$ $\qquad$ $AB(\cdot(Y = A(\cdot(Yb$
$X))CD = Xd))C$ $\qquad$ $X(\cdot(CD = Xd(\cdot(C$
$AB)\cdot(Y = A)\cdot(YB$ $\qquad$ $AB()Y = A()YB$
$AB(\cdot)Y = A(\cdot)YB$ $\qquad$ $AB)(Y = A)(YB$.]

[3] [Indismissible, transposible: dismissible, intransposible.]

[4] [Indismissible, intransposible: dismissible, transposible.

In propositions of unlike quantity, transposition is always by contraversion:)) ((,)·) (·(.

In propositions of like quantity, transposition is always direct:)·((), (·))(.—9 February 1861.]

Thus in *X*)) *Y*, *Y* is of vague extent; if it be (*A*, *B*), its aggregant *A* is transposible, the proposition being affirmative, by contraversion: that is *X*))*A*, *B* is identical with *Xa*))*B*. The rules are for comparison and generalization, not for use.[1] Nothing can be more evident than that if every *X* be either *A* or *B*, every *X* which is not *A* is *B*.

217. It has in effect been noticed that for every full term in a proposition a term of as much or less tension may be substituted; and for every vague term a term of as much or more tension. This is the whole principle of onymatic syllogism, or rather may be made so: for the varieties of principle upon which all onymatic inference may be systematically introduced are numerous. Thus in *X*()*Y*)·(*Z*, giving *X*(·(*Z*, all we do is to substitute for *Y* used vaguely in extent, the as extensive or more extensive term *z*. Or thus;—for *Y* of full intent, we substitute the as intensive or less intensive term *z*. For *Y*)·(*Z* or *Y*))*z*, shows that *z*, if anything, is of greater extent and less intent than *Y*.

218. There are processes which appear like transpositions, but are not so in reality. Thus *X*))*PQ* certainly gives *XP*))*Q*: here is a universal proposition, in which the element of a full tension is transposible. But not transposible within the description in § 216, in which it is affirmed that the proposition after transposition is identical with the proposition before transposition. This is not the case here; for though *X*))*PQ* gives *XP*))*Q*, yet *XP*))*Q* does not give *X*))*PQ*. Here, since *X*))*PQ* gives *X*))*Q* and *X*))*P*, the term *XP* is really *X*. And further, since *X*))*PQ* gives *X*))*Q* from whence *XR*))*Q*, be *R* what it may so long as *XR* has existence, the deduction of *XP*))*Q* from *X*))*PQ* is a case of something different from mere transposition: for *P*, in *XP*))*Q*, may be changed into anything else.

219. The dismissal of the elements of terms comes under what may be called the *decomposition of propositions*. When the elements of both terms are of the full tension, the proposition is a compound of $m \times n$ propositions, if *m* and *n* be the numbers of elements in the two terms. Thus *A*, *B*))*CD* gives and is given by the four propositions *A*))*C*, *A*))*D*, *B*))*C*, *B*))*D*.

220. Species, external, deficient, coinadequate
Dependent, repugnant, inessential, inalternative

must carry the notion of full extent and vague intent. For example, the universe being *England*, *farmer* is a deficient of *landowner*: of all the class[2] *farmer*, no part is identical with a certain part of the class *land-*

[1] [*U*, universal; *V*, vague;
P, particular; *F*, full.
Transposition, *UVPF* (cognate letters go together).—9 February 1861.]

[2] The student must, in any one proposition, be on his guard against thinking inconsistently of *class* and of *attribute*. Either of these modes of thought may be chosen, but not both together, unless the attribute be made to distinguish the class,

owner. To know this by extent I must know the whole class *farmer*: but to know it by intent, I need not know all the attributes of the notion *farmer*. Let there be *but one* of these attributes which is not an essential of *landowner*, and the proposition is established.

Genus, complement, exient, partient
Essential, alternative, independent, irrepugnant

must carry the notion of vague extent and full intent. The symbols will here help the memory of those who have fully connected them with the words.

221. The rules of § 50–52 must be translated as follows. A vague term in the conclusion takes extent or intent (scope or force) as follows.

i. In *universal syllogisms*, if one term of conclusion be of vague scope or force, it has the scope or force of the other; if both, one has the scope or force of the whole middle term, the other of its whole contrary.

ii. In *fundamental particular syllogisms*, the vague term or terms of the conclusion take scope or force from the vague premise.

iii. In *strengthened particular syllogisms*, the vague term or terms of conclusion take scope or force from the whole middle term or from its whole contrary, according to which is of full scope or force in both premises.

222. For example, (actual) farming depends on occupation of land (see the caution in § 191, often wanted in reference to this very instance); and occupation of land is an essential of county respectability: therefore farming and such respectability are inalternative. Here the terms of conclusion are both of vague intent or force, and the middle term of full intent: the force is precisely so much as is contained in the notion of *occupying land*. Any component either of actual farming or of county respectability which can be possessed by a non-occupier of land is of no import in the conclusion as from the above premises.

Take the mathematical form of the above:—Farmers are a species of occupiers of land; the county respectables are a species of occupiers; whence the farmer is a coinadequate of the county respectable, or both together do not make up the whole universe (that is, as implied, the population of the county). Here the contrary of the middle term, the class of *non-occupiers* of land, forms the extent of coinadequacy of the terms of conclusion implied in the premises.

223. The admission of complex terms, and of copular relations more general than the word of identification *is*, enable us to include in

without exceptions. For a remarkable instance, take the word *gentleman*: what different things people usually mean, according as they are speaking by notion of class or of attribute; the common attribute excludes a percentage of the class, and admits many who are not of the class. The reader may be puzzled to make out the text, unless his *character* of landowner correspond to his *class*.

common syllogism all the cases known as hypothetical syllogisms, conditional syllogisms, disjunctive syllogisms, dilemmas, &c. I shall merely take a few cases of these.

If P be true, Q is true; but P *is* true, therefore Q is true. This is an *hypothetical* syllogism, so called. To reduce it to a common syllogism between 'Q', 'true', and a middle term, we have 'Q' is 'a proposition true when P is true'; 'A proposition true when P is true' is 'true' (because P is true); therefore Q is true. Many other ways might be given. In truth, though the reduction is possible, the law of thought connecting hypothesis with necessary consequence is of a character which may claim to stand before syllogism, and to be employed in it, rather than the converse. But the discussion of this subject is not for a syllabus: see § 226. In a similar way may be treated 'If P be true, Q is true; Q is not true: therefore P is not true'.

224. Say that P is either A, or B, or C; A is not X, B is not X, C is not X; then P is not X. This is the syllogism

$$P))A,\ B,\ C)\cdot(X \text{ giving } P)\cdot(X$$

a common syllogism with the middle term an aggregate.

225. Either P is true, or Q; if P be true, X is true; if Q be true, Y is true; therefore either X or Y is true. The truth is the alternative of the truth of P or Q; which is the alternative of the truth of X or Y; therefore the truth is the truth of the alternative of X or Y.

Various other instances will be found in my *Formal Logic*, pp. 115–125.

226. In all syllogisms the *existence* of the middle term is a *datum*. If the conclusion be false, the syllogism being logically valid, and the premises true if the terms exist, then the nonexistence of one of the terms is the error. And if the terms which remain in the conclusion be existent, the nonexistence of the middle term may be inferred. When the syllogism is subjective in character, the transition into the objective syllogism frequently hinges on this point. Suppose success in a certain undertaking, such success being *conceivable*, depends both upon X and upon Z; then X and Z are not subjectively repugnant. Suppose that in objective reality they are repugnant: their coexistence being a thing wholly unknown and incredible. It follows then that success is objectively unattainable; impossible as things are, people say. The metaphysical premises $X((Y))Z$, X, Y, Z, being conceivable, give $X()Z$: and if X and Z have objective existence, and $X)\cdot(Z$, it follows that Y does not exist; for if it did, the premises $X((Y))Z$ would give $X()Z$. Suppose a qualification which depends both upon natural talent and early training; and suppose the talent to be one which cannot be developed early, *as things go*; then, as things go, the qualification is unattainable.[1]

[1] [Some paragraphs on probability theory and belief are here omitted.—Ed.]

244. I end with a word on the new symbols which I have employed. Most writers on logic strongly object to all symbols except the venerable *Barbara, Celarent,* &c. in § 109. I should advise the reader not to make up his mind on this point until he has well weighed [both separately and in connexion] two facts which nobody disputes. First, logic is the only science which has made no progress since the revival of letters: secondly, logic is the only science which has produced no growth of symbols.

ON THE SYLLOGISM: IV

and on the Logic of Relations

[Dated 12 November 1859]
[Read 23 April 1860]

In my second and third papers on logic [pp. 56, 107] I insisted on the ordinary syllogism being one case, and one case only, of the *composition of relations*. In this fourth paper I enter further on the subject of *relation*, as a branch of logic.

Much has been written on relation in all its psychological aspects except the logical one, that is, the analysis of necessary laws of thought connected with the notion of relation. The logician has hitherto carefully excluded from his science the study of relation in general: he places it among those heterogeneous *categories* which turn the porch of his temple into a magazine of raw material mixed with refuse. Aristotle does not give this part of logic a very hopeful look when (Categories, ch. v. or vii.) he puts forward no better phrase[1] than πρός τι to denote his abstract idea of relation. And such hope as there is becomes wellnigh extinct when we learn that the rudder is not properly the rudder of the ship, because people do not say (οὐ λέγεται) that the ship is the ship of the rudder. Here, as occasionally elsewhere, Aristotle is rather too much the expositor of common language, too little the expositor of common thought. Surely the question, 'What ship does this rudder belong to?' must sometimes have been heard in an Athenian dockyard: and if this question were not equivalent to 'Which is the ship of this rudder?' in the common idiom, the equivalence ought to have been established by the logician so soon as wanted. Terms may be related, even though they have more meaning than just goes to the relation. A ship is 'the steered' and the rudder is 'the steerer:' that it happens to a *ship* to mean *more*

[1] When a noun is thus formed, it is a sign that the mind of the language has not possession of the idea. There is a useful piece of furniture called a *what-not*, a holder of miscellaneous articles: the word is of the same type as πρός τι. We are an orderly people, and the notion of unarranged deposit is not among those for which we find words of serious approval. Dr Roget can produce no nouns which come close to the point except the contemptuous term *medley*, the corruption of a legal term *hodge-podge*, also contemptuous out of law, and the best word of all, the only one which perfectly applies, *omnium gatherum*, contemptuous and not English. The applier of the term *what-not* probably was not aware that he had the authority of Aristotle for his mode of proceeding.

than 'a thing steered,' and to a *rudder* to mean *no* more than 'the thing which steers,' is a purely material concomitant of the words.

The logicians of our day seem to my mind to combine a want of memory by which they do their own literary ancestors less than justice with an assumption by which they take advantage of their own wrong. Their predecessors worked the modern languages into adequate vehicles of scientific thought. They greatly augmented what they found in the Latin of the power of the Greek: and the vernacular idioms, partly by abstraction and partly by imitation, acquired the increased power of the Latin. From the first growth of experimental science down to our own day the logicians have not shewn themselves aware of this: at least they have not known how to use it in efficient defence of 'the schoolman' from the sneers of the physical writers. A person who approaches mediaeval psychology fresh from a long course of thought on exact science, its language, its progress, and its impediments, finds the claim of the scholastic writers presented to him in a strong light. He seeks the old books to learn something about the 'trammels'—this is, I believe, the proper technical word—in which they bound the human mind: for the human mind, he has been implicitly instructed, is rapid and vigorous in abstract science, if only it take care to follow no leader. But he finds that very much of his own lingual power of expressing abstract thought is due to the action of these schoolmen upon his mother-tongue: he feels that he is at the fountain-head of his own scientific idiom: he learns that those who raised the seed have been ignorant enough to think lightly of those who dug and manured the ground: and he comes to know that *language capable of science* can only be the result of deep thought upon the mind in relation to words, and words in relation to things. He then remembers the sarcasm[1] of the

[1] Logicus araneae potest comparari,
Quae subtiles didicit telas operari,
Quae suis visceribus volunt consummari,
Est pretium musca—si forte queat laqueari.

When Bacon adopted this sarcasm, he left out the fly, and propounded the web as the end, not the means: and he has been followed by some original writers who have likened the schoolman to the spider, which spins all its own *nourishment* from its own bowels.

The web which caught the flies at last was a mathematical web: and in time an imitation of the mathematical web was applied to subjects over which the empire of pure calculation did not extend. Neither the mediaeval logicians nor the followers of Bacon ever constructed a physical science. Those who delight to call themselves the followers of Bacon are in reality followers of Galileo and of Newton—of Galileo, the predecessor of Bacon in his works, and of Newton, who cannot be *proved* to have known that there was such a person as Bacon. Again and again has it been asked *what discovery has ever been made by that method which Bacon recommended?* and always without answer. And for this reason, that the mythical Bacon cannot be supported by quotations from the *Novum Organum*. It is full time that those who actually read the great work—for such it really is—which is supposed to have taught

spider, and finds it a true description of a needful process: the web first, the fly afterwards.

The logician appeals to common thought in proof of his system being an exposition of the necessary laws of thought. In one sense he is right: his system contains the *necessary* laws of thought; for the actual thought of the lowest type of mankind must be the maximum of the *necessary* thought: so that, on the Ricardo theory, the logician has created a great deal of rent. But, meaning by a necessary law of thought that mode of action which must guide the thinker who comes up to the point at which the question of law or no law can arise, I affirm that all the difference between Aristotle or Occam and the lowest of the noble savages who ran wild in the woods is only part, and I believe a very small part, of the development of human power. If the logician could leaven his own mind with a full sense of what his foregoers did for thought and for language, a spontaneous admission would grow that if these same foregoers had worked themselves into the same familiarity with relation in general which they obtained with what I call *onymatic* relations, and still more if they had cultivated those yet wider fields which lie beyond, the common language would have now possessed facilities on the want of which[1] he founds his assertion of the sufficiency of the old logic. Though satisfied that the educated world is in advance of the current system of logic, I feel equally sure that a more extensive system would work a still greater progress.

The investigation of the subject of relation has kept before my thoughts, and with a *de te fabula narratur* of a most humiliating character, conclusions which instruction of young minds during more than thirty years has forced upon me. A person accustomed to teach mathematics from the earliest commencement to the highest theories, to pupils wholly unformed in inference upon matter with which they are not familiar, has a perception of the difficulties of the uneducated process of reasoning which few others can arrive at. And that which he cannot help seeing in the efforts of an unformed mind, decided in character and large in amount, he learns to detect in the more advanced student and in the educated man. At the same time he finds the reason why the deficiency need not be acknowledged, and may even be denied by any one

[1] An existing instrument always appeals to the fact—in justice I must say the established fact—that all which ever was done resulted from the use of then existing instruments. In our own day Brown Bess has asked the long range rifle how many battles she won in the Peninsula: to which the rifle has replied by asking Brown Bess how many battles *she* won forty years before she was invented.

---

experimental philosophy her rudiments, should either support the pretensions advanced in its favour, or aid in the substitution of others of a more correct character. Provided always that *Bacon's own method*—which is very easily propounded—be advanced in *Bacon's own words*.

who takes the proper ground. For it is not a deficiency which strikingly manifests itself in habitual faults of commission: habitual faults are only in habitual things. The evil is most patent when new and strange materials are submitted to the mind; and it bears fruit, though of course undetected by positive consequences, in the many cases in which want of power is a prohibition.

The uncultivated reason proceeds by a process almost[1] entirely material. Though the necessary law of thought must determine the conclusion of the plough-boy as much as that of Aristotle himself, the plough-boy's conclusion will only be tolerably sure when the matter of it is such as comes within his usual cognizance. He knows that geese being all birds does not make all birds geese, but mainly because there are ducks, chickens, partridges, &c. A beginner in geometry,[2] when asked what follows from 'Every *A* is *B*,' answers 'Every *B* is *A*, of course.' That is, the necessary laws of thought, except in minds which have examined their tools, are not very sure to work correct conclusions except upon familiar matter. And above all, *relation* is a difficulty when the related terms are unusual names, even in the most[3] common cases.

[1] The syllogism is complex, and so is the act of walking: but in both cases the mind produces the whole without a consciousness of parts. Several persons have thought I was carrying things too far when, in my first paper, I said that a person who calls out *John!* enunciates two propositions, 'John is the person I want,' and, 'You are John.' They will probably think that the author cited by Roger Bacon (*Opus Tertium*, p. 102) also went too far, in the following passage. 'Auctor Perspectivae ponit exemplum de puero qui cum ei offeruntur duo poma, quorum unum est pulchrius altero, ipse eligit pulchrius, et non nisi quia judicat pulchrius esse melius, et quod est melius est magis eligendum. Ergo de necessitate puer arguit sic apud se: quod est pulchrius est melius, et quod est melius est magis eligendum; ergo pomum pulchrius est magis eligendum. . . . Unde licet laici non habeant vocabula logicae quibus clerici utuntur, tamen habent suos modos solvendi omne argumentum falsum. Et ideo vocabula sola logicorum deficiunt laicis, non ipsa scientia logicae.'

It is very difficult to deny that both the premises and the conclusion are truly parts of the boy's mental act of choice: but quite impossible to admit that they are *separate* parts. We must distinguish between the compound act of the uneducated thinker, and the analysed compound of the logician; between the process guided by law, and the cognizance of the law which guides. It is not true that the law by which thought is governed must be part of the thought which is governed: though some writers against logic have spoken as if they would sanction the affirmative. And, similarly, some writers against gravitation are hardly intelligible except when taken as implying that Newton gave the particles of matter some mysterious cognizance of $m:r^2$.

It is also clear that the opinion of Roger Bacon's time tended to the conclusion that logic is a science of invented laws, not an analysis of the actual laws of thinking; the mistake is not yet defunct.

[2] He is thrown at once into forms of strict reasoning, with unusual matter on which to employ them. Either some logic ought to precede Geometry, with familiar instances; or some acquaintance with figure by measurement ought to precede the reasoning; or, better than either, both.

[3] Though I take the following only from a newspaper, yet I feel confident it really

As the cultivation of the individual increases, the laws of thought which are of most usual application are applied to familiar matter with tolerable safety. But difficulty and risk of error make a new appearance with a new subject; and this, in most cases, until new subjects are familiar things, unusual matter common, untried nomenclature habitual; that is, until it is a habit to be occupied upon a novelty. It is observed that many persons reason well in some things, and badly in others; and this is attributed to the consequences of employing the mind too much upon one or another subject. But those who know the truth of the preceding remarks will not be to seek for what is often, perhaps most often, the true reason.

Waiving all question about common matter being usually the subject of tolerably good inference, about the assertion that logic, though of some use, does not fully repay its labour, and about the observed fact—the like of which is true in regard to all studies—that learners of logic not infrequently reason no better after instruction than before,—*waiving* these things, not *admitting* them, I maintain that logic tends to make the power of reason over the unusual and unfamiliar more nearly equal to the power over the usual and familiar than it would otherwise be. The second is increased; but the first is almost created.

An attempt to investigate the forms of thought involved in combination of relations, the results of which are contained in the following pages, has given me personal experience of the truth of the preceding remarks. I have had to work my way through transformations as new to my own mind, so far as the separation of form is concerned, as the common moods of syllogism to a beginner in logic. If there be any person who can see at a glance, and with justifiable confidence, what classes of men, including women, are specified in 'the non-ancestors of all non-descendants of *Z*,' I should not like to submit to his criticism the confusions and blunders through which I arrived at the following results: unless indeed I were able to remind him of some of his own similar experiences. And this could be done with the greatest names in

happened: there is the truth of nature about it, and the enormity of the case is not incredible to those who have taught beginners in reasoning. The scene is a ragged school. TEACHER. Now, boys, Shem, Ham, and Japheth were Noah's sons; who was the father of Shem, Ham, and Japheth? No answer. TEACHER. Boys, you know Mr Smith, the carpenter, opposite; has he any sons? BOYS. Oh! yes, Sir! there's Bill and Ben. TEACHER. And who is the father of Bill and Ben Smith? BOYS. Why, Mr Smith, to be sure. TEACHER. Well, then, once more, Shem, Ham, and Japheth were *Noah's* sons; who was the father of Shem, Ham, and Japheth? A long pause; at last a boy, indignant at what he thought the attempted trick, cried out, It *couldn't* have been Mr Smith! These boys had never converted the relation of father and son, except under the material aid of a common surname: if Shem Arkwright, &c., had been described as the sons of Noah Arkwright, part of the difficulty, not all, would have been removed.

the history of abstract speculation. If Newton were the examiner of my failures, I could recall the occasion on which he lost his own connexion between the inverse square and the ellipse, because his casual diagram put conjugate diameters at right angles to one another, and seduced him into the belief that they were the principal axes. Were it Wallis, I could revive the time when he hesitated at $\sqrt{12} = 2\sqrt{3}$, sure of the theorem, but doubtful of the validity of the expression, for want of precedent. Were it Leibnitz, I could bring to his memory the co-inventor of the differential calculus, doubting whether to say yes or no to the equation $\frac{dy}{dx} = d\left(\frac{y}{x}\right)$, and working out the decision on paper. And so on.

The want of power which most persons feel in the treatment of combined relations, may be well illustrated by cases of the class of relationships which have almost appropriated the name, those of consanguinity and affinity. Many educated persons, and some acute logicians, would either pause for an unreasonable time, or would not give the right answer, if asked for *all* the conclusion[1] that follows about John and Thomas from 'William is not John's father, and Thomas is William's uncle.'

The only relations admitted into logic, down to the present time, are those which can be signified by *is* and denied by *is not*. Allowing to the substantive verb all its range of meaning—and that range is a wide one —and introducing *contrary* notions, all the relations which were styled *onymatic* in my last paper, whether arithmetical, mathematical, or metaphysical, are capable of inclusion. All other relation is avoided by the dictum that it shall be of the form of thought to consider the relation and the related predicate as *the* predicate, and the judgment as a declaration or denial of identity between this and the related subject.

Accordingly, all logical relation is affirmed to be reducible to *identity*, *A* is *A*, to *non-contradiction*, Nothing both *A* and not-*A*, and to *excluded middle*, Everything either *A* or not-*A*. These three principles, it is affirmed, dictate all the forms of inference, and evolve all the canons of syllogism. I am not prepared to deny the truth of either of these propositions, at least when *A* is not self-contradictory, but I cannot see how,

[1] The old riddle-books often propound the following query:—If Dick's father be Tom's son, what relation is Dick to Tom? When a boy, I heard the following classical and Protestant version of the puzzle, over which I have since made grown persons ponder, not always with success. An abbess observed that an elderly nun was often visited by a young gentleman, and asked what relation he was. 'A very near relation,' answered the nun; 'his mother was my mother's only child:' which answer, as was intended, satisfied the abbess that the visitor must be within the unprohibited degrees, without giving precise information. When this is proposed, the first answer often is, He was her grandchild; and if the story did not say that the visitor was young, he would sometimes be taken for her grandfather; the matter not preventing, $\phi\phi^{-1}$ might as well be mistaken into $\phi^{-1}\phi^{-1}$ as into $\phi\phi$.

alone, they are competent to the functions assigned. I see that they distinguish truth from falsehood: but I do not see that they, again alone, either distinguish or evolve one truth from another. Every transgression of these laws is an invalid inference: every valid inference is not a transgression of these laws. But I cannot admit that every thing which is not a transgression of these laws is a valid inference. And I cannot make out how just the only propositions which are true of all things conceivable can *be* or *lead to* any distinction between one thing and another. I believe these three principles to be of the soil, and not of the seed, though the seed may possess some materials of the soil; of the foundation, not of the building, though the bricks may partake of the nature of the foundation; of the rails, not of the locomotive, though both may have iron in their structure.

The canons of ordinary syllogism cannot be established without help from our knowledge of the *convertible* and *transitive* character of identification: that is, we must know and use the properties '*A* is *B* gives *B* is *A*' and '*A* is *B* and *B* is *C*, compounded, give *A* is *C*.' Can these principles be established by concession of '*A* is *A*, nothing is both *A* and not-*A*, and every thing is one or the other'? All my attempts at such establishment end in begging[1] the question, when closely scrutinized. The logicians do not make their deduction in perfectly precise and formal method, so that a lapse may be clearly pointed out. I suspect that the use of convertibility and transitiveness actually takes place, and must take place, in every attempt to deduce the legitimacy of the two laws, as necessary consequences of the three laws: and if my suspicion be correct, it follows that the *two* principles must be assumed independently of the *three*. I cannot argue the question until I find some more precise attempt to maintain the assertion: I suspect that 'it is *as plain as that A* is *A*' has been confounded with 'it is true *because A* is *A*.'

In the consideration of the proposition, *identification* of *objects* is in

[1] It is not lawful to employ syllogism in deducing syllogism from postulates which are affirmed to necessitate it: for if all syllogism be invalid—and whether or no is *the* question—it may establish *itself* on any basis. The quadrature of the circle may be deduced from the Habeas Corpus Act by a method which contains only one paralogism. I have heard logic called the science which *demonstrates demonstration*: it only *analyses* demonstration. So surely as no system of truths can be established upon no truth to begin with, so surely can no methods of *transition* or *inference* be established without methods of inference to start with. If then the *very earliest* demand the use of the transitive and convertible characters of the copula, these characters cannot be themselves inferred: consequently, unless non-inferentially and *im*mediately seen in the three principles, they must be adopted on their own security. The moment this is done, the whole of the common syllogism must be admitted under the extension to *every copula which is both transitive and convertible*; for transitiveness and convertibility once separated from the three principles of *identification*, and standing on their own footing, the restriction of the copula to the *identifying* verb 'is,' no matter how many its senses, is only arbitrary and lawless distinction.

truth a *relation* of *concepts*. In the ordinary books on logic, the relation before the mind is confusedly mixed up with the *judgment*, the assertion or denial of the relation. The word *is* has two different meanings: standing alone, it means *identity affirmed*; in the phrase *is not*, it means only *identity*. I claim to recognize the distinction between relation and judgment, and to assign to each notion its own symbol. Let X and Y be terms, and L a relation in which X may or may not stand to Y, let $X..LY$ signify the assertion of the relation, and $X.LY$ its denial. This separation of relation and judgment is an important step towards the treatment of syllogistic inference as an act of combination of relation; as also towards the knowledge that the ordinary canons of syllogism do actually embrace *every* case in which one relation only is used, and that relation transitive and convertible.

That all analysis of thought should be confined to expression under one class of relations is the defence of a system formed under limited views, and a defence which nothing but necessity could have originated. It is the *great principle of pebbles* invented for justification of arithmeticians who have never got beyond pebbles. Pure arithmetic, dealing with nothing but the notion of number, has all its processes reducible of course to making number more or less. The solution of a cubic[1] equation to 153 figures is within the reach of a *calculator* who has enough of *calculi*, life, and patience. And number is defined by the more or less of counting which has taken place in its formation; further counting onwards is the *process* required in addition; counting backwards is the process required in subtraction: and to these all other processes can be reduced. The last unit, or item[2] of numeration, tells the result of all that has been done. Suppose any one to contend that arithmetic should

[1] 'If the curiosity of any gentleman that has leisure' to use Halley's words when inviting to the calculation of the logarithms of all prime numbers under 100,000 to 25 or 30 places of figures, 'should prompt him to undertake' to verify this assertion, he ought to find the following as the solution of the celebrated equation $x^3 - 2x - 5 = 0$. I will not say, with Halley, 'I can assure him that the facility of this method will invite him thereto.'

$x =$ 2·09455 14815 42326 59148 23865 40579 30296 38573 06105 62823 91803 04128
52904 53121 89983 48366 71462 67281 77715 77578 60839 52118 90629 63459
84514 03984 20812 82370 08437 22349 91

This result, which will place the power of Horner's method in its proper light of evidence, was calculated in 1850 by my pupil Mr John Power Hicks, since of Lincoln College, Oxford, and has not been published till now. A hundred places had previously been calculated by another pupil, Mr William Harris Johnston (*Mathematician*, Vol. III, p. 289) whose solution was unknown to Mr Hicks. Neither solution was merely numerical exercise; both were performed upon a knowledge of, and by incitement of, the tardiness of mathematicians, as well abroad as at home, in recognizing the true place of Horner's discovery in *fundamental* arithmetical operation.

[2] In my last paper I criticized the phraseology of logicians when they say that the difference between one and another individual of the same species is *numerical*. An able defender referred me to the Greek original of the phrase: in Porphyry, &c.,

never transcend pure counting, and he would be a faithful imitator of argument about logic, as not infrequently expressed, and always implicitly maintained. The arithmetician I have supposed should argue from the fundamental character of the counting process: he should leave practice and progress out of sight, should refuse to allow the possibility of abstractions which might end in the differential calculus, and should contend for the pure form of arithmetical thought. Every merchant's clerk would laugh at his book of arithmetic, and would be joined by every speculator on that theory of numbers at which he could never arrive. But our arithmetician should stand firm upon the fact that men naturally count on their fingers. And though those who count on the fingers do not want him, and those who can do better will not have him, he can retire within himself, satisfied that he is the true philosopher of arithmetic, and the sole depository of the science. And, all unreasonable as he is, he would be more reasonable than the logician. For it *is* the truth that all arithmetical result can be obtained by counters: it is *not* the truth that all inference can be obtained by ordinary syllogism, in which the terms of the conclusion must be terms of the premises. If any one will by such syllogism prove that because every man is an animal, therefore every head of a man is a head of an animal, I shall be ready to—set him another question.

When the logician contends that a syllogism which is not onymatic can be reduced to one which is, he always proceeds by a statement of the combination of relations, for his major, and an assertion that the relations so introduced into his *principium* exist in the *exemplum* before him, for his minor. But though this evasion—it is nothing else—is practised, and serves to hide the insufficiency of the onymatic syllogism, it is not

things which, being different, do not differ εἴδει, differ ἀριθμῷ. My thorough conviction that the Greeks never altered the vernacular in scientific terms led me to an examination of the word ἀριθμός, the results of which appear in the *Transactions of the Philological Society* for 1859. The original meaning of ἀριθμός, never lost, though soon associated with the secondary sense of *total*, is the *item* of enumeration, the unit of a collection, which standing alone would be μονάς. Thus Aristotle, (*Metaphysics*, book xi or xii) speaking of the primary meaning, affirms that μονάς and ἀριθμός do not differ in *quantity*. When an ἀριθμός was spoken of as large, the departure from the original meaning is precisely that which takes place in our own language when a sale is said to be made at a *high figure*, meaning much money to count [to the end of]. The word *sum* gives occasion to similar remarks. *Summa* and *sum* meant number indicated by the *highest unit* of counting: neither had reference to addition more than to subtraction, number to be subtracted being also *sum* and *summa deducibilis*. The *totum* was *summa totalis*, and *sum total* still remains in use, sounding like tautology: but the fact is that *totalis*, when it dropped off, left its meaning fixed in *summa*. The school-word for arithmetic, *summing*, is not a derivation from the leading rule, *addition*, but means, or meant, numbering generally. Logicians would speak more to the purpose, in English, if they substituted *monadical* for *numerical*: nothing can make a numerical difference to an English ear except a difference of numerical quantity.

distinctly proclaimed, and universally applied. When I first challenged the reduction to an Aristotelian syllogism of the inference that *some* must have both coats and waistcoats if *most* have coats and *most* have waistcoats, I supposed that among the attempts to answer would be the following:—'Two terms each of which has more than half the extent of a third term are terms which have some common extent; the men who have coats and the men who have waistcoats are two terms each of which has more than half the extent of a third term; therefore the men who have coats and the men who have waistcoats are terms which have some common extent.' But this was not brought forward: though it had as much right to appear as the following. Reid denied that '$A = B$, $B = C$, therefore $A = C$' is a (common) syllogism. True, says one able expounder, because it is *elliptical*: true, says another, because it is *material*. Both render it into what they call true logical form as follows: —Things equal to the same are things equal to one another; A and B are things equal to the same; therefore A and B are things equal to one another. I pass over the assertion that $A = B$ &c. is an *ellipsis* of this last, as not worth answer: the imputed *material* character requires further consideration.

When it shall be clearly pointed out, by definite precept and sufficiently copious example, what the logicians really mean by the distinction of form and matter, I may be able to deal with the question more definitely than I can do at this time. Dr Thomson (*Outlines*, &c., § 15) remarks that they seldom or never talk much about the distinction without[1] confusion. I can but ask what is that notion of form as opposed to matter on which it can be denied that '$A = B$, $B = C$, $\therefore$ $A = C$' is

[1] Because there really is not *much* to talk about: the separation is soon conceived, and soon made; and the work begins when, after separation, the analysis of the things separated is attempted. There is much detail in cookery, much in shoe-making, if we start from the raw flesh and the raw hide. The separation of these parts of the animal is easily seen to be wanted and easily made; any very great talk about it can have no effect, unless it be to give a chance of leather steaks and beef shoes. One of the oldest of the schoolmen, John of Salisbury—whose date may be remembered by the record that *tacitus, sed maerens, continuo se subduxit*, when Thomas-à-Becket was killed by his side—says nearly as much as need be said, as follows:—'At qui lineam, aut superficiem attendit sine corpore, formam utique contemplationis oculo a materia disjungit: cum tamen sine materia forma esse non possit. Non tamen formam sine materia esse abstrahens hic concipit intellectus (compositus enim esset) sed simpliciter alterum sine altero, cum tamen sine altero esse non possit, intuetur. Nec hoc quidem simplicitati ejus praejudicat, sed eo simplicior est, quo simpliciora, sine aliorum admixtione, perspicit singulatim. Hoc autem naturae rerum non adversatur, quae ad sui investigationem hanc potestatem contulit intellectui, ut possit conjuncta disjungere, et disjuncta conjungere' (*Metalogicus*, Lib. II, cap. 20). Add to this illustration from the original meaning of the terms the extension of the words *matter* and *form* to any distinction between the *quod se habet* and the *modus se habendi*, as also to the distinction of *operation* and *operated on*, and the two words may then take leave of each other. But when form and matter are to be adapted to the defence of the existing mode of distinction, it is no wonder if they must be hammered until the anvil is hot.

as pure a form of thought, apart from matter, as '*A is B, B is C, ∴ A is C.*' In both there is matter implied in *A*, *B*, *C*: but in both this matter is vague, all that is definite being the sameness of the matter of *A*, &c. in all places in which the symbol occurs. In both there is a law of thought appealed to on primary subjective testimony of consciousness; 'equal of equal is equal' in the first; 'identical of identical is identical' in the second. These two laws are equally necessary, equally self-evident, equally incapable of demonstration out of more simple elements. Does the very notion of *equation* demand the identity of *A* and *A* to be conceded? just as much does the very notion of identification demand the *equality* of *A* and *A* to be conceded. We can think of nothing but what has some attributes which have quantity: and the very notion of identity, demanding identity of all attributes, demands equality of quantity in those which *have* quantity. On what definition, then, of form is 'equal of equal is equal' declared material, while 'identical of identical is identical' is declared formal?

In choosing the instance of *equality*, a very near relation of *identity*, I am rendering but a poor account of my own thesis. I maintain that there is no purely and entirely *formal* proposition except this:—'There is the probability α that *X* is in the relation *L* to *Y*.' Accordingly, I hold that the copula is as much materialized, when for *L* we read *identity*, as when for *L* we read *grandfather*. The mere notion of *materiality*, like that of quantity (see my last paper), *non suscipit magis et minus*. And I hold the supreme *form* of syllogism of one middle term to be as follows; —There is the probability α that *X* is in relation *L* to *Y*; there is the probability β that *Y* is in relation *M* to *Z*; whence there is the probability $\alpha\beta$ that *X* has been proved in these premises to be in relation *L* of *M* to *Z*. Here is nothing but *formal* representation, that is, expression of form without particular specification of matter. I now proceed to something of a less controversial character.

Any two objects of thought brought together by the mind, and thought together in one act of thought, are *in relation*. Should any one deny this by producing two notions of which he defies me to state the relation, I tell him that he has stated it himself: he has made me think the notions in the relation of *alleged impossibility of relation*; and has made his own objection commit suicide. Two thoughts cannot be brought together in thought except by a thought: which last thought contains their *relation*.

All our prepositions express relation, and indeed all our junctions of words: but the preposition *of* is the only word of which we can say that it is, or may be made, a part of the expression of every relation; though the same thing may nearly be said of the preposition *to*. When relation creates a *noun substantive*, *of* is unavoidable: if *A* by its relation to *B* be *C*, it is a *C* of *B*. A volume might be written on the idiom of relation:

but it would be of the matter, not of the form, of the subject. I add a few desultory remarks, because some readers would hardly, from the symbols themselves, form a notion of the wide extent of thought which the symbols embrace.

When two notions are components in one compound, as *white* and *ball* in the phrase *white ball*, we have one of the many cases in which the relation is not made prominent, and the compound, as a whole, is the notion on which thought fixes. So little is the relation thought of that its introduction may produce unusual idioms. In speaking of the appurtenance of *white* to *ball*, we have the *whiteness of the ball*, which is idiomatic: but in speaking of the appurtenance of the *ball* to the *white*, we have the *rotundity of the white*, which is not familiar, though intelligible. Here we are sensible of a difficulty which usage puts in the way of logic: language hesitates at *realizing* notions which are not objectively called *things*. The metaphysical distinction of the ball being a substance, of which the whiteness is an inherent accident, is extralogical: all we have to do with is the junction in one notion of matter, roundness, and whiteness. Whether whiteness and rotundity were given to matter, or material and whiteness to rotundity, is of no account: the turner can do only the first, the thinker can do either. The notion of metaphysical or physical *order of precedence* in the entrance of components, dictates the exclusion of forms of language which are necessary to logical precision. We may think of a *horse*, and then of the attributes *swift* or *slow*: we speak of the *speed of the horse*, correctly expressing what we have in thought as related by appurtenance to the animal. But we never *speak* of the *horseness of the speed*: do we ever *think* of it? Suppose a horse going a hundred miles an hour: such a thing was never known. Suppose one which goes a million of miles in a second: perhaps this is the first time such a thing was ever *heard of*. In the first case the speed attributed to the horse is no marvel: in the second case it is not in nature, that we know of. We object to both rates, as predicated of a horse: but to the first rate *only* as so predicated. That is, it is not the velocity of the horse, but the *equinity of the velocity*, that strikes us as unprecedented when we speak of a hundred miles an hour: and the logician may use his privilege of making language for every distinction which exists in thought.

Relations of appurtenance, and indeed all others, carry with them distinctions of which grammar takes no cognizance: they give *time* or *tense*, for example, to nouns. That which hangs in the butcher's shop under the name of a *calf's head*, hangs under that name with perfect propriety: but the noun has a past tense. I am not sure that we should have been so well off as we are if philosophers had invented our language: it may have been that in such a case we should have had less sense and no poetry: but assuredly our nouns would have had moods indicative and potential, as well as tenses, past, present and future.

The relation in a compound notion sometimes seeks emergence; and the word *of* demands entrance. When we hear that 'it was the most bloody battle,' we feel an unfinished sentence: what of? the Peloponnesian war? the Peninsular war? &c. If not one of these a separation is wanted which may throw into notice the relation of appurtenance; 'it was the most bloody *of* battles.'

Indefinite extension of one component is a bar to the conception of relation, and tends to fix thought upon the whole compound. Thus in *six sheep*, the relation of *six* to *sheep* is almost dormant, so long as the selective and separative force of *six* is applied to all possible sheep. Make the collection more definite, and the relation demands expression: six *of* the sheep, six *of* his sheep. Not that *six of sheep* is unintelligible: and, on the other hand, *six his sheep* is a form not unknown in old English. Largeness of selection, totality, has the effect of destroying the relating preposition: thus *all his sons* is as admissible as *all* of *his sons*. But let the expression of completeness be retarded ever so little, and the relating preposition demands entrance. We do not say 'All *of* men are animals:' but we do say, 'Of men, all are animals.' The habits of thought of a nation silently accomplish many changes which we call caprices of language. Our modern forms of thought tend to sharpen specification of relation, especially in distinguishing agency from other relations. We no more hear of a person forsaken *of* his friends; it is now always *by*. Neither does the active participle bear the expression of relation, except as a vulgarism: squires and hounds are no longer catching *of* foxes.

I now proceed to consider the formal laws of relation, so far as is necessary for the treatment of the syllogism. Let the names X, Y, Z, be singular: not only will this be sufficient when *class* is considered as a unit, but it will be easy to extend conclusions to quantified propositions. I do not use the mathematical symbols of functional relation, ϕ, ψ, &c.: there are more reasons than one why mathematical examples are not well suited for illustration. The most apposite instances are taken from the relations between human beings: among which the *relations* which have almost monopolized the name, those of consanguinity and affinity, are conspicuously convenient, as being in daily use.

Just as in ordinary logic *existence* is implicitly predicated for all the terms, so in this subject every relation employed will be considered as actually connecting the terms of which it is predicated. Let $X..LY$ signify that X is some one of the objects of thought which stand to Y in the relation L, or is one of the Ls of Y. Let $X.LY$ signify that X is not any one of the Ls of Y. Here X and Y are *subject* and *predicate*: these names having reference to the mode of entrance in the relation, not to order of mention. Thus Y is the predicate in $LY.X$, as well as in $X.LY$.

When the predicate is itself the subject of a relation, there may[1] be a composition: thus if *X..L(MY)*, if *X* be one of the *L*s of one of the *M*s of *Y*, we may think of *X* as an '*L* of *M*' of *Y*, expressed by *X..(LM)Y*, or simply by *X..LM Y*. A wider treatment of the subject would make it necessary to effect a symbolic distinction between '*X* is not any *L* of any *M* of *Y*' and '*X* is not any *L* of some of the *M*s of *Y*.' For my present purpose this is not necessary: so that *X.LM Y* may denote the first of the two. Neither do I at present find it necessary to use relations which are aggregates of other relations: as in *X..(L,M)Y*, *X* is either one of the *L*s of *Y* or one of the *M*s, or both.

We cannot proceed further without attention to forms in which *universal* quantity is an inherent part of the compound relation, as belonging to the notion of the relation itself, intelligible in the compound, unintelligible in the separated component.

First, let *LM′* signify[2] an *L* of *every M*, *LM′X* being an individual in the same relation to many. Here the accent is a sign of universal quantity which forms part of the description of the relation: *LM′* is not an aggregate of cases of *LM*. Next let *L,M* signify an *L* of an *M* in every way in which it is an *L* at all: an *L* of none but *M*s. Here the accent is also a sign of universal quantity: and logic seems to dictate to grammar that this should be read 'an every-*L* of *M*.'[3] The dictation however is of convenience; not of obligation, as in the case of the double negative. Either some horse or no horse; if not no horse, then some horse. The Greek[4] idiom refused this dilemma. There is no scrape that man does

[1] A mathematician may raise a moment's question as to whether *L* and *M* are properly said to be *compounded* in the sense in which *X* and *Y* are said to be compounded in the term *XY*. In the phrase *brother of parent*, are *brother* and *parent* compounded in the same manner as *white* and *ball* in the term *white ball*. I hold the affirmative, so far as concerns the distinction between *composition* and *aggregation*: not denying the essential distinction between *relation* and *attribute*. According to the conceptions by which *man* and *brute* are aggregated in *animal*, while *animal* and *reason* are compounded in *man*, one primary feature of the distinction is that an impossible component puts the compound out of existence, an impossible aggregant does not put the aggregate out of existence. In this particular the compound relation '*L* of *M*' classes with the compound term 'both *X* and *Y*.'

[2] Simple as the connexion with the rest of what I now proceed to may appear, it was long before the *quantified relation* suggested itself, and until this suggestion arrived, all my efforts to make a scheme of syllogism were wholly unsuccessful. The quantity was in my mind, but not *carried to the account of relation*. Thus *LX))MY*, or every *L* of *X* is an *M* of *Y*, has the notion of universal quantity attached in the common way to *LX*, not to *L*: its equivalents $X..L^{-1},MY$, and $Y..M^{-1}L'X$, shew *X* and *Y* as singular terms, and though expressing the same ideas of quantity as *LX))MY*, throw the quantity entirely into the description of the relations.

[3] [*L((M*
L))M
as *L*, always *L* of *M*].

[4] It would be worth the while of some one who has the requisite scholarship to examine the question how far the negatory power of the double negative in Greek

not get into: if we had no other way of knowing this, we have the assurance of Euripides; but he informs us that there is *not* no scrape that man does not get into. The *educated* English idiom follows logic, which here commands. Such a phrase as the 'every uncle of a sailor' has no meaning except in poetry, where it means the *sole* uncle. It would be highly convenient if the distinction between LM' and L,M could be made as in '*L* of every *M*' and 'every-*L* of *M*.'

The symbols $L'MX$ and LM,X, which I shall not need, analogically interpreted would mean 'every *L* of an *M* of *X*' and 'an *L* of an *M* of none but *X*.' The compound symbol $L,M'X$ means an *L* of every *M* of *X* and of nothing else; and is really the compound $(LM'X)$ $(L\ MX)$. No further notice will be taken of it.

We have thus three symbols of compound relation; LM, an *L* of an *M*; LM', an *L* of every *M*; L,M, an *L* of none but *M*s. No other compounds will be needed in syllogism, until the premises themselves contain compound relations.

In *every* case in which there is a first and a second, let the *first* be *minor*, the *second, major*. Thus if $X..LM\ Y$, let *X* and *Y* be its minor and major terms, and *L* and *M* its minor and major relations: if it be the *first* premise of a syllogism let it be the *minor* premise.

The *converse* relation of L, L^{-1}, is defined as usual: if $X..LY$, $Y..L^{-1}X$: if *X* be one of the *L*s of *Y*, *Y* is one of the L^{-1}s of *X*. And $L^{-1}X$ may be read '*L-verse* of *X*.' Those who dislike the mathematical symbol in L^{-1} might write L^{v}. This language would be very convenient in mathematics: $\phi^{-1}x$ might be the 'ϕ-verse of x,' read as 'ϕ-verse x.'

Relations are assumed to exist between any two terms whatsoever. If *X* be not any *L* of *Y*, *X* is to *Y* in some not-*L* relation: let this *contrary* relation be signified[1] by *l*; thus $X.LY$ gives and is given by $X..lY$. Con-

[1] The affirmative symbol (..) is derived from the junction of the two negatives (.)(.). Analogy would seem to require that the privative relation not-*L* should be denoted by (*.L*). Or thus:—Let *W* denote the affirmation, and *V* the denial: then $XWLY$ would denote that *X* is an *L* of *Y*, and $XVVLY$ that *X* is not a not-*L*

---

determined the course of Aristotle in regard to privative terms. In further reference to the dictating power of logic, I may observe that it does not go far: forms cannot dictate meaning to any but a very small extent. For instance: It is almost universal, but not quite, that transference of *not* from the copula to the predicate produces no change of meaning. 'He either will do it, or he will-not do it' means the same as 'He either will do it, or he will not-do it;' and the two of each set are alternatives. But 'He either can do it, or he cannot do it' has not identity of meaning with 'He either can do it or he can not-do it:' the first pair are repugnant alternatives, the second are not: the same person who can do it, usually can not-do it, or can let it alone, but not always. Again, the junction of *not* to the verb usually gives a contrary, or a repugnant alternative: he eats or he eats not, he has or he has not, he does or he does not. But we may not say, Either he must, or he must not; these are no necessary alternatives: we can only say, Either he must, or he need not, Either he must not, or he may. Many similar instances might be given.

trary relations may be compounded, though contrary terms cannot: Xx, both X and not-X, is impossible; but Llx, the L of a not-L of X, is conceivable. Thus a man may be the partisan of a non-partisan of X.

Contraries of converses are converses: thus not-L and not L^{-1} are converses. For $X..LY$ and $Y..L^{-1}X$ are identical; whence X..not-LY and Y..(not-L^{-1})X, their simple denials, are identical; whence not-L and not-L^{-1} are converses.

Converses of contraries are contraries: thus L^{-1} and (not-L)$^{-1}$ are contraries. For since $X..LY$ and X..not-LY are simple denials of each other, so are their converses $Y..L^{-1}X$ and Y..(not-L)^{-1}X; whence L^{-1} and (not-L)$^{-1}$ are contraries.

The contrary of a converse is the converse of the contrary: not-L^{-1} is (not-L)$^{-1}$. For $X..LY$ is identical with Y.not-$L^{-1}X$ and with X.(not-L)Y, which is also identical with Y.(not-L)^{-1}X. Hence the term not-L-verse is unambiguous in meaning, though ambiguous in form.

If a first relation be contained in a second, then the converse of the first is contained in the converse of the second: but the contrary of the *second* in the contrary of the *first*.

The conversion of a compound relation converts both components, and inverts their order. If X be an L of an M of Y, then an M of Y is an L^{-1} of X, and Y is an M^{-1} of an L^{-1} of X. Or $(LM)^{-1}$ is $M^{-1}L^{-1}$. The mark of inherent quantity is also changed in place. If X be[1] an L of every M of Y, then Y is an M^{-1} of none but L^{-1}s of X. And if X be an L of none but Ms of Y, then Y is an M^{-1} of every L^{-1} of X. For $X..LM'Y$ is $MY))L^{-1}X$ or $Y..M_{,}{}^{-1}L^{-1}X$: and $X..L,MY$ is $L^{-1}X))MY$ or $Y..M^{-1}L^{-1\prime}X$.

When there is a sign of inherent quantity, if each component be changed into its contrary, and the sign of quantity be shifted from one component to the other, there is no change in the meaning of the symbol. Thus an L of every M is a not-L of none but not-Ms; and *vice versa*: and an L of none but Ms is a not-L of every not-M; and *vice versa*.

When a compound has no inherent quantity, the contrary is found by taking the contrary of either component, and giving inherent quantity to the other. Thus, either L of an M or not-L of every M; either L of an M or L of none but not-Ms. But if there be a sign of inherent quantity in one component, the contrary is taken by dropping that sign, and taking the contrary of the other component. Thus, either L of every M or not-L of an M; either L of none but Ms, or L of a not-M.[2]

[1] A good instance of the difficulty of abstract propositions: it is easy enough on a concrete instance. If X be the superior of every ancestor of Y, then Y is the descendant of none but inferiors of X.

[2] [$L()M; L)\cdot(M; L((M; L))M$.]

---

of Y. But I do not at present find advantage in a notation which expresses $X..LY$ and its equivalent $X.lY$ in one symbol: I may possibly do so at a future time.

The following table contains[1] all these theorems:

Combination	*Converse*	*Contrary*	*Converse of contrary* *Contrary of converse*
LM	$M^{-1}L^{-1}$	lM' or L,m	$M,^{-1}l^{-1}$ or $m^{-1}L^{-1\prime}$
LM' or l,m	$M,^{-1}L^{-1}$ or $m^{-1}l^{-1\prime}$	lM	$M^{-1}l^{-1}$
L,M or lm'	$M^{-1}L^{-1\prime}$ or $m,^{-1}l^{-1}$	Lm	$m^{-1}L^{-1}$

If a compound relation be contained in another relation, by the nature of the relations and not by casualty of the predicate, the same may be said when either component is converted, and the contrary of the other component and of the compound change places. That is if, be Z what it may, every L of M of Z be an N of Z, say $LM))N$, then $L^{-1}n))m$, and $nM^{-1}))l$. If $LM))N$, then $n))lM'$ and $nM^{-1}))lM'M^{-1}$. But an l of *every* M of an M^{-1} of Z must be an l of Z: hence $nM^{-1}))l$. Again, if $LM))N$, then $n))L,m$, whence $L^{-1}n))L^{-1}L,m$. But an L^{-1} of an L of none but ms of Z must be an m of Z; whence $L^{-1}n))m$.

I shall call this result theorem K, in remembrance of the office of that letter in Baroko and Bokardo; it is the theorem on which the formation of what I called opponent syllogisms is founded. For example, the combination in one of the mathematical[2] syllogisms is Every deficient of an

[1] The resultant relation in onymatic syllogism is identical with the compound from which it results. Thus (.)).) is (), identically; every complement of a deficient is a partient; every partient is a complement of a deficient. The contraries then are identical; and this gives the key to the resulting meaning of quantified compound relations: as ,(()), a genus of none but species; or (())′, a genus of every species. The complete rule of interpretation of such symbols is as follows. Reject as incapable of meaning all cases in which two universals or two particulars have different middle quantities, or in which a universal and particular have the accent upon the particular. Thus there is no such thing as))))′, or ,(.((), or ((()′: a species of every species of a given genus is non-existing. In all other cases, invert the spicula nearest to the accent, erase the middle spiculae, and the result shows the relation identical with the given compound. Thus (.) (.)′ gives (..(or ((: a complement of every complement is a genus; and *vice versa*. Again, ,(.) ((gives).(: a complement of none but genera is an external, &c. Also, ,(( )(gives)(: a genus of none but coinadequates is a coinadequate, &c. A defective account of these transformations will be found in my third paper.

[Retain *same* quantity of proposition with *same* quantity of middle term: and different quantity of proposition with accent on the universal.

```
,() () ||))    ,)) ((||((    () ))′||((
() ()′||((     )) ((′||))    () (·)′||(·(
(·( )·)′||((
,(·( )·)||))                             ]
```

[2] In arithmetical form thus:—Some *Y*s are not any *X*s, no *Y* is *Z*, therefore some things are neither *X*s not *Z*s. Deny the conclusion, affirm the first premise, and we may deny the second, which gives some *Y*s are not any *X*s, everything is either *X* or *Z*, therefore some *Y*s are *Z*s.

external is a coinadequate: *external* and *coinadequate* have *partient* and *complement* for their contraries, and *deficient* has *exient* for its converse: hence every exient of a complement is a partient; which is one of the opponent syllogisms of that first given.

Identity, in theorem K, does not give identity; as will be observed by watching the demonstration. For an instance, *brother of parent* is identical with *uncle*, by mere definition. But *non-uncle of child* is not identical with *non-brother*: for though every non-uncle of child is non-brother (as by the theorem), yet it is not true that every non-brother is non-uncle of child.

If LM be identical with N, meaning that N is an L of an M and of no other signification, we have $LM\|N$, $LMM^{-1}\|NM^{-1}$, $L^{-1}LM\|L^{-1}N$. Now $MM^{-1}X$ and $L^{-1}LX$ are classes which contain X; so that we may affirm $L))NM^{-1}$ and $M))L^{-1}N$; but not $L\|NM^{-1}$ nor $M\|L^{-1}N$.

Having given $LM\|N$, it is natural to ask whether we can *deduce* identical expressions for L and M: the answer is that no such thing can be done. If by M we mean some one particular M left vague, the form of L can be deduced, as we shall see; but not when N is a name for, and only for, every L of *every M*. Take, for example, the word *uncle*: it is identical with *brother of parent*; either is the other. Can we now construct a definition of *brother* out of *uncle*, *parent*, and their converses. *Uncle of child* of X is no definition of *brother* of X; it includes the brothers of the other parent. *Uncle of every child* of X will not do,[1] for a similar reason: if X had as many wives as Solomon, and children by all, nothing in logic excludes the supposition that they were all sisters.

In mathematics we have much power of forcing $NM^{-1}\|L$ out of $LM\|N$ by extension of language: and in a science of truths necessary as to matter it is almost a proof of insufficient grasp when we find either of the forms above unaccompanied by the other. Common language has some degree of tendency towards the same sort of enlargement of meanings. As in the very example before us: the brothers of the other parent are called *brothers* (in law): and under this extension *uncle of child* is identical with *brother*: for the word *uncle* receives similar extensions.

A relation is said to be *convertible* (though it should rather be said that the subject and predicate are convertible) when it is its own converse; when $X..LY$ gives $Y..LX$. And, L being any relation whatever, LL^{-1} is convertible: but $LL^{-1\prime}$ and L,L^{-1} are each the converse of the other. So far as I can see, every convertible relation can be reduced to the form LL^{-1}. If two notions stand in the same relation to one another, they can always, I think, be made to stand in one and the same relation to some third notion. The converse is certainly true, namely, that two notions which stand in one relation to a third, stand in convertible relation to each other. But it cannot be proved that if $X..LY$ and $Y..LX$,

[1] [Uncle of every *possible* child? No.]

then L must be reducible to MM^{-1}, for some meaning or other of M: this is certainly a *material* proposition. But I can find no case in which material proof fails. Take *identity*, for example: it is the very notion of identity between X and Y that $X..LL^{-1}Y$ for *every possible* relation L in which X can stand to any third notion. Identification of objects of thought by *names* derives its convertibility from the idea of the names standing in relation of applicability to the same object. Identification in thought of unnamed objects can only be conceived as *convertible* by reference, as above, to other notions. Exclude names, and identify X with itself by 'this is this:' it would be absurd to repeat the process, and say that there is conversion by reason of the first *this* of one indication being the second *this* of the other: such conversion would be only the invention of *different names spelt the same way*.

Among the subjects of a convertible relation must usually come the predicate itself, unless it be forced out by express convention. If all convertible relation can be expressed by LL^{-1} this is obviously necessary: for $LL^{-1}X$ includes X. Is a man his own brother? It is commonly not so held: but we cannot make a definition which shall by its own power exclude him, unless under a clause expressly framed for the purpose. Is a brother the son[1] of the same father and mother with the man himself? Then is he pre-eminently his own brother: for there never lived one of whom we have not more reason to be sure that he was the son of his own father and mother than that any reputed brother had the same parents with him. If we want to exclude him we must stipulate that by brother of X we mean any man who, *not being X himself*, has the same father and mother. In common language the stipulation is or is not made, according to the casual presence or absence of the necessity for it. Put the question what relation to a man is his brother's brother, and most persons will answer, His brother: point out that the answer should be, Either his brother or himself, and a fair proportion will think that himself was included.[2] I shall hold, for logical purposes, that the predicate *is* included among its own convertible relatives.

A relation is *transitive* when a relative of a relative is a relative of the same kind; as symbolized in $LL))L$, whence $LLL))LL))L$; and so on.

[1] When the individual is but one among many, and is speaking generally of his class, there is an implication that *others* are intended, and the introduction of self produces for a moment that sense of incongruity which, if it could be made to last, would give an air of humour. Thus Hobbes, in a sentence which, altering *geometris* into *logicis*, might be said of himself by a person I ought to know, speaks as follows: —*In magno quidem periculo versari video existimationem meam, qui a geometris fere omnibus dissentio. Eorum enim qui de iisdem rebus mecum aliquid ediderunt, aut solus insanio ego aut solus non insanio; tertium enim non est, nisi (quod dicet forte aliquis) insaniamus omnes.* Undoubtedly a man is among those who have written on the same subjects with himself.

[2] [*Irish Bulls*, p. 158: Dominick says, 'I have no brothers but myself.']

A transitive relation has a transitive *converse*, but not necessarily a transitive *contrary*: for $L^{-1}L^{-1}$ is the converse of LL, so that $LL))L$ gives $L^{-1}L^{-1}))L^{-1}$. From these, by contraposition, and also by theorem K and its contrapositions, we obtain the following results.

L is contained in $LL^{-1\prime}$, l,l^{-1}, $l^{-1}l'$, $L,^{-1}L$	LL is contained in L
L^{-1} .... L,L^{-1}, $ll^{-1\prime}$, $l,^{-1}l$, $L^{-1}L'$	$L^{-1}L^{-1}$ .... L^{-1}
l .... lL', L,l	$L^{-1}l$, lL^{-1} l
l^{-1} .... $L,^{-1}l^{-1}$, $l^{-1}L^{-1\prime}$	Ll^{-1}, $l^{-1}L$ ...... l^{-1} [1]

I omit demonstration, but to prevent any doubt about correctness of printing I subjoin instances in words: L signifies *ancestor* and L^{-1} *descendant*.

An ancestor is always an ancestor of all descendants, a non-ancestor of none but non-descendants, a non-descendant of all non-ancestors, and a descendant of none but ancestors. A descendant is always an ancestor of none but descendants, a non-ancestor of all non-descendants, a non-descendant of none but non-ancestors, and a descendant of all ancestors. A non-ancestor is always a non-ancestor of all ancestors, and an ancestor of none but non-ancestors. A non-descendant is a descendant of none but non-descendants, and a non-descendant of all descendants. Among non-ancestors are contained all descendants of non-ancestors, and all non-ancestors of descendants. Among non-descendants are contained all ancestors of non-descendants, and all non-descendants of ancestors.

The mathematician forces the predicate itself among its own chain of successive relatives, whether the relation be transitive or not: x, as $\phi^0 x$, appears in the sequence . . . $\phi^{-2}x$, $\phi^{-1}x$, $\phi^0 x$, $\phi^1 x$, $\phi^2 x$, . . . There is a little tendency towards the same thing in ordinary language, especially when the relation is transitive. Milton, in calling Eve 'the fairest of her daughters,' meaning female descendants in general, allowed $\phi^0 x$ to be a case of $\phi^n x$. Nothing but circumlocution avoids the same thing in our day, and by it language loses much force, or some precision. If we say that Achilles was the strongest of all his enemies, we feel both definite meaning and force: if we say that he was stronger than any one, [or every one], of his enemies, we gain an enfeebling addition of logical accuracy: if that he was stronger than all his enemies, we introduce ambiguity.

I now proceed to the syllogism, taking first the case in which the terms are individual notions, units of thought. All syllogisms of second intention, whether mathematical or metaphysical, come under this case;

[1] [$LL))L$ $\quad$ $L^{-1}l))l$, $\quad$ $L))l^{-1}l'$
$l))lL'$ $\quad$ $l))L,l$ $\quad$ $L))L,^{-1}L$
$LL))L$ $\quad$ $lL^{-1}))l$ $\quad$ $L))LL^{-1\prime}$
$L))l,l^{-1}$]

and arithmetical syllogisms are but aggregates of singular syllogisms, each of which also comes under this case.

The supreme law of syllogism of three terms, the law which governs every possible case, and to which every variety of expression must be brought before inference can be made, is this;—any relation of *X* to *Y* compounded with any relation of *Y* to *Z* gives a relation of *X* to *Z*. This is very nearly the wording of Euclid's implied definition of compound ratio of magnitudes;—The ratio of *X* to *Z* is compounded of the ratios of *X* to *Y* and *Y* to *Z*. If I had now produced this principle for the first time, and in the present manner, it would surely have been imputed to me that I had made a fanciful definition of syllogism out of a mathematical analogy. But my second paper will bear witness that I enunciated the identity of inference with combination of relation at a time when I had not noted the extreme closeness of the analogy. For when I in that paper remarked that the generality of the notion of composition (of ratio) prevented the Greek geometers from needing to make separate treatment of *decomposition*, I made no allusion (having in truth none to make) to the analogous point of syllogism. But if I *had* generalized the mathematical notion, *from the Greek*, the process would have been both natural and valid. For ratio is no direct translation of *λόγος*: the Greek[1] word means *communication*; and the same turn of thought which made *λόγος* a technical term of geometry made it stand for *any* relation in one of its derived meanings; that is, any way in which we talk about one notion in terms of another. Any way of speaking of one notion with respect to a second, joined with a way of speaking of the second notion with respect to a third, must dictate a way of speaking of the first notion with respect to the third. And this is syllogism: it exhibits, in the most general form, the law of thought which connects two notions by their connexions with a third. The character of the connexions belongs as much to the *matter* of the syllogism as the character of the terms connected.

The universal and all containing form of syllogism is seen in the statement of *X..LMZ* as the necessary consequence of *X..LY* and *Y..MZ*. Whether the compound relation *LM* be capable of presentation to thought under a form in which the components are lost in the compound—in the same manner, to use Hartley's simile, as the odours

[1] Euclid's definition of *ratio*, most properly when most literally translated, is '*Communicating instrument* is a habitude of two magnitudes of the same kind to one another with respect to *quantuplicity*.' We talk about magnitude in terms of magnitude only by *how many times* one contains the other. On the meaning of *πηλικότης* see the *Penny Cyclopaedia* and the *Supplement*, articles *Ratio*. That the communicating instrument was called *communication* (*λόγος*) was a case of that feature of the Greek under which the *excessive* curve was called *excess* (*hyperbola*), the *defective* curve the *defect* (*ellipse*), the irregular angle the *irregularity* (*anomaly*), and so on. *Parabola* is another instance, of which elsewhere.

of the separate ingredients are not separately perceptible in the smell of the mixture—is entirely a question of matter.

In the Aristotelian syllogism, figure is a function of the *places* of the middle term; and its necessity arises from the nature of the proposition being also a function of the places of its terms: we cannot, in that system, say 'Every X is Y' without having Y for the predicate. Adopt Hamilton's expressed quantifications and, as he justly remarks, figure becomes an unessential variation. Introduce the general idea of relation, and figure resumes its importance: but not as connected with the *place* of the middle term. Whether we say $X..LY$ or $LY..X$, the figure is the same. Change of figure can be effected only by conversion of relation. The *first* figure is that of *direct transition*: X related to Z through X related to Y and Y related to Z. The *fourth* figure is that of *inverted transition*: X related to Z through Z related to Y and Y related to X. The *second* figure is that of *reference to* (the middle term): X related to Z through X and Z both related to Y. The *third* figure is that of *reference from* (the middle term): X related to Z through Y related to both X and Z.

Before generalization, whatever may be our preference for the first figure, we hardly feel inclined to admit that *inference takes place in no other figure*; that is, *demonstrated* inference: that premises in the second figure can only yield their result by seeing the first figure through the second. Say that X is Y, Z is not Y: how do we know that X is not Z? If X be Y, it is not anything that Y is not: at this point we are immediately aided by 'Y is not Z;' only mediately by 'Z is not Y.' The ease[1] of the transformation prevents our feeling that it takes place. But if we take for our premises $X..LY$ and $Z..MY$, the necessity of conversion of the major premise, that is, of reduction into the first figure, is sufficiently apparent: we cannot express our inference without it.

In my second paper I stated that no inference can be drawn from a negative premise, except by *decomposition* of a relation. This is perfectly true, so long as *contrary* relations and *inherent quantity* are excluded: but not true when they are admitted. The following comparison will illustrate this. Let the premises be $X.LY$, $Z..MY$. These premises are identical with $X..lY$ and $Y..M^{-1}Z$ of which all the inference is $X..lM^{-1}Z$, or either of its two identicals, $X.LM^{-1\prime}Z$, $X.l,m^{-1}Z$. Or thus; —X is not any L of Y: of Y we know no more than that it is a *certain* M^{-1} of Z; and as the M^{-1} in question is *vagum*—which in English we

[1] Nothing is so well adapted to exhibit the simplicity of the first figure, as the expression of the four in common language as follows:—

1. $X..LY$, $Y..MZ$, X is L of M of Z.
2. $X..LY$, $Z..MY$, X is L of that of which the M is Z.
3. $Y..LX$, $Y..MZ$, X is that of which the L is the M of Z.
4. $Y..LX$, $Z..MY$, X is that of which the L is that of which the M is Z.

Here 'that' and 'the' must be read as indefinites.

call *certain*—all we can say is that X is not any L of *all* the M^{-1}s of Z. Hence $X.LM^{-1\prime}Z$ is all the inference we can draw.

Next, let contraries be forbidden. To deduce the inference, without use of inherent quantity or of contraries, we are compelled to proceed by the old *reductio ad impossibile* by which *Baroko* and *Bokardo* were made to listen to reason: and this equally in all cases which contain one negative premise. Let $X.LY$ and $Z..MY$ give $X.NZ$: then $X..NZ$ and $Z..MY$, conjointly, must contradict $X.LY$; that is, $X..NMY$ must contradict $X.LY$. That is, one instance of NMY must be identical with one instance of LY, the MY in question being Z. Here N is to be determined by the decomposition of a relation, which is all that need be said until we come to the consideration of the forms of inference.

In the meantime I take a concrete instance. Let it be, X is not any uncle of Y, and Z is a parent of Y. The whole inference clearly is that X is not any uncle of a particular child of Z. We also know *which* child: but as we throw away all reference to the middle term—the question being how much can we know when the middle term is completely eliminated—the inference is that X is not the uncle of *all* the children of Z. Material[1] knowledge, in this instance, converts the conclusion into 'X is neither the brother of Z, nor the brother of *all* the wives who have had children by Z.' Again, let the conclusion be, X is not any N of Z. If then X be N of Z, and Z parent of Y, X must be uncle of Y: that is 'N of parent' is 'uncle,' and N is to be found by decomposition. *What* of parent is uncle? The aggregate of brother and brother-in-law. But to say that X is neither brother nor brother-in-law would be to suppose

[1] I shall certainly have to meet the old objection that the correlation of parent and child is not a logical but a material fact. It is undoubtedly material that $(\text{parent})^{-1}$ is spelt c-h-i-l-d: and the pure *form* of inference, independent of the meanings of u-n-c-l-e and p-a-r-e-n-t, is that X is not any $(\text{uncle})\,(\text{parent})^{-1\prime}$ of Z, in which all that is meant by *uncle* and *parent* is that they were the *symbols* we saw in the premises, all the rest of the force of inference being in the meaning of $(\ldots)\,(\ldots)^{-1\prime}$. Again, it is material that 'uncle of all children' is either 'brother,' or 'brother of all wives who have had children:' it is material that the universe of our propositions is strictly moral, so that brothers of paramours of X are not included: it is material that we hope there are no such persons: it is material that if Z be either Whiston or Dr Primrose, the brother of *the* wife would be sufficient. All this and more is conceded: matter makes its appearance the moment L and M mean more than 'certain relations which, and no others, are designated by these letters throughout the syllogism.' Again, when I am told that *Logic* does not provide the inference that 'Philip was Alexander's father' because 'Alexander was Philip's son,' and that it is our *material* knowledge of the relation of father and son that enables us to make the inference, I reply that it is certainly material that father and son are related in the manner of L and L^{-1}; but that the transition from $X..LY$ to $Y..L^{-1}X$ is a *form* of thought, and a more general form than any case of conversion admitted by the logician in the common syllogism. It is that which is *common* to the transitions 'X a genus of Y, therefore Y a species of X', 'X a parent of Y, therefore Y a child of X,' 'X an identical of Y, therefore Y an identical of X,' &c.: and is therefore more abstract than any of them, and equally *form without matter* to all of them.

that Y might be *any* child of Z: so that all we are to say is, X is neither brother, nor brother-in-law with reference to one particular child. Drop the vestige of the middle term, and we say that X is neither brother nor brother-in-law by every wife: which agrees with the preceding.

The mode of decomposition may be thus generalized. Let there be *one* negative premise, and, L and M being the premising relations, let N be the concluding relation denied. Write down the terms of the negative premise, and between them the remaining term, choosing such order as shall make X precede Z. Combine the relations of the two pairs seen, and the combination must be the direct or converted relation in the negative premise, provided that due attention be paid to the particular character in the affirmative premise. For example, let the negative premise be $Z.MY$. Take Y, Z, and between them write X, YXZ; in which YX, XZ, are seen. Let the affirmative premise be $X..LY$: then L^{-1} and N combine to give M^{-1}; or N must be deduced by making $L^{-1}N$ identical with M^{-1}, a certain L^{-1} being understood.

I have had occasion to notice the manner in which, by wilful renunciation of knowledge, the conclusion is made to express not quite all the possible inference. This happens also in the common syllogism. If from 'Some Xs are not Ys' and 'Everything is either Y or Z,' we deduce 'Some Xs are Zs' it is not true that this conclusion embraces the whole knowledge which the premises give. It is known that 'some Xs' mean all that are not Ys: the vague quantity is not so vague as it would be if the conclusion were the only thing known. It ought to be noticed that a universal (Hamilton's *definite* would be a better word) lurks in the conclusion of every particular syllogism: in the above $X()Z$ would be $Xy))Z$, if all that is known were expressed. The particular conclusion of a syllogism is the universal of a narrower name: one premise predicates *existence* for a new and compounded name: the conclusion substitutes that compound in the other premise in a legitimate manner.[1]

Reserving the word *mood* as irrevocably associated with details of quantity and quality combined, let each figure have four *phases*, determined by the quality only of the premises. The four phases, + meaning affirmative, and − meaning negative, are to be remembered[2] in the standard order

$$++ \qquad -+ \qquad +- \qquad --$$

Let these be the *primary* phases of the four figures. The order of the

[1] [$X((Y))Z = XY))Z \quad X))Y))Z \quad X))Z \quad X))Y)\cdot)Z \quad Zy)\cdot(X$].

[2] Some persons, of whom I am one, but whether it be a gift or a defect I do not know, cannot associate two things with two other things, each with each, merely by conventional distribution, unless the association be required every day or every hour. Though I have read music for forty years, I have never known the crotchet rest from the quaver rest, except by context. These two symbols turn their heads one backwards and the other forwards, a difference which bears no imaginable relation to one standing for twice as much time as the other. I shall remember it in future, having

phases, in the four figures, is determined by reading *from* the leading or primary phase, first backwards and then forwards. Thus the phases are as follows:

	1	2	3	4
Figure I.	+ +	− +	+ −	− −
II.	− +	+ +	+ −	− −
III.	+ −	− +	+ +	− −
IV.	− −	+ −	− +	+ +

The following is the table of forms of syllogism, afterwards explained.

<table>
<tr><th></th><th>1</th><th>2</th><th>3</th><th>4</th><th></th></tr>
<tr><td>I</td>
<td>$X..LY$
$Y..MZ$
———
$X..LMZ$

$X.lM'Z$
$X.L,mZ$

$LM\Vert N$</td>
<td>$X.LY$
$Y..MZ$
———
$X..lMZ$

$X.LM'Z$
$X.l,mZ$

$NM^{-1}\Vert L$</td>
<td>$X..LY$
$Y.MZ$
———
$X..LmZ$

$X.lm'Z$
$X.L,MZ$

$L^{-1}N\Vert M$</td>
<td>$X.LY$
$Y.MZ$
———
$X..lmZ$

$X.Lm'Z$
$X.l,MZ$

$lm\Vert N$</td>
<td>I</td></tr>
<tr><td>II</td>
<td>$X.LY$
$Z..MY$
———
$X..lM^{-1}Z$

$X.LM^{-1\prime}Z$
$X.l,m^{-1}Z$

$NM\Vert L$</td>
<td>$X..LY$
$Z..MY$
———
$X..LM^{-1}Z$

$X.lM^{-1\prime}Z$
$X.L,m^{-1}Z$

$LM^{-1}\Vert N$</td>
<td>$X..LY$
$Z.MY$
———
$X..Lm^{-1}Z$

$X.lm^{-1\prime}Z$
$X.L,M^{-1}Z$

$L^{-1}N\Vert M^{-1}$</td>
<td>$X.LY$
$Z.MY$
———
$X..lm^{-1}Z$

$X.Lm^{-1\prime}Z$
$X.l,M^{-1}Z$

$lm^{-1}\Vert N$</td>
<td>II</td></tr>
<tr><td>III</td>
<td>$Y..LX$
$Y.MZ$
———
$X..L^{-1}mZ$

$X.l^{-1}m'Z$
$X.L,^{-1}MZ$

$LN\Vert M$</td>
<td>$Y.LX$
$Y..MZ$
———
$X..l^{-1}MZ$

$X.L^{-1}M'Z$
$X.l,^{-1}mZ$

$NM^{-1}\Vert L^{-1}$</td>
<td>$Y..LX$
$Y..MZ$
———
$X..L^{-1}MZ$

$X.l^{-1}M'Z$
$X.L,^{-1}mZ$

$L^{-1}M\Vert N$</td>
<td>$Y.LX$
$Y.MZ$
———
$X..l^{-1}mZ$

$X.L^{-1}m'Z$
$X.l,^{-1}MZ$

$l^{-1}m\Vert N$</td>
<td>III</td></tr>
<tr><td>IV</td>
<td>$Y.LX$
$Z.MY$
———
$X..l^{-1}m^{-1}Z$

$X.L^{-1}m^{-1\prime}Z$
$X.l,^{-1}M^{-1}Z$

$l^{-1}m^{-1}\Vert N$</td>
<td>$Y..LX$
$Z.MY$
———
$X..L^{-1}m^{-1}Z$

$X.l^{-1}m^{-1\prime}Z$
$X.L,^{-1}M^{-1}Z$

$LN\Vert M^{-1}$</td>
<td>$Y.LX$
$Z..MY$
———
$X..l^{-1}M^{-1}Z$

$X.L^{-1}M^{-1\prime}Z$
$X.l,^{-1}m^{-1}Z$

$NM\Vert L^{-1}$</td>
<td>$Y..LX$
$Z..MY$
———
$X..L^{-1}M^{-1}Z$

$X.l^{-1}M^{-1\prime}Z$
$X.L,^{-1}m^{-1}Z$

$L^{-1}M^{-1}\Vert N$</td>
<td>IV</td></tr>
<tr><td></td><td>1</td><td>2</td><td>3</td><td>4</td><td></td></tr>
</table>

The Roman numerals refer to figure; the Arabic to phase. The first two lines in each compartment contain the premises. The third line contains the conclusion in affirmative form, derived from reduction into the primary phase of the first figure. The fourth and fifth lines show the two forms of negative conclusion. In the sixth line N is the concluding relation, affirmative or negative according as the premises are of similar or different qualities: and the connexion of N with the premising relations is seen, as obtained by simple composition when the premises are of the same quality, and from opponent syllogism, or from the rule above, when the premises are of different quality.

The sixth line is the only one which will need any detail of consideration. When the premises are of one quality, so that N is not to be disengaged by decomposition, it is enough that N should be identical with, or should contain, the relation set down opposite to it. Thus in III. 4, the inference is that X is one $l^{-1}m$ of Z, or one N of Z, if only $l^{-1}m$ be contained in N. The enlargement of course is a weakening of the inference, an addition of scope[1] and diminution of force.

Let the premises, as in II. 1, be $X.LY$ and $Z..MY$, L being any one L, and M some one M. The reduction to I. 1 gives $X..lY$ and $Y..M^{-1}Z$, whence $X..lM^{-1}Z$ is all the conclusion that can be drawn. Of this $X.LM^{-1'}Z$ and $X.l,m^{-1}Z$ are equivalents. Again, if the conclusion be $X.NZ$, it is clear that $X..NZ$ and $Z..MY$, M being still some one M, should give $X..LY$, and do give $X..NMY$, whence NM and L should be identical. If we examine $NM \| L$, upon the condition that M is some one M, left vague, but not any one M, we see that it gives $N \| LM^{-1}$. For L is to include in its meaning any N of a certain M, and nothing else: so that N is LM^{-1}, where that M^{-1} is used which is the correlative of the M in question. But in *denying* this LM^{-1}, or rather any L of this vague M^{-1}, we do but deny $LM^{-1'}$.

This point is well illustrated by relations in which degree or quantity is conceivable. For example, let $X.LY$ be 'X is not an external of Y;' and let $Z..MY$ be 'Z is a genus of Y'. The inference is that X is

[1] In my last paper, speaking of the world at large as rudely acquainted with the *intension* of a term under the name of its *force*, I omitted, by one of those pieces of forgetfulness which are hard to account for, to add that they are also acquainted with *extension* under the name of *scope*. And many cases occur in which writers choose their terms as if they felt that the greater the scope the less the force, and use them accordingly: but I cannot find anything like a direct statement of the theorem, though I should suppose it can hardly have been missed by all writers.

looked it up for the purpose of this note, by seeing that the crotchet rest turns its head forwards, the quaver rest backwards; and assuming that progress is worth twice as much as retrogradation. In the case before me, the difficulty of attaching $- +$ and $+ -$ to the figures of which they are the primary phases may be lessened to those who are constituted like myself by remembering that the second figure is that of reference *to*, and that in $- +$ we read *to* the chief sign $+$, while the third figure is that of reference *from*, and that in $+ -$ we read *from* the sign $+$.

not an external of *all* species of Z. Since the species may be as nearly the whole genus as we please, and even the whole genus itself, the only inference is that *X* is not an external of Z. Again, we ask *what* of a particular genus is an external, the genus in question being vague. If the particular genus were known, we should say that the required class is not *partient* of that genus to any extent except some or all of the exience of the genus: but as this exience is quite vague, possibly nothing, we can only say not partient at all or external. In both cases *X*.{}).(}*Y* and Z..{((}*Y* gives *X*.{}).(}Z, or *X*()*Y*))*Z* gives *X*()Z.

In the same way other cases may be treated. But the entrance of contrary relations renders the method of decomposition useless for every purpose except historical comparison.

Except when both premises are negative, the conclusion can always be expressed in terms of the premising relations, without contraries. Thus among the concluding forms of III. 2, we see $L^{-1}M'$. The following rules may be collected. First, the relations converted in the conclusions belong to those premises which must be converted when reduction is made into the first figure. Secondly, the mark of inherent quantity appears in the ordinary form of conclusion only when the premises are of different qualities. Thirdly, when the conclusion is expressed without contraries, this mark is always attached to the relation of the affirmative premise. These rules would give mechanical canons of inference, if such things were wanted: and it would be well to remember that in the *second* figure the middle term usually comes *second* in both premises, and the *second* premise is converted in reduction into the first figure.

I shall now proceed to the consideration of the quantified proposition and its syllogism, presuming the reader to be acquainted with the notation and classifications of my second and third papers. If we take the proposition 'Every *X* is an *L* of one or more *Y*s' we may denote it by *X*))*L Y*: and similarly *L Y*))*X* may denote 'Every *L* of any *Y* or *Y*s is an *X*.' And similarly for the other parts of the notation.

I enter on this part of the subject only so far as to illustrate the ancient or Aristotelian syllogism. Though of necessity a part of logic, as involving possible forms and necessary connexions, the quantified syllogism of relation is not of primary importance as an explanation of actual thought: for by the time we arrive at the consideration of relation in general we are clear of all necessity for quantification. And for this reason: quantification itself only expresses a relation. Thus if we say that some *X*s are connected with *Y*s, the relation of the class *X* to the class *Y* is that of *partial connexion*: that some at least, all it may be, are connected, is itself a connexion between the *classes*. Nevertheless, it may be useful to exhibit the modifying quantification as a component, not as inseparably thought of in the compound; though in this we must confine ourselves to what may be called the *Aristotelian* branch of the extended subject. If we would enter completely upon quantified forms, we must examine not only the relation and its contrary, but the relation of a term in connexion with the relation of the contrary term. And here we find that all universal connexion ceases. The repugnance of X and not-X or x, which, joined with alternance, is the notion the symbols X and x were invented to express, cannot be predicated of LX and Lx: for $Y..LX$ and $Y..Lx$ may coexist. The complete investigation would require subordinate notions of form, effecting subdivisions of matter.

This complete examination would also require the investigation of the manner in which quantity of relation acts upon quantity of term: and this whether the quantity of relation be inherent or not; including an examination of all syllogisms in which inherent quantity of relation *appears in the premises.* And thus in logic, as in mathematics, the horizon opens with the height gained: generalization suggests detail, which again suggests generalization, and so on *ad infinitum.* There is no more limit to the formulae of thought than to the formulae of algebra. The logician may, if it please him, reduce all thought to simple assertion or denial of identification, and the algebraist may define all his science as either $x = y$ or $x = y \pm a$: one reduction is as true as the other. There is identity or difference in every possible logical judgment: there is equation or inequation in every possible algebraical judgment.

In the Aristotelian syllogism, the premising forms are $X))Y$, $X).(Y$, $X()Y$, $X(.(Y$; X being the subject and Y the predicate. The forms $X((Y$ and $X).)Y$ cannot appear, unless we add so much of Hamilton's system as is seen in them. Nor can we avoid doing this here. For conversion from figure to figure is no longer conversion of order of terms. Thus $LX))Y$ and $Y).(MZ$, do not give the first figure, but the third: there being reference from the middle term in both premises; that is, the middle term being the subject of relation in both cases.

In all the syllogisms which do not involve the forms (.) and)(, that is, in all which are either Aristotelian or capable of being made so by simple conversion, each premise is a congeries or aggregation of propositions involving individual notions, such as we have hitherto considered. An adequate quantification of the middle term insures the collection of a number of pairs, one out of each premise, in which the same individual from the middle term appears in both the premises: and thus the ordinary laws of dependence upon the quantities of the terms may be established. The whole of the system of relations of quantity remains undisturbed if for the common copula '*is*' be substituted any other relation: so that the usual laws of quantity may be applied to the table of *unit-syllogisms* given above, precisely as if L and M only meant 'is.' Thus $X.LY$ and $Y..MZ$ giving $X..lMZ$ or $X.LM'Z$, we find that $X).(LY$ and $Y((MZ$ gives $X).(LM'Z$.

In the first three figures, the pure Aristotelian modes are derived entirely from the first and third phases, and in no case from the second or fourth. But all the phases of the fourth figure give such syllogisms except the first.

Every one of the thirty-two forms of onymatic syllogism may be made to give some conclusion, however the relations may be distributed: but the results are at present of inferior interest, for reasons already given. Thus $X))LY$, $M\,Y)(Z$ give $X))LY$, $M\,Y).)z$, or $X))LY$, $Y).)M^{-1}z$, or $X).)L,M^{-1}z$. But direct relation between X and Z is here unattainable, without reference to the matter of L and M.

I now proceed one step nearer to the common syllogism, as follows. Let only one relation and its converse appear in the premises; and let this relation be *transitive*. That is, each relation[1] is either L or L^{-1}, and LL is L, $L^{-1}L^{-1}$ is L^{-1}. The most convenient relations from which to form instances will be 'ancestor' and 'descendant.'

Every phase of every figure gives its conclusion: but our question will be to determine those cases in which the concluding relation is, or may be, the relation of the premises, L or L^{-1}. We *may* have a larger conclusion: if so, we throw away a part of it. To illustrate this, let us examine I. 3: let $X..LY$ be the minor premise, and let $Y.L^{-1}Z$ be the major. The full conclusion is $X.L,L^{-1}Z$. This contains $X.L^{-1}Z$: for, as before seen, when L is transitive, L,L^{-1} contains L^{-1}. Thus when X is an ancestor of Y, and Y not a descendant of Z, X is not a descendant of Z. This of course is easy: if X were a descendant of Z, then Y, a descendant of X, would also be a descendant of Z, which he is not. But this is not all the conclusion. The full conclusion is that X is not an ancestor of none but descendants of Z: not Z himself nor herself, not his wife nor her husband, not any descendant of Z, and not the wife nor the husband of any descendant; unless, in the cases where wife or husband is mentioned, there be another marriage and a fruitful one with a non-descendant.

Looking through the phases of the figures, and making L the minor relation in all cases, the major relation being L or L^{-1}, we have the following Table of cases in which L or L^{-1} is a legitimate conclusion.

	1	2	3	4
I	$X..LY$ $Y..LZ$ $X..LZ$	$X.LY$ $Y..L^{-1}Z$ $X.LZ$	$X..LY$ $Y.L^{-1}Z$ $X.L^{-1}Z$	—
II	$X.LY$ $Z..LY$ $X.LZ$	$X..LY$ $Z..L^{-1}Y$ $X..LZ$	$X..LY$ $Z.LY$ $X.L^{-1}Z$	—

[1] [13 July 1864. When M^{-1} has only one M, write it $\dot{M}^{-1}$. Then $M\dot{M}^{-1}X$ is X, and $\dot{M}^{-1}MX$ may be other than X, but is transitive. For $\dot{M}^{-1}M\ \dot{M}^{-1}MX$ is $\dot{M}^{-1}(M\dot{M}^{-1})MX$, or $\dot{M}^{-1}MX$. Are all transitive and convertible relations reducible to $\dot{M}^{-1}M$?]

III	$Y..LX$ $Y.LZ$ $X.LZ$	$Y.LX$ $Y..LZ$ $X.L^{-1}Z$	$Y..LX$ $Y..L^{-1}Z$ $X..L^{-1}Z$	—
IV	—	$Y..LX$ $Z.L^{-1}Y$ $X.LZ$	$Y.LX$ $Z..L^{-1}Y$ $X.L^{-1}Z$	$Y..LX$ $Z..LY$ $X..L^{-1}Z$

In rejecting all conclusions which do not contain L or L^{-1}, we must not forget that these conclusions exist: I was only, by such rejection, preparing the way for the complete analogues of the common syllogism. For instance $X..LY$, $Y..L^{-1}Z$, give $X..LL^{-1}Z$, not necessarily either LZ or $L^{-1}Z$, though possibly either. But still it *is* a conclusion, and to some persons an important one: for if L mean *descendant*, and therefore L^{-1} *ancestor*, then, Z being the Queen, X is entitled to an honorary degree.

In my second paper I pointed out the law according to which L and L^{-1} are distributed. The radical forms of the four figures are here $+\,+$, $-\,+$, $+\,-$, $-\,-$; in my former paper, in which, according to usual practice, the major premise was written first, the radical forms were $+\,+$, $+\,-$, $-\,+$, $-\,-$. The rule is, that the radical form does not admit the converse relation: but that when one premise differs in quality from the radical form, the converse relation is thrown upon the other; when both, upon the conclusion.

Agreeing with the logicians that all judgment either identifies or separates two objects of thought, I maintain against them that this great alternative, though a real form inherent in all *judgment*, does not give the whole basis of the fundamental act of *reasoning*, or comparison of judgments. The old logicians carried their system all the length which its pretensions justified: the modern logicians, without abating a jot of the pretension, have tacitly dropped greatly short of the length. The restorer of logical study in England, Archbishop Whately, directs against many of his predecessors the reproach that, strongly as they contend for the syllogism containing the whole form of inferential thought, they seem never to use it nor to care about it when they come to their so-called applications of logic. I suppose that the parties inculpated found that the ordinary syllogism does not very frequently contain the act of reasoning. And in truth, when it does appear, it is usually *Barbara* or *Celarent*, that is 'Species of species is species' or else 'Species of external is external:' both contained in the principle that the part follows the whole as to inclusion or exclusion. Of the common logical heads, the study of the term and of the proposition, of the aggregates and components of the term, and of the transformations of the proposition, is far more necessary, presents points of far more frequent occurrence, and holds out far greater occasion for warning, than the study of the syllogism, when limited to the arithmetical *abacus*.

If the ordinary syllogism deserved the character given of it, a certain chapter in the older books of logic, instead of dropping into desuetude, would have increased in size and importance, with good assurance of addition to both. I mean the chapter *De Inventione Medii Termini.* This part of the subject was enlarged into many heads by the latest of the older writers: but in those who most resemble the genuine schoolmen, as Sanderson for example, the pure heading above given is preserved and its subject treated within the limits of the phrase. If all reasoning be reducible to ordinary syllogism, it follows that any assertion *inferred* about two terms must arise from comparison of the two by aid of some middle term, which is therefore to be investigated. Accordingly, a universal negative can only be established by finding out a third, or middle, term, in which one of the terms of the conclusion is wholly contained, and from which the other is wholly excluded. So necessarily is this invention of a middle term the act of investigation, if the syllogism, as given, be what it is said to be, that the mode of arrival at the missing element is very properly formalized into memorial verses *Fecana, Cageti*, &c., which ought to have followed *Barbara, Celarent*, &c., as practice follows theory.

When by the word *syllogism* we agree to mean a composition of two relations into one, we open the field in such manner that the invention of the middle term, and of the component relations which give the compound relation of the conclusion, is seen to constitute the act of mind which is always occurring in the efforts of the reasoning power. Was an event the consequence of another? We know that consequence of consequence is consequence, and, *X* being a suspected consequence of *Z*, we examine various *Y*s, and try if for any one of them we can establish that *X* is a consequence of *Y* and *Y* of *Z*. We do not consciously refer our search after relation to the notion of relation, nor our act of composition to the notion of composition; so that our descriptions of mental processes, when exhibited in technical terms, are as strange as our daily syntax when explained in phrases of grammar to an uneducated but tolerably correct speaker. The person *X*, did he commit the act *Z*? Non-possession of motive is, taken alone, probable innocence: non-production of motive is probable non-possession. We try for a motive *Y*, to which *X* is related by possession, and *Y* to *Z* by sufficiency. Here are the premises—*X* is the possessor of the motive *Y*; *Y* is a sufficient motive to commit *Z*; therefore *X* is the possessor of a sufficient motive to commit *Z*; and this compound relation is extensively contained in—or intensively contains—the relation of 'sufficiently in connexion with the action to give the evidence of actual commission a claim to consideration under ordinary notions of probability.' A very complicated concluding relation: but very familiar in action both to judge, counsel, and jury. But all this is not ordinary syllogism. The old logicians were right in attaching importance to the invention of the middle term; but their right notion was deprived of efficient action by their determining that no connexion worthy of a logician's attention could exist between terms except *is* or *is not*.

Any two notions whatsoever may happen to possess relation to each other in the mind. Choose two notions at hazard: the chances are small that they are related by inclusion or exclusion, total or partial, in any manner worth consideration: but these chances are multiplied a thousand fold if we turn our thoughts to the likelihood of their existing in some other relation. Indeed, some relation *must* exist between any two things, over and above the relations, usually well settled, of identity or difference.

When we examine any book of ordinary reasoning, we find that the onymatic syllogism is not very frequent, the combination of relations much more frequent, and the introduction of composition of terms and transformation of propositions by far the most frequent of all. Syllogisms are *rather chapters than sentences*, in many cases. When the acts of inference follow one another very quickly, or the reasoning is very consecutive, people begin to cry mathematics. I have read and heard the statement that Fearne's celebrated work on *contingent remainders* is *algebra*: it is no more algebra than a remainder-man is $x - y$; but the reasoning, if I may speak from a very old recollection of a few chapters, is remarkably sustained and connected. Chillingworth is a writer who delights in the technical exhibition of a syllogism, when he gets one: but the instances exhibited do not come very thickly. Nothing that I know of can be written *all* in syllogism, except mathematics: and this merely because, out of mathematics, nearly all the writing is spent in loading the syllogism, and very little in firing it.

It has sometimes been made a reproach to logic that the mathematicians, who reason more consecutively than any others when about their mathematics, do not regard the syllogism with respect in theory, and disdain it in practice. I shall proceed to examine how this matter stands.

First, as to the merest *technical* exhibition of the syllogism, it is, or should be, evident to all parties that such display of form is no more necessary to a proficient than the spelling of every word as he reads it. Those who cannot exhibit their inferences syllogistically need to learn; but those who can do not need to practise: which is exactly what may be said of spelling. When I wrote this last word, I was quite unconscious of s-p-e-l-l-i-n-g: no perceptibly separate acts of my mind dictated the writing down of the separate letters. This is all that need be said in answer to those who despise the analysis which is good for the learner, because the logician himself ends, in practice, by using the composite process with which the learner began.

There is a useful but very limited field of exercise for the syllogism in geometry. There is hardly an instance, over and above the elimination of B from $A = B$, $B = C$, which is not an overt use of the *principium et exemplum*: whenever P is true, Q is true; in this case P is true; therefore in this case Q is true. The reduction into the pure technical form, except in a few instances at the commencement, would be useless. The attempt of Herlinus and Dasypodius, of which Mr Mansel (Appendix to *Aldrich*, note L) has reprinted one proposition, is of use to the learner when carried to the extent to which he and Mr John Mill have carried it, that is, the exhibition of one proposition, to be repeated a few times for practice. But there is a far better logical exercise in Euclid. This great leader has, equally with Aristotle, a style of his own, and one full of its own technicalities: but utterly divested of any the smallest distinction between form and matter. This is most fortunate for that student for whom a further guide is provided: the book before him is raw material on which the exercise of thought about form and matter can be far more profitably carried on than it could have been if Euclid had made the distinction. And this especially on two points.

First, a geometrical proposition may either be a purely *formal* consequence of those which precede, or it may require (as most do) a further infusion of geometrical *matter*. When Euclid has proved that a *non*-central point inside a circle, or outside, is *not* a point to which three equal lines can be drawn, he holds himself *not* to have completed the proof that a point to which three equal lines *can* be drawn *is* the centre. But his demonstration is nothing except his often repeated transition from one to the other of the contrapositive forms of a universal affirmative proposition. It is not in his system to establish a purely logical inference once for all: accordingly, 'not-X is always not-Y' is converted into 'Y is always X' by one and the same train of thought whenever it is wanted. That the common end of three equal lines *is* the centre follows equally from the *non*-centre *not* being such common end, whether or no the reasoner can say what a circle is, or a centre, or a common end.

Again, this same want of admission of what logicians call *contraposition* gives rise to the majority of the *ex absurdo* demonstrations: in fact the *reductio ad absurdum* is usually nothing more than the mode of making the passage from the direct to the contrapositive form. When (in I. 6) it is to be shown that equal angles give equal sides, what Euclid really shows—that is, the geometrical *matter* of his proposition—is that unequal sides give unequal angles. His unequal sides immediately produce unequal areas with a pair of sides equal, each to each: whence, by I. 4 contrapositively taken, the included angles are unequal. All that is *ex absurdo* serves only to show that 'unequal sides give unequal angles' is identical with 'equal angles give equal sides,' and to admit of the direct, instead of the contrapositive, form of I. 4.

From such instances, and many others, I derive my now long fixed opinion that geometry is of little, though some, account for technical exercise in the syllogism; of more for exercise in the transformations of the proposition; of most of all, and of very much, for exercise in the separation of form and matter.

It says but little for the truth of the views taken of logic that this science and geometry lived so long in the same family—the old school of arts—without any attention being paid to the bearing of the first upon the second. But it is to be remembered—to say nothing of Euclid being *κύριος στοιχειωτής* and above criticism—that the form of contraposition, though known and duly registered, was, by reason of the neglect of contrary or privative terms, very little used or thought about: and also that the distinction of form and matter was never completely *envisaged*, though influential. That the *logicians*—and it must be remembered that *logicus* meant student or graduate *in arts*, in all its intension —prone as they were to syllogize, never threw the propositions of Euclid into technical form, must be taken as a point in their favour. Perhaps it would have been asserted as a matter of course that they did so, omission of all mention being taken as equally a matter of course, if the publication of Herlinus and Dasypodius, the only one of its kind, had not come in as the exception which proves the rule.

It is to *algebra* that we must look for the most habitual use of logical forms. Not that onymatic relations are found in frequent occurrence: but so soon as the syllogism is considered under the aspect of combination of relations, it becomes clear that there is more of syllogism, and more of its variety, in algebra than in any other subject whatever, though the matter of the relations—pure quantity—is itself of small variety. And here the general idea of relation emerges, and for the first time in the history of knowledge, the notions of relation and *relation of relation* are symbolized. And here again is seen the scale of gradations of form, the manner in which what is difference of *form* at one step of the ascent, is difference of *matter* at the next. But the relation of algebra to the higher developments of logic is a subject of far too great extent to be treated here. It will hereafter be acknowledged that, though the geometer did not think it necessary to throw his ever recurring *principium et exemplum* into an imitation of '*Omnis homo est animal*, *Sortes est homo*, &c.,' yet the algebraist was living in the higher atmosphere of syllogism, the unceasing composition of relation, before it was admitted that such an atmosphere existed.

I expect agreement in what I have said neither from the logicians nor from the algebraists: but, for reasons given in my last paper, I do not submit myself to either class. Not that I by any means take it for granted that all those who have cultivated both sciences will agree with me. When two countries are first brought by the navigators into communication with each other, it is found that there are two kinds of perfect agreement, and one case of nothing but discordance. All the inhabitants of each of the countries are quite at one in believing a huge heap of mythical notions about the other. At first, the only persons who though similarly circumstanced nevertheless tell different stories are the very mariners who have passed from one land to the other. This will go on for a time, and for a time only: *multi pertransibunt, et augebitur scientia.*

Appendix: On Syllogisms of Transposed Quantity
(15 March 1860)

In my *Formal Logic*, and in my recently published *Syllabus of a proposed System of Logic*, I gave instances of the *syllogism of transposed quantity*: that is, the syllogism in which the whole quantity of one concluding term, or of its contrary, is applied in a premise to the other concluding term, or to its contrary. As in the following:—Some *X*s are not *Y*s; *for every X* there is a *Y* which is *Z*: from which it follows, to those who can see it, that *some Z*s (the *some* of the first premise) are not *X*s.

Such syllogisms occur in thought and in discussion. It also happens that the premises and conclusion are stated independently, and their connexion not seen. It may also happen that the premises are stated simultaneously with the contrary of the conclusion. The following sentences, though they will not pass current in a paper on logic which produces them as an example of fallacy, would be very likely to slip through without detection, as part of an ordinary page of writing:—

'To say nothing of those who achieved success by effort, there were not wanting others of whom it may rather be said that the end gained them than that they gained the end: for they made no attempt whatever. But for every one who was more fortunate than he deserved to be, as well as for every one who used his best exertions, one at least might be pointed out who abandoned the trial before the result was known. And yet, so strangely are the rewards of perseverance distributed in this world, there was not one of these fainthearted men but was as successful as any one of those who held on to the last.'

Might not many educated logicians pass this over, supposing it presented without warning, as containing nothing but what might be true, without seeing that, except under forced interpretation, it combines in one the assertions that *all are* and that *some are not*?

The syllogism of transposed quantity is essentially a case of the numerically definite syllogism, though the number of instances is in every case of the indefinite, or rather unspecified, character of the algebraical letter: and the same may be said of every onymatic syllogism. Those who have commented upon the arithmetical syllogism have for the most part missed this point: they have not seen that the *numerical* definiteness of the premises is the definiteness of general, not of particular, symbols. That is, they have not caught the distinction between the form and the matter of arithmetical definition. The following slight account of the numerical syllogism will be sufficient for the present purpose.

Let us understand by mXY that *m or more* Xs are Ys; and by $m:XY$ that *m or fewer* Xs are Ys. Then by mXY we also mean, if x and y be the whole numbers of Xs and Ys in the universe, both $(x - m):Xy$ and $(y - m):xY$. Let u be the number of instances in the universe; x, y, z, the numbers in X, Y, Z; and $x'\ y'\ z'$ the numbers in x, y, z. Then mXY is $(x - m):Xy$, or $(y' - x + m)\ xy$, or $(m + u - x - y)\ xy$. And mXy is $(m + u - x - u + y)\ xY$, or $(m + y - x)\ xY$.[1]

Let mXY and nYZ coexist: we infer $(m + n - y)\ XZ$, or $(m + n + u - x - y - z)\ xz$. Let mXy and nYZ coexist: these are mXy and $(n + u - y - z)\ yz$; from which we infer $(m + n + u - y - z - y')\ Xz$, or $(m + n - z)\ Xz$ and $(m + n - x)\ xZ$.

Call the number of instances the (logical) extent of the term or proposition. Then it appears that when the two premises have the middle term Y in both, or y in both, the two forms of conclusion take from the premises, the one both terms direct, the other both terms contraverted: but when the middle term enters in both forms, Y and y, the two forms of conclusion take each one term direct from the premises, and one term by contraversion. In the first, the *coefficients of extent* in the form of conclusion are the united extent of the premises diminished by that of the middle term, and the united extent of the premises and of the universal diminished by the united extent of the three terms. In the second, the coefficients of extent are both described by the united extent of the premises diminished by the extent of the contraverted term.

We can now deduce either the ordinary syllogisms or those of transposed quantity, belonging to any one case of the numerical syllogism. Let the premises be

$$mXY,\ nyz, \text{ so that } (m + n - x)\ xz,\ (m + n - z')\ XZ,$$

are the forms of the conclusion. From $m = x$, we deduce nxz and $(x + n - z')\ XZ$; of the second of which we can say nothing without further knowledge of the relations of extent. On the meaning and character of the second form I may refer to my *Formal Logic*. From xXY and nyz we have then nxz; that is, using the notation of my second and third papers, from $X))Y$ and $Y)(Z$ we deduce $X)(Z$. Similarly, from $m = x$, $n = z'$ we show that $X))Y))Z$ gives $X))Z$: from $n = z'$ alone, we deduce that $X()Y))Z$ gives $X()Z$.

To find such syllogisms of transposed quantity as this form gives,

[1] [$m + T$ if introduced; $- T$ if abandoned.

$$\begin{array}{l|l|l} m + & \overline{u - x} & - \overline{u - y} \\ m + & y - & \overline{u - x}.] \end{array}$$

let $n = x$: then mXY and xyz give mxz. That is from 'Some *X*s are *Y*s, and for every *X* there is something neither *Y* nor *Z*' we deduce 'Some things are neither *X*s nor *Z*s.' When one term imparts its quantity to another, let the imparting term have a symbol placed above its spicula of quantity, and the receiving term below. Thus what we have just arrived at is that *X*()*Y*)(*Z* gives *X*)(*Z*. It must be specially observed that the term which imparts is always particular: thus when we see *X*()*Y*)(*Z*, in which *Z* is universal and *z* particular, the meaning of *X*()*Y* is 'For every *z* there is an *X* which is *Y*.' It is also to be remembered that in the formation of the symbol of conclusion the spicula of the imparting term is always to be inverted: thus *X*()*Y*)(*Z* does not give *X*((*Z*, but *X*)(*Z*.

When a term takes the *whole quantity* of a term external to its proposition, it will be convenient still to call the proposition *universal*, and, for distinction, *externally* universal. The ordinary universal may be called *internal*. When a *conclusion* is spoken of as universal, it is meant as being internally universal.

The circumstances under which two premises have a valid conclusion are precisely those of the ordinary syllogism. Two universals, either or both of which are externally so, give a conclusion, universal or particular according as the middle term is of unlike or like quantities in the two premises. A universal and a particular with the middle term of unlike quantities give a particular conclusion. And, as before noted, the symbol of the conclusion is derived as in the ordinary syllogism, with this difference, that the quantity of each imparting term must be changed in forming the conclusion.

Let external and internal universality be denoted by *Y* and *U*; and sameness and opposition of the quantities of the middle terms by *S* and *D*. The ordinary syllogism is valid under the conditions expressed in *UDU*, *USU*, *UDP*, *PDU*: and each of these forms has eight varieties. The syllogism of transposed quantity is valid under any one of the forms *YDU*, *UDY*, *YDY*, *YSU*, *USY*, *YSY*, *YDP*, *PDY*: and each of these forms has also eight varieties. There are therefore 64 varieties of transposed syllogism; twice as many as there are of ordinary syllogism.

In the forms *YDU* and *UDY*, or whenever an external and internal universal give a universal, the internal universal is really a simple identity or contrariety of its terms. Thus in ())) which gives ((, or 'For every *Z* an *X* is *Y*, every *Y* is *Z*, give every *Z* is *X*,' the first premise tells us that there cannot be more *Z*s than *Y*s, and the second that there cannot be more *Y*s than *Z*s. Hence the *Y*s and *Z*s exist in equal numbers; that is, since every *Y* is *Z*, *Y* and *Z* are identical. But in ())·(, or *X*()*Y*)·(*Z*, which is *X*()*Y*))*z*, *Y* and *z* are identical by the same reasoning, or *Y* and *Z* are contraries.

When two external universals are conjoined, the concluding terms, or one concluding term and the contrary of the other, must be arithmetically of the same number of instances, though not necessarily identical and, it may be, even externals of each other. Thus in ()() or in 'For every *Z* an *X* is *Y*, and for every *X* a *Y* is *Z*' we see that there cannot be more *Z*s than *X*s, nor more *X*s than *Z*s. Hence *Z* and *X* are of the same numbers of instances. Again in ())(or 'for every *z* an *X* is *Y*, and for every *X* there is something neither *Y* nor *Z*' we see that there cannot be more *z*s than *X*s, nor more *X*s than *z*s. Hence *X* and *z* are of the same number of instances, though the conclusion *X*))*Z* shows that no two instances, one of each, are identical.

The vague quantity of a particular conclusion is the vague quantity of the particular premise, when there is such a thing: when there is no such thing, it is either the quantity of the middle term, or of its contrary, whichever is universal in both premises.

The following is the list of varieties of syllogism:—

UDY	*YDU*	*YDY*	*YSY*
((()))	())) ((	())( ))	()())(
)·(() (·)	())·((·)	)·))(·)	)·)() (·(
)))·) (·)	(·((((·)	)((·((.)	)()·) (·(
)))(((	)((( ))	)(() ((	)()(
)·((·(((	)·))·( ))	)·))·) ((	)·)(·(()
(((·( )·(	)·))))·(	())·))·(	()(·( )·)
(·))( )·(	)((·))·(	(·(())·(	(·()( )·)
(·))·)))	(·((·) ((	(·((·( ))	(·()·))(

PDY	*USY*	*YDP*	*YSU*
())( )(	(()( )(	())(()	()((()
)·))((·(	)·()((·(	)·))( )·)	)·)(( )·)
)((·((·(	))(·((·(	)((·( )·)	)()·( )·)
)(() ()	))() ()	)(())(	)()))(
)·))·) ()	)·()·) ()	)·))·))(	)·)(·))(
())·))·)	(()·))·)	())·) (·(	()(·) (·(
(·(())·)	(·)())·)	(·(() (·(	(·()) (·(
(·((·( )(	(·)(·( )(	(·((·(()	(·()·(()

We have here given the symbols of the premises, followed by the symbol of the conclusion: from which the syllogisms may be read at length. Thus the last syllogism under *YDY* is as follows;—For every *z* there is an *X* which is not *Y*; for every *X* there is a *Y* which is not *Z*: whence every *X* is *Z*.

The several cases in *UDY* and *YDU* are inverted readings each of the other: those in *YDY* and *YSY* are essentially different. The cases in *USY* and *YSU* are but strengthened forms of those in *PDY* and *YDP*; the particular in the second being converted into an internal universal which contains it by an alteration in the quantity of the middle term, without any accession to the conclusion. The forms in *YDY* are derived from those in *PDY* and from those in *YDP* by strengthening—or at least rendering less vague,—the particular proposition by giving it that quantity which makes it an external universal: and the conclusion is thereby strengthened into a universal.

The following comparison will illustrate and extend the preceding remarks. In ordinary syllogism, the existence of valid inference depends upon the presence of *U* and *D*; that is, either *U* must be present twice; or *U* once, and *D*. In *UDU*, the most powerful of valid forms, the inference is *U*: in *USU*, *PDU*, *UDP*, it is only *P*. In *USP*, *PSU*, *PDP*, *PSP*, there is no inference: of these the first three may be said to be one remove from inference, and the fourth two removes. All this may be said of the cases in which the external universal is allowed to enter. Thus *PSP*, now two removes from inference, is made valid by such accessions as make it *PDY*, *YDP*, or *YSY*: each accession being either a change from *S* to *D*, or alteration of *P* into *Y*.

Of all the transposed syllogisms, one half, being all in the first compartment, are either identical with, or contained in, syllogisms of the ordinary kind. Of those in *UDY*, the one marked (̄(() is contained in, and contains, ||)); and)̄·(() is similarly identical with |·|)). Of those in *YDU*, ())) is identical with ((||: and so on. Of those in *YDY*, (̱̄))̱̄) is contained in, but does not contain,))));)̱̄·))(̱̄ is contained in (·))); and so on. Of those in *YSY*, (̱̄)()̱̄ is contained in))((; and so on. Overlooking strengthened forms, it thus appears that the really new cases are all contained in *PDY* and *YDP*, of which either is but an inverted reading of the other.

LOGIC

[From the *English Cyclopaedia*, V (1860)][1]

. . . The study of logic in this country has [lately] undergone three important changes. First, much more attention is paid to the subject: secondly, innovations have been listened to in a spirit which seems to admit that Kant's dictum about the perfection of the Aristotelian logic may possibly be false: thirdly, a disposition has arisen to distinguish logic from metaphysics and psychology, without losing sight of the psychological and metaphysical discussion which is necessary to a sound view of the meaning, province, and first principles of the science. In such a state of transition the best thing to be done is . . . to devote the present article chiefly to some account of recent developments and current disputes . . . We also explain that we are not writing for (nor against) the competent disputant, but for the learner who has mastered the common elements; that we refer to England (meaning the three kingdoms) and English thought only; and that we treat of that part of logic which may be styled an exact science, without any discussion of the grounds on which its obvious postulates are founded.

The changes to which we have alluded arise from that revival of the taste for philosophy which has commenced and is continuing, both in England and France. So far as England is concerned this revival was preceded by the publication of Dr Whately's work, the first edition of which was an article in the *Encyclopaedia Metropolitana* (about 1826). The author had for years taught the subject at Oxford, and had trained some, at least, to see the low state into which logic had fallen; a state not exaggerated in the unfriendly criticism presently mentioned. This work placed logic, in a comparatively attractive form, within the reach of many out of Oxford, to whom all the attainable books had been sealed by the stamp of a current prejudice; and it had merits of its own. The Archbishop of Dublin possesses the talent which distinguished Paley from his predecessors; the talent of rendering a dry subject attractive in a sound form by style, illustration, and clearness combined. And to him is due the title of the restorer of logical study in England.

In 1836, ten years after the publication of Dr Whately's work, Sir William Hamilton was appointed professor of logic and metaphysics in the University of Edinburgh. The extraordinary character of his learning

[1] [This article has been shortened and adapted to its present context, chiefly by the omission of obsolete bibliographical material.—Ed.]

is [hardly to be] overrated. But it should be added, as necessary to be known by any one who enters on the logical controversies of the day, that his strange hatred of the mathematical sciences was owing to an unusual inaptitude for them, which prevented, probably any sufficient study, certainly any real understanding, even of their lowest branches. In 1829, he commenced that powerful series of articles in the *Edinburgh Review* by which his reputation was first established out of Edinburgh: these were republished with some additional notes, under the title of *Discussions on Philosophy*; and no higher logical student can dispense with them. In 1833 appeared the celebrated criticism on Dr Whately's Logic, of which the first thing to be said is that it is due to Dr Whately himself that it had an audience to listen to it: its history, philosophy, and philology, would have fallen dead upon the previous generation. Accordingly this criticism, though most valuable as a logical dissertation, and of a necessity to be read which does not lessen with time, is nothing as a criticism; for it neither is nor proceeds upon a true view of the place and office of the work criticized. Nevertheless, it was one of the stimulants of the revival.

The meaning of the word *logic* has undergone much variation in different hands. It has been what the writer pleases, from the whole of the inquiry into truth and falsehood down to the investigation of the Aristotelian syllogism. This diversity of signification is probably near its end. There is a growing disposition to admit Kant's definition, which describes it as the science of the *necessary laws of thought*: it is said to treat of the *form* of thought independently of its *matter*. Though neither Aristotle nor his followers confine themselves within this definition, nor even so much as distinctly conceive it, all will acknowledge that the definition singles out the most important distinctive feature of their system. A few words on the relation of *form* and *matter* will be requisite.

When many things are thought of in one way, which way is neither governed nor modified by the difference between one thing and another, there is a common *form* of thought about distinct *matters*. Thus arithmetic is a formal science with reference to concrete magnitude: that 8 and 4 make the same as 4 and 8 is a form, a law of thought, which is not affected by the objects counted being yards rather than sheep, or pints rather than men. Pass into algebra, and the differences which are formal in arithmetic become only material: thus $8 + 4 = 4 + 8$ is but one material instance of the form $a + b = b + a$. Are we therefore to say that arithmetic and algebra are parts of logic? Certainly not: logic deals with the pure form of thought, divested of every possible distinction of matter. There is a form of thought in the above which is not even confined to number, and not even confined to magnitude: namely, that the manner in which we think of *part* and *whole*, in every possible case in which these words can apply, is wholly independent of the order in which the parts are considered as coming together. For example, the notions *animal* and *rational* are joined together in the mind when we think of *man*, but by a mode of junction very different from that called addition in arithmetic. Nevertheless, it matters nothing as to the notion arrived at whether we think of *animal* as subsequently limited by the notion *rational*, or of *rational* as subsequently limited by the notion *animal*. The pure form of thought is that which belongs equally to the last instance and to $8 + 4 = 4 + 8$; different matters, different modes of junction, under the common law that order of junction is indifferent. . . .

The great points of elementary logical investigation are four in number: 1. The *name* or *term*, the representative of one object of thought, as distinguished from others, including a mode of thinking. 2. The *relation*, or mode of bringing two terms together, signified by a *copula* connecting two terms. 3. The *proposition* or *judgment*, a relation between two terms affirmed or denied. 4. The *syllogism*, deduction of a relation between two terms by means of the relations of the two to a third term. These points must needs include the consideration of all the laws of ratiocinative thought in action: surely, What? What else? What of them? and What then? are questions which point to all that can take place in a mental process by which thought leads to thought.[1] Nevertheless, by certain restrictions which we hold to be purely arbitrary, logicians have curtailed their science, and made it appear to contain but a very small part of the processes of actual thought. In placing before the student a mere sketch of disputed points, we remind him that many things must be left unstated, many objections unprovided for. He must look for full assurance, either for or against, in writings of more extended character, and in discussions which are fully guarded by the use of defined technicalities.

First, as to the term or name, which may be in one word or in many. The old logicians drew the distinction between a name used as simply denoting an external object, such as might be thought of as existing without any mind to think of it, and the name used as thinking of the object in its mental relation to other objects. A *man*, thought of as an individual pointed out, or a quality, as *white*, the white of a particular white ball, were called names of *first intention*, or *first notions*. But *man* as a class, or an individual thought of as a member of a class, and *white*, as an attribute of classes, were names of *second intention*, or *second notions*. The distinction is precisely that now known as objective and subjective: and accordingly, we propose to consider things—not material things only—and the qualities residing in them, as belonging

[1] [Four subdivisions hold the thoughts of men:
What first? What next? What of them? And what then?

—6 May 1866.]

to the objective use of names; and classes, and the attributes by which we define classes, as belonging to the subjective use. Now though the logicians have always professed to cultivate second intentions, or subjective uses, the forms and the language of the syllogism have been strictly fashioned on the objective use, and allowed to remain so.

Next, it is clear that a name excludes as well as includes: every object of thought is related to *man*, for instance, either as *in* the name or *out*. The logician has always excluded the privative name, *not-man*, for instance, as all but useless: a certain practice of his own really makes it so. For he will have no *universe*—or total sphere of thought—except the whole universe of possible existence; or, at narrowest, the whole universe of objective reality. He forgets that, more often than not, the universe of the existing topic of thought is limited. We are talking of animals, for example, and nothing else: *not-man* becomes so definitely significative that we have a separate name for it, *brute*. Logic ought to give us that command of thought which will prevent our mental vision from being obstructed by the casual absence of a name; and it ought to investigate the *actual* form of thought, as well as possible scientific generalization.

Thirdly, two names may be joined either as separate parts of a common whole, or as jointly separating the common part of two different wholes. Thus the class *animal* has the two separate sub-classes, *man* and *brute*: but *man*, under the name *rational animal*, is seen as belonging to the common part of the two wholes, *rational being* and *animal being*. We call the first procedure *aggregation*, the second *composition*. The first process is *mathematical*: *animal* is made up of *man* and *brute* after the same law of thought by which a square is made up of two triangles. The second process is deep in the nature of things, *metaphysical*: the combination of *rational* and *animal* into a being such as man is not conceivable as *aggregation* or *addition*, and no more. Nevertheless the logician does not admit this: he announces an object as the *sum* of all its attributes. The preceding distinction divides logic into two parts, which we call the mathematical and the metaphysical; not meaning that one part of logic is mathematics, and another metaphysics, but that the distinctive features of the two sides of logic are of prominent account, the one in mathematics, and the other in metaphysics.

The distinction of composition and aggregation was conveyed and implied in a few remarkable words of Aristotle, contained in his Metaphysics: 'The genus is said to be part of the species; but in another point of view the species is part of the genus.' Animal is part of man: the *whole* notion (all the attributes) of *animal* forms part (component) of the notion *man*. But *man* is part of *animal*: the whole class (all the individuals) of *man* forms part (aggregant) of the class *animal*. This is the heading of a chapter in logic which only begins to be written in full in our own day: the logicians always threw the idea of attributes compounded of attributes into metaphysics, and retained the mathematical notion of class aggregated of classes for logic. The attributes which compound into an attribute were said to form its *intension*: the classes which aggregate into a class were said to form its *extension*. This distinction of extension and intension—or extent and intent—is now often styled that of extension and comprehension; the Mills, father and son, call it that of denotation and connotation; Hamilton, that of breadth and depth. The revival of the distinction, in logic, and as a separation of the two sides of logic, is mainly due to Hamilton: but he and his followers have made a singular misconception. In the above explanation it appears clearly that the logical *quantities* change terms in the opposed modes of speaking. *All* animal (all the attributes) forms *part of* the notion man: *all* man (the whole of the class) forms *part of* the class animal. According to Hamilton, the quantities do *not* change places. He affirms that when we say 'All men are some animals,' we speak[1] in depth; and that when we say 'Some animals are all men' we speak in breadth. We shall not enlarge upon this distinction: we do not think it necessary to impress at length upon the reader that Hamilton's distinction is not the great distinction of the laws of thought. And such discussion would be the more inappropriate at this time, because Hamilton's logical lectures are on the eve of publication by Mr Mansel, who may be expected to defend his principal well, if defence be possible, and who must either defend or surrender. And we are glad of the opportunity of calling the reader's anticipation to a work which will most surely contain a vast breadth and depth of thought.

Lastly, every logical term is postulated as having existence in thought, or existence in external reality, according to the universe in question. It is only as representing existence that a term is used in logic. Thus, when from every X is Y, and every Y is Z, we infer every X is Z, our premises are supposed to imply the assertions that X, Y, Z exist.

We now come to the *copula* or relation by which terms are connected, and the *proposition* or *judgment*, which asserts or denies the connection. And here the logicians admit only one copula into the form of the proposition: that is, *identification*, affirmed by *is*, denied by *is not*. If we say A goes before B, they call this proposition a material connexion between A and B. They hold that the form of the above which is essential to its consideration in pure logic is 'A *is* a thing which goes

[1] Mr Mansel (*North Brit. Rev.*, May, 1851), inverts this mode of reading. He will have 'some A is all B' to mean that all the *attributes* of the concept B are some of the attributes of the concept A; and 'all B is some A' to mean that all the *things* possessing the mark (or name) B are a portion of those possessing the mark A. We must leave the Hamiltonian logicians to settle among themselves which is which: that is, to array the two propositions—'Some animal is all man,' and 'all man is some animal'—under their proper banners.

before *B*.' And they further maintain that there are three fundamental forms of thought, which they call the principles of *identity*, *difference*, and *excluded middle*. Of identity, *A* is *A*; of difference, *A* is not not-*A* (or *B*, other than *A*); of excluded middle (or of *nothing between*), *B* is either *A* or not-*A*. That every thought of our minds must be fashioned so as not to contradict either of these principles is most evident; as evident as the things themselves; as sure as eggs are eggs. But the logician assumes a right to say that only these propositions are of the pure form of thought, true by the form: and that all others are true by the matter and not by the form. Because all assertion identifies something with something, and all denial separates something from something, he lays it down that identity and difference constitute the only forms of comparison of ideas, or the whole form. For ourselves, we believe that there is matter in the proposition '*A* is *A*,' one specific relation, identity: we do not see why, except by arbitrary separation founded upon great importance, the process of identification and the relation of identity are declared to be of so different a nature from all other processes and relations as to make the difference of form and matter. To us the pure form of the proposition, divested of all matter, is the assertion or denial of the following:—*X* stands in relation *L* to *Y*. The proposition '*X* is *X*' is brought under the general form by two introductions of matter: *L* is identity, and *X* and *Y* are the same symbols.

What is the test of distinction between a consequence which is true by its form, and one which is only true by its matter? When the assertion is true by its form, it can only be refused admission by impossibility in its matter; and when it can only be refused admission by impossibility in its matter, it is true by its form: and by impossibility we mean incompatibility with the conditions of the universe understood. If the universe be the whole sphere of possible thought, the impossible is that which contradicts itself, and nothing else; a five-footed quadruped, for example. But if it be the terrestrial sphere of actual existence, the impossible is only the non-existent on earth; a rational quadruped, for example. If the universe be limited to the idea of animal, a stone is an impossibility. For instance, '*A* is *A*,' and '*A* is not not-*A*,' are true by form, in our view; how can they be denied? or rather, when can we doubt of admitting them? for assertion must be opposed to non-assertion, not to denial. Only when *A* contradicts itself. A horse which is not a horse, and a cow which is not a cow, are they the same things, or different? and must they be either one or the other? We leave the logicians to settle it; for ourselves we cannot tell: we do not see how to affirm, and we do not see how to deny. But we do see that '*A* is *A*' can only be questioned, whatever the result may be, when the matter of *A* is impossible; and we recognize it as therefore true in form.

Again, let *X* be an existing animal; it follows that the tail of *X* is the tail of an animal. Is this consequence formal or material? Formal, because this is true whatever a tail may be, so long as there *is* a tail; and it cannot be refused assertion except when *X* has no tail. A guinea-pig, for instance, puts this proposition out of the pale of assertion, and equally out of that of denial; the tail of a non-tailed animal is beyond us. There are those who will assert that the tail of a *non-tailed* animal is *no tail*; but we are satisfied that the *tail* of a non-tailed animal is just as much a *tail* as no-tail; and therein lies the contradiction and the impossibility. If we were clear that the tail of a non-tailed animal is no tail, we should know how to think of it; for we can think of every subject which comes under a predicate. This very guinea-pig is here produced by us because it has been brought forward by an acute thinker[1] to prove that the consequence above given *is material*, and *not* formal. It has been made to prove that '*X* is an animal, therefore the tail of *X* is the tail of an animal' is a special inference gained from our material knowledge of the thing thought about, and not a general inference necessitated by the universal laws of thinking. We answer that though the lack of tail in a guinea-pig is not a law of logic, but a material incident of the object, yet we know the *consequence* to be necessitated by the laws of thinking, because we must go to impossible matter, we must make the tail of *X* a non-existence, before we can refuse to assert it.

The establishment of ordinary syllogism requires two principles. First, the *convertibility* of the terms of a proposition: '*A* is *B*' gives '*B* is *A*.' Secondly, the *transitiveness* of the connecting relation: '*A* is *B*' and '*B* is *C*' gives '*A* is *C*.' The logicians affirm that the three principles of identity, difference, and excluded middle, are sufficient for the evolution of all the laws of syllogism. We are not aware that any one has ever made this good by actually deducing the two principles last named from the higher three. This must be done, if at all, without syllogism, for syllogism must not be taken for granted as a step towards its own establishment; and if, as we believe, it cannot be done, then the three principles do not possess that dominant and all-sufficient character which has been claimed for them.

The syllogism is the determination of the relation which exists between two objects of thought by means of the relation in which each of them stands to some third object, which is the *middle term.* In our view of the subject the pure form of the syllogism, when its premises are absolutely asserted, is as follows:—*X* is in the relation *L* to *Y*; *Y* is in the relation *M* to *Z*; therefore *X* is in the relation '*L* of *M*,' compounded of *L* and *M*, to *Z*. In ordinary logic, which admits only the relation of identity, the actual composition of the relation is made by our consciousness of its *transitive* character. Thus *X* is *Y* and *Y* is *Z*, tell us that *X* is that which is *Z*. But an identical of an identical is an identical; whence *X* is *Z*.

[1] [Mansel.—Ed.]

Again, *X* is *Y* and *Y* is not *Z*; here *X* is that which is not-*Z*: or *X* is not *Z*. The full syllogism is a collection of such singular cases: thus every *X* is *Y*, and no *Y* is *Z*, repeats '*X* is a *Y*, that *Y* is a not-*Z*,' as often as there are *X*s in existence, and gives 'every *X* is not-*Z*,' or no *X* is *Z*.[1]

The requisites of the copular relation, in the system of ordinary syllogism, are *transitiveness* and *convertibility*. *Any* relation which possesses these qualities may take the place of 'is' in the common syllogism, without impeachment of its validity. Thus the word 'fellow' may have transitive senses, and is always convertible: choose a transitive signification, under which we may say that when *X* is a fellow of *Y*, and *Y* of *Z*, then *X* is a fellow of *Z*. Take a common syllogism, such as—no *Y* is any *Z*, some *Y*s are *X*s; whence some *X*s are not any *Z*s. For 'is' read 'is a fellow of,' and for 'is not' read 'is not a fellow of;' the inference remains valid. Against admitting this extension it is argued that the inference is one of matter, not of form; but though every *instance* is material, or has its own matter, we maintain that the above inference depends for its validity only on those qualities which must be seen in *identity* before the *common* syllogism can be established.

The logicians are well aware that there are many copulae which give inference by comparison with a middle term, and which are not what *they* call syllogisms; for instance, '*A* equals *B*, *B* equals *C*, therefore *A* equals *C*.' They reduce such arguments to syllogism by stating the requisite combination of relation in a major premise, and affirming the case to come under the combination in a minor premise. As in 'An equal of an equal of *C* is an equal of *C*; *A* is an equal of an equal of *C*; whence *A* is an equal of *C*.' But *A* and *C* are really compared in the mind with a middle term *B*, and thence with one another. When $A = B$, $B = C$, are made to give $A = C$, the process of the human mind is guided by steps in which = is as truly a *copula*, or connecting relation, as 'is' in '*A* is *B*, *B* is *C*, whence *A* is *C*.' The *transitive* character of the copula is as much the dictator of the result in the first case as in the second.

Dismissing [for the present] the extension to wider relations than those contained under 'is,' we shall proceed to point out the questions which have arisen as to the common forms of enunciation, and the systems of enunciation and of syllogism which have been proposed. After a few words on the common system, we shall notice the different proposals of Mr Boole, Sir Wm. Hamilton, and Mr De Morgan.

[1] [The proposition itself is a blank syllogism, which becomes effective when charged with a known middle term. In *X*))*Y* we have *X*))∘))*Y* and *X*)·(∘(·)*Y*; in *X*)(*Y* we have *X*))∘)(*Y* and *X*)·(∘)·(*Y*, etc. If the conclusion exist, there exist middle terms: if *a* middle term exist, the conclusion exists.

Thus () is ((() or ()))
or (·((·) or (·))·)
or (( )) or (·) (·)]

The common proposition is derived from the notion of assertion or denial, applied to *all* or to *some*, giving the universal affirmative and negative, every *X* is *Y*, no *X* is *Y*; and the particular affirmative and negative, some *X*s are *Y*s, some *X*s are not *Y*s. Here *some*, as in all logical writings, means no more than *not-none*, one at least, many it may be, even all, possibly. When we say that some *X*s are not *Y*s, we only mean to deny that the class *X* is entirely included in the class *Y*; the exclusion may be partial or may be total. The logical opposition of quantity, then, is not that of whole and not-whole or part; but of quantity asserted to be the whole, and quantity not asserted to be the whole.

The old writers on logic hardly speak of universal and particular *terms*; they apply these adjectives to the *propositions*. They say that a *proposition* is made universal by prefixing the word *omnis* to the *subject*. Later writers *quantify* both subject and predicate. They find out that 'all *X*s are *Y*s' means that 'all *X*s are some *Y*s;' that 'no *X* is *Y*' means that 'every *X* is no one of all the *Y*s;' that 'some *X*s are *Y*s' is 'some *X*s are some *Y*s;' and that 'some *X*s are not *Y*s' is 'some *X*s are not any of all the *Y*s.' And hence the well-known rule that while the quantity of the subject is indicated, the quantity of the predicate is determined by the quality of the proposition; particular in affirmatives, universal in negatives. But conversion of term and quantity is not allowed: 'all *X*s are some *Y*s' is never seen as 'some *Y*s are all *X*s.' The usual forms of language are made to dictate restrictions to thought. We shall presently return to this point.

Mr Boole's generalization of the forms of logic is by far the boldest and most original of those of which we have to treat. It cannot be separated from Mathematics, since it not only demands algebra, but such taste for thought about the notation of algebra as is rarely acquired without much and deep practice. When the ideas thrown out by Mr Boole shall have borne their full fruit, algebra, though only founded on ideas of number in the first instance, will appear like a sectional model of the whole form of thought. Its forms, considered apart from their matter, will be seen to contain all the forms of thought in general. The anti-mathematical logician says that it makes thought a branch of algebra, instead of algebra a branch of thought. It *makes* nothing; it *finds*: and it finds the laws of thought symbolized in the forms of algebra. We cannot attempt, in this article, to do more than show, by one single case, how common algebraical operation is transformation from one logical equivalent to another. We shall choose the conversion of 'to be both not-*A* and not-*B* is impossible' into 'every thing is either *A* or *B* or both.' Let *A* and *B* represent two objects of thought. Let 1 represent the universe, all that exists; let 0 represent the impossible, something that does not exist. Let $=$ represent identity. Let $A + B$ represent the class containing both A and B, with all the common part, if any, counted twice; let $A - B$ signify what is left of the class A, when B, which it contains, is withdrawn. Let AB represent the common part of the notions A and B. Then $1 - A$ and $1 - B$ represent all that is not A and all that is not B; and the non-existence of everything which is both not A and not B is symbolized by

$$(1 - A)(1 - B) = 0$$

The common rules of algebra transform this into

$$A + B - AB = 1.$$

Now, $A + B - AB$ is simply the aggregate of A and B, without repetition, the part reckoned twice in $A + B$, if any, being withdrawn once. Accordingly the second equation means that A and B between them contain the whole universe; or that everything is either A or B, or both. We have put forward enough to enable an intelligent student to raise a string of difficulties; for the solution of most of which we must refer him to Mr Boole's writings.

We now proceed to the discussion of Sir William Hamilton's system. At the outset the learned author puts into words a postulate[1] which no one would suppose had been left to him to demand. It is 'that we be allowed to state in language what is contained in thought.' We may trust Hamilton's learning for the fact that this postulate was never *announced*: but surely we shall feel inclined to ask, who has ever been timid enough not to use it, as wanted? Aristotle, we may answer, and nearly all his followers. There are cases in which Aristotle himself appears to doubt the right, or at least to waive the right, of pushing thought beyond the bounds of usual expression; and to this day logic has been circumscribed by this want of clear apprehension that language was made to express and extend thought, not to circumscribe it. The postulate ought to be pushed further; the logician ought to be allowed to state all that *can be* contained in thought; unless indeed we are to construe *is* as a junction of the present and future tenses.

Among the cases in which language did not find expression for possible thought, was the quantity of the predicate of a common proposition. The logicians, Hamilton at least, and most others we believe,

[1] Besides this principle, Hamilton announced another, which had been quite as much neglected as the former: and by merely lending the weight which his acumen and learning gave him to these two fundamental requirements of logic, he will have done much to promote it, even though his practice be not quite abreast of his preaching. 'Whatever is operative in thought, must be taken into account, and consequently be overtly expressible in logic; for logic must be, as to be it professes, an unexclusive reflex of thought, and not merely an arbitrary selection—a series of elegant extracts—out of the forms of thinking. Whether the form that it exhibits as legitimate be stronger or weaker, be more or less frequently applied;—that, as a material and contingent consideration, is beyond its purview.'

affirm that thought *does* quantify the predicate; for ourselves, after much observation, we believe it does not. We believe that minds of ordinary cultivation, with whom logic has not been a study, when they have occasion to think that no quadruped is a fish, do *not* hold it in thought that they are speaking about *all* fishes, actual and possible. They may, by a process they never analysed, be able to *use* this implied truth; but we do not believe they ever held it in that way in which they hold the thought which is apt to find expression. Be this as it may, Hamilton believed, not only that a quantity is held in thought for the predicate of the ordinary proposition, but even that quantities *are* in thought which have never been expressed in language even by logicians. He accordingly applied—as had been done before him, though the results had not been worked into a logical system—*both* the quantities, universal and particular, to both subject and predicate. He thus put forward, as what *we have* in thought, eight forms of predication, to the statement of which we add some explanation, and some objection.

1. All *X* is all *Y*. This means that *X* and *Y* are coextensive terms; accordingly it is a complex[1] proposition, made by compounding 'every *X* is *Y*,' and 'every *Y* is *X*.' It is simply contradicted by the alternative of one or another of two other propositions of the system: Either 'some *X*s are not *Y*s' or 'some *Y*s are not *X*s.'
2. All *X* is some *Y*. This is the same as 'every *X* is *Y*.'
3. Some *X* is all *Y*. This is 'every *Y* is *X*.'
4. Some *X* is some *Y*. This is 'some *X*s are *Y*s.'
5. Any *X* is not any *Y*. In negatives, the word *any* takes the place of all, for the sake of grammar. We have here, 'no *X* is *Y*.'
6. Any *X* is not some *Y*. This is 'some *Y*s are not *X*s.'
7. Some *X* is not any *Y*. This is 'some *X*s are not *Y*s.'
8. Some *X* is not some *Y*. This proposition is not in ordinary use. It means that some of the *X*s are not some of the *Y*s, even if they be others. To contradict it we must affirm that there is but one *X* and one *Y*, and that *X* identical with the *Y*. Consequently, here is a proposition which does not find its denial in the system.

Dr Thomson (*Outlines*, &c.) admits the first seven of these propositions, but rejects the eighth: and constructs a system of syllogism accordingly.

That Hamilton really believed the above system to be in *common thought*,[2] and not the deduction of a postulated extension, is manifest.

[1] This is denied. But if, of propositions *A*, *B*, *C*, *A* always make *B* and *C* follow, and *B* and *C* always make *A* follow, surely *A* is identical with the junction of *B* and *C*. What does *A* contain more than is in *B* and *C* compounded? And what less? A proposition is contradicted by alternative junction of two different propositions, of which neither contains the other: is it simple or complex?

[2] He published to the world the requirements for a prize essay to be written by his pupils, among which was the following:—'The reasons why common language

To this we object: but our greater objection is to the system itself. We have not seen any defence of the following points which has a single respectable[1] element, except the character of its producers. The introduction 1, of a complex proposition; 2, of a proposition which is not simply contradicted by any *one* other proposition; 3, of a proposition which cannot be contradicted at all in the system; 4, of a proposition compounded of two others *already in the system.*

The notation of the system is as follows. Woodcuts[2] resembling — and + are used for assertion and denial; a comma signifies particular quantity; a colon signifies universal quantity. Thus $X, \dashv\!\vdash : Y$ signifies '*some* X is not *any* Y.' And the following diagram represents the syllogism, 'all X is all Y, some Y is all Z, therefore some X is all Z.'

$$X : - : Y, - : Z$$
$$\underline{\quad , \qquad\qquad\quad}$$

There is valid inference when the middle term is once at least taken universally, and one of the propositions at least is affirmative. We shall presently point out the canon of inference, when we have described a notation which we prefer. We refer the student to Sir W. Hamilton's own writings for the notation, &c. connected with his distinction of breadth

[1] To the objection that 'All X is all Y' has no single contradiction, an eminent defender replied that it *has* a contradiction; and he produced it; 'All X is not all Y'; and Sir Wm. Hamilton assented: and both are right under a little admission of unusual construction. But the assailant had only objected that there was no contradiction *in the system*: and both Hamilton and his defender forgot to explain how this contradiction did not find its way *into the system.* The true explanation is that the system itself was founded, not on the laws of thought, but on an arbitrary extension of the application of language: and the end of it is that the Hamiltonian logic is *not* allowed to find language for all that is contained in thought. For both Hamilton and his defender have to go *out of the system* to find language for what must be *in thought* to those who think of the system, namely, the denial, when wanted, of the first of the propositions in the system.

[2] It will amuse the mathematician to see that Hamilton, to whom all mathematics was repugnant, stumbles upon + for his sign of negation, and — for his sign of affirmation.

makes an *ellipsis* of the *expressed* quantity, frequently of the *subject*, and more frequently of the *predicate*, though both have always their quantities in thought.' In saying this, he was so fully satisfied that he had announced the principle of applying *every* quantity to the predicate of *every* proposition, that he made a charge of plagiarism of this principle against one who applied it after (as he supposed) seeing this announcement, and rested the proof on the (as he thought) obvious meaning of the sentence above. It is hardly requisite to say that 'both have *their* quantities' is not the same as 'both have *all* quantities,' but generally means that one has one and another another. If any one had said that two persons 'both have always their hobbies,' no one would have gathered that the pair keep a pair of hobbies for their joint use. The present point, however, is the statement that this takes place in *common language*, and that the *ellipsis*, as he calls it, is only *frequent*, implying that the full expression is not infrequent.

and depth. We hold it quite useless to enter on the comparison of 'all man is some animal,' and 'some animal is all man,' as cases of a fundamental subdivision[1] of logic into two parts; those who can may believe that, as asserted, one of these propositions is *metaphysical* and one *logical*.

Sir W. Hamilton invited the severest criticism: he challenged it to show that his system is not more correct[2] in theory than that of Aristotle, and not preferable in practice. He affirmed that his system was intended to 'place the key-stone on the Aristotelic arch,' and that it succeeded in so doing. We hold him to be almost a miracle of learning, and, in every sort of psychological or metaphysical notion, except only when it is mathematical, we feel him to have a true genius for conception, a mighty power of execution, and a rare talent of expression. But when quantity is in question, his power is gone. Almost in a breath he tells us, first, that his two quantities, breadth and depth, are in reality one and the same quantity; and next, that the greater the one the less is the other (*Discussions*, &c. 1st. ed., p. 644*, 2nd ed., p. 699). He confounds equation of quantity with identification of quantified matter: he asserts that a proposition is 'merely' equation of quantities. He uses the phrases 'equation of quantities' and 'coalescence of notions' as convertible; and the prize essay of an able student,[3] published with his sanction, announces that 'predication is nothing more or less than the expression of the relation of quantity in which a notion stands to an individual, or two notions to each other.'

[Hamilton's system, though completely quantified, fails in symmetrical distribution of quantification. This would be no defect, if it were founded on analysis of thought; but it suggests doubt and query when

[1] Sir W. Hamilton seems, *in logic*, to have nothing answering to the *attribute* which marks a *class*: he substitutes the concrete quality, treated as a class of individuals. He says that Leibnitz and Newton have *two* human natures, one apiece: that one attribute of Plato is '*some* Athenian.' This is quite true, and the treatment of the quality, under the notion of one quality for one individual, another for another, is good in its proper and very subordinate place. But it is not connected with the great distinction of comprehension and extension, hereinbefore noticed.

[2] His completely quantified predicate is maintained by him to be necessary to the perfect representation of common thought. A living lesson on this point was soon given. Shortly after Sir W. Hamilton's death, an ardent admirer published a manual of his system for the use of schools. But though he had seen the objection to the form 'All *X* is all *Y*' having no contradiction, and Hamilton's admission and defence, he actually took 'Some *X* is not some *Y*' to be the contradiction required. And when the error was pointed out in a review, he continued to maintain it, and appealed to common sense for its truth, and to Hamilton's pupils (one of whom set him right) to vouch for its correct representation of the system. The author of the manual showed no want of acuteness in other things, and his book is a valuable and well-timed proof that Hamilton's system demands more than *is* in common thought, though not more than *may be* in the thought of those who will gain it.

[3] [Baynes.—Ed.]

it is remembered that Hamilton is but an arbitrary extender of forms of language. Quantification by introduction of contraries gives us:

	U	*P*
Double Universal	)·(	)(
Particular and Universal	((	(·(
Universal and Particular	))	)·)
Double Particular	(·)	()

both in particular and universal propositions. Hamilton's system distributes as follows:

	U	*P*
Double Universal	)·( )(	—
Particular and Universal	((	(·(
Universal and Particular	))	)·)
Double Particular	—	(·) ()

The doubt is removed and the query answered when we come to the *exemplar system*, which, though similarly distributed, is self-consistent. —10 February 1861.]

We now proceed to state Mr De Morgan's views, and for brevity as well as for other reasons, we shall confine ourselves to mere statement, without proof or enforcement; referring to the works previously mentioned.

The proposition in its common form is objective, or, in old phrase, of first intention. It is also arithmetical in character: it either enumerates or speaks by total of enumeration, as in Every *X* is *Y*, All *X*s are *Y*s. It is so far not distinguishable in character from a numerically definite proposition: 'Some *X*s are *Y*s' and '70 *X*s are *Y*s' are forms which differ only by vague and definite enumeration.

The adoption of a definite universe, as already noticed, gives precision to the privative term, not-*X*, the rest of the universe when *X* is removed. Let not-*X* be denoted by *x*; not-*Y* by *y*, &c. And *X* and *x* are called contraries.[1] This introduction destroys the distinction of assertion and denial, except in a relative sense: the assertion that every *X* is *Y* is the denial that any *X* is *y*. Affirmation and negation must be distinguished as follows. A proposition true of *X* and *X*, false of *X* and *x*, is affirmative: a proposition true of *X* and *x*, false of *X* and *X*, is negative. Thus 'every thing is either *X* or *Y*' is negative, though assertive in this form: it is true of *X* and *x*, false of *X* and *X*. It is to be understood that no term used fills the universe: names which belong to the whole universe, to one part as much as to another, cannot be of any distinctive force or meaning within that universe.

[1] No distinction is drawn between the words *contrary* and *contradictory*, whether as to terms or propositions.

Let a proposition be called universal, when the whole universe must be examined to verify it: particular, when the examination of a portion of the universe may verify it. Let a term be called total, where every instance of it must be examined before the proposition can be verified: partial, when such complete examination may not be needed.

There are two forms of predication in use: the *cumular*, as in 'all *X*s are some *Y*s' and 'some *X*s are not *Y*s' (are distinct from all *Y*s); the *exemplar*, as in 'every (each, or any) *X* is some one *Y*', and 'some one *X* (perhaps not *any* one) is not any one *Y*'. The cumular proposition speaks by collection; the exemplar, by selection. Grammatical correctness (representing a usual tendency of thought, though not an absolute law) allows either mode of expression in affirmatives, but demands exemplar expression in negatives; as in 'all *X*s are not any *Y*s'. The cumular and exemplar modes of expression have differences which will presently be further seen.

We first take the cumular proposition and syllogism. Let a term totally used, as *X*, be denoted by *X*) or (*X*; partially, by *X*(or)*X*. Let affirmation be denoted by two dots, or none; negation by one dot. Let propositions be distinguished by the quantities of their terms and the *quality* (affirmative or negative): this is found to make complete distinction. Thus (·) means a negative proposition in which both terms are particular: and *X* (·) *Y* is that proposition enunciated in terms of *X* and *Y*. It turns out to be 'Everything is either *X* or *Y*.'

There are eight forms of cumular predication: four universal, with four contrary (usually called *contradictory*) particulars. These are now given, with their symbols and usual readings: and the correctness of the distribution of the words universal and particular, total and partial, may be gathered by the reader from the definitions. Each universal (*U*) is followed by its contrary particular (*P*).

U. *X*)) *Y*. Every *X* is *Y*.
P. *X*(·(*Y*. Some *X*s are not *Y*s.
U. *X*)·(*Y*. No *X* is *Y*.
P. *X*() *Y*. Some *X*s are *Y*s.
U. *X*(·) *Y*. Everything is either *X* or *Y*.
P. *X*)(*Y*. Some things are neither *X*s nor *Y*s.
U. *X*((*Y*. Some *X*s are all the *Y*s.
P. *X*)·) *Y*. All *X*s are not some *Y*s.

Contraversion—changing a name into its contrary—alters the quantity of the term, and the quality of the proposition: thus *X*)) *Y* is *X*)·(*y* and *x*((*y* and *x*(·) *Y*. And a term and its contrary always enter one proposition *with different quantities*. *Conversion* is simply writing the propositional symbol inverted: thus *X*)) *Y* is conversely *Y*((*X*. We shall now use the forms)) (·(&c. to signify the propositions.

Of contraries; one must be true and one false: either)) or (·(&c. Each universal simply contradicts one particular—the one with different quantities and quality; is inconsistent with, and therefore denies, the universals of different qualities; remains indifferent to the universal of different quantities and its contradictory; and contains the two particulars of the same quality. Thus)) contradicts (·(, that is, denies and is the only mode of denial; it denies)·(and (·) but not by simple contradiction; it co-exists with either ((or)·); and it contains and affirms () and)(.

Each universal proposition has what we call *terminal ambiguity*: thus 'every *X* is *Y*' may coexist with either 'Every *Y* is *X*' or 'some *Y*s are not *X*s.' The following is the list of propositions which, with reference to the ambiguity just noted, have what we call *terminal precision*. The symbols used to denote them are prefixed.

X)◦)*Y*, compounded of *X*))*Y* and *X*)·)*Y*. All *X*s and other things besides are *Y*s.

X||*Y*, compounded of *X*))*Y* and *X*((*Y*. All *X*s are all *Y*s: *X* and *Y* are identical terms.

X(◦(*Y*, compounded of *X*((*Y* and *X*(·(*Y*. The *X*s contain all the *Y*s and other things besides.

X)◦(*Y*, compounded of *X*)·(*Y* and *X*)(*Y*. Nothing is both *X* and *Y*, and some things are neither.

X|·|*Y*, compounded of *X*)·(*Y* and *X*(·)*Y*. Everything either *X* or *Y* and nothing both: *X* and *Y* are contraries.

X(◦)*Y*, compounded of *X*(·)*Y* and *X*()*Y*. Everything is either *X* or *Y*, and some things are both.

Each kind of proposition is either simple or complex with respect to the other, according as we think of alternation or conjunction. Thus)◦) is the junction of)) and)·); but)) is the alternative)◦) or ||. Conversion and contraversion are under the same rules as before.

The preceding forms are completely arithmetical, and are truly particular cases of the numerical proposition, of which it will now be convenient to say something, as well as of the corresponding syllogism.

Let mXY signify that m (or more) *X*s are *Y*s; then mXy signifies that m or more *X*s are not *Y*s. Let u be the number of instances in the universe; let x, y, z, be the numbers of *X*s, *Y*s, and *Z*s: then $u - x$, $u - y$, $u - z$, are the numbers of *x*s, *y*s, and *z*s. A *spurious* proposition may exist: that is, one which by the constitution of the universe *must* be true. Thus if $x + y$ be greater than u, $(x + y - u)XY$ must be true. Every proposition has two forms: thus

$$mXY \text{ is } (m + u - x - y)xy$$
$$mXy \text{ is } (m + y - x)xY$$
$$mxY \text{ is } (m + x - y)Xy$$
$$mxy \text{ is } (m + x + y - u)XY$$

When one of the forms is spurious, the other contains a negative quantity, and is[1] inconceivable.

The contradiction or contrary of mXY is $(x + 1 - m)Xy$. Hence deduce contradictions of the other forms. From mXY and nYZ we deduce $(m + n - y)XZ$. That is, there is inference when the quantities of the middle term in the two premises together exceed the whole[2] quantity of that term. The following forms of syllogism may easily be investigated.

Premises	*Forms of conclusion*
$mXY\ nYZ\ (m + n - y)XZ$	$(m + n + u - x - y - z)xz$
$mXy\ \ nYZ\ (m + n - x)xZ$	$(m + n - z)Xz$
$mXY\ nyZ\ \ (m + n - z)Xz$	$(m + n - x)xZ$
$mXy\ \ nyZ\ \ (m + n + y - x - z)xz$	$(m + n + y - u)XZ$

The proposition *X*)) *Y* is xXY: the proposition *X*)◦) *Y* is xXY joined with $(y - x)xY$. And so of the rest.

In the more subjective view of logic, that is, in the *mathematical* side of it, the one commonly cultivated to the exclusion of the other, the term becomes the word expressive of a *class*, and the relation of class to class is that of inclusion or exclusion, total or partial. Each term, *X*, divides the universe into two classes, *X* and *x*. The following names may be applied to the *relations* of class:—

X)) *Y* *X* is a *species*[3] of *Y*; *Y* is a *genus* of *X*
X(·(*Y* *X* is an *exient* of *Y*; *Y* is a *deficient* of *X*
X)·(*Y* *X* and *Y* are *externals* of each other, or *co-externals*
X() *Y* *X* and *Y* are *partients* of each other, or *co-partients*
X(·) *Y* *X* and *Y* are *complements* of each other
X)(*Y* *X* and *Y* are *co-inadequates* of each other
X((*Y* *X* is a *genus* of *Y*; *Y* is a *species* of *X*
X)·) *Y* *X* is a *deficient* of *Y*; *Y* is an *exient* of *X*.

[1] Not strictly inconceivable, to those who remember the full signification of the negative quantity as here defined. Thus (− 7) *XY* means that − 7 *or more X*s are *Y*s: begin at the point of *more* at which logical predication begins to be conceivable, and we have '0 or more *X*s are *Y*s,' a proposition which is simply spurious.

[2] This is what Hamilton calls the *ultra-total* quantification of the middle term. Lambert first thought of this principle: Mr De Morgan, without any knowledge of Lambert, reconceived it and extended its use. Sir W. Hamilton, who did not know of Lambert till after this, states first, that he had himself thought of the principle and thrown it away; secondly, that Mr De Morgan took it from Lambert: and this though Mr De Morgan had explicitly stated that he never knew of Lambert's work till after his own paper on the subject had been published.

[3] Here is a departure from the common language. Usually *X*)◦) *Y* is signified when we say that *X* is a species of *Y*, and *Y* a genus of *X*. We take the species as being, possibly, the whole genus: just as *some* is possibly *all*.

The propositions of terminal precision may now be stated under the following nomenclature:—

X)∘)*Y* *X* a *subidentical* of *Y*
X||*Y* *X* an *identical* of *Y*
X(∘(*Y* *X* a *superidentical* of *Y*
X)∘(*Y* *X* a *subcontrary* of *Y*
X|·|*Y* *X* a *contrary* of *Y*
X(∘)*Y* *X* a *supercontrary* of *Y*

We now return to propositions of terminal ambiguity. When two propositions are joined together, between *X* and *Y*, and *Y* and *Z*, there is a valid syllogism, that is, one which yields a necessary conclusion, 1, when both premises are universal; 2, when, one premise only being universal, the middle term has *different* quantities in the two; or when the *spiculae* turn the same way. And the conclusion is found by erasing the symbols of the middle term. Thus (·))·) gives a valid syllogism: for though)·) is particular, there is a universal and a particular quantity in the middle term. The conclusion is (··) or (). By this we mean that *X*(·)*Y*)·)*Z* gives *X*()*Z*, or that *X*(·)*Y* and *Y*)·)*Z* give *X*()*Z*. That is, if 'Every thing is either *X* or *Y*,' and 'Some *Z*s are not *Y*s,' it follows that 'Some *X*s are *Z*s.'

There are 32 valid forms. 1. Eight are *universal*, with universal premises and conclusion; being all which have differently quantified middle terms. They are as in)))),)))·(, &c. 2. Eight are *minor particulars*, with the *minor* (or first) premise particular, and a particular conclusion; as (·((·), ())), &c. 3. Eight are *major particulars*, with the *major* (or second) premise particular, and a particular conclusion; as (·))(, ((((), &c. 4. Eight are *strengthened particulars*, universal premises with the middle term similarly quantified in the two, and a particular conclusion; as in))((,)·()), &c.

In every syllogism, the terms being notions of class, there is a combination of premising relations in the concluding relation. Thus in 'No *X* is *Y*, some *Y*s are *Z*s, therefore some *Z*s are not *X*s,' or in '*X*)·(*Y*()*Z* gives *X*)·)*Z*,' we read that *X* is an external of *Y*, and *Y* a partient of *Z*, whence *X* is a deficient of *Z*. And we see that an external of a partient is a deficient. Apply this to all the cases. Thus in (·))·(, giving ((, we read that a complement of an external is a genus.

The propositions of terminal precision give syllogisms having conclusions also of terminal precision by joining two in which the middle term has different quantities; as in *X*(∘)*Y*)∘(*Z*, giving *X*(∘(*Z*. This means that if everything be *X* or *Y*, and some things both, and if nothing be both *Y* and *Z*, and some things neither, it follows that the *X*s contain all the *Z*s, and more. The combination of relations here seen is as follows: a supercontrary of a subcontrary is a superidentical.

When the notion of figure is taken into account, its force and meaning is best seen by stating the combination of relation in the different figures. Thus when we say a species of a species is a species, we speak in the first figure, and compare the minor with the major by the relation which the minor stands in to the middle and the middle to the major. When we read it thus—species and genus of the same are species and genus of one another,—we use the second figure, and compare both major and minor with the middle. When we say that those to which the same is genus and species are species and genus of one another, we use the third figure, and compare the middle term with both major and minor. And when we speak thus,—that to which another is species of species is a genus of that other,—we use the fourth figure, that is, the first figure with the concluding relation inverted.

We now come to the *exemplar* form, already spoken of. Let *X*) and (*X* signify *any one X*: let)*X* and *X*(signify *some one X*, it not being known, even if true, that we may say *any one*.

The list of propositions is as follows. Each universal is followed by its contradicting particular:—

U. *X*)(*Y* *Any* one *X* is *any* one *Y*. This means that there is but one *X* and one *Y*, and the *X* is the *Y*.

P. *X*(·)*Y* Some one *X* is not some one *Y*. Either *X* and *Y* are not both singular: or if both singular, not identical.

U. *X*))*Y* *Any* one *X* is some one *Y*; or every *X* is *Y*.

P. *X*(·(*Y* Some one *X* is not any one *Y*; or some *X*s are not *Y*s.

U. *X*((*Y* Some one *X* is *any* one *Y*; or every *Y* is *X*.

P. *X*)·)*Y* Any one *X* is not some one *Y*; or some *Y*s are not *X*s.

U. *X*)·(*Y* Any one *X* is not any one *Y*; or no *X* is *Y*.

P. *X*()*Y* Some one *X* is some one *Y*; or some *X*s are *Y*s.

Omit the word *one* throughout, for *any* read *all* when the word is in italics, and we have Hamilton's[1] system, provided the first pair be not read as contradictions.

There are 36 valid forms of syllogism, both in the exemplar reading and in Hamilton's reading. All that is required is one affirmative premise, and one total occurrence of the middle term. In the exemplar

[1] Sir W. Hamilton mixed the exemplar and cumular forms in obedience to grammar. His system suggested the one before us, which its proposer holds to be a correction. Hamilton himself rejected the correction with his usual piquant scorn, declaring that it stands alone—in badness, that is—in the whole history of science. Those, therefore, who comply with his wish, will hand it over *entire* to Mr De Morgan, who will accept it all, if given, but cannot claim it all.

[If Hamilton had been to the fore, he would have replied:

> 'Jack stole his discourse from the famed Dr Brown,
> But, by reading it damnably, made it his own'.

—24 February 1861.]

system, the rule of inference is as above described for the cumular system. In Hamilton's system there is this modification: when the middle terms are of different quantities, a concluding term which is total, with a spicula turning a different way from those of the middle term, must be altered from total to partial, if its proposition be affirmative. Thus,)(() in the exemplar system gives)), but in Hamilton's system it gives (). Or, 'Any one *X* is any one *Y*, and some one *Y* is some one *Z*,' gives 'Any one *X* is some one *Z*:' but 'All *X* is all *Y*, and some *Y* is some *Z*,' gives 'Some *X* is some *Z*.' Again,)((·(, in Hamilton's system, gives (·(, not)·(, as in the exemplar system. The reason of this difference will easily appear, on consideration.

The exemplar proposition is often used, as distinguished from the cumular. It is, for example, the proposition of geometry. When Euclid proves that *all* isosceles triangles are of equal angles at the bases, he shows that *any* isosceles triangle is so, and he demonstrates only to those who can see that nothing is assumed in his demonstration which limits the selection.

The numerical syllogism leads to a species of syllogism which is occasionally used, but cannot be reduced to a common syllogism. It is the syllogism of *transposed quantity*, in which one of the concluding terms enters with the whole quantity of the other, or of its contrary. For instance, 'For every man in the house there is a person who is aged; some of the men are not aged; therefore some of the persons in the house are not men.' Nothing has yet been printed on the laws of this syllogism of transposed quantity: the following brief rules will enable the reader to detect the cases, which are sixty-four in number.

Let a *particular* proposition which has a term of the whole quantity of an *external* term—that is, in another proposition—be called an *external universal*, the ordinary universal being called *internal*. The proposition has a *receiving* term; the other proposition has an *imparting* term. Let the receiving term be distinguished by a hyphen below its spicula; the imparting term by a hyphen above. Thus $X\overline{)})Y)\cdot\underline{)}Z$ means as follows:—Every *X* is *Y*; for every *X* there is a *Z* which is not *Y*. But there is no valid syllogism when a term taken totally imparts its quantity: in the case before us the only chance of a valid inference arises from allowing *X*, which enters partially, to impart its quantity; as in 'Every *X* is *Y*; for every *X* there is a *Z* which is not *Y*.' This being understood, and also that in forming the conclusion every imparting term must change its quantity, the rules for detecting valid syllogism are precisely those of the cumular syllogism already described. That is, any two universals, each of either kind, give a conclusion; and one universal of either kind and one particular, if the middle terms have different quantities in the two.

Then ()(·(, having two external universals, is valid, and gives)·). That is, from 'For every *Z* there is an *X* which is *Y*, and for every *X* there is a *Y* which is not *Z*,' we deduce 'Some *Z*s are not *Y*s.'

Again, ()))) has an external and an internal universal, and gives ((. 'For every *Z* there is an *X* which is *Y*, and every *Y* is *Z*' gives 'Every *Z* is *X*'. And)((·(, having an external universal and a particular, with middle term of different quantities in the two, is valid, and gives)·). That is, from 'For every *Z* there is something neither *X* nor *Y*; some *Y*s are not *Z*s,' we deduce 'Some *Z*s are not *X*s.'

Few propositions that ever come before the human mind require closer attention than these transposed syllogisms. They are easily demonstrated from the general forms of numerical syllogism; not so easily by independent thought.

We shall now proceed to compare the mathematical and metaphysical sides of logic. A term may be formed by junction of terms in two ways. 1. By *aggregation*, as in what we represent by (*A*, *B*, *C*), which stands for all that is in *A*, in *B*, in *C*, or in two or more. 2. By *composition*, as in what we represent by (*A*-*B*-*C*), or (*ABC*), meaning all that is common to all the three terms *A*, *B*, *C*. The contrary of an aggregate is the compound of the contraries of the aggregants: either (*A*, *B*) or (*ab*). The contrary of a compound is the aggregate of the contraries of the components: either (*AB*) or (*a*, *b*).

The term, considered as aggregated of aggregants, is viewed in *extent*; as a compound of components, in *intent*. For *total* and *partial* we now substitute the words *full* and *vague*, to get rid of the wrong opposition which total and partial suggest; for the term called *partial* is not necessarily partial at all, it is only not known to be total. And this ambiguity has led acute[1] logical writers into absolute mistake. In this matter we

[1] In Hamilton's system, 'Every *X* is *Y*' is read 'All *X* is some *Y*,' and 'Every *Y* is *X*' is read 'All *Y* is some *X*.' But (*Discussions*, &c., 2nd ed. p. 688,) he says that 'All *X* is some *Y*,' and 'Some *X* is all *Y*,' are incompossible, that is, cannot be true together, 'unless *some* be identified with *all*.' This supposition he treats as an absurdity: hard pushed in controversy, he was misled by the ambiguity on which this note is written. The *some*, even of his own system, is a *possibly-all*: how otherwise can he dare to render 'Every *X* is *Y*' by 'All *X* is some *Y*'? The junction of the two propositions determines the *universality* of the so-called *particular*. This looks very like nonsense; but the fault is in the language of the logicians. Substitute *full* and *vague*: the word *some* is *vague* in either proposition taken apart: but the junction restrains the *vagueness*, and turns the indefinite into a definite, *vague* into *full*. Just as in algebra one relation between two unknown quantities may leave a vagueness which a second relation turns into comparative definiteness. Our two propositions are xXY and yYX. The first gives $x =$ or $< y$; the second gives $y =$ or $\bar{<} x$, that is, $x - y$ and $y - x$ are neither of them negative; whence $x = y$, so that *Y* is full in the first proposition, and *X* in the second.

The word *incompossible*, [here] attributed to Sir W. Hamilton, is in truth only revived by him. It is a very useful word.

follow Hamilton, who justly and acutely remarked that 'It is only as indefinite that particular, it is only as definite that individual and general, quantities have any (and the same) logical avail.' The word *indefinite* completely describes the word *particular*, or *partial*, as commonly used: we only use *vague* as a shorter word. But the *universal* or *total* of logicians is more than *definite*: it is the maximum of definiteness, and we use *full* as more correctly descriptive. *Two-sevenths* is as *definite* as *all.*

Extent and intent are the two logical *tensions*. The elements of extent are aggregants; the elements of intent are components. When one tension is full, the other is vague; when one tension is vague, the other is full. Thus *X*) signifies that *X* is taken fully in extent, vaguely in intent; and)*X* signifies that *X* is taken vaguely in extent, and fully in intent. When a tension is full, an existing element may be dismissed, but a new one cannot be admitted; when a tension is vague, no element can be dismissed, but any new one may be admitted. Thus *A,B*)) *Y* and *X*))*AB* allow *A*)) *Y* and *X*))*A*; but not *A, B, C*)) *Y* nor *X*))*ABC*. Again, *AB*)) *Y* and *X*))*A, B* do not allow *A*)) *Y* nor *X*))*A*; but they do allow *ABC*)) *Y* and *X*))*A, B, C.*[1]

Elements may, under certain conditions, be transposed from one term to another, without alteration of the import of the proposition. Universal propositions allow the elements of vague terms to be transposed: particular propositions allow the elements of full terms to be transposed. In universal propositions the transposition is made directly in negatives, by contraversion in affirmatives. In particular propositions the transposition is made directly in affirmatives, by contraversion in negatives. As instances *X*))*A, B* gives *Xa*))*B*; *AB*)) *Y* gives *B*)) *Y, a*; *AB*)·(*Y* gives *B*)·(*A Y*; *AB*()*Y* gives *B*()*A Y*; *AB*(·(*Y* gives *B*(·(*Y, a*; *A, B*(·) *Y* gives *A*(·) *Y, B*, &c. And in all these cases the result of transposition is identical with the original.

Both extent and intent are to be considered in both sides of logic, the mathematical and the metaphysical. A class may be an aggregate or a compound; the class *animal* is aggregate of *man* and *brute*; the class *animal* is compound (common part of) the class *body* and the class *living*. An attribute may be an aggregate or a compound: the attribute *useful* is aggregate of the naturally and the artificially useful: the attribute *useful* is compounded of, or at least has *among* its components, *attainable* and *applicable*. But the conveniences of thought, though not its necessities, and whether by mere habit or by human constitution is not a question of logic, dictate an almost exclusive confinement of the notion of aggregation to that of class, and of the notion of composition to that of attribute. Accordingly, intent is of predominant importance in the metaphysical side of logic, and extent in the mathematical.

[1] [*F*, full; *V*, vague: *E*, extent; *I*, intent. *VIFE*)*FIVE* Oh!—10 February 1861.]

The mathematical form of thought builds upon the notions of *contained* and *excluded*: the metaphysical form upon the notions of *essential* and *repugnant*. The metaphysical form should be cultivated because, right or wrong, human beings are made to be metaphysicians, children most of all, uneducated persons more than educated. The *must be* and the *cannot be* are the strong points of our mental constitutions. We know all about *can* and *cannot* from our cradles: we never feel the same assurance about *is* and *is not*. A philosopher, in a dark age, may determine to set out with a knowledge of the naturally possible and impossible; but not even a philosopher ever pretended to set out with a knowledge of the existent and non-existent. Logic excludes actual metaphysics by declining to enter into the inquiry whether this or that use of the metaphysical *form of thought* be true or false in matter. But logic claims to interfere to give a *logical* correctness in the use of terms and relating notions: to prevent, for instance, a person who, rightly or wrongly, makes reason an *essential* of man, from pronouncing it to be *therefore* repugnant to the nature of brute.

Additional intent may diminish extent, but never increases it: additional extent may diminish intent, but never increases it. By continual introduction of new attributes we may, if speaking of things existing, not of possibilities of thought, curtail the widest class until we have brought it down to an individual. Thus *being* includes everything; material being is body; living body is animal; human animal is man; man of old time is ancient; go on thus until we come to ancient Roman general who conquered Gauls, and wrote his own campaigns, and we have the individual Julius Caesar.

If we read our cumular propositions by the notion of enumeration of attributes, we have the following arithmetical reading by enumeration of attributes, just as 'every *X* is *Y*,' &c., show arithmetical reading by enumeration of the smallest[1] possible classes, that is, individuals.

X)) *Y*. All the attributes of *Y* are attributes of *X*.

X(·(*Y*. Some attributes of *Y* are not attributes of *X*.

X)·(*Y*. Everything wants either some attribute of *Y*, or some attribute of *X*.

X() *Y*. Some things want neither any attribute of *Y*, nor any attribute of *X*.

X(·) *Y*. Everything has either all the attributes of *Y*, or all the attributes of *X*.

[1] There is a termination to disaggregative separation; we cannot subdivide individuals. But if there be a termination to decompositive separation, we know nothing about it. We can disaggregate the class *mankind* into its constituent non-interfering indivisibles, or individuals: we cannot decompose reason into attributes, which all will agree upon as being primary and non-interfering, and not further separable. But this distinction is of no *logical* importance.

X)(*Y*. Some things want either some attributes of *Y*, or some attributes of *X*.

X((*Y*. Some attributes of *Y* are all the attributes of *X*.

X)·)*Y*. Any attributes of *Y* are not some attributes of *X*.

The complete inversion of the quantities will be perceived. We now give a metaphysical nomenclature.

X))*Y*. *X* a dependent of *Y*; *Y* an essential of *X*.

X(·(*Y*. *X* an independent of *Y*; *Y* an inessential of *X*.

X)·(*Y*. *X* a repugnant of *Y*; and *Y* of *X*.

X()*Y*. *X* an irrepugnant of *Y*; and *Y* of *X*.

X(·)*Y*. *X* an alternative of *Y*; and *Y* of *X*.

X)(*Y*. *X* an inalternative of *Y*; and *Y* of *X*.

X((*Y*. *X* an essential of *Y*; *Y* a dependent of *X*.

X)·)*Y*. *X* an inessential of *Y*; *Y* an independent of *X*.

The syllogisms are now described in a way which will suggest itself: thus (·))·) giving (), which read mathematically exhibits the combination 'A complement of a deficient is a partient,' will, when read metaphysically, give 'an alternative of an inessential is an irrepugnant'. . . .

When reduced to so brief an abstract as we have here given, a system of logic appears like a string of names. But the more names the more ideas; provided only that every name has meaning which is not merely repeated in any other. So far as the invention of words is analysis of ideas, or signifies the completion of such analysis, and prevents it from being lost, so far it is augmentation of power over ideas. Dr Thomson well observes that 'as the distinctions between the relations of objects grow more numerous, involved, and subtle, it [language] becomes more analytic, to be able to express them: and, inversely, those who are born to be the heirs of a highly analytic language, must needs learn to *think up* to it, to observe and distinguish all the relations of objects, for which they find the expressions already formed, so that we have an instructor for the thinking powers in that speech which we are apt to deem no more than their handmaid and minister.'

It is very common to discuss the utility of the subject, in an article treating of it in general; but of all arguments, that about the utility of any branch of knowledge is the most useless. Allowing an infrequent exception here and there, those who have mastered the first difficulties of *any* branch of knowledge are all convinced of its utility; and with those who have not, and who have the boldness to form an opinion, there is no basis for an argument.[1]

[1] [Of De Morgan's other contributions to the *English Cyclopaedia*, the articles on Predicables, Probability, Ratio, Relation and Syllogism are of particular relevance here—Ed.]

ON THE SYLLOGISM: V

and on various points of the Onymatic System

[Dated 14 April 1862]

[Submitted 19 May 1862]

[Read 4 May 1863.]

This paper contains the following points:—1. A criticism of Hamilton's system, as further explained in his posthumous work. 2. An explanation of the character of the system of Aristotle and his followers, which I affirm to have been *exemplar*. 3. The misconception of the character of this system by recent writers. 4. Enforcement of the right of *both* correlatives in any *pair*, and of all in any set, to equal fulness of treatment. 5. Application to the distinction of affirmation and *non*-affirmation; syllogism of indecision. 6. Deduction of the eight onymatic forms from purely *onymatic* meaning; alleged demonstration of the necessity and completeness of these forms. 7. *Restrictive* propositions, their affirmation and denial introduced in every view except the purely onymatic view, *whenever complete treatment of all correlatives is allowed.* 8. Completion of the exemplar system. 9. Extended comparison of the onymatic relations. 10. System of primary and secondary relations by copula of identification. 11. The same when the copula is any one of the simple onymatic relations. 12. The full system at which the Hamiltonian quantification aims. 13. The logical basis of extension and comprehension. [14. Addition on a recent phase of the controversy. *December* 1862.]

The Society is by this time aware that any introduction of philosophy proper is also the introduction of controversy; which, though not necessarily *personal* in the modern sense, must be *ad hominem* in the old sense. Such dispute is now as nearly as possible excluded from mathematics and experimental physics: but it was not so of old. There was a time when the investigator in either was nearer to the foundation, and had more to do with the subject from the psychological point of view. It was then that Newton called philosophy—meaning physics,—a litigious lady, and said a man might as well be engaged in lawsuits as have to do with her. But though Newton and others—and Newton above all—have tamed this shrew in her dealings with mathematics and physics, she keeps her character as to all subjects in which first principles must still be probed, and questions of boundary must still be fought. And logic is a subject in which little more than a commencement of either has been made.

I have good hope that in this paper my personal part of a long discussion will come to an end. Since July 1860, when Hamilton's *Lectures on Logic* were ably published by Professors Mansel and Veitch, with various additions from the scattered papers of the author, I have had what till then I never had, the means of knowing with precision what the system is which has led me into fourteen years of controversial thought and writing: how this occurred will presently appear. The whole dispute differs from many others by an inversion of character. It often happens that a contest of principles degenerates into a duel: but that which I speak of took its rise in personal accusation, and was gradually refined and sublimated into a legitimate war of systems; perhaps because there was a mathematician on one side of it. Logic affirmed that Mathematics could not understand her principles, far less extend their development: that Mathematics was a cracker of shells who could not even so get at the kernels; having no more merit than belongs to those who walk straight in a ditch. Mathematics replied, in effect, that she could understand and would cultivate the field of Logic: that Philosophy, which confessedly could not bite the kernel, had settled nothing; while she had at least cracked the shell: and that, while she herself could either find or cut straight ditches, the only ditch in which Philosophy and Psychology had allowed Logic to walk—that into which the blind lead the blind—was one in which, for good reason, there was no walking straight at all. Such a suit is not abated by the death of one of the original parties: for it concerns undying things, and the undying part of persons. Hamilton's mode of controversy was conspicuously *ad hominem*: the adverse mind was his field of psychological observation: his ways and means lay very much in inference from his opponent's alleged errors to his opponent's intellectual organization. Though I need not follow the example all lengths, its existence will allow me a liberty of nearer approach than I should of my own mere motion have taken; and this liberty may be used with advantage to the subject. Character and motive being left untouched, I hardly see how such freedom can be entirely avoided: anatomists may fight a theory upon a third body; but psychologists are compelled to make some dissection of each other.

In order that I might finally dispose of Hamilton's system of enunciation and of syllogism, I found it expedient to challenge contradiction of a very curious assertion by appeal to a literary journal. It was necessary that I should somewhere state, and prove from the posthumous papers, that my distinguished opponent, the great logical teacher of his day, had actually laid down, as valid syllogisms, forms of argument which were mere paralogisms. I could not expect permission to *originate* such an assertion in these Transactions: though the Society may disavow all sanction of the facts and opinions to which it gives currency, leaving the responsibility on their authors, yet there are extremes both of fact and of opinion which the disavowal will not reach. Nor could I forget that my opponent had taken pains to put the Society and the University itself into the position of parties to the discussion, so far as it lay with him to compel their appearance. He had in fact refused, not merely to the Society, but to the whole academic body, from the Chancellor downwards, all escape from responsibility for my logical[1] heresies. I therefore addressed two letters to the *Athenaeum* journal (published 13 July and 17 August 1861) in which I exposed a curious apparent blunder relative to Aristotelian logic, and also one of the paralogisms above alluded to. I gave two months for denial, with notice that, if no denial were attempted, I should myself point out grounds of *extenuation.* I fully expected that editors, or pupils, or other disciples, would dispute my conclusions: but nothing whatever appeared. I accordingly wrote two other letters (published 2 November and 28 December 1861), in which I pointed out how hurry, illness, and halting between two systems, deprived the errors, which I then assumed to be undeniable, of the very gross and illiterate character which would have attached to them had they been deliberate. Further account of them will appear in the proper places. [Having waited more than a year, I again called the attention of the logical world to a point which nothing but testimony could settle, naming those from among whom I expected an answer. This plan was successful; and an account of the defence made will be found in an Addition. I have allowed the body of the paper to stand as it was written. December 1862.]

My knowledge of Hamilton's system is derived from the following sources. I. A *prospectus* of the intended *New Analytic* issued in 1846, with *Requirements for a prize Essay*; both reprinted, the first with some omissions, in the *Lectures on Logic*. II. My correspondence with Hamilton in 1846–7, printed by him in 1847, with notes and additions, as part of our personal controversy. III. Mr T. Spencer Baynes's *Essay on the new Analytic*, the prize Essay of 1846, published in 1850, with additions, including a note by Hamilton himself. IV. A review of Hamilton, myself, and others, afterwards acknowledged by Mr Mansel, in the *North British Review* of May 1851. V. A letter of Hamilton, dated 7 August 1850, forthwith published in the *Athenaeum*, and reprinted in the

[1] . . . I neither claim to represent the University, nor do I admit the alternative on which Hamilton risked himself: but, when I found I must prove that my opponent, though well knowing his alphabet, spelt new words incorrectly, I thought it right that the Society and the University should not give that faint appearance of sanction which this publication involves, until denial from Hamilton's followers had been challenged.

Discussions. VI. An article[1] in the *Discussions* (1852) inserted probably at the last moment, under asterisked paging (621*–652*) and not altered —except as to paging—in the second edition. To get the page of the second edition, add 55 to that of the first. VII. Various editions of Bishop Thomson's *Outlines*, beginning with the second in 1849. VIII. The late Professor Spalding's *Introduction to Logical Science*, 1857. IX. The Appendixes, *passim*, to Hamilton's *Lectures on Logic*, 1860. If there be any other writings[2] which treat Hamilton's system at all extensively I am not acquainted with them. I shall quote these works by the numbers prefixed.

Some preliminary remarks are wanted upon the quantifying words

[1] This *hurried article*, as I shall sometimes call it, contains those quantities which are one and the same quantity, but of which the greater the one the less the other, and the apparent assertion that 'some at least' is 'possibly none.' It seems to show excitement: its sarcastic photographs have stronger lights than those of preceding writings. As Hamilton had had the last word in the *Athenaeum* journal eighteen months before, this is presumption of some new call to action. I surmise, from a stray sentence at the end, that the writer was roused, when his work was all but published, by information of the effect which my objections had produced south of the Tweed.... Those who examine the whole discussion in time to come, will note the manner in which his instinct made him feel that mathematics would destroy his fabric, unless he could first destroy mathematics.

Every proof of hurry in this article is an act of charity: the following is worth notice. Hamilton knew well (IX. i. 43) that in respect of 'irrefragable certainty' . . . 'Logic and Mathematics stand alone among the sciences, and their peculiar certainty flows from the same source.' He knew just as well that the contest between him and me turned wholly on the 'forms of intelligence'—the necessary laws of thought—of an exact science. How then came he to object to me that a mathematician in 'contingent matter' is like an owl by daylight? How came he thus to assert, by implication, that he and I had been arguing contingent matter? How came he to imply that the logical half of exact science is contingent? Except under this implication his assertion, supposing it true, would not help him. The answer is that he was in a great hurry, and pelted the mathematician with whatever came uppermost.

There is also hurry in Hamilton's appeal for help to Warburton's remark, that in his time the oldest mathematician in England was the worst reasoner in it. The person alluded to was Whiston: and no man of letters, writing very deliberately, would have taken Warburton as sufficient authority against Whiston on the point in question. The two are now chiefly remembered by their several paradoxes: Warburton, by his maintenance of the absence of the doctrine of a future state from a permanent national religion being, *per se*, proof of Divine support; Whiston, by his acceptance of the Apostolical Constitutions as genuine and authoritative. Whiston seems to have reasoned well enough from his wrong estimate of certain writings: Warburton defended his peculiar thesis with great 'ingenuity', say his admirers; but the word is one which admirers often substitute for 'sophistry.' There is enough here to show that the condemnation of Whiston's *reasoning* upon the authority of Warburton, as a well-adjudged case, is probably nothing but hurry.

[2] There is an elementary work which is unfortunately spoiled by a misapprehension of the meaning of one of the forms of enunciation. But it will be a book of true method of inference to all who read the forms in the *exemplar* system of my second paper. The author's mistake consists in making 'Some X is not some Y' the simple contradiction of 'All X is all Y.'

some and *any*. The word *any* is affirmed by Hamilton (in V.) to be exclusively adapted to negatives. This cannot mean that *any* is unfit to be used in an affirmative: surely *any* one knows better than that. What is meant must be that no other word suits a negative, universally expressed, except *any*. I reply that all our quantifying words, though tolerably precise in affirmatives, are ambiguous in negatives. 'He has got some apples' is very clear: ask the meaning of 'he has not got some apples' in a company of educated men, and the apples will be those of discord. Some will think that he may have one apple; some that he has no apple at all; some that he has not got some particular apples or species of apples. Say 'he has not got all apples,' and some will take him as not possessing all the apples in existence, while others will understand that he has other fruit besides apples. 'An apple' and 'the apple' are perfectly clear: but 'he has not got any apple' is not free from occasional ambiguity.

The word *any*, when used *in a negative*, may have either a universal or a particular meaning: it may either stand for *any whatsoever*, or for a *certain or uncertain one or more*. It has been said that a healthy person who cannot eat *any* wholesome food does not deserve to have *any* food to eat. The first *any* is particular; it applies, *inter alios*, to a person who refuses cold mutton, though ready for any other digestible: the second *any* is universal, and excludes all victuals whatsoever. A person who has just dined heartily need not take *any* food (universal): a convalescent ought not to take *any* food (particular; beef tea, but not pickled salmon). Some will perhaps make it depend upon the verb used; they will see the universal in '*need* not take any food', and the particular in '*ought* not to take any food'. Some will make it a question of emphasis, laying stress on *any*, when the word is particular: but the ambiguity is there, let the grammarian and rhetorician treat it as they will. A logician may, if he please, postulate that *any* shall always have the universal sense in technical enunciation: Hamilton did not do so, but implicitly maintained that *any* is *always* universal. Accordingly, he asserted that 'No X is Y' is properly expressed by 'Any X is not any Y.' But though 'No fish is fish' be certainly false, 'Any fish is not any fish' is false or true, according as the second *any* is universal or particular. Choose what fish you please, it is not *any* fish: turbot is not trout. This is a slight error, easily prevented by a postulate.

The idioms of logical quantity have had very little consideration given to them. The word *some*, although it may have points on which logicians divide, has one case of subdivision upon which all logicians unite against the world at large. The distinction is that of *certain some*, and *some or other*: the first has an unknown definiteness, the second is truly indefinite. People in general incline to the unknown definite: the logician demands the true indefinite, but can in many cases follow the usual tendency. Whenever one term of a proposition is a definite, known or unknown, the *some* of the other term is the unknown definite. As in 'All men are [certain some] animals', or as in 'The men he spoke of were [certain some of those who were] here yesterday'. But when one term is truly indefinite, then *certain some* is not admissible in the other. Thus 'any men are [certain some] animals' is not true when 'any' implies unlimited selection out of 'all'. This is most obvious in the unusual exemplar forms: thus 'some animal is any man' would reduce mankind to an individual if 'certain' some were intended. In some subsequent parts of this paper the reader must watch himself on this point.

Logic may take liberties with language for the expression of thought: but she must not declare her alterations to be actual parts of speech. I fully understand and agree to the assertion that complete quantification may be made to allow simple conversion; that 'some X is not any Y' may infer 'Any Y is not some X'. Nevertheless, this cannot be admitted if *subjection* and *predication* remain notions attached to the subject and predicate: for predication is posterior to subjection; the subject comes *first* into thought, and the question of predication *follows*. For instance, 'some man is not any animal' is a falsehood: designate the man, and a search through the animals will find him. But 'any animal is not some man' is true: choose *any* animal, man or not man, and we can *then* show *some man* which he is not. In order to make this last proposition as false as its converse, the right of precedence must pass over to the second side with the term which originally had it. Of 'any animal', first chosen, 'some man' may be denied: of 'some man', first chosen, 'any animal' cannot be denied. The same thing in every case in which *some* comes into contact with *all* or *any*. Hamilton saw this, and it made him insist upon enunciation being pure *equation* or *non-equation* of subject and predicate, meaning identification or differentiation of simultaneously entering terms. But Hamilton had the faculty of fastening upon his whole species any use of language into which he had drilled himself. Thus (IX. ii. 294) he says—'Why, for example, may I say, as I think,—*Some animal is not any man*; and yet not say, convertibly, as I still think, *Any man is not some animal*? For this no reason, beyond the caprice of logicians, and the elisions of common language, can be assigned.' If *he* should think it, *he* may say it: but in *common language*, and this with no elisions, 'Any man is not some animal' does not contradict 'Every animal is man', as he intends it should. For though every animal had been man, yet any man would not have been some animal. Common language makes subjects of terms and then predicates of them.

The word *some* has three distinct uses. First, as *non-partitive*; here it is only *not-none*, some-at-least, some-may-be-all. And this is the old sense of the logicians. Secondly, as *singly partitive*; some-not-all, some-at-most, but without any assertion or denial about the rest, Thirdly, as *doubly partitive*; some-at-most, and the rest the other way. As Hamilton says, this[1] *some* is 'both affirmative and negative', meaning that it makes any proposition which contains it both affirm and deny.

I cannot find any notice of the distinction between non-partition and single partition. The logicians are much given to halt between the two. Perhaps they would defend their course, as follows:—When we say 'Some are', meaning 'Some-not-all are', we say nothing at all about the rest. Perhaps also 'the other some are'. In what way then, do we differ from those who say 'Some-perhaps-all are'. Not at all, I reply, in the expressed 'some' of particular subjects: but much in the implied 'some' of particular predicates [of a universal proposition], in which 'some not all' is of double partition by necessary inference. For example, say '*all* men are *some* animals'; some-perhaps-all and some-not-all no longer give equivalents. If it be some-not-all, even though nothing were intended about the rest, the exhaustion of *man* contained in *all* forces double partition: the rest of the animals are *not* men.[2]

Hamilton confronted *non*-partition, under the name of *indefinite definitude*, with *double* partition, under the name of *definite indefinitude*: the second phrase is defensible; the first is false contrast. Of *single* partition

[1] The common usage of mankind inclines to partition: even the affirmation of *none* is, whenever it can be so made, affirmation of *some* of the alternative kind. No person pays any respect to the doctrine that from negative premises nothing can follow: the negatives have their implied affirmatives. This happens from the earliest childhood: for example,

Jack Sprat could eat no fat,
His wife could eat no lean;
And *so*, betwixt them both,
They licked the platter clean.

How this arose we learn from the second verse, long lost to the nursery, but recovered by Mr Halliwell.

For (i.e. as implied) Jack ate all the lean,
And Joan ate all the fat,
The bone they picked quite clean,
And gave it to the cat.

[Two abstinences make complete consumption.]

The same ambiguity accompanies the mention of definite number. Thus 'four of them' may be any four, or certain four. The context only can decide. When we are told that a man had his horse out four times in one day, we must know what we are talking about before we can tell whether it was one or other horse, or one particular horse: and the same if the phrase were 'one of his horses.' If the statement be made in proof of his almost living on horseback, we shall certainly suppose various horses: if of his want of consideration for his poor beasts, we see that one only is meant. Here the difficulty is real: raise it upon a matter in which context is not required, and we pass into the region of jokes; as in the case of the man who is reported to have been reduced to despair of compliance with the prescription by seeing on the apothecary's label, 'Two of the pills to be taken three times a day.'

[2] ['Some *X*s are some-not-all *Y*s' allowable; no distinction.]

he takes no distinctive notice whatever. That his partition is really double cannot be doubted. His 'some' is 'both affirmative and negative'; he represents 'Some *X* is not any *Y*' as *inconsistent* with 'No *X* is *Y*'. This *must* mean that 'Some *X* is not any *Y*' tells us that the remaining *X is Y*. There is however no need to enlarge upon this: the diagrams and explanations (VI. 631*, 632*) are sufficient. Had Hamilton advocated single partition, all his syllogisms would have been valid; and my challenge would have had a host of respondents. One opponent nearly committed himself: he imagined that Hamilton really did adopt single partition; but he found out his mistake in time.

The system which was to form the base—or one of the bases, for Hamilton permitted the old system to exist alongside of his own—of the *New Analytic* consisted in applying the quantifiers '*some*' and '*all*'—in negatives '*any*' universally taken—in every way to both subject and predicate: the word '*some*' was intended to be doubly partitive, affirmation or denial of it was intended to convey denial or affirmation as to that 'other some' which in common language is 'all the rest'. The hypothesis was truly and consistently applied to every form of enunciation *except one*: and in that one, by a curious forgetfulness, the second side of the double partition remained unnoticed. According to Hamilton, 'Some *X* is not some *Y*' quadrates (VI. 632*) with *all* the other forms, is useful *only* to divide a class, and (IX. ii. 283) is consistent with *all* the other negatives; which is true of non-partition or single partition; but is false of double partition. It is a singular commentary on Hamilton's assertion of his system as *actually in thought* that his 'Some *X* is *not* some *Y*', systematically interpreted, is an equivalent of the Aristotelian 'Some *X is* some *Y*' being the simple contradiction of 'Any *X* is not any *Y*.' This I must prove at length.

Remembering that all Hamilton's propositions are simply convertible, and that his 'some' is both affirmative and negative, we see in 'Some *X* is not some *Y*' that all the other 'Some *X is* some *Y*', that 'Some *Y* is not some *X*', and that all the other 'some *Y* is some *X*'. Now all these four assertions are true when *X* and *Y* are[1] equivalents, when *X* is part of *Y*, when *Y* is part of *X*, and when *X* and *Y* have each part, and part only, in common with the other. Consequently 'Some *X* is not some *Y*' is true except only when *X* and *Y* are wholly external each to the other, and then false: it is therefore the simple contradiction of 'Any *X* is not any *Y*', and consequently the equivalent of the usual 'Some *X is* some *Y*'.

It would have caused but little alteration in the details of my criticism if this oversight had not been made. I now proceed to write down the forms of Hamilton's system, on all the three suppositions: the doubly

[1] Take notice that the mere application of *this* 'some' denies that its term is singular.

partitive case being closely taken from himself (VI. 631*, 632*) in what appears to be his latest exposition.

	Hamilton's forms	*Expressed in Aristotelian forms*		
	Affirmatives	when doubly partitive	when singly partitive	when non-partitive
Toto-total[1]	All *X* is all *Y* [*X*‖*Y*]	Every *X* is *Y*, Every *Y* is *X*	Every *X* is *Y*, Every *Y* is *X*	Every *X* is *Y*, Every *Y* is *X*.
Toto-partial	All *X* is some *Y* [*X*)∘)*Y*]	Every *X* is *Y*, Some *Y* is not *X*	Every *X* is *Y*, Some *Y* is not *X*	Every *X* is *Y*.
Parti-total	Some *X* is all *Y* [*X*(∘(*Y*]	Every *Y* is *X*, Some *X* is not *Y*	Every *Y* is *X*, Some *X* is not *Y*	Every *Y* is *X*.
Parti-partial	Some *X* is some *Y* [*X*(·()·)*Y*]	Some *X* is *Y*, Some *X* is not *Y*, Some *Y* is not *X*	Some *X* is *Y*	Some *X* is *Y*.
	Negatives			
Toto-total	Any *X* is not any *Y* [*X*)·(*Y*]	No *X* is *Y*	No *X* is *Y*	No *X* is *Y*.
Toto-partial[2]	Any *X* is not some *Y*	Either toto-partial or parti-partial affirmative: any affirmative which contains *Some Y is not X.*	Some *Y* is not *X*	Some *Y* is not *X*.
Parti-total[2]	Some *X* is not any *Y*	Either parti-total or parti-partial affirmative: any affirmative which contains *Some X is not Y.*	Some *X* is not *Y*	Some *X* is not *Y*.
Parti-partial	Some *X* is not some *Y*	Cannot be false except when *X* and *Y* are singular and identical. [Should have been 'anything but a toto-total negative']		

[1] This proposition was objected to by me as being only a compound of the toto-partial and the parti-total: this was when I supposed the partition to be wholly vague. Mr Mansel (IV. 116) declared 'all *X* is all *Y*' to be a simple act of thought; and Hamilton (VI. 633*) supports this view. I now quote Hamilton's cooler thoughts, written without an opponent in the field (IX. ii. 292). 'For example; if I think that the notion *triangle* contains the notion *trilateral*, and again that the notion *trilateral* contains the notion *triangle*; in other words if I think that each of these is inclusively and exclusively [or perhaps *includedly* should have been invented] applicable to the other; I formally say, and, if I speak as I think, must say—*all triangle is all trilateral.*' This is all I want: here is one proposition compounded of two. Hamilton remarks that when I declare this last to be compound (VI. 633*) I do not attempt to explain how *all* should be compound and *some* simple. I never said this, nor thought it: what I said was that the *proposition* *X*‖*Y* is a compound of two *propositions* *X*))*Y* and *X*((*Y*; true when both are true; false when either is false. It is important to note that two wholes may compound into a third, without the parts of the two compounding into the parts of the third: I never said that *all* is compound of *somes*: but only that a proposition having two *alls* is compounded of two propositions having each one *some*.

[2] That disjunctively joined affirmatives should have the logical import of negatives,

In the *hurried article* (VI. 635*) we are informed in the text that the Aristotelian '*some*' is '*possibly none*'; and, in a note, that the Aristotelian '*not-some*' does not definitely *exclude* '*none*'. I suppose that if there be a point in which all preceding logicians agree, it is that *not-some* is *none*, and *not-none* is *some*. But I do not wish to give further attention to this extraordinary product of haste: I pass on to its source. When Hamilton combines *some-at-least* and *some-at-most* in one word, *some*; *not-all* and *not-none* are then of course constituents of the meaning of one and the same proposition. The ordinary logician, if he should choose to take 'some-at-most, possibly none' into his system,—as from Hamilton's words I suspect some must have done—will see two new particulars emerge, *equivalents* of the old ones, but not *identical* with them. For 'some-at-least-possibly-all *X* is *Y*' is convertible with, 'Some-at-most-possibly-none *X* is not *Y*': and 'Some-at-least-possibly-all *X* is not *Y*' is convertible with 'Some-at-most-possibly-none *X* is *Y*'. If equivalence be for a moment confounded with identity, a person already accustomed to *not-none* and *not-all* in *one* proposition, might shape his language to the supposition that the logicians who use *none* and *all* in two *equivalent* propositions, *none* in one and *all* in the other, use them both in *one and the same* proposition. I have pointed out, in the fourth of the letters alluded to, how an insufficient summary (IX. ii. 281) probably led Hamilton into the erroneous language of the hurried article (VI. 635*): it is hardly worth repeating here.

I proceed to the further consideration of the system before us. I shall apply my own notation to Hamilton's forms: thus *X*(·(*Y* will designate 'Some *X* is not any *Y*'. It will be seen that, in the doubly partitive system, no one proposition simply contradicts another: though)·(and (·) would have done it if (·) had been truly brought under definition.

I shall take for granted that when any premises are given, *every* conclusion which those premises can yield must be drawn. I do not mean that in the common syllogism ***I*** must be noted as a conclusion whenever ***A*** is so: because ***I*** can be inferred from ***A***. I mean that every possible conclusion must be stated, either immediately or mediately. I will grant to the framer of a system the right to be governed by the hypotheses on which he sets out, in the acceptance or rejection of any premises. But, should he accept a certain pair of premises, I will not grant him the right

seems at first sight absurd: but other instances of it may be found; and I suspect that, under limitation at least, it is a true canon. For another instance, I may cite my own form (·). It is a remarkable instance of the want of perception of analogies which characterizes early speculation on all subjects—and which I look at with profit and amusement in my own earlier papers, nothing doubting that I shall in time do the same with this one—that Hamilton, who (VI. 650*) sneers at my disjunctively affirmative form of the negative (·), had not long before (VI. 632*) given two of his own negatives the same kind of form.

to stifle a part of the conclusion because he has no form in his system by which to express it: he ought to invent the form. Against any one who demands such a right I quote Hamilton, who insists upon it that language is to be found for all that is in thought: and I aver that when premises are put into the head, *all* the conclusion is in thought to all who can master it. There are two ways of offending against the reasonable principle stated above. First, by curtailing the conclusion to as much as can be expressed in the system. Secondly, by excluding combinations of premises because they have no conclusion except what cannot be expressed in the system, *and for no other reason*. Both these faults are committed: to which must be added the still greater fault of conclusions which do *not* follow from the premises.

The canon of validity laid down is that one premise must be affirmative (or both); and that one middle term must be universal (or both). I take this from the earlier writings, and by induction from the latest list of syllogisms: I shall not stop to consider the *general canon* (IX. ii. 285). It will be remembered that by affirmative and negative Hamilton refers to his own division, to his affirmatives which (all but one) contain negations, and to those negatives which are but disjunctively joined affirmatives. Speaking his language, and especially remembering that all his propositions are simply convertible, I affirm that both articles of his canon of validity are erroneous. As follows:

1. *Both premises may be negative*. Let us try)·( )·). If 'Any *X* is not any *Y*' and 'Any *Y* is not some *Z*', it follows that 'Some *Z* is not any *Y*', and the remaining *Z* is *Y*, and therefore not *X*. Consequently, we have a right to the Aristotelian conclusion, 'Some *Z* is not *X*'.

2. *Both middle terms may be particular*. Let us try)) (). If 'All *X* be some *Y*' and 'Some *Y* is some *Z*', whence 'Some *Z* (the rest) is not any *Y*', it follows that all this remaining *Z* is not any *X*. Hence we have the Aristotelian conclusion, 'Some *Z* is not *X*'.

Here we see pairs of premises yielding conclusions from which we are debarred, because those conclusions are not such as require the doubly partitive '*some*' to express them. I now pass on to the syllogisms which *are* allowed admission (IX. ii. 287).

Hamilton arranges these under twelve heads. Each head has three syllogisms: one with both premises affirmative; two others formed by making one premise negative without alteration of quantities. Thus)()) is accompanied by)·()) and)()·), as follows:

)()) All *X* is all *Y* and All *Y* is some *Z*.
)·()) Any *X* is not any *Y* and All *Y* is some *Z*.
)()·) All *X* is all *Y* and Any *Y* is not some *Z*.

The negative syllogisms take the number of the positive one from which they are derived, with the letters *a* and *b*. The canon of inference may be stated as follows:—When one premise is)(the form of the other is that of the conclusion: in every other case the erasure of the two middle spiculae shows the form of the conclusion. I now make a table, adding a word of necessary remark in certain cases.

			a		*b*	
I	)()(	*	)·()(	*	)()·(	*
II	(())	False	(·())	Incomplete	(()·)	Incomplete
III	)())	*	)·())	False	)()·)	*
IV	(()(	*	(·()(	*	(()·(	False
V	)(((	*	)·(((	‡	)((·(	*
VI	)))(	*	)·))(	*	)))·(	‡
VII	((()	False	(·(()	Incomplete	(((·)	†
VIII	()))	False	(·)))	†	()))·)	Incomplete
IX	)(()	*	)·(()	False	)((·)	*
X	())(	*	(·))(	*	())·(	False
XI	((((	‡	(·(((	False	(((·(	False
XII	))))	‡	)·)))	False	)))·)	False

Of 36 syllogisms, 21 have no error either of commission or omission: which arises as follows. Those marked (*), 15 in number, are safe because they contain)(, the sign of equivalence. Let the other signs have any degree of absurdity, or even of contradiction, any one of them joined with)(only means that one of the terms is to be extracted, and an equivalent inserted in its place: consequently *X*)(*Y*(·(*Z*, for example, must give *X*(·(*Z*, let (·(mean what it may. Two others, marked (†), contain and conclude with the vague form (·), which 'quadrates with all the rest'; and their principle is that some (when singly partitive) of the *part* is an equivalent of some of the *whole*. Remember that Hamilton did not intrude double partition into the meaning of (·). Four more, marked (‡), involve 'some' only in one term of a universal affirmative, in which double partition is of the same effect as single. All the rest—being precisely all those which give working effect to the peculiar *differentiae* of Hamilton's system,—*are either false or incomplete*: eleven false, four incomplete. [I proved this in detail, in due compliment to the reputation of the proposer: but I omit[1] the proofs, because I find that the point is not to be contested. December 1862.]

I now ask what is the real basis of this system? It is formed on what

[1] In the *Athenaeum* journal I took for my instance a case of IV. *b*, which I called the *Gorgon* syllogism. 'Some man is all lawyer; any lawyer is not any stone; therefore some man (i.e. lawyer) is not any stone (i.e. all the rest are stone).' [Mr Baynes (22 November 1862) cheerfully accepts this syllogism under the name I have given it, declares it valid, and will defend it if it be 'seriously assailed.' This is hasty writing: he means that he will defend what *he* supposes Hamilton to have meant, not what *I* suppose him to have let pass. But what Mr Baynes takes for Hamilton's meaning needs no defence; what I suppose him to have passed cannot be *seriously* assailed. December 1862.]

I call the *pepper-box* plan; *all* and *some* are shaken out upon subjects and predicates in every possible way. I am a decided advocate for this process, as a preliminary mode of collecting materials: and I have now before me 512 modes of enunciation—and this only an instalment—obtained by using the pepperbox with some of the pairs of correlative notions which are scattered through the systems. It would have been well for logic if Aristotle had followed this plan. But it is an error to assume that because certain junctions of correlative concepts give an incomplete system, therefore the introduction of all the remaining junctions must complete that system. Any person who makes this supposition may become liable to the remark made by Hamilton upon Aristotle —and which I now make upon himself—that he commenced his synthesis before he had completed his analysis.

As soon as the distribution of 'all' and 'some' had been made, and also introduction of the partitive sense of 'some', very slight attention would have shown that the enunciative forms present an imperfect system of the kind which I called *complex* in my *Formal Logic*, and *terminally precise* in my third paper. Contrary or privative terms being refused admission, it would have been seen that there are *five* terminally precise relations; or rather, three terminally precise, and two of which one terminal ambiguity is due to the refusal of privative terms, which refusal prevents statement of the relation in which one name stands to the contrary of another. On the principle—which I will not argue further, for with great personal respect for its deniers, I tell them their denial is absurd—that no *system* of enunciation can be admitted to the name until it is as powerful at denial as at assertion, and at assertion as at denial, five contradictions ought to have been introduced. The conjunctive propositions should have brought in their disjunctive denials; and the whole would then have stood as follows. I use both Hamilton's language and my own; but the symbols are now to express Aristotelian forms.

1. All *X* is some *Y*:*X* toto-partially inclusive of *Y*:*X* a sub-identical of *Y*:*X*)∘)*Y*, conjoined of *X*))*Y* and *X*)·)*Y*. The contradiction is 'Either *X*(·(*Y* or *X*((*Y*', which I denote by *X*(,(*Y*.

2. All *X* is all *Y*:*X* toto-totally inclusive of *Y*:*X* an identical of *Y*:*X*||*Y*, conjoined of *X*))*Y* and *X*((*Y*. The contradiction is 'Either *X*(·(*Y* or *X*)·)*Y*', denoted by *X*)·),(·(*Y*.

3. Some *X* is all *Y*:*X* parti-totally inclusive of *Y*:*X* a superidentical of *Y*:*X*(∘(*Y*, conjoined of *X*((*Y* and *X*(·(*Y*. The contradiction is 'Either *X*)·)*Y* or *X*))*Y*', denoted by *X*),)*Y*.

4. Any *X* is not any *Y*:*X* toto-totally exclusive of *Y*:*X* an external of *Y*: *X*)·(*Y*. The contradiction is *X*()*Y*, which, as explained, should have been the parti-partial negation, 'Some *X* is not some *Y*' of Hamilton's system.

5. Some *X* is some *Y*:*X* parti-partially inclusive of *Y*:*X* a *complete particular* (*Formal Logic*, p. 66) of *Y*: or *X*(·()·)*Y*, conjoined of *X*(·(*Y*, *X*()*Y*, *X*)·)*Y*. The contradiction is 'Either *X*))*Y*, or *X*)·(*Y*, or *X*((*Y*', denoted by *X*)); ((*Y*.

These enunciations constitute the system[1] at which Hamilton was aiming, but which permutations of 'some' and 'all' did not and could not reach. I do not think it worth while to set out all the syllogistic forms: these are best obtained by resolution into simple pairs of premises. I shall presently have occasion to exhibit a more perfect completion.

I now proceed to inquire how this system was received in the time preceding the publication of Hamilton's *Lectures*. The day will come when, but for such hints as I now give and the explanations which they will directly or indirectly produce, an inquirer into the early history of the expressed quantification of the predicate would be in serious difficulty. From 1847 to 1860 he will trace a stream of eulogy and controversy, of which Hamilton's quantification is the subject: but not a direct word does either advocate or opponent let fall about this quantification containing a very striking departure from Aristotle and his followers. Hamilton himself gives no information until 1852, when he announces his plan in terms which, to the inquirer I am supposing, will appear as clear as any terms could be: but still neither friend nor foe seems to know more about it than before. It is not until after 1860, when those remains were published which had for eight years been known by nearly sufficient extract, that all Hamilton's admirers are suddenly and publicly challenged to show that his real[2] system does not lead to mere

[1] It is clear that Hamilton never examined the syllogism upon the doubly partitive hypothesis. To my mind by far the most probable hypothesis is that, after the attack of illness from which he never wholly recovered, he really believed that he *had* examined the syllogism: a sudden interruption of this kind often has strange effects in the way of confusion between what had been done and what was to be done. This supposition receives some confirmation from the note at the end of the table of propositional relations—'The preceding table may not be quite accurate in details' (IX. ii. 284, VI. 637*). Such a memorandum in a private paper is for personal use: it was copied into the hurried article (VI.), which means that no deliberate examination had taken place up to 1852, even of the table of propositional forms. Now it is clear that a minute verification of the cases of syllogism must have either ended in, or been preceded by, such examination of the table of enunciations as would have led to the erasure of the note.

[2] There is another point, which I cannot decide. Hamilton taught his own system publicly from 1840 downwards. What use of 'some' did he adopt? Neither he himself, nor Mr Baynes in his *New Analytic*, nor Bishop Thomson in his *Outlines*, nor Mr Mansel in his edition of the *Lectures on Logic*, give any information on the point. I put the question in my letters to the *Athenaeum*, but no reply was made. I cannot bring myself to think that my acute opponent actually taught, year after year, a system of syllogism containing a cluster of paralogisms. I lean strongly to the supposition that he retained the Aristotelian sense, or made no further departure than

paralogism: which not one of them undertakes to do. What does all this mean? Is it reserve? Is it misapprehension?

Previously to 1852, Hamilton did not indicate intention to depart from Aristotle in the meaning of the quantifying designations. In his *Prospectus* (1846) he announces that he is to put the key-stone on the Aristotelic arch: not a hint is given that the buttresses are to be changed. In his correspondence with me, not a word of so much as allusion. In my *Formal Logic* (1847) I published my suspicions of what the system was, in which I made it clear that I supposed the non-partitive quantity to be the one adopted. This was soon followed by Bishop Thomson's second edition (1849) and by Mr Baynes's Essay (1850), the first containing information communicated by Hamilton himself, the second a student's account crowned—and augmented—by Hamilton himself. But, though both writers drop a sentence or two which seem to hint that their own system is the singly partitive—most writers, as already noticed, occasionally use at least a singly partitive phraseology in their preliminaries—not a doubly partitive syllable escapes from either. In my second paper (1850) I made it still more apparent that I attributed only the non-partitive sense. Hamilton made an indignant remonstrance (V.) against the use of 'all' which I attributed to him: but not a word about 'some': [it turns out (see Addition) that he took me to be using 'some' in his own new sense, which first appeared in print with his criticism on my supposed objections to it. He had forgotten his own previous silence.] His editors (IX. ii.) say that his notation had a uniform[1] import from 1839–40 onwards.

[1] They say that 'this' (p. 278) was his uniform import. By the preceding sentence it appears that 'this' is 'the meaning which the author attached to them [the symbols] on the new doctrine.' These symbols, therefore, never had more than one meaning; but they certainly were doubly partitive at last; therefore they were doubly partitive throughout. But the diagrams on which (and on their explanation) the note is made do not agree with the later diagrams (VI. 632*): the partial negatives, for example, are not disjoined affirmatives; and the whole gives more than a suspicion of the singly partitive sense. I hope that the second edition will be more precise on this point.

In the text I give nothing but facts. My own belief is that Hamilton neither publicly taught, nor privately communicated to any of those who have since acknowledged communication, any thing beyond the singly partitive system. If, as his editors seem

the singly partitive meaning: but if this be the fact, what hinders those who can from establishing it? I repeat the question again, and I trust that, if the point can be cleared up, those who have the means will not allow *me* to be the only person who shows interest in Hamilton's literary fame. For the honour of Scotland, a land noted for the logical turn of its sons, the question should be settled. Should judgment at last go by default, the decision must be that for sixteen years undetected paralogisms formed a third part of the system of syllogism taught in the University of Edinburgh as the 'key-stone of the Aristotelic arch.' [Mr Baynes replied satisfactorily on this point, as will appear in the Addition. I leave this note as showing what I thought on the subject when this paper was communicated. December 1862.]

Mr. Mansel (IV. 113, 116) gives evidence (1851) of having on his mind the impression that Hamilton differs from Aristotle: but not a syllable is there in his article from which we can infer more than single partition, or at most the double partition which single partition forces out of the universal affirmative. I feel justified in so much use of our private correspondence as to state that he has informed me that all his sources were in print. He makes no allusion to Hamilton's pamphlet (II.), probably because he did not, any more than myself, gain any knowledge of the system from this source. I rest perfectly satisfied, until contradicted, that Mr. Mansel had no complete idea of the double partition, nor of its consequences. As one editor, indeed, he has given me and others the means of arriving at knowledge of the whole case: but both editors, in their short preface, imply a *caveat* against being supposed to agree with their principal in all points. Mr. Mansel's article is a valuable repertory[1] of the non-mathematical logician's objections to

[1] I quote at length the chief point of reference:—'Before quitting this part of our subject, we will describe the principle of Mr De Morgan's complex syllogism, as that part of his system which comes in some degree into rivalry with the quantified predicate of Sir W. Hamilton, which we are about to examine. When we say that the latter accomplishes all the ends attained by Mr De Morgan, with a vast superiority in clearness and simplicity as well as in accuracy of thinking, we have said all that is necessary in the way of criticism. Mr De Morgan refuses to quantify [Mr Mansel means *partitively*] the predicate in a single affirmative proposition. Accordingly, the universal affirmative, "all *X* is *Y*", may form part of two complex propositions, either "all *X* is *Y*, and all *Y* is *X*", or "All *X* is *Y*, and some *Y* is not *X*". Hence a syllogism in Barbara which, in Sir W. Hamilton's system, would be expressed in the form "All *X* is some *Y*, all *Y* is some *Z*, therefore all *X* is some *Z*", becomes in Mr De Morgan's hands the following complex reasoning [a hasty word; *expression* must be meant: for Hamilton's syllogism contains all this *reasoning*; and this by the partitive force of "*some*"].

All *X* is *Y*, and some *Y* is not *X*.
All *Y* is *Z*, and some *Z* is not *Y*.
Therefore, All *X* is *Z*, and some *Z* is not *X*.

The reader who is desirous of further details must seek them in Mr De Morgan's own work. Those who will take the trouble of comparing his fourth and fifth chapters

to suppose,—and not against any presumption which I can bring forward—his double partition was elaborated by 1846, I feel almost sure that he intentionally reserved it. He had a perfect right to do so; the same right which Titus Oates's fox had to carry a stone over the brook to see if the ice would bear, before he attempted to carry over the goose. But such reserve always brings perplexity into history: Hamilton has made it easier to cook his goose than to write its biography.

The following gives a strong suspicion—even more—of reserve in 1850, abandoned in 1852. In (V.), he says, 'The language I use is that of the logicians; only the quantity of the predicate, contained in thought, is overtly expressed. . . .' In the reprint of this letter (VI. 626*) he adds to the words 'some is not', the following in brackets—'[*Some is* should, however, have been held its direct and natural result; for, as we shall see, two particulars in the affirmative and negative forms, ought to infer each other. Compare p. 635*, sq.]' [This makes the forgetfulness above noted very strange.]

the results of mathematical habit: and I confidently predict that it will often be cited as such when the number of those who stow both logic and mathematics in one head shall be greater than it now is. So far I have not produced a single hint of double partition. When I examined the late Professor Spalding's work (VIII; 1857) I could not trace a phrase which was not perfectly reconcilable with the Aristotelian sense, or at most with single partition. On re-examining my copy for the purposes of the present paper, I found inserted a number of the *Edinburgh Weekly Review* (18 July 1857) containing an account of Mr. Spalding's work, and citing[1] him as among the chief objectors to Hamilton's junction of 'some at least' and 'some at most.'

Lastly, I mention myself, who might have been expected to have read the whole riddle at once in the publication (VI.) of 1852. But I, at that time, had good reason to feel estopped, as the lawyers say, from all interpretation of Hamilton's meaning: the reason is described in the Appendix to my third paper. I found that, in spite of the most distinct assertions, as well on the part of Hamilton as of his expositors, that '*all*' is the exponent of universal quantity, I was wholly in the wrong for not divining that '*any*' must be used in every[2] negative proposition (V.

[1] 'Unless indeed objection be taken, as is done by some of them [his disciples], and particularly by Professor Spalding, to Sir William's employment of both the alternative meanings of the word "some", as "some at least" and "some at most". There seems good reason for suspecting that the acceptance of the latter interpretation would again open the door [how is this possible?] to extralogical considerations.' I again examined the work: and again without success. I then remembered that Mr Spalding himself had sent me this review, as written by a friend of his own: and I suppose his friend had mixed up reminiscences of conversation with those of the printed pages. I conclude that Mr Spalding did object to the doubly partitive system, but showed his objection only by suppression.

[2] Hamilton's editors have judiciously ignored the whole controversy. But on one point they have made an indirect reference, seemingly intended to intimate that any one who lays down '*all*' as the symbol of universal quantity, does *in fact* lay down '*any*' as its substitute in negatives. They say—'The comma (,) denotes *some*; the colon (:) *all*'; which is all that is given in explanation of the symbols of

with the system we are about to describe, will, we are convinced, discover abundant grounds to justify our preference for the latter. We have followed Mr De Morgan through a tedious journey, during which we have more than once had occasion to express our respect for his talents, and our regret at their perversion. We take leave of him in the words of an eminent logician and mathematician:—"Enimvero quae confuse tantum cognoscuntur, ea saepius confunduntur, ut adeo casus similes videantur quae sunt dissimiles, et secundum ideam confusam qui agit, facile omittit quibus vel maxime fuerat opus. Atque ideo logica naturali instructus in applicatione saepissime aberrat. Exemplo nobis sunt illi qui, in mathesi cum laude versati, methodum mathematicam extra eandem perperam applicant, etsi sibi rem acu tangere videantur." (Wolf, *Philosophia Rationalis, Proleg.* § 19).' I suspect that the text of the last two sentences is corrupt: and I propose conjectural emendations. Remember that all that relates to *quantity* is mathematical; for *naturali* read *sine mathematica*, for *cum laude* read *minus*, for *extra eandem* read *inscitia naturali.*

passim). The sarcastic pictures caused the article (VI.) to be to me, so long as its author lived, a joke and nothing else; I mean that whenever I sat down to read in earnest I was always captured by the fun. And when, at last, I gave it serious examination, my disinclination to interpret was augmented. When I saw that 'some at least' was 'possibly *none*', it presented itself as on the cards that 'some at most' might be 'possibly *all*', and the system in some unfathomable way Aristotelian.

It must be noted that a person might take 'some at most' to be *singly* partitive, by supposing that the limitation 'at most' refers to what are spoken of: thus 'some at most are . . .' might be read as 'we speak of some at most, be the rest what they may; of these we say they are . . .' But Hamilton takes pains to explain his meaning. His 'some' is laid down as both affirmative and negative; his 'some are' is declared inconsistent with 'all are', and his 'some are not' with 'none are', &c. [I have insisted on this, being in doubt whether it might not be denied: but I believe it is admitted. There is, however, a mode of speaking which may lead to error. It is said that Hamilton gives two systems, the 'some at least' of the older logicians, and his own 'some at most': and the headings of his own table (VI. 637*) adopt this distinction. But it must be remembered that the 'some' of the table is always 'not-none'; so that his new system is that of 'some at least *and* at most.' In no other way could IFI, or 'Some—is some—' be a combination of my ())·) (·(, as (VI. 632* diagram *d*) it certainly is. December 1862.]

I now come to the consideration of the genuine Aristotelian system: I mean the system which was sketched out by Aristotle and held its ground down to the end of the seventeenth century. When (1847) I began this long discussion I knew Aristotle only, or almost entirely, as a collection of books of reference. Now and then it became necessary to decide for myself which of two contradicting statements about an opinion of his was true: so soon as one or both were rejected, my business with the Organon was settled for the time. In all cases of agreement I took it for granted that the leader was correctly followed. This assumption lasted until I was shaken by the translation of ἀριθμὸς καὶ λόγος into number and *speech*[1] which I exposed in my second paper. Being

[1] Plato, in the *Phaedrus*, says that Τοῦτον δὲ τὸν Θεὺθ πρῶτον ἀριθμόν τε καὶ λογισμὸν εὑρεῖν: but whether Thoth is held to have invented speech I cannot say. Conic sections are for mathematicians only, or it might have been that Apollonius would have passed for the first inventor of curtailment and exaggeration. Smiglecius (*Disp*. 9, qu. 6) remarks that Aristotle does not count speech as quantity in the fifth

quantity. They then say—'Thus;— *C*:—, *A* is read *all C* is *some A*. *C*: +— :*D* is read, *No C is any D*.' (IX. ii. 277, 278.) The word *thus* implies exemplification. To read 'No *C* is any *D*' may be permitted: but he who *thuses* this reading of '*C*: +— :*D*' upon 'the colon denotes *all*' reminds me of my old French master, an unhorsed hussar of 1815, who gravely taught that 'All the French words are derived from the Latin: *thus* "Seigneur", which is "Lord," comes from the Latin "Dominus".'

thus led to suspect that the mathematician Aristotle had been but loosely read, and shamelessly interpolated, by unmathematical followers, I paid more attention to his text. I took for my principle of interpretation that he meant what he said: and truly he is a writer who deserves this compliment. And I found that, though the great bulk of his ancient followers are faithful translators, our modern logicians, though nominally his adherents, have drifted into a system of quantification of their own, and have towed his name after them.

When I discussed Hamilton's system in my second paper, imagining it to be non-partitive in quantity, after pointing out that two of its propositions were without contradiction in the system, I noticed that very slight change would produce perfect logical consistency. This change was nothing but the substitution of *any* for *all*, in affirmatives as well as negatives. I proposed, though this is not absolutely required, that the implicit singularity should become explicit, as in 'any one' and 'some one.' This gives to six of the eight propositions the meaning which they have in the common system; and makes them, as usual, three pairs of contradictories. The remaining pair 'any one *X* is any one *Y*' and 'some one *X* is not some one *Y*', are also contradictory: the first giving *X* and *Y* as singular and identical. This system I called *exemplar*: its form is that of enunciation by selected example, the unlimited right of selection being expressed by *any*, the possibly limited right by *some*. This mode of expression stands opposed to the *cumular* form in common use: 'All *X* is some *Y*' being the cumular of 'Any one *X* is some one *Y*'; the aggregate of all its cases. Hamilton's criticism on all this can be seen in V. and VI. At this moment I am concerned with only one sentence of it (V.): he is persuaded, he says, (VI. 627*), that my ' "Table of Exemplars" stands alone . . . in the history of science': he also (VI. 648*) calls it a 'still-born monstrosity.' I dispute his judgment in all that relates to quantification; I do not dispute his learning: I therefore quote these words as a strong testimony to my originality; and I highly value its definite character. But it only applies to half of the system: the remaining half does not stand alone in history as part of my paper. I assert that *the system of Aristotle and his followers consists of four* EXEMPLAR *propositions, with unquantified predicates*. I therefore maintain that the exemplar system which I gave in 1850, as a reduction to logical consistency of Hamilton's system, is a true[1] extension and step towards completion of the old system.

[1] Of this, as my second paper will show, I had not the least idea when I first gave

book of the *Metaphysics*: he will not allow it to be a quantity; and he says that Aristotle made it quantity in the Categories only as 'vulgarem ea de re opinionem secutus.' But when or how the world at large joined number and speech as cognate quantities he does not state: nor how a writer must be held to have concealed his own opinion from deference in an example freely chosen by himself, where another would have done as well.

This assertion is mere statement of a fact, and a very simple one. Do the old logicians use the singular, or do they use the plural? Do they say 'Every, each, any,—man', or do they say 'All men'? Do they say 'Some man', or 'Some men'? If the first, they are *exemplar*, they speak by selection of example: for Every, Each, Any (with singular noun), are Every one, Each one, Any one; and Some, with a singular noun, is Some one.

The modern logician says 'All man': he speaks of the extent of the *genus* 'man' as divisible into *species*: he means that the collection of individuals 'All men'—all that exist, or all that can be imagined to exist, according to the universe he is in for the time—is divisible into smaller collections. My assertion is that 'All man is animal', thus understood, is a glaringly wrong translation of the '*Omnis homo est animal*' used by his foregoers, and of the *πᾶς ἄνθρωπος ζῷον* of the leader. Our English word *all*, when singular, refers only to some whole divisible into parts: and '*all* man is animal', before the phrase undergoes logical technicalization, is false, for it means that man is animal in legs and arms, body and *soul*. But the Latin *omnis* means *each*, *every*, *any one*, as in *sine omni periclo*, *omnis parturit arbos*. The whole divisible into parts is *totus*, *totus ager*, *tota mens*, *totus in illis*. And *totus* may naturally[1] replace *omnis*, and does: while *omnis* does sometimes replace *totus*. Thus we have *omnis insula* for the whole island, *omnis sanguis* for the whole blood. But *omnis* in the singular may collect the *individual* from its parts, never the *class*; when it is *all*, it is all the individual, not the collected species. In Greek *πᾶς* is both *ὅλος* and *ἕκαστος*: but *πᾶς ἄνθρωπος* is *each* or *every* man, not the *whole* man. Should a point be raised upon any ambiguity, and advanced in opposition to the preceding, I suppose it will be conceded that the particular quantity, if free from the same ambiguity, will settle the matter.

A logician strong in ancient association naturally tends towards the Latin singular: modern habits tend towards consolidation of plurality of individuals into *pieces of extent*. Hamilton compromises as follows (VI. 636*). He wants to translate 'Some dogs do not bark' in fully quantified form. He does not say *Quidam canes sunt nulla latrantia*: this would offend the logical ear. Neither does he say *Quidam canis est nullum latrans*: this would be purely exemplar. He does say *Quoddam caninum est nullum latrans*: he speaks singularly of *an indefinite section of dog-nature*, [a certain amount of *caninity*], and so conciliates the ancient exemplarity of phrase and the modern cumularity of thought.

I take, beginning with Aristotle, a score or more of logicians of all

[1] In French the transposition is permanent, as in *tout*: the language derives no word from *omnis*. In Italian, *tutto* and *ogni* (singular) still translate *totus* and *omnis*.

it: in my mind the exemplar system was a derivation, from that of correction, by Hamilton, which certainly suggested it.

ages, and of every kind of note: I choose them merely because I happen to have access to them at the time of writing. I go direct to the places in which the technical propositional forms are laid down, and to the chapters on conversion. Some writers vary their phrases a little as they get deep into their subjects: but we know that they would all desire that their systems should be described by what they lay down in their fundamental explanations. Hamilton (VI. 626*) has collected a large number of quantifying words both in Greek and Latin; and might have got more: but it would have been difficult to have found any *early* writer who heaped his defining chapters with all this variety, or with any noteworthy amount of it.

Aristotle (*Analyt. Pr.* cap. 1, &c.) defines the *universal* as that which belongs to *every-one* or to *no-one*, *τὸ παντὶ ἢ μηδενὶ*: the *particular* as that which belongs to *some-one*, or not to *some-one*, or not to *every-one*, *τὸ τινὶ ἢ μὴ τινὶ ἢ μὴ παντί*. Instead of a long quotation from cap. 2, on conversion, I pick out *all* the quantitatives as they stand: they are *μηδεμία, οὐδὲν, πᾶσα, τι, τις, τι, τινὶ, τινὶ, μηδενὶ, οὐδενὶ, τινὶ, μηδενὶ, τι, παντὶ, τινὶ, μηδενὶ, οὐδενὶ, παντὶ, τινὶ, τινὶ, μηδενὶ, οὐδενὶ, τινὶ, τινὶ, παντὶ, παντὶ*: not a plural among them. If all this be not exemplar, it must be because Aristotle said *one* and meant *many*. But so (by inference) does every person who says 'Any one man is some one animal'; he means to speak of *all* men, and he does it. So that in what sense soever Aristotle is not exemplar, the exemplar system itself is not exemplar. Some will say that Aristotle only distributes: then the exemplar system distributes; and that in modern use does not.

Again, a person using cumular language would say that a universal negative is upset not only by predication of *all*, but of *some*: he would never say that 'none are' is contradicted by '*all* are' and also by 'some *one* is'; he would certainly find intermediate room for the indefinite plural *some*. Now Aristotle (*Anal. Pr.* cap. 26) says that the universal negative is destroyed if the predicate be affirmable of *πᾶς* or some *one*, *εἰ παντὶ καὶ εἰ τινί*: this must be *every-one* or *some one*. He had previously said that the universal affirmative is upset if the predicate can be said to belong to no *one* or not to some *one*; *καὶ γὰρ ἢν μηδενὶ καὶ ἢν τινὶ μὴ ὑπάρχῃ, ἀνῄρηται* [*τὸ καθόλου κατηγορικόν*].

Hamilton, in various[1] places, appends to the word *all* the parenthesis

[1] In one place (IX. ii. 303) there is a boldness of assertion which may be quoted as showing that genuine feeling of the sameness of *all* and *every* which, but for repeated illustration, my readers would hardly believe to have existed. Alexander Aphrodisiensis is quoted as saying that it is 'impossible that all man should be all animal, as that all man should be all risible.' Restoring *every* for *all*, the Greek will be seen to mean that whether the terms *A* and *B* be coextensive or no, 'Every *A* is every *B*' is *impossible*; for that, without any question about the *matter* of the terms, each individual would be many individuals. Hamilton, with his eyes quite shut to this point, will have him speak of material impossibility, which is clear in the assertion

'[or every]', thus making it appear that in his mind 'all man is all animal' and 'Every man is every animal' are precisely the same English, and require precisely the same comment. In one place (IX. ii. 300) he translates Aristotle thus:—'For *all* or *every* [πᾶς] does not indicate. . . .' Here, as elsewhere, he distinctly proclaims that he sees no difference between our English *all* and *every* in the two forms. But 'all man' has parts, which are species of the genus man: 'every man' has no parts, but makes assertions about the individuals of every species. I repeat that the modern logician has accustomed himself to the identification of two distinct things: he sees distribution in the cumular, and cumulation in the distributive, until the two readings are no longer distinct in his mind. He would speak of a country in which there are no single adults of either sex, as one in which all the Jacks are married to all the Joans: and, though not without ambiguity, he would be understood by mathematicians and other unlogical persons after a moment's thought. But he would also crave permission to say that every Jack is married to every Joan; which, to all but those whose English has been spoiled by modern logical technology, would enunciate the maximum of polygamy.

The expositors and translators, from Boethius to Thomas Taylor, B. St Hilaire, and O. F. Owen, give correct literal translation. I find exemplar language, to the exclusion of cumular, in Paulus Venetus, the Cologne regents, Isenach, Pacius, Burgersdicius, Keckermann,[1] Crackanthorpe, Sanderson, Aldrich, &c. On the other hand, Molinaeus, Wallis, Wendelinus, and the Port-Royal, out of about forty systems which I have examined, give more or less into plural forms. That most rigid[2] disciplinarian, Crackanthorpe, collected quantitative terms in

[1] [26 December 1862] From the list of those who lay down nothing but exemplar readings Keckermann must be excluded. His universals are all laid down in the singular (except *cuncti*), and his particulars all in the plural (except *non nemo*). And these are employed, for the most part, in his instances of syllogism; universals in the singular, particulars in the plural. But Ramus may be added to the exemplar list. I also find that *quidam* is not so uniformly excluded as Mr Spalding supposed: Stahl and Keckermann both give it.

[2] Hamilton generally calls him 'Oxford Crackanthorpe'. He was for some five years fellow of a college, but his University sympathies could not have been marked: 'Puritan Crackanthorpe' would have been a better name; Anthony Wood would have protested against the other epithet. His book on Logic, written probably about 1600, was first published in 1622.

that 'all man is all animal.' But seeing that there is no material impossibility in 'All man is all risible'—which was believed to be true—he mends the text, and will have Alexander to declare this proposition only *useless*. Hamilton's quotation accordingly runs thus:—'For it is *impossible* that *all man* should be *all animal*, as [*useless to say*, (ἄχρηστον εἰπεῖν must have dropt out)] that *all man is all risible*.' Boethius (IX. ii. 308; *Patrolog*. lxiv. col. 323) has certainly interpreted Aristotle in Hamilton's sense. If (IX. ii. 301–315) *omnis* be translated by *every* throughout, it will be seen that the *Greek* commentators take Aristotle in the sense I contend for, and that there is diversity among the others.

profusion, and would have admitted a plural or two if such a thing had been canonical. His universal signs are *omnis*, *quilibet*, *quicunque*, *quandocunque*, *nullus*, *nemo*, *nunquam*: his particulars are *aliquis*, *alius*, *unicus*, *alter*, *nonnullus*. One of his *singular* terms is *omnis quando collective sumitur non distributive*: that is to say, the cumular is with him referred to the non-distributive[1] singular. He describes particular quantity as '*individuum* incertum et vagum.'

But the strongest testimony to the preponderance of exemplar expression is indirectly given by Hamilton himself, who says (IX. ii. 296) that the objection to 'all man is all risible' because each man would then be all the class risible, 'is only respectable by authority, through the great, the all but unexclusive, number of its allegers'. Now the original is 'omnis homo est omne risibile': that is, the logicians are, almost to a man, exemplar. Let who will believe that they nearly all refused a form tantamount to 'the *class A* is the *class B*', because they thought that each individual in *A* would thereby be pronounced to be all the class *B*. They meant the proposition in the sense of its correct translation, 'Every man is every risible', at which they laughed because, in Latin, as in English, the form implies that every separate man is every risible animal.

I cannot here properly give the volume of proof which it is easy to collect of the old mode of enunciation being what I call exemplar. What I have given will be sufficient for unbiassed minds, so soon as it shall appear that no equal force of citation is to be produced on the other side. I affirm then that the exemplar table which I gave in 1850 is the Aristotelian system, fully quantified, and made as complete in its forms as it can be so long as privative terms are excluded. But it must be remarked,—

First, that the system is not originally derived from distributions of quantification and search after their meanings. The leading idea is that of assertion or denial of class being contained in class, and of class being excluded from class. Indications of this origin are not wanting. Particular negation is very frequently enunciated by *οὐ πᾶς ἔστι*, that is, by denial of total inclusion or agreement: the greatest interest in 'some are not' is seen in 'not every one is.' If *quantification* had been a leading idea in the mind of Aristotle, *he* would not have been unable to use the pepper-box: but to him[2] the signs of quantity were but incidents of expression.

[1] This sentence, the quotation from Pacius presently given, and other things, lead me to suspect that my word *exemplar* is a synonym of the word *distributive*, in its old sense.

[2] My belief is that, in the mind of Aristotle, the four forms were merely intended to signify, in common language, the affirmation and denial of total inclusion, and the affirmation and denial of total exclusion. The entrance of quantifying adjectives or pronouns was only a non-essential incident of common language. Hence the old

Secondly, when a term was a genus, the *exempla* were species taken individually, not ultimate individuals. Thus when the quantified term was *omne animal*, the *hic*, *iste*, *ille*, &c. of the distribution would be *homo, bos, asinus*, &c.: when *omnis homo*, if *homo* were *infima species*, the details would be *Plato*, *Socrates*, &c.

Hamilton disputes the rational existence of 'Any one *X* is any one *Y*', and affirms (VI. 628*) that '*any*' and '*any one*' *necessarily* imply that there are *more*. This is not true: we have but a strong presumption of more. My critic had arrived at a conviction that *some* ought to be doubly partitive: but this was his own exclusive possession. The examination of his argument will show that *any* has no difficulty about it except what applies equally to *all*. When it is clearly understood that *part* is that which may be the *whole*—that is, when partition is formally excluded—it will then be seen that if there be that which is *any* part of *Y*, there can be but one part of *Y*, the smallest part is the whole, the whole is an individual. *Any* does not *necessarily* imply more than one: speaking of existence at this moment, any Queen of England is any Queen of Scotland: every Queen of England that can be found is all the Queen of Scotland there are; it would be treason to deny it.

The following addition to my statement as to quantification appears to me so evidently the true reading of the ancients, that I see no means of proving it to any one who, having examined Aristotle, &c., entertains any doubt about it. Predication, the assertion made in an affirmative proposition, is not identification, far less equation, of subject and predicate, but simply declares the predicate notion to be true of the subject. This predicate has an adjective force, is rather an *attribute* of the subject —a frequent name in later times—than another and containing *superject*, and the proposition is very close to the character which in my third paper I have called *physical*. The predicate is applied *in its totality* to the individual of the subject class; and is distributed over as many individuals as the proposition speaks of, one by one, being given *whole* to each one of them. Thus 'Every man is mortal' says of each man *all* that it says of every other. No such image ever presented itself to the ancients as a notion which, instead of being applied whole, is itself cut piecemeal and assigned, bit by bit, to the bits of the subject. Such imagination is possible, because it is actual. We have before us (VI. 643*) the assertion that our attribute of mortality is divisible: that when we sum up men, we also sum up their *mortalities*: that Newton has this mortality, Leibnitz that, &c. But none of this is in the old notion of predication;

---

notion, so long retained, that the *proposition* was universal or particular, not the *subject*. The departure from principle, which gradually clouded the theory, was the expression of denial of totality by a destructive example: as denial of '*X* wholly in *Y*' by 'certain *X* not in *Y*'. But there is a vestige of creation in *οὐ πᾶς ἔστι*, as mentioned in the text.

and my present controversy is with those who arraign Aristotle and his followers at the bar of this principle, and declare that a plea to the jurisdiction must be overruled.

The Hamiltonians, and many others, read their great exemplar—as I may call Aristotle—in cumular sense, until they have lost[1] the perception of *τις*, *omnis*, *quidam*, being individuals: so that when a table of forms is presented in which singularity is enforced by the word *one*, enormous learning declares that it stands alone in history. A plain statement will show that the declarant read history through coloured glass.

Aristotle (*De Interpr.* cap. vii.) denies quantity to a predicate: he says that *no* affirmative could then be true—*οὐδεμία γὰρ κατάφασις ἀληθὴς ἔσται*. And he[2] instances *πᾶς ἄνθρωπος πᾶν ζῷον*. Wholly exemplar in his enunciation, quite ignorant that *πᾶς ἄνθρωπος* meant *all man*,—the whole *extent* of the term *man*,—he said a plain Greek thing in a plain Greek way to Greeks who knew Greek. He said it is false—formally false, apart from the matter—that every man is *every* living being, meaning that then Socrates would be every living being, so would Plato, &c. When he affirmed a certain *quantification* to be *always* false, he meant false *in quantity*. And he was perfectly right: for there never was man who was more than *one* living being. The proposition 'Every X is every Y' makes singular terms both of X and Y.

Now Hamilton, who could not read in any other than the cumular sense, and who was possessed of the quantified predicate not merely as that which could be, and ought to be, but as that which is and must be, —asserted (IX. ii. 263), positively for this occasion only, that his great leader[3] talked 'nonsense.' He misconceived the nature of the falsehood

[1] There is much interesting discussion in Mr Spalding's *Introduction to Logical Science* (1857), but one single sentence curiously instances the want of power to see the singular which marks the modern logical mind. It will clearly appear that Mr Spalding was a man of extensive reading and acute perception. He says (p. 63), that the logical *some* is always indeterminate, some or other, not certain definite objects: 'it is always *aliqui*, never *quidam*.' This is perfectly true; even the collector Crackanthorpe does not admit *quidam*. But it should have been 'it is always *aliquis*, never *quidam*,' *quidam* being singular.

The only remark on the subject which I know of, published since Hamilton's denial of the existence of the exemplar form, is in the third edition (p. 57) of Mr Mansel's edition of Aldrich (1856). Here *οὐ πᾶς*, when a substantive is put on, is translated *not all men*: another instance of the obliteration of the distinction between *every man* and *all men*.

[2] I noted in a former paper that the ordinary practice of translating *ζῷον* into *animal* has led to the representation that Aristotle ranked the immortal gods under animals. I have since found that Francis Patricius, when collecting his proofs that Plato was more orthodox (in the Christian sense) than Aristotle, cites this supposed opinion as one of his proofs. I hope none of the Greek Fathers have been belied in the same way.

[3] 'The whole doctrine of the non-quantification of the predicate is only another example of the passive sequacity of the logicians. They follow obediently in the

imputed to a universal predicate: he thought that Aristotle's objection to 'every man is every living being' arose out of horses and dogs, rats and mice, &c., not being men. He charges the founder of logic (*sic notus Ulysses?*) with rejecting a logical form on the ground of certain matter making it false. To the last he could not see that the Aristotelian proposition attributes the whole predicate to every example of the subject: to the last he fixes on Aristotle the '*all* man is all animal', of the modern school, the erroneous translation of '*Omnis homo est omne animal.*' And he totally omits to notice Aristotle's assertion that *not one* proposition of the form 'Every *A* is every *B*' can be true: from which, on his plan of interpretation, he ought to have accused his master of denying the existence of co-extensive terms.

Mr. Baynes's work (III.) gives links which had long been dropped in the history of this discussion: and its author is a decisive instance of the manner in which Hamilton's teaching made cumular quantity the only one known in the history of logic, and the only one which can result

---

footsteps of their great master . . . He prohibits once and again the annexation of the universal predesignation to the predicate. For why, he says, such predesignation would render the proposition absurd; giving as his only example and proof of this, the judgment,—*All man is all animal* . . . Yet this nonsense (be it spoken with all reverence of the Stagirite) has imposed the precept on the systems of Logic down to the present day' (IX. ii. 263). Again (IX. ii. 296), Hamilton declares that 'a general rule or postulate of logic is,—That in the same logical unity (proposition or syllogism), the same term or quantification should not be changed in import.' Hence he infers that if in 'All man is all risible' the first all be distributive, so is the second. Hamilton may lay down this postulate for himself and those who like it: but there never was such a postulate in logic. On the contrary, the universal practice, down to our own time, implies that in 'Every man is ——', *all* that follows the word *is* is predicated of *each man*. If we say 'some men are twenty men' the obvious falsehood drives us to metaphor: some men have *each* the power of twenty. But Hamilton would have it that it *has been* postulated that this proposition means a literal truth; i.e. this man is one, that man another, &c.—a certain *some* making up twenty. It *may be* so understood by postulation: but it never *has been.*

But though the charge against Aristotle is a mere misconception of his meaning, Hamilton fell into the very error of which he accused his leader, namely, that of rejecting a *form* because certain *matter* falsifies it. He is speaking (VI. 627*) of the use of *any* in affirmatives. 'Now, let us try "*any*" as an affirmative:—"Any triangle is any trilateral." This is simple nonsense: for we should thus confound every triangle with every other, pronouncing them all to be identical. Nor, in fact, does Mr De Morgan attempt this. He wisely omits the form. But what an omission!' I pass over the last assertion with the observation that the very first proposition in the table here criticized is 'Any one *X* is any one *Y*': these words are followed by '*giving* there is but one *X* and one *Y*, and *X* is *Y*.' What I have here to do with is Hamilton's distinct rejection of the form because it is false as applied to plural notions. It *is* false that 'any triangle is any trilateral': he who makes this assertion 'confounds every triangle with every other'; that is, asserts the existence of only one triangle. And it is false that 'every animal is a man': but this does not compel the rejection of 'Every *X* is *Y*' from the forms of enunciation, on the ground of the instance declaring horses and dogs to be men.

from scientific analysis. The ambiguity which misled Hamilton seems to have come into general discussion by the sixteenth century: for by that time, taking the common belief that only man can laugh, the disputants had completely substituted '*Omnis homo est omne risibile*' for Aristotle's instance, as placing the true issue in clear light. They then asserted, in plain and rational terms, that every man is not *every* laugher, for each man is only *one*. Mr. Baynes calls this 'the inconceivably inconsequent ground that if *all man* is all risible, then necessarily *each man* is all risible.' Here *omnis homo* is translated *all man*, and made to mean *all men*. Mr. Baynes proceeds thus '. . . to take a parallel example (one, however, which they do not take) that if *twelve inches* are one foot, then necessarily *each individual inch* is also one foot.' The example is clearly not a parallel, but it well illustrates the divergence. The parallelism of the *twelve inches* and the *all man* is so perfect, that they make the same angle—to a tenth of a second—with *omnis homo*. The reader who consults the whole of the rare and interesting matter which Mr Baynes[1] has

[1] Mr Baynes is particularly worthy of citation on this subject because, quite fresh from the teaching of his distinguished guide, he threw himself into the history of quantification, and made very valuable researches. It is curious to see how he speaks of cumular quantification, as both a logical and a vernacular necessity. Speaking of the exemplar grounds of objection to 'Every man is every risible,' which to him could be nothing but 'all man is all risible,' he says (p. 93), 'When we consider these grounds, and remember the real ability of the men by whom they were successively urged, we cannot but be struck with a wonder amounting to marvel, that they could remain satisfied with them, and that a truth so obvious on its first enunciation, so imperative on its fuller exposition, should have been so uniformly and so long thus rejected.' Nevertheless, the clear exposition of Pacius, so deservedly high among the expositors of Aristotle, would have stopped the wonder of any one who knew the exemplar sense: though somewhat long, I repeat it from Mr Baynes, 'Hunc errorem ut Aristoteles tollat, ostendit *universalem notam nunquam posse adjungi attributo*; quia tunc omnis affirmatio *falsa* esset. Quod declarat exemplo hujus enunciationis "omnis homo est omne animal," quae sine dubio falsa est: nam si homo esset omne animal, esset etiam asinus et bos. Sed notare hic oportet, alia attributa latius patere quam subjecta, alia vero reciprocari cum subjectis . . . Ubi igitur attributum latius patet, ut in exemplo Aristotelis, res dubitatione caret: certum enim est, affirmationem esse falsam, nec possi dici, "omnem hominem esse omne animal". Sed merito dubitatur de attributis, quae reciprocantur cum subjectis, veluti si quis dicat, "omne animal est omne sensu praeditum", et "omnis homo est omne aptum ad ridendum": nam hic absurditas illa non aeque apparet, ut in illa enunciatione, "omnis homo est omne animal". Sed ut intelligatur has quoque enunciationes esse falsas, in quibus attributum, quod reciprocatur, adnexam habet particulam *omnis*, notare oportet, hanc particulam *omnis*, habere vim quam in scholis vocant distributivam; ut omnis homo, proinde valeat atque quilibet homo, vel *singuli homines*; et similiter omne animal, idem valet, quod singula animalia, vel unumquodque animal seu quodlibet animal. Quapropter si vere diceretur, "omne animal est omne sensu praeditum" etiam homo esset omne sensu praeditum; nam qui dixit omne animal, non exclusit omnem hominem, homo igitur esset quodlibet sensu praeditum: proinde hac ratione fieret, ut homo esset equus, et bos, quandoquidem equus et bos sunt sensu praedita.' (Pacius *in Aristot. de Interpr.* cap. VII.) The reader will see how clearly Pacius has

produced will see much force in the following argument:—If the ancients had cumular meaning, and wrote as they did, they took inconceivably inconsequent grounds, and ought to have discovered that an inch is a foot. But it is very unlikely that so large a collection of acute thinkers should make puerile mistakes, and fail to see that a foot no longer than an inch follows from their principles, if it really did so. Therefore it is very unlikely that the ancients, writing as they did, had cumular meaning.

This preliminary argument could not be weighed in time still recent, because the possibility of anything except the *extended* term was not in thought. Some readers will perhaps never have seen, until they meet with it here, the assertion that when Aristotle and his long train of followers shaped enunciation in the singular number, it was because they were thinking as they spoke. Those readers may have learnt to see nothing but cumular in the exemplar form, nothing but plural in the singular; and they may attribute this lapse of vision to Aristotle. If so, I remind them that the singular and plural could hardly have been so easily confounded in a language which *had the dual interposed.* It is worth[1] a thought whether the possible ambiguity arising out of the dual and plural did or did not dictate adherence to the singular: the plural must have frequently taken in the dual, frequently not: that is, the plural must have frequently meant two or more, frequently more than two. If this be the *explanation*, it does not alter the *fact.* And to the fact must be joined the utter extinction of the exemplar form in the minds of modern logicians: an extinction so thorough that such a chart of logical history as Hamilton's mind had not that course laid down, even as a possibility. It was easier to him to imagine Aristotle talking such 'nonsense' as that a form must be rejected because it was not true of all matter, than meaning his *singular* number to speak of *one*: and a table of exemplar forms published in 1850, appeared to him to stand alone in history.

The exemplar form of statement is that both of geometry and of

[1] Were it only because it has hardly been thought of. In English the confusion of singular and plural has occurred. The proverb says, 'One's none; two's some'. That one should be *none* (*ne one*, *not one*) defies etymology: but as *not one*, and *only one*, both deny *some* with its ordinary plural implication, and *some* and *none* pass for alternatives in life as well as in logic, the way in which the confusion arises is seen.

laid down the difference between exemplar and cumular, and how distinctly he has stated that the exemplar, not the cumular, is the ancient reading.

Should a teacher be so accustomed to *read exemplar enunciation in cumular sense* that the first time an exemplar table is explicitly presented he declares it to stand alone in the history of science, that teacher and his pupils may well regard the above with 'a wonder amounting to marvel'. The issue is a simple one. Aristotle, Pacius, &c. say—We enunciate in the exemplar form of thought: the moderns reply—You do no such thing; or if you do, we have lost the power of seeing the distinction, whence there is no difference.

algebra. A proposition in Euclid assumes *some one* case of satisfaction of hypothesis, and the demonstration lies in the perception of the receiving mind that nothing in the reasoning is adverse to the implied assertion that this *some one* may be *any one*. But this form of exact science is more pointedly exemplar in phraseology than the system of Aristotle: its distributor is *quilibet*, not *omnis*. We have an exemplar ladder in English: its steps are *any one, each one, every one* (*quilibet, unusquisque, omnis*). The third is cèrtainly not *all*; for it is but *one*: but it is more truly the grammatical singular of *all* than either of the others, near as they are.[1] It would be difficult to describe the differences of meaning: that there are differences will appear by our being able to make sentences in which all three shall occur, without power of transposition. For example:—'If you feel able to cope with *any one*, try *each one*, and so you will master *every one*'—the order cannot here be altered. The first, *any one*, has a purer unitarian character than the others: the second and third are more nearly transposible. Without further inquiry, *any one* is the most proper for strict exemplar use, as being applicable in negative predicates.

The form 'any one *X* is any one *Y*' is much wanted in geometry. In my last paper I pointed out that many indirect demonstrations are only refusals of the knowledge of contraposition; others, far less excusable, arise from refusal of the right to convert 'any one *X* is any one *Y*.' When *X* and *Y* are of the same number of instances, the propositions 'Every *X* is *Y*' and 'Every *Y* is *X*' are equivalent: which is most evident, if there be any gradations of evidence, when *X* and *Y* are singular. Consequently, if there be but one *X* and one *Y*, and if the *X* be the *Y*, it need not be proved that the *Y* is the *X*. Suppose that a person, holding himself to have shown that Junius was an individual, and knowing that Philip Francis was an individual, and that Francis was Junius, were to proceed as follows to prove that Junius was Francis:—If not, let Junius be *X*, another than Francis: then because Francis is Junius, and Junius is *X*, it follows that Francis is *X*; that is, Francis is another than Francis, which is absurd. So it is, and so are you too, would be the answer of common sense to the proposer of such a proof: is the principle of difference so much clearer than that of identity, that any one has a right to suppose the sameness of '*X* is *Y*' and '*Y* is *X*' to want corroboration by help of *X* being no other than itself? But this is done in geometry. Not to insist on antiquity, let us take Legendre, a professed amender of Euclid: he knows that through a point can be drawn but one perpendicular to a plane, and one parallel to a line; yet (Book V. Prop. 7) having proved that *the* parallel to a certain line is *the* perpendicular, he

[1] ['Which faith, except *everyone* keep whole and undefiled, without doubt *he* . . .' Everyone does not agree with itself. We cannot say that unless everyone keep, etc., everyone shall perish.]

gives further proof, of the kind[1] above, that the perpendicular is the parallel. And this is supposed to be the climax of rigour; proof *by syllogism* that if the sole *A* be the sole *B*, the sole *B* is the sole *A*. But where would syllogism have been, if this had not been true?

It must not be forgotten, in defence of Euclid, and of geometry without logic, that the above procedure may give *evidence*. When thought has not been analysed, and those who teach are determined that it shall not be analysed, Euclid presents the perfection of the way of doing without. But the time must come when his rich mass of raw thought shall be the material of exercise for logical analysis; when it shall be employed to place the forms of thought in their due order of sequence; when it shall be the ground on which it shall be learnt that the conversion of identity by help of syllogism is reasoning in a circle.

I shall proceed to connect the exemplar form with others: but there are several points which it will first be desirable to notice.

By a *restrictive* proposition I mean one which, of its own nature, imposes some absolute condition, positive or negative, upon the quantity of one or both of its terms, or of one or both of the contraries of its terms. I say *absolute* condition: not *relative*, as in 'All *X* is *Y*', which demands that the *Y*s shall at least equal the *X*s in number. The only such propositions yet met with are 'Some *X* is not some *Y*', which requires that, when identical, *X* and *Y* are not singular: and 'Any *X* is any *Y*' which imposes on *X* and *Y* both singularity and identity. But besides *singular identity*, we shall find ourselves, so soon as we begin to carry every mode of enunciation into every case, obliged to recognize *penultimate identity*, in which the contraries of our two terms are singular and identical; also *singular and penultimate identity*, in which both[2] our

[1] We may laugh at the geometer establishing by syllogism the conversion of identity, but such is the force of habit that the logician may be a geometer without carrying away into logic the illustrations which lie nearest the surface. My opponent, Mr Mansel—out of formal logic—is a mathematician, and applies psychological thought to first principles. In formal logic he argues in favour of 'All *A* is all *B*' being a simple proposition, in opposition (IV. 116) to my assertion that it is complex; and Hamilton quotes his argument with approbation. Mr Mansel says 'I cannot assert "all *A* is *B* and all *B* is *A*" without having thought of *A* and *B* as coextensive, i.e. without having made the judgment "all *A* is all *B*".' Euclid (I. 5), the universe being *triangle*, proves that 'all isosceles is isogonal', and then (I. 6), proves that 'all isogonal is isosceles'; and then, and not till then, does his reader become aware that 'all isoceles is all isogonal.' Both the components are in thought before the compound. Geometry is the richest field of coextensive notions: it swarms with instances of coextension gained by synthesis of counter-inclusions. I admit that a compound cannot be decomposed except by those who have got it to decompose: but, on the other hand, those who have hold of the components may put them together. In the dining-room pudding may be treated as compound of flour and plums: but if before that, in the kitchen, flour and plums had not been treated as components of pudding, the dining-room process would have been Barmecide theory.

[2] I am duly sensible of the figure which a universe of two instances will cut: but

terms and their contraries are singular and identical; and *singular and penultimate contrariety*, in which two singular terms are each identical with the contrary of the other. The laws of thought will produce these forms[1] by the score, as we shall see.

The time is coming when no one of two correlatives will be introduced without as full an introduction of the other. Logic abounds in pairs[2] of which both must enter thought together, but of which one only has been allowed to become prominent in language. Of *converse* relations, and of *contrary* (or *contradictory*) relations, we generally see one embodied, while the other is but as a shadow. *Part* and *whole* give a marked instance: our language is familiar with a whole of several parts, but hardly knows such a phrase as 'a part of several wholes'.

How loosely the subject of correlation is considered may be seen in the case of *assertion* and *denial*. In logical writings these are—I do not say defined, but—treated as alternatives. In the wide world it is generally assumed that all which a person cannot assert he can and will deny: let any one hesitate at affirming, and four out of five of his hearers will report him as having contradicted; and the four will be precisely those who see no use in logic. The books on logic so far favour this inaccuracy that they take no notice of any intermediate[3] between affirmation and

[1] By introducing 'some *X* is not some *Y*', the denial of a restrictive, Hamilton, when non-partitively interpreted, has given a conclusion to two invalid forms (·()) and (()·). It will presently be pointed out that every one of the thirty-two invalid forms gives a conclusion, the denial of a restrictive.

[2] Many common words, when they represent material objects, have meaning of which relation to other objects is an essential part; whence arises some confusion. An *island* is land surrounded by water: is the surrounding water a part of the island? Yes, for no water, no island: no, for if you walk into the water, you quit the island. The ambiguity is easily explained in this case: there is the object named, and the relation by which it is named: the object does not extend into the water, but the droits of the notion do, perhaps as far as those of the crown. Again, what is a box? Is it a space bounded by an envelope of wood, or is it the envelope itself? Not the first, for we certainly move a box from town to town, which no one can do to a bit of space. And yet, when I asked a little girl what would happen if the nails used in fixing a card of address were too long, she answered that they would 'get *into the box*, and spoil the things.' We get over these ambiguities in common life; but they are sore puzzles in philosophy.

[3] 'But negation and affirmation must be contradictorily opposed; as Aristotle has expressed it—"Between affirmation and negation there is no mean" ' (Hamilton, VI. 636*). True enough so far as this, that of affirmation and negation one must be true and the other false; but not true of enunciation. I may not know which is true

I may say on my own behalf, that though I shook it out of the pepperbox, I did not put it in. The laws of thought, which did put it in, are solely responsible for this contempt of established authority. Nor can I even claim the invention of the mode of shaking which brought it out. Hamilton had used the method, and produced, if not singular identity, at least its denial: this was the first of the class of restrictives. I think that here, as elsewhere, it will be found that one instance is but ill understood until more arrive.

negation. The following brief summary will show how easily a sufficient notation of syllogism will enable us to collect all cases of what I shall call *indecision.* I mean *inferential* indecision; in which inability to affirm or deny a conclusion is a necessary consequence of inability to affirm or deny a premise.

When two premises, *A* and *B*, give a conclusion *C*, it follows from the usual law of *opponent* reduction, as I call it, that the *assertion* of either premise, with hesitation at *denial* of the other, is equal hesitation at *denial* of the conclusion. For one premise, with denial of the conclusion, *is* denial of the other premise. Hence any hesitation at affirmation of the contrary of the other premise, is equal hesitation at affirmation of the contrary of the conclusion. That is to say, there are syllogisms in which assertion and non-denial give non-denial; there are others in which assertion and non-assertion give non-assertion: of four possible forms these are the most systematic; each form including the other three.

The syllogisms of undecided denial, in which assertion and non-denial give non-denial, are precisely those in which assertion and assertion give assertion. Thus)))·) gives)·); or *X*))*Y*)·)*Z* gives *X*)·)*Z*. Assert either *X*))*Y* or *Y*)·)*Z*, and refuse to deny the other, and we must refuse to deny *X*)·)*Z*. This gives rise to two forms of the other kind. Assert *X*))*Y*, and refuse to affirm *Y*((*Z*, or assert *Y*)·)*Z*, and refuse to affirm *X*(·(*Y*; in either case we must refuse to affirm *X*((*Z*.

In syllogisms of undecided assertion, in which assertion and non-assertion give non-assertion, the law of validity is as follows. When one proposition only is particular, that particular must be the undecided assertion. Every form is valid in which a universal and a particular occur: but when both are universal, or both particular, the middle term must be *balanced*, that is, of the same quantity in both. The symbol of the conclusion is derived as in the ordinary syllogism, with this exception, that the spicula which we are to obtain from the decided proposition must be inverted. Thus, denoting want of power to assert by ˘ affixed, we may shew that))()˘ gives ()˘,)))·)˘ gives (·)˘, ()˘((gives ()˘, (·)˘(·) gives ((˘,)(˘)·) gives)·(˘, &c. But))))˘ and)·))·)˘ give no conclusion.

For example:—'We can hardly undertake to say that all men are responsible for the *effects* of their actions, independently of motive: for there are men who are really incapable of any consecutive tracing of consequences, a thing we must hesitate to affirm of beings whose responsibility is for consequences'. This form is (·()·)˘, giving))˘; as follows:

(·(Some men are not capable of tracing consequences.

---

and which is false; I may have the courage to avow it, and to follow Hamilton's principle of finding language for all that is in thought.

)·)˘ We will not affirm that there are beings responsible for consequences who are incapable of tracing consequences.
))˘ Therefore we will not affirm that all men are responsible for consequences.

For *will not*, we may read[1] *must not*, *cannot*, *ought not*, *need not*, &c., provided only that we make the conclusion follow the premise; all that is wanted is *non*-affirmation, be the restraining cause what it may. The forms of indecision are precisely those in which affirmation and denial give denial: but the mere presentation of indecision would have been a valuable addition to the logic of the middle ages. Here there was nothing but sharp assertion and denial: and theology, the science in which the word *dogmatism* got its evil sense, was made to look even more positive than she really was. Forbearance is not categorical; and the syllogism of charity is the syllogism of indecision.

The portion of all possible thought within which our concepts are and are[2] to be contained is the *universe*. When that universe is in any

[1] The terms of relation can be applied: and it will be good exercise to learn to see the combinations. If we call 'that which we cannot affirm to be a species' an *unaffirmed* species, we may read as follows. In *X*)) *Y*((˘*Z*, or *X*((˘*Z*, we see that a species of an unaffirmed genus of *Z* is itself an unaffirmed genus of *Z*. In))˘((, giving))˘, we see that an unaffirmed species of a genus is an unaffirmed species. In (()·)˘, giving)·)˘, we see that the genus of an unaffirmed deficient is itself an unaffirmed deficient. In)(˘)·(, giving)·)˘, we see that the unaffirmed coinadequate of an external is an unaffirmed deficient.

[2] Falling asleep while I was considering how to answer this objection—that a definite universe is material—in the most elementary form, I found Logicus, Mathematicus, and Neuter, in the middle of an argument upon the very point. L. In 'All *X* is *Y*' we have a pure form of thought, divested of matter: we see *how* we think, independently of *what*. N. It's not true, though. M. He does not mean that whenever he *says X* he *says Y*. L. By no means: *X* and *Y* are names; and my proposition asserts that whatever I may name *X*, I may name *Y*. N. Why, so may I, or so many any man; but— L. Nay! I meant with truth, according to received meanings: *X* and *Y* are representations of concepts, and the concept *X* is asserted as what ought never to be in thought without the concept *Y*. M. But concepts are *matter* of thought, are they not? L. Yes: but *X* and *Y* are but concepts as concepts, recognized as different concepts by difference of symbol, stated to be thought as included and including by the proposition. M. But if your form contain concepts as concepts, and if concept be matter, surely your form contains matter as matter. N. You won't get out of that, I see, let concept be which it will, Greek or Hebrew; it may be one or the other for me. L. You confirm me entirely in what I was going to say, that the goodness of formal inference may be perceived independently of the meaning of the terms; *concept* is to you as would be *X* or *Y*. M. Then my remark is admitted to be just? L. Certainly: matter as matter is present in every enunciation; but the perception of the formal force of a proposition is independent of the material *differences* between the *different matters* which it contains or might contain. M. That is to say, you treat *concept* as algebra treats *number*? L. Precisely: logic preceded algebra in the use of general terms. M. But algebra never talks about a *pure form* of numbering from which *matter* of number is excluded. With us numbers lie hid in sealed packets, marked outside with letters: but they *are* numbers, whether before or after assignment

way divided into two parts, the name by which the individuals in one part are distinguished from those in the other is a *term*. All terms are names; but some names are not terms. When [*living*] *animal* is the universe, *hairy* is a *term*, a divider of the universe: *mineral* is not a term, but a *vacuous* name; *sentient*, *sensu praeditus*, is not a term, but an *omnitenent* name; *mineral* and *sentient* equally fail to divide the universe, the first by *non-continence*, the second by *non-exclusion*. These contraries, the vacuous and the omnitenent, must stand or fall together. When we speak of *terms* only, we see as clearly that contrary terms have no *term* which is a *common whole* as that they have *no common part*; for nothing less than the universe contains both: no *term* contains both. To what I have said (in former papers) on the exclusion of omnitenent[1] names, I add that, even in the prevailing system, the predicate of a negative must not be of universal extent, for then some of the subject would be shut out of the universe in which it is to be: and that if the predicate of an affirmative be a universal, the proposition asserts no more than is held to be asserted of the subject by its mere presence.

In order fairly to put the exemplar and cumular forms into connexion, it is necessary to examine them with the fullest introduction of both sides of every correlation which makes any appearance at all. Until lately I have never felt assured that they were not two different systems, presenting points of agreement. But before making the investigation, it may be shown that neither one system nor the other can claim to *dictate* the precise forms of enunciation. That claim is made by another system, more fundamental than either; and is made demonstratively.

The logicians have admitted only one idea of relation: the connexion between terms *as terms*: I call the system thus produced by the name of *onymatic*. They make what appears to me a confusion between the term and the objects of thought which it represents: they identify terms which

[1] This universe is sometimes all that exists objectively, and sometimes all that can exist in thought. If there be any one who demands yet more, and wants room for that which cannot be in thought, whether as possible or impossible, he invades the universe of a higher power, and will perhaps square the circle; a problem which a speculator of the last century reduced to the following,—*Construere mundum divinae menti analogum*.

or discovery of their *values*; differences of value exist or may exist, though ignored as to amount so long as only the consequences of difference as difference are in question. L. It is, I dare say, not quite correct to affirm that the form of the proposition is void of matter: we introduce different matters, leaving the differences unsymbolized, except *as* differences. But for this, the form should rather be 'Every is ' than 'Every X is Y'. M. Then what objection do you make, looking at the way in which man thinks his thought and says his say, to the introduction of a sphere or universe, say U, on the same terms as X or Y: as material as they are, as unspecified with reference to *this* or *that* as they are; allowing full right to consider, as one case, what I might perhaps denote by $U = \infty$? What Logicus answered I could not even dream; so I awoke.

are not identical as terms, whenever they can identify the objects represented. Now two terms, as terms, whatever may be the case in etymology, cannot have any relation to each other in logic except what they gain by their relations to things signified or excluded. And the only relation of a term to a thing is that of *applicable* or *not applicable*. And a term, as a term, has its contrary: a term[1] without a contrary is no term. The relations between terms, the only ones admissible because they *are* terms and for no other reason, are those of *applicable to some the same object*, and *not applicable to any the same object*. If *X* and *Y* be two terms, *x* and *y* their contraries, then, making full use of all our correlative alternatives,—namely *X* or *x*, *Y* or *y*, of joint application or not of joint application,—we shall obtain what must be all the forms of enunciation admissible into the system of relations between terms *as terms*. And from our purely onymatic enunciations we may decipher the common forms of identification, or of discrimination, in which the distinction of *term* and *designated object of thought* is afterwards lost to language[2] by the application of *is* and *is not* to the *terms*. The results are as follows:

Onymatic relation between terms	*Proposition*	*Relation*	*Symbol*
X, *Y* have joint application	Some *X*s are *Y*s	*X* [co-]partient of *Y*	*X*( ) *Y*[3]
X, *Y* have no joint application	No *X* is *Y*	*X* [co-]external of *Y*	*X*)·(*Y*
X, *y* have joint application	Some *X*s are not *Y*s	*X* exient of *Y*	*X*(·(*Y*
X, *y* have no joint application	Every *X* is *Y*	*X* species of *Y*	*X*)) *Y*
x, *y* have joint application	Some things neither *X*s nor *Y*s	*X* coinadequate of *Y*	*X*)(*Y*
x, *y* have no joint application	Everything either *X* or *Y*	*X* complement of *Y*	*X*(·) *Y*
x, *Y* have joint application	Some *Y*s are not *X*s	*X* deficient of *Y*	*X*)·) *Y*
x, *Y* have no joint application	Every *Y* is *X*	*X* genus of *Y*	*X*((*Y*

[1] When Aristotle practically dismissed the privative term under the name of *aorist*, he had previously denied it to be the name of anything. My belief is that he was inclined to deny that it is a *term*; he thought that *not-man*, for instance, takes in so much, and shuts out so little, that it is hardly distinctive. If such were his idea, he would have refused, *à fortiori*, the title of *name* to a word which designates the whole universe, both *man* and *not-man*; which shuts out nothing whatever.

As to the aorist character, I should like to know, supposing a name to include just half the universe, which is the aorist, that name, or its privative? This is the most nicely balanced question in logic, just as the following, which even *Notes and Queries* cannot answer, is the most nicely balanced question in geography. If all the northern hemisphere were land, and all the southern hemisphere water, which should we have to say, that the northern hemisphere is an island, or the southern hemisphere a lake? I am Buridan's ass in respect to both questions.

[2] This distinction is usually obliterated in all cases in which the term has *meaning*. But let abstraction be placed before an unpractised mind without warning, and reason may, properly enough, refuse the identification of the *terms* by the substantive verb. A book on logic was presented to a young person of my acquaintance: after some time an account of progress was asked for. 'Oh!' was the answer, 'I read as far as '*Every X is Y*', but I knew *that* wasn't true, so I left off.' Assuredly 'no *X* is *Y*': every child who learns the alphabet is plagued with 650 such negations. But it may chance that every [thing signified by] *X is* [also one of the things signified by] *Y*.

[3] [26 June 1864: *X*, *Y* exists, or *X*, *Y* does not take all. The system equally deducible from: *X*, *Y* not none; *X*, *Y* not all.]

The moment we begin to speak of *part* of a term, we are no longer using the term in the purest onymatic sense: we have made it stand for the collective group to each individual of which it applies as a designation. Before we introduce the word *part*, I observe that, as every relation has both its converse and its contrary, it is advisable in every case to examine both conversion and contradiction. One converse of '*X*, *Y*, have joint application' is 'there are objects to which both of the terms, *X*, *Y*, are applicable'. We have nothing to remark about *this* conversion except that it furnishes the most natural mode of reading the new propositions (·) and)(.

The above table exhausts, I think demonstratively, all purely onymatic relation; that is, all in which the terms are names to be applied or not applied, not names used *for objects* by conventional substitution. There is no notion of quantity in this system: the affirmatives—the assertions of joint application out of which the particulars spring—demand 'one or more' objects to which joint application is made. But this is only tantamount to 'There exists that which . . .' and its quantity is only the notion of *one* which precedes numeration in *Omne quod est, eo quod est, singulare est*. I have not space to develop the objections which the pure onymatic system, as well as other views, furnish against the Hamiltonian doctrine that all enunciation is equation of quantity: but even those who would not admit their force will guess what they are.

Let us now introduce the notion of multitude of objects which, considered as having a common designation, give the idea of *class*, part of the universe separated from the rest. Each class—except when singular—has sub-classes which are its parts, and—except when penultimate—is a sub-class of classes which are its *wholes*. Any collection of objects which is itself only part of the universe may be called a class, as capable of receiving a common designation which is also distinctive. We shall find the eight onymatic forms starting up in the following simple appearance, without the reality, of system: this I say because, as shall be shewn, we have only a systematic selection from a complete system. The remainder, after the selection is made, will contain *restrictive* propositions, or their denials. And this will happen in all attempts to systematize which involve quantity, and which make a full use of all correlatives which are admitted at all. Observe that we do not admit the universe as distinctively a *whole*, because it is a whole of all terms, and not itself a term.

Some class is part of both *X* and *Y*	*X* partient of *Y*	()
No class is part of both *X* and *Y*	*X* external of *Y*	)·(
Some class is whole of both *X* and *Y*	*X* coinadequate of *Y*	)(
No class is whole of both *X* and *Y*	*X* complement of *Y*	(·)
Some class is whole of *X* and part of *Y*	*X* species of *Y*	))
No class is whole of *X* and part of *Y*	*X* exient of *Y*	(·(
Some class is part of *X* and whole of *Y*	*X* genus of *Y*	((
No class is part of *X* and whole of *Y*	*X* deficient of *Y*	)·)

Here we see terms without their contraries; '*some*' with one terminal extreme, '*none*', but without the other, '*every*'; conjunctions, as 'both part of X and part of Y', without the corresponding disjunctions, as in 'either part of X or part of Y'; conjunctions of affirmations only, without the corresponding cases of one affirmation and one negation, or of two negations. If the whole system were formed, every case which does not reproduce one of the above, would either require terms coextensive with the universe, or penultimate, or singular; or would deny propositions requiring such terms. But as this point will presently receive sufficient illustration, I shall proceed no further with it at present: I shall also presently have occasion to go some way into the extension.

Both the preceding systems of enunciation have an exemplar character: in both the forms we see 'there does exist an instance of . . .' denied by 'there does not exist any instance of . . .' I will now proceed to an exemplar system in which part or whole of one term is in affirmation identified with part or whole of the other; the unlimited selection *any*, and the possibly limited selection *some*, either or both, being used in all combinations. The restrictive propositions will be denoted as follows: singular identity by (:=); penultimate identity by (=:); singular and penultimate identity by (:8); singular and penultimate contrariety (°:o). And that singular identity in which one term and the contrary of the other are singular and identical, may be denoted by (·—) or by (—·), as convenient.

Part and Part	*Whole and Whole*
Any part of X is any part of Y :=	Any whole of X is any whole of Y =:
Some part of X is not some part of Y := denied	Some whole of X is not some whole of Y =: denied
Any part of X is some part of Y))	Any whole of X is some whole of Y ((
Some part of X is not any part of Y (·(	Some whole of X is not any whole of Y)·)
Some part of X is any part of Y ((	Some whole of X is any whole of Y))
Any part of X is not some part of Y)·)	Any whole of X is not some whole of Y (·(
Some part of X is some part of Y ()	Some whole of X is some whole of Y)(
Any part of X is not any part of Y)·(	Any whole of X is not any whole of Y (·)
Only (·))(excluded.	Only)·(() excluded.

Part and Whole	*Whole and Part*
Any part of X is any whole of Y 8:	Any whole of X is any part of Y 8:
Some part of X is not some whole of Y 8: denied	Some whole of X is not some part of Y 8: denied
Any part of X is some whole of Y :=	Any whole of X is some part of Y =:
Some part of X is not any whole of Y := denied	Some whole of X is not any part of Y =: denied
Some part of X is any whole of Y =:	Some whole of X is any part of Y :=
Any part of X is not some whole of Y =: denied	Any whole of X is not some part of Y := denied
Some part of X is some whole of Y ((	Some whole of X is some part of Y))
Any part of X is not any whole of Y)·)	Any whole of X is not any part of Y (·(
Only (( )·) included.	Only)) (·(included.

The symmetry and compensation of this table is an instance of what we shall always find whenever correlatives are fairly and equally used. By carrying the whole through Xy, xy, and xY, as well as XY, we produce the main system eight times, and complete the system of restrictives. We may call the system of *part and part* and of *whole and whole* by the name of *balanced*;[1] the others being *unbalanced*. The rules of distinction and identification of forms are as follows:—1. Balanced readings *exclude* from the general system nothing but *any affirmed of any* and *some denied of some*: unbalanced readings *admit* nothing but *some affirmed of some* and *any denied of any*. 2. When exclusion is not thereby made admission, or *vice versa*, 'any part' and 'some whole' are convertible, as also 'any whole' and 'some part'. Thus '*Some part* of *X* is some whole of *Y*' is the same proposition as '*Any whole* of *X* is some whole of *Y*'.

There are two positions which have, alone or together, been expressed or implied in several distinct quarters. First, that the mere completed distribution of the *quantifying words* is the completion of a true logical system, dictated by the laws of thought. Secondly, that the eight forms first obtained by complete distribution of *contrary terms* through the old forms is an arbitrary system, which might have been something else if the framer had so pleased. I contend that these descriptions should be exchanged: that the arbitrary character, but not to so great an extent as asserted of the other, belongs to Hamilton's system before the correction which makes it simply the true extension of the real Aristotelian system; and that the extended cumular system is not in any sense arbitrary. Take what plan we please, carry the correlations fairly out, and we arrive at the eight onymatic forms, together with restrictives and their denials. I shall take two more cases, observing that *restrictives* have appeared in every system except the original, in which nothing appears except *terms* as distinctive *names*, under the relation to objects of *applicable* or *not applicable*.

First, I take the exemplar form in which some or other extent, or any extent—*some class* or *any class*—is identified, conjunctively or disjunctively, with both whole or part of *X* and whole or part of *Y*. This is that portion of extension which I previously announced that I should give. I write down only the apparent affirmatives, leaving the reader to construct the negatives: for brevity, I also write 'some *X*' for 'some one part of *X*', and 'any *X*' for 'any one part of *X*'. And first of conjunctive comparisons.

Any class is both any *X* and any *Y*	Universe of one individual. No terms
Some class is both any *X* and any *Y*	*X* and *Y* singular and identical
Any class is both any *X* and some *Y*	Universe of one individual. No terms
Some class is both any *X* and some *Y*	*X* species of *Y*.))
Any class is both some *X* and some *Y*	*X* and *Y* universal. No terms
Some class is both some *X* and some *Y*	*X* partient of *Y*. ()
Any class is both some *X* and any *Y*	Universe of one individual. No terms
Some class is both some *X* and any *Y*	*X* genus of *Y*. ((

[1] These useful terms, suggested by Hamilton, may be used in reference to any pair of correlatives.

Among these assertions and their denials we have the Aristotelian forms complete: and our assertions give the affirmatives, our denials the negatives. The disjunctive forms may now follow: *either* meaning *either or both*, the true[1] contrary of *neither*. For '*both*' and '*and*' substitute '*either*' and '*or*': none[2] but restrictives will be found. In going through all the varieties of application of *part* and *whole*, we come upon the *complement*, yet unseen, among the correlative affirmations of exclusion: as in 'Any class is either not any whole of *X* or not any whole of *Y*'. But the view opens as we proceed. *Part* and *whole* are but synonyms of *species* and *genus*: at our present point we may ask what would result if we were to examine all the cases of 'Any [or some] class is both—of *X* and—of *Y*' when either blank may be filled up with any of the eight names of relation? I certainly should not have asked this question if the answer had required me to exhibit to the reader such a shaking of the pepperbox as would seem necessary. The truth is that I have all but answered the question in previous writings, as shall presently appear.

I positively assert that the first of the preceding views[3] contains demonstration that the relations between terms, derived from their relations to objects, must be the eight forms, and no others. The postulates are that by a *term* we mean a *distinguishing* mark, the sign of some object or objects, not the sign of others; and that to any collection of objects which is not the whole universe, we have a right to assign a term. I contend, as in my last paper, for the right and duty of logic to treat of other relations between terms, derived from the relations of objects to one another: but my present concern is with onymatic relations only. I proceed to a more systematic connexion of the eight forms than I have yet given.

Each universal is in two ways of a universal character, one of an *active* meaning, the other of a *passive*. Thus,

X))*Y*	*X* wholly included in and wholly incompletive of *Y*
X((*Y*	*X* wholly including and wholly uncompleted by *Y*
X)·(*Y*	*X* wholly excluding and wholly excluded from *Y*
X(·)*Y*	*X* wholly completive of and wholly completed by *Y*

Each particular has also two characters: and by each character is inferentially attached to a universal. Thus *X*()*Y* affirms that *X* is partially or wholly included in *Y*, and that *X* partially or wholly includes *Y*:

[1] 'Shall I bring both?—No need, either will do.' Here the *either* is *either or both*.

[2] If *individual* were used instead of *class*, the restriction would be removed from some propositions. Thus 'any class is either some *X* or some *Y*' enunciates a universe of two individuals, one *X* and one *Y*: but 'any individual is either some *X* or some *Y*' means *X*(·)*Y*, without restriction.

[3] The first idea of this mode of derivation is in my *Formal Logic* (p. 105): but I did not then see either the import or the importance of what was there given.

and $X(\cdot(Y$ affirms that X is partially or wholly excluded from Y, and is partially or wholly completive of Y.

Again, four of the relations may be called *greater*, and four *less*. A greater relation is one which cannot be changed into its contrary without subtraction: a lesser relation is one which cannot be changed into its contrary without addition. The greater relations are ((, (·), (·(, (), being all of which the minor term is particular: the lesser relations are)),)·(,)·),)(, being all of which the minor term is universal. The Aristotelian collection includes the lesser universals and the greater particulars.

Each universal has a *contranominal*, with which it may coexist; and two *extreme*[1] *contraries* or *extreme contradictories*. Thus $X))Y$ has the contranominal $X((Y = x))y$ and the extreme contraries $X)\cdot(Y$ and $X(\cdot)Y$.

Hence we see the connexion of each universal with two inferred particulars. Each partial proposition asserts the existence of an indefinite share of the extreme extent by which the universal is *toto orbe divisum* from one of its extreme contraries. Thus 'wholly included in' which is also 'wholly incompletive of', or)), necessarily contains 'partially included in' and 'partially incompletive of', () and)(, which are indefinite contraries (commonly called *contradictories*) of)·(and (·), of each which)) is an extreme contradiction. The connexion of the contranominals, through their extreme contraries and the particulars, is illustrated in the adjacent table (*W*., wholly; *P*., partially). The lines may also be read backwards, the spicular symbols being still read forwards.

)).............(·(<   )·(>   )·)............((
W. included in — *P*. excluded from — *W*. excluded from = *W*. excluding — *P*. excluding — *W*. including

((.............)·)   <   (·)   >   (·(............))
W. uncompleted by — *P*. completed by — *W*. completed by = *W*. completive of — *P*. completive of — *W*. incompletive of

))   >   ()................)·(..................()   <   ((
W. included in — *P*. included in — *W*. excluded from = *W*. excluding — *P*. including — *W*. including

((>   )(................(·)..................)(<   ))
W. uncompleted by — *P*. uncompleted by — *W*. completed by = *W*. completive of — *P*. incompletive of — *W*. incompletive of

)·(............()   <   ))   >   )(............(·)
W. excluded from — *P*. included in — *W*. included in = *W*. incompletive of — *P*. incompletive of — *W*. completive of

(·)............)(<   ((>   ()............)·(
W completed by — *P*. uncompleted by — *W*. uncompleted by = *W*. including — *P*. including — *W*. excluding

)·(>   (·(................))..................(·(<   (·)
W. excluded from — *P*. excluded from — *W*. included in = *W*. incompletive of — *P*. completive of — *W*. completive of

(·)   >   )·)................((..................)·)   <   )·(
W. completed by — *P*. completed by — *W*. uncompleted by = *W*. including — *P*. excluding — *W*. excluding

[1] I hold by the amalgamation of the words *contradictory* and *contrary*, in spite of the disapprobation of some who have approved various points of my system. And this I do first, because the common language makes synonyms of the two: he who

In this table contradiction is denoted by a dotted line; and ascent or descent by the algebraic signs for *less* and *greater*.

Common language proceeds as if the part were more worthy than the whole, as a notion on which to base enunciation. Accordingly, we are familiar with *inclusion*, *exclusion*, and *partience* of both: but *completion*[1] and *coinadequacy* are strange and heretical. I have somewhere read of a speculator who maintained that every world has, in some other part of space, a counterpart world of defects equal and opposite to its own. If his system be true—all questions about other stars or planets are quite open—there is somewhere a planet in which thought fixes upon *whole* in preference to *part*; in which the concept of *penultimacy* is more familiar than that of *singularity*; in which the demonstrative pronoun is not *this*, but some word of the force of *all else*; and in which, at this moment, some antimathematical logician—for the mathematical tendency is in excess in the logic of *our* counterpart—endeavours to force attention to *exclusion* and *partience* upon a community which is too exclusively familiar with *completion* and *coinadequacy*. I have amused myself with constructing enunciations and syllogisms as they are in the exemplar-counterpart forms of our counterpart planet; from which planet I myself may have come, if there be any truth in the doctrine of transmigration. If any of those who are too firmly rooted in our common notions will do the same, they will derive the same sort of benefit which your arithmeticians—who all think that 10 *must* be *ten*—

[1] Mr Spalding (VIII. 166) says that all the *eight* forms are set forth by Boethius. I cannot find them. Boethius does indeed apply the *four* to privatives, and so obtains equivalents of the eight onymatic forms: but I cannot detect him evolving relations *between the given terms* by help of their privatives. But he is rather prolix; and perhaps some reader may favour me with a definite reference to something which will support Mr Spalding's assertion. If not, that assertion is one of a very numerous class, of the bad consequence of which no one can form an idea who is not familiar with the history of discovery. Two things are affirmed to be the same because the passage from one to the other is easy in the mind of the affirmant, after study of both: they are *virtually* the same, one *amounts* to the other, &c. This was Solomon's practice, or he never would have said that there is nothing new under the sun. I once had a private discussion of several long letters which might have been spared if my correspondent had said at first what he said at last, that certain two methods were the same *to all intents and purposes*: he began by saying they were *the same*; which is quite a different thing.

---

contradicts maintains the contrary. And this even from the mouths of persons versed in technical logic. Dr Clarke said of Collier the idealist 'he can neither prove his point himself, nor can the *contrary* be proved against him.' Secondly, the etymology does not support the distinction. Thirdly, the true opposition is that of any contradiction and the extreme or total contradiction. 'All are'; contradiction, some (perhaps all) are not; extreme contradiction, *none are*. [Particular *and* universal contradiction.] Fourthly, the existing terms hide the distinction, and give a notion which makes a logician say, 'so far from being the contradictory, it is not *even* the contrary.'

derive from constructing systems on another radix. We want a better balance of logical correlatives. The original tendencies of language, partial, one-sided, stopping at just enough, have tied some of our mental muscles until they only act by special volition and a good deal of it. And we appeal to the defect in proof of the necessary character of the ligatures; to the incapacity of the slave in proof of the inexpediency of emancipation. As to untying a ligature, that would be extralogical and *material*.

Every *universe of objects* has its *universe of relations*, to which I now come. At the outset I am met by a difficulty which is shared by writers on perspective, and no way of escape is better than theirs. They cannot put solid objects into a book: so they draw a perspective figure to be the object, and then draw a tablet, a painter, and a collection of rays projecting the object on the tablet. Imitating this plan, let the symbols 1, 2, 3, 4, &c. be attached to the objects of the universe as, in the strictest sense, *proper names*: it being understood that these names imply no quality, and are assigned to the objects at hazard. Objects are thus distinguished by their *ἀριθμοί*, the word being used in the true Greek sense described in my last paper. What are commonly called *proper* names are frequently nothing but *singular* names, derived from notions of class; Horatius Flaccus shews both genus—or at least *gens*—and difference.

We have a right to treat *any* collection of objects, from one inclusive upwards, as a class; to be distinguished from the contrary class, containing all other objects, by a *mark*. I am not afraid, at this time, of being met by the old dictum that the differentia of a species[1] must be

[1] This is a question on which heretics have differed. Cicero affirmed *Trojan* and *Theban* to be species of man. Ludovicus Vives, heretic, and Johannes Rivius, orthodox, declare Cicero wrong, on the ground that the species must have an *essential* difference. Marius Nizolius, a worse heretic, describes them as 'quorum uterque audet reprehendere Ciceronem', forgetting that Aristotle, on various points, is described by himself through four long books (*De veris principiis et vera ratione philosophandi, contra Pseudo-philosophos*, 1553), as Philosophaster and Pseudo-philosophus. I give his distinction of species, husk and all:—'Quis te docuit, O inepte grammaticule, hominem, etiam si extra ordinem substantiae non egrediamur, non posse esse verum genus Thebani et Trojani . . . Quare tu quoque disce verum esse id quod dicit Cicero, Trojanum et Thebanum esse veras hominis species, si non essentiales at certe accidentales, et cognosce ea, quae tu ex sterquilinio dialecticorum hauriens contra Ciceronem nugaris, nihil aliud esse nisi meras insanias.'

Nizolius, great as the author of the *Thesaurus Ciceronianus*,—we have seen how sensitive he was on Cicero—is in logic a small handler of a large theme; and very scurrilous withal. G. L. (whom Tiraboschi and others assert to be Leibnitz, whose initials were G. G. L.) republished the *De veris Principiis* in 1674, with a preface. But G. L. according to the Bodleian catalogue, altered the title into 'Antibarbarus philosophicus; sive philosophia scholasticorum impugnata': in other words, Leibnitz (?) saw that Nizolius was more useful against the schoolmen than in favour of truth. Tiraboschi leaves every one to decide for himself whether he will judge by the

of the essence: but a little of the spirit of this demand may yet be left. Some may be disposed to think that *selections* exist—they will not say *classes*—the individuals of which really have no common difference, nothing which distinguishes them, and them alone, from all other things. I challenge such a selection. While awaiting an answer I imagine an acceptor; and I think I do nearly as well for him as he could do for himself, if I suppose him to select from the universe 'material object, past or present', as a lot which he defies me to difference from all other things, the following miscellany:—all men who have killed their brothers, the hundred largest ink-stands that ever were made, and Aristotle's dinner on his twenty-first birthday. What is the class-mark of these objects? I answer that to them alone belongs the epithet—'Selected by the fancy of (*here insert name and date*) in unsuccessful impeachment of the unlimited right of logical division'. I am willing to go further than Nizolius, and to divide species into essential, accidental, and perverse; affirming that the difference is extralogical. The more absurd such an instance as mine, the better does it make the claim asserted; Hamilton implied the like when he presented Newton and Leibnitz with their wigs awry.

If the number of objects in the universe be *n*, the number of possible collections which can be the selections denoted by *terms* is 2^n-2, the number of pairs of collections is $(2^{n-1}-1)(2^n-3)$ and the whole *universe of relations*, true and false, has $8(2^{n-1}-1)(2^n-3)$ instances, equally divided between true and false. Let the relations *species*, *exient*, &c. be denoted by the symbols)), (·(&c.: thus))*X* and *X*((both denote 'species of *X*'. When a symbol of relation is placed between two others, let it be read in the singular exemplar method; and let the two extremes be read *from* the middle term. Thus (((·))·(or *X*(((·))·(*Y* means to assert that 'Any one class is either species of *X* or external of *Y*': and *X*))))))*Y* means 'Any one genus of *X* is some one species of *Y*'. Of such possible readings there are 8.8.8, or 512, of which half are restrictives, and half are not.

I may be asked whether such methods of stating propositions are actually in use? I answer yes, sometimes in grave writing, and more often in rhetorical flourish, a kind of appeal to assent in which a little study of the characters of fallacy is not obviously needless. A certain sort of speaker wants to say that *all* Englishmen are lovers of liberty:

approbation of Leibnitz, or the disparagement of a modern writer, who expresses great surprise that Leibnitz should have published an edition. I judge by the book itself, which appears to me that of an emancipated slave, who made a new master of his liberty. Nizolius, arguing against what he supposes to be the scholastic doctrine, namely, that a genus contains only things present, strengthens the opposite opinion by the authority (*idem quoque confirmatur ab auctoritate*) of Julius Pollux, who, in what he says περὶ γένους, includes both ancestors and posterity.

for your stump-orator deals in nothing but universals, be the name of his stump what it may; a proceeding forced upon him by the lovers of his style, who consider a man of rules with exceptions as an equivocator and a loophole-monger. He declaims as follows:—'Show me any number of men, and I will say with confidence either that they will with one accord raise their voices for liberty, or that there are aliens among them.' This figure of speech is *X*((*Z* expressed as *X*(((·) (·(*Z*, where *X* is 'lover of liberty' and *Z* is 'Englishman'.

Every proposition is a *blank syllogism*: that is, every true proposition is a conclusion which has *middle extents*, whether the *terms* exist for them or not. Thus *X*)) *Y* is *X*))0)) *Y*, where for 0 may be written any genus of *X* which is also species of *Y*. It is also *X*)·(0(·) *Y*, where for 0 may be written the contrary of any such intermediate class. Even the useless extreme *X*))*X* may be written *X*))*X*))*X*. And the *blank* syllogism and the conclusion are convertible: thus *X*)) *Y* is *X*))0)) *Y*, and *X*))0)) *Y* is *X*)) *Y*. When the concrete middle term is inserted, this convertibility ceases: thus *X*)) *Y* is deducible from *X*))*A*)) *Y*, but not *X*))*A*)) *Y* from *X*)) *Y*. The essential of syllogism is the *existence* of the middle term, not its being this or that. The conclusion, as I have observed in a former paper, renounces all knowledge of the middle except its existence. That 'all man is mortal' is established by every one who shall prove that a genus of a man is a species of mortal: the physiologist may have to think of the middle term 'animal', the theologian of the middle term 'sinner'; but to both it is enough for the conclusion that a middle term exists. This explicit reduction of the middle term to mere existence is, I think, essential to the *formal* consideration of the syllogism.

In such a proposition as)))·((·(, the spiculae being, 12, 34, 56, let 12, 56, be *primary* relations, 34 the *secondary* relation, relation of the second order, or relation of relations. Let the spiculae 3, 4, be *means*; 2, 5, *adjacents*; 1, 6, *extremes*. Take notice that the secondary relation is the common identification, or its denial: thus 12))56 is not '21 *X* species of 56 *Y*', but 'Any 21 *X* *is* one 56 *Y*, some 56 *Y*'.

Of 512 secondary propositions, 256 are valid representations of unrestricted onymatic forms: the remaining 256 are either assertions or denials of restrictives. The unrestricted forms may[1] be obtained as follows: 32 of them are the forms of syllogism, with blank middle terms, and the secondary (); 32 more are the contradictions which deny that a middle term can be found, with the secondary)·(. Three other sets of 64 each are found by varying the readings of the first 64 in the same manner as *X*() *Y* and *X*)·(*Y* are varied by use of *x* and *y*

[1] I did not obtain them so easily, for I worked through the 512 cases separately and independently, before I saw what, when seen, was also seen to be what ought to have been seen. The reader may thus be made more sure of the completeness of my investigation.

for *X* and *Y*. Thus, the proposition *X*((Z being a necessary consequence of *X*(·) *Y*)·(Z is an equivalent of *X*(·) 0)·(Z, and of *X*(·) ())·(Z. That is, '*X* genus of Z' is an equivalent of 'Some complement of *X* is some external of Z'. The denial is 'Any complement of *X* is not any external of Z', *X*(·))·( )·(Z, which is denial of *X*((Z, or an equivalent of *X*)·)Z, or '*X* deficient of Z'. The eight varieties, four of each proposition, are as follows, relaxing the exemplar form into ordinary reading.

X(·) ())·(Z Some complement of *X* is external of Z
X(·) (·(()Z Some complement of *X* is not partient of Z
X)( )(()Z Some class is neither coinadequate of *X* nor partient of Z
X)( )·))·(Z Some external of Z is not coinadequate of *X*.

Here are four secondary ways of saying '*X* is genus of Z'. Again,

X(·))·( )·(Z No complement of *X* is external of Z
X(·))) ()Z Every complement of *X* is partient of Z
X)((·) ()Z Every class is either coinadequate of *X* or partient oı Z
X)((( )·(Z Every external of Z is coinadequate of *X*.

Here are four secondary ways of saying '*X* is deficient of Z'.

We can now give meaning to the 32 compositions which fail to show valid conclusion: they are all denials of restrictives. For instance *X*(·(*Y*))Z gives no conclusion: and this is *X*(·(()))Z. There is a term, says the proposition, which is both deficient of *X* and species of Z. Of course there is, will be the first reply; must *every* species of Z fill up *X*? Certainly not, unless every individual of Z be *all X*; that is, unless Z and *X* be singular and identical. Consequently, *X*(·(*Y*))Z has a conclusion; it denies 'Any *X* is any Z'; and we have one of Hamilton's syllogisms, when the non-partitive 'some' is used. The secondary form *X*(·( )·( ))Z affirms that no deficient of *X* is a species of Z, and affirms 'any *X* is any Z', or denies that 'Some *X* is not some Z'.

Again, *X*(·(())·)Z expresses that some class is deficient both of *X* and Z. To deny it is to say that *every* class is genus either of *X* or of Z, which gives only two individuals to the universe, one *X* and one Z.

The law which regulates these cases is very easily given. First, when the invalid form is either a universal and a particular, or two particulars of unbalanced middle terms, as))(),)·()·), or)·))·), ())(. Let there be two singular and identical terms, of course with penultimate and identical contraries. When *X* is particular, let it be one of the singular terms; when *X* is universal, let it be one of the contraries: and the same for Z. The proposition which the (hitherto) invalid form denies is then constructed. Thus, writing down the instances of the universe, with their designations, we have four cases, under which are written all the combinations which deny them.

[(·)] *X x x x x*...	[))] *x X X X X*...	])·(] *x X X X X*...	[((] *X x x x x*...
Z z z z z...	*Z z z z z*...	*z Z Z Z Z*...	*z Z Z Z Z*...
(()·) (·)() (·()) ()(·) ())·) (·(() deny :===	))())·()·))()))·)(·))(())·))·) deny —·	))(·( )·()( )·)(( )()·( )((·( )·))(deny =:	(()((·)(·(()(((·()·(())((·((·(deny ·—

Thus *X*))()*Z*, or 'a middle term is both genus of *X* and partient of *Z*' denies that *Z* is singular and *X* its contrary: and the same of five others,)·()·) &c. Secondly, when the invalid form has two particulars with balanced middle terms, let terms and contraries be both singular; the cases in which *X* and *Z* have balanced quantities deny that *X* and *Z* are contraries, the cases in which *X* and *Z* have unbalanced quantities deny that *X* and *Z* are identical. Thus

:: or $\frac{X\,x}{z\,Z}$ is denied by ()(),)()(, (·()·),)·)(·([())(deny —· —· in form of :: ::]

:: or $\frac{X\,x}{Z\,z}$ is denied by ()(·(,)()·), (·()(,)·)(). [(·()·) deny := =: in form of :: ::][1]

To produce the forms which *affirm* the restrictives, we must have recourse to the secondary)·(.

I return to the cases which are without restriction. There are three balances, which I shall call primary, secondary, and tertiary. The primary balance is even when the primary relations are both universal or both particular; uneven in other cases. The secondary balance is even when the spiculae of the secondary relation are both universal or both particular; uneven in other cases. The tertiary balance is even when the primary relations are both Aristotelian,[2] or both otherwise; uneven in other cases.

1. When the *primary* and *secondary* balances are of the *same* name, both even or both uneven, the primaries *agree* with their adjacent means or *differ* from them, according as the *secondary* is *universal* or *particular*. Thus (( )) () is admissible; both balances uneven, universal secondary, primaries of the same name as their mean adjacent spiculae. If *U* and *P* denote *universal* and *particular* propositions, *u* and *p* similar *spiculae*, so that, for instance, *uUp* denotes a universal proposition of universal and particular spiculae, as)), then the legitimate combinations in which the primary and secondary balances are of the same name are *U, uUu, U*; *P, pUp, P*: *U, uUp, P*; *P, pUu, U*; *P, uPu, P*; *U, pPp, U*; *P, uPp, U*; *U, pPu, P*.

[1] [Additions dated 5 July 1864.—Ed.]

[2] These are species, exient, external, partient;)), (·(,)·(, (); lesser universal or greater particular; the first spicula of the same name as the proposition.

2. When the *primary* and *secondary* balances are of *different* names, the *tertiary* balance must be *even.*

3. To determine the *product*, or resulting simple relation, take the extreme spiculae, invert each one which has a universal mean nearest to it, and make the result negative when the data show one or three negatives.

4. Given a product, to determine all the cases of which it is the product. Choose a secondary; treat the given spiculae as in the last rule; distribute signs of negation so as to have none, two or four, in all (product included); and supply adjacents in any manner which will satisfy the rules.[1]

For example () (·) () is valid; universal secondary, primary and secondary balances both even, and particular primaries with particular mean spiculae; and (·) results. That is '*X* complement of *Y*' means that 'Any term is either partient of *X* or of *Y*'. Again, (·) (·( )·) is valid: secondary relation particular, primary and secondary balances both uneven, universal and particular primaries with particular and universal mean spiculae; the result is (·(. Also, (·) (·(((is valid, for the primary and secondary balances are of different characters, and the tertiary balance is even, neither primary being Aristotelian; and the same of (((·( )·(in which both primaries are Aristotelian. It must be remembered that the primaries are read *from* the secondary spiculae. Thus the last is 'some *species* of *X* is not any external of *Y*'.

These rules are not complicated, considered as selecting 256 out of 512, and deciding on their results. But any one acquainted with the canons of onymatic syllogism will find it easier to change the secondary into)·(or (), according as it is universal or particular, and then to try the primaries by the rules of syllogism. For instance (((·((). If we contravert the right-hand mean spicula and primary, we have ((())·(: and *X*((*Y*)·(*Z* is a pair of premises with the valid conclusion *X*(·(*Z*.

If space would permit, much might be said on the relations of the forms of syllogism in which the secondaries are () and)·(. The first must be used in practice, almost exclusively; namely, the proof of the existence of a middle term by its actual production. The second is well known in thought, though its method of procedure, the denial of the

[1] [23 December 1864. Secondaries

()	)·(		
UU	$\dot{U}P$	$\dot{P}U$	
)(	(·)		
PP	$\dot{P}U$	$\dot{U}P$	
)·)		((	
PU	$\dot{P}\dot{P}$	$\dot{U}\dot{U}$	
(·(	))		. = unbalanced
UP	$\dot{U}\dot{U}$	$\dot{P}\dot{P}$	.. = balanced]

existence of any middle term whatsoever, can but seldom be a direct means of establishing a conclusion. Thus *X*)·(*Z*, presented as *X*(()·())*Z*, is a familiar type of thought: instead of 'no *X* is *Z*', we see that '*X* and *Z* have no species in common'. The assumption that inference must proceed upon a comparison of two terms with a third is shown to be only an incident of that bisection of system which begins in the refusal of privative terms. That there is *no* middle term which will do might be made the regulator of our forms of inference. Thus *Barbara*, or)))))), as commonly presented, is equally represented by (( )·( )·(, which affirms that no species of the minor term is an external of the major. And this last is but a strengthened form of ())·( )·(, which affirms that no partient of the minor is an external of the major.

When the middle term is only an *intermediary*, *some* term wholly indefinite, or *any term*, a notation which, for good reasons, I had dropped, may be amended and re-established. We may say)))) =)), (((·) (·(= ((, &c. Such notation as *X*))*Y* + *Y*))*Z* = *X*))*Z* is faulty in two[1] respects. First, the sign = is applied to an inconvertible relation:

[1] Mr Mansel (IV. 119) takes the following objection:—'As little [as of Euler's geometrical syllogism-figures] do we approve of the algebraical method adopted by Mr De Morgan, in which the premises of a syllogism are connected by a *plus*, and their relation to the conclusion expressed by the sign of equality, a method too redolent of the computation-theory noticed above, [either Hobbes or the arithmetically definite syllogism], and tending to confound the intuitive judgments of Arithmetic with the discursive inferences of logic. The algebraical equation proper does not represent a syllogism, but a proposition which, like any other, may form part of a logical reasoning, but cannot with any propriety represent the whole.' To this I say first, that + and = are not signs peculiar either to arithmetic or to algebra: +, −, and = are *in genere* aggregative, disaggregative, and equivalential. A person who has no counting, and as yet no symbols, might be introduced at once to the symbolic aggregation of concrete lengths, which is seen in

—— + ———— = ——————.

Secondly, a syllogism *is* a proposition; for it affirms that a certain proposition is the necessary consequence of certain others. An affirmation is not the less an affirmation because it affirms about other affirmations. Mr Mansel will not deny that the following *propositions* are premises giving a valid conclusion. *Minor:* 'Every case in which all *X* is *Y* and all *Y* is *Z* is a case in which all *X* is *Z*'. *Major:* 'Every case in which all *X* is *Z* is a case in which all not-*Z* is not-*X*'; therefore &c. What is the first of these *propositions* but a *syllogism*?

In the *Athenaeum* Journal (10 and 24 November 1860) appeared reviews of Hamilton's *Lectures*, which Mr Mansel at once attributed to me: in which he was correct, so far as any one can be correct in giving to a contributor an article which, appearing under editorial responsibility, passes through editorial hands before it is made public. Certain mathematical errors were pointed out, which it appeared were mostly copied from others, though some of them were read to the class for twenty years together. Such as that Euclid (I. 1) *shows* that his three lines *constitute* a triangle, and that the circles meet; such as mention of two lines which divaricate at an acute angle, 'like a pyramid'; such as an inch equal to a foot, because both have an infinity of parts, and one infinity is not larger than another, set down as a 'contradiction proving the psychological theory of the conditioned'! The first of these was in a Lecture, with

for, though $X))Y + Y))Z$ gives $X))Z$, $X))Z$ does not give $X))Y + Y))Z$, but only $X))? + ?))Z$, where both queries may be answered by the same term, when that term is known. Secondly, the premises are *compounded*, not *aggregated*. For both these errors I was indebted to the suggestion of the school of logicians, who not only aggregate concepts into concepts, but who sometimes go as far as animal + rational = man.

I now assert that every onymatic syllogism can be announced in eight forms: and each conclusion has 24 ways in which it can be announced with a secondary of its own quantity; and 8 ways with a secondary of the other quantity. I write down all the ways of announcing the conclusions)) and ().

Conclusion))

(())())·)(()·((()·()·( )·)(·)()	))())) (·()((·( ))(·((·((·()·)))
(·))))·))(((((·))·((( )((·))·)	)·(()(·) ()))()( )·((·()(())·)(·)
())))())·((()·(()))·()·( )·((·)()	
(·()))·)))(((((·()·((( ))(·))·)	
(())))))·)(((·((()·((·( )·)(·)))	
(·)))(·))((()((·))·()( )((·)(·)	

other things resembling it; the second and third were private notes. Mr Mansel replied (1 and 8 December 1860), resting mainly on the fact that Hamilton had taken the errors from others. He also asks why Hamilton is to 'be tied down to an exactness in the use of mathematical illustrations which professed mathematicians have not held themselves bound to observe.' His instance is as follows:—'I find in Prof. De Morgan's "Formal Logic" (p. 131) a syllogism in *Barbara*, expressed in the form $Y)Z + X)Y = X)Z$; an expression with which I shall not quarrel, as an algebraical metaphor, so to speak, though I fancy that the author himself will hardly maintain that the relation between the premises and the conclusion of a syllogism is, literally, identical with that between the two sides of an equation.' To which I reply that, so soon as I quarrel with the *literal* application of a symbolic relation, I quarrel with the *metaphor* too. I rejected both in my third paper, for the reasons in the text. When I became master of the distinction between *aggregation* and *composition*, which the logicians do not admit, I saw that there is generic agreement, with specific differences, between the connexion of two premises in a syllogism, and the operation symbolized in $A \times B$ (not $A + B$). Accordingly, depriving $\times$ of the specific character, and retaining only the generic, I now affirm the convertibility of (·) ×)·) and (), and I say (·) ×)·) = (), or, using the usual abbreviation, (·))·) = ().

With regard to the question why a person ignorant of mathematics is to be tied down to a correctness of illustration which the proficient does not observe, the answer is easy: the ignorant man is pretty sure to darken counsel, the proficient will probably illustrate the matter in hand, even though his parallel be inaccurate with respect to what is not in hand. Let any one look at the manner in which Sir W. *Rowan* Hamilton produced systematic truth out of the true side of my symbol, as shewn in my third paper; and then let him take the resemblance between an *acute angle* and a *pyramid*, and see what he can make of that: he will come out with some notion why Sir William Hamilton is to be tied down much tighter than Sir William Rowan Hamilton.

Conclusion ()

((())))·))((·(((·((·( )·))·)))	))))() (·((()·( )))·()·((·((·)()
(·)()(·))()()((·)(·()( )()·)(·)	)·()))·) ().(((( )·()·(((()(·))·)
()())))·() ((·(()(·((·( )·()·)))	
(·(()(·))))()((·((·()( )))·)(·)	
((()())·))()·(((·()·( )·))·)()	
(·())·))()((((·)(·((( )()·)))·)	

The common syllogism has a *conjunctive* relation of premises: as in)) ())) which asserts terms—generally proved by assigning one—which are both genus of the minor and species of the major; or as in)·(() (·), i.e. there are terms which are both external of the minor and complement of the major. But there are *disjunctive* relations of premises: as)·((·) (), any term is either external of the minor or partient of the major. When the secondary is thus disjunctive, the canon of validity is simply inverted as to universal and particular, and the canon of inference as to affirmative and negative. Thus (·((·))·) gives inference, because both premises *are* particular; and the conclusion is negative, (·): if *every* term be deficient, either of the major or the minor, these last are complements. Similar observations may be made on the secondary)(. The eight methods offer a crowd of analogies which I shall not describe. Taking () for a standard secondary, the universal syllogisms comprise all the cases in which the primary and secondary balances are of the same character, and the tertiary balance uneven: when this last becomes even, we have the strengthened syllogisms. In the particular syllogisms, there is even tertiary balance. The fourth case, uneven tertiary balance accompanied by difference of character in the other two, does not give any unrestricted forms.

I now make a selection from the 512 identifications, in illustration of the danger of asserting completeness without a very cautious examination. No one will deny, whatever he may think of the system, that it *is a system*, and that no portion of it could be selected as complete in itself with reference to all correlatives employed. Should any one object, his objection must affirm that the system is not yet complete, and that some higher power of 2 than 512 is the true number of cases. I take only one out of 32, as follows:—

X(( ))))*Y* = *X*))*Y* Any part of *X* is some part of *Y*

X)) ((((*Y* = *X*))*Y* Some whole of *X* is any whole of *Y*

X(((·( ))*Y* = *X*(·(*Y* Some part of *X* is not any part of *Y*

X)))·) ((*Y* = *X*(·(*Y* Any whole of *X* is not some whole of *Y*

X(((( ))*Y* = *X*((*Y* Some part of *X* is any part of *Y*

X)))) ((*Y* = *X*((*Y* Any whole of *X* is some whole of *Y*

X(( )·)))*Y* = *X*)·)*Y* Any part of *X* is not some part of *Y*

X)) (·(((*Y* = *X*)·)*Y* Some whole of *X* is not any whole of *Y*

X(( )·( )) Y = X)·(Y Any part of X is not any part of Y
X)) (·) ((Y = ∴ Every class is either some whole of X or of Y
X((())) Y = X() Y Some part of X is some part of Y
X)))(((Y denies ∴ Some class is neither whole of X nor of Y
X(((·))) Y = ∴ Every class is either some part of X or of Y
X)))·(((Y = X(·) Y Any whole of X is not any whole of Y
X(( )( )) Y denies ∴ Some class is neither part of X nor of Y
X)) (( )) Y = X)(Y Some whole of X is some whole of Y[1]

This table selects all the cases in which the primaries are either genus and genus, or species and species; genus and species are called whole and part. The readings by *part and part* form a system analogous to that of Hamilton, and differing only from it in this, that the restrictive affirmed and denied is singular and penultimate contrariety, instead of singular identity. Both systems are only portions of larger wholes; and in both, other sections balance the irregularities of the sections here under review. And both give this lesson, that no system is complete until all its circumstances exhibit complete balance; any appearance of irregularity in one of the aliquot parts being thrown into symmetry by an inverted irregularity in another part.

Taking the last table as a whole, and dismissing the restrictives to their proper sphere, we see that each unbalanced proposition has a reading of either kind; while each balanced proposition has only one reading. And we see—*again*, having seen the same in the full exemplar system,—that)X or X(is '*some* part' or '*any* whole'; while X) or (X is '*any* part' or '*some* whole'.

In the preceding method the process of thought is absolute identification; or its denial: thus X(( )))) Y affirms of any species of X that it is strictly identical, coextensive with, some species of Y. There is another set, of 512 cases, in which the comparison is made by assertion or denial of one class being the precise external complement, or contrary, of another: one instance would be 'Any species of X is the contrary of some species of Y'. This system needs no more than a mention. I proceed to readings in which the copular notion no longer insists on complete identification or its extreme contrary, but assumes one of the eight terminally ambiguous forms: as seen in the presentation of 'Every X is Y' under the form 'Any species of X is a species of any genus of Y'. I shall not lengthen this paper by a full discussion of the whole of this system: I shall confine myself to the cases in which the primary relations are *genus* and *species*. And these words may be dispensed with, since their correlatives are not to be employed: *part* and *whole*

[1] [In May 1863, December 1864 and January 1865, various notational amendments were added to this and the preceding table, but it has not been thought necessary to include them.—Ed.]

will be sufficient for the purpose. Over and above the reinforcement of preceding notions, that purpose is the comparison of extension and comprehension, or, as I prefer to say, of extent and intent. With the above limitations the following table, to be immediately explained, contains all that is necessary.

I	II	III	IV
))))	)) ((	((((	(( ))
((·((	((·))	))·))	))·((
( )) (pw D ∵ wp ::	( ) ( ) pp D ∵ ww =:	) (( ) pw :: wp D ∵	) ( ) (pp := ww D
) (·( ) pw ∵ wp D ::	) (·) (pp ∵ ww D =:	( )·) (pw D :: wp ∵	( )·( ) pp D := ww
( ))) wp : ww =:	( ) ((pp D ∵ pw D· –	) (((pp := pw :=	) ( )) wp D –·ww D
) (·((wp D =: ww D =:	) (·)) pp ∵ pw · –	( )·)) pp D := pw D :=	( )·((wp –· ww
))) (pp := wp :=	)) ( ) pp D ∵ wp D –·	((( ) pw =: ww =:	(( ) (pw D· – ww D
((·( ) pp D := wp D :=	((·) (pp ∵ wp –·	))·) (pw D =:ww D =:	))·( ) pw · – ww

Take one of these readings, for instance I. 6) (·((, say *X*) (·((*Y*, where *X*) may be either 'Any part of *X*' or 'some whole of *X*' and the same of (*Y*. There are four readings; *ww* (whole and whole), *wp*, *pw*, and *pp*. Of these *pp* and *pw*, about which no remark follows, are unrestrictive readings, and give) (·((with the middle spiculae erased, or *X*)·(*Y*. That is, 'Any part of *X* is *exient of* [not wholly contained in] any part of *Y*' and 'Any part of *X* is exient of some whole of *Y*' mean simply that '*X* is external of *Y*', or that 'no *X* is *Y*'; and the converse. But *wp* and *ww* are denials of a restrictive, and both simply deny (*D*) that *X* and *Y* are penultimately identical. That is, 'some whole of *X* is exient of any part of *Y*', and 'some whole of *X* is exient of some whole of *Y*', simply say, 'It is not true that *X* and *Y* are coextensive and each taking up all the universe except one individual object.' When *X* and *Y* are anything but coextensive, or, being coextensive, anything but penultimate, some whole of *X*, *X* or *X* and more, is not wholly within any part of *Y*.

Take the symbol IV. 4 as an example, *X* ()·() *Y*. Omit the secondary spiculae: we have *X* (·) *Y*, which is the proposition symbolized. Read the secondary)·(as 'is out of', 'is entirely excluded from', or 'entirely excludes'. Four readings are possible, from part to part, *pp*, &c. These four readings are

> *pp*, Some part of *X* is out of some part of *Y*;
> *ww*, Any whole of *X* is out of any whole of *Y*;
> *pw*, Some part of *X* is out of any whole of *Y*;
> *wp*, Any whole of *X* is out of some part of *Y*.

Of these the table tells us that only *pw* and *wp* are unrestrictive: that *pp* merely denies (*D*) that *X* and *Y* are singular and identical; and *ww* merely affirms that *X* and *Y* are singular and contrary. But *pw*, which affirms that *Y* and anything, up to penultimacy, leaves out some part of *X*, affirms, as we see, that all which is not *Y* is *X*.

The rules for detecting unrestricted readings are as follows:—

1. (Lines 1 and 2.) When the primary and secondary spiculae are alike, as in)))),))·((, all the four readings are unrestricted. Thus *X*(·(*Y* follows from *X*((·((*Y* in every case of

some part		any part	
	of *X* is not in		of *Y*
any whole		some whole	
(	(·(	(	

2. (Lines 3 and 4.) When the primary and secondary spiculae are both balanced, there are two unrestricted readings, both unbalanced: when both unbalanced, two unrestricted readings, both balanced. Thus)()(and)(·)(have the readings *pw*, *wp*, unrestricted: but)(() and)(·((have *pp* and *ww* unrestricted.

3. (Lines 5, 6, 7, 8.) When the primary and secondary spiculae are one balanced, and the other unbalanced, one of the extreme spiculae is of a different curvature from its neighbour: let this be the *detached* spicula. Two readings are unrestricted; and the detached spicula has the same reading (part or whole) in both. That common reading is by *part* when the other extreme is particular in an affirmative, or universal in a negative; by whole, when the other extreme is universal in an affirmative, or particular in a negative. Take notice that the most *Aristotelian* combinations go together; part, particular affirmative, universal negative. Thus ())) has the first extreme spicula detached, the second particular in an affirmative: accordingly, ())) gives () in the readings *pp*, *pw*. But ()·)) gives (·) in the readings *wp*, *ww*. And))·)(, in which the second spicula is detached has the readings *pp*, *wp*.

Interchange of primary and secondary spiculae produces no effect in any case on the modes of unrestricted reading: thus)(·((and ()·((both give *pp*, *pw*, for unrestricted readings.

[26 December 1862. The restricted readings may be easily connected with the peculiar pairs in page 307, in which *pp* goes with (·),)(; *ww* with)·(, (); *pw* with ((,)·); *wp* with)), (·(. Take the secondary and concluding relation from any case in which restrictions exist; the letters to which they are attached in the last sentence point out the *restricted* readings. Thus ()·((, giving)·(and (·(, has *ww* and *wp* for restricted readings:)(·)), giving)·), (·), has *pw*, *pp*, restricted.]

Each relation is enunciated in *ten* ways; by secondary relation of its own name in four ways, and in two ways by each remaining relation of the same quality. Thus *species* enunciates *species* in four ways, and *genus*, *partient*, *coinadequate*, enunciate *species* in two ways each. The following are the ways of announcing[1] that *X* is a species of *Y*.

Any part of *X* is in some part of *Y*	Any part of *X* does not complete any whole of *Y*
Any part of *X* is in any whole of *Y*	Any whole of *X* does not complete any whole of *Y*
Some whole of *X* is in any whole of *Y*	Any part of *X* takes in some part of *Y*
Some whole of *X* is in some part of *Y*	Some whole of *X* takes in any whole of *Y*
	Any part of *X* is not out of some part of *Y*
	Any part of *X* is not out of any whole of *Y*

I finish this part of the subject by noticing that in any proposition one spicula[2] may be read as a verb, subject to rejections on account of the production of restrictives asserted or denied. The modes of reading are:—

X), *X* is in; *X*(, *X* takes in; *X*(·, *X* is not in; *X*)·, *X* does not take in.
(*X*, takes in *X*;)*X*, is in *X*; ·)*X*, does not take in *X*; ·(*X*, is not in *X*.

[1] I use simple English verbs for the universal relations; *is in, takes in, is out of, makes up* or *completes*. To *eke out* is the purest English for to *make up all the rest*: but it has in our time too much the implication of *pis aller* and *succedaneum*. The particulars are merely the negations of the universals: I doubt if they ought ever to be anything else. I have made great use of these simple verbs, and with a feeling of relief from the state trappings of technical terms; like the post-boy's horse in John Gilpin, I felt

. . . right glad to miss
The lumbering of the wheels.

[2] The 'mysterious spiculae' make a powerful language. In using one symbol,), as in *X*)*Y*, to denote both the total quantity of the subject and the particular quantity of the predicate, I followed the plan by which a fraction is represented, in which one symbol distinguishes both numerator and denominator: and I ultimately marked the symbol twice. If a fraction had been denoted by $\frac{a}{b}$, $\underline{a}$ and $\bar{b}$ would have been convenient symbols for *a* as a numerator and *b* as a denominator; and might be made useful even as it is. Forgetting that I was not writing wholly for mathematicians, I used expressions on this subject which were misunderstood. In my magazine of animadversions (VI. 650*) there is a spirited criticism of my notation, the colouring of which is heightened by assuming to be *one* my *two* syllogistic notations, pictorial and arbitrary; the first only a study, the second a language for use. In it we find—'We need hardly, therefore, be surprised, that, in the end, Mr De Morgan should actually laud the farrago for expressing *diametrically opposite* things ("the universality of the subject," "the particularity of the predicate") by the *self-same* representation.' Had I held, with the logicians, the exclusive right of the onymatic relations to be logical forms, I should now have dropped the word *spicular*, already borrowed from Hamilton, and have substituted *farraginal*, with the motto

Quicquid agunt homines nostri est farrago libelli.

If, as I suspect, I am on the way to a much wider use of the complex forms)), (·(, &c. the second adjective may yet find an introduction.

Examples are seen in

X)) *Y*, All *X* is in *Y*; *X*(·(*Y*, Some *X* is not in *Y*;
X(·) *Y*, Any whole of *X* does not take in *Y*,

and so on.

I shall now sketch out the whole of which the Hamiltonian attempt is a part. It will not be worth while to reduce it to tables, because the complex syllogisms to which it leads are easily reduced to compositions of simple ones, and would really appear in this way, except only when they show the junctions of universals which are seen in the system of terminal precision. The particulars of this system are of very infrequent occurrence compared with the universals. My object in giving this account is not to detail the system as for use, but to make it a lesson upon the necessity of giving full action and equal prominence to all sides of every correlation: and further, to show that the defects of an incomplete system are magnified when the part selected from the whole system is not an *aliquot part*. The Aristotelian table of enunciation, for instance, is a true bisection of system: it selects the lesser universals and the greater particulars. But the system of syllogism is not a true bisection: *nineteen* syllogisms cannot be a real aliquot part of any system. I postulate—in my own mind I say I have demonstrated—that the eight onymatic forms are essential to any complete system of enunciation.

We are to take in both *all* and *some-not-all* as quantifiers: that is, 'some affirmed to be all', and 'some denied to be all'. At the outset then we are asked to select two out of three alternatives, without allusion to the third. We know that *X*s, if *X*s enter into thought at all, enter as *some*; and this some is either affirmed as all, or neither affirmed nor denied as all, or denied as all. Any *some* must appear in enunciation under one, and only one, of these three relations to *all*. The Aristotelian system makes a fair bisection of this set of alternatives. When there are three alternatives of which one is equally and symmetrically related to both of the others, that one may be repeated twice, once in relation to each extreme: and either extreme, with the common mean, is a symmetrical bisection of system. The Aristotelian plan confines itself to 'some affirmed to be all' and 'some not [denied] to be all': one extreme, and the mean in relation to it. But if we take the *two* extremes, we must also take the mean in its relation to both. Again, as contrary terms must enter, whatever subdivisions we make of 'some *X*' we must also make the same of 'some *x*'. Accordingly, since a universal term gives a particular contrary, there is no proposition but must enter in four different ways. A term being universal, we must distinguish the case in which the particular contrary is to be *some-or-all* from that in which it is to be *some-not-all*. Denoting *all* and *some-or-all* in my usual way, I shall denote by an accent that the particular term indicated is *some-not-all*, or else that the universal indicated has *some-not-all* for its contrary. There are then, besides the *eight* usual forms, 3 × 8 or 24 others, all formed, as we shall see, by conjunctions of two of the eight, or three. These last, by equivalences, are reduced to *twelve*; which with twelve disjunctive denials, make a total of 32. Of these I shall, for brevity, consider only the common forms and the 12 conjunctives: syllogisms containing disjunctions can be dealt with by opponent reduction.

First, a universal, such as)), is accompanied by))′,)′), and)′)′. The three last are equivalent, and equivalent to the form)) joined with)·); or to)∘). And the same of the others. So that the system of universals contains the *simple* universals)), ((,)·(, (·), and the *double* universals)∘), (∘(,)∘(, (∘).

Secondly, a particular, such as (), is accompanied by ()′, (′) and (′)′. These three have the following meaning. Each one consists of the proposition without the accent, joined to the proposition in which the unaccented term is contraverted. Thus ()′ is () and)·); (′) is () and (·(; (′)′ is () and)·) and (·(. These may be denoted by ()·), (·(), and (·()·). Accordingly, we have

()′	and	)·)′	mean	()·)	(′)′	means	(·()·)
(′)	and	(′·(	mean	(·()	(′·(′	means	)(·()
)(′	and	(·(′	mean	)(·(	)′·)′	means	()·)(
)′(	and	)′·)	mean	)·)(	)′(′	means	)·)(·(

Remember that)·)(·(is the triple junction of)·),)(, (·(, &c. Contranominals do not appear in any double proposition: thus we have not equivalence,)) and ((, nor contrariety,)·(and (·), nor ()(, nor (·(and)·).

The denials may be represented by the disjunctive comma: thus the denial of)′(′ is 'either ((or (·) or))', represented by {((, (·),))}. Of the whole number, Hamilton's plan selects *seven*, when 'Some *X* is not some *Y*' is properly treated, and adds the assertion of equivalence 'All *X* is all *Y*'. The seven are

)∘), (∘(, (′)′,)·(, (), (′·(,)·)′;

being two simple propositions, four double, and one triple. It thus includes all the cases in which the new forms, (·) and)(, are absent. To these it adds the equivalence, or junction of)) and ((, without adding the junction of (·(and)·), the denial of {)), ((}. The junction of contranominals is, in every one of its four cases, excluded from separate enunciation by the main principle of this system. If Hamilton had expressly started on the principle of allowing every Aristotelian proposition, every possible junction, and every disjunctive denial, with simple conversion, he would have come very near a system.

The syllogisms of this system are, when it is fully taken,—1. The 32 forms with two single premises each. 2. Eight universal forms with double premises and double conclusion, being those I have called syllogisms of terminal precision; and 16 opponents, having one disjunctive premise and a disjunctive conclusion. 3. Various forms in which a single universal—or a double one, which gives only a strengthened form with the same conclusion,—with a double particular, give a double particular. 4. Various forms in which premises one or both of which are more than single give only a single conclusion. On these it is not necessary to dwell: any case is resolved at a glance by any one familiar with my notation.

I cannot undertake, in the present paper, to give a full account, in relation to aggregation[1] and composition, of the distinction of *extent* and *intent*. I shall therefore confine myself to what I expect will be a termination of my controversy on this point, followed by a brief account of what I hold to be the true logical foundation of the distinction.

No part of Hamilton's system has received a more ready assent from his followers than his mode of making the distinction—I say his substitute for the distinction—which Aristotle announced when he divided *genus in species*—attribute in attribute—, from *species in genus*—class in class. I shall not, after what is said in my third paper, offer any further proof that there *is* a substitution. It will be enough here to quote (VI. 642*) his governing[2] principle—'the predicate of the predicate is,

[1] This distinction is not yet seen, nor, I fear, will it be seen until the logician is restricted to puddings which are only *aggregates*, and not *compounds*. It is remarkable that we have no word of pure English which designates the part as a component: *element*, *constituent*, *ingredient*, *component*, *material*, are all foreign. Shakespeare's witches talk of *ingredients*; but they were scientific characters: the word can be distinctly shown to have been limited to medicines, charms, &c. What would a housewife of the time of Elizabeth have said, when she told her servant not to forget the —— for one of those puddings which I would withhold from the logician. The *things* or the *stuff* will suggest themselves; but they only prove the absence of the truly distinctive word. For *things* may be aggregants as well as components: and *stuff* is the proper term when there is but one kind of material; though, for want of better, it occurs in such words as garden-stuff, kitchen-stuff. And the word applies equally to aggregants and components.

[2] The word predicate is here loosely used. The first time it occurs it means 'predicate affirmed': in the two other cases it means 'predicate affirmed or denied'. Hamilton's readers must be cautioned as to the very positive way in which he puts forward brand new principles as though they were generally received, and convicts those who deny them of mistake, by appeal to the principles themselves. For example, (VI. 642*):—'This suffices to show how completely Mr De Morgan mistakes the great principle:—*The predicate of the predicate is, with the predicate, affirmed or denied of the subject.*' Would not any one suppose it to be notorious that this great principle had been previously announced by others? Be this as it may—I assert no negative, but I cannot find it—I had denied this principle, in effect, though I had never heard it, by proceeding on principles repugnant to it. When I say a horse has four legs, I ought to be taken as *denying* the great principle of bipedality, not as counting each leg twice in an attempt to *apply* it. In the point before us the Port Royal logicians

with the predicate, affirmed or denied of the subject'—which ushers in the form of *depth*, or comprehension, 'All *X* is some *Y*', as distinguished from that of breadth, or extension, 'Some *Y* is all *X*'. When we say, says Hamilton, that Leibnitz, a mathematician, is not Newton, we deny 'mathematician' of Newton; not 'any' mathematician, but the mathematician incorporated in Leibnitz; Newton is not the LmaEtheImaBNtiIciTanZ who is here spoken of. He means that each quality residing, inhering, in a subject is an object of thought, *per se*, as a quality, distinct from, though a component of, the subject of inhesion, and from the same quality in any other subject. All this can be thought: what is its force as a distinct mode of enunciation? and what is its utility in logic? Show me the first, and I can undertake to find the second.

Two objects are in a certain particular alike, so that if they were as much alike in all particulars they would be the same object. If Leibnitz, besides mathematician, had been English, Fellow of Trinity, Lucasian professor, &c. &c. &c. he would have been Newton: and the proper name Leibnitz would have been but an alias of Newton. What! it will be asked, do you deny that in thought you can conceive two men, fac-similes in body and mind, thinking, speaking, and acting, exactly in the same way, &c. &c. &c., all through their lives? If the querist mean that they are to differ in *place* or in *time*, I can conceive two *different* men, each the double of the other in all things except place or time. But if, among the other samenesses, they be to occupy the same place at the same time, I cannot call them *two* men. If I could, I should say there is no such thing as an individual; that each one man is a hundred, or a thousand, agreeing in all things, place included, at all times, and therefore without distinction. Suppose one individual to differ from another only in one quality, the first being $AXYZ$... and the second $BXYZ$..., A and B being repugnant. Hamilton says they have two different X qualities, X_1 and X_2: let it be so; the individuals are then $AX_1Y_1Z_1$... and $BX_2Y_2Z_2$... If A and B had chanced to be the same, these two individuals would have been wholly without distinction—would have been the same.

have *repugned* the 'great principle' as well as myself, and to all appearance with no more knowledge of its existence than myself; and Hamilton proves his knowledge of their opinion by citing them—very correctly, I believe,—as the restorers of the distinction of extension and intension. I may slightly mention another point. Hamilton thinks it sufficient to answer his opponent's meaning by fixing another meaning on his opponent's words. I designated a proposition of his as *spurious*, referring to a page of my own book for my own technical use of that word. Hamilton (VI. 639*) begins his answer thus, '*Spurious* in law means a bad kind of *bastard*:' and on this definition he easily convicts me of absurdity. If, under a definition of my own, I had called his proposition *goniometrical* instead of *spurious*, he might well have impeached my Greek; but it would have been of coequal absurdity if he had answered me by solemnly proving that he had not enunciated a theodelite.

Remember that we are supposed to have enumerated *every* concept under which either is viewed or which either receives or creates. If then, which I do not deny, X_1 and X_2 be really different examples of the same quality, all knowledge of this difference—the very difference itself, as to the *esse quod habet in anima*—is due to the difference of A and B. What then is the logical import of a method by which, because there are differences which distinguish, we read samenesses into *different samenesses*, and contend that agreements, as such, have differences of which only disagreements wholly independent of the agreements make us cognizant.

Again, why do we give a class-mark, a term-name? to distinguish the objects of the class from all others, and (*pro tanto*) to *confound them with one another*. As against all other species, each is *signatum* by the class-mark; thus, though there be many *men*, I distinguish Newton and Leibnitz by the attribute *humanity* from each and every *brute*. But as against each other, this common class-mark is *vagum*: though I know each to be *man*, I do not know them to be *different men* till I have found another class-mark, the property of one, but not of the other. When the Irishman had caught the cluricaune, and made him show under which thistle out of many acres of them the treasure was buried, he tied his garter round the thistle—he added one[1] additional class-mark—and ran home for a spade. But the imp, while he was gone, tied a garter of exactly the same form and colour over every thistle in the field. When the poor man came back, he was made sadly sensible of the impossibility of distinguishing two individuals by the difference of their points of agreement. Hamilton would have described the situation to him as follows (VI. 643*):—'Let us consider what is meant by the proposition, —"This thistle has a garter." "A garter" does not here imply *all*, *every*, or even *any* garter, but *some* garter,—*a certain* garter; and this *particulare*, —be it *vagum*, be it *signatum*,—this *some* or *certain* garter which we affirm to be on this thistle, we do deny to be on that, in denying this to be that.' To which the Irishman might reply;—'True for you, your honour! but what will I be the better of that? Sure it's the *signatum* I'm wanting, and the *vagums* are of no use at all at all.' And this is the true answer. If we only know that the garter on this thistle is not the garter on that, by (otherwise) knowing that *this* is not *that*, we have nothing that we can enunciate about garters as giving knowledge of this and that. Any one who can make a *formal* profit of the *differentiae* of undistinguishable class-marks, may make a *material* profit of the cluricaune, if he can catch the creature. In the mean time, he may employ himself in

[1] The logician must not say that he merely distinguished an individual, and did not include in a class: independently of the truth, sometimes denied, that a class may consist of one individual only, his own remaining leg, and many other legs, were fellow-members with the designated thistle.

studying how to advise the little boy who had two shillings, and was puzzled to find out which he ought to spend first, to make his money go farthest.

I hold this distinction between 'Every man is in the class animal' and 'Every man is an object in which inheres one quality animal' to be of small meaning and no use. To make it the great distinction between the two sides of logic seems to me solemn trifling: to symbolize it by the inversion of phrase in 'Some animal is all man' and 'All man is some animal' is to bring distinction without difference in aid of difference without distinction.

In my third paper I gave a generalization of the old distinction of extension and comprehension (or intension) as the foundation of what I called the mathematical and metaphysical sides of logic. To all there laid down I adhere; but I add that the logical skeleton of the metaphysical side is connected with *whole in relation to part* just in the same manner as that of the mathematical side is connected with *part in relation to whole*. Every *attribute*, or concept by which a class is distinguished, makes many portions of the universe to be so many *wholes* in relation to contained parts. If the class X be a part of the class Y, the class Y is a whole of the class X, the attribute Y is a component of the attribute X, whenever we mean by the attribute X the *total attribute*, the compound of all possible attributes, possessed by X. The proposition is 'X and every part of X'—not merely its *distinct* parts, but all possible parts—comes under Y and all its wholes. The correlation of part and whole has been so little examined that further detail may be necessary.

There are classes, X and Y, containing 20 and 30 individuals: they aggregate into a class of not less than 30 nor more than 50 individuals; and I must know how many individuals belong to *both* classes before I can assign the aggregate number; that is, before I can ascertain the *common whole* of which X and Y are *parts* I must know the *common part*, if any, of which X and Y are *wholes*: this common part may be of any number of individuals not exceeding 20. This is the principle which Mr Boole has formulized in $X + Y - XY$ for the aggregate of X and Y; and which determined my use of (X, Y) instead of $X + Y$ in my *Formal Logic*. I call the common whole of two parts their *aggregate*; the common part of two wholes their *compound*.

Suppose a universe of six individuals, of which the proper names, the representatives of singular attributes, are 1, 2, 3, 4, 5, 6. Let us consider the class X, or 1, 2, 3. This class has the parts, 1, 2, 3, 12, 23, 31, 123. It has the wholes, 123, 1234, 1235, 1236, 12345, 12356, 12346. But 123456, though a whole of 123, is not a term dividing the universe, which has six lowest parts, 1, 2, &c., and six highest wholes 23456, 13456, &c. Every selection is to have its name, which may equally designate the class and the attribute by which the class is distinguished; being at once the instrument of cumulation and of distinction: of cumulation, when one individual of the class is coupled with another; of distinction, when one in the class is separated from one of the externals.

Every point of correlation is seen, or will[1] be seen, to be perfect. The individuals being non-partient of each other, we may designate the class 1, 2, 3, by $1 + 2 + 3$. We have no symbol in mathematics which may by analogy be employed to designate the attribute of this class; nothing which suggests 'the common mark of 1, 2, 3, and of them alone': except so far as this, that A_{123} is sometimes used in such a sense, *inter alia*; which may therefore denote the common attribute. Suppose we describe the class $1 + 2 + 3$ as the *aggregate* of $1 + 2$ and 3: what is the correlative mode of describing its attribute in terms of the compound of two? The answer is that a class may be described by its contrary, and that 'the alternative attribute of A_{3456} A_{12456}' is the description of the attribute required. The relations of aggregation and composition are closely connected with those of direct and contrary: thus the propositions '*C* is aggregate of *A* and *B*' and 'not-*C* is compound of not-*A* and not-*B*' are convertible.

The following is an example of the correlation of propositions.

X)·(*Y*. No *X* is *Y*; everything either *x* or *y*: *X* and *Y* have no common part: but, if not complements, have common wholes. Every individual is in some of the parts either of *x* or of *y*: and is either not in some whole of *X*, or not in some whole of *Y*. That is, no junction of a new attribute selects any part of one out of the other: everything wants some attribute of one or the other.

X(·)*Y*. No *x* is *y*: everything either *X* or *Y*: *X* and *Y* have no common[2] whole: but, if not externals, have common parts. Every individual is in all the wholes either of *X* or of *Y*, and is either not any part of *x*, or not any part of *y*. That is, no dismissal of an existing attribute makes any whole of one a whole of the other: everything has all the attributes of one or the other.

[1] A qualification rendered necessary by the smallness of the number who think of such distinctions. That *esse* is *percipi* is especially true of the *esse in anima*. The logical eye of the mathematician, and the mathematical eye of the logician, are yet to be opened. The cultivators of both the sides of exact science seem to proceed upon the notion that distinct vision is not possible with both eyes together. Some contend for the right eye, some for the left: and the voice of mankind finds no utterance; for *parmi les aveugles un borgne est roi*, let him have which eye he may.

[2] One word more on this stumblingblock. All terms have a common *whole*, the universe: but this is not a *whole term*. The logician does not see why the universe is to be excluded, nor can he see until his mathematical eye is open. But he excludes it in his own system, and very easily, by never inventing a name for it. 'Every thing that exists', 'the *omne cogitabile*', are opposed in thought to their contraries, the non-existing, and the *incogitabile*. Where is the name that includes both the existing and the non-existing, the thinkable and the unthinkable? Let this name be shown, and shown in use, and then I shall be open to the charge of correcting the old logic: but I think I have only imitated it. In a full work on logic, the universal name might be discussed in the chapter which treats of *restrictives* and other extremes, not forgetting *vacuous* names. But in the logic of the term—*distinctive name*—the garter is as useless when all the thistles have it as it would be if none had it.

I shall be asked whether, when the intensive proposition is thus reduced to its skeleton form, as a relation between wholes, I do not abandon the distinction of *mathematical* and *metaphysical*, as designative of the two sides of logic. Is not the idea of a whole including a smaller whole as mathematical as that of a part contained in a larger part? Certainly it is, but nevertheless I do not abandon the nomenclature, which loses none of its truth and none of its utility: but the names must be held designative of a subsequent distinction. The proposition of extent remains mathematical to the end; the proposition of intent becomes metaphysical in application. Even when *man* and *brute* are clothed with all their qualificative concepts, they make up *animal* just as the items of a tradesman's bill make up the total of goods furnished. The individuals are plain counters in the formal enunciation, and painted counters in the material: but never anything except counters. But when, in the proposition of intent, the whole is recognized by its separating attribute, that attribute coalesces with others in each individual by a process of which we hide our ignorance when we call it ontological or metaphysical. The whole *rational* contains the whole *man*; the attribute *rational* goes to the composition of the attribute *human*: but, in spite of the logician, there is more than *summing up* in this second process. Extensive quantity has *partes extra partes*, as they once said, and some will admit no other kind of quantity: *de essentia quantitatis est habere partes extra partes*, says Smiglecius (*Disp*. ix, qu. 3). But extensive quantity has this quality objectively, permanently, and *de essentia*: intensive quantity has it only subjectively, *pro re nata*, as an accident of the thoughts. We *can separate* the rational in man from the animal in man, for the mind, by an act of the mind: we *cannot but separate* this man from that, save only when we think of the class as a unit, a process as subjective as that of separating the individual into concepts. First intentions give individuals which are compounds not yet decomposed, and aggregants not yet aggregated. Second intentions exhibit component attributes, and aggregate classes. The basis[1] of these

[1] Mr Mansel (IV. pp. 117–119) has some remarks on extension and intension, hinting opposition to Hamilton's doctrine, and *recognizing the change of the quantities* in passage from one to the other. With him 'some *A* is all *B*' gives all the attributes of *B* as some of those of *A*; while 'all *A* is some *B*' classes *A* under *B*. This mode of enunciation is very confusing: and from it follows that I owe Mr Mansel reparation for all but absolute misrepresentation in my article *Logic* [p. 251] in the *English Cyclopaedia*; an inattentive reader would suppose I make him *merely* change the places of Hamilton's forms, whereas he does more. Mr Mansel says (p. 119)—'The problem which we wish to see satisfactorily solved by the advocates of Sir W. Hamilton's doctrine may be stated as follows: To construct a synthetical proposition containing an *equation* or *identification* of subject and predicate in any other respect than that of the objects thought under the compared concepts.' My position is, either that this question is now solved, or that the given problem is not the one which should have been given.

oppositions is seen in *X*)) *Y* under the forms '*X* and all its parts are parts of *Y*'—'*Y* and all its wholes are wholes of *X*.'

This basis of thought may now be introduced in my former papers as the mathematical substratum of the metaphysical notion: I need not enter into details. Both the systems of secondary relations may be adapted to it. In the second of the systems given above *pp* is the mathematical reading; *ww* the metaphysical; *pw* the physical; and *wp* the contraphysical: according to the phraseology of my third paper.

I need hardly say that, in like manner as any individuals may be selected, and constituted a class, so those same individuals may be distinguished by a term which denotes an attribute: we cannot put on a class-mark without acquiring a right to treat that mark as designative of a concept. When we pass from the arithmetical abacus to the use of terms of relation, mathematical or metaphysical, as *species*, *dependent*, &c. we shake ourselves free of many of the questions which I have discussed. Before we come to this point we feel a want as to (·) and)(of which we are inclined to complain until we see that only defective correlation prevented our feeling the corresponding want as to)·(and () in another wing of the subject. I have frequently heard it made an objection to *X*(·) *Y* that it appears as 'Everything is either *X* or *Y*', of disjunctive character and apparently affirmative quality. So long as we have a copula either of identification or inclusion, we cannot read either (·) or)(by *part and part*. For this objection, as an objection, I have never cared: those who acknowledge the existence, and admit the entrance, of a privative term must needs confess that *X*)) *Y* and *x*(·) *Y* are equivalent. But I have always respected the complaint as merely directed against a blemish, and have awaited the time when further consideration would provide further explanation. The reader will see that this time has now

Mr Mansel criticizes Bishop Thomson for not taking sufficient account of *constitutive* attributes as distinguished from simple *characteristics*: I hold that Dr Thomson—and others, including the author of my second paper—had taken too much account of this extralogical distinction; extralogical, so far as entrance into enunciation is concerned. For a term is held to be divided from its contrary before enunciation: while, in the proposition, an attribute is of the same import whether it be constitutive, or only characteristic. Hamilton, from whom I seldom differ in principle as to what is and is not logic—though in application we sometimes so widely disagree that, like a professor I have mentioned elsewhere, I do not grant him that the whole is greater than its part until I see what use he wants to make of it—replies as follows:—'. . . In reference to Breadth and Depth, there is no difference whatever between "constitutive" and "attributive", between necessary and contingent, between peculiar and common. It is of no consequence, what has antecedently been *known*, what is newly *discovered*. These are merely material affections. We have only to consider what it is we formally *think*,' (VI. 643*). With reference to the quantities, Mr Mansel is answered by (644*, note)—'As others, besides Mr De Morgan, have misunderstood this matter . . .' followed by a clear and dogmatical exposition of Hamilton's doctrine of breadth and depth, never till then given, and placing his error of quantity in broad daylight.

arrived: the forms)·(and () are subject to precisely the same difficulties with reference to *whole and whole.* The following table of correlative readings will illustrate this.

X)·(*Y*.	*X*(·)*Y*.
No part of *X* is any part of *Y*.	No whole of *X* is any whole of *Y*.
Any part of *X* is not included in (and does not include) any part of *Y*.	Any whole of *X* does not include (and is not included in) any whole of *Y*.
Some whole of *X* is external of some whole of *Y*.	Some part of *X* is complement of some part of *Y*.
Every penultimate is whole either of *X* or of *Y*.	Every individual is part either of *X* or of *Y*.
Every penultimate includes either *X* or *Y*.	Every individual is included in either *X* or *Y*.
Every individual is not included in some penultimate either of *X* or of *Y*.	Every penultimate does not include some individual either of *X* or of *Y*.

And so we might proceed, never failing to translate a reading of either proposition into a reading of the other, strictly correlative in every detail.

I shall close this paper by attempting to procure for the quantification of the predicate an honourable acquittal from the charge of having disturbed the peace of the logical world. It has never been the subject of discussion, except by myself in the investigation of the numerical syllogism; an investigation of which the truth remains unquestioned, and in which all quantification of the predicate is proved superfluous. Another notion, under the name of *quantification*, has stirred up controversy. I say nothing here about the mere question whether the quantity of the predicate should be *expressed.* The explicit demand for this expression was first made by Hamilton: it is a great step; and the logical world is pretty well agreed that its merit is quite distinct from the merit or demerit of the particular mode of quantifying which he adopted.

What is *quantification*? It means, or should mean, the giving or expressing of quantity; and as quantity is essentially a *more* or a *less*, the giving of quantity cannot exist without the giving of a more or a less. But the quantity of the predicate, be it more or less, is always the quantity of the subject, or its complement, as well in negatives as in affirmatives; that is, so far as it is more or less. I postulate that a proposition is only a proposition, a propounder, a challenger of assent or denial, in so far as, and with reference to, its assertion of what might have been deniable, or its denial of what might have been assertable. For example, in 'Every *X* is *Y*', it is a clear matter of affirmation, and so intended, that each *X* is *X*, and each *X* not more than one *Y*: but these are not put forward as parts of the proposition, because they are not *distinctive* parts. In propositions, as in terms, all that belongs to the whole universe of propositions is to be tacitly rejected: I claim to make the rejection explicit, because it is sometimes tacitly refused. This being conceded, if I say '*X*s are *Y*s' it is clear that the number of *Y*s spoken of is the same as the number of *X*s: if that number be ten at most, then ten (or fewer) *X*s are ten (or fewer) *Y*s. If I say '*X*s are not *Y*s', what I deny is that the ten (or fewer) *X*s are any ten (or fewer) *Y*s: I do not mean to deny that the ten are *nine* or *eleven*; for that I can deny by the form of thought, let *X* and *Y* be what they may. If I say 'Everything is either *X* or *Y*' neither *X* nor *Y* has quantity until quantity is assigned to the other: in a universe of 100 instances, if 40 *X*s go to the verification of this proposition, the number of *Y*s required for the same purpose is 60.

In treating the numerical syllogism, it appears that 'm *X*s are found among n *Y*s' is a proposition importing no more and no less than 'm *X*s are *Y*s'. Also that 'm *X*s are not found among n *Y*s', *X*s and *Y*s being x and y in number, is *spurious*—that is, true independently of which are *X*s and which are *Y*s—if $m + n$ be less than y or less than x; and otherwise, of the same import as '$m + n - y$ *X*s are not *Y*s' and $m + n - x$ *Y*s are not *X*s.

Neither is the predicate of an affirmative more or less definite than the subject, as to *quiddity*,[1] to revive an old term. If I say 'All *X*s are *Y*s', I only fail to know whether this or that *Y* is spoken of by failure of definite knowledge of the *X*s. If I say 'all man is animal', and cannot say that I have spoken of *that* animal, it is only because I do not know whether *that* object was spoken of under 'man'.[2]

What notion, then, has been brought forward and discussed under the name of *quantity*? Distinction between affirmation and non-affirmation of *all* or *any*: totality affirmed, totality not affirmed, without any reference to the *quantity* of the *totum*, the more or fewer individuals existent in the class. To speak of *X* at all is to speak of the whole class, to speak of all *X* as a class, or not to speak of it as a class. 'Man is

[1] This word, which was but badly replaced by *essentia*, has been selected as a joke against the old logicians: but *quantity* and *quality* are in honourable use. The joke may be retorted upon a discerning public, which, while treating the word with ridicule, fell into the error of theory which it may be supposed to favour, to every extent short of the absolute maximum. All we know of *quid* is derived from *quantum* and *quale*: if mankind had discarded *quiddity* on this ground, the race would have vindicated reason against philosophy with honour to itself, or at least would have shown an appearance of it. But, on the contrary, men in general assume a knowledge of things, *res ipsae*, entities, essences, substances, natures, &c.; and they claim to assert much about quiddity upon any the least knowledge of quantity and quality. One exception, indeed, their modesty does reserve: it is admitted, enforced, and made pulpit doctrine, that the Almighty is known only by his attributes, in a manner which implies that his creatures can be otherwise known. There was a time when educated persons, in numbers, had never heard of *attributes* in any other way; some may still be left. When a boy, I remember hearing murmured charges of irreverence against a person in company who spoke of the attributes of the vegetable world: my impression was that some of those present had a vague idea that the speaker might be a worshipper of leeks and onions.

[2] [But about negatives?]

animal': do you speak of man as a whole class? yes; do you speak of animal as a whole class? I say nothing about it; you are to take this proposition for purposes of inference without knowing whether I speak totally or partially; there is neither assertion nor denial, but reserve; it may be that I know the truth; it may be that you know the truth; but this proposition says nothing about it, and is intended to say nothing. This is all that is meant by 'animal' being *particular*.

If this view had been taken from the beginning, the difficulties of the singular proposition and of the indefinite proposition would never have appeared. All the confusion which has arisen from want of care in stating the meaning of 'some' would have been avoided. The Hamiltonian quantification, if it had appeared at all, would have appeared in a sound form. It would have been remembered that affirmation and denial are not alternatives; and the three quantifiers of which I have shown the united effect would have been allowed full operation. To this I may add that Hamilton would never, even while denying its utility, have allowed 'most' (half plus some) to have been *legitimate*. This importation from truly arithmetical quantification would have remained in its proper sphere, in company with other fractions.

In my third paper I closed the controversy with my late opponent, as to every strictly personal matter: in this paper I hope to do the same with the purely logical questions, so far as his criticism on my own views is concerned. What remains of a polemical character—save only the question treated in the addition—concerns neither this logician nor that mathematician, but *the* logician and *the* mathematician. I believe that the necessary laws of thought constitute as wide a study as the necessary matter of thought: and that Kant's opinion on the finality of the Aristotelian system has as much truth and sense as any similar opinion —if any such were ever held—about the finality of the elements of Euclid.

To the logician I say that the system which he owes to a mathematician, Aristotle by name, is a system of which none but mathematicians have ever shown a disposition to extend or vary the forms which has been followed by general respect: as Boethius, Ramus, Leibnitz, Lambert, Kant. There is but one logician of great note who, not having mathematical habit, has attempted to depart from routine in the construction of a system of inference. It is not for me, appointed by himself his most prominent opponent, to pass sentence upon his system: but I suspect I have shown that system to be none the better for its author's ignorance of the other branch of exact science. The growth of logic has been stunted by its separation from mathematics: I feel certain that my learned and acute antagonist will be cited in time to come as the great champion of reunion, though appearing and intending to fight on the other side.

To the mathematician I assert that from the time when logical study was neglected by his class, the accuracy of mathematical reasoning declined. An inverse process seems likely to restore logic to its old place. The present school of mathematicians is far more rigorous in demonstration than that of the early part of the century: and it may be expected that this revival will be followed by a renewal of logical study, as the only sure preservative against a relapse.

Addition [26 *December* 1862]

Since the communication of the preceding paper I have obtained some notice of my criticisms from Mr T. Spencer Baynes, who I hoped might have been able to give evidence from his own personal recollections of Hamilton's conversation and public teaching: this he does only on one of the points, referring the others to Hamilton's printed works. Some account of his remarks is necessary: they do not induce me to *alter* anything I have written; but, as noticed, I *omit* the detailed proof of the falsehood and incompleteness of many of the syllogisms, because I find that no opposition will be made on this point. I remain of opinion, and must so remain until further showing, of which I entertain no hope, that Hamilton did leave one set of syllogistic forms as recipients of both senses of 'some', the old non-partitive sense, and his own doubly-partitive sense. That the neglect to make the necessary comparisons was a consequence of illness[1] I have no doubt. All the letters referred to appeared in the *Athenaeum* journal: the dates are those of publication. As stated in the paper, I had brought forward Hamilton's phrase '*some at least* (possibly therefore *all* or *none*)': failing all attempt at defence, I had (28 December 1861) given my own method of excusing its occurrence. Mr Baynes defends Hamilton (22 November 1862): I abide by my explanation; and the matter is now left to opinion. The

[1] Mr Baynes took no notice of my expressed conviction (2 November 1861) that 'as to his [Hamilton's] passing what I have called the Gorgon syllogism as valid inference, after actual examination, there is no need to say that it was impossible he should have done it.' My whole position was that he had allowed himself, without examination—and this probably owing to his illness—to take the whole application to syllogism for granted. I said (2 November 1861), 'I have no doubt that when he returned to his studies after the seizure, he imagined that he had tested the whole system of syllogism upon his most recent definitions of the quantifying words.' According to Mr Baynes I have charged Hamilton with false reasoning: the preceding quotations will show the sense in which the charge was made. Be it remembered that these quotations are no afterthoughts, but actual accompaniments of what is called the 'charge'. But I regret to say that the last proof of my view of the subject, given near the end of this addition as very recently discovered, shakes my confidence in Hamilton's want of examination, though I still hold that it is the more probable hypothesis.

phrase carries its own condemnation with it; to those who cannot see this I have really nothing to say. But as my object in producing it was only to show the hurry of the article in which it appears; and as it belongs, not to Hamilton's system, but to his account of the old one; and as I have omitted my own explanatory excuse from the preceding paper,—I omit Mr Baynes's defence from this addition. I may hereafter compare it with my own excuse, when something arises which the comparison will illustrate. I also asked (2 November 1861) for information as to whether Hamilton had given his own sense of 'some' *from his chair*. The silence of all his pupils on this point obliged me to think he might actually have taught this sense of 'some' as to be applied to the only forms of syllogism which I could—or can—ascertain that he had given. I therefore (18 October 1862) put the question in stronger terms, and by name to Mr Baynes, to Hamilton's editors, and to his successor. In taking up this point, Mr Baynes of course felt it necessary to take up the others; but on this point his answer (22 November 1862) was explicit and satisfactory; as follows. 'Within my experience of his class-teaching (up to the close of session 1853–4), Sir William did not, that I remember, depart from the ordinary meaning of "some" in teaching the syllogism. But for years before this he was accustomed to expound briefly from the chair his doctrine of immediate inference [in which one proposition only is concerned], and of course as a part of it the different meanings of "some".' This is to the purpose; and Mr Baynes is the best living witness on the matter.

The remaining point is that of the application of the new meaning of 'some' to syllogism. On this Mr Baynes speaks—but without a single reference in proof of his statements—as follows: I put some words in Italics (22 November 1862).

'The alleged invalidity of these syllogisms wholly depends on the use of the quantifying term "some" in *a special sense*. But Prof. De Morgan offers *no proof whatever* that it is so employed in the scheme he criticizes. He states, indeed, what is perfectly true, that Sir William Hamilton signalized this particular meaning and *contended for its partial use*. [This statement is not mine.] Sir William Hamilton, in applying his new doctrine to propositional forms, discusses the vague generality of "some" in its ordinary use as a mark of quantity, points out that it may be taken in a narrower or more definite sense, and proposes the introduction of this new meaning "alongside of the other" *in particular cases and for special objects*. These objects, as Sir William defines them, *all* relate to propositional forms. The *partial* use of the narrower "some" not only yields a complete and consistent scheme of opposition, but supplies certain valuable forms of immediate inference. For these reasons, Sir William introduces alongside the ordinary and vaguer "some" (some at least) the more definite "some" (some at most) as a mark of quantity;

but *he carefully defines the condition of its use, and specifies the instances in which it is actually employed.* From this *partial* and *well-defined* use of the more definite "some" in the treatment of propositional forms, Prof. De Morgan *assumes* that Sir William Hamilton not only carries it over into his scheme of syllogism, but applies it to every detail of that scheme.'

In my reply (29 November 1862) I disposed of two of the Italic phrases by pointing out that I had given references to the successive papers on proposition and syllogism, which, writing to persons who had the book in their hands, and power to follow an implied argument in their heads, I took to be quite enough. I challenged Mr Baynes to support the remaining words in Italics from Hamilton's writings, stating that this present paper was going to the printer, and desiring to couple with my statements the fullest account of his answer. Mr Baynes, acknowledging my references by substituting want of 'definite proof' for statement that I had made only 'simple assertion', refused (6 December 1862) to give any support whatever to what he admitted were his own unsupported assertions, until after the appearance of this memoir. He then pledged himself to reply if I should support my case by 'definite evidence', by 'anything like proof', by 'anything indeed approaching to a plausible reason'. It would require, he said, 'not only a detailed statement, but a number of extracts'. I take Mr Baynes as admitting that no single extract, and no two extracts put together, would make a *prima facie* appearance of contradiction to my hypothesis. I fear I shall never see this defence: the mode of proceeding does not promise much. In Mr Baynes's short opening letter (1 November 1862), he thinks his reply 'may be put into very moderate compass'; and that it 'may be easily shown that Prof. De Morgan's chief difficulties arise from a complete, though perhaps not very unnatural, misunderstanding of Sir W. Hamilton's condensed form of expression'. Here the words 'easily shown' can hardly have meant that all the showing was to be assertion, without one single supporting reference to Hamilton's writings. But when Mr Baynes finds that simple assertion will not be taken as showing anything, and that substantiating references are called for, and when he is told that I shall handle his reply in this paper, the moderate compass becomes detailed statement too long for the journal, and the tone becomes more sarcastic. In pointing this out I direct attention to all[1] that

[1] Perhaps not quite all. The assertions being dismissed which are to be established 'some' day at latest (perhaps therefore never?) there remains the fact proved by Mr Baynes's evidence, that Hamilton explained to his class the doubly partitive 'some,' and (IX. ii. 268) the *immediate* inference thence arising. There is also the fact proved by Mr Baynes's silence, that Hamilton did not therewith tell his hearers that the doubly partitive enunciations would not validate the only syllogistic forms which he had given them. In my mind this adds probability to the hypothesis that Hamilton had never tested the point: it was his habit to go on year after year without making

Mr Baynes will allow to be shown: high confidence with good humoured condescension changing, on demand for proof of statements, into what must be interpreted as confession of difficulty, with disparagements and ironies which seem intended to avenge the difficulty upon him who put it in the way. I am quite content that Mr Baynes's imitation of his great teacher's tone of controversy shall continue, provided only that he will demand respectable references from every statement which applies for admission. Should he really attempt to redeem his conditional pledge, I shall be much pleased: for I confidently expect that my views will be positively confirmed. But should I and the public hear nothing more from him, which from his recent retreat is too much to be feared, I must be content with the negative confirmation which his silence will inevitably be taken to afford. But I hope better things.

I now proceed to point out how I came to arrive at so strange a conclusion as that Hamilton's *own new* propositional forms, emerging out of his *own new* use of 'some', were intended to be used, as well as the old ones, in his *own new* system of syllogistic forms. In every book of logic the treatment of the proposition precedes that of the syllogism: and the forms of enunciation treated in the chapter on propositions are those used in the chapter on syllogism. This of course; for usually there is but one system of propositions. When, for the first time, we see two systems of propositional forms, of which the new one is declared to be placed 'alongside' of the old[1] one, we must needs infer—unless the contrary be

[1] 'Though it may not supersede' the other: not 'must not,' nor 'ought not to;' but only 'may not.' The phrase is no more than permissive to the old system to remain, if others insist on it. That this was the leaning of Hamilton's mind—nay more, that disapprobation accompanied the permission—is evidenced, I think, throughout his discussion. For instance, by his interpolation quoted in the body of the paper, to his reprint of the letter in the *Athenaeum* journal: here he says that 'as we shall see, two particulars in the affirmative and negative forms, *ought* to infer each other'. To this it must be added that (IX. ii. 254) he, in January 1850, demands it as a *postulate of Logic* that 'the *some*, if not otherwise qualified, means *some only*—this by presumption.' If we accept Mr Baynes's statement, that *some only* (= *some at most*) was not intended to be introduced into syllogism, and if *some*, without qualification, be to mean *some only*, it follows that there is to be no formal syllogism in which the quantifying word 'some' stands alone. That the old forms can be well spared, is clearly in Hamilton's meaning: and if they go, what have we left? The new forms, without any syllogism?

---

any alterations. If he began to explain doubly partitive enunciation to his class, with an intention of soon proceeding to investigate the syllogism belonging to it, there is good reason to suppose that, though the execution of the intention were delayed, he would still continue his imperfect statement. The third Lecture on Logic has pages beginning with 'I would interpolate some observations which I ought, in my last Lecture, to have made before leaving. . . .' These lectures were read for twenty years without the alteration being made.

expressly stated—that both sets of forms are to be used in syllogism. If we be to have a thing so completely unheard of as a set of propositions which have no syllogisms in which they combine, we feel that the writer will certainly give us warning of what we are not to expect: especially when the new system is to stand alongside of the old one, side by side, in the same rank. Hamilton, writing on his own system, left a rough but very elaborate sketch of propositional forms, and another of syllogisms (*Logic*, II. 277–84, 285–9, appendixes (*d*) and (*e*)). These are given consecutively[1] by his editors, without a word indicating that it had passed through their minds that, of the two sets of propositional forms given, the new one was, or might be, unconnected with the one system of syllogism which appears to belong to both, for aught that Hamilton says to the contrary. These volumes are edited, as was said of them in a review, 'in the best style of laborious and conscientious workmanship': and they contain much more than a casual reader can appreciate of unpretending reference and comparison. The additional papers, on which this discussion arises, are put together in a manner which makes it clear that the trouble they cost must have left the editors in close possession of their details.

Finding that the new sense of 'some' made syllogistic forms invalid, and having searched in vain for anything even congruent with the notion that this new sense was not to be used in syllogism, I publicly applied to Hamilton's followers for information. None was given for a year.

[1] It weighed much with me that one of the editors, Mr Mansel (IV. 113) came to his task with the conviction that Hamilton had a use of 'some' different from that of Aristotle; and that this new sense of 'some' was applied to some sort of syllogism. The quotation given in the body of the paper shows this. When the unpublished papers came into Mr Mansel's hands, he, without any editorial remark, allowed the syllogisms in appendix (*e*) to follow the new and additional sense of 'some' propounded in appendix (*d*). I took it that he—who had shown his belief that Hamilton did apply *some* new 'some' to syllogism—had no reason to doubt that the syllogisms which he presented as editor were those which he had opposed to mine as reviewer. I divided the responsibility between Hamilton and the editors in the following words (17 August 1861)—'I do not say that Hamilton himself would have admitted this syllogism. But I do say that those who will accept his writings as they stand must admit it.' Mr Mansel did not impeach either my interpretation of Hamilton, or my implied interpretation of his own editorial proceeding. I consequently became fixed in the belief, which I still hold, that I had construed the editors rightly: and I believe that they were right as well as I. Though they had examined (*e*), which it was *not* their business to do, with reference to the validity of the connexion, they would not have been justified in deviating from the course they have taken. They might have taken up my suspicion that Hamilton forgot, after his seizure, that he had not finished his investigation. They might have suggested what Mr Baynes asserts, but refuses to prove in time for this paper, that the new propositions were never intended to walk the world in pairs. But, whatever they might have thought, it would have been their duty to put the *new* syllogisms into that connexion with the *new* propositions which the state of the papers seemed to require; leaving their caveat, if they had given one, to work its own effect on the reader's judgment.

The editors[1] and Mr Baynes, who was Hamilton's substitute during illness, remained silent. Another appeal, relating to what Hamilton had orally taught, of a pointed and personal character, brought out Mr Baynes on the whole question, with assertions which are—if he should see any plausibility[2] in my reasoning—to be substantiated so soon as my most appropriate opportunity of discussing them shall have passed away. These things speak for themselves: I fully anticipate that any attempt to invalidate my conclusion will speak more plainly still. Something I have got; I have extracted the defence which is to be set up: namely, that the new sense of 'some' is to be *asyllogistic*. Should any one point out to me, publicly or privately, any passage in Hamilton's writings on his sense of 'some' which expresses or implies that this was the case in his mind, or even agrees better with this supposition than with its contradiction, I will discuss that passage when I next take up the subject. In the mean time, I cannot too distinctly affirm that the most attentive consideration[3] has not enabled me to detect such a passage.

[1] Mr Mansel, and Professor Fraser, Hamilton's successor, have a right to the statement that they privately, in reply to applications from me, made after my letters were published, informed me that they had no more means of information than were open to myself in print. It was not for me to ask what opinion they had formed from these materials. The reader will understand that the second public application, especially made to four persons, was not on a question of opinion, but on a question of fact; namely, as to what sense of 'some' Hamilton taught from his chair: this question could be decided only by testimony.

[2] Since the bulk of this addition was written, Mr Baynes (20 December) has given an *unconditional* assurance that he will attempt to substantiate his statements. It was drawn out by a letter of mine (13 December) in which I administered what I call a rebuke, and he calls a personality, upon the tone of his preceding letter. Here I need only say that I think my remark was richly deserved, and that I know it was meant to be directly personal. I have much reason to be pleased with the result, namely, the withdrawal of the condition which left Mr Baynes at liberty to attempt proof of his statements, or to leave it alone, as should seem fit. I expect good from the discussion, which is really that of the question, argued upon an instance, whether one who is *not* of a mathematical turn can safely attempt to meddle with the forms of logic. My opponents—all at least who follow Hamilton—will hold that the word in Italics ought to be omitted; and I readily accept this as the issue, should it please them to take it.

[3] The latest account which Hamilton gave of the propositions furnished by his own 'some' is in the *Discussions* (VI. 631*): to me it is also the clearest. After distinctly relegating the old system, *indefinite definitude*, to subsequent pages, he proceeds to explain his diagrams, in which parallel straight lines denote coextension so far as they run together, and coexclusion so far as they separate. Letters stand for terms, as usual: *D* and Δ for coextensives; *Z* and *Ω* for total coexclusives; *B* and *C* for includent and included; *C* and *K* for partially co-including and co-excluding; and something I am not sure I understand for 'Some—is not some—'. This I must explain to show that he is really symbolizing his own peculiar forms. Then follows 'the rationale of the letters is manifest; . . .'; it is so, and it is manifest that, so far as the different letters are distinctively symbolic, they typify circumstances peculiar to Hamilton's own system. The sentence then runs on thus: 'and it is likewise manifest,

I now come to a proof which I cannot claim as one of my original grounds, for I never noticed it until after this addition had been dated and signed. I can easily understand how I came to miss it. I always read Hamilton's paper (VI.) in the *Discussions* as his defence of himself: I gave it comparatively little of sharp scrutiny as his attack on me. I recommend to every one who has to read a mixed polemical argument to give separate readings, some treating it solely as attack without reference to defence, some treating it solely as defence without reference to attack. The article (VI.) was written against my *second* paper. In that paper I had no notion[1] whatever that Hamilton had any other sense of 'some' than that of the logicians; this will be very apparent. I state that *six* of his propositions agree with those of the old school; which is not true of any *one*; I add that the remaining two are 'peculiar propositions.' I set out the list of syllogisms symbolically: I point out the differences between Hamilton's system and my *exemplar* derivation from it; especially the failure of the canon of inference. Hamilton sees all this (VI. 630*), speaks of my treatment of his syllogism, reprehends me for my alleged mistake about his canon of inference, &c. But what of all this? Hamilton had the old system as well as the new. This is the point. He goes on to show that his head is so full of his own new plan that he cannot read an opponent in any other sense; that he cannot understand an opponent who knows nothing of his 'some at most', which he was then giving *for the first time in print*. He goes on to say (VI. 631*) 'I shall first consider the objections [i.e. my objections] to the *propositional forms*, which I have peculiarly adopted. But it is proper to premise a general enumeration of these . . .;' He then proceeds to lay down what I have already called his clearest explanation of the forms involving his new sense of 'some'. Having done this, he proceeds with 'Of the four propositional forms specially recognized by me (1, 3, 6, 8) Mr De Morgan questions only two . . .;' Surely, because I took the other two, as I said, to be converted Aristotelians; but Hamilton clearly supposes that I had taken him in his own peculiar sense throughout. Thus when he comes (VI. 633*) to assail me for compounding 'All *X*s are all *Y*s' out of 'all *X*s are some *Y*s' and 'Some *X*s are all *Y*s' he charges me with compounding '*incompossible* propositions': that is, he supposes me to be taking his own propositions in his own sense. He proceeds thus—'But unless *some* be identified with

[1] 'But Sir William Hamilton is the first who published the idea of taking all phases of usual quantification, and making them the basis of a system of syllogism' (§ 4 of my second paper, p. 42). The word *usual* implies antithesis, not to any other meaning of '*some*,' but to the numerical quantification.

that this principle of notation may be carried out into syllogistic.' Here is an express reference to syllogism in connexion with the new sense of 'some.' Any one who denies that the new propositions are meant to be applied to syllogism must rebut from elsewhere, the presumption which this passage raises.

all [as it may be in the old system], if either of the latter propositions is true the other must be false;—nay, in fact, if either be true, the very proposition which they are supposed to concur in generating is false likewise.' I now see what all this means: it says in effect—'You pretend to argue about *my* propositions and their connexion, while you are advancing objections which are valid only on the supposition that some of *my* forms are the *old ones*.'

It would have been absurd in Hamilton to have argued against me that my conjunction required *some* to be identified with *all*, unless he had supposed me to be employing a 'some' which could not be so identified. It stands thus. I was representing Hamilton's system to the best of my knowledge. Hamilton had not, so far as I knew, any but the common meaning of 'some'. But he had another meaning, of which his own head was so full that he took it as of course that in my representation of him I adopted that meaning. He did not object to my collection of syllogistic forms—and they are identical with those on which this discussion has arisen. By failure of objection he accepts these forms, and quarrels with nothing but the form I had given of the canon of inference. If Mr Baynes be correct, Hamilton ought to have told me that his own new use of 'some' was partial; that it is for particular cases and for special objects; that it is only for isolated propositions and *immediate* inference; that I was wrong in assuming it intended for syllogism at all, and still more wrong in carrying it into every detail. Instead of all this, he opens his fire by charging me with having taken the rule of *mediate* inference from Ploucquet, and then proceeds to a detailed exposition of his own new forms, of which he makes me receive six, and object to two. It is now for Mr Baynes to make Hamilton contradict me without making him contradict himself.

There is one point which many persons may misconceive: and on which I therefore notice Mr Baynes again. Wishing to give an account of all the strength of his answer, I reminded him of the difficulty which would exist, a hundred years hence, in confronting the weekly journal with the scientific quarto; and I suggested that he should substantiate certain assertions in time for me to present his whole case in this addition. In reply[1] he is jocose upon the idea of posterity knowing anything

[1] Mr Baynes derives innocent amusement from the words 'scientific quarto.' It may be worth while to inform those who do not know it that the scientific transactions are, almost without exception, printed in quarto form; while separate works are almost always in octavo. Hence a reference to *quarto* is—in the United Kingdom—rapidly coming to mean allusion to publication in one of the sets of transactions. I have, a hundred times, heard such a phrase as 'That is not in his work; that is in the quarto memoir;' meaning that the author had not published in his separate writing something he had previously given in a memoir inserted in the transactions of some scientific body. I fell into the phrase 'scientific quarto' as briefer than 'transactions of a scientific body.' It may be useful to foreigners, who have more separate writings in quarto than ourselves, to notice this growing idiom of our language.

about the matter.[1] He may think, as perhaps many do, that the whole question is about Hamilton and myself; I, from the beginning, in 1847, have never considered it in this light. I believe, and I am joined by many reflecting persons, among students both of logic and of mathematics, that as the increasing number of those who attend to both becomes larger and larger still, a serious discussion will arise upon the connexion of the two great branches of exact science, the study of the necessary laws of thought, the study of the necessary matter of thought. The severance which has been widening ever since physical philosophy discovered how to make mathematics her own especial instrument will be examined, and the history of it will be written. A great contest of that future day will be seen to have had its origin in our day; the details of the controversy which began in 1847 will be sought for as matters of its early history; the questions which have arisen between Hamilton and myself will be renewed between writers who will have a small public versed in both sciences to judge them. Let all else end how it may, it is clear that the great change to which Hamilton's name must be attached, the *expressed* quantification of the predicate, must have its history. To every one of our day his own opinion as to how the questions will be settled, or as to whether they will ever be settled at all: but I find that the reflecting of all sides are prescient of a discussion to come. Among them I doubt not I may place the administrators of our Society for the last twelve years: I cannot in any other way explain the publicity given by them to the controversial parts of this series of papers. While such anticipations exist among so large a number of thinking men, there is no reason to quail before those who joke the jokes which are stereotyped against all who avow that they take posterity into their calculations: there is as good a retort, not quite so commonplace. I have over them this undeniable advantage: if right, I shall be known to have been right; if wrong, I shall not be known to have been wrong.

[1] ['Let me add . . . that although in this particular matter I can hardly claim to share the lively concern for posterity he appears to feel, still the interests of logical inquiries in the year 1962 will not be altogether neglected.' (Baynes: *Athenaeum*, 6 December 1862.)]

APPENDIX

ON THE SYLLOGISM: VI

On Quantity and Location; on Identity in relation to the Syllogism; on the History of the Mnemonic Words, of the Fourth Figure, of Logic at Cambridge, of the Occult Quality; on the Triadic System of Enunciation

[An unpublished memoir, dated 27 August 1868.
De Morgan's own summary is given.]

This paper contains as follows:—*Section 1.* Discussion of quantity, ending in proposal of *equilibration of vagueness* of universal and particular; the separation of *quantity* and *location,* as elements of enunciation; locative forms of enunciation; separation of the systems in which the universal quantities are *semper* and *nunquam*; demonstration of the laws of syllogism; which becomes practicable under the separation of quantity and location; *eductive* form of enunciation, for extrication of the predicate of a relation; the four eductive systems.

Section 2. Expression of propositions by identification of extents, or by denial; corresponding expression and proof of a system of syllogism; proof that this is not the common syllogism, which requires the additional principle 'part of part is part', an equivalent of the *dictum de omni*; discussion of the three principles, identity, non-contradiction, excluded middle; relation of the second and third to each other; connexion with the *individuation* of the Schoolmen.

Section 3. Remarks on the history of logic; connexion of Petrus Hispanus with the mnemonic words; discussion of the text-sources of P.H., with doubts as to his having left more than a compendium, like that of Aldrich; connexion of Paulus Venetus with the mnemonics; points in the history of the fourth figure, from Averroes, the Cologne Masters, and J. J. Isenach; the Cambridge writers, Seton, Carter, Downame, Milton; the books affected by the visitation of the University in 1535; the mnemonics for invention of middle terms; other attempts at symbolical logic; attempts at mnemonics in English; the occult qualities of the Schoolmen.

Section 4. Triadic system of enunciation, a simplified view of the *secondary relation* of the last paper, a general—probably the most general—form of onymatic enunciation; structure and laws, establishment of non-restrictive cases; + and − relations of the onymatic forms; reduction of locative and eductive to triadic readings; full connexion of *name* and *thing* given by those readings; hint of a theory on which every pair of repugnant alternatives is inseparably connected with the signs + and −, the same to the same.

INDEX OF NAMES

Names and references of a merely illustrative character are given in italics.

INDEX OF SUBJECTS

Major references are given in bold type.